Studien zum
Handels-, Arbeits- und Wirtschaftsrecht

edited by

Prof. Dr. Barbara Dauner-Lieb
Prof. Dr. Dr. Dr. h.c. mult. Klaus J. Hopt
Prof. Dr. Dres. h.c. Harm Peter Westermann

Band 167

Martin Wilhelm

Business Rescue in South Africa

A Comparative and Functional Approach

Nomos

The Deutsche Nationalbibliothek lists this publication in the Deutsche Nationalbibliografie; detailed bibliographic data are available on the Internet at http://dnb.d-nb.de

a.t..: Hamburg, Univ., Diss. 2016

ISBN 978-3-8487-3980-6 (Print)
978-3-8452-8320-3 (ePDF)

British Library Cataloguing-in-Publication Data
A catalogue record for this book is available from the British Library.

ISBN 978-3-8487-3980-6 (Print)
978-3-8452-8320-3 (ePDF)

Library of Congress Cataloging-in-Publication Data
Wilhelm, Martin
Business Rescue in South Africa
A Comparative and Functional Approach
Martin Wilhelm
469 p.
Includes bibliographic references and index.

ISBN 978-3-8487-3980-6 (Print)
978-3-8452-8320-3 (ePDF)

1st Edition 2017

For Anneke and Sarah
&
my Parents

Preface

When the idea for my doctoral thesis which has resulted in this book arose soon after the inception of the new business rescue regime in South Africa, it was meant to take a fairly straightforward approach: to provide a comprehensive overview of this novel corporate insolvency procedure in South Africa and an analysis of selected problems from a comparative perspective. What this book has eventually turned into however was something I could not have imagined at the time: a functional (and comparative) study from a law and economics perspective. Despite the pain and agony of having to venture into a method of analysis largely unfamiliar to me at the time, using the economic analysis of law as a functional tool for examining the South African business rescue law has fascinated me throughout writing this book. In fact, it was probably the main reason that prevented me from losing focus at difficult stages of my thesis. I hope sincerely that this book will contribute meaningfully to the development of business rescue law in South Africa and to law and economics scholarship in the area of corporate insolvency law generally.

This book would not have been possible without the contribution and support of many people. First and foremost, I would like to thank my supervisor, Prof. Dr. Dr. Dr. h.c. mult. Klaus J. Hopt for his excellent guidance, advice and support throughout the doctorate and for his speedy review of the final manuscript. His rigour of thought and his positive and energetic attitude during our conversations were always a source of inspiration for me. I further thank Professor Hopt, as co-editor of the publication series *Studien zum Handels-, Arbeits- und Wirtschaftsrecht* of the *Nomos Verlag* as well as his fellow co-editors, for the inclusion of my thesis; this is indeed a great honour for me. I also thank the second reviewer of my thesis, Prof. Dr. Heribert Hirte, for his insights on aspects of my thesis. His swift review of the final manuscript of my thesis contributed considerably to the completion of the final stage of my doctorate.

I also received valuable scholarly support from a number of institutions and people. A big thank you to Prof. Dr. Markus Roth at the law faculty of the University of Marburg for providing me with a position as a research assistant and his general advice and support in relation to my thesis. I thank the Konrad Adenauer Foundation for their financial and ideational support and Prof. Dr. Dr. h.c. mult. Reinhard Zimmermann for allowing me to spend a year as a research assistant at the Max Planck Institute for Comparative and International Private Law in Hamburg. Thank you also to the department of commercial law at the University of Cape Town for enabling me to use their facilities to do research and especially Associate Professor Graham Bradfield for his helpful advice and kind support. I further thank Dr. Felix Steffek of the University of Cambridge, Professor Dale Hutchison of ENSafria and the University of Cape Town, Professor Philipp Sutherland of the University of Stellenbosch, Professors André Boraine and Piet Delport of the University of Pretoria, Hans Klopper of Independent Advisory (Corporate Recovery Advisors), Robin Taggart of Nedbank and Etienne Swanepoel of the commercial law faculty at the University of Cape Town for the insightful discussions on the topic of my thesis. Thank you also to Jeremy Fenner and Barbara Wood for proofreading earlier drafts of the manuscript.

I further greatly appreciate the support given by my previous employers, White & Case LLP and ENSafrica, by allowing me to take additional leave for purposes of working on my thesis.

On a personal level, I would like to thank with all my heart my parents for their unconditional investment in, and support throughout, my education. Their contribution to this book is greater than they will ever know.

The most important contribution to this book however has come from my beloved wife, Anneke. I cannot imagine how I would have completed this project without her unquestioning support and care, her encouragement, patience, and words of comfort in difficult stages of writing this book. By taking on the editorial work of the manuscript in the final stages of the thesis despite her own busy professional schedule, and then again before submission to the publisher despite her commitments as a mother after the arrival of our daughter, she made a sacrifice for me that I could never have asked for and that has deeply touched my heart. Thank you!

This book has attempted to state the law as at January 2017.

Frankfurt am Main, August 2017 *Martin Wilhelm*

Abbreviated Table of Contents

Table of Contents

List of Abbreviations

AABIP	Association for the Advancement of Black Insolvency Practitioners
AIPSA	Association of Insolvency Practitioners of South Africa
ARITA	Australian Restructuring Insolvency and Turnaround Association
ASIC	Australian Securities and Investments Commission
Auditing Profession Act	Auditing Profession Act 26 of 2005
CALDB	Companies Auditors and Liquidators Disciplinary Board
CBM	Creditors' Bargain Model
Cf	Compare
Ch	Chapter
CIPC	Companies and Intellectual Property Commission Report
Close Corporations Act	Close Corporations Act 69 of 1984
Commission	Companies and Intellectual Property Commission
Companies Act 1926	Companies Act of 1926
Companies Act 1973	Companies Act 61 of 1973
Companies Act 2008	Companies Act 71 of 2008
Companies Amendment Act 2011	Companies Amendment Act 3 of 2011
Company controllers	Shareholders of closely held companies and directors through whom such shareholders act
Cramdown	The ability of a voting majority of creditors to impose the rescue plan on the contractual rights of the minority creditors
Critical point	The point in time at which the shareholders lose their economic interest in the company and the risk of continued trading shifts from the company's shareholders to its creditors
CVA	Company voluntary arrangement
CVL	Creditors voluntary liquidation

Debt consolidation scheme	A particular form of the scheme of arrangement under the previous Company law regime in South Africa in which typically an insider acquired the debt claims of the existing creditors
DTI	Department of Trade and Industry
Economic distress	A financial state of a company where its assets are worth more broken up than kept together as a going concern
Economic distress entry ground	An entry ground of rescue proceedings commonly found in management-displacing rescue regimes which requires that there be a reasonable likelihood that the statutory rescue objectives will be achieved
ed	Editor
edn	Edition
Enforcement enhancing actions/transactions	Certain actions taken typically by secured creditors in the vicinity of insolveny seeking to avoid formal insolvency or rescue proceedings or placing themselves in a stronger position than unsecured creditors in the event that the company is placed under formal insolvency proceedings
Entry of economically distressed companies	The entry into rescue proceedings of companies that are economically distressed
GmbH	Gesellschaft mit beschränkter Haftung (Private limited company)
Guide	Guide on Trading Whilst Factually Insolvent by the South African Institute of Chartered Accountants
Impending insolvency entry ground	An entry ground of rescue proceedings commonly found in management-displacing rescue regimes which requires that the company be in a financial state close to insolvency
Income Tax Act	Income Tax Act 58 of 1962
Insolvency Act 1936	Insolvency Act 24 of 1936
Insolvency Act	Insolvency Act 24 of 1973
IoDSA	Institute of Directors in Southern Africa
JIC	Joint Insolvency Committee

Jurisdictional requirement	The requirement that the South African scheme of arrangement be between the company and the existing creditors
Legislative scheme	The South African scheme of arrangement
LRA	Labour Relations Act 66 of 1995
man ed	Managing editor
Management-displacing system of governance	A system of governance of rescue proceedings where a third party office holder replaces the existing board of directors during rescue proceedings
MoMiG	Gesetz zur Modernisierung des GmbH-Rechts und zur Bekämpfung von Missbräuchen (Law for the Modernisation of the German Limited Liability Company Law and the Prevention of Misuse)
n	Footnote
PAA Act	Public Accountants' and Auditors' Act 51 of 1951
para	paragraph
Preferential claw-back provisions	The claw back of antecedent transactions by the office holder of a company during insolvency proceedings which preferred certain creditors over others
Preferred procedure actions	The use of secured creditors of their right to place the company under insolvency proceedings favouring one insolvency procedure over the other in a value-diminishing fashion
Premature entry	The entry into rescue proceedings where the assets of the company would in fact have been placed to their highest value use if the company had been restructured outside formal rescue proceedings
Premature entry opportunism	The perverse incentive giving rise to premature entry
Pt	Part
Reg	Regulation
Reorganisation	Restructuring of the company's capital
Rescuability entry ground/ Rescuability	An entry ground of rescue proceedings found under the South Africa rescue law requiring that there be a reasonable prospect of rescuing the company

Risk-shifting incentive	A perverse incentive of company controllers to pursue excessively risky corporate projects in the vicinity of insolvency
RPBs	Recognised Professional Bodies
s 389-arrangement	An arrangement under Section 389 of the Companies Act 1973
s/ss	Section/sections
SAICA	South African Institute of Chartered Accountants
SARS	South African Revenue Service
SCA	Supreme Court of Appeal
Sch	Schedule
SIP	Statement of Insolvency Practice
UK	United Kingdom
US	United States

PART A
THEORETICAL FOUNDATIONS

Chapter 1 General Introduction

I. Introduction of topic; methodology, objectives and structure of study

The new business rescue law[1] introduced in 2011 has shaken up corporate insolvency law in South Africa. It has replaced a largely archaic and unworkable rescue procedure, judicial management,[2] which had been in place since 1926. The new rescue law has so far received considerable attention in academia and it has been subject to a fair amount of litigation since its inception. The fact that it is a novel approach to South African corporate insolvency law, that it has occasionally introduced legal concepts foreign to South African law,[3] that it is in certain respects not the most consistently drafted piece of legislation[4] and that its focus on rescue does not sit well with the largely pro-liquidation and pro-secured creditor legal insolvency culture have given ample material for the courts and academia to grapple with.

The responses in academia to the new business rescue law have so far largely relied on a conventional or doctrinal approach, at times adopting a comparative methodology.[5] In contrast, this study will undertake to analyse the new rescue law from a functional perspective. The 'function' against which the South African rescue law will be tested is the extent to which it is successful in reducing so-called 'agency costs'.

Based on the study of new institutional economics,[6] a 'principal-agent problem' or 'agency problem' arises whenever the furtherance of the inter-

---

1 The relevant procedures are contained in Chapter 6 Companies Act 71 of 2008 (hereafter, '*Companies Act 2008*').

2 Ss 427–440 Companies Act 61 of 1973 (hereafter, '*Companies Act 1973*').

3 See, eg, the term 'voidable transactions' in s 141(2)(c) Companies Act 2008.

4 See, eg, the interchangeable use of the term 'provisions' and 'obligations of the company' and 'entire agreements' under s 136 Companies Act 2008.

5 See, eg, Loubser, *Some Comparative Aspects of Corporate Rescue in South African Company Law* (LLD thesis, University of South Africa 2010).

6 On the study of new institutional economics generally see, eg, Milgrom and Roberts, *Economics, Organization and Management* (2nd edn, Prentice-Hall 1992); Coase, 'The New Institutional Economics' (1998) 88(2) Americ. Econ. Rev. 72; Williamson, 'The New Institutional Economics: Taking Stock, Looking Ahead' (2000) 38(3) J. Econ. Lit. 59.

ests of one party (referred to as the '*principal*') depends on the actions of another party (referred to as the '*agent*').[7] A principal-agent relationship in the economic sense does not require a legal relationship between the parties; a mere *factual* dependency by the principal on the agent's actions is sufficient.

The problem arises because the agent tends to not exert himself as much in maximising wealth for the principal as where all the benefits were to flow to the agent. Where the agent has an information advantage over the principal in respect of the relevant facts (so-called 'asymmetric information'), the agent is tempted to shirk on his promised performance or take for himself some of the value that the principal is entitled to. This is referred to in economics literature as a 'perverse incentive' or 'opportunism'[8] of the agent. Of course, the principal could monitor the agent to ensure that he receives the full value of what is promised to him. However, such monitoring is costly. Accordingly, the value of the agent's performance to the principal would be reduced, irrespective of whether the principal monitors the agent, generating so-called 'agency costs'.[9]

The agency cost theory has largely been employed in the analysis of company law, where three so-called 'agency relationships' (or 'conflicts') have been identified, namely (i) the manager-owner conflict; (ii) the majority owner-minority owner conflict; and (iii) the company-creditor conflict. Based on these three relationships in company law, the following three agency conflicts emerge in rescue law: (i) the manager-owner conflict becomes an office holder-creditor conflict; (ii) the majority-minority conflict becomes a secured creditor-unsecured creditor conflict; and (iii) the company-creditor conflict is the same in relation to rescue law since as in company law, it arises outside formal rescue proceedings.

It will be shown that the perverse incentives of the agent in each of these agency conflicts give rise to certain principal-harming actions,

---

7 See generally, eg, Furubotn and Richter, *Institutions and Economic Theory: The Contribution of the New Institutional Economics* (2nd edn, University of Michigan Press 2005).

8 The term 'opportunism' refers to self-interested behaviour that involves some element of guile, deception, misrepresentation or bad faith; Williamson, *The Economic Institution of Capitalism* (The Free Press 1985) 47–9; Armour, Hansmann and Kraakman, 'Agency Problems and Legal Strategies' in Kraakman and others (eds), *Anatomy of Corporate Law – A Comparative and Functional Approach* (2nd edn, Oxford University Press 2009) 35.

9 Armour, Hansmann and Kraakman, 'Agency Problems' (n 8) 35–7.

which the law can be seen to respond to by means of so-called legal strategies – that is, substantive law rules that can be seen to ameliorate agency costs. Due to the large scope of the topic, this study will only deal with agency costs-generating actions arising under the company-creditor conflict.

To be sure, the generation of agency costs is not the only type of inefficiency that may arise in the context of corporate insolvency law. Other important types of inefficiencies are the costs of the insolvency procedure and the costs of an adverse reaction of market participants to financial distress (referred to as 'direct' and 'indirect' costs of insolvency, respectively). Although such other types of costs are relevant to a functional understanding of rescue law, only the agency costs theory has proved to be capable of general application across the entire set of rules making up rescue law. It is for this reason that the agency costs theory will be used as the primary analytical methodology.

In analysing the South African rescue law, regard will also be had to the corporate insolvency law of foreign jurisdictions. Given the common legal heritage of South African law with the laws of the UK, the US and Australia particularly in respect of commercial law, those jurisdictions will primarily be drawn on. To the extent that German law provides interesting perspectives for purposes of comparison, it will also be consulted occasionally.

Consistent with the functional approach, the applicable foreign law rules will be scrutinised primarily insofar as they can be seen to respond to the applicable agency costs-generating actions.

It should be noted that this study does not intend to provide an exhaustive account of each of the mentioned jurisdictions. The aim is rather to pick out legal responses of the foreign jurisdictions that provide particularly useful insights to the discussion.

The agency cost and comparative analysis of the South African business rescue law is the primary objective of this study, but it is not its only one. Given the novelty of the new rescue law, it is thought appropriate that an overview of the new procedure be provided and selected problems be examined. This discussion will have regard to the historical and cultural context within which the new rescue law is set.

This study will be structured as follows. Section II. in this Chapter will expand on the explanation of the principal-agent conflict and the common legal responses to principal-harming actions.

Chapter 2 will examine the theoretical foundations of corporate insolvency law primarily from a law and economics perspective. This will provide a sound foundation for the agency costs analysis later on.

The general overview and analysis of selected problems of the South African rescue law is contained in PART B. Chapter 3 sets out the previous rescue law, while Chapter 4 deals with the new rescue law having regard to its historical and legal cultural context.

The functional and comparative analysis of the legal responses to the agency costs-generating actions arising under the company-creditor conflict will be discussed in PART C. The Chapters in this part are structured according to the three actions arising under the company-creditor conflict and identified as being particularly pertinent to rescue law, namely: (i) the perverse incentive of company controllers to delay the invocation of rescue proceedings or pursue excessively risky projects in the vicinity of insolvency (Chapter 5); (ii) the extension of shareholder loans to the company in the vicinity of insolvency (Chapter 6); (iii) and the strategic invocation of formal rescue proceedings (Chapter 7).

An Overall Summary and Outlook will conclude the discussion.

II. The principal-agent model and legal strategies

1. Basic elements of the principal-agent theory, agency problems in company law and an introduction to the role of the law in addressing agency costs

Economists distinguish between two types of opportunism of the agent, depending on whether such opportunism arises before the principal-agent relationship is established (*ex ante* opportunism) or afterwards (*ex post* opportunism). The problem of *ex post* opportunism, which economists also refer to as 'moral hazard', follows the pattern explained above. *Ex ante* opportunism, on the other hand, is where the agent furnishes the principal with misleading particulars about his competence and intentions because of asymmetric information, which reduces the ability of the principal to determine the agent's credentials. *Ex ante* opportunism is also referred to in the economics literature as an 'adverse selection' problem.

The extent of the agency costs often depends on the complexity of the tasks the agent is mandated to undertake and the degree of discretion the agent is given – more of both would potentially increase the agency costs for the principal. The reason for this is that both factors make it more difficult for the principal to assure himself of the quality of the agent's performance, thereby giving the agent a greater incentive to act opportunistically, skimp on the quality of his performance or even divert to himself some of the fruits that were promised to the principal.[10]

By extending the theory to relationships involving multiple parties (ie, where an agent acts on behalf of several principals), as is typically the case in a company, two related factors will influence the extent of the agency costs, namely the number of the principals and the extent to which their interests diverge. The higher their number and the more divergent their interests – or 'heterogeneous preferences', as economists would say – the more difficult it is for them to agree on a single set of goals. This causes the principals to incur 'co-ordination costs', which can frustrate the principals' efforts to engage in collective action. As this would increase the costs of each individual principal of monitoring the agent, the agent has a greater incentive to act opportunistically, resulting in higher agency costs.[11] An illustration of this can be found in a particular principal-agent conflict that will be discussed below, where the managers act as agents of the owners of the company. In this agency conflict, the agency costs are likely to be higher in respect of companies with dispersed ownership than companies with concentrated ownership.

A further reason for the presence of higher agency costs in widely-held companies than in closely-held companies is that asymmetric information between managers (acting as agents) and owners (acting as principals) is expected to be higher in widely-held companies than in closely-held companies. The first explanation for this is that majority owners could lose a greater percentage of their total investment than dispersed owners in the case of insolvency of the company or companies in which the majority and minority owners have invested. This gives majority owners a stronger incentive to monitor their investment more closely than dispersed owners. The second explanation for the different levels of asymmetric information between closely-held and widely-held companies is that the monitoring costs of majority shareholders are likely to be lower than those of minority shareholders. This is because majority shareholders typically have a more concentrated portfolio than minority shareholders. This means that majori-

10 Armour, Hansmann and Kraakman, 'Agency Problems' (n 8) 35–6.
11 Ibid 36–37.

ty shareholders are able to devote their entire monitoring costs or at least a large portion of their monitoring costs on the management of the only company or few companies that they own, whereas dispersed shareholders would need to divide their monitoring costs between the many companies in which they have invested.

The generation of agency costs is problematic both on a micro-level and on a macro-level. On a micro-level, agency costs result in an inappropriate wealth transfer from the principal to the agent. On a macro-level, it results in the inefficient allocation of resources and thus in the reduction of the aggregate welfare of all the constituents affected by the applicable activities.[12]

The concern underlying all of the above-mentioned (undesirable) effects of agency costs from a law and economics perspective, is to ensure that the affairs of the company are conducted in the most efficient (and least wasteful) manner. The most widely accepted meaning in economics of 'efficiency' is that provided by the British economists Kaldor and Hicks (1939) and is thus commonly referred to as 'Kaldor-Hicks efficiency'. The authors claimed that a transaction between multiple parties is efficient if the gains to the parties that are better off after the conclusion of the transactions, on aggregate, are larger than the losses of the parties who are worse off.[13] However, Kaldor-Hicks efficiency has been criticised on various grounds, which will not be set out here,[14] suffice it to say that the attacks on Kaldor-Hicks efficiency and more generally on the economic

12 Indeed, the advancement or maximisation of social aggregate welfare is regarded by sympathisers of the theory of law and economics as the main goal of company law; Armour, Hansmann and Kraakman, 'What is Corporate law?' in Kraakman and others (eds), *Anatomy of Corporate Law – A Comparative and Functional Approach* (2nd edn, Oxford University Press 2009) 1, 28.

13 Kaldor, 'Welfare propositions of economics and interpersonal comparisons of utility' (1939) 49 Econ. J. 549 and Hicks, 'The foundations of welfare economics' (1939) 49 Econ. J. 696. The fact that under Kaldor-Hicks efficiency the 'winners' of the transaction do not actually have to compensate the 'losers' for there to be an optimal outcome, distinguishes it from a previous conception of efficiency advanced by Pareto (see Pareto, *Manual of Political Economy* (Schwier tr, Schwier and Page (eds), A. M. Kelly 1971) 26); Mokal, *Consistency of Principle in Corporate Insolvency* (Doctoral thesis, University College London 2001) 34–5.

14 For relevant criticism, see eg Coleman, *Markets, Morals and the Law* (Cambridge University Press 1988) 138; Lawson, 'Efficiency and individualism' (1992) 42 Duke L.J. 53. Kornhauser, 'Constrained optimisation: Corporate law and the maximisation of social welfare' in Kraus and Walt (eds), *The Jurisprudential Founda-*

analysis of law, have cast some doubt on the normative merits of the concept of efficiency in the law.[15] Nevertheless, efficiency does appear to play a meaningful role in the analysis of at least some areas of the law, perhaps not as the ultimate justification thereof, but at least as a legitimate means of attaining the normative goals of the law. Seen in this way, efficiency would ensure that the normative goals of the law are achieved in the least wasteful (or cheapest)[16] way possible.[17]

As mentioned above, the principal-agent theory has, so far, featured most prominently in the field of company law,[18] where three agency problems have been identified. The first agency problem is where the managers act as agents of the owners (hereafter, the '*manager-owner conflict*'). Here the danger is that the managers skimp on the quality of their performance or take for themselves some of the value that was promised to the owners. The second agency problem is where controlling shareholders – in so far as they are able to direct the decision-making of the management of the company – act as agents for non-controlling shareholders (hereafter, the '*majority-minority conflict*'). Here the danger is that the

---

tions of Corporate and Commercial Law (Cambridge University Press 2000), 87, 98–110.

15 In the context of corporate insolvency law, see Mokal, 'Consistency of Principles' (n 13) 35–8. See generally Dworkin, 'Why Efficiency? A Response to Professor Calabresi and Posner' (1981) 8 Hofstra L. Rev. 563; Coleman (n 14); Lawson (n 14) 53.

16 This should be understood in the economic sense insofar as the value expended in achieving the normative goals of law include non-monetary costs.

17 See, chiefly, Mokal, 'Consistency of Principles' (n 13) 37–9. See also Williamson and Masten, *Transaction Cost Economics* (Edward Elgar 1995); Milgrom and Roberts (n 6) 22–30.

18 The theory first emerged in the US; see Berle and Means, *The Modern Corporation and Private Property* (Macmillan 1932) and the *locus classicus* Jensen and Meckling, 'Theory of the Firm: Managerial Behaviour, Agency Costs and Ownership Structure' (1976) 3 J. Finan. Econ. 305. For more recent examples, see also Easterbrook and Fischel, *The Economic Structure of Corporate Law* (Harvard University Press 1996). For the UK, see, eg, Davies, *An Introduction to Company Law* (2nd edn, Clarendon Press 2010) 110ff and Germany, eg, Fleischer, 'Grundfragen der ökonomischen Theorie im Gesellschafts- und Kapitalmarktrecht' (2001) 30 ZGR 1. For evidence of the theory's wide acceptance, see Kraakman and others (eds), *Anatomy of Corporate Law – A Comparative and Functional Approach* (2nd edn, Oxford University Press 2009), in which scholars from the US, UK, Germany, Italy, Switzerland and Japan use the principal-agent theory in analysing the company laws of the respective jurisdictions.

majority (often acting through managers) expropriates the minority. The third agency problem is where the company acts as agent for its contractual partners, such as the employees, the creditors[19]of the company (hereafter, the '*company-creditor*' and the '*company-employee conflict*', as applicable).[20] Here the danger is that the company might expropriate creditors, exploit workers or mislead consumers.[21]

2. Legal Strategies for the amelioration of agency costs

The law can play an important role in mitigating agency costs by employing so-called 'legal strategies' – ie, substantive law rules that can be seen to ameliorate agency costs.[22] In saying that, legal strategies need not necessarily be restricted to legal norms (or mandatory law); agency costs could also be addressed by contract.[23] Legal strategies benefit both principals and agents insofar as principals are willing to compensate the agent

---

19 This principal-agent relationship also exists between the company and non-contractual claimants (so-called involuntary creditors or non-adjusting creditors) against the company's assets, in particular victims of delicts committed by the company.

20 The positions in this agency relationship could also be reversed. Eg, to the extent that the company's profits depend on the performance of employees and to the extent that the company relies on debt equity to finance its business projects, the employees and the creditors could be seen to act as agents of the company; in relation to employees, see Cheffins, *Company Law – Theory, Structure and Operation* (Clarendon Press 1997) 92.

21 Armour, Hansmann and Kraakman, 'Agency Problems' (n 8) 36. The bulk of the literature relates to the manager-owner and the majority-minority agency problems in company law. On the company-creditor problem, see, eg, Armour, Hertig and Kanda, 'Transactions with Creditors' in Kraakman and others (eds), *Anatomy of Corporate Law – A Comparative and Functional Approach* (2nd edn, Oxford University Press 2009) 115; Cheffins (n 20) 521ff. For a comparison of creditor protection under German law and UK law from a principal-agent perspective, see Steffek, *Gläubigerschutz in der Kapitalgesellschaft* (Mohr Siebeck 2011). On the company-employee relationship, see, eg, Enriques, Hansmann and Kraakman, 'The Basic Governance Structure: Minority Shareholders and Non-Shareholder Constituencies' in Kraakman and others (eds), *Anatomy of Corporate Law – A Comparative and Functional Approach* (2nd edn, Oxford University Press 2009) 89, 100–4.

22 Armour, Hansmann and Kraakman, 'Agency Problems' (n 8) 37.

23 The constitutional document of a company is an obvious example in the context of company law; Armour, Hansmann and Kraakman, 'Agency Problems' (n 8) 37–8.

for the assurance of honest and high-quality performance by the agent. An example of this would be mechanisms addressing opportunistic behaviour by directors, acting on behalf of the company's shareholders (who as owners represent the company's interests at least while it is solvent), at the expense of the body of creditors,[24] by reducing the risk for creditors of lending money to the company. The creditors (acting as principal) are willing to compensate the company (acting as agent) for the existence of such agency costs-reducing measures (usually imposed by way of contract), by reducing the costs at which they are prepared to lend to the company, thus benefitting principal and agent alike.[25]

We will now set out the different types of legal strategies relevant to rescue law.

a. The legal strategies explained

aa. General

The range of legal strategies that address the agency problems can be divided into two broad categories: on the one hand, substantive terms that constrain the agent's behaviour directly, referred to as 'regulatory strategies' and, on the other hand, mechanisms that seek to facilitate the principal's control over the agent, referred to as 'governance strategies'.

The success of governance strategies depends on the ability of the principals to co-ordinate their efforts in monitoring the agent and on exercising their control rights. High co-ordination costs thus reduce the effectiveness of governance strategies. Regulatory strategies, on the other hand, rely on strong institutions – notably courts and regulatory bodies – for their enforcement and strong disclosure of information to enable institutions to determine compliance with applicable legal norms by agents.[26]

Regulatory and governance strategies take effect either *ex ante* (that is, before the agent acts) or *ex post* (that is, after the agent acts). Although not always clear or analytically sound, the distinction between whether legal strategies operate *ex ante* or *ex post* is nevertheless a useful tool for

---

24 As we will see later, the company-creditor agency conflict indeed plays an important role in the context of this study.

25 Armour, Hansmann and Kraakman, 'Agency Problems' (n 8) 37.

26 Ibid 38.

demonstrating and exploring the role of the law in mitigating agency costs.[27]

It should be noted at the outset that the demarcations between different legal strategies are not always clear and a legal mechanism sometimes could be seen as an instance of more than one legal strategy. Moreover, the matrix of legal strategies as set out below is not intended as an authoritative classification of legal responses to company affairs, but rather as a tool to explore the functional role of corporate and corporate insolvency law. Nor is the functional role of the law presented here intended to displace traditional doctrines of company law and corporate insolvency law.[28]

Regulatory and governance strategies can be divided into further subsets of legal strategies, as set out below.

bb. Regulatory strategies

Regulatory strategies comprise 'rules' and 'standards' (collectively referred to as the 'agent constraints' strategy) and 'entry' and 'exit' strategies (collectively referred to as the 'affiliation terms' strategy).

Rules and standards are legal norms that direct agents to refrain from actions that harm their principals. The difference between the two is that rules clearly prescribe what the agent must do or refrain from doing *ex ante*, while standards give more flexible guidance on the actions of agents that are to be determined by the courts *ex post*. Standards are usually found where the content of the harmful action by the agent and the potential harm done to the principal is easily determinable. Common examples of rules are minimum capital requirements and, to a lesser extent, restrictions on distributions and related transactions, which are all aimed at constraining actions by the shareholders (acting through the management) that harm creditors generally.[29] Sometimes, however, the content of the agent's actions and the way in which this might harm the principal is more complex. Here the use of standards is more appropriate since this allows for the agency costs to be addressed with greater sensitivity and flexibility. A conspicuous example of a standard relevant to rescue law is the imposition

27 Ibid 44–5.

28 Ibid 38–9, 45.

29 We will touch upon such creditor protection mechanisms in the context of the company-creditor agency conflict at PART A, Chapter 1, II., 3., a below.

of liability on directors for inappropriately delaying the invocation of formal insolvency or rescue proceedings. Here the courts have to determine *ex post* whether, loosely stated, the directors continued trading when there was no reasonable prospect that the company would be able to avoid a general default on its debts to creditors.[30] The efficacy of both rules and standards depends, to a large extent, on the quality of their enforcement. Standards, which require adjudicators to interpret and, occasionally, develop the law in respect of the amelioration of agency problems, require particularly strong and high quality institutions, the main characteristics of which are expertise and integrity.[31]

The other regulatory strategy regulates the terms of the relationship (or 'affiliation')[32] between the principal and the agent, in respect of either the principal entering into such relationship *ex ante*, or exiting such relationship *ex post*. A typical entry term is the requirement that a company disclose information relevant to its promised performance before contracting with principals. Such requirements are frequently found in capital markets law, for example, prospectus disclosure for initial public offerings of listed companies. Common examples of exit strategies are the minority shareholder's appraisal rights in respect of a fundamental transaction.[33] A rare example of the *affiliation rights strategy* in the context of corporate insolvency and rescue law is found in jurisdictions, such as the US, which allow the trading of claims of the debtor during Chapter 11 proceedings. Here the right of the existing creditor to sell their claims constitutes an *exit strategy*. The investor buying the claims is not protected by entry strategies as such and must accordingly protect himself through, for example, doing a due diligence on the creditor selling the claims to him.[34]

30 This is considered at PART A, Chapter 1, II., 3., a., bb and PART C, Chapter 5 below.

31 This paraphrases Armour, Hansmann and Kraakman, 'Agency Problems' (n 8) 38, 39–40.

32 Which explains why this legal strategy is referred to as the 'affiliation terms' strategy.

33 This paraphrases Armour, Hansmann and Kraakman, 'Agency Problems' (n 8) 40–2.

34 Rich and Moser, 'Bankruptcy Claims Trading: Basic Concepts' (2013) Practical Law Company <http://www.r3mlaw.com/Articles/Bankruptcy-Claims-Trading-Basic-Concepts.pdf> accessed 14 January 2017.

cc. Governance strategies

The three sets of governance strategies are selection and removal rights (collectively referred to as the 'appointment rights strategy'), initiation and veto rights (collectively referred to as the 'decision rights strategy') and *trusteeship* and *reward strategies* (collectively referred to as the 'agent incentives strategy').

The selection *ex ante* and removal *ex post* of directors by shareholders and sometimes also non-shareholder constituents, such as employees, is one of the key corporate governance mechanisms in company law. To the extent that the delegated management structure of companies transforms into rescue proceedings – where the office holder or incumbent directors manage the companies on behalf of the body of creditors –, equivalent selection and removal rights can be found in rescue law.[35]

Initiation and ratification rights allow the principal to initiate and ratify managerial decisions entrusted to the agent. Initiation rarely occurs in company law, given the efficiencies of delegating decision-making to a few specialists, and the same reasoning would in principle apply in rescue law.[36] Ratification *ex post* is more common, but only in relation to fundamental decisions. The standard example of this in rescue proceedings is the right of creditors to vote on the rescue plan.

The final set of governance strategies is the trusteeship and reward strategies that provide the agent with incentives to refrain from acting opportunistically. The *reward strategy*, as the name suggests, rewards the agent *ex post*, typically in monetary terms, for furthering the interests of the agent. The option provided under the South African rescue procedure that the company and the rescue practitioner can agree to an additional, contingency-based fee for the rescue practitioner for attaining certain

35 This paraphrases Armour, Hansmann and Kraakman, 'Agency Problems' (n 8) 42.

36 Armour and Mokal, 'Reforming the Governance of Corporate Rescue: The Enterprise Act 2002' (2004) ESRC Centre for Business Research Working Paper 288 <http://papers.ssrn.com/sol3/papers.cfm?abstract_id=567306> accessed 16 January 2017. See generally Easterbrook and Fischel (n 18) Chs 1 and 2; Davies, 'An Introduction to Company Law' (n 18) 9. However, an important exception to this principle is found, eg, in the UK, Australia and South Africa where creditors are sometimes placed in a position to initiate formal rescue proceedings in advance of insolvency, which will be touched upon later in this Chapter and further discussed in Chapter 5.

specified milestones constitutes an example of this strategy.[37] The *trusteeship strategy* provides the agent not with 'high-powered' monetary incentives as under the *reward strategy*, but rather with 'low-powered' incentives *ex ante*, such as conscience, pride and reputation. A conspicuous example in company law is the requirement that self-dealing transactions be approved by independent directors, which is now required in some jurisdictions. Examples of the *trusteeship strategy* in rescue law are (i) where the court (acting as trustee) is called upon to approve a scheme of arrangement between the company and a class of, or all of, its creditors[38] and (ii) where office holders may be motivated by reputational concerns when managing companies during rescue proceedings, given that they rely on new appointments for their monetary and professional advancement. The effectiveness of such reputational concerns, however, will depend to a large degree on the competitiveness of the market for office holders.

b. Enforcement

The efficacy of the legal strategies depends on whether they induce compliance by the agent, which in turn, depends on the quality of enforcement. Strong enforcement is particularly important for the success of regulatory strategies, given that they, by definition, rely solely on regulatory institutions for their enforcement. The quality of enforcement depends on effective legal institutions, such as courts, regulators and procedural rules. Governance strategies, by contrast, rely chiefly on the intervention by the principals to ensure the compliance of agents and are thus less reliant on the quality and effectiveness of legal institutions.[39]

---

37 S 143(2) to (4) Companies Act 2008.

38 A scheme of arrangement is an alternative rescue procedure in South Africa, the UK and Australia. For South Africa, see s 155(7) Companies Act 2008; for the UK, see Pt 26 Companies Act 2006; for Australia, see Pt 5.1 Corporations Act 2001. A rare example of where the plan is required to be approved by the court under the main rescue procedure is France; see Armour, Hertig and Kanda (n 21) 145–6.

39 Schwartz, 'Relational Contracts in the Courts: An Analysis of Incomplete Agreements and Judicial Strategies' (1992) 21 J. Legal Stud. 271; Rock and Wachter, 'Islands of Conscious Power: Law, Norms, and the Self-Governing Corporation' (2001) 149 U. Pa. L. Rev. 1619. See generally, Armour, Hansmann and Kraakman, 'Agency Problems' (n 8) 45–6.

Three modes of enforcement can be distinguished: public enforcement, private enforcement and 'gatekeeper control'. Public enforcement refers to all enforcement action brought by organs of state, such as courts and regulatory authorities,[40] which can induce compliance *ex ante* or impose sanctions for non-compliance *ex post*.

Private enforcement refers to enforcement action brought by private individuals and includes informal sanctions, such as the possible reputational harm suffered by agents as a result of sanctions brought by principals. Private enforcement largely induces compliance by the agent by means of the deterrence effect of imposition of penalties *ex post*. A rare example of where private enforcement allows for regulatory approval *ex ante* is the requirement of court approval of the scheme of arrangement in the UK, Australia and South Africa.[41]

The third mode of enforcement – 'gatekeeper control' – is the recruitment of corporate outsiders, such as accountants, to monitor the conduct of, and ensure compliance by, agents. Gatekeeper control generally operates *ex ante*, for example, where parties refrain from concluding contracts with a distressed company that are at risk of being set aside by the insolvency office holder (hereafter, the '*office holder*') *ex post*. Proper performance by gatekeepers is generally ensured by the threat of sanctions, such as civil and criminal liability of auditors for providing a faulty audit of the company or, in the example mentioned above, the costs of the contractual counterparty of the company of the reversal of the contract when it is set aside in insolvency proceedings. The employment of gatekeepers does, however, result in the creation of a new agency relationship – where the gatekeeper acts as agent for the company –, which is addressed by the legal strategies applicable to the relevant gatekeeper.[42]

c. Disclosure

Disclosure duties of agents are an effective mechanism for ameliorating agency costs, given that they assist in reducing information asymmetries

40 The relevant regulatory authority in respect companies in South Africa is the Companies and Intellectual Property Commission (hereafter, '*Commission*').

41 See n 38 above and accompanying text.

42 The text under this heading paraphrases Armour, Hansmann and Kraakman, 'Agency Problems' (n 8) 46–9.

between agents and principals, which is, as we have seen above, an important reason for the generation of agency costs.

We have already seen the important role of disclosure duties in relation to the *affiliation terms strategy*.[43] However, disclosure is also important in relation to the other types of legal strategies. For example, under the South African rescue law, the directors have a duty to disclose to creditors, shareholders, employees or trade unions representing employees that the company is 'financially distressed'.[44] This enables the principals to assess whether to intervene by using their *initiation right* to place the company under rescue proceedings.[45] Moreover, the rescue practitioner has extensive duties to disclose information relating to the development of a rescue plan to creditors and employees.[46] This improves the principals' decision when exercising their *ratification right* on the approval of the rescue plan.[47]

Ensuring compliance with disclosure duties themselves poses a real challenge. The legal approach to this depends on whether the disclosure is periodic, ie where the type of information is expected but the content is unknown (so-called 'known unknowns'), or where the disclosure is *ad hoc*, ie where the disclosure itself is unexpected (so-called 'unknown unknowns'). In relation to periodic disclosure, given that the principals expect the disclosure to be made, enforcement of the fact that disclosure is, in fact, made is not the difficulty; rather, the quality of the disclosure needs to be ensured, which gatekeepers, in the form of auditors, typically enforce.

By contrast, vigorous legal enforcement seems to be the only means of ensuring compliance with *ad hoc* disclosure duties, given that principals do not expect disclosure in advance.[48]

---

43 See PART A, Chapter 1, II., 2., a., bb above.

44 'Financial distress' is a technical term under the South African rescue law and denotes a state of impending insolvency; see s 129(7) read with s 128(1)(f) Companies Act 2008.

45 However, as we will see in Chapter 5, this *initiation rights strategy* is problematic.

46 Such duties of disclosure under the South African rescue procedure are discussed in Chapter 4 below.

47 The developing of, and voting on, the rescue plan is contained in Part D of Chapter 6 Companies Act 2008.

48 The text under this heading paraphrases Armour, Hansmann and Kraakman, 'Agency Problems' (n 8) 49–50.

3. Agency problems in relation to corporate insolvency law and rescue law

The three agency problems described above also arise in relation to corporate insolvency law in general and rescue law in particular. The company-creditor conflict in company law – namely where the company expropriates the creditors in various forms to benefit the shareholders – finds similar application in corporate insolvency and rescue law (discussed at a. below). As such, it arises outside formal insolvency proceedings. Another agency problem that could occur outside formal insolvency proceedings is an analogous form of the majority-minority conflict mentioned above. Here it is not the majority shareholders who act as agents for the minority shareholders, but rather one class of creditors, generally secured creditors, who act as agents of another class of creditors, generally non-secured creditors (hereafter, the '*inter-creditor conflict*'). The conflict in the inter-creditor conflict arises over the deployment of the company's assets in respect of companies that have defaulted on their obligations to creditors generally (discussed at b. below).[49]

An analogous form of the manager-owner conflict arises once a company has been placed under formal insolvency proceedings (discussed at c. below). Here the persons that are given managerial powers of the company in rescue proceedings – for example, the office holder under the South African, the British and Australian rescue laws – act as agents for the persons who have claims against the company during rescue proceedings[50] The agency costs in this agency conflict arise as a result of the incentive of the managers to shirk their duties to the company's claimants under the formal insolvency or rescue procedure. The inter-creditor conflict does not only occur in the vicinity of insolvency, but it could also arise within formal insolvency proceedings. Here the conflict is essentially over the deployment of the company's assets among the options of distribution pro-

49 On the operation of the inter-creditor agency conflict during formal rescue proceedings, see below under this heading.

50 The company's claimants in formal insolvency proceedings generally comprise only creditors, given that in practice, the equity is generally wiped out in companies that have defaulted on their debts generally and has as a consequence been placed under formal insolvency proceedings; Armour, Hertig and Kanda (n 21) 121.

vided under the formal insolvency and rescue procedure (discussed at d. below).

a. Company-creditor conflict in the vicinity of insolvency

aa. General

Company-creditor conflict is greater in distressed companies — Although the company-creditor conflict arises in respect of both solvent companies and financially distressed companies, the company – or to be more precise, the shareholders acting through (the shareholder-regarding) managers (hereafter, '*company controllers*') – have a much stronger perverse incentive to harm creditors in respect of distressed companies than in respect of solvent companies. This is largely because when the shareholders' equity has evaporated or has been reduced to negligible levels and the company's business model is not sufficiently established to repair this financial position, the risk of continued trading shifts from the company's shareholders to its creditors (hereafter, '*critical point*'). Since the doctrine of limited liability protects the shareholders' personal assets from the consequences of the company's failure, the shareholder-regarding directors can focus solely on the potential upside of the prospective actions taken by the company. Put differently, if such actions fail, shareholders cannot lose more than they already have, but if such actions succeed, shareholders will reap all the benefits. The position of the creditors, however, is reversed: corporate actions that would diminish the company's net asset position further will fall solely on the creditors, while creditors' financial positions would not correspondingly improve if the corporate actions succeeded, given that the creditors' returns are fixed.

This explains why, from the critical point, company controllers have a perverse incentive to continue trading, even where the company's assets would have been placed to their highest value use if the company were placed under formal liquidation or rescue proceedings.[51] This harms the

51 There are further supplementary factors that explain the company controller opportunism to delay the invocation of formal rescue and liquidation proceedings inappropriately. Chief among such factors are the loss of control of the company by the directors (and majority shareholders) during formal liquidation and rescue proceedings in jurisdictions that employ a management-displacing system of gover-

creditors of the company, as the continued trading reduces the pool of assets available to the creditors in insolvency.[52]

A (distressed) company's assets would be placed to their highest value use under liquidation proceedings if the company's assets are worth more broken up than kept together (in which case such company is said to be 'economically distressed'). This is because generally the objective of liquidation proceedings is to sell off companies' assets piecemeal. Where a (distressed) company's assets are worth more kept together than broken up (in which case it is said to be 'economically viable'), such company's assets are placed to their highest value use if they were retained as a going concern.[53] Whether the assets of economically viable companies are placed to their highest value use if such companies' financial problems were attempted to be resolved outside, rather than within, formal rescue proceedings depends on the costs of each restructuring option, which vary according to the particular circumstances of each case. The primary types of costs of formal rescue measures are (i) the costs of the formal procedure itself, including the costs of the office holder and court proceedings (direct costs of rescue proceedings) and (ii) the reduction in value of the company's assets largely as a result of the market downgrading its expectations of the company's commitment to performance (indirect costs of rescue proceedings).[54] On the other hand, the primary types of costs of informal

---

nance (eg, South Africa, the UK and Australia) and a psychological state of 'irrational optimism' of company controllers of the chances of survival of distressed companies; see the discussion and applicable references in nn 130ff and accompanying text below.

52 Eidenmüller, 'Die GmbH im Wettbewerb der Rechtsformen' [2007] ZGR 181, 193.

53 See generally Crystal and Mokal, 'The Valuation of Distressed Companies – A Conceptual Framework' (2006) SSRN <http://papers.ssrn.com/sol3/papers.cfm?abstract_id=877155> accessed 16 January 2017. It should be noted that the economic literature generally refers to the situation where a company's assets are worth more as a going concern than broken up as 'financial distress; see, eg, Andrade and Kaplan, 'How Costly is Financial (not Economic) Distress? Evidence from Highly Leveraged Transactions that Became Distressed' (1998) 53 J. Finance 1443, 1443–44. However, since the South African rescue law uses the same term for the impending insolvency entry ground, we will refer to the economic state of 'financial distress' as 'economic viability' to avoid confusion.

54 Armour, Hertig and Kanda (n 21) 122.

rescue measures are holdout and free-rider problems as well as transaction costs.[55]

Apart from the company controller opportunism to simply continue trading after the critical point, they also have a perverse incentive to actively pursue excessively risky projects (ie, projects with a negative net value). This is because the shareholders no longer carry the risk of such projects after the critical point, and can therefore look solely to their potential upside, regardless of how probable their success may be.[56]

Conversely, while the shareholders' funds in the company are still sufficient, the shareholders would bear the losses of unsuccessful projects first. Accordingly, the company controllers would have an incentive to pursue only appropriately risky projects. Furthermore, the company would be reluctant to jeopardise its reputation as a borrower and its prospects of obtaining further credit particularly in the public debt market and in relation to short term creditors.[57] This explains why the perverse incentive of company controllers to harm creditors is much stronger in respect of distressed companies than in solvent companies and, accordingly, why the law generally refrains from regulating this problem in solvent companies.[58]

Company-creditor problems in solvent companies—However, company controllers are, nevertheless, tempted to take creditor-harming actions when the company is solvent. One such action occurs when the company raises new debt funding. Here the company controllers may present to potential creditors an inflated value of its assets as this would enable the

55 Eidenmüller, 'Trading in Times of Crisis: Formal Insolvency Proceedings, Workouts and the Incentives for Shareholders/Managers' (2006) 7 EBOR 239, 254ff.

56 Indeed, much of the relevant economic literature generally focuses on the company controllers' perverse incentive to pursue risky projects as opposed to the mere continued trading of the company. However, there is no reason why the mere continued trading could not also be regarded as a manifestation of the company controller opportunism in question for the reasons mentioned above. It is also clear that it reduces the company's value and thus harms the creditors (see text to n 52 above).

57 In relation to the public debt markets, see Armour, Cheffins and Skeel Jr, 'Corporate Ownership Structure and the Evolution of Bankruptcy Law: Lessons from the United Kingdom' (2002) 55 Vand.L.Rev. 1699, 1764. In relation to short term creditors, see Davies, 'Directors' Creditor-Regarding Duties in Respect of Trading Decisions Taken in the Vicinity of Insolvency' (2006) 7 EBOR 301, 305.

58 The text under this heading 3.a., save where indicated otherwise, paraphrases Davies, 'Directors' Creditor-Regarding Duties' (n 57) 301–7.

company to obtain debt funding at lower costs than it would have been able to, given its risk profile.[59]

A further creditor-harming action is when the company controllers siphon assets out of the company typically to themselves or 'connected' persons, which results in the reduction of the pool of assets available to creditors in the event of the company's insolvency. This type of transaction is often referred to as 'asset dilution'.[60]

Company controllers are also tempted to exchange assets originally used for low-risk/low-return business activities for assets used in high-risk/high-return projects, a phenomenon that has been referred to as 'asset substitution'. Shareholders benefit from the potential upside resulting from the increase in the riskiness of the company's cash flows, while the potential losses – in an expected-value sense – fall on the creditors. This is because the shareholders' losses are limited due to the principle of limited liability and the creditors' gains from their investments are fixed, as explained above.[61] However, since this perverse incentive generally arises at the point at which the risk of continued trading of the company shifts from the shareholders to the creditors, the problem of 'asset substitution' is expected to feature rarely in respect of solvent companies.

A final situation in which the company-creditor conflict arises in respect of solvent companies is the extension of new loans. Since the 'old' creditors would have to share the company's assets with the 'new' creditors if the company goes insolvent, the old creditors' investments become riskier. To the extent that this risk is not priced into the loan terms with the old creditor or the old creditors have not protected themselves by appropriate contractual covenants, the new creditors are effectively subsidised by the old creditors, which could give the new creditors an incentive to

59 Armour, Hertig and Kanda (n 21) 115–6.

60 Armour, Hertig and Kanda (n 21) 116.

61 See generally Jensen and Meckling (n 16) 334–47; Galai and Masulis, 'The Option Pricing Model and the Risk Factor of Stock' (1976) 3 J. Finan. Econ. 53. See also Armour, 'Transactions at an Undervalue' in Armour and Bennett (eds), *Vulnerable Transactions in Corporate Insolvency* (Hart Publishing 2003) 37, paras 2.28–2.29; Armour, Hertig and Kanda (n 21) 116–7. For empirical evidence of 'asset substitution', see Daigle and Maloney, 'Residual Claims in Bankruptcy: An Agency Theory Explanation' (1994) 37 J.L. & Econ. 157, 182–7; Andrade and Kaplan (n 61); Eisdorfer, 'Empirical Evidence of Risk Shifting in Financially Distressed Firms (2008) 63 J. Finance 609.

fund value-decreasing projects. This action sometimes is referred to as 'debt dilution'.[62]

Company law generally leaves it largely to the relevant parties to protect themselves by way of contract against company-creditor agency costs arising in solvent companies. As the extent of the agency problems might vary according to the particular business models of companies and the varying levels of heterogeneous preferences of creditors of companies, contractual self-regulation allows the parties to address agency costs with greater sensitivity and flexibility than mandatory law. Moreover, the content of the agency problems might evolve over time, which would require changes to the creditor-protective terms. The costs of renegotiating such terms contractually would seem to be much lower than having to make applicable changes to the law governing creditor relations.[63]

Notwithstanding the prevalence of creditor self-help mechanisms in relation to the company-creditor conflict in solvent companies, some legal mechanisms are nevertheless found in this regard. One common legal strategy that mainly addresses the problem where company controllers misrepresent their financial positions in order to obtain 'cheap' debt funding, is mandatory disclosure requirements. One example would be the mandatory preparation and disclosure of financial statements, and the enhancement of the quality of such disclosure through the use of trusted third parties (so-called 'gatekeepers'), such as auditors.[64] This is supplemented by voluntary disclosures by companies through private credit bu-

---

62 For early accounts of this agency problem, see Myers, 'Determinants of Corporate Borrowing' (1977) 5 J. Finan. Econ. 147; Smith and Warner, 'On Financial Contracting: An Analysis of Bond Covenants' (1979) 7 J. Finan. Econ. 117; see also Schwartz, A Theory of Loan Priorities (1989) 18 J. Legal Stud. 209. For a useful summary in recent times, see Bratton, 'Bond Covenants and Creditor Protection: Economics and Law, Theory and Practice, Substance and Process' (2006) 7 EBOR 39, 46–7. See generally Armour, Hertig and Kanda (n 21) 117.

63 Acharya, Amihud and Litov, 'Creditor Rights and Corporate Risk Taking' (2008) SSRN <http://papers.ssrn.com/sol3/papers.cfm?abstract_id=1085195> accessed 16 January 2017; Kanda, 'Debtholders and Equityholders' (1992) 21 J. Legal Stud. 431, 440–1, 444–5; Kahan, 'The Qualified case Against Mandatory Terms in Bonds' (1995) 89 Nw. U. L. Rev. 565, 609–10; Armour, 'Legal Capital: An Outdated Concept?' (2006) 7 EBOR 5, 21–2. See generally Armour, Hertig and Kanda (n 21) 119.

64 See PART A, Chapter 1, II., 2., b above. See generally Armour, Hertig and Kanda (n 21) 123ff. For the requirement that annual financial statements be audited in South Africa, see s 30 Companies Act 2008.

reaus and the employment of market gatekeepers in the form of credit rating agencies in respect of public companies.[65]

A further common legal strategy that could, in a sense, be seen to respond to all of the above-mentioned problems is mandatory minimum capital requirements,[66] albeit arguably for the limited purpose of indicating to creditors the 'seriousness' of the relevant entrepreneurs in their business ventures, given that the minimum capital initially required will generally have been used up long before the company's financial situation reaches a creditor-harming state.[67] Minimum capital requirements are often supplemented by capital maintenance rules. These broadly take the form of restrictions on so-called distributions and related transactions, such as the distribution of dividends to shareholders[68] and certain measures that must be taken in the event of a capital reduction, such as placing the company into formal insolvency proceedings, as is the case in Germany for example.[69] Capital maintenance rules or in jurisdictions without minimum capital requirements, general restrictions on distributions and related transactions could be seen to address in particular the problem of asset dilution.

A further legal strategy that has the effect of controlling asset dilution is the right of a company to set aside *ex post* certain transactions concluded in the vicinity of insolvency that have the effect of harming creditors.

65 See generally Armour, Hertig and Kanda (n 21) 125, 128ff.

66 In South Africa, mandatory minimum capital requirements and the related capital maintenance regime have been abandoned for a more modern and flexible distribution restrictions and related transactions regime under the Companies Act 2008.

67 Hudson, 'The Limited Liability Company: Success, Failure and Future' (2008) 161 Royal Bank of Scotland Review 26; Eidenmüller, Grunewald and Noack, 'Minimum Capital and the System of legal Capital' in Lutter (ed) *Legal Capital in Europe* (De Gruyter 2006) 1, 25–7. In setting a minimum capital amount, the law needs to balance the need of creditor protection with the need of entrepreneurship; Armour, 'Legal Capital' (n 63) 5. See generally Armour, Hertig and Kanda (n 21) 131.

68 Generally Armour, Hertig and Kanda (n 21) 131ff. For an overview of dividend restriction rules in various jurisdictions, see Cheffins (n 20) 534–5; Fleischer, 'Disguised Distributions and Capital Maintenance in European Company Law in Lutter (ed) *Legal Capital in Europe* (De Gruyter 2006) 94. In South Africa, the system of minimum capital requirements and capital maintenance rules under the Companies Act 1973 was replaced by a system of distribution and financial assistance restrictions coupled with a solvency and liquidity test, see s 44–46 read with s 4 of the Companies Act 2008.

69 §§ 15 and 19 *Insolvenzordnung*. See generally Armour, Hertig and Kanda (n 21) 133ff.

The problem of asset dilution also arises in respect of distressed companies and the applicable legal strategies will be considered in greater detail at bb. below.

The company-creditor conflict and the above-mentioned legal strategies that control such conflict[70] fall outside the scope of this book, as its purpose is the efficient deployment of assets in distressed, rather than solvent, companies.

Company-creditor conflict in distressed companies and its impact on involuntary creditors—In contrast to the creditor-harming actions taken by company controllers in solvent companies, such actions taken in distressed companies do impact on the use of rescue proceedings as a value-maximising option in restructuring a company's assets, and such actions are accordingly relevant for this study. There are broadly two actions that could harm the interests of creditors. One action is when the company controllers continue trading in situations in which the assets of the company actually would have been placed to their highest-value use if the company had been restructured under formal rescue proceedings. The other action is, in a sense, the opposite of the first-mentioned action. Here the company controllers indeed invoke formal rescue proceedings either (i) in a situation in which the assets of the company in fact would have been placed to their highest-value use if the company had been restructured outside formal rescue proceedings or (ii) in a situation in which the assets of the company would have been placed to their highest-value use if the company had been placed under liquidation proceedings. We will consider the two above-mentioned forms of the manager-owner conflict in relation to distressed companies at bb. and cc., respectively.

A final form of company controller opportunism concerns creditors that have claims against the company not on the basis of a contract concluded with the company, but rather as victims of corporate delicts and breaches of regulatory and environmental law committed by the company. Such creditors are often referred to as 'non-adjusting' or 'involuntary' creditors. Company controllers, including those of solvent companies, have a particularly strong incentive to expropriate involuntary creditors. The primary

---

70 Save for the ones that could also arise in the vicinity of insolvency, namely 'asset substitution'. To be sure, the problem of asset dilution may also sometimes arise in respect of distressed companies; however, the legal strategies that ameliorate asset dilution fall outside the scope of this study for other reasons, as indicated below.

sources of this perverse incentive is the general insulation of shareholders from personal liability for delicts and applicable regulatory violations committed by the company. The reason for such insulation of personal liability is the company law doctrine of limited liability and the inability of involuntary creditors to cater for the risk of their exposure to the company *ex ante* due to the absence of a contractual relationship between them and the company. This allows the company controllers to effectively shift the company's costs of compliance with the applicable legal requirements to the victim of its non-compliance, ie, the involuntary creditor. This form of company controller opportunism gives rise to two types of actions that could harm involuntary creditors.

First, company controllers may undercapitalise companies that are at a particular high risk of delictual or regulatory liability claims *ex ante* (referred to by economists as an adverse selection problem) or shift assets out of the company (often to other entities within the same corporate group) after the commission of the delict or regulatory violation *ex post* (referred to by economists as a 'moral hazard' problem).[71]

Second, where a large contingent claim by involuntary creditors arises that could jeopardise the company's continued existence (instances of which have been reported most frequently in the US), company controllers might be tempted to place the company under formal rescue proceedings. The moratorium under such proceedings prevents the enforcement of the claim by the affected involuntary creditor, and since the involuntary creditor is unsecured and would therefore rank last in rescue proceedings, the company is in a position to effectively expropriate the affected involuntary creditor.[72] This second-mentioned problem concerning involuntary creditors could be seen to fall within the company controller opportunism giving rise to value-minimising invocations of formal rescue proceedings, and the general legal strategies employed to protect involuntary creditors will accordingly be discussed in that context.

The fact that the perverse incentive of company controllers is particularly strong in the vicinity of insolvency and in relation to involuntary

71 See generally Bebchuk and Fried, 'The Uneasy Case for the Priority of Secured Claims in Bankruptcy', (1996) 105 Yale L.J. 857; Armour, Hertig and Kanda (n 21) 120–1. For empirical evidence of the 'opting out' of shareholders of claims by involuntary creditors in hazardous industries, see Ringleb and Wiggins, 'Liability and Large-Scale, Long-Term Hazards' (1990) 98 J. Polit. Economy 574.

72 Davies, 'Directors' Creditor-Regarding Duties' (n 57) 305.

creditors justifies the response to such problems by mandatory law, despite its relative costs as compared to contractual self-regulation by the applicable parties.[73]

The legal strategies commonly employed to ameliorate the company-creditor agency problems in the vicinity of insolvency, and to protect involuntary creditors, will be briefly considered when we elucidate these problems generally at bb and cc, respectively and then again in greater detail in PART C.

The role of behavioural economics in explaining value-minimising directorial behaviour in the vicinity of insolvency—The agency theory assumes that value-minimising actions by company controllers in the vicinity of insolvency is based on rational and self-interested behaviour of the agent (ie, the agent is regarded to act as a *homo economicus*). However, research from the field of behavioural economics, particularly in respect of explaining why company controllers frequently delay the invocation of formal insolvency proceedings inefficiently, suggests that this may also result from distortions of perception and psychological biases in judgment of the company controllers. First, company controllers tend to be overly optimistic and resort to wishful thinking in assessing the company's chances of survival.[74] Closely related thereto is an 'overconfidence bias' of company controllers of overestimating the likelihood of survival of the company and, conversely, underestimating the likelihood of failure of the company.[75] Likewise, especially company controllers that have been successful in their careers, frequently overestimate their ability to control events in their lives and their decision-making abilities.[76] Second, company controllers tend to ignore signs that indicate that the company may be in financial difficulties and overestimate information that purportedly confirms their decision that the company is able to trade out of its financial difficulties ('confirmation bias').[77] Third, company controllers tend to take overly excessive risks when it comes to avoiding anticipated losses (in which

73 Armour, Hertig and Kanda (n 21) 119.

74 Klöhn, '§ 15a' in Kirchhof, Eidenmüller and Stürner (eds), *Münchener Kommentar zur Insolvenzordnung* (3rd edn, C.H. Beck 2013) recital 38 and further references cited in n 94.

75 Dickerson, 'A Behavioral Approach to Analyzing Corporate Failures' (2003) 38 Wake Forest L. Rev. 1, 5 and further references cited therein.

76 Ibid.

77 Klöhn (n 74) recital 38 and further references cited in n 95.

case they are referred to as being 'loss averse').[78] And finally, company controllers tend to refuse to accept when they have made a wrong decision and increase their commitments to support it even if it becomes evident that they have made a wrong decision ('escalation of commitments').[79]

Although the field of behavioural economics presents different explanations for the value-minimising actions of company controllers to those provided by the agency theory, both theories appear to generally predict the same type of perverse incentive in relation to the value-minimising actions by company controllers in the vicinity of insolvency. Both theories thus seem to have their place in analysing this form of opportunism.

bb. Value-minimising postponement of formal business rescue proceedings

Company controllers have a perverse incentive to inappropriately delay the invocation of rescue proceedings due to the above-mentioned shift in the risk from shareholders to creditors, which arises when the shareholders' funds have been used up. This perverse incentive will be referred to as the 'risk-shifting incentive'. We will now discuss the three primary manifestations of the risk-shifting incentive.

Value-minimising continued trading and pursuance of risky projects—The first manifestation of the risk-shifting incentive is that the company controllers might simply continue trading inappropriately or actively pursue excessively risky projects. A subtle form of the pursuance of overly risky projects is what we have referred to above as 'asset substitution', namely the sale of assets used for low risk activities and the use of the proceeds for the acquisition of assets used in high risk activities.

The legal strategies in this regard vary according to the system of governance that is used during rescue proceedings. In jurisdictions in which an independent third party replaces the management of the company during formal insolvency proceedings (hereafter, '*management-displacing system of governance*'), a *standards strategy* is generally used in the form of the imposition of liability on directors for delaying the invocation of formal insolvency proceedings *ex post*, as is found in South Africa, the

78 Klöhn (n 74) recital 38 and further references cited in n 96.

79 Klöhn (n 74) recital 38 and further references cited in n 97.

UK, Australia and Germany, for example.[80] By contrast, jurisdictions in which the incumbent managers remain in office during formal rescue proceedings, such as under Chapter 11 proceedings in the US[81] (referred to in the US as 'debtor-in-possession', a term which will, for the sake of convenience, be adopted herein to refer to such governance systems generally) rely primarily on a *reward strategy*.[82] Here the managers (acting as agent for the company's creditors), apart from staying in control of the company during Chapter 11, may place companies under Chapter 11 proceedings

---

80 See the discussion in Chapter 5.

81 11 U.S.C. 1101(1). An independent third party (referred to as a trustee or examiner) may only be appointed in exceptional circumstances; 11 USC § 1104. Examples of jurisdictions that provide for an option that the incumbent management remain in office during rescue proceedings is (i) Germany (referred to as *Eigenverwaltung*), although the incumbent management remains under the supervision of an independent trustee (*Sachverwalter*) (see generally § 270ff Insolvenzordnung) and (ii) Japan (see Armour, Hertig and Kanda (n 21) 146).

82 It should be noted that some States appear to recognise an *ex post* delictual cause of action against company controllers exercising quasi-directorial functions for causing loss to the company as a result of fraudulenty (and possibly also negligently) making the company incur further debt and continuing to trade after it has become insolvent (see, eg, *NCP Litigation Trust v. KPMG*, 945 A.2d 132, 144 (N. J. Super. L. 2007); *In re Norvergence, Inc.*, 2009 WL 1346049 (Bankr. D. New Jersey 2009); *Official Committee of Unsecured Creditors v. Baldwin (In re Lemington Home for the Aged)*, F.3d 2011 WL 4375676 (3d Pa. Cir. 2011); *Official Committee of Unsecured Creditors v. Baldwin (In re Lemington Home for the Aged)*, 777 F.3d 620, 2015 BL 16998 (3d. Cir. 2015). This is referred to as the tort of 'deepening insolvency'. Other States merely recognise deepening insolvency as a theory for calculating damages arising on a separate cause of action, notably directorial breach of fiduciary duties (*In re The Brown Schools*, 386 B. R. 37, 48 (Bankr. D. Del. 2008); *In re Worldwide Wholesale Lumber, Inc.*, 378 B. R. 120, 127 (Bankr. D. S. C. 2007); see also *Thabault v. Chait*, 541 F.3d 512, 523 (3d Cir. 2008) and *Federal Nat. Mortgage Assoc. v. Olympia Mortage Corp.*, 04-CV-4971 (NG MDG), 2014 WL 2594340 (E. D. N. Y. June 10, 2014). However, after the rather rapid development of the cause of action of the deepening insolvency under tort law from its emergence in the 1980s until the early 2000s, it has generally failed to establish itself in practice and some States have even rejected it outright (eg, *Trenwick America Litigation Trust v. Billett*, 931 A.2d 438 (Del. Supr. 2007) 781; *Trenwick America Litigation Trust v. Ernst & Young, LLP* 902 A.2d 168, 204 (Del. Ch. 2006). For an overiew and critical analysis from a comparative perspective, see Frastanlis, *Insolvenzverschleppungshaftung und Gläubigerschutz in der Insolvenzkrise – Ein rechtsvergleichender Blick aus Sicht des deutschen, griechischen und US-amerikanischen Rechts* (unpublished doctoral thesis, copy on file with author, University of Hamburg 2015) 44ff.

when they are still solvent, as there is no entry requirement that the company be close to insolvency. The managers are furthermore entitled to propose a rescue plan in the first 120 days after the commencement of Chapter 11 proceedings, referred to in the US as the 'exclusivity period'.[83] These powers afforded to the managers could be seen to *reward* the shareholders (in whose interests the managers act) for placing the company under Chapter 11 early. This is because it increases the chances that the shareholders maintain their stake in the company after the company emerges from Chapter 11 proceedings,[84] which, in turn, discourages the (shareholder-regarding) managers from embarking on overly risky projects and engaging in asset dilution in the vicinity of insolvency.[85] However, in practice managers are often replaced by persons appointed by secured creditors immediately before or during Chapter 11 proceedings and frequently struggle to find equivalent positions subsequently.[86] Moreover, it seems that an increase in creditor bargaining in respect of distressed companies in recent years has weakened the position of sharehold-

83 11 U.S.C. 1121(b). This period may be extended to 180 days by the court. In Germany, the 'debtor-in-possession' (referred to as '*Eigenverwaltung'*) is entitled to propose a rescue plan for a maximum period of 3 months under the fairly recently introduced reorganisation procedure preceding formal insolvency proceedings (see § 270b(1)(2nd sentence) *Insolvenzordnung*, which is referred to as the '*Schutzschirmverfahren*' (see the explanatory memorandum to the enabling statute, the Act for the Further Facilitation of the Restructuring of Enterprises ('*Gesetz zur weiteren Erleichterung der Sanierung von Unternehmen (ESUG)*', RegE-ESUG, BT-Drucks. 17/5712, 40ff, 70ff)).

84 Weiss, 'Bankruptcy Resolution: Direct Costs and Violation of Priority Claims' (1990) 27 J. Finan. Econ. 285; Franks and Torous, 'An Empirical Investigation of US Firms in Reorganization' (1989) 44 J. Finance 747.

85 Armour, Hertig and Kanda (n 21) 146.

86 LoPucki and Whitford, 'Corporate Governance in the Bankruptcy Reorganisation of Large, Publicly Held Companies' (1993) 141 U.Pa.L.Rev. 669; Gilson, 'Bankruptcy, Boards, Banks, and Blockholders: Evidence on Changes in Corporate Ownership and Control When Firms Default' (1990) 27 J. Finan. Econ. 355, 386; Gilson, 'Management Turnover and Financial Distress' (1989) 25 J. Finan. Econ. 241; Hotchkiss, 'Post-Bankruptcy Performance and Management Turnover' (1995) 50 J. Finance 21; Ayotte and Morrison, 'Creditor Control and Conflict in Chapter 11' (2008) Columbia Law and Economics Research Paper No. 321 <http://ssrn.com/abstract=1081661> accessed 16 January 2017.

ers generally.[87] The prospect that managers might not remain in control during Chapter 11 and propose the rescue plan during the exclusivity period (due to their frequent removal in practice) and the generally declining power of shareholders (due to the increase in creditor bargaining), could well have reduced the effect of the reward to the shareholders in re-balancing the above-mentioned value-reducing actions in the vicinity of insolvency.[88]

Another mechanism that could be seen to curb the perverse incentive in question is the right of creditors to place the company under formal insolvency proceedings, which could be seen as an *initiation rights strategy*. Here the creditors (acting as principals) are entitled to intervene in management decisions, which actually is a mechanism rarely used in company law given the high costs of collective decision-making.[89] The threat of the initiation of formal insolvency proceedings by creditors gives the managers an incentive either to seek to restructure the company outside of formal insolvency proceedings or to place the company under rescue proceedings sooner. In the UK and Australia, secured creditors (so-called 'floating charge-holders') have particularly strong rights in relation to the initiation and control of formal administration, namely that they may appoint an administrator of their choice (in the UK) or insist that the company be managed and the company's assets realised solely in their interest in a procedure designed specifically for that purpose (in Australia).[90] Such strong rights of secured creditors in the UK and Australia is expected to

87 Weiss and Capkun, 'Bankruptcy Resolution: Priority of Claims with the Secured Creditor in Control' (2007) American Law & Economics Association Annual Meetings <http://law.bepress.com/cgi/viewcontent.cgi?article=1929&context=alea> accessed 16 January 2017; Barath, Panchapagesan and Werner, 'The Changing Nature of Chapter 11' (2010) Fisher College of Business Working Paper No. 2008-03-003 <http://ssrn.com/abstract=1102366> accessed 16 January 2017.

88 Armour, Hertig and Kanda (n 21) 146.

89 Such decision-making rights are given to principals only for the most fundamental managerial decisions, such as takeovers, mergers and changes to the constitutional documents of the company and, even in those cases, the shareholders (acting as principals) do not get to make the decision themselves, but rather have the right to ratify the applicable managerial decision *ex post*; Armour, Hansmann and Kraakman, 'Agency Problems' (n 8) 42.

90 For the UK, Insolvency Act 1986, Sch B1, para 26(1); for Australia, s 450A(3) read with s 441A Corporations Act 2001. In Australia, the floating charge-holder's security will typically be over all of the assets of the company and the floating charge-holder (or a receiver on his behalf) will accordingly be entitled to take con-

encourage managers to pursue informal rescue measures outside of the formal rescue procedure to a greater degree than in other rescue regimes that also use a management-displacing system of governance, since in such latter jurisdictions there are no similar rights for secured creditors.[91]

Shareholder loans—The second manifestation of the risk-shifting incentive is the extension of loans from the company's shareholders to the company in the vicinity of insolvency. A shareholder might, from the critical point, be tempted to extend a loan to a distressed company and thereby enable the company to continue trading for longer than it would have been able to, had it not received such a loan. This can be the case even in situations where the company's assets would have been placed to their highest value use if the company had been placed under formal liquidation or rescue proceedings and the reduction in value of the company as a result of its continued trading falls on the company's (unsecured) creditors.[92] As with the pursuance of risky projects in the vicinity of insolvency, the shareholder loan, apart from inappropriately enabling the company to continue trading, may also allow the company to pursue excessively risky projects.[93] However, the shareholder's perverse incentive is counteracted by the fact that he also becomes a creditor (to the extent of the amount of the loan), and, in that capacity, also shares in the downside risk of the company's projects.[94] For reasons that will be set out in Chapter 6 however, the shareholder's percentage share in the upside benefits (as shareholder) generally outweigh his percentage share in the downside risk (as creditor), meaning that his perverse incentive (in relevant circumstances) generally prevails.

Common legal strategies that could be seen to counteract this problem are the automatic subordination of shareholder loans when it is advanced

---

trol of all the assets of the company; Crutchfield, *Annotated Corporate Voluntary Administration Law* (The Law Book Company 1994) 9–10.

91 Armour, Cheffins and Skeel Jr (n 57).

92 Skeel Jr. and Krause-Vilmar, 'Recharacterization and the Non-Hindrance of Creditors' (2006) 7 EBOR 259, 270–1.

93 Ibid. From a German perspective, see Eidenmüller, 'Gesellschafterdarlehen in der Insolvenz' in Heldrich and others (eds), *Festschrift für Claus-Wilhelm Canaris zum 70. Geburtstag Band II* (C.H. Beck 2007) 49, 55–6; Engert, 'Die ökonomische Begründung der Grundsätze ordnungsgemäßer Unternehmensfinanzierung' [2004] ZGR 824, 826.

94 Eidenmüller (n 93) 56; Engert (n 93) 825.

ex ante, as found in Germany and the recharacterisation of shareholder loans as equity by the courts *ex post*, as found in the US.[95]

Asset dilution—The third manifestation of the risk-shifting incentive is an action that we have termed above as 'asset dilution'. This is where the company controllers siphon assets out of the company typically to themselves or 'connected' persons. Unlike with asset substitution and the extension of shareholder loans, when invoking asset dilution, the company controllers do not intend to keep the going concern intact,[96] but rather plan to expedite the company's demise.[97]

Asset dilution is commonly addressed by two legal strategies. One such legal strategy is the imposition of mandatory restrictions on distributions *ex ante* – that is, before the applicable distribution is made. An example of this can be found under the new South African company law regime in the form of the 'solvency and liquidity test',[98] which the board and, in some cases, the shareholders must consider and apply when approving certain transactions that could functionally be regarded as furthering asset dilution. Such transactions include 'distributions' (a term that is widely defined and includes the payment of dividends, payments instead of the

95 See the discussion in Chapter 6.

96 A further instance in which the risk-shifting incentive operates so as to accelerate the arrival of insolvency is in respect of company groups, which will be discussed below.

97 A common variant of asset dilution that is particularly prevalent in the UK, but has apparently not featured in South Africa, is where the company's business is sold as a going concern – often at an undervalue – to a new company controlled by the same directors and trading under the same or a similar name as the transferor company. This is commonly referred to in the UK as the 'Phoenix syndrome'. By using the same name as, or a similar name to, the transferor company, the transferee company exploits the goodwill and business opportunities of the transferor company, while concealing to the public its troubled past. The creditors of the transferor company are deprived of the true value of the company, while the creditors of the transferee company are potentially misled about the transferee company's creditworthiness. The main legal strategy employed in the UK to curb Phoenix trading is the imposition of criminal and civil liability on directors of an insolvent company (including persons who were directors of the insolvent company in the period of 12 months before its insolvency), who become directors of another company with the same or a similar name as the insolvent company within 5 years of the insolvency of the insolvent company (S 216 Insolvency Act 1986). See generally in this regard Davies and Worthington, *Gower and Davies Principles of Modern Company Law* (10th edn, Sweet & Maxwell 2016) paras 9-16ff.

98 The liquidity and solvency test is regulated in s 4 Companies Act 2008.

awarding of capitalisation or treasury shares and payments as consideration for share buy-backs)[99] and the provision of financial assistance to related companies and for purposes of the subscription of the company's shares.[100] This *ex ante* mechanism is reinforced by the imposition on directors of personal liability *ex post*, in the form of civil liability for the failure to vote against a relevant resolution adopted contrary to the legislative requirements, including consideration and application of the solvency and liquidity test.[101]

Another standard legal strategy that could be seen to partially address asset dilution is the recruitment of persons transacting with companies in the vicinity of insolvency as 'gatekeepers' *ex ante*. Such persons have an incentive to monitor the company and the transactions closely, given the risk that their transactions could be set aside during the insolvency of the company *ex post*.[102] Such provisions are often referred to as 'claw-back provisions' in that they allow the office holder to 'claw back' assets that the company had disposed of prior to insolvency.

The type of claw-back provisions in the US and Germany that set aside transactions made by the company to 'insiders', including transactions made to subsidiaries and related companies, and 'persons with a close relationship to the company' address the problem of asset dilution directly.[103] A further type of claw-back provision that has the effect of reducing asset dilution is the one that impugns antecedent transactions made in fraud of creditors.[104]

No doubt, in theory, the problem of asset dilution is relevant to an examination of rescue law since it prevents the efficient allocation of the assets of a company not only in respect of solvent companies, but also in respect of distressed companies. Nevertheless, the legal strategies in this regard will not be examined, since the legal strategies addressing the other

---

99 See s 1 Companies Act 2008.

100 Ss 44–46 read with ss 1 and 4 Companies Act 2008.

101 S 77(3)(e)(iv-vii) Companies Act 2008.

102 On the recruitment of gatekeepers in this context, see Armour, 'Transactions at an Undervalue' (n 61) 46–7; Armour, Hertig and Kanda (n 21) 128ff, 141.

103 For the US, see 11 USC § 548(a)(1). Further requirements are that the debtor must have been 'insolvent' (as defined) when it concluded the transaction. For Germany, see § 133(2) *Insolvenzordung*.

104 For South Africa, see, eg, the common law remedy of *actio Pauliana*. For Germany, see § 133(1) *Insolvenzordnung*. For the UK, see the transactions defrauding creditors under ss 423–425 Insolvency Act 1986.

two problems stemming from the risk-shifting incentive – ie, the pursuance of risky projects and the extension of shareholder loans – are more important in the context of rescue law, and such legal strategies exhaust the scope of this study in relation to the agency conflict outside of formal insolvency proceedings.

Factors determining the intensity of agency problem—There are, broadly speaking, two factors that determine the intensity of company controllers' risk-shifting incentive in the vicinity of insolvency: the management structure during formal rescue proceedings and the ownership structure while the company is still trading. The perverse incentive in relation to the management structure in rescue proceedings would appear to be stronger in rescue laws using a management-displacing governance system. The prospect of company controllers that they would largely relinquish their control over the management of the company to an independent office holder during rescue proceedings gives such company controllers a stronger incentive to take on risky projects in the vicinity of insolvency than under rescue laws that employ a debtor-in-possession governance system.[105]

We have already explained how the second-mentioned factor – the ownership structure of companies – affects agency costs: more dispersed owners have higher monitoring costs and greater information deficits than concentrated owners and are therefore in a weaker position to impose their interests on the managers than concentrated owners.[106]

It has been argued that the interests of managers who hold shares or share options in widely-held companies would, *qua* owners, also participate in the upside benefit of corporate projects and would accordingly, to an extent, also be subject to the risk-shifting incentive.[107] On the other hand, such managers are likely to be poorly diversified, which makes them more risk-averse than (ordinary) shareholders.[108]

Notwithstanding the lower prevalence of the risk-shifting incentive in widely-held companies in which managers hold no shares in general, managers of such companies may nevertheless be tempted to take on risky

105 Davies, 'Directors' Creditor-Regarding Duties' (n 57) 308; Crystal and Mokal (n 53).

106 Armour, Hertig and Kanda (n 21) 117–8.

107 Mokal, *Corporate Insolvency Law-Theory and Application* (Oxford University Press 2005) 289–92.

108 Armour, Hertig and Kanda (n 21) 115, 118 note 10.

projects in the vicinity of insolvency, given that the initiation of formal insolvency proceedings would generally generate significant costs for directors, namely reputational costs and the costs of re-employment.[109] This explains why particularly in management-displacing governance systems of rescue, managers are expected to share some of the shareholders' interest to avoid the onset of formal insolvency proceedings.

A further argument has been advanced that the credit market might, in the long run, reward widely-held companies that appoint directors with a reputation of dealing responsibly with corporate failure. This would enable such companies to obtain debt capital at lower costs in the future, which would ultimately benefit shareholders.[110] It is not clear, however, whether this long-term reward will typically be sufficiently tangible to rebalance the risk-shifting incentive of managers.[111]

One important exception to the general rule that the manager-owner agency problem is stronger in closely-held companies than in widely-held companies, is owner-managed companies. This is because the owner-managers of such companies are likely to be poorly diversified because such managers would likely have invested most, if not all, of their personal funds in such companies. This means that the liability of such owner-managers of their personal assets would no longer be truly limited in the event of the insolvency and such owner-managers would accordingly not be able to focus solely on the upside of corporate projects of the company once their equity has been dissipated. Such liability should make owner-managers more risk-averse in respect of corporate projects in the vicinity of insolvency.[112]

Corporate groups—The company-creditor conflict operates differently in corporate groups than in free-standing companies. First, the identity of the agent is different in corporate groups. Where a subsidiary of a corporate group encounters financial difficulties, it is the parent company's board (rather than the ailing subsidiary's board) that could be seen to act as

---

109 See also Davies, 'Directors' Creditor-Regarding Duties' (n 57) 308. It should be noted, however, that the extent of such costs may depend on legal culture and market dynamics: eg, the entrepreneurially-minded US market may be more forgiving to failed directors than the more liquidation-oriented South African market.

110 Mokal, 'Corporate Insolvency Law' (n 107) 285–8.

111 Davies, 'Directors' Creditor-Regarding Duties' (n 57) 308.

112 Armour, Hertig and Kanda (n 21) 135.

agents of the creditors of the ailing subsidiary. This is because the controllers of the parent company would use their majority stake in the subsidiary and their general control over the group to direct the subsidiary's management.

Second, the parent company's board (acting as agent) are tempted to take a different value-minimising action than in a free-standing company. To be sure, the source of the perverse incentive in corporate groups is, as with free-standing companies, that the risk of continued trading in the vicinity of insolvency falls on the creditors once the shareholders' funds in the distressed subsidiary have evaporated. However, because the economic interest of the company controllers of the holding company is reflected by the performance of the group as a whole, the losses suffered by an individual group entity – or in the worst case, its insolvency – must be seen in the context of the financial health of the group as a whole. Accordingly, it could sometimes make more business sense for the group as a whole that the ailing subsidiary be placed under insolvency proceedings despite the group having sufficient funds to save it.[113] This would, of course, leave the creditors of the ailing subsidiary worse off than the creditors of the other group members.[114]

It should be noted that the agent in a corporate group is tempted to take the opposite action than in a free-standing company: while the agents in a free-standing company are tempted to trade the company out of trouble in situations in which the assets of the company would be placed to their highest value use if the company were restructured during formal insolvency proceedings, in a corporate group context, they are tempted to abandon the ailing subsidiary notwithstanding that the subsidiary might still be economically viable as an autonomous entity.[115]

None of the jurisdictions canvassed appear to tackle the problem where a parent company abandons a subsidiary by means of mandatory law, leaving it to creditors to protect themselves by contract *ex ante*.[116] The rationale for this approach is the difficulties of justifying that the insolvency

113 See Davies and Worthington (n 97) para 9-21.

114 Ibid.

115 Ibid.

116 However, some opportunistic actions in corporate groups that harm minority shareholders and creditors in corporate groups, other than the abandonment of an ailing subsidiary, are commonly addressed by mandatory law. The most common example of such actions is where the parent company instructs the subsidiary to

of a subsidiary, which has complied with the general creditor-protection mechanisms, should be allowed to jeopardise the economic viability of the entire group.[117] Moreover, creditor self-help arguably strikes the balance between the need for creditor protection in a distressed group scenario and the commercial advantages of the doctrine of limited liability with greater sensitivity than mandatory law.

cc. Value-minimising invocation of formal business rescue proceedings

General—As noted above, company controllers might, in certain situations, be tempted to initiate formal rescue proceedings in cases where the assets of the company would in fact have been placed to their highest value use if the company had been restructured outside formal rescue proceedings (hereafter, '*premature entry*'). Company controllers might also be tempted to place a company under formal rescue proceedings in cases where the company would have been placed to their highest value use if

---

pursue projects that are not in its best interests, but which advance the interests of the group as a whole. The general legal approach to this problem among jurisdictions differs between the extension of general company law mechanisms to corporate groups and a set of rules specifically designed to apply to corporate groups, such as the German *Konzernrecht*. According to this, a parent company must indemnify subsidiaries for losses incurred as a result of acting in the group's interests (in respect of a contractual group – *Vertragskonzern*) or the parent must compensate any subsidiary which it causes to act contrary to the subsidiary's own interests (in respect of a *de facto* group – *faktischer Konzern*); see *Drittes Buch, Aktiengesetz*; see generally Emmerich and Habersack, *Konzernrecht* (10th edn, C.H. Beck 2013); Hommelhoff, Hopt and Lutter (eds), *Konzernrecht und Kapitalmarktrecht* (Stämpfli 2001); Armour, Hertig and Kanda (n 21) 140–1. Common company law mechanisms that have been applied to the context of groups are the extension of directorial liability to controlling shareholders through the doctrine of shadow and *de facto* directors, as in the UK (see Armour, Hertig and Kanda (n 21) 138) and the imposition of personal liability on controlling shareholders through piercing of the corporate veil, as under the US doctrine of 'substantive consolidation', which allows the bankruptcy courts to consolidate the assets and liabilities of two related corporations; see, eg, *In Re Augie/Restivio Baking Co* 860 Federal Reporter 2d 506 (2d Cir.1988); see generally Baird, 'Substantive Consolidation Today' (2005) 47 B.C. L. Rev. 5; Mevorach, 'The Appropriate Treatment of Corporate Groups in Insolvency' (2007) 8 EBOR 179; Armour, Hertig and Kanda (n 21) 140.

117 Davies and Worthington (n 97) para 9-21.

the company had been liquidated under liquidation proceedings – namely, where the company is economically distressed, and where, provided the formal rescue procedure permits break-up sales, the costs of such a sale would be lower under liquidation than under rescue proceedings[118] (hereafter, '*the entry of economically distressed companies*'). A further form of the company controller opportunism in question arose under the scheme of arrangement procedure under the previous South African company law regime (and has presumably continued under the current company law regime), which, as we will see below, does not fall within either of the two above-mentioned forms of company controller opportunism, and will therefore be discussed separately.

These three mentioned forms of opportunism will now be considered in greater detail.

Premature entry—Three common features of rescue law are a moratorium in respect of claims against the company that has been placed under rescue proceedings, the ability of such company to withhold the performance of some of its contractual obligations for the duration of the rescue proceedings and the ability of the company to impose the rescue plan on a creditor minority. Although such features are indispensable to rescue law, they could, somewhat ironically, also give rise to the problem of premature entry in certain situations. An example of such a situation is where the company faces a contingent claim, which, although the company might still be technically solvent when such claim arises, would by itself threaten the company's continued existence if such claim were to arise (a phenomenon which has so far most frequently occurred in the US).[119] The same action has also been reported in the Netherlands, where the company is faced with particularly onerous prospective claims under an employee redundancy scheme[120] (which has apparently not yet occurred in any of the jurisdictions that are analysed in this book).

Whether or not the invocation of rescue proceedings in, for example, the above-mentioned situations is value-minimising, and therefore undesirable, is a complex matter and will depend on the particular circum-

118 On the question whether the South African rescue procedure permits break-up sales, see Chapter 4 below.

119 Davies, 'Directors' Creditor-Regarding Duties' (n 57).

120 See Faber and Vermunt, National Report for the Netherlands in Faber, Vermunt and Kilborn (eds), *Commencement of Insolvency Proceedings* (Oxford University Press 2012) 425, 439.

stances of each case. Useful considerations in this regard are the size of the prospective claim against the company; the significance of the threat that the claim poses to the company's continued existence; the number of classes of creditors that would be affected by a potential restructuring outside of formal rescue proceedings (the fewer the number of creditor classes affected, the lower the potential costs of restructuring informally, as this would entail lower bargaining and co-ordination costs); and lastly a comparison of the likely costs of dealing with such threat outside, as opposed to within, formal rescue proceedings. Again, a helpful indicator for this last mentioned consideration is the number and heterogeneity of the company's creditors: the greater the number and heterogeneity of the affected creditors, the higher the costs of bargaining and co-ordination in dealing with the threat outside of formal rescue proceedings, and the greater the likelihood that dealing with the contingent claim within formal rescue proceedings would be value-maximising.[121]

Debtor-in-possession governance systems, such as the US, are, in principle, more vulnerable to the problem of premature entry, given the absence of an entry ground for Chapter 11 filings that requires the company to be close to the state of insolvency.[122] Furthermore, managers are encouraged to file early by the fact that the incumbent management stays in control of the company during Chapter 11 proceedings and the right to propose a rescue plan during the exclusivity period.[123] It is thus not surprising that some of the best-known cases in the literature of premature entry have occurred in the US, for example, the Chapter 11 filings induced by asbestos-related liability claims, a trend that started in the 1980s by the notorious Johns-Manville Corporation case.[124]

---

121 Gilson, John and Lang, 'Troubled Debt Restructurings: An Empirical Study of Private Reorganisations of Firms in Default' (1990) 27 J. Finan. Econ. 315, 354; Asquith, Gertner and Scharfstein, 'Anatomy of Financial Distress: An Examination of Junk Bond Issuers' (1994) 109 Quart. J. Econ. 625, 655; Brunner and Krahnan, 'Multiple Lenders and Corporate Distress: Evidence on Debt Restructuring' (2008) 75 Rev. Econ. Stud. 415. See generally Armour, Hertig and Kanda (n 21) 122–3.

122 However, we will see below that the US makes use of a *standards strategy ex post* to counteract premature entry.

123 However, as we have seen above, such 'rewards' have been undermined by recent developments in practice in respect of distressed companies in the US.

124 *In re Johns-Manville Corp.*, 68 B.R. 618, 634 (Bankr. S.D.N.Y. 1986). See generally Davies, 'Directors' Creditor-Regarding Duties' (n 57) 305.

South Africa, the UK and Australia, on the one hand and the US, on the other hand rely on different legal approaches to control the problem of premature entry. The three first-mentioned jurisdictions rely primarily on a requirement for the entry of companies into rescue proceedings *ex ante*, namely that the company be in a state of impending insolvency (hereafter, '*impending insolvency entry ground*'). The impending insolvency entry ground could be seen to address premature entry to the extent that it often occurs in solvent companies.[125] It seems that the reason for this, from an economics perspective, is that because the company is not in general default of its debt obligations while it is solvent, the resolution of the threatened risk to the company's existence should, in principle, require bargaining by the company with fewer classes of creditors than if the company were in general default. This would mean that the costs of bargaining and negotiation should typically be lower outside formal rescue proceedings than within rescue proceedings, particularly given the relatively high direct and indirect costs of formal rescue proceedings.

There is a risk that the impending insolvency entry ground may not sufficiently re-balance the company controller opportunism in question, particularly where companies have entered rescue proceedings outside a formal court procedure (which is allowed under the South African, British and Australian rescue laws, for example). This is because in such entry route there is no external and independent control of whether this requirement has been met. This risk is mitigated in South Africa and the UK by the *ex ante* effect on the directors' perverse incentive by means of the imposition of civil and criminal sanctions on directors *ex post* for failure to meet the impending insolvency ground.

All three above-mentioned jurisdictions, of course, also provide for the release of the company from rescue proceedings should it be found that the company does not meet the impending insolvency entry ground. As we will see in greater detail in Chapter 7, two primary legal strategies are employed in this regard: the company's claimants are entitled to challenge the invocation of rescue proceedings by the directors *ex post* (which could be seen as a *decision rights strategy*) and the office holder is saddled with duties of investigating the financial affairs of the company and taking rele-

125 However, we will see in Chapter 7 that the company's solvency is not the source of the relevant perverse incentive of the company controllers, which is why the impending insolvency entry ground is ultimately insufficient in controlling the problem of premature entry.

vant steps where he finds that the company does not meet the impending insolvency entry ground (which could be seen as a *trusteeship strategy*).

In contrast to the above-mentioned approach of the three jurisdictions in question, in the US, the problem of premature entry is addressed by the power of the court to dismiss strategic Chapter 11 filings *ex post*, on the grounds that such filings were not made in good faith. Since one of the general policies of Chapter 11 is to encourage companies to utilise such procedure[126] (which is evidenced, for example, by the fact that the incumbent management stays in control of the company during Chapter 11 proceedings and that there are no entry requirements), it is not surprising that the legal intervention in this regard has come from the courts.

In relation to the above discussed problem faced by involuntary creditors, the legal strategy that is adopted by a number of jurisdictions in Europe and Japan, but apparently not in South Africa, is the imposition of mandatory insurance schemes on companies operating in particularly hazardous industries, which face a particularly high risk of committing applicable delictual or regulatory liability. This is often supplemented by requirements that allow the victim of the liability to claim directly from the insurance company on the insolvency of the company that has committed the delict or violated the regulatory requirements.[127] Together, these legal mechanisms prevent the company controllers from shifting the costs of relevant violations to the involuntary creditors, and instead placing such costs on the companies committing the relevant violations. Further legal strategies that lie within corporate insolvency law and company law have been proposed in academic writing, most notably the giving of priority of involuntary creditors over other unsecured creditors in the insolvency of the company[128] and the imposition of personal liability on shareholders for delictual liability of companies (which is, in effect, an instance of piercing the corporate veil).[129] We will not elaborate on the above-mentioned legal strategies that protect involuntary creditors. The reader is encouraged to

126 Armour, Hertig and Kanda (n 21) 146.

127 Ibid 121.

128 Leebron, 'Limited Liability, Torts Victims, and Creditors' (1991) 91 Colum. L. Rev. 1565; Finch, 'Security, Insolvency and Risk: Who Pays the Price? (1999) 62 MLR 633, 657.

129 Hansmann and Kraakman, 'Toward Unlimited Shareholder Liability for Corporate Torts' (1991) 100 Yale L.J. 1879; Mendelson, 'A Control-Based Approach to Shareholder Liability' (2002) 102 Colum. L. Rev. 1203. See generally Armour, Hertig and Kanda (n 21) 120–1.

consult the applicable literature cited above for further reading on that topic.

Entry of economically distressed companies—Company controllers may also be tempted to place companies under rescue proceedings (rather than under liquidation proceedings) when such companies are 'economically distressed'[130] for two main reasons. First, the financial state of an economically distressed company is likely to have deteriorated to a degree where rescue measures outside of formal insolvency proceedings may no longer be feasible. Second, just as company controllers may tend to be overly optimistic in respect of the chances of the company's survival,[131] they may likewise often tend to be overly optimistic about the chances of a turnaround of the company; the literature refers to such company controllers as being 'hard-wired for optimism'.[132] It would appear that company controllers of owner-managed companies who have invested most of their personal funds in the company and would in the event of the liquidation of the company lose a larger percentage of their total assets than directors of widely-held companies, would be particularly amenable to this irrational optimism.

As with the problem of premature entries, there is a smaller risk of entries of economically distressed companies in management-displacing, than in debtor-in-possession, rescue regimes.

The standard response to the entry of economically distressed companies in South Africa and the UK (but not in Australia), is the provision of an entry ground *ex ante* requiring that there be a prospect that the company meet the prescribed objectives of rescue (hereafter, the '*economic distress entry ground*').[133] At the stage when the company commences for-

130 The term of 'economic distress' was explained in the text to n 53 above.

131 See the discussion in text to n 74 above.

132 Damodaran, *The Dark Side of Valuations: Valuing Young, Distressed and Complex Business* (2nd edn, Financial Times Press 2010) cited in Harvey, 'The valuation of a business facing distress or decline' in Harvey (ed), *Turnaround Management and Corporate Renewal – A South African Perspective* (Wits University Press 2011) 180, 186. Although this state of 'irrational optimism' is specifically mentioned in the context of the valuation of businesses that are in distress (where it leads to an overvaluation of such businesses), it seems that such irrational optimism could equally apply to the way in which company controllers assess the chances of their companies in distressed situations.

133 For South Africa, see s 129(1)(a) read with s 128(1)(b) and (h) Companies Act 2008; for the UK, see Insolvency Act 1986, Sch B1, para 29(3)(b).

mal rescue proceedings, this determination must be made by the board of directors (by way of a board resolution) in South Africa and by the administrator (by way of a public statement) in the UK.[134]

As with the premature entry problem, South Africa, the UK and Australia provide for both *ex post* challenges to the commencement of rescue proceedings where the company does not meet the objectives of rescue (which makes up the economically distressed entry ground) and whether, therefore, rescue proceedings should be converted to liquidation proceedings (which is a *decision rights strategy*). It thus imposes a duty on the office holder to investigate whether the same scenario exists and take the appropriate measure (which is a *trusteeship strategy*).

As with the problem of premature entries, the US addresses the entry of economically distressed companies with the judge-made good faith requirement *ex post*.

Predictably, all the above-mentioned jurisdictions provide that rescue proceedings be converted to liquidation proceedings if the company is found to be economically distressed on the economic distress entry ground, however, as we will see in Chapter 7, the person in which the power vests differs in some of these jurisdictions.[135]

The risk of the appointment of a 'friendly' office holder—In rescue regimes that use a management-displacing system of governance, the effectiveness of the above-mentioned legal strategies addressing the perverse incentive of company controllers that gives rise to the two types of value-minimising invocations of formal rescue proceedings could be undermined by the risk that directors appoint an office holder who is related, or sympathetic, to the directors or the shareholders of the company.

The standard legal strategies relied on in the applicable jurisdictions are (i) relevant *ex ante* minimum qualification requirements that relate generally to office holders' independence of, *inter alia*, the shareholders and directors of the company; (ii) duties of disclosure of office holders of their independence *ex ante* (with both ((i) and (ii)) being supplemented by applicable *ex post* sanctions for non-compliance with such requirements);

---

134 However, unlike with the impending insolvency entry ground, neither South Africa nor the UK imposes *ex post* sanctions on the decision-takers as to whether the company meets the economic distress entry ground.

135 For South Africa, s 130(5) Companies Act 2008; for the UK, Insolvency Act 1986, Sch B1, para 83(1)(a) and (b); for Australia, s 446A Corporations Act 2001; for the US, 11 USC § 1112.

(iii) and the *ex post* removal of office holders, *inter alia*, in situations where the office holder is unable to exercise independent and unfettered judgment.

Specific form of abuse under the previous South African scheme of arrangement—A practice emerged under the South African scheme of arrangement procedure under the Companies Act 1973 where a third party would acquire the claims of all existing creditors of the company mainly for purposes of using the assessed loss of the company for tax purposes. The acquirer ordinarily bought the claims of the existing creditors at an undervalue. Moreover, after the release of the company from the scheme of arrangement he refrained from restoring the company's profitability and solvency, while continuing to extend credit to trade creditors on terms that were unfavourable to them in light of the company's reduced creditworthiness; in economic terms, this is referred to as an adverse selection problem.

Because the acquirer of the company's debt was often either an existing shareholder or was connected to the company and typically became the sole shareholder of the company after the implementation of the scheme, he could in a sense be seen as a company controller. Accordingly, the company, acting through the acquirer, could be seen to act as the agent of the existing creditors (in relation to the undervalue acquisition of their debt claims) and acting as agent for the new creditors in the post-scheme period (in relation to the adverse selection problem). Since under this form of the scheme the acquirer used the scheme for purposes of extracting value from both the existing creditors and the new creditors for himself, it could be seen as a value-reducing abuse of a formal rescue procedure.

b. Inter-creditor agency conflict outside formal insolvency proceedings

Under the creditor-harming actions by company controllers discussed above, the creditors' relationship to the company is that of a contractual counterparty. However, once the company defaults on its debts generally, and assuming that at that stage, as is common in practice, the equity of the company has evaporated, the creditors become entitled by virtue of their contractual rights to determine the distribution of the company's assets. In other words, the creditors become – in a functional rather than a legal sense – the 'owners' of the company's assets.[136] Once the creditors' role changes from being a contractual counterparty of the company to becoming the 'owners' of the company's assets, the company-creditor conflict, in principle, changes to a conflict between different classes of creditors essentially over the distribution of the company's assets.[137]

The two classes of creditors that generally stand on opposite sides of the inter-creditor conflict are secured creditors and unsecured creditors.[138] As under the analogous majority-minority conflict in solvent companies, the source of the perverse incentives of the secured creditors (acting as agent) and the unsecured creditors (acting as principal) is that the secured creditors generally have better information than the unsecured creditors of the relevant facts in relation to the enforcement of their claims. The reason for this information advantage is twofold. First, secured creditors have a stronger incentive to monitor the company than unsecured creditors, given that their claims generally make up a higher percentage of their total investments compared to those of unsecured creditors. And second, secured creditors' monitoring costs are lower than those of unsecured creditors, given that secured creditors typically have fewer debtors to monitor than unsecured creditors.[139]

This information advantage gives secured creditors a perverse incentive to take certain actions that place them in a better position than unsecured creditors in relation to the recovery of the outstanding claims of such creditors against the debtor-company. Such opportunistic actions fall into two broad categories, depending on whether they are taken outside formal insolvency proceedings or consist of the choice of placing the company un-

136 Triantis, 'The Interplay between Liquidation and Reorganization in Bankruptcy: The role of screens, gatekeepers, and guillotines' (1996) 16 Int. Rev. Law Econ. 101; Baird and Rasmussen, 'Control Rights, Property Rights and the Conceptual Foundations of Corporate Reorganizations' (2001) 87 Va. L. Rev. 921; Rasmussen, 'Secured Debts, Control Rights and Options' (2004) 25 Cardozo L. Rev. 1935. See generally Armour, Hertig and Kanda (n 21) 115–6, 121.

137 Armour, Hertig and Kanda (n 21) 116.

138 The term 'unsecured creditors' is used here to include all persons with (debt) claims against the company that are not secured regardless of whether the insolvency law prefers some unsecured creditors over others, eg, employees and the State in relation to tax claims against the debtor-company.

139 Armour and Frisby, 'Rethinking Receivership' (2001) 21 ojls 73, 82ff. These reasons are, in principle, the same as for the information advantage of concentrated owners compared to dispersed owners of solvent companies discussed above.

der a particular insolvency proceeding. Under the first-mentioned category, secured creditors might seek to utilise their information advantage to either enforce on their claims in preference to the claims of unsecured creditors[140] or ensure that their position would be safeguarded during formal insolvency proceedings (for example, by taking security over existing debt).[141] (This category of actions will hereafter be referred to as '*enforcement enhancing actions/transactions*'.)

Under the second-mentioned category of opportunistic actions secured creditors generally use their rights to initiate formal insolvency proceedings (which is allowed under most jurisdictions) to favour one insolvency procedure over the other in a value-diminishing fashion (hereafter, '*preferred procedure actions*'). This perverse incentive arises because of the contractual hierarchy of creditors' claims which are reinforced in formal insolvency proceedings, on the one hand and the different goals of the two main insolvency proceedings, namely liquidation and rescue proceedings, on the other hand. The claims of secured creditors generally either fall outside of the collective distributional regime of, or rank ahead of all the other creditors' claims during, insolvency proceedings. The objective of liquidation proceedings is typically a swift fire sale of the company's assets, while the rescue procedure typically aims at the reorganisation of the company's capital structure (hereafter, simply '*reorganisation*') or the sale of the company as a going concern. There is thus a smaller risk that the collateral of the secured creditors will be exposed to changing trading conditions under liquidation proceedings than under rescue proceedings. This explains their general preference for liquidation over rescue proceedings.[142] However, this preference of secured creditors for placing a company under liquidation proceedings rather than rescue proceedings is value-diminishing if the company's assets are worth more kept together than broken up – that is, where the company is 'economically viable'.[143]

---

140 See, eg, Walters, 'Preferences' in Armour and Bennett (eds), *Vulnerable Transactions in Corporate Insolvency* (Hart Publishing 2003) 123, para 4.22.

141 Wood, *Principles of International Insolvency* (2nd edn, Sweet & Maxwell 2007) para 17-057.

142 Armour and Mokal (n 36).

143 Crystal and Mokal (n 53). See also Roe, 'Bankruptcy and Debt: A Model for Corporate Reorganization' (1983) 83 Colum. L. Rev. 527; Bebchuk, 'A New Approach to Corporate Reorganizations' (1988) 101 Harv. L. Rev. 775. The principal-agent conflict between different classes of creditors could also be reversed. To the extent that unsecured creditors and constituents other than contractual or

There are, broadly speaking, four types of legal strategies that address the above-mentioned value-reducing actions that arise as a result of secured creditors opportunism. The first type is the 'claw-back' by companies located in formal insolvency proceedings of transactions concluded in the vicinity of insolvency that favoured one creditor over the general body of creditors (hereafter, '*preferential claw-back provisions*'). Such provisions are found in all jurisdictions examined.[144] The preferential

---

involuntary creditors, such as employees, are entitled to trigger liquidation or rescue proceedings, such persons could be seen to act as agents of the general body of creditors. In contrast to secured creditors, unsecured creditors and employees would favour rescue proceedings over liquidation proceedings. In relation to unsecured creditors, this is because they have everything to gain from rescue proceedings and everything to lose from liquidation proceedings, given that rescue holds out the prospect of a higher recovery of their claims than they would receive in a liquidation. Employees would likewise generally favour rescue over liquidation to the extent that employees' rights are generally stronger under rescue proceedings compared to liquidation proceedings, as is the case, eg, in South Africa. A further important advantage of rescue over liquidation for employees is the possibility that a reorganisation can be pursued under rescue proceedings, which would provide employees with a prospect of retaining their jobs. The preference of unsecured creditors and employees of rescue over liquidation would be value-diminishing if the company was economically distressed. However, the danger that unsecured creditors and employees would place economically distressed companies into rescue proceedings is minimal in practice, given that such constituents generally lack the necessary information to determine that the company is eligible to be placed under formal insolvency proceedings. Moreover, since none of the jurisdictions examined in this study allow the commencement of rescue proceedings by such constituents outside formal court proceedings, the prospect of court scrutiny would appear to operate as a significant deterrent for such actions.

144 For South Africa, ss 29 and 30 Insolvency Act 1936; for the UK, s 239 Insolvency Act 1986; for the US, eg, 11 USC § 547; for Australia, s 565 Corporations Act 2001; for Germany, §§ 130, 131 *Insolvenzordnung*. For a different justification of such claw-back provisions (as well as the taking of security over pre-existing debt in the vicinity of Insolvency, which is sometimes referred to as '*Rückschlagsperre*' under German law (§ 88 *Insolvenzordung*), see Grünewald, *Mehrheitsherrschaft und insolvenzrechtliche Vorauswirkung in der Unternehmenskrise* (Mohr Siebeck 2015) 358ff. He argues that these provisions are justified on the basis of the pre-insolvency application ('*insolvenzrechtliche Vorauswirkung*') of a duty of loyalty ('*Treuepflicht*') or, more precisely, a binding obligation ('*Pflichtbindung*') as between creditors which is based on the principle of equal treatment of creditors ('*Gläubigergleichbehandlung*') and the safeguarding of the relative weighting of interests of creditors ('*Wahrung der relativen Interessengewichte*') within a group of creditors ('*Gruppensituation*').

claw-back provisions constitute an *ex post standards strategy*, insofar as particular enforcement enhancing transactions may be set aside *ex post* (usually in the debtor-company's insolvency) according to general legal standards, the chief one being that the transaction must be shown to have benefitted the creditor concerned.[145]

The second legal mechanism is the imposition of personal liability *ex post* on creditors (usually banks) found to have influenced directorial decision-making to favour their interests at the expense of the other creditors. This mechanism also constitutes an *ex post standards strategy*. The general approach in the UK (and possibly also South Africa) is the extension of directorial liability to lenders in certain instances to the extent that the banks are found to have acted as *de facto* or 'shadow' directors.[146] A further approach relied on in both these countries is the explicit statutory extension of liability to 'any person' (which would include creditors) found liable for carrying on the company's business with the intent to defraud the general body of creditors.[147] Germany, on the other hand, imposes liability on banks primarily through the extension of delictual liability to an accessory (§§ 830, 840 *BGB* – '*Teilnehmerhaftung*')[148] and on the intentional damage to another contrary to public policy under (§ 826 *BGB* –

---

145 Jurisdictions differ, however, first, as to whether the creditor favoured by the transaction needs to act in bad faith, which is required in Germany, but not, eg, in the US and the UK; and second, whether merely the effect of the transactions improves the creditor's position (eg, in the US). Other jurisdictions require an intention of the *company* to favour the creditor (eg, the UK, South Africa (in relation to 'voidable preferences' under s 30 Insolvency Act 1936) and Australia). South Africa requires, in a separate provision, that the transaction was not in the ordinary course of business ('undue preferences') under s 29 Insolvency Act 1936).

146 For the UK, see ss 214(7) and the definition of 'director' in s 251 Insolvency Act 1986, s 251 Companies Act 2006. For South Africa, see R Cassim, 'Governance and the Board of Directors' in FHI Cassim (man. ed), *Contemporary Company Law* (2nd edn, Juta 2012) 372, 375–6; Idensohn, 'The Regulation of Shadow Directors' (2010) 22 SA Merc LJ 326. See further the discussion in the context of the directors' creditor-regarding statutory duties at PART C, Chapter 5, II., 1., a. below.

147 For the UK, see s 213 Insolvency Act 1986; *Morris v Bank of India* [2005] 2 Butterworths Company Law Cases 328. For South Africa, see s 214(1)(c) Companies Act 2008.

148 §§ 830, 840 *BGB*. See generally Steffek (n 21) 507.

'*sittenwidrige vorsätzliche Schädigung*')[149] under the general civil law statutory rules.[150]

The third legal mechanism is an *ex post reward strategy* found in the strong rights given to specific types of secured creditors, namely the floating charge-holders, to control insolvency proceedings in the UK. Accordingly, as briefly mentioned before,[151] floating charge-holders in the UK are encouraged to place a company under formal insolvency proceedings by means of their right to appoint an administrator out-of-court, without having to demonstrate the entry grounds.[152] Moreover, where any other party with standing to apply for the commencement of administration proceedings intends to appoint an administrator, the floating charge-holder has to be notified and has the opportunity to appoint an administrator of its choice.[153]

Here the floating charge-holder (acting as the agent) is effectively *rewarded ex post* for transferring the resolution of the inter-creditor conflict to formal rescue proceedings (where such conflicts can arguably be resolved more effectively), by granting the floating charge-holder greater control over the formal rescue proceedings. The effect of this incentive given to floating charge-holders to invoke formal insolvency proceedings timeously is that it reduces the risk that they will embark on enforcement advancing and preferred procedure actions in the vicinity of insolvency.[154]

---

149 Hopt, 'Bankgeschäfte' in Hopt (ed), *Baumbach/Hopt Handelsgesetzbuch Kommentar* (36th edn, C.H. Beck 2014) recitals G6, G31–2.

150 Grünewald (n 144) 366 proposes a further *ex post standards strategy* under German law in the form of liability for the breach of a duty of loyalty ('*Treuepflicht*') or, more precisely, a binding obligation ('*Pflichtbindung*') owed by creditors to each other which is imposed particularly on creditors with a contractually and structurally strong bargaining power, such as major creditors and strategic investors, for exercising their bargaining power in disregard of the principle of equal treatment of creditors ('*Gläubigergleichbehandlung*') and the safeguarding of the relative weighting of interests of creditors ('*Wahrung der relativen Interessengewichte*') during negotiations in the vicinity of insolvency or within the debtor-in-possession reorganisation procedure preceding formal insolvency proceedings under § 270b I*nsolvenzordnung* (which is referred to as the '*Schutzschirmverfahren*') in preparation of formal rescue or insolvency proceedings.

151 See text to n 90 above.

152 Insolvency Act 1986, Sch B1, para 35(2)(a).

153 Insolvency Act 1986, Sch B1, para 12, 26, 36.

154 However, the control rights of floating charge-holders during formal rescue proceedings could transfer the inter-creditor agency problems to the formal rescue

The final legal strategy which counteracts specifically preferred procedure actions by secured creditors is that liquidation proceedings are sometimes allowed to be converted to rescue proceedings by the court either of its own accord, or upon application by creditors.[155] Where the court converts liquidation proceedings to rescue proceedings of its own accord, the conversion is best described as a *trusteeship strategy*, as the courts (acting as trustee) is largely driven by low-powered incentives in safeguarding the interests of the principal. By contrast, where the conversion is instigated by a court application by individual claimants, it constitutes a *veto* or *ratification strategy*, to the extent that the decision under which insolvency forum the company should be placed constitutes a management decision. The possibility of conversion allows economically viable companies that have been placed under liquidation proceedings opportunistically to be moved to the more value-enhancing rescue proceedings for economically viable companies.

To be sure, the inter-creditor conflict in the vicinity of insolvency affects the efficient deployment of the assets of distressed companies in the vicinity of insolvency, and would therefore, in principle, be relevant for our analysis. Nevertheless, the legal strategies that mitigate the inter-creditor conflict in the vicinity of insolvency will not be the primary focus of this study. This is because it is thought that there is a greater risk of the generation of company-creditor agency costs than inter-creditor agency costs in the vicinity of insolvency, and the scope of this study is already exhausted by an analysis of the legal strategies reducing the former. The reason for the lower risk of inter-creditor-generating agency costs is that secured creditors would generally have to act through the company's management, at least in respect of the above-mentioned enforcement enhancing actions, and the interests of directors are generally not aligned with secured creditors.

---

procedure. We will consider the inter-creditor conflict during rescue proceedings further below in this Chapter. In Australia, floating charge-holders are entitled to 'bypass' the collective procedure by their right to realise their claims without regard for other creditors' interests in a separate procedure designed for that purpose (see text to n 90 above).

155 See, eg, in South Africa, liquidation proceedings may be converted to rescue proceedings either by 'affected persons' (which comprise creditors, employees, trade unions and shareholders) by means of court application or by the court of its own accord (s 129(6) and (7) Companies Act 2008).

In saying that, the legal strategies that specifically curb the preferred procedure actions by secured creditors, such as the conversion of winding-up proceedings to rescue proceedings and, to a certain degree, the *reward strategy* found in the UK and Australia in relation to the floating charge-holders, will be touched upon where appropriate, since such mechanisms are located squarely within rescue law and are sufficiently limited in scope. To the extent that the statutory creditor-regarding directorial duties are extended to banks, they will also be mentioned briefly in that context.

c. The office holder-creditor conflict during business rescue proceedings

As indicated above, the manager-owner conflict arises in an analogous form in rescue proceedings. Here the office holder (in management-displacing rescue regimes) or the incumbent management (in debtor-in-possession rescue regimes) acts as agent for the body of claimants of the company. Since the equity of a company is likely to be wiped out once it has been placed under rescue proceedings, the claimants of the company generally comprise creditors and employees.[156]

The governance structure of putting the decision-making of the company in the hands of a few specialists is used in rescue proceedings for the same reason as in companies outside of rescue proceedings: it reduces the cost of decision-making.[157] As under the owner-manager conflict outside of insolvency proceedings, the office holder, often with the assistance of the incumbent directors (in management-displacing rescue regimes), and the incumbent management (in debtor-in possession rescue regimes) are likely to have an information advantage over creditors, giving them an incentive to shirk on the quality of their performance promised to the creditors.[158]

The main concern in rescue law, as is the case in company law, is thus to ensure that the office holder is accountable to the body of creditors, par-

156 Armour and Mokal (n 36).

157 This is largely as a result of the directors' expertise and lower costs of resolving disagreement; Armour and Mokal (n 36). The principal sources of the costs of resolving disagreement are so-called 'free riding' and 'holdout' behaviour; see Easterbrook and Fischel (n 18) Ch 12.

158 Armour and Mokal (n 36).

ticularly in respect of the office holders' competence and efficiency.[159] Obvious legal strategies to this end are the office holder's duties (in management-displacing governance systems) and the creditors' rights to participate in the development of the rescue proposal, usually through creditors' committees. Due to the large scope of the company-creditor agency problems in the vicinity of insolvency, the office holder-creditor conflict will not be examined in this study.

d. The inter-creditor conflict during business rescue proceedings

The inter-creditor conflict during rescue proceedings is an analogous form of the majority-minority shareholder conflict in companies outside of insolvency proceedings. In solvent companies, the majority-minority conflict generally arises where the majority owners are able to dictate the way in which the company is run, primarily through appointing themselves or connected persons to the board, and in doing so, expropriating the minority shareholders.[160]

As already explained, upon a general default by the company (and, therefore, typically also in rescue proceedings), the creditors of the company replace the shareholders as the residual claimants, and thus, in a functional sense, as the 'owners' of the company. As under the inter-creditor conflict in the vicinity of insolvency, in rescue proceedings, the conflict is between the different classes of creditors – generally between secured creditors and unsecured creditors. In deviation from the analogous majority-minority shareholder conflict, however, the inter-creditor conflict is specifically over how the assets of the company should be deployed (ie, between reorganisation and a going concern sale) and given the scarce resources of the company and the time constraints within which the rescue objectives need to be implemented, how long the office holder should spend pursuing the favoured option.[161] The length of time spent on pursuing a rescue objective could be relevant for both classes of creditors: for secured creditors, insofar as changing trading conditions could affect the value of the company's assets encumbered by the security; for unsecured

159 Ibid.

160 See generally Armour and Mokal (n 36); Armour, Hansmann and Kraakman, 'Agency Problems' (n 8) 36.

161 Armour and Mokal (n 36).

creditors, insofar as the costs of the proceedings and any further trading losses while the company is in formal rescue proceedings usually rank above unsecured creditors' claims in rescue proceedings, meaning that such costs and losses will primarily fall on them.

A further difference to the analogous majority-minority conflict in solvent companies is that one class of creditors is able to shape the management of the company during rescue proceedings. It could do so not by the appointment of themselves or representatives to the management organ of the company,[162] but rather by various other, more indirect, measures. One is the degree of involvement in the development of the rescue proposal. Secured creditors are generally in a stronger position than other classes of creditors to exert influence over the office holder for two primary reasons: (i) due to pre-commencement monitoring of the company (which, in turn, is due to low monitoring costs),[163] they have better information about the company than other classes of creditors and (ii) since secured creditors are generally fewer in number than other classes of creditors, they can impose their interests on the management of the company at lower co-ordination costs.[164]

The other way in which influence could be exerted over the office holder is through having a strong bargaining position during rescue proceedings. This could be due to superior rights afforded mostly to secured creditors by rescue law itself, such as the ability of secured creditors to vote the secured portion of their claim against the company under the South

---

162 However, an exception to this can be found in Australia (and before the far-reaching changes brought about by the Enterprise Act in 2002, also the UK). Under the Australian rescue procedure, a secured creditor holding a security interest (usually made up of a mixture of fixed and floating charges) over the whole, or substantially the whole, of the property of the company is allowed, within 13 business days of the beginning of voluntary administration, to appoint a representative (referred to as 'receiver or controller'). It is the duty of such representative to realise the company's assets in the sole interest of the secured creditor (see ss 441A and 442D read with the definition of 'decision period' in s 9 and Pt 5.2 Corporations Act 2009). Indeed, the secured creditor is able to exercise even greater control over the management of the company during voluntary administration than majority shareholders over the management in solvent companies. This is becaus the receiver and controller owes his duties solely to the secured creditor, while directors owe their duties to the shareholders generally, and not specifically to the majority shareholder.

163 See text to n 139 above.

164 Armour and Frisby (n 139).

African rescue procedure[165] or the super-preference status afforded to post-commencement secured finance in the US,[166] which is often provided by existing secured creditors. The strong bargaining position could also arise due to the enforcement of pre-commencement contractual terms.

Since the inter-creditor conflict does not, unlike in solvent companies, generally arise as a result of the right to appoint the persons to the management organ of the company (with the effect that in solvent companies the manager-owner conflict often morphs into a majority-minority owner conflict),[167] it is more common for the inter-creditor conflict and the practitioner-company conflict to exist alongside each other. This is in contrast with the equivalent manager-owner and majority-minority conflict in solvent companies, which are mutually exclusive.

The primary reason for the conflict between the different classes of creditors is – as indicated in respect of the perverse incentive of secured creditors in the inter-creditor conflict outside insolvency proceedings – differences in risk profiles of the different classes of creditors in respect of the means of asset deployment. This typically depends on the extent of the 'economic' interest of a class of creditors in the assets of the company at a particular time in such company's financial decline.[168] Accordingly, given that the claims of secured creditors are generally either excluded from, or rank highest in, rescue proceedings, secured creditors would favour the option that would ensure that their collateral is realised as swiftly as possible to prevent it from being exposed to changing trading conditions.[169] This explains why secured creditors would generally favour a going concern sale over a reorganisation of the company's assets.[170] By the same token, since security agreements are generally upheld in rescue proceedings, they do not, in the first instance, carry the risk of the failure

165 By virtue of s 145(4)(a) Companies Act 2008.

166 11 USC § 364(c). See generally, Skeel Jr, 'The Past, Present and Future of Debtor-in-Possession Finance' [2004] Cardozo L.Rev. 1905.

167 Armour, Hansmann and Kraakman, 'Agency Problems' (n 8) 36.

168 See text to nn 142 and 143 above.

169 Armour and Mokal (n 36).

170 This is particularly so where the value of the collateral is higher than the claims of the secured creditors (ie, where the secured creditor is over-secured). In saying that, where the secured creditor is 'under-secured', the risk of a further reduction in value of the collateral in a reorganisation and, to a lesser extent, a going concern sale would mean that the secured creditor may well still favour the option which realises its collateral the quickest.

of a rescue attempt. One consequence of this is that the direct costs of rescue proceedings do not, in the first instance, fall on the secured creditors.

The incentive of unsecured creditors in respect of the deployment of assets differs from that of secured creditors because the claims of unsecured creditors rank lowest in rescue proceedings. The preferred method of asset deployment in rescue proceedings of unsecured creditors depends on the extent of their 'economic interest' in the company. Typically, the 'fire-sale' value or 'liquidation' value of a company placed under rescue proceedings would be lower than the sum of all claims against the company or, in the worst case, would not cover the claims of unsecured creditors. A class of unsecured creditors would have an 'economic interest' in the company to the extent that the liquidation value of the company exceeds the claims of such class of creditors. The one end of the scale is where the class of unsecured creditors has no economic interest in the company (ie, where the claims of that class of creditors are not covered by the liquidation value of the company).[171] Here the class of unsecured creditors bears no risk of the failure of a rescue attempt and, accordingly, would favour reorganisation over a going concern sale, given that this option holds out the prospect of the 'resurrection' of the claims of that class of creditors.

Where the economic interest of a class of creditors is somewhere between the two extremes, the incentive structure is as follows: the lower the economic interest of a class of creditors (ie, the smaller the difference between the claims of that class of creditors and the company's liquidation value), the more it can look to the upside benefits of a reorganisation; by contrast, the higher the economic interests of a class of unsecured creditors (ie, the bigger the difference between the claims of that class of creditors and the company's liquidation value), the higher the downside risk of a reorganisation (in particular, its higher costs compared to a going concern sale),[172] and the higher the upside benefits of a going concern sale.[173]

171 The opposite end of the scale – ie, where the liquidation value of the company fully covers the claims of that class of unsecured creditors – is not relevant in this context, given that in such a case the company would be solvent.

172 The costs of the proceedings – which usually have a super-preference over unsecured creditors' claims – and any further trading losses while the company is in formal rescue proceedings will diminish the economic interest of unsecured creditors even further.

173 For the same principle, see Baird and Jackson, 'Corporate Reorganisations and the Treatment of Diverse Ownership Interests: A Comment on Adequate Protection of Secured Creditors in Bankruptcy' (1984) 51 U. Chi. L. Rev. 97, 106ff. The

On the other hand, the incentive of employees in respect of the objectives of rescue cannot be fully explained by the likely return of their claims, given that employees also have non-monetary interests in the company. Employees are expected to generally favour a reorganisation over a going concern sale as this increases the chances of the retention of their jobs and, at the same time, reduces the chances of relocation, which employees may have an interest to avoid due to non-financial interests, such as emotional and social attachments to the location of the company in which they work.[174] Given that such non-financial considerations are not attributed to a rational actor in the principal-agent model, the economic analysis of law has its limitations in explaining the incentive structure of employees in this regard.

Under most modern corporate insolvency procedures employees are provided with stronger protection than general unsecured creditors. We will consider possible justifications for this at III. below.

Although it has become clear from the above discussion on the incentive structures of the three major types of creditors that all three types of creditors could have a perverse incentive in respect of the deployment of the company's assets, we have also seen earlier that it is secured creditors that are in the strongest position to implement their perverse incentive.[175]

The standard legal strategy that controls the conflict over the deployment of the company's assets is the statutory hierarchy of the rescue objectives (ie, a *rules-based strategy ex ante*), which is reinforced by relevant office holders' duties (ie, a *standard-based strategy ex post*). Such duties deter office holders from selecting a value-minimising rescue objective and ensure that the office holder is not wasteful in pursuing such rescue objective. A further important legal strategy in this regard is the voting requirements of creditors on the rescue plan (ie, a *decision rights strategy*). Such requirements seek to address inter-creditor agency costs by stipulating which classes of creditors are allowed to vote on which decisions

---

incentive of shareholders is the same as unsecured creditors. However, shareholders are unlikely to have an economic interest in a company that has been placed under rescue proceedings. An exception to this used to be companies that were placed under Chapter 11 proceedings. However, this trend has stopped in recent years; see nn 85 to 88 and accompanying text above.

174 See generally Finch, *Corporate Insolvency Law – Perspectives and Principles* (2nd edn, Cambridge University Press 2009) 607ff, 775ff.

175 See text to nn 163 to 166 above.

and altering the strength of the vote of certain classes of creditors in certain circumstances. This legal strategy thus particularly addresses the above-mentioned opportunism that arises due to the ability of creditors to have a say in the future of the company through voting on the rescue plan in cases where they lack an economic interest in the company. This is illustrated pertinently by the approach in the UK. Where the administrator concludes that the company can be rescued (either through reorganisation or a going concern sale), only unsecured creditors are entitled to vote,[176] while secured creditors are only allowed to vote the value of the unsecured portion of their claim.[177] However, where the administrator concludes either that the company is so hopelessly insolvent that unsecured creditors will not receive a return,[178] or that the company cannot be rescued, and will therefore need to be liquidated, then no vote is required,[179] ie, unsecured creditors will not get to have a say in the deployment of the assets.

Due to the large scope of the company-creditor agency conflict, we will not be able to explore the above-mentioned legal strategies addressing the inter-creditor conflict during rescue proceedings.

III. The protection of employees in insolvency proceedings

Employees are typically provided with legal protections during liquidation and rescue proceedings that go beyond the protections afforded to general unsecured creditors. Common examples of such special legal protections of employees are that relevant employee claims rank ahead of general unsecured creditors in insolvency,[180] that employee contracts are given

176 Insolvency Act 1986, Sch B1, para 51(1) read with para 52(1).

177 Rule 2.24 Insolvency Rules 1986.

178 Beyond the ring-fenced fund in accordance with s 176A(2)(a) Insolvency Act 1986.

179 Except if requested by creditors holding at least 10% of the value of the company's total debts (Insolvency Act 1986, Sch B1, para 52(2)).

180 For South Africa (in rescue proceedings), see s 135 Companies Act 2008 and the discussion in PART B, Chapter 4, IV., 7. below. For the UK (in administration), see Insolvency Act 1986, Sch B1, para 99(5), Sch 6. Interestingly, in the UK, certain employee claims and entitlements, including certain claims following dismissal of employment contracts, such as redundancy pay and a basic award of compensation for unfair dismissal, can be claimed directly from the National Insurance Fund, and thus fall outside the administration procedure completely. This is then statutorily subrogated to the relevant rights of the employees against the

stronger protection than contracts of general unsecured creditors against the office holder's general right to terminate uncompleted contracts, particularly during rescue proceedings,[181] and that in some jurisdictions, notably South Africa, employees are given stronger procedural rights of participation in the development of the rescue proposal than other unsecured creditors.[182]

The above-mentioned types of mechanisms that afford special rights to employees in insolvency proceedings cannot be explained by the principal-agent theory. Of course, because employees would, in the absence of their statutory preferred ranking, rank last in insolvency, together with the general unsecured creditors, employees are, like unsecured creditors, exposed to the risk of expropriation, for example, in cases of premature entry. However, employees do not appear to be at a greater risk of company controller opportunism than the general (commercial) unsecured creditors.

The rationale for the special treatment of employees, rather, is found elsewhere. First, employees are in a weaker position than commercial unsecured creditors to spread the risk of their loss in case the company fails. This is essentially due to differences in the nature of the relationship of employees and commercial unsecured creditors to the company: the latter are commercial partners, for example, a supplier of goods to a company is likely to supply goods to many companies; employees, by contrast, are required, by virtue of the employment relationship, to invest most of their

---

employer in administration (ss 185ff Employment Rights Act 1996). For the US (in bankruptcy proceedings generally), see 11 USC § 503(b)(1)(A), § 507(a)(4); see further, eg, *In re Mammoth Mart, Inc.*, 536 F.2d 955, 955 (1st Cir.1976); *Rodman v. Rinier (In re WT Grant Co)*, 620 F.2d 319, 321 (2d Cir.). On the priority of employee claims in the US generally, see Korobkin, 'Employee Interests in Bankruptcy' (1996) 4 Am. Bankr. Inst. L. Rev. 5, 7ff, 14.

181 For South Africa, see s 136 Companies Act 2008 and the discussion in PART B, Chapter 4, IV., 6., e. below. In the UK, a company is generally required to consult with employees where proposing to dismiss more than 20 employees (s 188 Trade Union and Labour Relations (Consolidation) Act 1992) and in the US where proposing to terminate collective bargaining agreements (11 USC § 1113).

182 See, eg, (i) the fact that employees are entitled to form an employees' committee separate from the creditors' committee (s 144(3)(c) Companies Act 2008), (ii) that the rescue practitioner is required to call a separate first meeting of employees' representatives (s 148 Companies Act 2008) and (iii) that employees' representatives (but not creditors' representatives) are entitled to address the meeting called for purposes of considering the rescue plan (s 152(1)(c) Companies Act 2008). Equivalent rights are not found, eg, in the UK or the US.

(human) capital into the company that employs them.[183] Moreover, employee benefits not related to wages, such as pensions, are often contractually tied to the employer.

The second justification often advanced for the special protection of employees in insolvency is that the working commitment by employees to their employer is a contribution deserving of superior moral claims against the employer.[184] Moreover, the special relationship between employees and their employer creates expectations on the part of the employees which go beyond concerns relating to the risk of non-payment by the debtor (which are typical for commercial unsecured creditors), such as building a career with the employer, continuing prospects of a regular income and the provision for old-age.[185]

The legal strategies in the applicable jurisdictions briefly touched upon above will not be elaborated on.

---

183 This is because employment with multiple employers is generally either difficult due to time-constraints or contractually prohibited by employers.

184 Villiers, 'Employees as Creditors: A Challenge for Justice in Insolvency Law' (1999) 20 Co. Law. 222, 229; Korobkin, 'Rehabilitating Values: A Jurisprudence of Bankruptcy' (1991) 91 Colum. L. Rev. 717; Korobkin, 'Contractarianism and the Normative Foundations of Bankruptcy Law' (1993) 71 Tex. L. Rev. 541; Korobkin, 'The Role of Normative Theory in Bankruptcy Debate' (1996–7) 82 Iowa L. Rev. 75; Walzer, *Spheres of Justice* (Basil Blackwell 1995); Finnis, *Natural Law and Natural Rights* (Clarendon Press 1980); Shuchmann, 'An Attempt at a "Philosophy of Bankruptcy"' (1973) 21 UCLA. L. Rev. 403; Gewirth, *The Community of Rights* (University of Chicago Press 1996). See generally Finch, 'Corporate Insolvency Law' (n 174) 775–6.

185 Van Wezel and Stone, 'Labour Markets, Employment Contracts and Corporate Change' in McCahery, Picciotto and Scott (eds), *Corporate Control and Accountability* (Clarendon Press 1993); O'Connor, 'Restructuring the Corporation's Nexus of Contracts: Recognizing a Fiduciary Duty to Protect Displaced Workers' (1991) 69 North Car. L. Rev. 1189. See generally Finch, 'Corporate Insolvency Law' (n 174) 776.

Chapter 2 Justification of Mandatory Rescue Law and the Role of Contractual Restructuring Mechanisms

I. Introduction

Over the last few decades, starting in the 1980s, various scholars have sought to provide a coherent set of principles that explain why it is desirable for insolvent companies to be dealt with in a collective and statutorily regulated procedure, rather than leaving it to creditors to distribute the assets of such companies among themselves by contract.

Although this study does not take a normative approach to rescue law, an analysis of the normative theories is nevertheless a worthwhile exercise for two primary reasons. First, and as a general point, a thesis of this nature would be incomplete without a consideration of the theoretical foundations of corporate insolvency law. And second, although the normative theory of corporate insolvency law that derives from the law and economics school of thought has serious weaknesses, the scholarly debates and theories provide an appropriate starting point for the law and economics analysis employed in this study. This is because it introduces, and 'sensitises' the reader to, fundamental economic concepts of corporate insolvency law, which will become important later on in the discussion.

Apart from the question why we ought to have a collective insolvency procedure in the first place (discussed in II below), there are two further fundamental theoretical issues in respect of corporate insolvency. One question concerns the most appropriate means by which a company's assets should be deployed by the collective procedure – ie, whether the law should focus primarily on preserving the company as a going concern or whether it should allow for, or even prioritise, the sale of the company's business. This question will be considered in III. below.

The other question explores possibilities of contractual solutions to financial distress that could reduce the reliance of distressed companies on the mandatory procedure, given its high direct and indirect costs. This issue will be considered in IV. below.

II. Normative theories of corporate insolvency law

1. The Creditors' Bargain Model ('CBM')

a. The CBM in a nutshell

The first – and probably most influential – comprehensive and principled theory of corporate insolvency law advanced is the 'Creditors' Bargain Model' (hereafter, '*CBM*') by Thomas Jackson in collaboration with Douglas Baird and later Robert Scott in a series of papers in the 1980s.[186] This theory attributes to insolvency law a single purpose: to distribute the company's pool of assets among creditors according to their pre-insolvency entitlements; as Jackson famously stated, 'bankruptcy, at its core, is debt-collection law'.[187] Three claims follow from this fundamental purpose attributed to corporate insolvency law, namely: (i) corporate insolvency law should only be concerned with the interests of creditors; (ii) its only goal should be to maximise the returns of creditors; and (iii) it should leave the pre-insolvency entitlements of creditors intact.

Before considering the justificatory basis of the CBM, it should be pointed out that most modern insolvency law regimes do not (fully) reflect the three claims above. One telling example contradicting claim (iii) is insolvency law's willingness to alter creditors' pre-insolvency entitlements, notably the ranking of certain employees' claims ahead of unsecured creditors.[188] A further example of current rescue law that might be at odds

---

186 Jackson, 'Bankruptcy, Non-Bankruptcy Entitlements and the Creditors' Bargain' (1982) 91 Yale L.J. 857; Baird and Jackson, 'Corporate Reorganisations and the Treatment of Diverse Ownership Interests: A Comment on Adequate Protection of Secured Creditors in Bankruptcy' (1984) 51 U. Chi. L. Rev. 97; Baird, 'The Uneasy Case for Corporate Reorganisations' (1986) 15 J. Legal Stud. 127; Jackson, *The Logics and Limits of Bankruptcy Law* (Harvard University Press 1986); Baird, 'A World without Bankruptcy' (1987) 50 Law & Contemp. Probs. 173; Baird, 'Loss Distribution, Forum Shopping, and Bankruptcy: A Reply to Warren' (1987) 54 U. Chi. L. Rev. 815; Jackson and Scott, 'On the Nature of Bankruptcy: An Essay on Bankruptcy Sharing and the Creditors' Bargain' (1989) 75 Va. L. Rev. 155.

187 Jackson, 'Logics and Limits' (n 186) 3.

188 For South Africa, see s 98A Insolvency Act 1936; for the UK, see Insolvency Act 1986, ss 40, 175; for the US, see 11 USC § 507(a)(4), (5); for Australia, see s 444DA read with ss 556, 560, 561 Corporations Act 2001. See also Warren, 'Bankruptcy Policy' (1987) 54 U. Chi. L. Rev. 775; Warren, 'Bankruptcy Policy

with claims (i) and (ii) is the objectives of most rescue laws. Typically the primary goal of rescue proceedings is the preservation of the corporate entity as such (which we have termed 'reorganisation'), rather than the going concern sale of the company's business (or part thereof).[189] Depending on how onerous the requirements are for the office holder of the debtor-company (or the incumbent management in the case of Chapter 11 in the US) when pursuing the secondary goal instead of the primary goal, the law may be seen to endorse a goal other than creditor wealth maximisation, and to take into account interests other than those of the creditors. This is particularly true for Chapter 11 in the US (at least up until the early to mid-2000s) where it has been argued that 'bankruptcy' judges exhibited a clear bias for reorganisation, presumably as an end in itself, regardless of whether this would be more cost-beneficial to creditors as a whole.[190] Moreover, the fact that in the US the incumbent management does not only remain in control of the company during Chapter 11 ('debtor in possession'), but also has the exclusive right to propose a reorganisation plan in the first 120 days of the proceedings,[191] puts equity-holders in a strong bargaining position, allowing them to extract value from creditors as a *quid pro quo* for placing the company under Chapter 11 proceedings timeously.[192] Indeed, empirical evidence from the late 1980s and 1990s shows that under Chapter 11 proceedings equity-holders sometimes do re-

---

in an Imperfect World' (1993) 92 Mich. L. Rev. 336; Garrido, 'The Distributional Question in Insolvency: Comparative Aspects' (1995) 4 i.i.r. 25, 28; Goode, *Principles of Corporate Insolvency Law* (3rd edn, Sweet & Maxwell 2005) 60–3; Finch, 'The Measures of Insolvency Law' (1997) 17 OJLS 227.

189 For South Africa, see s 128(1)(b)(iii); for the UK, Insolvency Act 1986, Sch B1, para 3; for Australia, see s 435A Corporations Act 2001. Although there is no provision in US Chapter 11 that sets out an order of priority of the two main methods of rescuing a company, 'reorganisation' is widely understood to be the procedure's primary goal; eg, Warren and Westbrook, *The Law of Debtors and Creditors* (6th edn, Aspen 2009) 387, 404.

190 See, eg, Triantis, 'Financial Slack Policy and the Law of Secured Transactions' (2000) 29 J. Legal Stud. 35, 67–8.

191 11 USC § 1121(b).

192 At least this was the perception up until the early to mid-2000s; Meckling, 'Financial Markets, Default and Bankruptcy: The Role of the State' (1977) 41 Law & Contemp. Probs. 13, 33–7; Bebchuk and Chang, 'Bargaining and the Division of Value in Corporate Reorganization' (1992) 8 J.L. Econ. & Org. 253; Bebchuk, 'Ch 11' in Newman (ed), *The New Palgrave Dictionary of Economics and the Law* (Palgrave Macmillan 1998).

ceive claims in the reorganised companies.[193] This implies that Chapter 11 is neither concerned solely with the interests of creditors (disproving claim (i)), nor interested only in creditor wealth maximisation (refuting claim (ii)).[194] Accordingly, given that all three claims are at odds with current law, it becomes clear that the CBM is a normative, not a positive, theory of corporate insolvency law.[195]

The CBM's justificatory basis for the collective insolvency procedure is that creditors would agree to such a procedure if they were able to bargain with each other *ex ante* (ie, at some time before advancing the loan to the company) and assuming zero transaction costs.[196] It is clear that the notion of consent is the primary normative source of the CBM. This is because the enforcement of principles that the creditors would have hypothetically consented to would violate their autonomy and freedom of choice,[197] which is *per se* undesirable. However, the notion of consent must be seen in conjunction with the *ex ante* position from which creditors agree on the collective procedure. To this end, Jackson applies the Rawlsian notion of

---

193 LoPucki and Whitford, 'Bargaining over Equity's Share in the Bankruptcy Reorganization of Large, Public Held Companies' (1990) 139 U. Pa. L. Rev. 125; Weiss, 'Bankruptcy Resolution: Direct Costs and Violation of Priority Claims' (1990) 27 J. Finan. Econ. 285; J White, 'The Ex Ante Effects of Bankruptcy Reform on Investment Incentives' (1994) 72 Wash. U. L.Q. 1159.

194 An example of a feature of the South African rescue law that contradicts all three claims is that the rescue procedure is willing to discriminate against the general body of creditors in favour of protecting the rights of employees in the form of the special protection of employee contracts (s 136(2A)(b) Companies Act 2008) and granting of a super-preference of post-commencement employees' claims against the company (s 135(1)(a) Companies Act 2008). For a discussion of the applicable protections of employee rights under the current South African rescue law, see Chapter 4 below.

195 Armour, 'The Law and Economics of Corporate Insolvency Law: A Review' (2001) ESRC Centre for Business Research Working Paper 197 <http://disciplinas.stoa.usp.br/pluginfile.php/35886/mod_resource/content/1/CHY%20The%20Law%20and%20Economics%20of%20Corporate%20Insolvency.pdf> accessed 16 January 2017.

196 This explains why the theory is referred to as the 'creditors' *bargain*.'

197 In particular, Jackson and Scott (n 186). This idea was developed shortly before the emergence of the CBM by a leading scholar on law and economics, Richard Posner. See Posner, 'The Ethical and Political Basis of the Efficiency Norm in Common Law Adjudication' (1980) 8 Hofstra L.R. 487. On consent in law and economics generally, see Brudney, 'Hypothetical Consent and Moral Force' (1991) 10 Law & Phil. 235.

the 'original position' to his model,[198] in which creditors are placed behind 'a veil of ignorance'.[199]

According to the CBM, there are essentially two reasons why a rational and self-interested creditor (*homo economicus*) would agree to a bargain as proposed by Jackson. First, creditors would realise that a collective and orderly distribution of their pre-insolvency claims against the company would be more efficient than if each creditor were to enforce their claim individually under the general law. The prisoner's dilemma, deriving from 'game theory' in economics,[200] provides the starting point for this claim. It explains why rational and self-interested creditors would not agree to a contractual solution that would in most circumstances be more efficient (which is the second explanation for creditors' decision). This is because not knowing whether the other creditors are willing to co-operate, and given the first-come-first-served approach of the general law, each creditor would be better off enforcing on their claims, regardless of what the other creditors are inclined to do. Here enforcement is the 'dominant strategy', as economists would say. This would result, as Jackson famously claimed, in an inefficient 'race to collect'. However, individual enforcement would also be inefficient as it would create duplicative and wasteful collection costs, which would be harmful to all creditors and the debtor. The race to collect would also generate duplicative and wasteful monitoring costs: to avoid not being the last one to become aware of the event of default, each creditor would have an incentive to spend significant costs on monitoring the debtor, which a collective procedure would reduce significantly. Finally, the absence of a collective debt collection procedure could result in an inefficient use of the company's assets. This would be the case where the company's assets are worth more when kept together as a going concern than if they are broken up piecemeal by way of liquidation (ie, where the company is essentially 'economically viable'). However, due to the prisoners' dilemma, creditors would *always* liquidate a company's assets, thus

198 As deriving from the seminal work, Rawls, *A Theory of Justice* (Harvard University Press 1971).

199 Jackson, 'Logics and Limits' (n 186) 17 n 22, 236–7.

200 On the prisoner's dilemma generally, see Rasmusen, *Games and Information: An Introduction to Game Theory* (4th edn, Blackwell 2007).

placing the company's assets to their lowest value use.[201] Therefore, the primary function of the automatic stay on (unsecured) creditor enforcement under collective insolvency law, according to the CBM, is to overcome this problem.[202]

It might be argued that the prisoner's dilemma is a somewhat crude explanation for the race to collect, as it assumes that creditors have no information about each other, which is not true in reality. Nevertheless, according to the CBM, co-ordination between creditors would be unlikely because the transaction costs of doing so would be prohibitively high. This is particularly the case where there are a large number of creditors with widely dispersed interests, resulting in a 'collective action problem', as economists would put it.[203] Moreover, bargaining among creditors gives rise to the problem that (rational and self-interested) creditors may have a perverse incentive to refuse agreeing to a (value-maximising) bargain in order to extract value for themselves relative to other creditors that participate in the bargain – referred to as 'hold-up' or 'holdout' behaviour.[204]

---

201 See, eg, Baird, 'Bankruptcies Uncontested Axioms' (1998) 108 Yale L.J. 573, 580–2. Of course, the inefficiencies would – to use a theme central to the study of law and economics – also be harmful to society as a whole (social costs); M White, 'The Corporate Bankruptcy Decision' (1989) 3 J. Econ. Perspect. 129; M White, 'Corporate Bankruptcy as a Filtering Device': Ch 11 Reorganization and Out-of-Court Restructuring' (1994) 10 J.L. Econ. & Org. 268; White, 'The Costs of Corporate Bankruptcy: A US-European Comparison' in Bhandari and Weiss (eds), *Corporate Bankruptcy: Economic and Legal Perspectives* (Cambridge University Press 1996) 467. However, this justificatory device cannot, and has not been claimed to, be available to the CBM, given that the theory derives its normative force from the self-interested preferences of creditors, who would not be interested in any societal interests that do not directly benefit them.

202 This summarises Jackson, 'Logics and Limits' (n 186) Ch 2; see also Baird, 'World without Bankruptcy' (n 186).

203 See, eg, Morrison, 'The Economics of Bankruptcy: An Introduction to the Literature' (2009), Columbia Law and Economics Working Paper No. 366, 2 <http://papers.ssrn.com/sol3/papers.cfm?abstract_id=1529822> accessed 16 January 2017.

204 See, eg, Gilson, 'Managing default: Some Evidence on how Firms choose between Workouts and Chapter 11' in Bhandari and Weiss (eds), *Corporate Bankruptcy – Economic and Legal Perspectives* (Cambridge University Press 1996) 308, 316–7. It should also be noted that the holdout problem and the problem of 'free-riding' (the perverse incentive to reap the benefits of an arrangement without contributing to its establishment and maintenance) are often used interchangeably. However, drawing a conceptual distinction between the two, see Cohen, 'Holdouts and Free Riders' (1991) 20 J. Legal Stud. 351.

Majority consent in formal insolvency proceedings might be seen to address this problem in particular.[205] Jackson argues that the inefficiencies resulting from the above two problems constitute a 'market failure', which creditors in the *ex ante* position would realise and conclude that only insolvency law would be able to remedy.[206]

b. Distribution of the assets in insolvency proceedings – perspectives from the CBM and financial economics

The third of the above-mentioned claims of the CBM provides that the creditors' pre-insolvency entitlements should be maintained in insolvency proceedings. In other words, formal insolvency proceedings should divorce the questions of the *distribution* from the *deployment* of the 'common pool' of assets.[207] Consequently, insolvency law should only allow for the sale of the company' assets to third parties (in US parlance, 'auc-

---

205 Armour (n 195).

206 See, eg, Jackson, 'Creditors' Bargain' (n 186). This argument must be understood against the background that the CBM is essentially based in law and economics in the context of corporate and commercial law, which – to put it in the most general terms – sees legal regulation (merely) as a mechanism to provide a structure for the markets to function smoothly; Kornhausen, 'Constrained Optimization – Corporate Law and the Maximization of Social Welfare' in Kraus and Walt (eds), *The Jurisprudential Foundations of Corporate and Commercial Law* (Cambridge University Press 2000) 83, 88.

207 The 'common pool problem' is well-known concept in law and economics; Kammel, 'Economics of Corporate Insolvency' in Omar (ed), *International Insolvency Law – Themes and Perspectives* (Ashgate 2008) 61, 69 n 25, referring to Hardin, 'The Tragedy of the Commons' (1968) 162 Science 1243. See also generally Friedman, 'The Economics of the Common Pool: Property Rights in Exhaustible Resources' (1971) 18 UCLA L. Rev. 855; Sweeney, Tollison, and Willett, 'Market Failure, The Common Pool Problem, and Ocean Resource Exploitation' (1974) 17 J.L. & Econ. 179. For the argument that the 'common pool of assets' is flawed because it does not accord with basic economic facts and legal structures, see Flessner, 'Philosophies of Business Bankruptcy Law: An International Overview' in Ziegel (ed), *Current Developments in International and Comparative Corporate Insolvency Law* (Oxford University Press 1994) 19, 25–6.

tions'), but not for the reorganisation of the company's capital with the intention of preserving the corporate entity.[208]

The CBM advances several reasons for this claim. First, it argues, rather formalistically, that substantive rights in the general law should not be treated differently in insolvency. This is based on the well-established principle in corporate finance that financing decisions and investment decisions should be clearly separated.[209]

Second, it asserts that any disruption of secured credit's non-insolvency priority in insolvency would raise the costs of borrowing at the expense of debtors.[210]

Third, the fact that the collective insolvency procedure rearranges the creditors' contractual rights gives rise to the opportunistic invocation of the collective insolvency procedure by company controllers or unsecured creditors to capture gains for themselves at the expense of the common pool ('forum shopping').[211]

And finally, it contends that permitting collective decision-making on the optimal deployment of the company's assets in insolvency proceedings is inefficient. For a start, heterogeneous preferences among the various classes of creditors gives parties a perverse incentive to support a decision which serves their interests,[212] giving rise to inter-creditor agency costs. For example, unsecured creditors, knowing they rank behind secured creditors and particularly where they have lost their economic interest in the company, would tend to favour high-risk rescue outcomes. Moreover, because unsecured creditors would in that case not bear the direct costs of a prolonged procedure, they have an incentive to draw out the procedure at

---

208 See, eg, Baird, 'Uneasy Case' (n 186) 139; Baird, 'Revisiting Auctions in Ch 11' (1993) 36 J.L. & Econ. 633, 638ff. However, it is not entirely clear whether going concern sales are indeed more efficient than reorganisations; see PART A, Chapter 2, III., 1 below.

209 In particular, Baird, 'Loss Distribution' (n 186) 822ff.

210 See, eg, Jackson, 'Creditors' Bargain' (n 186) 868–9; Jackson and Kronman, 'Secured Financing and Priorities Among Creditors' (1979) 88 Yale L.J. 1143. See also Levmore, 'Monitors and Freeriders in Commercial and Corporate Settings' (1982) 92 Yale L.J. 49. For a critique of the efficiency premise of secured credit, see Schwartz, 'Security Interests and Bankruptcy Priorities: A Review of Current Theories' (1981) 10 J. Legal Stud. 1, 7ff.

211 See, eg, Baird and Jackson, 'Adequate protection of secured creditors' (n 186) 101; Baird, 'Loss Distribution' (n 186) 824ff.

212 See, eg, Baird and Jackson, 'Adequate protection of secured creditors' (n 186) 104 n 22, 107 n 39; Baird, 'Uneasy Case' (n 186).

the expense of the entire body of creditors. The opposite is true for senior (secured) creditors: since they bear the downside risk of a decline of the company's value in insolvency, they would have an incentive to realise their collateral as swiftly as possible, regardless of whether the company may be worth more as a going concern than broken up.[213]

The CBM argues that auctions would avoid many of the inefficiencies of collective decision-making by creditors in that third party bidders would have the right incentives to value the company appropriately.[214]

2. Problems of the CBM and alternative theories of corporate insolvency law

a. General

The CBM has been subject to vigorous attacks on various levels. One type of objection questions the possibility and desirability of comprehensive and principled theories of corporate insolvency law. Elizabeth Warren – one of the first scholars to react to the CBM – found such an enterprise futile and undesirable, preferring analyses that are 'dirty, complex, elastic, interconnected', and which can 'neither predict outcomes nor even necessarily fully articulate all the factors relevant to a policy decision'.[215]

There have also been objections and rival theories that go to the actual content of the CBM. One set of criticisms comes from within the field of

213 See, eg, Baird and Jackson, 'Adequate protection of secured creditors' (n 186) 106ff. See also generally on this argument Roe, 'Bankruptcy and Debt: A Model for Corporate Reorganization' (1983) 83 Colum. L. Rev. 527; Bebchuk, 'A New Approach to Corporate Reorganizations' (1988) 101 Harv. L. Rev. 775. Moreover, though not particularly emphasised by proponents of the CBM, information asymmetries among creditors would increase the scope for differing views on, and disputes over, the optimal deployment decision, raising the (direct) costs of insolvency proceedings; Armour (n 195).

214 Baird, 'Uneasy Case' (n 186) 139. See also Roe (n 213). See generally Armour (n 195). More recently, it has been argued by Baird and Rasmussen that in the New Economy, companies will seldom have a going concern surplus, since assets of companies are increasingly 'industry-specific', and less 'firm-specific'. An exception to this could be small companies, since in such companies the human capital could still be tied up in the company; see Baird and Rasmussen, 'The End of Bankruptcy' (2002) 55 Stan L Rev 751, 788ff.

215 Warren, 'Bankruptcy Policy' (n 188) 811.

law and economics. It challenges the central assumption of the CBM that insolvency law is indispensable because the costs of contracting for collective debt-collection *ex ante* would be prohibitively high.[216] The expositors of this strand of criticism of the CBM theorise about contractual solutions to the prisoner's dilemma, calling into question the need for mandatory insolvency law. Another source of opposition to the CBM has its origins outside of law and economics. The commentators of this category of criticism of the CBM all appear to reject, in one way or another, the normative force of the underlying law and economics sentiment that the law should reflect a solution that is based entirely on the self-interest of the 'affected' parties and on efficiencies. Based on this general idea, alternative theories to the CBM have been advanced. We will now examine these two strands of criticism of, and the alternative theories to, the CBM in turn.

b. Ex ante bargaining solutions to the prisoner's dilemma

The basis for the law and economics attack on the CBM is the assertion that the prisoner's dilemma only becomes relevant when the company has defaulted on its debts, and not at the time funds are advanced to the company.[217] Expositors of this school of thought explore contractual solutions at the time funds are advanced to the company to overcome the co-ordination costs of bargaining for a collective procedure outside formal insolvency proceedings, particularly the collective action problem and holdout behaviour.[218]

---

216 See text to nn 203–206 above.

217 See, in particular, Rasmussen, 'Debtor's Choice: A Menu Approach to Corporate Bankruptcy' (1992) 71 Tex. L. Rev. 51; Adler, 'Financial and Political Theories of American Corporate Bankruptcy' (1993) 45 Stan. L. Rev. 311; Schwartz, 'A Contract Theory Approach to Bankruptcy' (1998) 107 Yale L.J. 1807. Indeed, even after funds have been advanced, and when financial distress is imminent, the costs of resolving the debtor's troubles may not always be prohibitive to a bargaining solution. This is one reason why informal rescue mechanisms may be a powerful mechanism; see generally PART A, Chapter 2, IV., 1. below.

218 See text to nn 203–204.

aa. 'Chameleon equity' structure

One such solution, proposed by Barry Adler, seeks to pre-empt the problem of co-ordination costs by designing a special type of capital structure coupled with a contractual prohibition on enforcement remedies. Instead of enforcement against the debtor in the event of default, there is an automatic rearrangement of priorities of claims: previous shareholders' claims are cancelled and the lowest ranking creditors become the company's residual claimants.[219] That is why this model is referred to as 'chameleon equity'.

However, Adler concedes that even if the current law allowed for creditors and debtors to contract out of the insolvency regime, we would still not see chameleon equity structures in practice. This is because of uncoordinated tax, commercial, corporate and tort laws. This constitutes the fundamental difference to the CBM: Adler saw the need for insolvency law as a result of legal failure, while Jackson and others saw it as a market failure.[220]

bb. Provision of a 'menu' of insolvency procedures

An inherent practical problem for contractual solutions *ex ante* is that current law does not allow for the 'contracting out' of the formal insolvency regime.[221] This means that any creditor who commits himself to a contractual collective regime would be vulnerable to being 'expropriated' if the debtor subsequently borrows 'traditional' debt.[222] A mechanism is thus needed that binds all creditors to the contractual solution to financial distress.

Such a mechanism has been proposed by Robert Rasmussen, according to which the company's constitution could provide for a menu of insolvency procedures that would 'lock in' each creditor contracting with the company. This would allow a company to select the insolvency procedures that would, for example, best suit its capital structure, thereby reducing

219 Adler (n 217).

220 See Morrison (n 203).

221 Schwartz, 'Bankruptcy Workouts and Debt Contracts' (1993) 36 J.L. & Econ. 595.

222 See Armour (n 195).

creditors' monitoring costs and strategic behaviour by company controllers. According to this theory, only non-contractual creditors, such as tort victims, should be protected by mandatory provisions.[223]

However, this theory has some problems. In inefficient capital markets, the company may not choose the most efficient insolvency option. This increases the risk of company controller opportunism.[224] There is also a danger that company controllers would choose a sub-optimal choice of insolvency procedure due to their potential fear of an adverse market reaction to certain terms that may be perceived to signal a high risk investment.[225] Probably the most problematic feature of this theory is that a company's business, finance and organisational structure may evolve over time, which would likely require a different insolvency option. However, a change to the insolvency regime would require consent from all creditors, allowing for a collective action problem to re-emerge.[226]

c. Alternative theories from outside the field of law and economics

aa. Immanent values and communitarianism

Elizabeth Warren, having initially questioned the merits of a comprehensive normative theory of corporate insolvency law,[227] some years later actually suggested what appears to be an alternative theory to the CBM. She argued that corporate insolvency law does, and ought to, reflect the values of the general law[228] – that is, the law's immanent values.[229]

However, although neatly solving problems of implementation of the underlying principles to the law, the theory provides little guidance on resolving tough questions, such as where different interests conflict.[230]

A further objection has been advanced to the CBM's *homo economicus* premise, and particularly to one of the necessary implications of this assumption, namely that corporate insolvency law should only concern itself

223 Rasmussen, 'Debtor's Choice' (n 217).
224 Armour (n 195).
225 Roe (n 213).
226 Armour (n 195); Morrison (n 203).
227 Text to n 215.
228 Warren, 'Bankruptcy Policy-Making in an Imperfect World' (n 188) 36.
229 For the expression, see Armour (n 195).
230 Ibid.

with the interests of creditors. The main expositor of this challenge to the CBM, Karen Gross, argued that corporate insolvency law ought to rather take into account broader interests, notably those of the community, which are based on 'multiple intuitive factors' drawn from internal reflection on human nature and fairness.[231] She argued that people are essentially altruistic, and would be 'willing to forego certain self-interests to accomplish larger goals.[232]

However, the theory suffers from problems of internal logic. Altruism in itself does not justify a collective insolvency procedure; surely the bailing-out of an insolvent company by the local communities or by the government would be equally compatible with the notion of altruism.[233] Moreover, like the immanent values principle, the standard of community interests suffers from problems of indeterminacy:[234] how is one to select between the many community interests and how are the selected interests to be weighed?[235] The theory provides no answers to these questions.

bb. Broad-based contractarianism

Another rival theory to the CBM, expounded by Donald Korobkin,[236] uses the CBM's hypothetical bargain device,[237] but expands the conditions under which the parties are placed in the 'original position'. Under the CBM's version of the *ex ante* position, creditors are merely stripped of the knowledge of what would happen to their particular debtor and how well-positioned they would be in that particular transaction, but not of their personal characteristics, notably their personal skills and experiences in debt-

231 See, generally Gross, *Failure and Forgiveness: Rebalancing the Bankruptcy System* (Yale University Press 1997) and Gross, 'Taking Community Interests into Account in Bankruptcy: An Essay' (1994) 72 Wash. U. L. Q. 1031.

232 Gross, 'Failure and Forgiveness' (n 231) 200.

233 Armour (n 195).

234 This is apart from the difficulties of defining the community; Schermer, 'Response to Professor Gross: Taking the Interests of the Community into Account in Bankruptcy' (1994) 72 Wash. U. L. Q. 1049, 1051.

235 Finch, *Corporate Insolvency Law – Perspectives and Principles* (2nd edn, CUP 2009) 42.

236 See in particular Korobkin, 'Rehabilitating Values: A Jurisprudence of Bankruptcy' (1991) 91 Colum. L. Rev. 717; Korobkin, 'Contractarianism and the Normative Foundations of Bankruptcy Law' (1993) 71 Tex. L. Rev. 541.

237 Like the CBM, this theory is essentially a contractarian theory of law.

collection, their relative bargaining power, and how they are related to the debtor (referred to as 'Natural Ignorance'[238]).[239] By contrast, under Korobkin's more expanded version of the original position, the parties are not permitted to know their real-world positions and personal attributes – that is, any characteristics that might lead them to advance personal interests (referred to as 'Dramatic Ignorance'[240]).[241] Moreover, unlike the CBM, all parties that might be affected by a company's failure, and not only creditors, are placed behind the 'veil of ignorance'. Korobkin argued that in this position the parties would opt for a collective insolvency procedure that consisted of two fundamental principles: first, a principle of 'inclusiveness', meaning that the interests of all parties potentially affected by the company's decline will be taken into account; and second, a principle of 'rational planning', which would ensure that the parties would agree on 'aims' that would best promote the 'long-term' interests of the company, and where this is not possible, would choose the 'aims' that protect the interests of the most vulnerable parties (which is akin to Rawls' 'difference principle').[242]

However, Korobkin's broad-based contractarian theory suffers from two defects. First, and similar to all alternative theories to the CBM discussed so far, Korobkin's theory fails to provide a convincing basis on which to choose between competing interests.[243] His suggestion that the most vulnerable should be given special protection might be considered

238 See Jackson (n 202) 499.

239 Mokal, *Corporate Insolvency Law – Theory and Application* (Oxford University Press 2005) 37ff cites passages from the writings of Jackson and Baird that confirms this is indeed the level of 'ignorance' the CBM attributes to creditors, eg, Jackson and Scott (n 186) 160; Jackson, 'Logics and Limits' (n 186) 15, 30, 59, 80. Mokal also argues convincingly that any other level of ignorance would be inconsistent with the CBM (at 75ff, 87ff).

240 Mokal (n 239) 61, 73.

241 This is closer than Jackson's or Posner's version to the veil of ignorance as understood by its progenitor, John Rawls; see Armour (n 195). In fact, Jackson's and Posner's theory have been categorised instead as part of what is known in political philosophy as 'mutual advantage' theories; a contemporary proponent of this theory is Gauthier, *Morals and Agreement* (Clarendon Press 1986); see Mokal (n 239) 36, 62, 75–6.

242 This summarises Korobkin, 'Contractarianism' (n 236) 572–89.

243 Drawing on Rawls, Korobkin provides some tentative guidelines for determining what is 'rational' in the insolvency context, eg, that parties would choose those aims that could be achieved 'with the least expenditure of means and to the

sufficiently tangible, but Korobkin then has difficulties providing how one might determine the most vulnerable among '*all*[244] persons in society [who] should', according to Korobkin, 'have representation in the choice of [insolvency law] principles'.[245]

Second, Korobkin cannot explain how his distributional principles relate to issues of wealth. As Finch correctly argues, the sheer size of the interests that are to be weighed up, and uncertainties in undertaking that exercise, would result in soaring, and hardly sustainable, costs of borrowing.[246]

d. Misconception of the characteristics of the parties in the CBM's ex ante position

Rizwaan Mokal[247] has exposed a limitation of Jackson's hypothetical bargain, from which the theory can hardly recover. The problem with the CBM, he argues, is that the persons in the CBM's *ex ante* position have certain characteristics that give them no reason to agree to a collective insolvency procedure. Let us consider Mokal's reasoning in this regard.

The CBM's proponents argue that the persons in the *ex ante* position are unaware of what would happen to their particular debtor and how well positioned they would be in that particular transaction. However, they are nevertheless taken to be 'real' and are aware of their personal attributes, 'native endowments', strength, intelligence and bargaining savvy. Thus, in

---

fullest extent' or a set of rules which allows the realisation of more rather than less of the aims, or the realisation of the more important aims, even if it might frustrate less important ones; Korobkin, 'Contractarianism' (n 236) 581–2, in each case citing Rawls, 'Theory of Justice' (n 198). However, it is doubtful whether these guidelines are sufficiently concrete for making tough choices between competing interests.

244 Emphasis added.

245 Korobkin, 'Contractarianism' (n 236) 541, 554. See Finch, 'Corporate Insolvency Law' (n 235) 40.

246 Finch, 'Corporate Insolvency Law' (n 235) 40.

247 Mokal (n 239) Ch 2. Mokal's attack mirrors Ronald Dworkin's (Dworkin, 'Why Efficiency? A Response to Professor Calabresi and Posner' (1981) 8 Hofstra L. Rev. 563) attack on Richard Posner's attempt to demonstrate the normative force of efficiency by means of consent from an *ex ante perspective*; Posner (n 197). A further critic of the CBM is David Carlson; see Carlson, 'Philosophy in Bankruptcy' (1987) 85 Mich. L. Rev. 1341.

expressing their antecedent self-interest in the *ex ante* position, the creditors must know their relative debt collection skills, bargaining power, ability to diversify the risk of losing a race to collect and their relation to the debtor.[248] This implies that the creditors in the *ex ante* position must be heterogeneous.[249]

Moreover, preferences depend on the knowledge of the participants and the time at which it is expressed. However, the CBM does not specify a time at which the self-interest (or preference) of creditors should be determined. It thus offers nothing that makes the assessment of any given creditor's self-interest, say, at the time when that creditor is still new to the business of lending, morally more desirable than when he has gained more experience and skills in individual debt collection.[250]

Accordingly, knowing he is a repeat player at debt-collection, and thus knowing he has a more than even chance of winning the race to collect, a creditor would simply have no reason to agree to a collective procedure.[251]

Admitting that this is a 'troublesome' feature of his theory,[252] Jackson tried to argue around this problem by suggesting that duplicate enforcement and monitoring costs would even disadvantage the strong creditors and that the collective regime would eliminate 'residual elements of uncertainty of relative ranking [...] to the benefit of all creditors'.[253] Mokal disproves both arguments on the grounds that collection and monitoring costs for better-resourced creditors and repeat players in debt collection are lower because such creditors have the ability to position themselves better for the race to collect, for example through economies of scale. Moreover, such creditors may be in the position to diversify the risk of uncertainty of relative ranking, making it more cost-beneficial for such creditors to eliminate this risk in the general law than in a collective insolvency procedure.[254]

---

248 Text to n 239 above.

249 Mokal (n 239) 52.

250 Ibid 50–1.

251 Ibid 52–3; Carlson, 'Philosophy in Bankruptcy' (1987) 85 Mich. L. Rev. 1341, 1349.

252 Jackson, 'Creditors' Bargain' (n 186) 863–4; Jackson, 'Logics and Limits' (n 186) 15.

253 Jackson, 'Logics and Limits' (n 186) 15 n 18.

254 Mokal (n 239) 57.

III. The appropriate means of asset deployment – reorganisations vs. going concern sales

1. Inefficiencies of auctions

As seen above, the CBM has argued that collective insolvency law should only allow for auctions, not reorganisation, largely due to problems of collective decision-making by creditors.[255]

However, this assertion has been challenged on several grounds. First, due to failures in the market for distressed companies, going concern sales may significantly undervalue the company's assets. This is because companies' assets are often industry-specific, and therefore worth more to members of the same industry than to members of other industries. However, where the company's decline is a result of an industry-wide downturn, as is frequently the case, the market for the distressed assets may be highly illiquid, preventing an effective reallocation of the debtor-company's resources.[256]

Second, the value of a debtor-company's assets may be undermined by the adverse market signals of insolvency. Potential buyers may believe that only low-quality companies in distress would be offered for sale to the market, and lacking appropriate information, would therefore undervalue the company's assets[257] (which, in economic parlance, constitutes an adverse selection problem).[258]

---

255 See PART A, Chapter 2, II., 1., b. above.

256 Shleifer and Vishny, 'Liquidation Values and Debt Capacity: A Market Equilibrium Approach' (1992) 47 J. Finance 1343. This source of this effect could be both on the demand-side and on the supply-side of the market (as to the latter, see Pulvino, 'Effects of Bankruptcy Court Protection on Asset Sales' (1999) 52 J. Finan. Econ. 151). This is supported by empirical evidence, showing that the higher the extent of the industry shock and the more specific the assets to an industry, the lower the selling price fetched for the debtor-company's assets (Pulvino, 'Do Asset Fire-sales Exist? An Empirical Investigation of Commercial Aircraft Transactions' (1998) 53 J. Finance 939; D Brown, 'Liquidity and Liquidation: Evidence from Real Estate Investment Trusts' (2000) 55 J. Finance 469; Strömberg, 'Conflicts of Interest and Market Illiquidity in Bankruptcy Auctions: Theory and Tests' (2000) 55 J. Finance 2641).

257 Webb, 'An Economic Evaluation of Insolvency Procedures in the United Kingdom: Does the 1986 Insolvency Act Satisfy the Creditors' Bargain?' (1991) 43 Oxford Econ. Pap. 139, 147ff. See generally Armour (n 195).

258 Armour (n 195).

By contrast, because the pre-commencement owners have superior information of the company's financial affairs and are less vulnerable to adverse market reactions, they are likely to put a higher value on the company's assets.[259] The same might be true for significant creditors, for example, banks, as they are likely to have monitored the company throughout its decline.[260] Here it might therefore be more efficient either for the company to remain in the hands of the previous owners and that the debt be restructured, or that ownership be transferred to the existing (secured) creditors by means of a debt for equity swap, for example.[261]

What is more, auctions could also give rise to agency costs. This is because of uncertainties of the appropriate person to oversee the auction process. Normally the residual claimants will have the appropriate incentives to maximise value for the company, as they bear the utimate risk of any losses incurred. Yet there is a catch-22 situation in that until a valuation of the company has been conducted, it is impossible to know who the residual claimants are.[262] Thus, even an auction requires oversight by an 'agent', and the person placed in charge of the company (ie, the agent) is prone to act opportunistically, generating agency costs.[263]

A good example of this was the oversight granted to floating charge-holders under a particular (quasi-contractual) form of a restructuring procedure in the UK, administrative receivership (which has however been practically abrogated by the Enterprise Act of 2002). Here the person in control of the company's assets, ie the administrative receiver, owed his duties primarily to the person who appointed him, ie the floating charge-holder. Where the floating charge-holder was oversecured, the administrative receiver lacked an incentive to sell the assets for the highest possible price, so long as the price covered the floating charge-holder's outstanding debt claim against the company.[264]

---

259 Crystal and Mokal, 'The Valuation of Distressed Companies – A Conceptual Framework' (2006) SSRN <http://papers.ssrn.com/sol3/papers.cfm?abstract_id=877155> accessed 16 January 2017.

260 Ibid.

261 Ibid.

262 Armour (n 195).

263 Easterbrook, 'Is Corporate Bankruptcy Efficient? (1990) 27 J. Finan. Econ. 411. See generally Armour (n 195).

264 Mokal (n 239) 210ff; Aghion, Hart and Moore, 'A Proposal for Bankruptcy Reform in the UK' (1993) 9 I.L. & P. 103, 103ff. For a defence of administrative receivership, see Armour and Frisby, 'Rethinking Receivership' (2001) 21 ojls

Given these conflicting arguments of the merits of reorganisation and auctions, there is no clear answer as to which of the two goals is generally preferable. It would seem that it would depend on the circumstances of each situation.[265]

Particularly the above problems of auctions have prompted scholars to consider alternative auction models, which we will now consider in greater detail.

2. Alternatives to conventional auctions

a. The Bebchuk model

One such auction variant stems from Lucian Bebchuk.[266] It seeks to address the problem of creditor heterogeneity by means of the homogenisation of claims,[267] and the problem of the market undervaluation by making existing claimants the bidders for the company's assets. In that model, all claims are converted to equity, ensuring commonality of interests. Moreover, the pre-insolvency priorities are retained by the automatic allocation to the claimants of options at an exercise price that takes account of such priorities.[268]

However, under Bebchuk's model, in order for the claimants to make an informed decisions whether they should exercise their options, they need to know the value of the company. This re-introduces the problems associated with valuations.[269] Moreover, there is a potential for the model to discriminate against unsecured creditors, as they may not have the required liquidity to exercise their options.[270]

---

73. For empirical evidence, see Franks and Sussman, 'Financial Distress and Bank Restructuring of Small to Medium Size UK Companies' (2005) 9 Review Of Finance 65.

265 Eidenmüller, *Unternehmenssanierung zwischen Markt und Gesetz: Mechanismen der Unternehmensreorganisation und Kooperationspflichten im Reorganisationsrecht* (Otto Schmidt 1999) 48.

266 Bebchuk, 'Corporate Reorganizations'(n 213).

267 See Armour (n 195).

268 For an example of how the exercise price would be calculated, see Bebchuk, 'Corporate Reorganizations' 'Corporate Reorganizations'(n 213) 800 n 46.

269 Armour (n 195); Morrison (n 203).

270 Armour (n 195).

b. The Aghion, Hart and Moore model

Aghion, Hart and Moore put forward another alternative to conventional auctions ('AHM model'), seeking to address the pitfalls under Bebchuk's model.[271] The AHM model involves three steps: (i) the solicitation of bids for the company (cash and non-cash); (ii) the allocation of (voting) rights to the company by an insolvency judge among the existing creditors (using largely Bebchuk's model) and the exercise of options on the basis of the bids; and (iii) voting on the desired bid by the residual claimants.[272] The AHM improves on Bebchuk's model in three main respects. First, it reduces valuation costs by enabling existing creditors to base their decision on whether to exercise their options on the bids. Second, the entire procedure removes management from control unless they are voted in at the end, thereby reducing company-creditor agency costs. Nor are any particular classes of creditors in a strong position to influence the procedure, reducing the scope for inter-creditor agency costs. And third, although by allowing for outside bids, the AHM model introduces a potential danger that Bebchuk's model avoids, namely undervaluation due to market-failures, this problem is mitigated by the permission of non-cash bids.[273] The general appeal of the AHM model is that ultimately the asset deployment decision is placed in the hands of the residual claimants, reducing decision-making costs.[274]

A potential limitation of the AHM model is that it could probably not be used by most of the companies under insolvency proceedings (smaller and medium-sized non-listed companies), as such company forms are generally not suited for the trading of options as required under the model. Moreover, although the AHM model goes a long way in reducing the collective decision-making costs of creditors, it is unable to prevent another major source of inefficiencies of formal rescue proceedings, namely negative market (over-)reactions to companies being placed under formal rescue proceedings which typically result in less favourable financing conditions (ie, the indirect costs of insolvency).[275] This emphasises the impor-

271 Aghion, Hart and Moore, 'The Economics of Bankruptcy Reform' (1992) 8 J.L. Econ. & Org. 523.

272 Ibid 532ff.

273 Ibid 536ff.

274 Armour (n 195).

275 Eidenmüller, 'Unternehmenssanierung' (n 265) 122.

tance of pre-insolvency bargaining solutions to financial distress, which will be discussed in the next section.

IV. Pre-insolvency bargaining solutions to financial distress – informal rescue mechanisms and pre-packaged plans

1. General, advantages of informal rescue mechanisms

Above, we dealt with normative challenges to the CBM's claim that a formal insolvency procedure is indispensable because the costs of bargaining *ex ante* would be prohibitively high.[276] These insolvency law theorists proposed contractual devices at the time when funds are advanced to creditors that seek to overcome such bargaining costs.[277] In contrast, bargaining solutions in the shadows of insolvency law ('workouts') are neither normative (in the sense of questioning the justification of the formal procedure), nor do they occur before or at the time when funds are advanced. Instead, the case for workouts is that under certain circumstances, contractual bargaining by creditors after the advancement of the funds to the company, but before the need for filing for formal proceedings arises,[278] is both possible and desirable.

Generally, the main advantage of workouts is the avoidance of the costs of formal insolvency proceedings. There are three primary sources of such costs. One is the 'direct costs' of implementing the formal procedure, primarily the costs of court proceedings,[279] the costs of the insolvency office holder (hereafter, the '*office holder*') and the co-ordination costs of creditors.[280] Thus formal proceedings tend to take longer than workouts and

276 See PART A, Chapter 2, II., 1., a. above.

277 Ibid.

278 Which typically occurs when the debtor-company meets the tests of impending insolvency under corporate insolvency law.

279 These may, of course, vary depending on how court-reliant the formal procedure is. Thus, such costs might be higher in the court-driven US Chapter 11 procedure than in Australia's largely court-exclusive voluntary administration.

280 Wood, *Principles of International Insolvency* (2nd edn, Sweet & Maxwell 2007) para 2-028; Eidenmüller, 'Unternehmenssanierung' (n 265) 74.

professional fees in formal proceedings tend to be higher than in workouts.[281]

The other source of costs is a negative market reaction to the invocation of insolvency proceedings, resulting in a devaluation of the company's assets (which we have termed 'indirect costs of insolvency proceedings').[282] In contrast, to the extent that a workout is kept secret from the commercial public, a similar adverse market reaction is unlikely to occur in workouts.[283]

The final source of costs are foregone investment opportunities, so-called 'opportunity costs'. The fact that formal proceedings generally take longer, and typically commence later than workouts, means that the com-

281 For empirical evidence from the 1980s that Chapter 11 proceedings in the US take longer than workouts, see Gilson, John and Lang, 'Troubled debt restructurings – An empirical study of Private Reorganisation of Firms in Default' (1990) 27 J. Finan. Econ. 315. Claiming that there is a causal relationship between time and professional fees in a US context, see LoPucki and Doherty, 'The Determinants of Professional Fees in Large Bankruptcy Reorganization Cases' (2004) 1 J. Emp. L. Stud. 111, 120; see also Altman, 'Evaluating the Chapter 11 Bankruptcy-Reorganization Process' [1993] Colum. Bus. L. Rev. 1, 2–4; Gilson (n 204) 310ff; Franks and Torous, 'An Empirical Investigation of U.S. Firms in Reorganization' (1989) 44 J. Finance 747, 747–8, 751; Rasmussen and Thomas, 'Whither the Race? A Comment on the Effects of the Delawarization of Corporate Reorganizations' (2001) 54 Vand. L. Rev. 283, 295; J White, 'Harvey's Silence' (1995) 69 Am. Bankr. L.J. 467, 473–4. Denying such a causal relationship with the aid of empirical evidence and claiming that the key determinants for costs are rather the complexity of the restructuring and compensation structure of the professionals retained, see Lubben, 'What we "Know" about Chapter 11 Cost is Wrong' (2012) 17 Fordham J. Corp. & Fin. L. 142, 147, 153ff. See also Lubben, 'Chapter 11 Professional Fee Study' (2007) Am. Bankr. Ins. <http://ssrn.com/abstract=1020477> accessed 16 January 2017; Lubben, 'Corporate Reorganization & Professional Fees' (2008) 82 Am. Bankr. L.J. 77.

282 See, eg, Wood (n 280) para 2-004; Finch, 'Corporate Insolvency Law' (n 235) 251–2; D Brown, *Corporate Rescue – Insolvency Law in Practice* (John Wiley & Sons 1996) para 1.35ff; Segal, 'Rehabilitation and Approaches other than Formal Insolvency Procedure' in Cranston (ed), *Banks and Remedies* (Oxford University Press 1992) 133. However, even the extent of such costs may vary depending on the 'rescue-friendliness' of a jurisdiction. Accordingly, such costs may be lower in the pro-rescue US where a market for 'distressed assets' might have developed to a greater extent than, eg, in the presumably (still) pro-liquidation South Africa context. On the legal culture of the South African corporate insolvency law, see PART B, Chapter 4, VI. below.

283 Eidenmüller, 'Unternehmenssanierung' (n 265) 74ff, 122, 331ff.

pany foregoes investment opportunities that it would have been able to take, had it resolved its distress informally.[284]

2. Conditions reducing the costs of pre-insolvency bargaining

a. Debt capital structure of companies

Of course, given the absence of a moratorium and procedural rules to 'co-ordinate' creditors' bargaining, the costs of bargaining – primarily co-ordination costs and holdout behaviour/free-riding – make workouts difficult, particularly where the debt capital of the company is widely dispersed.[285] Nevertheless, there are certain factors or conditions that reduce such bargaining costs. One condition is the number and type of creditors involved: the smaller the number and the less heterogeneous their interest, the lower the costs.[286] Indeed, there is some empirical evidence supporting this claim in respect of SMEs in the UK, which are typically financed by a single bank.[287] This is encouraged by British law allowing lenders to take security by way of a package of fixed and floating charges over the debtor's assets.[288] However, even for companies that have creditors with homogeneous interests, the type of creditor might matter. Empirical evidence from the US shows that companies whose private debt comprises mainly bank

---

284 Gilson (n 204) 313.

285 See n 204 and accompanying text above.

286 Gilson, John and Lang (n 281) 315, 321ff; McConnell and Servaes, 'The economics of pre-packaged bankruptcy' in Bhandari and Weiss (eds), *Corporate Bankruptcy – Economic and Legal Perspectives* (Cambridge University Press 1996) 322, 323; Wood (n 280) para 2-005; D Brown (n 282) para 1.43. On how a company's capital structure (notably dispersed or concentrated debt) could be seen as a response to the collective action problem, see Picker, 'Security Interests, Misbehaviour and Common Pools' (1992) 59 U. Chi. L. Rev. 64. On how capital structures could overcome the costs of resolving financial distress, see Bolton and Scharfstein, 'Optimal Debt Structure and the Number of Creditors' (1996) 104 J. Polit. Economy 1; Bris and Welch, 'The Optimal Concentration of Creditors' (2005) 60 J. Finance 2193.

287 See generally Franks and Sussman (n 264) 65. On the impact of this loan structure on workouts by comparison to Germany and France, see Davydenko and Franks, 'Do Bankruptcy Codes Matter? A Study of Defaults in France, Germany, and the UK' (2008) 63 J. Finance 565.

288 Ibid.

lenders tend to be more successful in implementing workouts.[289] This might be either because of information asymmetries[290] or because trade creditors' claims are too small to justify the costs of bargaining *ex ante*.[291]

b. The development of non-binding principles of informal rescue measures

Non-binding principles facilitating workouts also play an important role in reducing the costs of resolving distress outside of formal insolvency proceedings. Probably the best-known example of such set of principles is the so-called 'London Approach'.[292] Founded by the Bank of England in response to the multibank restructuring of the secondary banking crisis of the 1970s,[293] it facilitates co-operation, co-ordination, information sharing, and pro-rata cost/loss-sharing among lending banks of a distressed debtor.[294] Costs are specifically reduced through a contractual moratorium among the banks ('standstill' agreement); the facilitation of bargaining through the establishment of a committee of members of participating banks ('steering committee'); the appointment of a 'lead bank' of the steering committee to co-ordinate the workout and reduce information asymmetries and free-riding through the gathering and distribution of information to all steering committee members, which also ensures that costs are shared;[295] and the reduction of holdout behaviour or free-riding

---

289 Gilson, John and Lang (n 281) 315, 323.

290 For a comprehensive account of which factors may influence the participation of different classes of creditors in workouts, see Wood (n 280) para 21-003.

291 Wood (n 280) para 2-005.

292 There is no single documentation of the principles, but rather a series of papers by Bank officials; Kent, 'The London Approach' (1993) 8 J.I.B.L. 81; Kent, 'The London Approach: Distressed Debt Trading' (1994) B.E.Q.B. 110; Kent, 'Corporate Workouts: A UK Perspective' (1997) 6 I.I.R. 165. A further set of principles is INSOL International, 'Statement of Principles for a Global Approach to Multi-Creditor Workouts' (2000) <https://www.insol.org/pdf/Lenders.pdf> accessed 14 January 2017.

293 Segal, 'Corporate Recovery and Rescue – Mastering the Key Strategies Necessary for Successful Cross Border Workouts' (2000) 13 Ins. Int. 17, 20.

294 Belcher, 'The Economic Implications of Attempting to Rescue Companies' in Rajak (ed), *Insolvency Law: Theory and Practice* (Sweet & Maxwell 1993) 235.

295 Segal, 'Corporate Recovery and Rescue' (n 293) 20; Finch, 'Corporate Insolvency Law' (n 235) 309. The role of the steering committee and the lead banks are

of the participating banks through reputational and future business damage for not co-operating or engaging in holdout behaviour.[296]

Further typical steps after a standstill have been agreed are the immediate pro-rata provision of new facilities, where necessary, the gathering of information about the debtor-company, and the devising of a restructuring plan. The Bank of England may be involved as an intermediary, where necessary.[297]

However, apart from the inherent problems of contractual solutions to corporate distress,[298] utility of the London Approach is usually limited to large companies to which banks have extended significant loans.[299] This is because only in such cases the reputational and commercial concerns would probably justify the high costs of implementing a workout.[300]

Principles based on the London Approach have been established throughout advanced economies.[301] It is conjectured that the new formal rescue procedure in South Africa will provide an impetus particularly to banks to pay more attention to workouts.

It has been argued that in order to overcome the inherent limitations of arrangements, such as the London Approach, in ameliorating particularly the holdout/free-rider problems, mandatory duties of creditors and/or the company to co-operate in contractual workouts could be developed from the general law.[302] Examples of such co-operation duties could be duties

---

among the issues documented in the 'inter-creditor agreement'; Segal 'Corporate Recovery and Rescue' (n 293) 27.

296 Wood (n 280) para 21-025; Finch, 'Corporate Insolvency Law' (n 235) 309; Armour and Deakin, 'Norms in Private Insolvency Procedures: The "London Approach" to the Resolution of Financial Distress' (2001) 1 JCLS 21, 45.

297 Segal, 'Corporate Recovery and Rescue' (n 293) 20.

298 Text to nn 203–206 above.

299 There were only around 150 London Approach workouts in the UK in the late 1980s and 1990s; Flood and others, 'The Professional Restructuring of Corporate Rescue: Company Voluntary Arrangements and the London Approach' (1995) ACCA Research Report 45 < http://johnflood.com/pdfs/Prof_Restructuring_of_Corp_Rescue_1995.pdf> accessed 16 January 2017; Pointon, 'London Approach: A Look at its Application and its Alternatives' [1994] Insolv. B. 5.

300 Finch, 'Corporate Insolvency Law' (n 235) 309–10. On the high implementation costs, see Flood and others (n 299).

301 Segal, 'Corporate Recovery and Rescue' (n 293) 25.

302 Eidenmüller, 'Unternehmenssanierung' (n 265) Ch 6; Eidenmüller, 'Trading in Times of Crisis: Formal Insolvency Proceedings, Workouts and the Incentives for Shareholders/Managers' (2006) 7 EBOR 239, 254ff.

to *negotiate* or duties to *agree* to certain reorganisation measures or even duties of creditors to grant a bridging loan or to participate in an out-of-court debt restructuring.[303] Given their potential advantages for rescue, it would be worthwhile considering the development of such co-operations duties in South Africa. However, this topic falls outside the scope of this study and is thus left to be analysed by future research.

3. A hybrid procedure – pre-packaged plans

Having emerged in the US in the mid-1980s, pre-packaged plans ('pre-packs') are by now widely used both in the US and the UK.[304] In a pre-pack – as the name suggests – the terms of a restructuring plan are usually devised by management with its major creditors[305] prior to formal insolvency proceedings, and the majority voting provision of the formal procedure is then used to have the plan passed. Conducting most of the negotiations on the plan outside the formal insolvency procedure reduces the di-

303 Eidenmüller, 'Trading in Times of Crisis' (n 302) 256.

304 See, eg, Vilaplana, 'A Pre-Pack Bankruptcy Primer' (1998) 44 Ali-Aba The Practical Lawyer 33; Skeel Jr, *Debt's Dominion: A History of Bankruptcy Law in America* (Princeton University Press 2001). For the UK, in 2004, it is claimed that a pre-pack was involved in 44% of all formal rescues; Katz and Mumford, *Report to the Insolvency Service: Study of Administration Cases* (Insolvency Service 2006). In 2006–7 at least a third and perhaps half of all going concern sales are estimated to have involved a pre-pack; Frisby, 'A Preliminary Analysis of Pre-packaged Administrations: Report to R3 – The Association of Business Recovery Professionals' 2007 R3 <https://www.r3.org.uk/media/documents/publications/press/preliminary_analysis_of_pre-packed_administrations.pdf> accessed 30 December 2016.

305 For an argument that German law imposes a duty primarily on creditors with a contractually and structurally strong bargaining power, such as major creditors and strategic investors, to initiate, or participate in, negotiations with the debtor and possibly other types of creditors as part of a pre-pack on the basis of the pre-insolvency application ('*insolvenzrechtliche Vorauswirkung*') of a duty of loyalty ('*Treuepflicht*') or, more precisely, a binding obligation ('*Pflichtbindung*') as between creditors which is based on the principle of equal treatment of creditors ('*Gläubigergleichbehandlung*') and the safeguarding of the relative weighting of interests of creditors ('*Wahrung der relativen Interessengewichte*') within a group of creditors ('*Gruppensituation*'), see Grünewald, *Mehrheitsherrschaft und insolvenzrechtliche Vorauswirkung in der Unternehmenskrise* (Mohr Siebeck 2015) 250ff, 370-1.

rect costs of implementing formal proceedings, which is supported by empirical evidence in the US.[306] Moreover, the fact that the formal insolvency procedure might be perceived by the market merely as a 'necessary evil' to rescue a financially distressed, but otherwise viable business, might also reduce the indirect costs of insolvency.[307] Holdout and free-riding costs during the pre-insolvency negotiations of the plan are controlled through the 'threat' that holdout and free-riding creditors will be outvoted during formal insolvency proceedings.[308]

However, these cost-savings of pre-packs must be weighed up against their costs that primarily fall on unsecured creditors. Inevitably, the proposal in a pre-pack will be a going concern sale of (part of) the company's business. As the pre-pack negotiations on the rescue plan prior to the opening of formal insolvency proceedings are typically kept confidential in order to avoid the adverse consequences of creditor enforcement and a negative market reaction, the market might not be properly tested when searching for a buyer of the company's assets,[309] resulting in the sale of the company's business at an undervalue.[310]

The constituents most likely to benefit from a quick sale are primarily secured creditors, notably banks. So long as the proceeds of the sale cover

306 Tashjian, Lease and McConnel, 'Prepacks: An Empirical Analysis of Prepackaged Bankruptcies' (1996) 40 J. Finan. Econ. 135, 155; Vilaplana (n 304) 34; Ayer, Bernstein and Friedland, 'Ch 11 – "101": Out-of-Court Workouts, Prepacks and Pre-arranged Cases: A Primer' (2005) 24 Abi Journal 16. But see Lubben, 'Chapter 11 Costs' (n 279) 146–7, 153ff, 169, showing empirical evidence to the contrary, arguing that there is merely a shifting of such costs to the pre-bankruptcy period.

307 Finch, 'Corporate Insolvency Law' (n 235) 457; Cranston, *Pre-packaged Business Disposals: White Knight or Thief in the Night?* (ILA Annual Conference 2006).

308 Particularly in respect of 'vulture fund' creditors, see Viliplana (n 304) 33.

309 Empirical evidence on pre-packs in the UK from 2007 show that only in 7.9% of pre-packs was the company marketed compared to 55.6% in non-pre-packed going concern sales; Frisby (n 304); S Davies, 'Pre-pack – He Who Pays the Piper Calls the Tune' [2006] Recovery 16, 17.

310 On this problem in the UK, see Flynn, 'Pre-pack Administrations' – A Regulatory Perspective' [2006] Recovery 3. Empirical evidence on pre-packs in the UK from 2007 show that returns to unsecured creditors are only one half in pre-packaged sales in administration than in non-pre-packed sales pre-Enterprise Act 2002, and only one eleventh in the post-Enterprise Act 2002 period. By contrast, secured creditors do much better in pre-packaged sales (59.1% to 27.5%); Frisby (n 304).

the outstanding portion of their claims, secured creditors' interests are much better served by a quick sale that might be (slightly) undervalued, since this would likewise reduce the risk that a long and protracted formal procedure and changing trading conditions might reduce the value of their collateral. This gives rise to an inter-creditor agency problem.

Moreover, there have also been reports from the UK of planned proposals that provide for the incumbent management buying the company's business (referred to as 'management buy-outs' ('MBOs')), bringing with it a risk of the 'phoenix syndrome'.[311] This is where the company's business is sold as a going concern at a knock-down price to a new company established by the former management for this purpose and usually carrying the same or similar name as the first company, with the sale price being effectively 'subsidised' by unsecured creditors.[312] This effectively amounts to a form of asset dilution.[313]

Although the legal controls ensuring the protection of creditors are available under the formal procedure, it has been reported in the UK that the proposal would often be treated as a *fait accompli*, and the office holder would be reluctant to traverse the plan proposal in a manner consistent with his statutory duties,[314] let alone consider the primary rescue method, namely preservation of the going concern.[315]

It is not clear whether professionals involved in the negotiations of the pre-pack should be allowed to be appointed as the office holder in formal rescue proceedings. This is because, on the one hand, it could raise concerns about the person's independence. On the other hand, it could discourage the use of pre-packs, as the office holder might be reluctant to impose the pre-pack without having investigated the affairs of the company, thereby raising the direct costs of the procedure, which is precisely what the pre-pack seeks to avoid.[316]

---

311 S Davies (n 309) 16, 17.

312 Sealy and Milman, *Annotated Guide to the Insolvency Legislation* (10th edn, Thomson/Sweet & Maxwell 2007).

313 See Chapter 1 for the meaning of 'asset dilution'.

314 Finch, 'Corporate Insolvency Law' (n 235) 464; Moulton, 'The Uncomfortable Edge of Propriety – Pre-packs or Just Stitch-ups?' [2005] Recovery 2.

315 Walton, 'Pre-packaged Administrations – 'Trick or Treat' (2006) 19 Ins. Int. 113, 116.

316 Whether or not professionals having acted for the company are entitled to be appointed as a rescue practitioner is not clear under South African law, as will be discussed in Chapter 4 below.

The challenge in regulating pre-packs – as in relation to the question whether advisors of the company are independent of the company, and may thus be appointed as an office holder – is to avoid that such legal intervention undermines the cost-advantages of pre-packs. For example, an introduction of legal controls prior to the filing of insolvency – such as disclosure requirements and even voting, as in the US[317] – could re-introduce the very costs that the pre-pack seeks to reduce and which make it such an attractive option.[318]

An alternative to shifting some insolvency regulation to the pre-insolvency period is 'self-regulation' of professional bodies – that is, through professional ethical rules applying to the professionals conducting the pre-packaged negotiations.[319] However, the major weaknesses of self-regulation would be its limited reach (in that it only applies to the regulated profession) and questions about its rigour.[320]

V. Summary and conclusion

This Chapter considered three aspects of the theoretical foundations of corporate insolvency law, namely: (i) attempted justifications of the mandatory collective insolvency procedure primarily from the perspective of the field of law and economics; (ii) the most appropriate means of applying the company's assets in insolvency proceedings; (iii) and the possibilities of contractual solutions to financial distress that could reduce the reliance of distressed companies on the mandatory procedure, given its high direct and indirect costs.

The Creditors' Bargain Model ('CBM') is the first comprehensive theory seeking to justify collective insolvency law. According to the CBM, collective insolvency law is justified because creditors would agree to it if they were placed behind a veil of ignorance. This is because they would realise that the prisoners' dilemma would prevent them from co-ordinating

317 11 USC § 1126(b); rules 3017–3018 Federal Rules of Bankruptcy Procedure (1983). This probably also accounts for Lubben's finding (n 281) 169 that in pre-packs in the US there is merely a shift of the Chapter 11 costs to the pre-insolvency period.

318 Finch, 'Corporate Insolvency Law' (n 235) 477.

319 Ibid 466–7.

320 Ibid 473–4.

their actions efficiently if they had to resolve the financial distress of their debtors by contract (duplicative enforcement costs, high monitoring costs, high co-ordination costs and holdout behaviour).

The CBM further claims that collective insolvency law should only distribute the common pool of assets of the debtor and leave pre-insolvency contractual rights intact. Consequently, auctions are the only acceptable form of deploying the company's assets. The main reason advanced is that this would reduce the collective decision-making costs of creditors (mostly inter-creditor agency costs).

The CBM has been subject to various attacks. One line of criticism has been advanced from within the field of law and economics. It explores ways of overcoming co-ordination costs and holdout problems of bargaining for a contractual solution to financial distress at the time funds are advanced to debtors.

One theory suggests designing a special type of capital structure indirectly proportional to the ranking in insolvency which kicks in when the debtor defaults on his debts (Adler's 'chameleon equity'). However, for chameleon equity to be feasible, applicable areas of law would need to be co-ordinated, the costs of which would be prohibitively high.

Another theory suggests that the company's constitution provide for a 'menu' of insolvency procedures to which every creditor would be bound upon contracting with the company. This would allow companies to choose an insolvency procedure that would be suited to its capital structure, thereby reducing strategic behaviour and monitoring costs (Rasmussen's 'menu of insolvency proceedings'). However, in inefficient capital markets, company controllers may not choose the most efficient insolvency option, giving rise to company-creditor agency costs. Moreover, changing finance and business conditions would require the insolvency options to be adapted, thus raising co-ordination costs.

Further rival theories have been advanced from outside the field of law and economics, namely: (i) Warren's immanent values theory (ie, that insolvency law should reflect values of the general law); (ii) Gross' communitarian theory (ie, that insolvency law should take into account community interests); and (iii) Korobkin's broad-based contractarianism (ie, that insolvency law should be inclusive of all interests potentially affected by the company's decline and promote the long-term interests of the company or, failing that, the most vulnerable in society). However, all of these theories essentially fail to provide for a convincing basis for choosing between competing interests.

Mokal convincingly argues that the biggest problem with the CBM is that the persons in the *ex ante* position have certain characteristics that give them no reason to agree to a collective insolvency procedure, thereby stripping the CBM of much of its theoretical basis.

With regard to the question of the most appropriate means of applying the company's assets in insolvency proceedings, the assertion of the CBM that auctions will always place the debtor's assets to their highest value use is questionable. This is because the market could often undervalue the assets (illiquidity of market in industry-wide downturn and negative market signals of insolvency) and that a person is required to oversee the auction, potentially generating agency costs.

It would thus seem that there is no clear answer as to whether reorganisation or auctions should be preferred. This will depend on the circumstances of each situation.

Alternative auction models (proposed by Bebchuk, on the one hand and by Aghion, Hart and Moore, on the other hand) have been developed that seek to overcome the aforementioned problems of conventional auctions. They do so by homogenising creditors' claims through converting them to equity, while retaining the pre-insolvency priorities through the allocation of options to the existing creditors at an exercise price that takes account of such priorities.

Both models are potentially limited, however, as their requirement of trading options makes the models unsuitable for smaller and medium-sized (non-listed) companies, which make up most of the companies under insolvency proceedings. Moreover, the models are unable to prevent the indirect costs of insolvency.

Informal rescue mechanisms have the advantage of avoiding the high direct and indirect costs and the opportunity costs of insolvency proceedings.

However, their use is made difficult by holdout/free-rider problems and transaction costs. These problems are less pronounced where companies' debt structure is concentrated and where the creditors are largely banks, as this reduces co-ordination costs.

Non-binding arrangements between banks, such as the London Approach, could promote the use of workouts. However the utility of the London Approach seems to be limited to large companies to which banks have extended large loans, since only in such cases the reputational and commercial concerns would probably justify the high costs of implementing a workout.

In ameliorating particularly the holdout/free-rider problems, mandatory duties of creditors and/or the company to co-operate in contractual workouts could be developed from the general law. Given their potential advantages for rescue, it would be worthwhile considering the development of such co-operation duties in South Africa.

A hybrid procedure between workouts and formal insolvency proceedings is a pre-packaged plan ('pre-packs'). Pre-packs combine the low direct costs of informal workouts with the ability to impose the plan on a minority under the formal procedure.

The advantages of pre-packs are that they (i) save on the direct costs (creditor negotiations conducted outside insolvency proceedings) and indirect costs of insolvency (market might regard opening of insolvency proceedings as 'necessary evil' to rescue) and (ii) reduce holdout behaviour by the 'threat' of a vote on the prepackaged plan during insolvency proceedings.

However, pre-packs might give rise to inter-creditors agency costs (undervalue sales) and forms of asset dilution (the Phoenix syndrome in MBOs, particularly in the UK).

In regulating this matters, the law needs to strike a balance between protecting unsecured creditors from abuses by company controllers and maintaining the cost advantages of pre-packs.

An alternative to shifting some insolvency regulation to the pre-insolvency period is 'self-regulation' of professional bodies – that is, through professional ethical rules applicable to the professionals conducting the pre-packaged negotiations. Major weaknesses of self-regulation would be its limited reach and questions about its rigour.

PART B
DEVELOPMENT AND CENTRAL FEATURES OF THE SOUTH AFRICAN RESCUE LAW

Chapter 3 The Previous South African Rescue Law

I. Introduction

The aim of this Chapter is to place the new rescue regime into its historical context. The historical evolution of rescue law plays an important role in understanding the current rescue regime. Against the background that the new rescue law has only been in effect since mid-2011, the benefits of having regard to the previous rescue regime are primarily twofold. First, it provides context to amendments to the regulatory framework of insolvency law and to provisions under the new rescue law to the extent that such amendments specifically address problems of the previous rescue procedures. Examples would be the broadening of the objectives of business rescue proceedings, the softening of the entry requirements and the regulation of the rescue practitioners' profession under the new law.[321] By the same token, where previous legal concepts that are idiosyncratic to the South African corporate insolvency law have been retained under the new rescue law, such as the just and equitable ground for the commencement of rescue proceedings, an understanding of the context within which such concepts have been developed could be instructive for their meaning under the new law.[322]

The second benefit of an historical approach lies in providing the reader with a better understanding of the South African 'legal culture' in the area of (corporate) insolvency law. As will become clear from our discussion in this Chapter, the South African corporate insolvency law has traditionally been biased in favour of the liquidation, as opposed to the rescue, of dis-

---

321 These will be discussed in greater detail in Chapter 4.

322 See, eg, s 427 (passage before sub-s (2) Companies Act 1973 and ss 130(5)(a)(ii) and 131(4)(a)(iii) Companies Act 2008. Unless otherwise indicated, any provisions cited in this Chapter refer to the Companies Act 1973. Moreover, unless otherwise indicated, the term 'companies' is used instead of the more cumbersome 'entities falling under the Companies Act 1973' and 'entities falling under the Companies Act 2008', as the context requires. On the range of entities falling under the Companies Act 1973, see the definition of 'company' in s 1 read with ss 19ff, and in the context of the Companies Act 2008, see the definition of 'company' in s 1 read with s 8 of the Companies Act 2008.

tressed companies.[323] A bias for liquidations usually goes hand in hand with a preference for the rights of secured creditors over other classes of creditors. This is primarily because secured creditors typically benefit from a quick break-up sale of a company's assets because of the higher risk of the devaluation of their collateral under a protracted rescue procedure due to changing trading conditions.[324]

As with the relevant law-on-the-books, an understanding of the legal culture of the South African corporate insolvency law is important for providing context to possible changes under the new rescue law that are specifically aimed at promoting a stronger rescue culture. Examples of such amendments are the expansion of the objectives of rescue proceedings and the introduction of a plan procedure and a cramdown mechanism under the new rescue regime. By the same token, it may sometimes take time before general attitudes in society change in accordance with amendments to the law-on-the-books,[325] particularly in respect of legal requirements that leave room for interpretation. In such instances an understanding of the legal context within which that legal culture arose will be instructive to explaining judicial interpretation.

The previous company law regime provided for four alternative procedures to liquidation proceedings for distressed companies. These are the already mentioned judicial management,[326] the scheme of arrangement or compromise[327] (hereafter, '*legislative scheme*'), the 'arrangement and binding of dissentient creditors' under s 389 (hereafter, '*s 389-arrangement*')[328] and the statutory composition under s 72 Close Corporations Act 69 of 1984 (hereafter, '*Close Corporations Act*'), which applies to close corporations (which is the popular corporate form for small businesses in South Africa).

323 On the impact of legal culture on the South African corporate insolvency law generally, see the discussion in PART B, Chapter 4, VI. below.

324 Armour and Mokal, 'Reforming the Governance of Corporate Rescue: The Enterprise Act 2002' (2004) ESRC Centre for Business Research Working Paper 288 <http://papers.ssrn.com/sol3/papers.cfm?abstract_id=567306> accessed 16 January 2017.

325 Martin, 'Common-Law Bankruptcy Systems: Similarities and Differences' (2003) 11 Am. Bankr. Inst. L. Rev. 367, 374–5.

326 Ch 15.

327 Ch 12.

328 S 66(1) Close Corporations Act specifically excluded the applications of the three procedures mentioned.

Of the four mentioned procedures, judicial management (broadly-speaking, a procedure providing for a court-imposed moratorium that enabled companies to trade out of their financial problems) and the legislative scheme (broadly-speaking, a capital restructuring procedure imposed by a majority vote of creditors or shareholders) played a meaningful role as rescue mechanisms, while the s 389-arrangement and the statutory composition were and will be of lesser or no relevance in practice. It is for this reason that the last two mentioned procedures will not form part of the discussion below, but will rather briefly be dealt with in this Introduction.

The s 389-arrangement entitled a company that was able to pay its debts and was about to be, or was in the course of being, wound up, to enter into an 'arrangement' with its creditors, provided that 75% of all creditors in value and number or a special resolution of members approved thereof.[329] One of the reasons why the s 389-arrangement was of little relevance in practice was that the range of measures that were allowed to be agreed on by the parties in deviation of (minority) creditors' contractual rights by the term 'arrangement' (as opposed to, for example, by the term 'compromise')[330] was too narrow to allow for significant debt restructuring measures.[331] It appears that the scope of use of the s 389-arrangement was further limited by the fact that it was only available to cash flow solvent companies[332] and thus at a stage in a company's decline where the company and creditors might not see the need for any action. Finally, the fact that the ability of dissenting creditors to have the arrangement reviewed by the court could increase the costs of the procedure and the fact that the required majority of creditors needed to be in relation to *all* creditors, regardless of whether they were present at the meeting or voted on the pro-

329 S 389(1).

330 On the distinction between the two terms, see PART B, Chapter 3, IV., 1 below.

331 See, eg, the term arrangement was held to preclude any measures 'materially modifying creditors' rights' (Delport and others, *Henochsberg on the Companies Act 71 of 2008* (loose-leaf) (Lexis Nexis 2015) s 389, 835). If any measures beyond that were necessary, the legislative scheme had to be resorted to (see British case law authorities on the equivalent British provision (s 306 Companies Act 1948): *In re Contal Radio Ltd* [1932] 2 Ch 66, 69; *Re Trix Ltd* [1970] 3 All ER 397 (Ch)).

332 Though it has been argued that this form of (in)solvency was not determined according to s 345, which provides for the test of cash flow insolvency; *Henochsberg Companies Act* (n 331) s 389, 835.

posal,[333] were also seen as significant hindrances to its use in practice.[334] The s 389-arrangement has been abolished under the Companies Act 2008.

The statutory composition applicable to close corporations is based on the composition procedure for natural persons[335] and is only available during liquidation proceedings.[336] The majority required for passing a composition is two-thirds in value and number of creditors who proved claims against the close corporation.[337]

The statutory composition had several shortcomings. First, it was generally quite limited as a restructuring facility as it merely allowed for debt reductions[338] and, possibly extensions of the term of loans,[339] but no other restructuring mechanisms. Moreover, the statutory composition could only be concluded with unsecured creditors, not with statutorily preferred creditors and secured creditors, much less with shareholders.[340]

And second, the liquidator had a discretion to submit the composition proposal to creditors,[341] but is conjectured to have had little incentive to do so, given that he received a time-based remuneration.

Since the new scheme of arrangement procedure under the Companies Act 2008 will also apply to close corporations,[342] it would seem that the more flexible scheme or arrangement procedure[343] will make the composition procedure even less relevant in practice than under the previous Companies Act.

---

333 S 389(2).

334 See Gower, *Modern Company Law* (2nd edn, Sweet & Maxwell 1957) 555 in relation to a similar provision in Britain at the time, s 306 Companies Act of 1948.

335 See s 119ff Insolvency Act 1936. See generally Boraine and others, *Meskin Insolvency Law and its Operation in Winding-up* (loose-leaf) (Lexis Nexis Butterworths 2006) para 72.1.

336 S 72(1) Close Corporations Act.

337 S 72(7) Close Corporation Act.

338 *Vlachos v Supermeats Mtuba (Pty) Ltd* 1968 (4) SA 35 (D) 41–2; *Ottawa Rhodesia (Pvt) Ltd v Burger* 1975 (1) SA 462, 464.

339 *Henochsberg Close Corporations Act* (n 335) para 72.1.

340 S 72(7)(c) Close Corporations Act. See also *Ilic v Parginos* 1985 (1) SA 795 (AD) 802.

341 Cilliers and Benade, *Commentary on the Close Corporations Act 1984* (Butterworths 1986) para 14.03.

342 Item A, 7 Sch 3 Companies Act 2008.

343 On the greater flexibility of the legislative scheme than the composition under the previous Act, see *Henochsberg Close Corporations Act* (n 335) para 72.1.

This Chapter will proceed by first setting out selected issues of the regulatory framework of insolvency law under the Companies Act 1973 (at II. below) and thereafter provide an overview of judicial management (at III. below) and the legislative scheme (at IV. below). The problems under the previous rescue regime will be discussed at the beginning of Chapter 4 in order to provide for a smooth transition to the responses under the new rescue law to such problems.

II. Regulatory framework of insolvency law under the Companies Act 61 of 1973

1. The regulatory system of insolvency law

Consistent with the general reception of British commercial law and the structural and institutional framework into South African law,[344] the British insolvency law tradition that separating the legal and institutional framework for insolvencies of natural and legal persons found its way into South African law.[345] Thus insolvency law for natural persons has traditionally been regulated by the Insolvency Act 24 of 1936 (hereafter, '*Insolvency Act 1936*'), while insolvency law for corporate entities has been governed by the respective enabling company law legislation. However, unlike the Australian approach,[346] for example, the South African legislative framework did not provide for a complete legislative separation between personal and corporate insolvencies. Instead, the law relating to personal insolvencies – ie, the Insolvency Act 1936 as well as the applicable

344 See generally Bodenstein, 'English Influences on the Common Law of South Africa' (1915) 32 SALJ 337; Botha, 'The Early Influence of the English Law Upon the Roman-Dutch Law in South Africa' (1923) 40 SALJ 396; Zimmermann, *Das römisch-holländische Recht in Südafrika – Einführung in die Grundlagen und usus hodiernus* (Wissenschaftliche Buchgesellschaft 1983).

345 Burdette, *A Framework for Corporate Law Reform in South Africa* (LLD thesis, University of Pretoria 2002) 56. Before the insolvency law was unified in the UK in 1985/1986 and consolidated in the Insolvency Act 1986, the insolvency law of natural persons was contained in the Bankruptcy Act 1914 and of companies in the respective company law legislation.

346 The Corporations Act 50 of 2001 comprehensively deals with the insolvencies of the corporate forms incorporated under it, leaving any gaps in the statute to be filled only by case law and not by the general insolvency statute, the Bankruptcy Act 1966.

common law[347] – applied to the winding-up of companies[348] to the extent that the winding-up provisions under the Companies Act 1973 did not provide for a particular matter.[349] On the other hand, any alternative insolvency procedures to winding-up, notably the rescue-like procedures discussed above, were governed solely by the Companies Act 1973.

The winding-up provision under the Companies Act 1973[350] also applied to the winding-up of close corporations.[351]

It should be noted, however, that the winding-up and rescue provisions for certain special types of entities are contained in the respective legislation pertaining to such entity, for example co-operatives,[352] friendly societies,[353] banks,[354] insurance companies,[355] pension funds,[356] medical schemes,[357] financial exchanges[358] and collective investment schemes.[359]

---

347 The South African 'common law' denotes non-statutory law in South Africa, which was received from Roman Dutch law as it was applied in the 15th and 16th centuries in the province of Holland and subsequently developed by South African courts; see generally, eg, Hosten and others, *Introduction to South African Law and Legal Theory* (2nd edn, Butterworths 1995).

348 See Ch 14.

349 S 339.

350 See s 66 Close Corporations Act.

351 See Pt 9 Close Corporations Act.

352 Ss 71–76 of the Co-operatives Act 14 of 2005. The Act almost reproduces all of the provisions of the Insolvency Act 1936 and is thus closer to the Australian approach mentioned above; see Burdette, 'LLD thesis' (n 345) 183 n 15.

353 S 35 Friendly Societies Act 25 of 1956.

354 S 68 Banks Act 94 of 1990 (as amended by the Banks Amendment Act 36 of 2000) and ss 74–5 Mutual Banks Act 124 of 1993. See also Patrikis, 'Role and Functions of Authorities: Supervision, Insolvency Prevention and Liquidation' in Giovanoli and Heinrich (eds), *International Bank Insolvencies, A Central Bank Perspective* (Kluwer Law International 1999) 283.

355 Ss 42–3 Long-term Insurance Act 52 of 1998 and ss 41–2 Short-term Insurance Act 53 of 1998. See generally in this regard Burdette, 'Legislative framework for the facilitation of turnarounds in South Africa' in Harvey (ed), *Turnaround Management & Corporate Renewal – A South African Perspective* (Wits University Press 2011) 185–99.

356 S 29 Pension Funds Act 24 of 1956.

357 S 27 Medical Schemes Act 131 of 1998.

358 S 33 Financial Markets Control Act 55 of 1989.

359 Ss 34–8 Collective Investment Schemes Act 45 of 2002.

2. Procedural interaction of insolvency procedures

The Companies Act 1973 provided for separate and self-contained insolvency procedures, ie, winding-up and the rescue-like procedures discussed above, and each procedure provided for a separate avenue of entry and, to a certain degree, different procedural mechanisms. This contrasts with the German *Einheitsverfahren*, for example, which has a uniform and co-ordinated set of procedural rules governing both rescue and liquidation proceedings.[360] Moving from one procedure to the other would appear to create greater procedural costs in a multiple-procedure system than in the *Einheitsverfahren*.

3. Institutional setting – jurisdiction over insolvency law and regulation of insolvency profession

The High Court in the area of a company's registered office or main place of business had jurisdiction over winding-up and rescue-like proceedings of companies[361] and over the composition of close corporations.[362] The Magistrates' Court in the area in which a close corporations' registered office or main place of business was situated had jurisdiction over the winding-up of close corporations.[363]

Unlike, for example, the US court system, South Africa did not have specialist insolvency courts or specialist corporate or insolvency law divisions within the generalist courts.[364] The advantages of specialised courts are that they are generally likely to create efficiencies as hearings are likely to be shorter, decisions are likely to be taken faster and are less likely to be taken on appeal and case backlogs of generalist courts and the chances

360 Stürner, 'Einleitung' in Kirchhof, Eidenmüller and Stürner (eds), *Münchener Kommentar zur Insolvenzordnung* (3rd edn, C.H. Beck 2013) recital 6.

361 S 12.

362 S 7 read with s 72 Close Corporations Act.

363 S 7 Close Corporations Act read with s 29(1)(fA) Magistrates' Court Act 32 of 1944. See also *Henochsberg Close Corporations Act* (n 335) paras 7.1., 66.2.13.

364 For the US, see, eg, Zimmer, 'Overview of Specialized Courts' [August 2009] International Journal for Court Administration <http://www.iaca.ws/files/LWB-SpecializedCourts.pdf> accessed 30 December 2016.

of forum-shopping is likely to be reduced.[365] It would seem that insolvency and rescue law are sufficiently complex and distinguishable from the general commercial law and give rise to sufficient litigation to justify serious consideration of establishing specialised courts or at least specialised division or judges within the generalist courts.

The insolvency profession was not regulated under the Companies Act 1973.[366] However, there is at least some anecdotal evidence that in practice only persons who were registered with the Master's office (in a register referred to as the 'Master's Panel')[367] were appointed as liquidators or judicial managers.[368] In order to be placed on the Master's Panel, the applicant had to submit basic documentation[369] and was interviewed by the Master and one or two members of the two voluntary member organisations representing the interests of insolvency office holders (hereafter, the '*office holders'*): the Association of Insolvency Practitioners of South Africa ('*AIPSA*') and the Association for the Advancement of Black Insolvency Practitioners ('*AABIP*').[370]

Administrative tasks in the winding-up procedure and judicial management of companies were performed by the Master (a civil servant) of the

365 Ibid. On the other hand, the establishment of specialised courts could create inefficiencies insofar as it could itself give rise to forum-shopping (from the specialised court to generalist courts). Specialised courts could further lead to judicial isolation in the development of the law; to lower access to justices, as specialised courts are likely to be concentrated in one particular geographical area; and to the appointment of low quality judges, as positions in specialised courts carry less prestige.

366 See, eg, Calitz and Burdette, 'The Appointment of Insolvency Practitioners in South Africa: Time for a Change?' (2006) 4 TSAR 721, 721 (including n 4) 732; Loubser, *Some Comparative Aspects of Corporate Rescue in South African Company Law* (LLD thesis, University of South Africa 2010) 37; Loubser, 'An International Perspective on the Regulation of Insolvency Practitioners' (2007) 19 SA Merc LJ 123; Loubser, 'The Insolvency Practitioner – Professional Status at Last?' (1999) 7 JBL 53.

367 Calitz and Burdette (n 366) 732.

368 Ibid. See also Loubser, 'LLD thesis' (n 366) 34.

369 Including a *curriculum vitae* containing, *inter alia*, formal and other qualification and experience in the field of insolvency, proof of the appropriate infrastructure (ie, office space and personnel, etc.), and proof of the applicant's ability to provide security; Calitz and Burdette (n 366) 732.

370 Calitz and Burdette (n 366) 732.

High Court having jurisdiction over the particular matter.[371] Among the Master's tasks were the appointment of the liquidator (in relation to winding-up proceedings)[372] and the judicial manager (in relation to judicial management).[373]

III. Judicial management

1. General

Drawing on the British law on receivers and managers and the US equity receivership,[374] judicial management was introduced as early as 1926 under the first national legislation on company law (the Companies Act of 1926 (hereafter, '*Companies Act 1926*')).[375] The objective and structure of the procedure was fairly straightforward. Having been initially introduced to prevent the demise of large industrial companies vital to the young South African economy at the time of the inception of judicial management,[376] its sole objective was to enable ailing companies to 'trade' out of

371 See the definition of 'Master' in s 1 read with the relevant winding-up (Ch 14) and judicial management provisions (Ch 15). For a historical perspective on the role of the Master, see Calitz and Burdette 722ff.

372 S 367ff.

373 S 428(b)(i).

374 Union of South Africa House of Assembly Debates 25 Feb 1926, vol. 6, col 996–7. See also Olver, *Judicial Management in South Africa* (PhD thesis, University of Cape Town 1980) 2ff.

375 Before the passing of the Companies Act of 1926 (hereafter, '*Companies Act 1926*'), the four provinces at that time (Cape, Transvaal, Natal and Orange Free State) as well as Griqualand West had the sole jurisdiction to regulate company law within their provinces; de la Rey, 'Aspekte van die Vroeë Maatskapyereg: 'n Vergelykende Oorsig (Deel 1)' (1986) 27 Codicillus 4, 13ff and de la Rey, 'Aspekte van die Vroeë Maatskapyereg: 'n Vergelykende Oorsig (Slot)' (1986) 27 Codicillus 18, 18ff. The Companies Act 1926 was based on the Companies Act 1909 of the Transvaal province, which, in turn, had borrowed heavily from the British Companies Act 1908; Olver, 'PhD thesis' (n 374) 1.

376 See the relevant Parliamentary debate in Union of South Africa House of Assembly Debates 25 February 1926, vol. 6, col 996–7 cited in Olver, 'PhD thesis' (n 374) 2–3; Olver, 'Judicial Management – A Case For Law Reform' 1986 (49) THRHR 84, 84.

their financial difficulties, if need be, through the implementation of operational measures.[377]

Judicial management had two further central features. First, during the subsistence of judicial management a court-imposed – as opposed to a mandatory – moratorium prevented creditors from enforcing on their claims.[378] And second, judicial management provided for a management-displacing system of governance according to which the incumbent directors, who were presumably often thought to have caused the company's problems in the first place,[379] were replaced with an independent office holder, referred to as the judicial manager.[380]

Judicial management, like the winding-up procedure, proceeded in two stages: a provisional stage, essentially verifying the debtor-company's eligibility for judicial management;[381] and a final stage, during which the measures to turn around the debtor-company (if any) were carried out.[382]

The court was generally heavily involved in the proceedings. Every important decision had to be approved by the court, such as the ordering of the moratorium, whether to grant the order for the commencement of the provisional stage[383] and the final stage[384] and any variation of the final judicial management order.[385]

Despite the fact that judicial management was in effect for 85 years (from 1926 until its replacement by business rescue under the Companies

---

377 See further the discussion in 2. below.

378 S 428(2) (passage after para (c)). Interestingly, the moratorium was only introduced by the first set of amendments of the Companies Act 1926 in 1932 (Companies Amendment Act 11 of 1932 amending s 196(1) Companies Act 1926). This amendment appears to have been intended to protect farmers whose mortgage loans were at risk of being terminated as a result of the demise of the lending institutions during the economic depression of the late 1920s; see the relevant Parliamentary debates: Union of South Africa House of Assembly Debates 1932, vol 18, col 1867 cited in Olver, 'PhD thesis' (n 374) 6. See also Rajak and Henning, 'Business Rescue for South Africa' (1999) 115 SALJ 262, 265.

379 This is hinted at by the fact that one of the entry grounds for judicial management specifically mentions mismanagement as one of the reasons for the company being unable to pay its debts (s 427(1)(passage before para (a)).

380 S 428(2)(a) and s 432(3)(a).

381 S 428ff.

382 S 432ff. For the two-stage process of the winding-up procedure, see ss 368, 431(2)(a) and (b).

383 S 428(1).

384 S 432(2)(passage after para (e)).

385 S 432(4).

Act 2008, which only came into operation in 2011), it was not only rarely utilised in practice,[386] but where it was so utilised, it led to very few successful cases.[387] It has generally been regarded as a failure.[388]

We will now consider selected matters of the procedure in more detail.

2. The objectives of judicial management

The fact that one of the grounds for the commencement of judicial management provided that it had to be reasonably possible that the company would be restored to full solvency if placed under judicial management,[389] implies that judicial management did not allow for the preservation of the company's business through the sale of the company as a going concern, much less for the piecemeal sale of its assets.[390] Nor did judicial management allow for any capital restructuring mechanisms that addressed the

---

386 See The Department of Trade and Industry's ('*DTI*') Policy Framework, *South African Company Law for the 21st Century: Guidelines for Corporate Law Reform* (GG 26493, Notice 1183, 2004) 45.

387 The latest available empirical data from 1980 (Olver, 'PhD thesis' (n 374)) 286), shows a meagre success rate of just over 12% (rounded to the nearest whole number). The Reports of all Commissions of Enquiries prior to each amendment of the Companies Act until the Companies Act 1973, confirmed this low success rate for judicial management; see Olver, 'PhD thesis' (n 374) 286, 287. For recent (non-empirical) evidence, see the DTI (n 387) 45.

388 See, eg, Olver, 'Judicial Management' (n 376) 86–7; Burdette, 'Unified Insolvency Legislation in South Africa: Obstacles in the Path of the Unification Process' (1999) 32 DJ 44, 57; Kloppers, 'Judicial Management – A Corporate Rescue Mechanism in Need of Reform?' (1999) 10 Stell LR 417, 423; Rajak and Henning (378) 267–8; Smits, 'Corporate Administration: A Proposed Model' (1999) 32 DJ 80, 85–6; Kloppers, 'Judicial Management Reform – Steps to Initiate a Business Rescue' (2001) 13 SA Merc LJ 359, 371ff; Burdette, 'Some Initial Thoughts on the Development of a Modern and Effective Business Rescue Model for South Africa (Part 1)' (2004) 16 SA Merc LJ 241, 248–50.

389 See the discussion in c. below.

390 Denying that a more advantageous sale of assets in judicial management than in liquidation was an objective of the procedure, see *Irvin and Johnson Ltd v Oelofse Fisheries Ltd* 1954 (1) SA 231 (E) 238; *Millman NO* v *Swartland Huis Meubileerders (Edms) Bpk* 1972 (1) SA 741 (C) 744–745 and cases cited therein, *Tenowitz* v *Tenny Investments (Pty) Ltd; Spur Steak Ranches (Pty) Ltd v Tenny Investments (Pty) Ltd* 1979 (2) SA 680 (E) 684. See also Loubser, 'Judicial Management as a Business Rescue Procedure in South African Corporate Law' (2004) 16 SA Merc LJ 137, 146.

company's financial problems. This is because the procedure lacked legal mechanisms that allowed for such measures, such as the ability to amend the terms of the debt agreements of the company and the ability to impose (or 'cram down') such amendments on the applicable creditors. Instead, the only mechanisms available to the judicial manager in restoring the company to full solvency were operational measures. It is mainly for this reasons that judicial management cannot be seen as a modern rescue procedure.

To be sure, because the legislative scheme was available under judicial management,[391] a compromise and arrangement of a company's debt and equity imposed by a 75% majority of creditors or shareholders, as contemplated under the legislative scheme, was effectively available under judicial management. However, it is conjectured that the legislative scheme was used very seldom during judicial management for two primary reasons.[392] First, where it was clear at the entry stage of judicial management that a company could only be saved by capital restructuring mechanisms under a legislative scheme, a purposive reading of the aforementioned entry ground together with the just and equitable ground of entry, arguably denied companies access to judicial management. According to the just and equitable entry ground, judicial management was regarded as an extraordinary procedure, as discussed further below.[393] Second, because judicial managers received a time-based remuneration and had to consent to the scheme,[394] they had a strong disincentive to end judicial management prematurely by entering into a legislative scheme.

391 By virtue of the reference to 'judicial management order' under s 311(1).

392 The last available empirical data date back to 1980, showing that 15% (rounded to the nearest whole number) of the cases resulted in a legislative scheme. This percentage has been calculated from the figures given by Olver, 'PhD thesis' (n 374) 286.

393 See the discussion in c. below.

394 *International Contract Co (Hankey's case)* (1862) 26 LT 358; *Re Guardian Assurance Co* [1917] 1 Ch 431 441; *Re Anglo-Continental Supply Co Ltd* [1922] 2 Ch 723 731; *Re Norfolk Island & Byron Bay Whaling Co* (1969) 90 WN (Pt 1) (NSW) 351 354; *Re Savoy Hotel Ltd* [1981] 3 All ER 656; *Ex parte NBSA Centre Ltd* 1987 (2) SA 783 (T) 787; *Ex parte Lomati Landgoed Beherende (Edms) Bpk* 1985 (2) SA 517 (W) 521; *Ex parte Mielie-Kip Ltd* 1991 (3) SA 449 (W) 454.

3. Entry into judicial management

a. Routes of entry and parties entitled to enter

Judicial management could only be commenced by court order, not by the company itself by board resolution.[395] The parties entitled to apply to court for a provisional judicial management order were the company, individual creditors, individual shareholders or the Master of the High Court.[396] The majority view is that only the general meeting of shareholders, and not the board of directors, was entitled to act on behalf of the company for the purpose of commencing winding-up proceedings and judicial management.[397]

b. Appointment of judicial manager

Although the procedure provided for a separate appointment of a judicial manager for the provisional and the final stage of the proceedings,[398] in practice the person appointed as provisional judicial manager was usually also appointed as final judicial manager.[399] This might be seen to benefit

---

395 Out-of-court entry by board reslolution is available under the new procedure; s 129 Companies Act 2008.

396 S 427(2) read with s 346.

397 See *Ex parte New Seasons Auto Holdings (Pty) Ltd* 2008 (4) SA 341 (WLD); *Hlobane Building & Mining Supplies (Pty) Ltd* 1984 (3) SA 270 (N) 273; *Ex parte Russlyn Construction (Pty) Ltd* 1987 (1) SA 33 (D); *Ex parte Screen Media Ltd* 1991 (3) SA 462 (W). See also, *Re Emmadart Ltd* [1979] 1 All ER 599. See also Blackman, Everingham and Jooste, *Commentary on the Companies Act* (loose-leaf) (Juta 2002) Ch 14, 149–50. For the opposite view, see the older authorities *Ex parte Voorligter Drukkery Beperkt* 1922 EDL 315; *Ex parte Edenvale Wholesalers and General Suppliers (Pty) Ltd* 1959 (2) SA 477 (W); *Ex parte Umtentweni Motels (Pty) Ltd* 1968 (1) SA 144 (D). For more recent authorities, see *Ex parte Tangent Sheeting (Pty) Ltd* 1993 (3) SA 488 (W); *Ex parte Graaff-Reinet Rollermeule (Edms) Bpk* 2000 (4) SA 670 (E). See also McLennan, 'Powers of Directors to Winding Up Insolvent Companies' (1987) 104 SALJ 232; *Henochsberg Companies Act* (n 331) s 427, 928. See generally Larkin, 'A Question of Management: Does it Include Ceasing to Manage?' (1987) 16 Businessman's Law 165; Havenga, 'Directors May Not – or May They? – Apply for the Liquidation of Their Company' (1993) 1 JBL 183.

398 See s 429(b)(i) and s 431(2)(c).

399 See, eg, Loubser, 'LLD thesis' (n 366) 36.

the creditors of the debtor-company, as the final judicial manager did not have to spend scarce resources and time in examining the company's affairs afresh.

However, concerns were raised about the independence of judicial managers. The procedure for the appointment of a judicial manager followed that of the appointment of a liquidator in winding-up proceedings,[400] where the Master would accept nominations (or 'requisitions' – hence the name 'requisition system')[401] by the majority of creditors for the appointment of a provisional liquidator. The purpose of the requisition system was presumably to ensure that the same person was nominated both at the preliminary and the final stages of the proceedings, thus ensuring continuity in the appointments of the provisional and final liquidator.[402]

However, there were serious problems with the requisition system, as the person appointed as provisional liquidator was not the person who necessarily enjoyed the support of the majority of creditors for two primary reasons. First, the fact that the Master was not bound by the nomination of the majority of creditors apparently resulted in corrupt appointments.[403] And second, at the stage when creditors voted on a nominee for the position as provisional judicial manager they had not proved their claims, meaning that it was not clear whether the 'majority' of creditors had been properly constituted.[404]

The aforementioned irregularities left scope for the appointment of judicial managers who lacked the required independence and partiality.

Apparently partly in reaction to this concern, a provision was added to the Companies Act 1973 in 2003 authorising the Minister of Justice and Constitutional Development to determine a policy for the appointment of

400 Ibid 34.

401 On the history and reasons for introducing this system back in 1977, see *Meskin Insolvency Law and its Operation in Winding-up,* paras 4.1–4.2 (issue 19).

402 S 431(4) read with s 369. See also, eg, Loubser, 'LLD thesis' (n 366) 34 (including n 120); Calitz and Burdette 733.

403 *Beinash & Co v Nathan (Standard Bank of SA Ltd Intervening)* 1998 (3) SA 540 (W) 545D. See also South African Law Reform Commission, *Review of the Law of Insolvency: Draft Insolvency Bill and Explanatory Memorandum* (Discussion Paper 66 Project 63, 1999) paras 2.2., 4.5. See generally Loubser, 'Insolvency Practitioner' (n 366) 54 and Loubser, 'LLD thesis' (n 366) 75.

404 See, eg, Calitz and Burdette 734–5 (including n 117).

provisional managers and other office holders,[405] however, such policy was never implemented.[406]

c. Entry grounds

Judicial management could be commenced on three grounds. First, the applicant had to show that the company, by reason of mismanagement or for any other cause, is unable to pay its debts or was probably unable to meet its obligations,[407] and has not become or is prevented from becoming a successful concern.[408] Second, there had to be a reasonable probability that judicial management would enable the company to pay its debts or to meet its obligations and to become a successful concern.[409] And third, even if a company met these requirements, the court could still refuse to grant a provisional judicial management order on grounds that it would be just and equitable to do so.[410]

The person applying for a judicial management order bore the onus of proof.[411]

The entry requirements applied to both the application for a provisional judicial management and to the granting of a final judicial management order.[412]

The requirement that the company be unable to pay its debts has been held to require proof of cash flow insolvency. However, the provisions ap-

405 S 15(1A), which was introduced by the Judicial Matters Amendment Act 16 of 2003. On the motive for introducing this provision, see Business Day (28 August 2002) <http:// www.businesslive.co.za/> accessed 30 December 2016 cited in Loubser, 'LLD thesis' (n 366) 34.

406 Loubser, 'LLD thesis' (n 366) 35.

407 S 427(1)(a).

408 S 427(1)(b).

409 S 427(1)(passage after para (b)).

410 S 427(1)(passage after para (b)).

411 *Irvin and Johnson Ltd v Oelofse Fisheries Ltd* 1954 (1) SA 231 (E); *De Jager v Karoo Koeldranke en Roomys (Edms) Bpk* 1956 (3) SA 594 (C) 601; *Kotze v Tylryk* 1977 (3) SA 118 (T) 122; *Bahnemann v Fitzmore Exploration (Pty) Ltd* 1963 (2) SA 249 (T); *Tenowitz v Tenny Investments Pty Ltd; Spur Steak Ranches (Pty) Ltd v Tenny Investments (Pty) Ltd* 1979 (2) SA 680 (E) 685; *Ben-Tovim v Ben-Tovim* 2000 (3) SA 325 (C) 331; *Porterstraat 69 Eiendomme (Pty) Ltd v P A Venter Worcester (Pty) Ltd* 2000 (4) SA 598 (C) 615.

412 See s 432(2) in respect of the final judicial management order.

plicable to an application for winding-up when a company is deemed to be unable to pay its debts,[413] making the proof of cash flow insolvency easier, appeared not to apply to the commencement of judicial management.[414] This is rather surprising, as the deeming provisions would have had the effect of enabling companies to enter into judicial management earlier. This would have been helpful, since companies have a greater chance of being rescued if they are placed under formal rescue proceedings at a stage before they are cash flow insolvent.[415]

The entry requirement that the company probably be unable to meet its obligations appears to have been slightly broader than cash flow insolvency in two respects. First, it mentions obligations (rather than debts), which must refer to contractual obligations other than the payment of debts, for example to supply goods or provide services. And second, the word 'probably' indicates that the inability to perform these contractual obligations was allowed to be a mere threat, yet the use of the present tense ('is') required this threat to be foreseeable in the immediate future.[416]

The entry ground that the company has not become, or is prevented from becoming, a successful concern seems to have had no technical meaning, and was thus considered to be a more general statement of the requirements demonstrating the company's financial difficulties.[417]

The entry requirement that there be a reasonable probability that the company would be able to pay its debts or meet its obligations if placed under judicial management, has been held to mean that the company is viable and capable of ultimate solvency.[418] At the very least, there had to be a reasonable probability – ie, less than a *strong* probability,[419] but more

413 See s 345.

414 See Loubser, 'Judicial Management' (n 390) 143; *Henochsberg Companies Act* (n 331) s 427, 926.

415 Wood, *Principles of International Insolvency* (2nd edn, Sweet & Maxwell 2007) para 9-005.

416 See also Loubser, 'Judicial Management' (n 390) 143.

417 For a criticism of this requirement and reading it, and the ability to pay debts, as one requirement, see Loubser, 'Judicial Management' (n 390) 143–4.

418 *Millman NO v Swartland Huis Meubileerders (Edms) Bpk* 1972 (1) SA 741 (C) 744; *Porterstraat 69 Eiendomme (Pty) Ltd v PA Venter Worcester (Pty) Ltd* 2000 (4) SA 598 (C) 616, 620.

419 *Kotzé* v *Tulryk Bpk* 1977 (3) SA 118 (T) 122.

than a *mere* possibility[420] – that *all* debts of the company[421] would be paid *within a reasonable time*. Any time frame less restrictive than this was held to infringe the just and equitable ground of entry into judicial management discussed below.[422]

As in relation to the financial difficulties entry ground discussed above, the requirement that the company become a *successful concern* does not appear to have been a stand-alone requirement.[423]

In interpreting the just and equitable ground, the courts took as the point of departure the fundamental principle in the South African insolvency law that any unpaid creditor has a right *ex debito justitiae* to wind-up the company (provided the requirements for winding-up are met).[424] This was the basis for arguing that it would seldom be just and equitable

---

420 *Kotzé* v *Tulryk Bpk* 1977 (3) SA 118 (T) 122; *Noordkaap Lewendehawe Kooperasie Bpk v Schreuder* 1974 (3) SA 102 (AD) at 109–110; *Ben-Tovim v Ben-Tovim* 2000 (3) SA 325 (C) at 333 and cases cited therein. Because the requirement in the final order that the company must become a successful concern did not use the phrase 'reasonable probable', but rather the seemingly more demanding phrase 'will' (s 432), some courts believed this to indicate the test was more stringent for the final order than for the provisional order; see *Tenowitz and Another v Tenny Investments (Pty) Ltd; Spur Steak Ranches (Pty) Ltd v Tenny Investments (Pty) Ltd* 1979 SA 680 (E) 683. However, this reading of the provision was rejected in *Ex Parte Onus* 1980 4 SA 63 (O) 66 (finding support for this position in the earlier decisions of *Kotzé v Tulryk Bpk en Andere* 1977 3 SA 118 (T) and *Ladybrand Hotel (Pty) Ltd v Segal and Another* 1975 2 SA 357 (O)), on the basis that s 432's purpose is to give the court authority to grant a final order and not to lay down the entry requirements.

421 *Millman NO* v *Swartland Huis Meubileerders (Edms) Bpk* 1972 (1) SA 741 (C) 744.

422 *Irvin & Johnson Ltd* v *Oelofse Fisheries Ltd* 1954 (1) SA 231 (E) 237; *Ex parte Mayhew* 1959 (1) PH E9 (SR); *Tenowitz* v *Tenny Investments (Pty) Ltd; Spur Steak Ranches (Pty) Ltd v Tenny Investments (Pty) Ltd* 1979 (2) SA 680 (E) 684.

423 The fact that the granting of a final judicial management order refers only to the company becoming a successful concern and not the ability to pay debts or meet obligations (s 432(2)), suggests that these two requirements are interchangeable; see Loubser, 'Judicial Management' (n 390) 146.

424 *Tenowitz and Another v Tenny Investments (Pty) Ltd; Spur Steak Ranches (Pty) Ltd v Tenny Investments (Pty) Ltd* 1979 SA 680 (E) 683. Another interpretation of the just and equitable ground is that a judicial management order is only to be granted if there is no other remedy available; *Makhuva and Others v Lukhoto Bus Service (Pty) Ltd and Others* 1987 (3) SA 376 (V); *Repp v Ondundu Goldfields Ltd* 1937 CPD 375, 379–380; *Ben-Tovim v Ben-Tovim and Others* 2000 (3) SA 325 (C).

to grant a judicial management order against the wishes of any creditor unless this interest was superseded by the interests of the creditors and members as a whole,[425] particularly where there was no unanimity among the other creditors and members in favour of judicial management.[426] Factors that weighed against the granting of a judicial management order on the basis that it might not be just and equitable to do so were, *inter alia*, a long delay in discharging unpaid debts,[427] the effects of the moratorium on the rights of creditors[428] and the nature of the company's difficulties.[429] This resulted in courts generally treating judicial management as an extraordinary procedure, which could only be granted in exceptional circumstances.[430]

The just and equitable entry ground thus demonstrates the clear bias for the liquidation of companies under the previous rescue regime.

---

425 *De Jager v Karoo Koeldranke en Roomys (Edms) Bpk* 1956 (3) SA 594 (C) 602; *Guttman v Sunlands Township (Pty) Ltd* 1962 (2) SA 348 (C) 351–2; *Tobacco Auctions Ltd v AW Hamilton (Pvt) Ltd* 1966 (2) SA 451 (R) 453.

426 *Marsh v Plows (SA) Ltd* 1949 1 PH E4 (C).

427 *Guttman v Sunlands Township (Pty) Ltd* 1962 (2) SA 348 (C) 352.

428 *Irvin and Johnson Ltd v Oelofse Fisheries Ltd* 1954 (1) SA 231 (E) 237; *Porterstraat 69 Eiendomme (Pty) Ltd v P A Venter Worcester (Pty) Ltd* 2000 (4) SA 598 (C) 615.

429 *Tobacco Auctions Ltd v AW Hamilton (Pvt) Ltd* 1966 (2) SA 451 (R) 453; *Kotze v Tylryk* 1977 (3) SA 118 (T) 123.

430 *Silverman v Doornhoek Mines Ltd* 1935 TPD 349; *Pax Clothing Co Ltd v Vaskis Tailoring (Pty) Ltd* 1953 2 PH E13 (T); *Sammel v President Brand GM Co Ltd* 1969 (3) SA 629 (A) 663; *Ladybrand Hotel (Pty) Ltd v Segal* 1975 (2) SA 357 (O) 359; *Tenowitz and Another v Tenny Investments (Pty) Ltd; Spur Steak Ranches (Pty) Ltd v Tenny Investments (Pty) Ltd* 1979 SA 680 (E) 683; *Ben-Tovim v Ben Tovim* 2000 (3) SA 325 (C) 331; *Porterstraat 69 Eiendomme (Pty) Ltd v P A Venter Worcester (Pty) Ltd* 2000 (4) SA 598 (C) 615; *Le Roux Hotel Management (Pty) Ltd v E Rand (Pty) Ltd* [2001] 1 All SA 223 (C) 233; *Gushman v TT Gushman & Son (Pty) Ltd and Others* [2009] JOL 23589 (ECM) 24. Interestingly, and somewhat ironically, it appears as though there were concerns about the courts in general being too lenient in granting judicial management orders under the Companies Act 1926, primarily due to insufficient facts and low creditor turnouts at the relevant court hearings; see Millin Commission, *Report of the Commission of Enquiry on the Amendment of the Companies Act* (UG No. 69 of 1948) 93 and the van Wyk de Vries Commission, *Main Report of the Companies Act Commission of Enquiry* (RP 45 1970) 145.

4. The moratorium, treatment of security and quasi-security interests, uncompleted contracts and set off

According to the moratorium, 'all actions, proceedings, the execution of all writs, summonses and other processes against the company' were stayed.[431] This definition generally included the right of secured creditors to realise their security in the company. However, it appears as though one form of real security – the cession *in securitatem debiti* – was exempt from the moratorium, at least where the debtor-company ('cedent') ceded to its creditors ('cessionary') its book debts in security of its obligations to the creditor. Accordingly, the cessionary was entitled to enforce against the cedent's debtors while the cedent was under judicial management. However, where the cedent's debtors were not informed of the cession and continued to make payment to the cedent, the proceeds of such payments were not subject to the cessionary's security interest.[432]

It seems that property subject to so-called quasi-security agreements (security in substance, but not in form), such as a retention of title, hire-purchase or sale and leaseback, was in principle also caught by the moratorium.[433] However, since in liquidation proceedings such property ordinarily does not form part of the insolvent estate,[434] the court in judicial management, in exercising its discretion, only precluded the third-party owner from exercising its rights to the property if the objective of judicial management would be impossible to achieve without such property.[435]

---

431 S 428(2)(passage after para (c)).

432 *Goode Durrant & Murray (SA) ltd v Glen and Wright NNO* 1961 (4) SA 617 (C) 622.

433 Under South African law, such property is generally referred to as property purchased subject to a condition, which in turn, falls under the broader heading of 'property possessed, but not owned by the debtor-company'; see, eg, Bertelsmann and others, *Mars: The Law of Insolvency in South Africa* (9th edn, Juta 2008) 203–5.

434 Save where the third-party owner notifies the liquidator of his ownership right in the applicable asset before it is auctioned off; s 36(5) Insolvency Act 1936. Where the third-party owner fails to so notify the liquidator and the said property is liquidated, the third-party owner is entitled to the proceeds of the sale; s 36(6) Insolvency Act 1936.

435 *Henochsberg Companies Act* (n 331) s 428, 933. For an example where the court allowed the creditor to repossess its property, see *Samuel Osborne (SA) (Pty) Ltd v United Stones Crushing Co (Pty) Ltd* 1938 WLD 229, 234; however, the oppo-

As under liquidation proceedings, the judicial manager was able to rid the company of onerous contracts through the right to terminate any uncompleted contracts, in which case the counterparty was entitled to claim damages for the unperformed part under the contract.[436]

Since judicial management did not bring about a *concursus creditorum*, the court was not entitled to preclude the operation of set-off.[437]

5. Disposal of assets, post-commencement finance and governance of judicial management

The ability of the judicial manager to dispose of assets during judicial management was closely circumscribed presumably because in the early years of judicial management, judicial managers were said to have often used the procedure to liquidate assets.[438] First, the judicial manager was allowed to sell assets only with the leave of the court and in the ordinary course of business.[439] And second, the judicial manager was not allowed to pay off pre-commencement creditors before paying the costs of the procedure.[440]

Judicial management did not provide for a super-preference for post-commencement finance. However, pre-commencement unsecured creditors could agree that post-commencement debt financing rank ahead of their claims, thereby enabling the company to borrow at lower costs.[441] Moreover, the judicial manager was entitled to raise funds without the authority of shareholderswhere it obtained the permission of the court.[442]

---

site conclusion was reached in *Western Bank Ltd v Laurie Fossati Construction (Pty) Ltd* 1974 (4) SA 607, 611.

436 *CCA Little & Sons v Niven* 1965 (3) SA 517 (SRA). See generally Loubser, 'LLD thesis' (n 366) 89–90.

437 *Wire Industries Steel Products and Engineering Co (Coastal) Ltd v Surtees and Heath* 1953 (2) SA 531 (A); *Transkei Development Corporation Ltd v Oshkosh Africa (Pty) Ltd* 1986 (1) SA 150 (C) 155.

438 See the Millin Commission (n 430); see also Olver, 'PhD thesis' (n 374) 8–12.

439 S 434(1).

440 S 433(2).

441 S 434(1)(a). This preference remained in force if the judicial management was converted into winding-up proceedings (S 435(1)(b)(i)). See also Olver, 'PhD thesis' (n 374) 140.

442 S 432(3)(c).

With regard to the governance mechanisms under judicial management, the judicial manager had full managerial powers of the company,[443] while there were no duties on the directors to provide information to the judicial manager in respect of the company's affairs to assist in reducing information asymmetries of the judicial manager.

The judicial manager had general duties to provide information to creditors and members, particularly in relation to the financial position of the company.[444]

It has been held that judicial managers owed the general common law fiduciary duties to the company, including the duties to (i) act *bona fide* in the best interests of the company – which may have provided a remedy for the statutory duty to manage the company in a manner he deems most economic and promotive of the interests of the creditors and members of the company, (ii) avoid a conflict of interests and (iii) refrain from making a profit from his position.[445] Moreover, it has been argued that the judicial manager owed the common law duty of care and skill to the company, meaning that he could not be negligent and tardy in the performance of his duties.[446] However, no cases could be found in which liability was imposed on judicial managers for breaching their fiduciary duties and the duty of care and skill.

The only statutory requirement that sought to ensure the judicial manager's integrity and competence was that neither the auditor of the applicable company, nor any disqualified liquidators, could be appointed as judicial managers.[447] These requirements were complemented by the common law principle that judicial managers could be removed from office for mismanagement, complete incompetence or dishonesty.[448]

---

443 S 428(2)(a) and s 432(3)(a).

444 See, eg, s 430(c) read with 429(b) and s 433(h).

445 *Blackman Companies Act* (n 397) s 433, ch15, pp24–25.

446 *The Master of the Supreme Court v Bell* 1955 (3) SA 100 (T) 103; and see *Venter v Williams* 1982 (2) SA 310 (N) 315. See generally *Blackman Companies Act* (n 397) s 433, ch15, p25.

447 S 429(b)(i) read with ss 372 and 373.

448 *Samuels v Nicholls and another* 1948 (2) SA 255 (W).

It has been held that the court had an inherent power to remove a judicial manager from office;[449] however, again, no cases could be found in which the court made use of such power.

Since the only outcome of the procedure was that the company be in a position to resume trading and fully pay its debts, there was little need for requirements that regulate the bargaining between creditors.

IV. The scheme of arrangement

1. Scope of restructuring mechanisms available

Unlike judicial management, the legislative scheme provided for the restructuring of the capital of companies by means of a 'compromise' or 'arrangement' between the company and the creditors and/or shareholders. Although a 'compromise' is conceptually narrower than an 'arrangement',[450] it was not necessary to draw a distinction between these two concepts for purposes of the legislative scheme,[451] as the procedure allowed for both concepts. This resulted in the tendency to assimilate both concepts under the term 'scheme'.[452]

---

449 *The Master of the Supreme Court v Bell* 1954 2 PH E21 (T); *The Master of the Supreme Court v Bell* 1955 3 SA 100 (T). See generally *Blackman Companies Act* (n 397) s 433, Ch15, p 25.

450 First, a compromise requires that there be some difficulty in the enforcement of the rights to be compromised (*Sneath v Valley Gold Ltd* [1893] 1 Ch 477 494 (CA); *Mercantile Investments and General Trust Co v International Co of Mexico* (1891) [1893] 1 Ch 484n 489 491 (CA); *Re Guardian Assurance Co* [1917] 1 Ch 431 432–4 (CA); *Ex parte Cyrildene Heights (Pty) Ltd* 1966 (1) SA 307 (W) 308; *Ex parte Bruyns: In re Coverite (Pty) Ltd* 1968 (1) SA 51 (W) 52). An arrangement, by contrast, can be invoked merely for the purpose of getting the parties to agree (*Re Guardian Assurance Co* [1917] 1 Ch 431 441 (CA); *Ex parte Cyrildene Heights (Pty) Ltd* 1966 (1) SA 307 (W) 308). And second, a 'compromise' requires a reduction in the creditors' claim (de la Rey, *Skikkings in die Suid-Afrikaanse Maatskappyereg* (LLD thesis, University of Pretoria 1983) 33–4), whereas a rearrangement of the creditors' rights is sufficient for an arrangement (*Ex parte Satbel (Edms) Bpk: In re Meyer v Satbel (Edms) Bpk* 1984 (4) SA 347 (W) 359–360; see generally, de la Rey, 'LLD thesis' (n 450) 33–4).

451 De la Rey, 'LLD thesis' (n 450) 33.

452 See, eg, *Ex parte Bruyns: In re Coverite (Pty) Ltd* 1968 (1) SA 51 (W) 52, cited in de la Rey, 'LLD thesis' (n 450) 32–3 (including n 25).

Presumably because of the commercial usefulness of the legislative scheme, there has been a tendency to give the terms 'compromise' and 'arrangement' a wide meaning. For example, some courts have held that the only limitation on the scope of a legislative scheme is that it must not be contrary to the general law or *ultra vires* of the company.[453] There are nevertheless some limitations on the scope of the types of restructuring mechanisms that are permitted under legislative schemes. First, there must be an element of give and take and thus, a mere expropriation or waiver of rights would therefore not qualify as a scheme.[454]

Second, and related to the first requirement, a scheme must affect the rights and obligations of the parties to it – that is, the company and the creditors (or shareholders) whose interests are affected by the agreement.[455]

---

453 *Du Preez* v *Garber: In re Die Boerebank Bpk* 1963 (1) SA 806 (W) 813. See also *Ex parte Provisional Liquidator Hugo Franco (Pty) Ltd* 1958 (4) SA 397 (W) 399–400; *Re Savoy Hotel Ltd* [1981] 3 All ER 646 (Ch) 652. On the general law and *ultra vires* requirements, see *Re Oceanic Steam Navigation Co Ltd* 1939 Ch 41; [1938] 3 All ER 740; *Ex parte Provisional Liquidator Hugo Franco (Pty) Ltd* 399–400; *Du Preez v Garber: In re Die Boerebank Bpk* 812; *Ex parte Cyrildene Heights (Pty) Ltd* 1966 (1) SA 307 (W) 309; *Re NFU Development Trust Ltd* [1973] 1 All ER 135; *Ex parte Federale Nywerhede Bpk* 1975 (1) SA 826 (W) 834; *Re Savoy Hotel Ltd* [1981] 3 All ER 646 (Ch) 652; *Ex parte Natal Coal Exploration Co Ltd* 1985 (4) SA 279 (W) 283; *Ex parte Suiderland Development Corporation; Ex parte Kaap-Kunene Beleggings Bpk* 1986 (2) SA 442 (C); *Ex parte NBSA Centre Ltd* 1987 (2) SA 783 (T) 808; *Ex parte Millman: In re Multi-Bou (Pty) Ltd* 1987 (4) SA 405 (C) 410; *Mercian Investments (Pty) Ltd v Johannesburg City Council* 1990 (1) SA 560 (W) 573; *Ex parte Mielie-Kip Ltd* 1991 (3) SA 449 (W) 451; *Namex (Edms) Bpk v Kommissaris van Binnelandse Inkomste* 1994 (2) SA 265 (A) 283–8.

454 *Re Alabama, New Orleans, Texas and Pacific Junction Railway Co* [1891] 1 Ch 213 243 (CA); *Re Alabama, New Orleans, Texas & Pacific Junction Railway Co* [1973] 1 All ER 135, 140; *Re NFU Development Trust Ltd* [1973] 1 All ER 135; *Ex parte Federale Nywerhede Bpk* 1975 (1) SA 826 (W) 834; *Kleena Industries (Pty) Ltd v Senator Insurance Co Ltd* 1982 (2) SA 458 (W) 462; *Ex parte Suiderland Development Corporation: Ex parte Kaap-Kunene Beleggings Bpk* 1986 (2) SA 442 (C); *Ex parte Satbel* 1987 (3) SA 440 (W); *Ex parte Garlick Ltd* 1990 (4) SA 324 (C) 331; *Re Sonodyne International Ltd* (1994) 15 ACSR 494 497–8 SC(Vic). However, see the dissenting minority judgment of Goldstone J in *Ex parte NBSA Centre Ltd* 1987 (2) SA 783 (T) 811–2.

455 *Ex parte NBSA Centre Ltd* 1987 (2) SA 783 (T) 786–9; *Standard Bank Group Ltd and Liberty Group Ltd, Ex Parte* [2007] 4 All SA 1298 (W) 1303–4. As we will

Third, the subject matter of a scheme must be impossible to achieve by independent agreement between the company and each individual creditor. This includes situations where at least one creditor would not agree to the scheme, albeit due to apathy,[456] or where the reaching of an agreement with all creditors individually would be practically impossible.[457] In the insolvency context, this requirement appears to be easily satisfied.

Finally, a scheme cannot be used to supplant any (other) procedures prescribed by the Companies Act 1973.[458] However, the courts have interpreted this requirement very broadly,[459] allowing, for example, schemes that provided for what could be seen as alternative means of liquidation,[460] notwithstanding that this could arguably circumvent mechanisms that protect unsecured creditors under the liquidation procedure.[461] The general reasoning of the courts for softening this requirement appears to be a gen-

---

see below, it was not clear whether this requirement was met in a particular form of the legislative scheme.

456 De la Rey, 'LLD thesis' (n 450) 35.

457 *Ex parte Cyrildene Heights (Pty) Ltd* 1966 (1) SA 307 (W) 309; *Kleena Industries (Pty) Ltd v Senator Insurance Co Ltd* 1982 (2) SA 458 (W) 464, 770; *Ex parte Lomati Landgoed Beherende (Edms) Bpk* 1985 (2) SA 517 (W) 521; *Ex parte NBSA Centre Ltd* 1987 (2) SA 783 (T) 795–6, 801; *Ex parte Mielie-Kip Ltd* 1991 (3) SA 449 (W) 454; *Ex parte Standard Bank Group Ltd and Liberty Group Ltd* [2007] 4 All SA 1298 (W) 1302–3.

458 *Ex parte NBSA Centre Ltd* 1987 (2) SA 783 (T).

459 See, eg, *Ex parte Federale Nywerhede Bpk* 1975 (1) SA 826 (W). See generally de la Rey, 'LLD thesis' (n 450) 39.

460 Notably, (i) providing for a stay on legal proceedings and distribution by a receiver of the proceeds from a break-up sale of the assets (*Ex parte Klopper and Another NNO: In re Rena Finansieringsmaatskappy (Pty) Ltd* (*In Provisional Liquidation*) 1979 (1) SA 254 (T) 255–56), (ii) a going concern sale of the company's business (*Ex parte Bruyns: In re Coverite (Pty) Ltd* 1968 (1) SA 51 (W) 52–3) or the company's future earnings (*Ex parte Meer: In re Indent Wholesalers v Meer's Retailers (Pty) Ltd* 1950 (3) SA 780 (D)) and (iii) a share (and debt) sale to a third party (*Lansdown NO* v *Baldwins Ltd* 1973 (3) SA 908 (W); *Du Preez v Garber: In re Die Boerebank Bpk* 1963 (1) SA 806 (W) 808–9). See also *Ex parte Cronjé NO* case no 12119/82 TPA (unreported). In the UK and New Zealand there is evidence of schemes amounting to debt-for-equity-swaps; see *In re Empire Mining Company* (1890) 44 ChD 402; *In re Milne and Choyce Ltd* (1953) NZLR 724. See generally de la Rey, 'LLD thesis' (n 450) 47–9.

461 De la Rey, 'LLD thesis' (n 450) 53.

eral reluctance to impose the court's view on what would be in the best commercial interests of the creditors.[462]

2. Procedural requirements

In order to invoke a legislative scheme, a liquidator (where the company was in winding-up proceedings), a judicial manager (where the company was in judicial management), a creditor or a shareholder (where applicable)[463] had to apply to court with a proposal for a scheme for leave to conduct meetings of creditors to consider and vote on the scheme proposal.[464]

The court had wide discretion as to whether or not to grant the convening of meetings of creditors and/or members, taking into account, *inter alia*, (i) the probability that the requisite majority would be obtained,[465]

462 *In re English Scottish & Australian Chartered Bank* [1893] 3 Ch 385 (CA) 409. See also *Du Preez v Garber: In re Die Boerebank Bpk* 1963 (1) SA 806 (W) 813; *Lordan v Dusky Dawn Investments (In Liquidation)* 1998 (4) SA 519 (SEC).

463 S 311(1).

464 S 312(1).

465 *Ex parte Turkstra* 1941 TPD 169; *Liquidator Dainty Foods Ltd v Glenton and Mitchell* 1942 EDL 26; *Bagus Allie v Meer-Onia (Pty) Ltd* 1948 (4) SA 550 (C); *Ex parte Bruyns: In re Mammoth Construction & Drilling Co (Pty) Ltd* 1973 (3) SA 721 (T) 722; *Ensor NO v South Pine Properties (Pty) Ltd* 1978 (2) SA 755 (N) 767–8; *E Sacks Futeran and Co Pty Ltd v Linorama (Pty) Ltd: Ex parte Linorama (Pty) Ltd* 1985 (4) SA 686 (C) 687 690; *Ex parte De Villiers NO: In re MSL Publications (Pty) Ltd (in liq)* 1990 (4) SA 59 (W) 68; *Ex parte De Villiers & Another NNO: In re Carbon Developments (Pty) Ltd (in liq)* 1993 (1) SA 493 (A) 508.

(ii) the fairness and equity of the scheme,[466] (iii) the business merits of the legislative scheme[467] and (iv) the sincerity of the scheme proposal.[468]

In order to ensure that creditors came to an informed and sensible decision when voting on the scheme, the court usually required that a comprehensive circular be prepared and made available to creditors by an independent person (ordinarily a legal practitioner) appointed to chair the meetings of creditors.[469] Moreover, the court order had to be published in local and national newspapers to ensure that all creditors were informed of the meetings.[470]

For purposes of voting on the scheme proposal, the creditors had to be placed into their respective classes. The test for determining the classes of creditors was whether the creditors had a 'commonality of rights' rather

---

466 *Liquidator, Dainty Foods Ltd v Glenton and Mitchell* 1942 EDL 26; *Ex parte Singh (Pty) Ltd: In re Orkin Brothers (Pretoria) Ltd under judicial management* 1950 (1) SA 471 (T) 475–6; *Ex parte Wells NO* 1968 (4) SA 391 (W); *Ex parte Barnes* 1973 (2) SA 201 (W); *Ex parte De Wet: In re Atlas Motion Picture Co (Pty) Ltd* 1978 (1) SA 375 (W) 376; *E Sacks Futeran and Co (Pty) Ltd v Linorama (Pty) Ltd; Ex parte Linorama Pty Ltd* 1985 (4) SA 686 (C) 688; *Ex parte Strydom NO: In re Central Plumbing Works (Natal) (Pty) Ltd* 1988 (1) SA 616 (D) 624; *Ex parte Lebowa Development Corporation Ltd* 1989 (3) SA 71 (T) 91; *Ex parte De Villiers NO: In re MSL Publications (Pty) Ltd (in liq)* 1990 (4) SA 59 (W) 69.

467 *Ex parte Turkstra & Others* 1941 TPD 169; *Bagus Allie v Meer-Onia (Pty) Ltd* 1948 (4) SA 550 (C); *Ex parte Bruyns* 1973 (1) SA 815 (T) 816; *Ex parte Lebowa Development Corporation Ltd* 1989 (3) SA 71 (T) 90–1; *Ex parte De Villiers NO: In re MSL Publications (Pty) Ltd (in liq)* 1990 (4) SA 59 (W) 69.

468 *Ex parte de Villiers NO*: *In re MSL Publications (Pty) Ltd (in liq)* 1990 (4) SA 59 (W) 68.

469 *Re National Bank Ltd* [1966] 1 All ER 1006 1012; *Ex parte Ruskin NO: In re Peace Distributors (Pty) Ltd* 1959 (2) SA 747 (W) 749–1; *Du Preez v Garber: In re Die Boerebank Bpk* 1963 (1) SA 806 (W) 823–8; *Ex parte Seafare Investments Ltd* 1970 (2) SA 417 (C); *Dundas & Miller (Pty) Ltd v Borton NO* 1971 (1) SA 106 (E) 108; *Rennie v Ruca Styles (Pty) Ltd* 1973 (4) SA 266 (C) 269–1; *Ensor NO v South Pine Properties (Pty) Ltd* 1978 (2) SA 755 (N) 760; *Ex parte Strydom NO: In re Central Plumbing Works (Natal) (Pty) Ltd* 1988 (1) SA 616 (D) 618; *Borgelt v Millman NO* 1983 (1) SA 757 (C) 770–1; *Ex parte Lebowa Development Corporation Ltd* 1989 (3) SA 71 (T) 80–1; *Ex parte De Villiers NO: In re MSL Publications (Pty) Ltd (in liq)* 1990 (4) SA 59 (W) 68–9; *Ex parte Garlick Ltd* 1990 (4) SA 324 (C) 733; *Ex parte De Villiers & Another NNO: In re Carbon Developments (Pty) Ltd (in liq)* 1993 (1) SA 493 (A) 508.

470 Klopper and Bradstreet, 'Averting Liquidations with Business Rescue: Does a Section 155 Compromise Place the Bar too High?' (2014) 3 Stell LR 549, 557.

than 'interests'. It seems that the default rule was to classify creditors according to their statutory ranking in insolvency.[471] However, narrower divisions were possible,[472] according to whether the rights of the creditors are so 'dissimilar as to make it impossible for them to consult together with a view to their common interests.'[473] Where the scheme affected more than one class of creditors, separate meetings of the classes had to be held.[474]

The majority that was required for the scheme to be passed was 75% of all creditors in a class present and voting[475] and the vote bound only the creditors of each class.[476]

Where the requisite majority for the scheme had been obtained, the court was required to sanction the scheme.[477] In exercising its discretion, the court considered the extent to which the vote exceeded the majority, the likelihood that the directors of the company would be held personally liable for reckless and fraudulent trading or damages in delict[478] and whether the scheme was consistent with notions of commercial morality[479] and public policy.[480] Finally, the court had to satisfy itself that the pre-

471 *Blackman Companies Act* (n 397) Ch 12, 16-1.

472 See *Ensor NO v South Pine Properties (Pty) Ltd* 1978 (2) SA 755 (N) 763.

473 See *Borgelt v Millman NO* 1983 (1) SA 757 (C) 763; see *Henochsberg Companies Act* (n 331) s 311, 607–8.

474 See *Ensor NO v South Pine Properties (Pty) Ltd* 1978 (2) SA 755 (N) 763. See also *Sovereign Life Assurance Co v Dodd* (1892) 2 QB 573 = [1891-94] All ER 246 (CA); *Ex parte Milne NO: In re Khandaan Drive-in Cinema (Pty) Ltd* 1959 (1) SA 13 (D); *Ex parte Venter NO: In re Rapid Mining Supplies (Pty) Ltd, African Gate & Fence Works Ltd (Intervening)* 1976 (3) SA 267 (O) 275;

475 S 311(2).

476 *Du Preez v Garber: In re Die Boerebank Bpk* 1963 (1) SA 806 (W) 816; *Investment Pty (Ltd) v Crown Furniture Manufacturers (Pty) Ltd* 1963 (2) SA 271 (W) 272.

477 *Re Saratoga Investments (Pty) Ltd* 1941 NPD 117 141–2; *Mahomed v Kazi's Agencies (Pty) Ltd* 1949 (1) SA 1162 (N) 1172. See also *Ex parte Judicial Managers Goldfields Building Society and Another* 1943 WLD 45 47.

478 S 311(5).

479 *Ex parte Lebowa Development Corporation Ltd* 1989 3 SA 71 (T); *Ex parte De Villiers NO: In re MSL Publications (Pty) Ltd (In Liquidation)* 1990 4 SA 59 (W); *Ex parte De Villiers & another NNO: In re Carbon Developments (Pty) Ltd (In Liquidation)* 1992 (2) SA 95 (W).

480 *Ex parte Kaplan & Others NNO: In re Robin Consolidated Industries Ltd* 1987 (3) SA 413 (W).

scribed formalities were substantially complied with,[481] particularly those that could have had a direct impact on the outcome of the vote, such as whether the information provided to creditors on the subject matter of the scheme had been sufficient,[482] creditors had been properly notified of the meetings,[483] separate meetings had been called and, by implication, creditors had been placed in the correct classes.[484]

It would seem that the close involvement of the court and the elaborate procedural requirements set out above were generally meant to protect minority creditors and shareholders.

3. The debt consolidation scheme

a. General

A certain form of the legislative scheme developed in practice over the years, typically in respect of closely-held private companies, pursuant to which a third party acquired the claims of all creditors against a company in financial difficulties, and thereby removed the need for the co-operation of the existing creditors in the post-scheme period. (Since the debt of the company was in this way effectively 'consolidated' in the hands of the ac-

---

481 *Ex parte Chenille Corporation of SA (Pty) Ltd*: *In re Chenille Industries (Pty) Ltd* 1962 (4) SA 459 (T) 461–2; *Du Preez v Garber*: *In re Die Boerebank Bpk supra* 814; *Rosen v Bruyns* NO 1973 (1) SA 815 (T) 818–19; *Ex parte Venter NO*: *In re Rapid Mining Supplies (Pty) Ltd*: *African Gate & Fence Works Ltd (Intervening)* supra 279-8; *Ensor NO v South Pine Properties (Pty) Ltd* 1978 (2) SA 755 (N) 760. And see *Ex parte Meer*: *In re Indent Wholesalers v Meer's Retailers (Pty) Ltd* 1950 (3) SA 780 (D); *Ex parte Simjee*: *In re RA Simjee (Pty) Ltd (in liq)* 1956 (4) SA 733 (N); *Ex parte Milne NO*: *In re Khandaan Drive-in Cinema (Pty) Ltd* 1959 (1) SA 13 (N).

482 See, eg, *Ex parte Borton NO* 1970 (1) SA 190 (E).

483 *Ex parte Cornelissen NO* 1976 (3) SA 286 (O).

484 *Ensor NO v South Pine Properties (Pty) Ltd* 1978 (2) SA 755 (N) 763; *Rapid Mining Supplies (Pty) Ltd* 1976 (3) SA 267 (O) 227; *In re Unity Motors (Pty) Ltd* 1956 (4) SA 14 (W); *Ex parte Ruskin NO*: *In re Peace Distributers (Pty) Ltd* 1959 (2) SA 747 (W); *Ex parte Borton NO* 1970 (1) SA 190 (E); *Ex parte Venter NO: In re Ensor NO v South Pine Properties (Pty) Ltd* 1978 (2) SA 755 (N) 764. See also *Re Unity Motors (Pty) Ltd* 1956 (4) SA 14 (W); *Re Hellenic and General Trust* [1975] 3 All ER 382 385; *Ex parte Simjee: In re RA Simjee (Pty) Ltd* 1956 (4) SA 733 (N) 734; *Ex parte Milne: In re Khandaan Drive-in Cinema (Pty) Ltd* 1959 (1) SA 13 (D).

quirer, this form of the legislative scheme will hereafter be referred to as the '*debt consolidation scheme*'.) Moreover, the acquirer was often an existing shareholder of the company or a connected person to such a shareholder (hereafter, '*insider*'),[485] and normally made the transaction conditional on him becoming the sole shareholder of the company.[486]

The debt consolidation scheme typically took place while the company was under provisional liquidation proceedings,[487] as the *concursus creditorum* effectively protected the company from creditor enforcement.[488] Due to the risk of further depletion of the claims of existing creditors due to the direct costs of the liquidation proceedings, it made sense for the existing creditors to sell their claims to the acquirer under the debt consolidation scheme.[489] The acquirer normally bought the creditors' claims at their liquidation value.[490]

The acquirer was primarily interested in the debt consolidation scheme for tax reasons, as the company's assessed loss could be set off against any future income of the acquirer's existing business.[491] This gave rise to a perverse incentive of the acquirer that the company continue trading at a loss after such scheme had been sanctioned and the company had been released from liquidation proceedings.[492] Moreover, given that companies typically entered debt consolidation schemes during liquidation proceedings, they were ordinarily balance sheet insolvent when the scheme was

485 See, eg, *Ex parte Kaplan & Others NNO: In re Robin Consolidated Industries Ltd* 1987 (3) SA 413 (W) 424. See generally; Kloppers, *Judicial management as a technique for corporate rescue: a comparison with English and Australian law* (LLM thesis, University of Stellenbosch 2000).

486 On the debt consolidation scheme generally, see Getz and Jooste, 'S 311 of the Companies Act: Preserving the Assessed Loss' [1995] AJ 58; Anonymous, 'Company Schemes of Arrangement: Preserving the Assessed Loss' [1989] The Taxpayer 26; Jooste, 'Schemes of Arrangement – a new Development' (1989) 28 Income Tax Reporter 7; Delport, 'Die Appèlhof en Standaardskemas in die Maatskappyereg' [1996] SA Merc LJ 377, 385; Kloppers, 'LLM thesis' (n 485) 192ff; Willimse, 'Het die Klokke Gelui vir Skikkings Ingevolge a 311 van die Maatskappywet?' [1989] De Rebus 205.

487 See *Namex (Pty) Ltd v Kommissaris van Binnelandse Inkomste* 1994 (2) SA 265 (A) 278. See generally Kloppers, 'LLM thesis' (n 485) 193.

488 Klopper and Bradstreet (n 470) 554, 557.

489 Getz and Jooste (n 486) 56.

490 Ibid.

491 S 20(1)(a) Income Tax Act 58 of 1962 (hereafter, '*Income Tax Act*').

492 See, eg, *Cooper v A & G Fashions (Pty) Ltd* 1991 (4) SA 204 (K) 213.

proposed,[493] and the lack of any minimum capital requirements meant that the acquirer had no incentive to restore the company's solvency.[494]

However, particularly trade creditors of such companies would typically lack the resources to justify the costs of monitoring such companies. They would therefore typically continue supplying goods or providing services on credit to such companies on the same terms as in the pre-scheme period, notwithstanding that such terms would seem too favourable in light of the company's decreased creditworthiness due to its continued insolvency in the post-scheme period.[495] This gave rise to what economists would refer to as an adverse selection problem.

The primary question which the courts had to grapple with was whether the post-scheme creditors, as a matter of policy, required any (additional) legal protection at all and, if the answer was in the affirmative, the appropriate legal response to that problem.[496]

From the acquirer's perspective, the success and efficacy of the debt consolidation scheme depended on whether it met two fundamental requirements, namely: (i) that the scheme was between the *company* and the existing creditors (and not between the *acquirer* and the existing creditors (hereafter, '*jurisdictional requirement*'[497])); and (ii) that the underlying transaction fell outside of the tax law requirement that the assessed loss is reduced by any amount compromised by, or concession granted to, the company by the relevant creditors,[498] since in that case the tax benefit – and hence the appeal of the debt consolidation scheme as such – would have been significantly reduced to the acquirer.[499]

---

493 *Henochsberg Companies Act* (n 331) s 155, 536.

494 See *Ex parte Lebowa Development Corporation Ltd* 1989 3 SA 71 (T); *Ex parte De Villiers NO: In re MSL Publications (Pty) Ltd (In Liquidation)* 1990 4 SA 59 (W); *Cooper v A & G Fashions (Pty) Ltd* 1991 4 SA 204 (K); *Ex parte De Villiers & another NNO: In re Carbon Developments (Pty) Ltd (In Liquidation)* 1993 1 SA 493 (A). See also Willimse (n 486) 205; Getz and Jooste (n 486) 56; Kloppers, 'LLM thesis' (n 485) 196ff.

495 *Ex parte De Villiers & another NNO: In re Carbon Developments (Pty) Ltd (In Liquidation)* 1992 (2) SA 95 (W) 103I–J; *Ex parte Lebowa Corporation Ltd* 1989 (3) SA 71 (T) 98. See generally McLennan, 'Abuse of Limited Liability, "Insider" Debts and Subordination Agreements' 110 (1993) SALJ 686, 703–4.

496 This questions will be considered in greater detail at PART B, Chapter 3, IV., 3., b. below.

497 Getz and Jooste (n 486) 58.

498 S 20(1)(a)(ii) Income Tax Act.

499 Getz and Jooste (n 486) 56.

It is largely the attempts of the transacting parties to satisfy these two requirements that gave rise to the emergence of innovative variants of the debt consolidation scheme, with each new variant attempting to avoid the pitfalls of the previous one, resulting in a significant body of case law.[500] In order for the reader to get a sense of the basic construction of these variants, it is sufficient if we briefly set out the earliest variant, which is referred to as the 'standard scheme'.

Under the standard scheme, the acquirer made a sum of money available to be distributed by a 'receiver' to the existing creditors of the company as a dividend in return for which such creditors ceded or deemed to have ceded their claims against the company to the acquirer.[501] The jurisdictional requirement was addressed by the fact that the dividend paid over to the creditors was nominally lower – for example, one cent in the rand – than the creditors' total liquidation interest in the company, which was believed to ensure an adjustment of the rights between the creditors and the *company* rather than between the creditors and the *acquirer*.[502] Moreover, since the diminution of the creditors' claims was only nominal, the reduction in the company's assessed loss was negligible, thereby largely preserving the tax benefits to the acquirer.[503]

b. The continued insolvency of the company in the post-scheme period

The courts were split over the question whether the adverse selection problem of post-scheme trade creditors required a legal response. Deciding over whether to sanction a scheme, some courts relied on the private autonomy of the parties, and concluded that no legal response was re-

500 For a comprehensive account of the variants of this form of the legislative scheme and applicable case law, see *Blackman Companies Act* (n 397) Ch 12, 17–30; Getz and Jooste (n 486) 56.

501 For a useful summary of this variant of the scheme, see *Namex (Pty) Ltd v Commissioner for Inland Revenue* 1992 (2) SA 761 (C) 767–8; generally Getz and Jooste (n 486) 58.

502 See, eg, *Namex (Pty) Ltd v Commissioner for Inland Revenue* 1992 (2) SA 761 (C) 767–8. See generally, Getz and Jooste (n 486) 58.

503 Getz and Jooste (n 486) 58.

quired, on the grounds that it was open to post-scheme trade creditors to simply refrain from contracting with the company.[504]

It was further argued that such creditors were in any event sufficiently protected by s 26(3) Public Accountants' and Auditors' Act 51 of 1951 (hereafter, '*PAA Act*').[505] This provision required the auditor of a company to report to the directors of any 'reportable irregularity' that such auditor was satisfied or believed to have taken place in the conduct of the affairs of a company which has caused or would be likely to cause financial loss. The term 'reportable irregularity' was argued to encompass a situation in which a company was incurring debt while being balance sheet insolvent and this was causing, or was likely to cause, loss to the company or any shareholder or creditor of such company, which was regularly the case in the post-scheme period. In practice, the auditor would often require that the company and the insider conclude a subordination agreement, according to which the debt claim of the insider would be subordinated to the debt claims of all other unsecured creditors, as this was believed to remove the reportable irregularity of the company's credit transactions.[506]

Other courts adjudicating over sanctioning a scheme, however, did not believe that s 26(3) PAA Act was sufficient to protect post-scheme trade creditors, and insisted that the parties enter into an appropriately worded subordination agreement.[507] This was presumably on the grounds that the subordination of the insider's debt claims would reduce the likelihood that the continued trading of the company in the post-scheme period would give rise to directorial liability for reckless and fraudulent trading, and

504 See in particular *Ex parte Strydom NO: In re Central Plumbing Works (Natal) (Pty) Ltd; Ex parte Spendiff NO: In re Candida Footwear Manufacturers (Pty) Ltd; Ex parte Spendiff NO: In re Jerseytex (Pty) Ltd* 1988 (1) SA 616 (D) 623.

505 This Act has in the meantime been superseded by the Auditing Profession Act 26 of 2005.

506 *Ex parte Strydom NO: In re Central Plumbing Works (Natal) (Pty) Ltd; Ex parte Spendiff NO: In re Candida Footwear Manufacturers (Pty) Ltd; Ex parte Spendiff NO: In re Jerseytex (Pty) Ltd* 1988 (1) SA 616 (D) 623.

507 Although some courts have insisted on the conversion of the insider's debt claim to equity (eg, *Ex parte Kaplan & Others NNO: In re Robin Consolidated Industries Ltd* 1987 (3) SA 413 (W) 427), contractual subordination has prevailed; see *Ex parte De Villiers & another NNO: In re Carbon Developments (Pty) Ltd (In Liquidation)* 1993 1 SA 493 (A) 505; see also *Cooper v A & G Fashions (Pty) Ltd* 1991 (4) SA 204 (K).

thus ensuring that the court was approving a scheme of arrangement that was not in violation of the law.[508]

V. Summary and conclusion

The regulation of corporate insolvencies and rescue mechanisms was partially separated between the Insolvency Act 1936 and the relevant company law statutes: while the respective rescue-like procedures (most importantly, judicial management and the legislative scheme) were dealt with exhaustively in the relevant company law statutes, the winding-up of companies was partly regulated in the applicable company law statutes and partly in the Insolvency Act 1936.

The winding-up and rescue-like procedures were separate and self-contained. An important disadvantage of such an approach, as opposed to a more co-ordinated and integrated procedure (such as the German *Einheitsverfahren*), is that moving between different insolvency procedures generates higher procedural costs.

Unlike in the US, for example, the South African court system did not provide for specialist insolvency or rescue courts, or specialised insolvency or rescue divisions or judges within the generalist courts. An important advantage of specialised courts is that they are likely to generate greater efficiencies in the adjudication of disputes.

Office holders were generally unregulated. In saying that, some *de facto* control over the persons acting as office holder was exercised by the Master in conjunction with relevant voluntary professional organisations for office holders.

Judicial management was passed as part of the Companies Act 1926 primarily for purposes of protecting the large industrial companies that were considered important to the young South African economy at the time. However, judicial management cannot be seen as a modern rescue procedure. This is because it merely allowed for ailing companies to trade

508 The main authority is *Ex parte De Villiers & another NNO: In re Carbon Developments (Pty) Ltd (In Liquidation)* 1993 1 SA 493 (A) 505. Other courts based their decision on the grounds that the removal of the company's balance sheet insolvency in the post-scheme period reduced the risk of the extension of credit to the company by future trade creditors; *Cooper v A & G Fashions (Pty) Ltd* 1991 (4) SA 204 (K) 207ff.

out of their financial problems without the possibility of effecting capital restructuring mechanisms, let alone the saving of the company's business through a going concern sale.

Although capital restructuring was effectively available through the use of the legislative scheme during judicial management, it is conjectured that this occurred rarely. The reasons for this are a purposive interpretation of the applicable entry grounds of judicial management and an incentive of judicial managers to delay judicial management in order to bring about the company's ultimate liquidation.

Two further important features of judicial management were that the court could impose a moratorium, *inter alia*, on enforcement actions by creditors and that an independent office holder – referred to as the judicial manager – assumed management powers of the company *in lieu* of the incumbent directors.

Judicial management proceeded in two stages – a provisional stage, which functioned essentially to verify the debtor-company's eligibility for judicial management; and a final stage, during which the measures to restore the company to solvency were carried out.

Consistent with the fact that judicial management was strongly court-driven, it could only be commenced by court order and not by the board of directors out-of-court.

The requisition system of appointment of judicial managers, although well intended, left scope for the appointment of office holders who lacked competence, independence and partiality.

The grounds of entry into judicial management were rather restrictive in general. First, companies could only be placed under judicial management when they were cash flow insolvent or where there was an immediate threat of them failing to meet their obligations. This meant judicial management was generally commenced at a fairly late stage in the companies' financial decline. Second, there had to be a reasonable probability that the companies would be restored to full solvency. And third, the just and equitable ground ensured that judicial management was only granted in extraordinary circumstances.

The moratorium generally prevented enforcement action under security and quasi-security agreements, save for a few exceptions, while the judicial manager was entitled to terminate uncompleted contracts, subject to the rights of the counterparty to claim damages for the unperformed part of the contract.

The ability of judicial managers to dispose of assets of the company was very limited in order to prevent use of the procedure to effect liquidations, which had been a problem earlier on during the existence of judicial management.

Judicial management lacked meaningful incentives for post-commencement finance, for example, through providing such funding with a super-preference.

Although a few mechanisms existed that sought to ensure the accountability of judicial managers to the body of creditors, including, arguably, the common law fiduciary duties and the duty of care and skill as well as the ability of the court to remove judicial managers from office, such remedies appear not to have played a big role in practice.

The fact that the procedure did not envisage any variation of the terms of credit agreements, explains the absence of requirements regulating the bargaining of creditors.

Unlike judicial management, the legislative scheme provided for capital restructuring mechanisms by means of a 'compromise' or 'arrangement' between the company and its creditors. The courts have given both these concepts a very wide meaning, providing the parties with maximum flexibility to restructure the capital of the company.

Two court applications were required under the legislative scheme – one for convening the meetings of creditors to vote on the scheme; and, if a majority of creditors and/or shareholders for the scheme had voted for the scheme, another for the sanctioning of the scheme.

The court had wide discretion in relation to both decisions. It was entitled to take into account a wide range of factors, the purpose of which, in principle, was the protection of minority creditors from expropriation by the majority.

The court normally required an independent person appointed to chair over the creditors' meetings to prepare and make available to creditors a comprehensive circular and to ensure that the court order convening the meetings of creditors was published in local and national newspapers.

Creditors voted on the scheme in separate classes, which were generally determined by a commonality of the 'rights', rather than the 'interests', of creditors.

The majority required for passing a scheme was 75% of creditors in a class present and voting and the vote bound only the creditors of each class.

Over the years, a particular form of the legislative scheme developed where a third party – often an insider – acquired the entire debt, and often also became the sole shareholder, of the company ('debt consolidation scheme'). The primary motivation for the debt consolidation scheme was that the acquirer could set off the assessed loss of the company from any future income from the acquirer's existing business for tax purposes. This gave rise to a perverse incentive of the acquirer that the company continue trading at a loss and refrain from removing its balance sheet insolvency in the post-scheme period. Since trade creditors generally lacked the resources to monitor their debtors, they generally continued providing goods and services to such companies in the post-scheme period on terms that would not price in the increased risk stemming from the lower creditworthiness of the company. This gave rise to an adverse selection problem.

For the debt consolidation scheme to fulfil the aforementioned tax purpose, it had to be between the company and the existing creditors, and not the acquirer, and it needed to avoid the tax requirement that the assessed loss would be reduced by any amount compromised. Both these criteria gave rise to several variants of the debt consolidation scheme over the years.

The courts were split on the question as to whether the post-scheme trade creditors required protection at all. Some courts, deciding over whether to sanction a legislative scheme, argued that the private autonomy of the contractant required the trade creditors to protect themselves against the aforementioned risk by simply refraining from contracting with the companies in the post-scheme period. Such courts further held that post-scheme trade creditors were in any event protected by the auditors' duty to report to the directors of any reportable irregularity causing loss to the company, shareholders or creditors. This requirement ordinarily caught the incurrence of debt by companies in the post-scheme period when being balance sheet insolvent.

Other courts, however, held that the auditors' duty to report was not sufficient to protect trade creditors and insisted that the company and the acquirer conclude a subordination agreement, pursuant to which the acquirer subordinated his claim to the claims of post-scheme trade creditors.

Chapter 4 Selected Issues of the New South African Rescue Law

I. Introduction

The Companies Act 2008 has completely overhauled the South African rescue law. The new rescue procedure, referred to as 'business rescue', has replaced, and fundamentally changed, judicial management. The scheme of arrangement procedure, on the other hand, has been retained under the Companies Act 2008, though some important changes have been made to it.

As mentioned in the General Introduction, the objective of this Chapter is to provide an overview of the new rescue law, acquaint the reader with changes to the previous rescue law, highlight new concepts and consider selected interpretational problems under the new rescue law. This should be of interest primarily to law students, practitioners and the judiciary alike.

Consistent with this objective, the main focus of this Chapter is not to analyse the new rescue law from a principal-agent perspective. Accordingly, to the extent that certain legal provisions under the new rescue procedure are of interest for the aforementioned reasons, such provisions will still form part of the analysis in this Chapter, notwithstanding that they may fall outside the legal strategies dealing with the three manifestations of the company-creditor conflict in the vicinity of insolvency discussed in PART C. A pertinent example of this is the inclusion of the post-commencement finance and the governance regimes of the new business rescue procedure in this Chapter (in IV.7 and IV.8, respectively), despite the fact that the applicable provisions fall squarely within the office holder-company and the majority creditors-minority creditors agency problems, and thus outside the scope of the functional analysis in PART C.

Due to the fairly broad scope of this Chapter, foreign jurisdictions will only be consulted where it is thought to make a particularly insightful contribution to the discussion.

The discussion of the previous rescue law in Chapter 3 has provided the historical context for the consideration of the new rescue law. For this reason, a brief analysis of the main problems of the previous rescue law at the beginning of this Chapter (in II. below) is thought to provide an appropriate starting point for the discussion of the new rescue law. That will be followed by an examination of the regulatory framework of insolvency law (in III. below). We will then analyse the rescue procedure (in IV. below) and conclude with a consideration of the new scheme of arrangement procedure (in V. below).

II. Evaluation of main problems under the previous rescue regime

1. Objectives and entry requirements of judicial management too narrow

The only objective of judicial management seems to have been to provide companies with an opportunity to 'trade' themselves out of their financial difficulties. This means that judicial management did not cater for temporarily distressed but economically viable companies that required more than operational measures to be turned around, namely where the company's capital structure needed to be reorganised or its business needed to be transferred as a going concern.

Moreover, the fact that companies had to be very close to being cash flow insolvent before being entitled to invoke judicial management, meant that by the time companies were eligible to be placed under judicial management, there was limited scope for trading them out of their financial difficulties.[509]

Accordingly, it is conjectured that only a small percentage of temporarily distressed but economically viable companies were either granted access to the provisional stage of judicial management and, where they had been granted access, ended up being placed under liquidation proceedings. This contributed to the general failure of the South African rescue law to place the assets of economically viable but temporarily distressed companies to their highest value use.

2. High direct costs of judicial management and the legislative scheme

Certain features of the previous rescue regime gave rise to rather high direct costs. First, both judicial management and the legislative scheme were

509 See the discussion in PART B, Chapter 3, III., 2 and PART B, Chapter 3, III., 3 above.

heavily court-driven. Under judicial management, the court had to approve certain important decisions and actions, such as the granting of the provisional and the final judicial management order,[510] the sale of the company's assets and the application of moneys received by the company during judicial management.[511] The legislative scheme required two court applications – one for ordering the meetings of creditors and another for sanctioning the scheme after it had been approved by the majority of creditors. It is questionable whether the high costs of court proceedings were always justified in the aforementioned instances for purposes of protecting the creditors' interests, as there are several alternative legal responses that might be equally effective. Examples of these would be relevant duties of the judicial manager in relation to judicial management and approval of the more fundamental decisions by the creditors' meeting.[512]

Second, the legislative scheme provided for further cumbersome procedural requirements, namely the preparation of the circular for the benefit of creditors by the independent persons appointed to preside over the creditors' meetings (the so-called 'Chairperson'), the placing of the court order in local and national newspapers and the fees of the Chairperson.[513]

Third, the fact that the different rescue-like procedures were self-contained made moving from one to the other rather costly.[514] Moreover, the lack of specialised insolvency and rescue courts or judges arguably resulted in procedural inefficiencies.[515]

The aforementioned requirements resulted in fairly high direct costs of the two formal rescue procedures, discouraging particularly smaller companies from utilising the two formal rescue procedures.[516]

510 See the discussion in PART B, Chapter 3, III., 1 above.

511 See the discussion in PART B, Chapter 3, III., 5 above.

512 See, eg, Loubser, *Some Comparative Aspects of Corporate Rescue in South African Company Law* (LLD thesis, University of South Africa 2010) 43, 161.

513 On the requirements themselves, see PART B, Chapter 3, IV., 2 above. For a criticism of such requirements, see Klopper and Bradstreet, 'Averting Liquidations with Business Rescue: Does a Section 155 Compromise Place the Bar too High?' (2014) 3 Stell LR 549, 557.

514 See the discussion in PART B, Chapter 3, II., 2.

515 See the discussion in PART B, Chapter 3, II., 3.

516 See, eg, Rajak and Henning, 'Business Rescue for South Africa' (1999) 115 SALJ 262, 268; Olver, *Judicial Management in South Africa* (PhD thesis, University of Cape Town 1980) 87; Klopper and Bradstreet (n 513) 555, 557; Loubser, 'LLD thesis' (n 512) 148.

3. Incompetence, lack of independence and perverse incentives of judicial managers

There were grave concerns about the competence of, and abuses by, judicial managers under the previous rescue regime. First, persons who acted as judicial managers were not regulated.[517] As a result of this, persons who primarily possessed the skills required and the mindsets of a liquidator – ie, the break-up sale of the company's assets and its ultimate dissolution – were usually appointed as judicial managers. However, the management of companies under judicial management required measures that were, in a sense, diametrically opposed to this, namely turning around the companies through operational adjustments. Thus, the persons who were generally appointed as judicial managers generally lacked the expertise and inclination required by the goal of judicial management.[518]

Second, the competence, impartiality and independence of practitioners was generally called into doubt, first by the lack of regulation of the judicial managers' profession[519] and, second, by the irregularities under the requisition system for the appointment of a judicial manager, as it failed to ensure that the judicial manager was supported by the majority of creditors.[520] This concern was exacerbated by the weak governance regime under judicial management to ensure the accountability of the judicial manager to the body of claimants.[521]

Finally, the inadequacies of judicial management as a corporate rescue procedure generated perverse incentives of judicial managers. Because of the onerous entry requirements of judicial management, notably the ones relating to the restoration of the company to full solvency and the just and equitable ground,[522] many provisional judicial management orders would not be made final, and the proceedings would inevitably be converted to liquidation proceedings. However, it became common in practice that the person who had been appointed as judicial manager would also be appointed as a liquidator following the conversion of judicial management to liquidation. This practice gave rise to a perverse incentive on the part of

---

517 See the discussion in PART B, Chapter 3, II., 3. above.

518 See Olver (n 516) 86; Rajak and Henning (n 516) 282–5.

519 See, eg, Loubser, 'LLD thesis' (n 512) 43.

520 See the discussion in PART B, Chapter 3, III., 3., b. above.

521 See the discussion in PART B, Chapter 3, III., 5. above.

522 See the discussion in PART B, Chapter 3, III., 3., c. above

professional insolvency office holders (hereafter, the 'office holders') to paint a rosy picture to directors about the company's chances of being granted a final judicial management order, and to suggest such course of action even in hopeless cases. Office holders effectively used judicial management to secure appointments in order to avoid competing with other candidates for the appointments as a liquidator of the company.[523]

In general, the above-mentioned concerns with the competence, impartiality and independence of judicial managers contributed to a general lack of confidence in judicial management as a rescue procedure in the eyes of the commercial public,[524] presumably resulting in a reluctance of companies to make use of that procedure.

4. Problems under the debt consolidation scheme

The debt consolidation scheme gave rise to three value-reducing actions, namely: (i) the underpayment of the existing creditors by the acquirer when acquiring the company's entire debt under the debt consolidation scheme; (ii) the failure of the acquirer to apply the company's assets to their highest value use in the post-scheme period; and (iii) the already-discussed adverse selection problem in the post-scheme period. Since the adverse selection problem has already been dealt with in Chapter 3,[525] we will only consider the first two mentioned actions here.

With regard to the underpayment of the existing creditors under the debt consolidation scheme, the acquirer ordinarily acquired the claims of the existing creditors at the liquidation value of their claims. Where the companies were economically viable, the liquidation value clearly undervalued the creditors' claims, amounting to an effective expropriation of such creditors.

It is conjectured that existing creditors of economically viable companies were often willing to sell their claims at an undervalue because the liquidation value may nevertheless often have constituted a reasonable price for the claims. There are several reasons for this conjecture. First, since the debt consolidation scheme was normally concluded during liqui-

523 Olver (n 516) 86.
524 Rajak and Henning (n 516) 267.
525 See the discussion in PART B, Chapter 3, IV., 3., b. above.

dation proceedings,[526] it would generally have been invoked at a very late stage in the cycle of decline of companies. At such a late stage there is generally little scope for capital reorganisation measures. In any event, the general shortcomings of the legislative scheme as a capital restructuring procedure, including its high direct costs and the absence of an effective governance regime, would have made such measures very costly.

Second, due to the aforementioned difficulties of resolving economically viable companies' temporary financial problems by means of capital restructuring, a going concern sale would often have been a more feasible option. However, going concern sales did not seem to be prevalent, as that was not the primary goal of the legislative scheme. In any event, there was a low demand for such assets in South Africa, as the market for distressed businesses was generally quite weak.[527]

With regard to the undervalue deployment of companies' assets under the debt consolidation scheme, the acquirers normally continued trading but refrained from rescuing the companies in the post-scheme period, even though the companies were ordinarily unprofitable and balance sheet insolvent. This constituted a value-reducing deployment of the companies' assets, both in respect of economically viable companies and economically distressed companies: in respect of economically viable companies, the company's assets would have been worth more if applied to productive uses (referred to by economists as an 'underinvestment problem'),[528] while in respect of economically distressed companies, the company's assets would have been worth more if liquidated.

526 See PART B, Chapter 3, IV., 3., a. above. For the reasons for the conjecture that the legislative scheme generally was not invoked regularly during judicial management, see PART B, Chapter 3, III., 2. above.

527 Both aforementioned arguments may also explain why, from the perspective of the acquirer, the monetary value of the tax benefit may often have exceeded the economic viable companies' going-concern value, giving the acquirer an incentive to pursue the debt consolidation scheme.

528 'Underinvestment' occurs where an overindebted company has growth opportunities that require further funding, but shareholders may be reluctant to provide such funding, as their returns will have to be shared with creditors. The opposite problem – referred to as 'overinvestment' – is the investment of funds in projects a rational investor would have rejected because the returns are too low; Armour, Hertig and Kanda, 'Transactions with Creditors' in Kraakman and others (eds), *Anatomy of Corporate Law – A Comparative and Functional Approach* (2nd edn, Oxford University Press 2009) 115, 117 n 7; Myers, 'Determinants of Corporate Borrowing' (1977) 5 J. Fin. Econ. 147.

The aforementioned shortcomings of the legislative scheme and the weakness of the South African market for distressed businesses also explain why the monetary value of the tax benefit may often have exceeded the company's going-concern value and break-up value to the acquirer, giving him a disincentive to rescue economically viable companies and to liquidate economically distressed companies, respectively.

A further cause for the problems under the debt consolidation scheme was the general deficiency of judicial management as a modern corporate rescue procedure.[529] As a result, many temporarily distressed but economically viable companies ended up being placed under liquidation proceedings, where such companies were more vulnerable to the three value-minimising actions discussed above.

As the problems arising under the debt consolidation scheme could be seen as manifestations of the value-minimising use of formal rescue proceedings, the legal responses to such problems will be considered in Chapter 7.[530]

III. Regulatory framework of insolvency law under the Companies Act 71 of 2008

1. The regulatory system of insolvency law

The Companies Act 2008 has made significant changes to the corporate insolvency law procedures. Judicial management has been replaced with a new rescue procedure[531] and the s 389-arrangement has been repealed. Furthermore, the scheme of arrangement, which under the Companies Act 1973 provided for arrangements both between shareholders (and thus in respect of solvent companies) and between creditors (and thus in respect of distressed companies) has been separated under the Companies Act 2008 and certain amendments have also been made to both procedures.[532]

---

529 See generally the discussion in PART B, Chapter 3, III. above.

530 For an explanation of why this action falls within this agency problem, see PART A, Chapter 1, II., 3., a., cc. above.

531 Which is contained in Chapter 6 Parts A to D Companies Act 2008.

532 The arrangement between shareholders is contained in s 114 (which has retained the previous name 'scheme of arrangement') and the arrangement between creditors in s 155 (which is referred to as 'compromise with creditors'). We will consider changes made to the compromise with creditors procedure discussed further

The winding-up procedure for *insolvent* companies has been retained under the Companies Act 1973 pending the outcome of the proposed reforms of insolvency law,[533] which has been under discussion for quite some time,[534] and does not appear to be driven with any conviction by the legislature at present. Such reforms propose that new unified insolvency legislation replace the current Insolvency Act 1936, which is proposed to regulate insolvencies of both natural and legal persons, including the provisions governing the winding-up of companies that have been retained under the Companies Act 1973 in the interim.[535] The winding-up provisions for *solvent* companies, however, have been moved to the Companies Act 2008.[536] This is an appropriate change, as the winding-up of solvent companies is a company law, and not a corporate insolvency law, procedure. It remains to be seen whether the business rescue and compromise with creditors procedures will, in the spirit of complete unification of insolvency law, be moved to the proposed unified insolvency legislation.[537]

---

below in this Chapter. (Each section cited in this Chapter, both in the body of the text and in the footnotes, will be a section of the Companies Act 2008, unless otherwise indicated.)

533 And the relevant Chapter under the Companies Act 1973 that contains the winding-up of companies and therefore remains in force despite the repeal of the Companies Act 1973 (see Sch 5 item 9). The previous winding-up provisions for *insolvent* close corporations also remain in force until the new insolvency legislation is enacted (see s 66(1) Close Corporations Act as amended by Sch 3 item 7(1)). This implies that such provisions are also intended to be moved to the proposed uniform insolvency legislation.

534 For a useful overview of the insolvency law reform process, see Burdette, 'Some Initial Thoughts on the Development of a Modern and Effective Business Rescue Model for South Africa' (Part 1) (2004) 16 SA Merc LJ 241, 242–3.

535 South African Law Reform Commission, *Review of the Law of Insolvency: Draft Insolvency Bill and Explanatory Memorandum* (Discussion Paper 68 Project 63, 1999) 6. This is a radical change in policy from the DTI's position in 2004: DTI Policy Framework, *South African Company Law for the 21st Century: Guidelines for Corporate Law Reform* (GG 26493, Notice 1183, 2004) 43.

536 Ch 2 item 7(2)).

537 On the merits and demerits of unifying a dual regulatory system of insolvency law generally, see Keay, 'To Unify or not to Unify Insolvency Legislation: International Experience and the Latest South African Proposals' (1999) 32 De Jure 62, 71–4. For a proponent of unified insolvency legislation, see Burdette, *A Framework for Corporate Insolvency Law Reform in South Africa* (LLD thesis, University of Pretoria 2002)). Interestingly, it is being proposed that a rescue regime applicable to natural persons, including partnerships and business trusts,

Interestingly, in contrast to the position under the Companies Act 1973, both business rescue and the compromise procedures apply to close corporations.[538]

2. Procedural interaction of insolvency procedures

a. The costs of moving between insolvency procedures

The Companies Act 2008 has retained the procedural separation and self-containment of the various insolvency and rescue procedures that existed under the Companies Act 1973. The primary concern with this is that switching between different procedures may generate high procedural costs. The extent of such procedural costs in a situation where a company switches from rescue proceedings to winding-up proceedings appear to depend on two factors: (i) the institutional body that is required to decide on whether rescue proceedings are to be converted to winding-up proceedings; and (ii) whether the person who acted as office holder in rescue proceedings is allowed to be appointed as liquidator in a subsequent liquidation.

In South Africa, the decision whether rescue proceedings may be converted to winding-up proceedings is taken by the court,[539] which appears to generate higher costs than if the decision was placed with the office holder (as in the UK).[540] Moreover, the body of creditors might also be better positioned than the court to decide on the conversion, provided they

be contained under unified insolvency legislation; Ch 24 Draft Insolvency and Business Recovery Bill (unofficial working copy, June 2011, on file with author).

538 See s 66(1A) Close Corporations Act (as inserted by Sch 3 item 6(1)).

539 See s 141(2)(a)(ii) and (b)(i). However, there are three exceptions to this. One is where rescue proceedings had been commenced out-of-court and in the rather unlikely event that the company has been restored to financial health without the need of a rescue plan. In that case, the rescue practitioner can end rescue proceedings by filing a notice of termination; s 141(2)(b)(ii). Another exception is where the board resolution to begin rescue proceedings failed to comply with the formalities in s 129(3) and (4), in which case the board can resolve to place the company under winding-up proceedings; s 129(6). The final exception is where the company's business has been sold as a going concern as part of the rescue plan, in which case the subsequent liquidation of the original corporate entity can be initiated by board resolution; s 129(6) read with s 132(2)(c)(ii).

540 Insolvency Act 1986, Sch B1, para 83(1) and (6)(b).

do so by majority vote (as in Australia),[541] as they bear the ultimate risk of the decision, and therefore have the right incentive to maximise value for the company.[542] On the other hand, the UK approach may generate 'agency costs', as administrators might be tempted to delay the conversion, given that they generally receive a time-based remuneration. However, this temptation may be mitigated if the office holder is entitled to be appointed as liquidator in a subsequent winding-up, as is the case in the UK[543] and Australia[544], but not in South Africa.[545]

Whether or not an office holder is entitled to be appointed as a liquidator also has an impact on the direct costs of the subsequent liquidation proceedings, as a new person would have no prior knowledge of the company's affairs and will have to expend significant costs in familiarising himself with the relevant facts. The South African approach of prohibiting a rescue practitioner from being appointed as liquidator after a conversion of rescue proceedings to winding-up proceedings is probably a reaction to the abuses associated with this practice under judicial management.[546] However, the main reason for such abuse – namely that professional liquidators had a reasonable expectation that a final judicial management order would not be granted due to the onerous entry requirements of judicial management – would not seem to be relevant under the new rescue procedure, as its entry requirements have been relaxed significantly.[547] In light of that, the familiarisation costs imposed on unsecured creditors as a result of the company having to appoint a new person as liquidator seem to be unjustified.

541 S 446A(1)(a) Corporations Act 2001.
542 This is however only true insofar as secured creditors are excluded from the vote, as they will generally not be the residual claimants in that situation; see the discussion in PART C, Chapter 7, II., 1., c below.
543 Insolvency Act 1986, Sch B1, para 83(7)(b).
544 S 446A Corporations Act 2001.
545 S 136(4). For a comprehensive comparative analysis of the conversion of rescue proceedings, see the discussion generally in PART C, Chapter 7, II., 1., c. below.
546 See PART B, Chapter 4, II., 3. above.
547 See PART B, Chapter 4, IV., 2., b. below.

b. Separation of the scheme of arrangement between shareholders and between creditors

The separation of the compromise procedure and the scheme of arrangement with holders of a company's securities[548], although appearing to be doctrinally sound at first glance, could raise the costs of capital restructuring arrangements in distressed situations. [549] This is because where a distressed company would require capital restructuring measures that would affect the company's securities within the meaning of the type of arrangements set out in s 114(1),[550] the company would be required to also invoke the separate scheme of arrangement procedure. Particularly the requirement under a scheme of arrangement that a report by an independent expert be prepared,[551] could lead to a wasteful duplication of procedural costs, given that the compromise procedure already provides for the preparation of a proposal for the debt restructuring measures.

Moreover, the fact that the scheme of arrangement is not available under liquidation proceedings,[552] means that the scope of restructuring mechanisms available to distressed companies under the compromise procedure has been limited in practice. This is because the compromise procedure may well be used frequently during liquidation proceedings, given the lack of a moratorium under the compromise procedure.

c. Need for a less onerous rescue procedure for small companies?

Since small companies, by definition, have simpler borrowing structures, less dispersed creditors, fewer employees and less complex corporate

548 Securities are defined in s 1 as 'any shares, debentures or other instruments, irrespective of their form or title, issued or authorised to be issued by a profit company'.

549 See also Loubser, 'LLD thesis' (n 512) 149–50.

550 Namely, a consolidation of securities of different classes; a division of securities into different classes; an expropriation of securities from the holders; exchanging any of its securities for other securities; a re-acquisition by the company of its securities; or a combination of the methods contemplated in s 114(1). This list is not exhaustive (as indicated by the words 'among other things' in s 114(1) (passage before para (a))).

551 S 114(2) and (3).

552 S 114(1).

structures than larger companies, inter-creditor agency and co-ordination costs in developing a rescue plan during rescue proceedings are typically lower than for larger companies. Accordingly, certain procedural safeguards that may be important for larger companies to control such costs, may not be required for smaller companies. In fact, the potential that such procedural safeguards may raise the direct costs of the proceedings, could discourage small companies from utilising the formal rescue procedure.[553] For example, certain procedural safeguards of the South African rescue procedure might be considered unnecessary for small companies, such as the requirement that two separate meetings be held for creditors and employees and that creditors and employees[554] are entitled to form separate committees.[555]

The compromise with creditors procedure – although arguably lighter on procedural requirements,[556] and thus generally more cost-effective than business rescue[557] – has structural limitations that undermine its effectiveness as a restructuring procedure. Examples would be the fact that it does not provide for a moratorium[558] and that it arguably does not allow for going concern sales of companies' assets (unless where such sales are effected in combination with an arrangement or compromise).

553 Loubser, 'LLD thesis' (n 512) 50.

554 See ss 147, 148 and 151.

555 S 144(3)(c) (employees) and s 145(3) (creditors).

556 Eg, the compromise procedure requires only one creditors' meeting (see s 155(6)), lacks the fairly extensive disclosure and consultation requirements by the rescue practitioner (eg, providing reports on the progress of rescue proceedings to creditors' and employees' committees (s 149(1)(b)) and does not provide for equivalent duties of the rescue practitioner to investigate the company's affairs (s 141). On the other hand, the compromise procedure requires separate voting for each class of creditors (which is implied by the reference to 'class' (of creditors) in s 155(6)) and for the compromise to be approved by the court before it can be made binding on minority creditors (s 155(7)(a)). Both of these factors could potentially raise the direct costs of the procedure. On a comparison of the direct costs of the compromise and business rescue procedures, see Klopper and Bradstreet (n 513) 561ff.

557 Klopper and Bradstreet (n 513) 558.

558 And unlike, eg, in the UK, the compromise procedure is not available while companies are under rescue proceedings (s 151(1)), and is thus not protected from creditor enforcement by the moratorium of the main rescue procedure.

It might thus be asked whether there would be a need for an alternative, more streamlined, simpler and more flexible formal rescue mechanism for small companies in South Africa than the two current procedures.

Two possible legislative approaches could be considered for introducing such an alternative rescue mechanism: (i) a separate and self-contained procedure, as in the UK, namely the 'company voluntary arrangement' ('*CVA*'), which is less court driven and, crucially, provides for a moratorium);[559] or (ii) provisions that specifically apply to small companies contained within the main rescue procedure, as in the US.[560]

Criteria for purposes of determining the eligibility of companies for an alternative rescue procedure for small companies could be based on the existing criteria used for determining the level of accounting standards that are to apply to the different categories of companies under the Companies Act 2008.[561] These are (i) the number of employees, (ii) the extent of third party liability, (iii) the annual turnover and (iv) the number of persons holding a 'beneficial interest'[562] in the company's issued securities.[563] Similar criteria are used in the UK for determining the size of a company for purposes of its eligibility for the CVA procedure,[564] whereas the US uses the amount of the debts of the debtor for determining whether the

559 Insolvency Act 1986, Pt 1.

560 See, eg, 11 USC §§ 362(n)(1)(D), 1116, 1121(e), 1125(f). For a criticism of these provisions on policy grounds, see Warren and Westbrook, *The Law of Debtors and Creditors* (6th edn, Aspen 2009) 687, 690–2.

561 Regs 26(2), 27(4) Companies Regulations, 2011. (Each regulation cited in this Chapter, both in the body of the text and in the footnotes, will be a regulation of the Companies Regulations, 2011, unless indicated otherwise indicated.)

562 A person has a beneficial interest in the company's securities if that person is entitled to any of the rights in such securities, but whose name does not appear in the securities register; definition in s 1 read with s 57. See also Sigwadi, 'The Registration of Securities under the Companies Act 71 of 2008' in Mongalo (ed), *Modern Company Law for a competitive South African economy* (Juta 2010) 73, 85ff.

563 Reg 26(2). The same four criteria are required for determining the size of a company ('large', 'medium' and 'small' (reg 127(2)(b)) for purposes of ascertaining which of the three categories of rescue practitioners ('senior', 'experienced' or 'junior', which are determined according to the number of years of experience as a rescue practitioner) (reg 27(2)(c)) are entitled to be appointed to act as rescue practitioners for the respective sizes of companies during rescue proceedings (reg 127(3)-(5)).

564 Insolvency Act 1986, Sch A1, para 3(2) read with s 382(3) Companies Act 2006.

provisions applicable to small creditors under Chapter 11 proceedings should apply.[565]

3. Institutional setting – jurisdiction over insolvency law and regulation of insolvency profession

Although the Companies Act 2008, unlike in the US, for example,[566] has not introduced either specialist insolvency courts, specialist corporate or insolvency law divisions or specialist judges within any particular generalist court, the Judge President of each High Court (which have jurisdiction over business rescue and compromise with creditors matters)[567] may designate a specialist judge for commercial, commercial insolvencies and business rescue issues.[568] However, no such specialist judge has been appointed yet.

A further change from the previous rescue regime is that the 'requisition system' under the old regime for the appointment of *judicial managers* – and the role of the Master of the High Court in the appointment process[569] – has been largely abolished.[570] Instead, a rescue practitioner is now appointed by the applicant for the commencement of rescue proceedings out-of-court by the the board of directors[571] or by the court in the case of commencement by court order. This is done upon nomination by the applicant[572] and ratification by the majority of 'independent creditors'[573] in the first creditors' meeting.[574]

---

565 11 USC § 101(51D).

566 See PART B, Chapter 3, II., 3 and applicable references cited therein.

567 S 128(1)(e).

568 S 128(3) read with s 128(1)(e).

569 On the role of the Master in the appointment of judicial managers under the previous regime, see PART B, Chapter 3, III., 3., b above.

570 However, the requisition system is presumably still used for the appointment of liquidators for winding-up proceedings, at least until the insolvency law reforms have been implemented.

571 S 129(3)(b).

572 On the persons who have *locus standi* to apply for commencement by court order, see PART B, Chapter 4, IV., 2., a., aa. below.

573 For an explanation of this term, see PART B, Chapter 4, IV., 2., a., bb below.

574 S 131(5) read with s 147. On the meaning of 'independent creditors', see PART B, Chapter 4, IV., 2., a., bb. below.

The Companies Act 2008 brings South African law in line with international trends in relation to the regulation of the rescue practitioners' profession.[575] The legislature has ultimately opted for a two-tier system of regulation – partial licensing and partial accreditation of certain professions.[576] Accordingly, only persons who are not members in good standing of the legal, accounting and business management professions have to obtain the required licence to practice as a rescue practitioner.[577] Members of the three mentioned professions are exempted from having to obtain a licence as a rescue practitioner, provided such professions have been accredited by the Commission.[578]

The requirements for obtaining a licence to act as rescue practitioner is that the applicant is of good character and integrity,[579] has sufficient education and experience[580] and may not be subject to an order of probation under s 162(7) or meet the grounds of disqualification from acting as a director under s 69(8).[581] The Commission may withdraw such licence should a rescue practitioner no longer fulfil the above-mentioned requirements.[582]

When considering an application for the accreditation of a profession, the Commission must have due regard for the qualifications and experience that are set as conditions for membership of such profession and the ability of such profession to discipline its members.[583] The Commission may revoke an accreditation if it has reasonable grounds to believe that the profession is no longer able to properly monitor or discipline its members.[584]

575 The regulation of the insolvency profession has been on the agenda for quite some time; see Explanatory Memorandum to the Insolvency Bill (n 535) 122ff.

576 S 138(1)(a) and (b). See also Boraine and others, *Meskin Insolvency Law and its Operation in Winding-up* (loose-leaf) (Lexis Nexis Butterworths 2006) para 18.14.2.1. Earlier versions of the Companies Act 2008 had not provided for the exemption from licensing for certain profession, and had instead required that all rescue practitioners be licensed; see the versions of the Companies Act 2008 before the amendment under s 38 of Act 3 of 2011.

577 S 138(1)(a), (b). See also reg 126(1)(b) Companies Regulations, 2011.

578 Reg 126(1)(a).

579 Reg 126(4)(a).

580 Reg 126(4)(b).

581 S 138(1)(c) and (d), respectively.

582 Reg 126(7).

583 Reg 126(1)(a).

584 Reg 126(1)(a).

However, the above-mentioned licensing of rescue practitioners and the accreditation of the specified professions has not yet been implemented.[585] Instead, the Commission is currently granting licences on an *ad hoc* and conditional basis[586] until the Commission has 'thoroughly investigated turnaround practices locally and internationally' in order to determine an appropriate licensing and accreditation approach.[587] A further measure of control over the quality of the services provided by rescue practitioners is that the level of experience of a rescue practitioner determines the size of the company[588] for which he may be appointed.[589]

It remains to be seen whether the liquidators' profession will be regulated, and if so, which body will be made responsible for the regulation. Currently, there is a clear institutional separation between the rescue practitioners' and liquidators' professions, which is unusual from a comparative perspective.[590]

IV. The rescue procedure (Chapter 6 Parts A to D)

1. The objectives of business rescue

a. General

An appropriate starting point for the discussion of the new South African rescue procedure is the term 'business rescue' itself, which is defined in s 128(1)(b) as follows

---

585 Lotheringen, unpublished Power Point Presentation, 21 September 2012, slide 10 (on file with the author).

586 Reg 126(6)(b).

587 Lotheringen (n 585) slide 11.

588 See regs 127(2)(c)(i), (ii), (iii).

589 On the calculation of the size of companies, see reg 26(2).

590 In the UK and Australia, both liquidators and administrators are subject to the same regulatory requirements. For the UK, see s 388(1) Insolvency Act 1986 and see generally Pt 13. In Australia administrators are included in the term 'registered liquidator' under s 1282 Corporations Act 2001 (which, together with s 1283, sets out the regulation of the insolvency profession); D Brown and Symes, 'Insolvency Practitioner Regulation: Providing Practice Standards Through the Use of Codes of Conduct' [2013] 3 (hard copy on file with author).

> 'Proceedings to facilitate the rehabilitation of a company that is financially distressed by providing for—
>
> (i) the temporary supervision of the company, and of the management of its affairs, business and property;
> (ii) a temporary moratorium on the rights of claimants against the company or in respect of property in its possession; and
> (iii) the development and implementation, if approved, of a plan to rescue the company by restructuring its affairs, business, property, debt and other liabilities, and equity in a manner that maximises the likelihood of the company continuing in existence on a solvent basis or, if it is not possible for the company to so continue in existence, results in a better return for the company's creditors or shareholders than would result from the immediate liquidation of the company.'[591]

Three fundamental characteristics of the South African rescue procedure arise from this definition. First, the South African rescue procedure relies on a management-displacing system of governance (see sub-para (i) of the definition).[592] This contrasts with a debtor-in-possession system of governance, as employed under Chapter 11 of the US Bankruptcy Code for example.[593]

Second, in contrast to the reliance on a *discretionary* moratorium imposed by the court under judicial management, business rescue now provides for a *mandatory* statutory moratorium (see sub-para (ii) of the definition).[594]

And third, the rescue objectives – which are referred to under the Companies Act 2008 as 'goals' of rescue[595] – are clearly set out (see sub-para (iii) of the definition). Thus, the rescue procedure provides for two objectives, which are structured in an order of preference.

The primary objective is referred to as 'to rescue the company by restructuring its affairs, business, property, debt and other liabilities, and eq-

---

591 S 128(1)(b).

592 This follows from the phrase 'the temporary *supervision* of the company' read together with s 140(1) ('General Powers and duties of practitioners'). 'Supervision' is defined as 'the oversight imposed on a company during its business rescue proceedings' (s 128(1)(i)). For the definition of 'rescue practitioner', see s 128(1)(d). See generally Delport and others, *Henochsberg on the Companies Act 71 of 2008* (loose-leaf) (Lexis Nexis 2015) s 128, 447.

593 See the discussion in n 81 at Chapter 1 and accompanying text.

594 The moratorium will be considered in greater detail at PART B, Chapter 4, IV., 3 below.

595 See, eg, s 128(1)(h).

uity in a manner that maximises the likelihood of the company continuing in existence on a solvent basis'. The phrase 'company continuing in existence on a solvent basis' implies that this objective envisages the preservation of the corporate entity.[596] The reference in sub-para (iii) to the restructuring of, *inter alia*, the company's debt, liabilities and equity as methods of achieving the primary objective makes clear that in contrast to judicial management, capital restructuring measures (hereafter, '*reorganisation*') are now permitted under the new rescue procedure.[597]

The secondary objective is referred to as any outcome that 'results in a better return for the company's creditors or shareholders than would result from the company's immediate liquidation'. The fact that this rescue objective may only be pursued if reorganisation is 'not possible' to achieve, clarifies that it is merely of secondary importance to the primary objective.[598] Since the secondary objective becomes relevant when it is not possible that the company '[continues] in existence on a solvent basis', the secondary objective must necessarily envisage an outcome where the original corporate entity does not survive.[599]

---

596 See also *Henochsberg Companies Act* (n 592) s 128, 446.

597 This conclusion is further implied by the requirement that the proposal for a rescue plan must provide information on the extent to which the company is to be released from the payment of its debts and any debt is proposed to be converted to equity (s 150(2)(b)(ii)).

598 See also *Oakdene Square Properties (Pty) Ltd v Farm Bothasfontein (Kyalami) (Pty) Ltd* [2013] JOL 30498 (SCA) para 23ff (citing the Australian case *Dallinger v Halcha Holdings* (1996) 14 ACLC 263, 268 (at para 24) on the equivalent Australian provision, s 435A Corporations Act 2001); and see the court in the first instance: *Oakdene Square Properties (Pty) Ltd v Farm Bothasfontein (Kyalami) (Pty) Ltd* [2013] JOL 30498 (SCA) para 49(7); *Southern Palace Investments 265 (Pty) Ltd v Midnight Storm Investments 386 Ltd* 2012 (2) SA 423 (WCC) paras 3, 25, 27. See also generally *Henochsberg Companies Act* (n 592) s 128, 446.

599 See, eg, *Oakdene Square Properties (Pty) Ltd v Farm Bothasfontein (Kyalami) (Pty) Ltd* [2013] JOL 30498 (SCA) para 28 stating, correctly, that the word 'rehabilitate' (which in its ordinary meaning means restoration to a normal healthy state) must be read in the context of the secondary objective, which necessarily precludes a rehabilitation in the ordinary sense (at para 25); *Francis Edward Gormley v West City Precinct Properties (Pty) Ltd* 19076/11 (WCC): 18 April 2012 para 13; *Southern Palace Investments 265 (Pty) Ltd v Midnight Storm Investments 386 Ltd* 2012 (2) SA 423 (WCC) para 25. See also Loubser, 'LLD thesis' (n 512) 45–6. The interpretation of the secondary objective as merely constituting an extension of the primary objective in *Anthonie Welman v Mar-*

Moreover, the fact that under the secondary objective it is sufficient that the creditors as a whole would obtain higher returns than in an immediate liquidation, implies that this objective does not require that all creditors be paid in full from the proceeds of the (going concern) sale of the company's assets. The secondary objective of rescue accordingly further broadens the scope of companies that were eligible to avail themselves of judicial management.[600]

Pertinent issues that arise in relation to the objectives of rescue will now be discussed in b. and c. below.

b. Pertinent issues under the secondary objective of rescue

aa. The content of the secondary objective

The first question that arises in relation to the secondary objective is how higher returns to the company's creditors and shareholders[601] may be achieved in rescue than in winding-up. There appear to be two possibilities. The first possibility is where the company's business (or part of it) is sold to a third party. Here the proceeds of the sale are paid out to the company's claimants and the original corporate entity of the debtor is wound-up and eventually dissolved. This method of achieving the secondary objective of rescue is appropriate where a company is still 'economically viable' – that is, where its assets are worth more kept together than where they were sold piecemeal. In this instance, the creditors would receive higher returns from a going concern sale than if the assets were liquidated.

It is appropriate that going concern sales are permitted in rescue proceedings, notwithstanding that they may be permitted under winding-up proceedings as well,[602] as the rescue procedure provides a more suitable

celle Props 193 CC 33958/2011 (GSJ): 24 February 2012 para 12 must respectfully be considered incorrect.

600 Further on this argument, see PART B, Chapter 4, IV., 2., b., dd below. See Chapter 3 on the purpose of judicial management.

601 Provided, of course, shareholders still have an economic interest in the company, which is expected rarely to be the case in practice, as rightly pointed out by Loubser, 'LLD thesis' (n 512) 46.

602 Which is facilitated by a liquidator having the power to carry on the company's business if this is beneficial for its liquidation; s 386(4)(f) Companies Act 1973; see Loubser, 'LLD thesis' (n 512) 46.

framework for effecting going concern sales.[603] This is primarily because secured creditors are in principle not stayed from enforcing their security interests in winding-up,[604] while the moratorium blocks enforcement by secured creditors in rescue proceedings.[605] Further mechanisms of rescue proceedings that favour going concern sales are the mandatory priority on post-commencement finance[606] and the fact that the rescue practitioner has greater powers than the liquidator under winding-up proceedings to suspend or cancel uncompleted contracts, which would leave the counterparty merely with a claim for damages against the company.[607] The first-mentioned mechanism might provide the rescue practitioner with more time to prepare the business for a sale and the second-mentioned mechanism enables the rescue practitioner to rid the company of onerous contracts, thereby potentially increasing the value of the company.[608] And finally, there is a better chance that a market for distressed businesses will develop if going concern sales are effected from rescue proceedings rather than from winding-up proceedings, as the market is likely to consider the assets of companies in rescue proceedings in a more positive light than assets of companies in winding-up proceedings.

bb. Compatibility of break-up sales with the secondary objective

However, a better return for creditors in rescue proceedings than in liquidation proceedings might also be achieved if a company's break-up value exceeds its going-concern value (in which case it is said to be 'economically distressed'), where the break-up sale or the 'trading out' of existing contracts can be effected at lower costs in rescue proceedings than in liquidation proceedings.[609] Such an outcome is expressly permitted under the British administration procedure in cases where it is not 'reasonably prac-

---

603 For a contrary view, see Loubser, 'LLD thesis' (n 512) 46–7, 49.

604 S 366(1)(c) Companies Act 1973 read with s 83 Insolvency Act 1936.

605 S 133(1).

606 S 135(2) and (3)(b).

607 Compare s 136(2) and (3) with, eg, s 386(4)(g) Companies Act 1973 read with s 35 Insolvency Act 1936.

608 On the advantages of both mechanisms generally, see *Henochsberg Companies Act* (n 592) s 131, 465.

609 On the 'trading out' alternative, see Armour and Mokal, 'Reforming the Governance of Corporate Rescue: The Enterprise Act 2002' (2004) ESRC Centre for

ticable' to achieve a reorganisation and a going concern sale.[610] The fact that s 128(1)(b)(iii) provides that rescue proceedings constitute the '*rehabilitation* of companies'[611] could be argued to presuppose some form of restoration to former privileges.[612], This would certainly contradict an outcome where the company is liquidated and eventually dissolved.

It may even be argued that the meaning of 'rehabilitation' is not compatible with the preservation of a company's business through a going concern sale to a third party. A going concern sale is more a 'saving' or 'preservation' than a 'restoration'; and not of the 'company' (as required by s 128(1)(b)(iii)), but of the company's 'business', which are technically not the same. To the extent that it is correct that 'rehabilitation' on its ordinary meaning cannot contemplate going concern sales, but such a mechanism is clearly envisaged by the secondary objective, the 'ordinary' meaning of rehabilitation loses its force as a benchmark for interpreting the objectives of rescue under s 128(1)(b)(iii).[613]

Indeed, by considering whether a break-up sale during rescue proceedings would result in higher returns than if it were effected during liquidation proceedings, some courts have implicitly accepted that liquidations fall within the secondary objective of rescue.[614] On the other hand, Judge Brand in the *Oakdene Square* case[615] held that he did not believe that the liquidation of companies was contemplated by business rescue. He then went on to consider whether higher returns would be obtained by creditors if the company's assets were liquidated in rescue proceedings,[616] which would not have been necessary if company liquidations were prohibited

---

Business Research Working Paper 288 <http://papers.ssrn.com/sol3/papers.cfm?abstract_id=567306> accessed 16 January 2017.

610 Insolvency Act 1986, Sch B1, para 3(4) read with para 3(1)(c). See also Armour and Mokal (n 609).

611 S 128(1)(b)(passage before para (a)).

612 Oxford Online Dictionary <http://www.oxforddictionaries.com> accessed 10 January 2017.

613 See, by implication, *Oakdene Square Properties (Pty) Ltd v Farm Bothasfontein (Kyalami) (Pty) Ltd* [2013] JOL 30498 (SCA) para 25.

614 See, eg, *CSARS v Beginsel* 2013 (1) SA 307 (WCC) para 58ff; *Nedbank Ltd v Bestvest 153 (Pty) Ltd*; *Essa and Another v Bestvest 153 (Pty) Ltd* 2012 (5) SA 497 (WCC) para 53ff; *Oakdene Square Properties (Pty) Ltd v Farm Bothasfontein (Kyalami) (Pty) Ltd* [2013] JOL 30498 (SCA) para 48ff.

615 *Oakdene Square Properties (Pty) Ltd v Farm Bothasfontein (Kyalami) (Pty) Ltd* [2013] JOL 30498 (SCA) para 33.

616 At 34ff.

under rescue proceedings. It thus seems as though the last word is yet to be spoken on this matter. From a policy perspective, it would seem that as long as there is a good chance that creditors could receive higher returns from a liquidation of companies during rescue proceedings rather than if such companies were liquidated during winding-up proceedings, there would certainly be no reason why creditors should be deprived of such higher returns.

cc. Tension between the mandatory nature of the development of a rescue plan and the secondary objective of rescue

A strict reading of the definition of 'business rescue' suggests that the objectives of rescue may only be implemented by means of the development, adoption and implementation of a rescue plan.[617] This conclusion is supported further by the fact that the entire scheme of business rescue is geared towards an inclusive and participatory procedure[618] and that the authority for whether, and the means by which, the company be rescued vests in the group of (eligible) claimants of the company, which they exercise through voting on the rescue plan.[619]

However, a situation could arise where the company is made a market-related offer for the acquisition of the entire or significant part of the company's business as a going concern shortly after the commencement of rescue proceedings and the transaction would, for commercial reasons, fail if it was delayed until a rescue plan is developed and adopted in accordance with the prescribed procedure.[620] In such a situation, the rescue practitioner could, in principle, be seen to violate his duty to act in the best interests

617 See the reference to 'the development and implementation, if approved, of a plan to rescue the company by [...]' in s 128(1)(b)(iii).

618 As demonstrated, eg, by the strong participation rights of creditors in the development of the rescue plan under Part C of Chapter 6 Companies Act 2008. The plan procedure is regulated under ss 150 to 154 generally and will be discussed in more detail below.

619 S 152(2) read with s 128(1)(j) and s 145(4)-(6).

620 To be sure, the relevant time periods in rescue proceedings are typically maximum, rather than minimum, time periods. (Eg, the first meeting of creditors has to take place within 10 business days and the rescue plan must be published within 25 business days of the appointment of the rescue practitioner (s 147(1)(passage before para (a), s 148(1), passage before para (a) and s 150(5), passage be-

of the company (ie, the entire body of eligible claimants against the company) for failing to maximise the returns for such claimants as a result of refraining from accepting the offer of the potential purchaser for the acquisition of the company's business.[621]

The resolution of this conflict generally depends on the ultimate source of the rescue practitioners' powers. Under the British administration procedure, a going concern sale without the approval of creditors has been allowed in applicable circumstances (including arguably a situation as contemplated above).[622] Here the administrator's power appears to be derived, to a much greater extent than under the South African rescue law, from the statutory objectives of rescue, as reinforced by the applicable administrators' duties *ex post*.[623] Under the South African rescue law, by contrast, the plan procedure – including the claimants' vote – forms a much more integral part of the rescue procedure, suggesting that the primary source of the rescue practitioners' powers is the claimants' meeting.[624] Accordingly, it appears as though in South Africa, the rescue practitioner does not have the authority to conclude a sale of the above-mentioned type without the

fore para (a), respectively) and the claimants' meeting to vote on the plan must be convened within 10 business days of publishing the plan pursuant to s150 (s151(1)). Accordingly, it is possible that a rescue plan be adopted in a shorter space of time than the statutory time periods. However, rescue proceedings may be delayed for practical reasons, eg, where the company has a complicated (debt) capital structure, resulting in more time-consuming bargaining between the company and the various classes of claimants. Indeed, according to recent statistics for the period between the inception of business rescue on 1 May 2011 until 31 March 2015, the vast majority of active business rescue cases have exceeded the statutory minimum default period of 3 months (see s 132(3)) and approximately 61% of the active cases have been under business rescue for longer than 1 year, 11.5% even for up to, and possibly beyond, 3 years; see Companies and Intellectual Property Commission Report (*CIPC*), 'Status of Business Rescue Proceedings in South Africa (March 2015)' (2015) <http://www.cipc.co.za/files/1914/3377/1988/Status_of_Business_Rescue_in_South_Africa_version1_0.pdf> accessed 10 January 2017.

621 The rescue practitioner's duty to act in the best interest of the company derives from s 140(3)(b), read with s 76(3)(b). For further discussion on the rescue practitioners' best interests duty, see PART B, Chapter 4, IV., 8., b below.

622 *Re T & D Industries plc and another* [1999] All ER (D) 1239.

623 Insolvency Act 1986, Sch B1, para 3. See also Armour and Mokal (n 609).

624 This follows from the reasons mentioned at nn 617, 618 and 619 and accompanying text above.

approval of the claimants' meeting as part of the voting on the rescue plan.[625]

c. The dual role of the rescue objectives

The rescue objectives perform a dual role. The first role is to determine which companies are eligible to enter rescue proceedings. One of the two primary grounds of entering rescue proceedings is that there must be 'a reasonable prospect of rescuing the company'.[626] 'Rescuing the company' is defined as achieving the objectives set out in the definition of business rescue,[627] which, as we saw above, includes reorganisation, a going concern sale and possibly a break-up sale.

The second role of the rescue objectives is that the order of priority in which the objectives should be achieved binds the rescue practitioner when performing his responsibility of developing a business rescue plan. It achieves this by providing guidance on which method of deploying the company's assets the practitioner is to give priority to and together with the minimum time periods of the different stages of rescue proceedings how long the practitioner is required to spend in trying to achieve the different asset deployment methods.[628] This second role of the rescue objectives is not specifically mentioned by the business rescue provisions under the Companies Act 2008; however, it follows by implication.[629] Although there is no express provision that holds the rescue practitioner accountable

625 However, the potential adverse consequences for the maximisation of value for the company resulting from the rescue practitioner's prohibition from concluding a transaction as contemplated above, could be somewhat alleviated in respect of small companies with a simple capital structure, insofar as such companies are more likely to adopt and implement a plan in a shorter space of time.

626 For out-of-court entry, see s 129(1)(b) and for entry by court application, see s 131(4)(a)(ii).

627 See definition in s 128(1)(h). As noted in Chapter 1, this entry ground could be seen as a legal strategy to reduce 'agency costs' arising from perverse incentives of company controllers to place the company under rescue proceedings for strategic purposes. This problem will be considered in Chapter 7.

628 S 140(1)(d)(i).

629 It is also consistent with the function of the objectives of rescue under the Australian and British rescue procedures: for Australia, see s 435A Corporations Act 2001 and for the UK, see Insolvency Act 1986, Sch B1, para 3; see also Armour and Mokal (n 609).

to the creditors to comply with the statutory order of priority of the rescue objectives, it would seem that this responsibility should be mediated through the rescue practitioners' duty to act in the best interests of the company or his duty of care, skill and diligence. The rescue practitioner owes both of these duties to the company by virtue of s 140(3)(b) read with ss 75 to 77.[630]

2. Entry into business rescue proceedings

a. Pertinent features of the entry requirements

aa. Routes of entry, parties entitled to enter and point in time when the moratorium is effective

Like the British administration procedure, the South African rescue regime provides for a 'dual gateway' into rescue proceedings.[631] Rescue proceedings can accordingly be commenced either out-of-court by the board of directors by the filing of a resolution to that effect with the Companies and Intellectual Property Commission (hereafter, '*Commission*')[632] or by court order.[633] A single shareholder, single creditor, a registered trade union representing employees or their representatives (where they are not represented by trade unions) (together referred to as 'affected persons')[634] have *locus standi* to apply to commence rescue proceedings by court order.[635] In addition, winding-up proceedings may be converted to

---

630 See the discussion in PART B, Chapter 4, IV., 8., b., cc. below.

631 For out-of-court entry under administration, see Insolvency Act 1986, Sch B1, paras 14ff and 22ff; for entry by court application, see paras 10ff. For the expression 'dual gateway', see *Henochsberg Companies Act* (n 592) s 129, 450. By contrast, entry into the Australian voluntary administration is only possible out-of-court (ss 436A(1), 436B(1), 436C(1) Corporations Act 2001), while in the US commencement of Chapter 11 is possible only by court filing; 11 USC §§ 301(a) and 303(b).

632 S 129(1) read with sub-s 3.

633 S 131.

634 S 128(1)(a).

635 S 131(1).

rescue proceedings even after a *final* liquidation order has been granted[636] via the court entry route, either by the application to court by an affected person[637] or by the court on its own motion.[638] According to s 131(6), a conversion to rescue proceedings will however only suspend the liquidation proceedings from the granting of a provisional or final liquidation order and not any proceedings prior to the granting of such order.[639] By contrast, liquidation proceedings may not be converted to rescue proceedings via the out-of-court entry route.[640]

It is not specified which constituents have *locus standi* to bring an application for a conversion of winding-up proceedings to rescue proceedings. The fact that the 'company' does not have *locus standi* to apply to court for the commencement of rescue proceedings generally, would seem to suggest that the liquidator – in whom the general directorial and managerial powers of the company are vested during winding-up proceedings (and who is accordingly entitled to take legal actions on behalf of the company)[641] – likewise lacks *locus standi* to apply to court for the commencement of rescue proceedings while the company is under winding-up proceedings. This contrasts with the position in the UK and Australia, where

636 This matter was settled by the Supreme Court of Appeal ('SCA') in *Richter v Absa Bank Ltd* (20181/2014) [2015] ZASCA 100 (1 June 2015) after some courts had previously held that a conversion from winding-up proceedings to business rescue proceedings was only possible up until the granting of a final winding-up order; see *Richter v Bloempro CC and Others* 2014(6) SA 38 (GP) and *R J C Molyneux & Another v M I Patel & Others* (14618/2014) [2014] ZAWCHC 191 (27 November 2014). Prior to *Richter v Absa Bank*, the majority of the decisions on this matter had already come to the same conclusion; see *Van Staden v Angel Ozone Products CC* (in liquidation) and others 2013(4) SA 630 (GNP); *Absa Bank Ltd v Summer Lodge (Pty) Ltd* 2014(3) SA 90 (GP); *Absa Bank Ltd v Summer Lodge (Pty) Ltd* 2013(5) SA 444 (GNP); *Absa Bank Ltd v Makuna Farm CC* 2014(3) SA 86 (GJ); *Van Der Merwe and Others v Zonnekus Mansion (Pty) Ltd and Others* (4653/2015) [2015] ZAWCHC 90 (10 June 2015) (coming to such conclusion on the application of the *stare decisis* principle, rather than on an interpretation of the relevant provision (see para 17)).

637 S 131(6).

638 S 131(7).

639 This follows from an interpretation of the word 'liquidation proceedings' in s 131(6); see *Absa Bank Ltd v Summer Lodge (Pty) Ltd* 2014(3) SA 90 (GP); *Absa Bank Ltd v Summer Lodge (Pty) Ltd* 2013(5) SA 444 (GNP); *Absa Bank Ltd v Makuna Farm CC* 2014(3) SA 86 (GJ).

640 S 129(2)(a).

641 See s 386 Companies Act 1973.

the liquidator can convert liquidation proceedings to rescue proceedings.[642] A further unusual provision from a comparative perspective is the court's power (presumably on its own motion) to grant an order for the commencement of rescue proceedings in the course of proceedings to enforce any security against the company.[643] The court may also (again presumably on its own motion) grant an order placing the company under rescue proceedings when considering an application brought by a director or shareholder for relief from oppressive or prejudicial conduct by the company or any director that unfairly disregards the interests of the applicant or that abuses the separate personality of the company.[644]

Out-of-court entry of rescue proceedings begins when the resolution is filed with the Commission,[645] while entry by court order begins when an application to this effect is made to the court.[646] Application to the court has been held to mean on the launching of the application to court rather than (retrospectively) on the making of the court order.[647] Where the rescue practitioner is appointed by the board in an out-of-court entry, this appointment can be challenged by an affected person *ex post* on the grounds specified in s 139(1)(b) up until the adoption of a business rescue plan.[648]

---

642 UK: Insolvency Act 1986, Sch B1, paras 37, 38; Australia: s 436B Corporations Act 2001.

643 S 131(7).

644 S 163(2)(c).

645 S 132(1)(a)(i). If, pursuant to s 129(5)(a), the resolution to commence rescue proceedings has lapsed and becomes a nullity as a result of the company failing to comply with the procedural requirements under s 129(3) and (4), the company may, pursuant to s 129(5)(b), apply to court for approval to file a further resolution to commence rescue proceedings within three months of the adoption of the lapsed resolution. During this period, the company is generally precluded from filing a further resolution. If the court grants the approval in such an application, rescue proceedings commence when the application to the court is made (s 132(1)(a)(ii)).

646 S 132(1)(b).

647 See *Taboo Trading 232 (Pty) Ltd v Pro Wreck Scrap Metal CC; Joubert v Pro Wreck Scrap Metal CC* 2013 (6) SA 141 (KZP) para 11 (stating that the precise point at which rescue proceedings commence is once the application has been lodged with the Registrar, a copy of the application has been served on the Commission and each affected person has been properly notified). See also Standard Bank of South Africa Ltd v Gas 2 Liquids (Pty) Ltd (45543/2012) [2016] GJ (10 March 2016). See generally *Meskin Insolvency Law* (n 576) para 18.5.1.

648 S 130(1)(passage before sub-s (1)). See also *African Banking Corporation of Botswana Ltd v Kariba Furniture Manufacturers (Pty) Ltd and Others* 2013 (6)

bb. Ratification of nominated rescue practitioner in entry by court order and concept of 'independent creditors'

In an entry by court order, the court appoints the rescue practitioner upon the nomination by the affected person having applied for the commencement of rescue proceedings, and subject to the ratification by the 'independent creditors' voting interest'.[649] Independent creditors are defined as creditors who are not related to the company, a director or the rescue practitioner in a manner contemplated by the definition of 'related' in s 1 as read with s 2(1)(a) to (c).[650] According to these provisions, two natural persons are related to each other if they are married, or live together in a relationship similar to marriage and are separated by no more than two degrees of natural and adopted consanguinity and affinity.[651] A legal and a natural person and two legal persons are related to each other if the one has 'direct or indirect control' over the other legal person. 'Control' effectively means the ability of one person (also together with any related or

SA 471 (GNP) at para 62. A rescue plan has been adopted once the requisite majority of creditors' votes and the requisite majority of the security holders' vote (if applicable) has been obtained (s 152(3)(b) and sub-para (c), respectively). 'Adoption' of the plan is different from the 'implementation' of the plan; implementation is the carrying out of the plan as adopted (see, eg, s 152(5)(b) and subss 7-9). Rescue proceedings only end after the implementation of the plan (ie, once the rescue practitioner has filed a notice of substantial implementation of the plan) (see s 132(2)(c)(ii)).

649 S 131(5). The rescue practitioner's appointment only becomes final when it is ratified by a vote of the independent creditors.

650 S 128(1)(g)(i) and (ii). Under this provision, the term 'creditor' includes certain persons that do not have a debt claim against the company, such as employees, insofar as they have a pre-commencement claim as contemplated in s 144(2) (see s 128(1)(g)(i)) as well as creditors whose claims are contractually subordinated and insofar as such subordinated creditors would have a claim against the liquidation value of the company (see s 145(4)(b)). Shareholders, by contrast, do not appear to fall within the meaning of 'creditors', irrespective of whether they have an economic interest in the company (see, by implication, s 152(3)(b) and (c)).

651 S 2(1)(a)(i) and (ii). This manifestation of the meaning of 'related persons' is relevant in applicable situations where any creditor is a natural person and the relationship under scrutiny is between such creditor and the rescue practitioner or a director.

'inter-related' persons)[652] to 'materially influence the policy of the other legal person'. This could be (i) through a holding-subsidiary relationship (as defined),[653] (ii) by holding the majority of general voting rights of the other person, (iii) through being entitled to appoint the directors who hold the majority of the votes at a meeting of the board of the other person or (iv) by any other comparable means.[654]

cc. Entry grounds

There are two grounds for entry that apply to both avenues into rescue proceedings. The first is that there 'is' – or in the case of out-of-court entry, 'appears to be' – a reasonable prospect of rescuing the company (hereafter, '*rescuability entry ground*' or simply '*rescuability*').[655] As indicated above, 'rescuing the company' is defined as 'achieving the goals set out in the definition of 'business rescue' in (s 128(1)(b))'[656] (which is the section that includes the two objectives of rescue discussed above). This entry ground thus requires that there be a reasonable prospect that, in the very least, rescue proceedings would result in a better return for the company's creditors or shareholders than in a hypothetical liquidation.[657]

The other entry ground that applies to both modes of entry is that of 'financial distress', which is a technical term under the Companies Act 2008. Companies are defined as being 'financially distressed' when

652 For the definition of 'inter-related persons', see s 1. According to that definition, inter-related means where 3 or more persons are related to each other in an unbroken chain of 'related' relationships.

653 See s 3.

654 See s 2(2). This manifestation of the meaning of the term 'related persons' is relevant in situations where the creditor is either a natural person or a legal person and the directors and the rescue practitioner are legal persons. (The third person from whom a creditor must be independent in order for such creditor to fall within the definition of 'independent creditors' voting rights' is the company, which is by definition a legal person.)

655 Ss 129(1)(b), 131(4)(a)(passage after sub-para (iii)).

656 S 128(1)(h).

657 Given this clear meaning, it is rather perplexing that the court in *AG Petzakis International Holdings Ltd v Petzakis Africa (Pty) Ltd and Others (Marley Pipe Systems (Pty) Ltd and Another (Intervening))* 2012 (5) SA 515 (GSJ) para 17 concluded that s 131(4) does not 'incorporate' the secondary objective of rescue; see also *Henochsberg Companies Act* (n 592) s 131, 462.

> '(i) it appears to be reasonably unlikely that the company will be able to pay all of its debts as they become due and payable within the immediately ensuing six months; or
> (ii) it appears to be reasonably likely that the company will become insolvent within the immediately ensuing six months.'[658]

The first limb of the definition refers to impending cash flow insolvency, while the second limb appears to refer to impending balance sheet insolvency. This is supported by the fact that the balance sheet test under s 4 for purposes of determining whether distributions are permitted is also referred to as 'solvency'.[659] The use of both tests of (impending) insolvency arguably moves the trigger for the commencement of rescue proceedings to an earlier stage than if only impending cash flow insolvency had been used, as has been the traditional position under South African law.[660]

A rather unusual provision is found in s 129(7). S 129(7) provides that if the board has reasonable grounds to believe that the company is financially distressed, but it has not adopted a resolution to commence rescue proceedings, it must notify each affected person of the fact that the company is financially distressed and provide reasons for not placing the company under rescue proceedings. S 129(7) arguably seeks to reduce information deficits of affected persons, thereby enabling them to utilise their

---

658 S 128(1)(f).

659 See also *Henochsberg Companies Act* (n 592) s 128, 448(1), 452.

660 The use of both tests of insolvency for purposes of the definition of 'financial distress' is arguably a departure from the position under the South African corporate insolvency law under the Companies Act 1973. This is because the test of insolvency has traditionally been cash flow insolvency, while balance sheet insolvency operated merely as a factor to be taken into account when deciding whether to place a company under winding-up proceedings (though, admittedly, the position has never been finally settled); see s 344(f) read with s 345 Companies Act 1973; see also, eg, *Ex Parte De Villiers and Another NNO: In re Carbon Developments* 1993 (1) SA 493 (A) 502. The position in relation to winding-up proceedings is arguably the same under the Companies Act 2008; see, eg, *Boschpoort Ondernemings (Pty) Ltd v Absa Bank Ltd* 2014 (2) SA 518 (SCA) [2014] JOL 31202 (SCA)) para 21; *Standard Bank of SA Ltd v R-Bay Logistics CC* 2013 (2) SA 295 (KZD) para 37; *Firstrand Bank Limited v Wayrail Investments (Pty) Ltd* [2013] 2 All SA 295 (KZD) para 15; *Firstrand Bank Ltd v Lodhi 5 Properties Investment CC and Another* 2013 (3) SA 212 (GNP) para 30. The current state of play is conveniently summarised in *Henochsberg Companies Act* (n 592) s 80, 313ff.

right to apply to court for an order to commence rescue proceedings under s 131.[661]

It should be noted that the better view of the provision that sets out the entry grounds for entry by court order, s 131(4)(a), is that the financial distress entry ground is not mandatory for the commencement of rescue proceedings by court order. A company is eligible to be placed under rescue proceedings by court order regardless of whether it is financially distressed where '(it) has failed to pay over any amount in terms of an obligation under or in terms of a public regulation, or contract, with respect to employment-related matters' (s 131(4)(a)(ii)) or where 'it is otherwise just and equitable to do so for financial reasons'(s 131(4)(a)(iii)).[662] The reasons for this are as follows. With regard to s 131(4)(a)(ii), failure to pay an employment-related obligation cannot constitute a mandatory entry ground, as this would unduly restrict the ability of affected persons to place temporarily distressed but economically viable companies under formal rescue proceedings. This would be inconsistent with the legislative scheme that business rescue provide for the efficient rescue and recovery of financially distressed companies in a manner that balances the rights and interests of all relevant stakeholders.[663]

With regard to s 131(4)(a)(iii), the word 'or' at the end of s 131(4)(a)(ii) suggests that the just and equitable ground is a further alternative to the financial distress entry ground. To be sure, the courts have in the past frequently read 'or' to mean 'and'.[664] In the context of s 131(4)(a)(ii) however, this would not be warranted. Replacing 'or' with 'and' in s 131(4)(a)(ii) would mean that entry into rescue proceedings would need to be just

661 This provision will be revisited in Chapter 5, as it could be seen as a legal strategy controlling company controller opportunism to delay the invocation of rescue proceedings inappropriately and to pursue excessively risky projects in the vicinity of insolvency.

662 See also Loubser, 'LLD thesis' (n 512) 60–1. For a contrary interpretation, see Bradstreet, 'Business Rescue Proves to be Creditor-friendly: Claassen J's Analysis of the New Business Rescue Procedure in *Oakdene Square Properties*' (2013) 130 SALJ 44.

663 S 7(2)(k). By virtue of s 5, the provisions in the Companies Act 2008 should be interepreted in such a manner to give effect to the purposes set out in s 7.

664 See, eg, *Barlin v Licencing Court for the Cape* 1924 AD 472, 478; *Ngcobo v Salimba CC; Ngcobo v Van Rensburg* 1999 (2) SA 1057 (SCA) para 11; *SATAWU v Garvas* 2013 (1) SA 83 (CC) para 143; *S v Sengama* 2013 (2) SACR 377 (SCA); and, recently, *Panamo Properties (Pty) Ltd and Another v Nel and Others NNO* 2015 (5) SA 63 (SCA) para 31.

and equitable for financial reasons *in addition to* the failure to pay employment-related obligations and the financial distress of the company, but not *in addition to* its rescuability. There would be no rational reason for this distinction.

Moreover, in comparable provisions in the Companies Act 2008, it would seem that the legislature was mindful of the difference between 'or' and 'and', and used each of these words to convey their correct meaning. First, in s 81(1)(c), which deals with the grounds of the compulsory winding-up of solvent companies upon the application to court by creditors, the just and equitable concept in sub-para (i) is preceded by 'and', while the just and equitable concept in sub-para (ii) is preceded by 'or'. There is no dout that in that context 'and' is used to convey *in addition to* and 'or' to convey *independently from*. This supports the view that the word 'or' should also convey its correct meaning in s 131(4)(a)(ii), particularly since the wording and the structure of the respective provisions are almost identical. Second, the word 'and' would seem to be used in its correct meaning in s 131(4)(a)(iii) iself to indicate that the rescuability entry ground is mandatory. As with the failure to pay employment-related obligations, this interpretation of the rescuability entry ground is reinforced by the underlying purpose of business rescue in s 7. It would hardly be efficient and equitable as between the interests of all stakeholders if companies were granted access to business rescue proceedings without there being reasonable grounds that they are rescuable, nor that this should only be required in the out-of-court entry route (where it is clearly a mandatory requirement),[665] but not in the court entry route.[666] The correct and deliberate use

665 This follows from the use of the word 'and' in s 129(1).

666 For entry by court order, see, eg, *Koen v Wedgewood Village Golf and Country Estate (Pty) Ltd* 2012 (2) SA 378 (WCC) para 17; *Oakdene Square Properties (Pty) Ltd v Farm Bothasfontein (Kyalami) (Pty) Ltd* [2013] JOL 30498 (SCA) (by implication, since it accepts the presence of financial distress (para 5, 49(3)) and yet bases its decision to dismiss the application for the commencement of business rescue on the reasonable prospect of success-ground (para 49(7)). See also *Henochsberg Companies Act* (n 592) s 131, 463; Loubser, 'LLD thesis' (n 512) 61. However, see Bradstreet (n 662) 5, who reads the grounds in s 131(4)(a)(iii) and (iv) as alternatives to sub-paras (i) and (ii). Although there is some scope for such an interpretation because of the word 'or' in sub-para (ii), the fact that the deeming provision in sub-para (ii) only makes sense as an alternative of the financial distress entry ground in sub-para (i) (as explained above), would preclude such an interpretation. The confusion on this is due, in large part, to the clumsy drafting of this provision.

of 'and' with respect to the rescuability ground in s 131(4)(a)(iii) would again strengthen the argument that the same is true for the use of 'or' in s 131(4)(a)(ii) with respect to the just and equitable ground.

Reading the failure to pay employment-related obligations as an alternative, rather than cumulative, to the financial distress entry ground has the effect of making it easier for affected persons to prove the existence of financial distress. All that an affected person needs to show is that the company has in fact not paid over any employment-related claim. In other words, s 131(4)(a)(ii) essentially operates as a deeming provision for the financial distress of the company. A similar approach is found in winding-up law: the actual failure to pay a debt also operates as a deeming provision for cash flow insolvency in respect of winding-up.[667] It might be asked why a similar deeming provision relating to unpaid debts other than employment-related obligations has not been included in s 131(4).

It should be noted that unlike entry by court order,[668] the just and equitable concept does not constitute an alternative entry ground to financial distress in out-of-court entry. The just and equitable concept in s 130(5)(a)(ii) is only available to affected persons for challenging the commencement of rescue proceedings by the board, and not to the board for placing the company under rescue proceedings.

dd. Standard of proof of reasonable prospect of success of rescue entry ground

Possibly the most controversial and heavily litigated issue under the new rescue procedure so far has been the standard of proof contemplated by the phrase a 'reasonable prospect' (of rescuing the company). It appears that the reason for this uncertainty has partly been the novelty of the phrase 'reasonable prospect' in the South African corporate insolvency law and partly the difficulty of the policy issue underlying this question. The right balance between promoting a rescue culture and preventing the abuse of rescue proceedings needs to be found.[669]

---

667 S 345 Companies Act 1973.

668 See above under this heading.

669 As noted in Chapter 1, the rescuability entry ground can be seen as a legal strategy to prevent the entry into rescue proceedings of economically distressed companies, which will be considered in Chapter 7.

After some conflicting decisions, the Supreme Court of Appeal ('*SCA*') in the case of *Oakdene Square*[670] has largely settled the matter.[671] The court held that a reasonable prospect requires more than a mere *prima facie* case, an arguable possibility or speculative suggestion[672] as to the likelihood of success of rescue, but rather 'a prospect based on reasonable grounds'.[673] Moreover, the court held that the allegation of the existence of a reasonable prospect that the rescue will be successful must be supported by a cogent evidential foundation.[674]

This standard of proof is lower than that of the equivalent found under judicial management, which required that there be a 'reasonable probability' that the company would become a successful concern. A 'reasonable probability' was held to mean more than a mere possibility.[675] It is clear that something that is 'possible' is less sure to happen than something that

---

670 *Oakdene Square Properties (Pty) Ltd v Farm Bothasfontein (Kyalami) (Pty) Ltd* [2013] JOL 30498 (SCA) para 29.

671 For a comprehensive review of the case law on the meaning of the existence of 'a reasonable prospect of rescuing a company', see *Henochsberg Companies Act* (n 592) s 131, 465ff; *Meskin Insolvency Law* (n 576) para 18.43.

672 See also, eg, *Koen v Wedgewood Village Golf and Country Estate (Pty) Ltd* 2012 (2) SA 378 (WCC) para 19; *Eveleigh v Dowmont Snacks (Pty) Ltd and Others* (11982/2013) [2014] ZAKZPHC 1 (22 January 2014) para 24.

673 At para 29. This description is, with respect, somewhat circular. Arguably a more useful formulation as to the meaning of 'reasonable prospect' is a possibility that rests on objectively reasonable grounds'; see *Propsec Investments (Pty) Ltd v Pacific Coast Investments 97 Ltd and Another* 2013 1 SA 542 (FB) para 12. See also *Zoneska Investments (Pty) Ltd/Bonatla Properties (Pty) Ltd v Midnight Storm Investments 386 Ltd (Registration No. 2007/019270/06)* and *Another (Grayhaven Riches 9 Ltd and Others as Interested Parties; First Rand Bank Limited as Intervening Creditor)* [2012] 4 All SA 590 (WCC) paras 39–40.

674 At para 30–1, citing *Propspec Investments v Pacific Coasts Investments 97 Ltd* 2013 (1) SA 542 (FB) para 11. Interestingly, the court endorsed the view of earlier judgments holding that where a major lender holding a majority share of the votes on the rescue plan has declared its opposition to the invocation of rescue proceedings, this should constitute a factor in determining whether or not to grant an order placing the company under rescue proceedings (at para 38). However, holding that the opposition of a major lender should not be a factor in determining whether the objectives of rescue would be achieved, see *Employees of Solar Spectrum Trading 83 (Pty) Ltd v Afgri Operations Ltd* unreported Case Nos. 6418/2011, 18624/11, 66226/11 8 May 2012 (GNP) paras 36–7. See also *Nedbank Ltd v Bestvest 153 (Pty) Ltd; Essa and Another v Bestvest 153 (Pty) Ltd* 2012 (5) SA 497 (WCC).

675 See PART B, Chapter 3, III., 3., c. above.

is 'probable'. Therefore, the burden of proof is accordingly lighter under business rescue than it was under judicial management.[676]

To the relief of many scholars fearing that this requirement would prevent the promotion of a rescue culture,[677] the SCA in *Oakdene Square* departed from the more exacting interpretations of the earlier decisions in holding (i) that the method of showing a reasonable prospect need not be prescribed,[678] (ii) that the matters on which certain minimum information must be given need not be specified[679] and (iii) that at the stage of commencement of rescue proceedings, a detailed rescue plan need not be set out.[680]

---

676 See in a company law context under the South African Companies Act 46 of 1926 *Noordkaap Lewendhawe Ko-operasie Bpk v Schreuder* 1974 3 SA 102 (A). See generally in this regard T Joubert, '"Reasonable possibility" versus "reasonable prospect": Did business rescue succeed in creating a better test than judicial management?' 2013 (76) THRHR 550, 552. Expressly holding that 'reasonable prospect' is a lesser requirement than 'resonable probability' under judicial management, see *Oakdene Square Properties (Pty) Ltd v Farm Bothasfontein (Kyalami) (Pty) Ltd* [2013] JOL 30498 (SCA) para 29. See also *Southern Palace Investments 265 (Pty) Ltd v Midnight Storm Investments 386 Limited and Others* 2012 (2) SA 423, para 21.

677 See, eg, *Henochsberg Companies Act* (n 592) s 131, 465ff.

678 See, eg, *Southern Palace Investments 265 (Pty) Ltd v Midnight Storm Investments 386 Limited and Others* 2012 (2) SA.

679 Examples of matters on which certain information was held to be provided in the earlier judgment of *Southern Palace Investments 265 (Pty) Ltd v Midnight Storm Investments 386 Limited and Others* 2012 (2) SA 423 are, *inter alia*, the likely costs of formal rescue proceedings; the likely availability of funds to meet the day-to-day expenses; and the availability of 'any necessary resource' (at para 24). See also *Nedbank Ltd v Bestvest 153 (Pty) Ltd; Essa and Another v Bestvest 153 (Pty) Ltd* 2012 (5) SA 497 (WCC).

680 The SCA in *Oakdene Square* pointed out, correctly, that it is more appropriate to leave the development of a rescue plan to the rescue practitioner as part of his investigatory duties of the company's affairs under s 141 (at para 31). This was held to be required, eg, by *Francis Edward Gormley v West City Precinct Properties (Pty) Ltd* 19076/11 (WCC): 18 April 2012 para 13.

ee. Challenges to out-of-court entry into business rescue proceedings

Any affected person can challenge the board resolution to commence rescue proceedings in court on at least three, if not four,[681] grounds.[682] The two obvious grounds of challenge are that the company does not fulfil the financial distress and rescuability entry grounds.[683] If the court sets aside the board resolution to commence rescue proceedings on the grounds that the company was not financially distressed, and the court finds 'that there were no reasonable grounds for believing that the company would be unlikely to pay all its debts as they became due and payable',[684] the court may grant a costs order against any director who voted for the resolution to commence rescue proceedings.[685]

A further ground for challenging the board resolution is that the company has failed to meet the procedural requirements set out in s 129(3) and (4).[686] However, at first glance, there is an anomaly between two provisions relating to this ground of challenge, namely s 129(5)(a) and s 130(5)(a). Non-compliance with any of the procedural requirements – no matter how trivial they may have been, according to some courts[687] – leads to business rescue proceedings automatically lapsing and becoming a nullity under s 129(5)(a), while non-compliance with the substantive financial distress and rescuability entry grounds require a court application by an affected person and a setting aside by the court under s 130(5)(a).[688] This distinction is not sustainable.

681 For a discussion on whether a fourth ground of challenge exists, see further below under this heading.

682 S 130(1)(passage before sub-s (1)).

683 S 130(1)(i), (ii).

684 Which is a slightly amended form of the impending cash flow insolvency test.

685 S 130(5)(c)(ii).

686 S 130(5)(a)(iii).

687 See *Advanced Technologies and Engineering Company (Pty) Ltd v Aeronautique et Technologies Embarquées SAS* (GNP case no 72522/11); *Madodza (Pty) Ltd (in business rescue) v ABSA Bank Ltd* (GNP Case 38906/12); *Homez Trailers and Bodies (Pty) Ltd (under supervision) v Standard Bank of South Africa Ltd* (GNP case no 35201/2013);*ABSA Bank Ltd v Ikageng Construction (Pty) Ltd* (GNP Case no 61235/2014).

688 Indeed, s 129(5)(a) and s 130(5)(a)(iii) are in direct conflict with respect to noncompliance with the procedural requirements under s 129(3) and (4) themselves.

The SCA in *Panamo Properties (Pty) Ltd and Another v Nel and Others NNO*[689] resolved this anomaly by interpreting s 129(5)(a) to provide for an automatic lapsing only of the board resolution that placed the company under rescue proceedings, and not the rescue proceedings themselves. According to the SCA, rescue proceedings would terminate only upon a court order setting aside such a board resolution, even where the ground upon which this is based is non-compliance with the procedural grounds under s 129(3) and (4). The court came to this conclusion on a purposive and contextual reading of the relevant provisions, including s 132(2)(a)(i). This provision provides, in relevant parts, that rescue proceedings end when the court sets aside the resolution or order that began those proceedings.[690]

The SCA in the *Panamo Properties* case ventured to provide its interpretation of another aspect of s 130(5)(a) that has been subject to uncertainty, namely whether the ground on which a court can set aside a board resolution commencing rescue proceedings in sub-para (ii) of that section is in the alternative, or rather cumulative, to the three entry grounds mentioned in s 130(1)(a).[691] Sub-para (ii) provides that the court may set aside a resolution where it would be 'otherwise just and equitable' to do so. The word 'or' between sub-paras (i) and (ii) could be interpreted to suggest that the just and equitable ground is in the alternative to the three entry grounds mentioned in s 130(1)(a). Such a reading of s 130(5)(a) would mean that the just and equitable ground constitutes an additional ground of challenging an out-of-court entry into rescue proceedings.[692] The SCA in *Panamo Properties* contended, however, that introducing an entry ground

689 2015 (5) SA 63 (SCA) paras 20ff. For similar sentiments in previous decisions, see *Ex Parte Van den Steen NO (Credit Suisse Group AG Intervening)* 2014 (6) SA 29 (GJ)M; *ABSA Bank Ltd v Caine NO, In Re: Absa Bank Ltd v Caine NO* [2014] ZAFSHC 46. See also *MAN Financial Services SA (Pty) Ltd v Blouwater Boerdery CC* (GNP case no 72522/2012).

690 See, in particular, paras 28–9.

691 As we will see in PART C, Chapter 7, II., 1., c., aa, the answer to this question is relevant for whether the just and equitable ground of challenging the out-of-court commencement of rescue proceedings could be seen to reduce agency costs arising from company controller opportunisms to invoke rescue proceedings prematurely.

692 Favouring this interpretation, see *DH Brothers Industries (Pty) Ltd v Gribnitz NO and Others* [2014] 1 All SA 173 (KZP) paras 17–8. See also *The Commissioner for the South African Revenue Service v The Business Zone 983 CC* (9673/2015) [2015] WCC (7 September 2015).

in s 130(5)(a) that is not contained in the enabling provision (ie, in s 130(1)(a)) constitutes an untenable inconsistency.[693] This inconsistency the court resolved by reading 'or' in s 131(4)(a)(ii) as 'and',[694] and thus changing the just and equitable concept from constituting an additional ground of challenge to a requirement that would need to be satisified *in addition to* each of the three entry grounds mentioned in s 130(1)(a).

Although the SCA's approach certainly puts the grounds of out-of-court challenge in a better systematic light, it is nevertheless not entirely convincing. First, as shown above, there is strong support from other provisions in the Companies Act 2008 that deal with the just and equitable ground that the word 'or' should be afforded its correct meaning in 130(5)(a) as well.[695] Second, against that background, reading the just and equitable ground into the enabling provision does not constitute a significantly greater encroachment (if greater at all) on the plain meaning of the text than replacing the word 'or' with 'and', as suggested by the SCA. And third, a further supporting argument the SCA raised for its approach is that the just and equitable ground would largely preclude lititgants from exploiting technical issues to turn the business rescue provisions to their advantage, which had indeed been the case on the facts of the case the SCA had to decide. The just and equitable ground no doubt has this effect. However, if there are strong reasons for a different interpretation, as advocated by this author, this effect of the just and equitable concept cannot *ipso facto* justify the SCA's approach; in other words, it is an inductive, not a deductive, argument.

b. Changes to entry requirements under judicial management

aa. General

The entry requirements under the new rescue procedure depart from those of its predecessor in three significant respects. First, while judicial management could only be commenced by court order and presumably not by

693 At para 30.

694 The court pointed out that this is not a novel approach taken by South African courts; see the cases cited in n 664 above.

695 See cc above.

the board,[696] the new rescue procedure provides for the commencement of rescue proceedings by the board[697] in addition to entry by court order.[698] Second, the grounds of entry are triggered earlier under business rescue than judicial management. And third, since under the new rescue regime the objectives of rescue are broader than under judicial management, a wider range of companies in financial difficulties can now avail themselves of formal rescue proceedings.

These three departures from the entry requirements under judicial management will now be considered in turn.

bb. Addition of an out-of-court entry route by the company's board

The addition of out-of-court entry by the board of directors is expected to encourage earlier entry into formal rescue proceedings than under judicial management, thereby enhancing the chances of success of rescue and preventing further losses primarily to unsecured creditors. Earlier entry may be encouraged under out-of-court entry for two reasons.

First, because the directors typically have the best information about the company's financial affairs, they are typically the first constituents to become aware of the need for rescue proceedings. Accordingly, directors are in the best position to place the company under formal rescue proceedings timeously.[699]

And second,[700] the out-of-court entry route places the costs of enforcement of denying ineligible companies access to formal rescue proceedings

---

696 See PART B, Chapter 3, III., 3., a. above.

697 S 129.

698 S 131.

699 *Henochsberg Companies Act* (n 592) s 129, 450. See also, eg, Posner, 'Introduction' in Bhandari and Weiss (eds), *Corporate Bankruptcy – Economic and Legal Perspectives* (Cambridge University Press 1996) xiff.

700 For the same argument, though for reasons other than the favourable effects on management incentives, see Loubser, 'LLD thesis' (n 512) 50–1. However, as mentioned in Chapter 1, the directors (acting in the interests of shareholders) typically have a perverse incentive to pursue excessively risky projects in the vicinity of insolvency. Legal strategies that could be seen to control this problem will be explored from a comparative perspective in Chapter 5. By contrast, directors may in exceptional circumstances be tempted to place a company under formal rescue proceedings prematurely. The comparative analysis of the legal responses to this problem will be considered in Chapter 7.

on affected persons *ex post*,as opposed to on the court *ex ante*, as under the court entry route. Accordingly, the direct costs of enforcement were certain to occur regardless of the merits of the application under judicial management. By contrast, such costs are more likely to occur only in cases where there is a reasonable chance of success in the out-of-court entry route, given that the costs are borne by the persons bringing the application. As this reduces the chances of the imposition of unjustified costs on the company at the entry stage, directors are encouraged to place companies under rescue proceedings earlier. This 'carrot' could be seen to counteract the perverse incentive of company controllers to delay the invocation of rescue proceedings inappropriately.

cc. Earlier trigger of business rescue proceedings than under judicial management

Earlier entry into formal rescue proceedings is also promoted by the addition of the financial distress entry ground under rescue proceedings. That entry ground is triggered when either of the two tests of insolvency appears 'reasonably likely to occur within the next six months'. This places the trigger of formal rescue proceedings well in advance of insolvency.

To be sure, the entry ground that the company 'probably' be unable to meet its obligations[701] also placed the trigger of judicial management in advance of a state of insolvency. However, it would seem that the requirement that the inability to meet obligations must be foreseeable in the immediate future[702] placed the trigger of judicial management well within the six months period as contemplated by the financial distress entry ground.

To the extent that the company controller opportunism to inappropriately delay formal insolvency proceedings typically arises in advance of insolvency,[703] and a company's financial situation may often be beyond repair by the time it reaches a state of insolvency, the financial distress entry

701 S 427(1)(a) Companies Act 1973.

702 See PART B, Chapter 3, III., 3., c. above.

703 See Chapter 1 above.

ground could be seen to counteract both such problems. It is therefore a welcome introduction to the new rescue regime.[704]

The standard of determining whether the company is in financial distress is rather low in that there must be a mere 'appearance' of a 'reasonable likelihood' of financial distress.[705] The enquiry as to the existence of financial distress in respect of out-of-court entry by directors is objective, as it is required that there must be 'reasonable grounds to believe that the company is in financial distress.'[706]

dd. Wider range of companies eligible for formal rescue than under judicial management

Since the rescuability entry ground incorporates the two objectives of rescue (for both commencement modes), and the objectives of the new rescue procedure are broader than those of judicial management,[707] a wider range of companies will have access to formal rescue proceedings under the new rescue procedure.[708] Accordingly, while companies were denied access to

---

704 It should be noted that, as explained in Chapter 1, the financial distress entry ground could be seen as a legal strategy reducing agency costs arising from company controller opportunism to place companies under formal rescue proceedings prematurely, which will be discussed in Chapter 7.

705 S 128(1)(f)(i) and (ii).

706 S 129(1), s 130(1)(a)(i), s 130(5)(c)(ii). It has been argued that the enabling provision, s 129(1), hints at a combination of an objective and a subjective test, as it provides that '*the board* has reasonable grounds to believe [...]', meaning that whether or not a director's grounds were reasonable will be judged from the perspective of the knowledge, skill and experience of that director (Loubser, 'LLD thesis' (n 512) 56. However, in respect of challenges to the board resolution commencing rescue proceedings on the financial distress entry ground (s 130(1)(a)(i)) and costs orders against directors for applying the financial distress entry ground incorrectly (s 130(5)(c)(ii)), the test for the existence of financial distress is clearly objective. It is expected that courts will read the objective standard of s 130(1)(a)(i), s 130(5)(c)(ii) into s 129(1).

707 For the objectives of judicial management, see PART B, Chapter 3, III., 2. above.

708 Some courts have held that the general policy under the Companies Act 2008 has shifted from favouring the liquidation of companies under the Companies Act 1973 to the saving of companies' businesses; see, eg, *Absa Bank Ltd v Newcity Group (Pty) Ltd, Cohen v Newcity Group (Pty) Ltd and Another* [2013] 3 All SA 146 (GSJ) paras 29–33 and *Dippenaar NO & Others v Business Venture Investments No 134 (Pty) Ltd* [2014] 2 All SA 162 (WCC) paras 45–6.

judicial management unless it was shown that *all* creditors would be paid in full, companies are now granted access even if it is clear that some creditors are not likely to recover the full value of their claims, provided the creditors as a group would receive better returns than in (a hypothetical) liquidation.[709] This explains the need for a majority vote by the company's claimants on a rescue plan under the new rescue procedure. As mentioned above, this was not necessary under judicial management, as such procedure contemplated that the position of all creditors would be restored to their pre-judicial management position.

c. Comparative perspectives of certain aspects of the out-of-court entry route with the UK and Australia

The addition of the out-of-court entry route of rescue accords with international practice. For example, it is also found under both the British and the Australian procedures.[710] However, there are two relevant differences between the three jurisdictions on the parties that are entitled to enter. First, unlike the British main rescue procedure, the Australian and the South African procedures do not entitle the general meeting to place the company under rescue proceedings.[711] This is rather surprising, given that the decision to commence rescue proceedings would appear to belong to the category of fundamental decisions for which the South African company law generally requires mandatory shareholder approval.[712] However, the likely

---

709 This follows from the secondary objective of rescue (see PART B, Chapter 4, IV., 1., b above). It is for this reason that any reference to the entry grounds under judicial management (s 427(1) Companies Act 1973) in interpreting the entry grounds under the new procedure should be resisted (however, see, eg, *Swart v Beagles Run Investments 25 (Pty) Ltd* 2011 (5) SA 422 (GNP) paras 23–5).

710 For the UK, Insolvency Act 1986, Sch B1, para 22(1); for Australia, see s 436A Corporations Act 2001.

711 On the general meeting's power to appoint an administrator in the UK, see, for out-of-court entry Insolvency Act 1986, Sch B1, para 22(1); for entry by court order, see Insolvency Act 1986, Sch B1, paras 12(1)(a). Interestingly, the first South African Draft Companies Bill of 2007 still allowed the general meeting to enter recue proceedings out-of-court; clause 132(1).

712 The most pertinent example for our purposes is the decision to voluntarily wind-up an insolvent company (s 350 Companies Act 1973) and a solvent company (s 80). Other transactions requiring shareholder approval are, eg, certain 'fundamental transactions' (Ch 5 pt A).

costs and delay of calling a meeting of shareholders and the possible adverse effects of the likely publicity of such a meeting, may, as a practical matter, undermine the effectiveness of granting the general meeting the power to commence rescue proceedings.[713]

The second difference is that the British and Australian procedures entitle a special type of secured creditor, who holds a so-called floating charge over the whole or substantially the whole of the company's property, to appoint an administrator of their choice.[714] Appointments of administrators by floating charge-holders are encouraged under the British administration procedure by the fact that floating charge-holders are not required to meet any grounds of entry.[715] Furthermore, where any other party entitled to place a company under administration intends to appoint an administrator, the floating charge-holder has to be notified and is given the opportunity to appoint an administrator of their choice.[716]

Until the sweeping changes brought about by the Enterprise Act 2002, the UK provided for a corporate insolvency procedure that enabled the floating charge-holder to realise his security largely to the exclusion of

---

713 See also Loubser, 'LLD thesis' (n 512) 50–1. In relation to the British administration procedure, see Fletcher, *The Law of Insolvency* (4th edn, Sweet & Maxwell 2009) para 16-034.

714 For the UK, see Insolvency Act 1986, Sch B1, paras 14ff; for Australia, see s 436C Corporations Act 2001. A floating charge is a security device over present and future assets, which in the ordinary course of business change from time to time, and which the debtor/chargor-company is free to continue to deal with in the ordinary course of business (*Yorkshire Woolcombers Association Ltd, Re,* [1903] 2 Ch. 284, 294; *Illingworth v Holdsworth* [1904] A.C. 355, H.L. See also Fletcher (n 713) para 14-004). This has the practical advantage for the chargor-company of enabling it to raise secured finance while being able to use the encumbered assets for routine trading activities. The floating charge becomes 'real' security (in British law parlance, a 'fixed charge') on the happening of some enforcement event. On this event, the charge is said to 'crystallise'. See generally Davies and Worthington, *Gower and Davies Principles of Modern Company Law* (10th edn, Sweet & Maxwell 2016) para 32-5ff.

715 Insolvency Act 1986, Sch B1, para 35(2)(a).

716 Insolvency Act 1986, Sch B1, para 12, 26, 36.

other types of creditors, referred to as administrative receivership.[717] This is still effectively the position in Australia.[718]

This ability of floating charge-holders to effectively take control of the formal rescue procedure in the UK and Australia appears to exacerbate inter-creditor agency costs during rescue proceedings, and its justification might be questioned on that basis. We have seen in Chapter 1 that one justification could be that it might ameliorate secured creditors' opportunism to embark on enforcement enhancing or preferred procedure actions in the vicinity of insolvency, by *rewarding* them with greater control rights during formal rescue proceedings.[719]

Another argument in favour of the power afforded to floating charge-holders, is that it might facilitate a more effective running of the company during administration. A considerable number of companies' financial decline is attributable to poor management.[720] In such cases, the board's ability to appoint an administrator might simply transfer the cause of the company's problems to administration proceedings, as the administrator might find it too unpleasant to completely side-line the directors who have appointed him. This problem is overcome where the floating charge-holder is entitled to appoint the administrator.[721]

Floating charge-holders are usually significant banks that commonly monitor their debtor-companies' customers closely.[722] Accordingly, they have the information and expertise to determine whether or not the company's problems are management-related at fairly low costs. Moreover, their appointment of an administrator ensures there is no allegiance of the administrator with the incumbent directors.[723] Moreover, the risk of oppor-

---

717 The floating charge-holder used to have much greater control over rescue proceedings under the administrative receivership procedure. This procedure entitled the floating charge-holder to appoint an administrative receiver, who was accountable to an overwhelming extent to the floating charge-holder, and had wide-ranging powers to manage the company and sell off the company's assets (either as a going concern or as a fire-sale) to satisfy the floating charge-holder's outstanding claim against the company. See generally Armour and Frisby, 'Rethinking Receivership' (2001) 21 OJLS 75.

718 See Pt 5.2 Corporations Act 2001.

719 See the discussion in PART A, Chapter 1, II., 3., b. above.

720 Armour and Mokal (n 609).

721 Ibid.

722 Ibid.

723 Ibid.

tunistic behaviour by the floating charge-holder during administration proceedings is controlled by such procedure's governance mechanisms.[724] These policy arguments may account for the British legislature's clear preference for the appointment of administrators by floating charge-holders.

There is no equivalent security device to the floating charge in South Africa. Holders of the two revolving security devices in South African law – the general notarial bond and the cession in security (*cession in securitatem debiti*) – have never enjoyed the exclusive right of realising their security in insolvency as the floating charge-holder under administrative receivership.

3. The statutory moratorium (s 133)

a. General

Unlike under judicial management, which provided for a discretionary moratorium,[725] the new rescue procedure provides for a statutory (and automatic) moratorium once rescue proceedings are triggered.[726] The moratorium is contained in s 133(1)[727] and reads as follows:

> 'During business rescue proceedings, no legal proceeding, including enforcement action, against the company, or in relation to any property belonging to the company, or lawfully in its possession, may be commenced or proceeded within any forum'.

The requirement that 'no legal proceeding' be brought against the company during rescue proceedings makes the scope of the moratorium potentially very broad,[728] which is consistent with international trends; in the UK for example, the moratorium precludes all 'legal process',[729] in Australia, 'proceeding in a court' and, as a separate ground, 'enforcement pro-

---

724 Ibid.

725 See PART B, Chapter 3, III., 1. above.

726 S 128(1)(b)(ii).

727 Passage before para (a).

728 On the wide scope of the moratorium generally, see also *Meskin Insolvency Law* (n 576) para 18.6.

729 Insolvency Act 1986, Sch B1, para 43(6). More specific grounds are contained in para 43.

cess'[730] and in the US, 'judicial, administrative or other action or proceeding'.[731]

A few questions arise in relation to the scope of the moratorium under the South African rescue procedure. First, the requirement that the moratorium only prevents legal proceedings that are brought 'within any forum' might reduce the scope of the moratorium, a question that will be considered further at b.aa. below. Second, the moratorium stays legal proceedings 'against the company, or in relation to any property belonging to the company, or lawfully in its possession'. The type of property that falls within these formulations will be explored at b.bb. and b.cc below. Third, although proceedings against the company where it has stood surety or given a guarantee to a creditor for the obligations of a third-party debtor are expressly exempted from the moratorium,[732] the position in respect of the opposite scenario – ie, where a creditor of a company proceeds against a third party surety or guarantor of the company's obligations owed to the creditor – is not provided for. The question is whether the creditor is entitled to proceed directly against the third party surety or whether the moratorium on enforcement against the principal obligation extends to the accessory obligation. This question was settled by the court in *Investec Bank Ltd v Bruyns*[733] in favour of the creditor. Drawing on the old authorities[734] and relevant case law,[735] the court held that a moratorium constitutes a defence *in personam* (being purely personal to the debtor and, as such, does not affect the enforceability of the underlying obligation), rather than a defence *in rem* (which attaches to the underlying obligation itself).[736] The surety was therefore not entitled to raise a defence against the creditor when he proceeded directly against the surety.[737]

---

730 S 440D and 440F Corporations Act 2001.

731 11 USC § 362(a)(1). More specific grounds are contained in § 362 generally.

732 S 133(2).

733 19449/11 (WCC): 14 November 2011.

734 The court mentions Voet and Van Leeuwen in respect of the legal institutions of *letters of inductie* and *atterminatie*, but refrained from providing precise references.

735 In particular, *Worthington v Wilson* 1918 TPD 104.

736 Scholtz, 'Suretyship' LAWSA (2nd edn repl. vol, 2015) vol 26, para 201; *Standard Bank of SA Ltd v SA Fire Equipment (Pty) Ltd & Another* 1984 (2) SA 693 (C).

737 Paras 17–9. See also *Business Partners Ltd v Tsakiroglou and Others* 2016 (4) SA 390 (WCC). See also *Henochsberg Companies Act* (n 592) s 133, 475–6.

Certain exceptions to the moratorium are set out in s 133(1)(a) to (f), which can be divided broadly into general exceptions to be granted at the discretion of the rescue practitioner and the court (paras (a) and (b), respectively) and specific exceptions (paras (c) to (f)). These include criminal proceedings both against the company and its directors; proceedings against property or rights over which the company exercises the powers of a trustee; and proceedings or the assertion of any other claim against the company by a regulatory authority. Moreover, in contrast to the position in winding-up,[738] but consistent with the position under judicial management,[739] the operation of set-off is allowed to operate during rescue proceedings. The automatic exemption of set-off from the moratorium is of great practical relevance to creditors, as creditors against whom the company has counter-claims effectively fall outside the collective procedure of rescue proceedings.[740] Set-off is also desirable from an efficiency perspective in that it reduces transactions costs.[741]

Finally, the broad scope of the moratorium means that s 133 might overlap with provisions that place restrictions on creditors to exercise certain rights against assets owned or lawfully possessed by the company (which is dealt with under s 134). There might further be an overlap with powers of the rescue practitioner to suspend and the court to cancel contracts of the company with third parties that had been concluded before the commencement of rescue proceedings and continue to exist after the commencement of rescue proceedings (which is regulated by s 136). The relationship between s 133 with these two provisions will be considered at 4.a and 6.b, respectively.

738 For the position in winding-up, see s 339 Companies Act 1973 read with s 46 Insolvency Act 1936; see also *Henochsberg Companies Act* (n 592) s 133, 477.

739 See PART B, Chapter 3, III., 4 above.

740 Wood, *Principles of International Insolvency* (2nd edn, Sweet & Maxwell 2007) para 17-012.

741 Van der Merwe and others, *Contract – General Principles* (2nd edn, Juta 2003) 515.

b. Scope of the moratorium

aa. The meaning of any 'legal proceeding, including enforcement action, […] in any forum'

Does parate executie enforcement fall within s 133(1)?—The action that is stayed by the moratorium under s 133(1) is any 'legal proceeding, including enforcement action, […] *in any forum*'.[742] The term 'forum' could be interpreted to restrict the ambit of s 133(1) to enforcement action through any institution in which a dispute is heard, including a court and any other judicial or quasi-judicial tribunal,[743] and perhaps even through a court official, such as the sheriff or the registrar of the High Court.

On this reading of the word 'forum', enforcement action agreed between the parties to a contract to take place privately – referred to in South African law as *parate executie* – falls outside the scope of s 133(1), and would accordingly be allowed, notwithstanding the general moratorium on legal proceedings against the company.[744] Relevant practical examples of where *parate executie* enforcement is often contracted for by the parties are where the debtor pledges corporeal movable assets or cedes incorporeal assets (referred to in South African law as 'cessions *in securitatem debiti*') to the creditor in security for the debtor's obligations to the creditor. Here a *parate executie* clause in the applicable security agreement would entitle the creditor to sell the pledged or ceded assets in security and satisfy its outstanding claim against the debtor, without recourse to the court.

This reading seems to be reinforced by the plain meaning of 'legal proceeding', which would appear to exclude any proceedings outside the type of judicial or quasi-judicial institutions mentioned above or statutory insti-

---

742 Note that the moratorium applies to any legal proceeding that is both 'commenced' and 'proceeded with' during rescue proceedings (s 133(1)). This means that the moratorium, quite sensibly, applies even to legal proceedings that had been initiated, but not concluded, *before* the commencement of rescue proceedings.

743 *Cloete Murray and Another NNO v FirstRand Bank Ltd t/a Wesbank* 2015 (3) SA 438 (SCA) para 32 has held that a forum is normally defined as a court or tribunal.

744 ENS opinion 28 April 2010, paras 17–8, 55.3. *Chetty v Hart* 2015 (6) SA 424 (SCA) has confirmed that arbitration proceedings fall within the moratorium under s 133(1).

tutions that largely perform administrative functions, such as the Commission.[745]

However, the practical effect of this interpretation of s 133(1) could be undermined where a debtor approaches the court to compel the creditor to abstain from the private enforcement of its security, on the ground that the private enforcement action would prejudice the debtor.[746] Should the court rule in favour of the debtor, then the enforcement action would no longer be outside a 'forum', and accordingly fall within s 133(1).[747]

Moreover, the power of the rescue practitioner to suspend, and the power of the court to cancel, existing agreements during rescue proceedings under s 136(2), might be broad enough to allow the rescue practitioner to suspend, or the court to cancel, a *paratie executie* provision under a contract. The uncertainty of the scope of s 136(2) arises from the fact that it is not clear whether it allows for the suspension and cancellation of entire agreements or just 'obligations of the company'.[748] The suspension and possibly also the cancellation of *parate executie* enforcement would only be permitted on the former, not the latter, interpretation. This is because *paratie executie* enforcement would appear to be a contractual right of the creditor that does not appear to have a corresponding 'obligation of the company', and would, accordingly, not fall outside the ambit of s 136(2)

---

745 See the definition of 'proceeding' in Black's Law Dictionary <http://thelawdictionary.org/> accessed 16 January 2017. For the functions of the Commission, see s 187. The court in *Cloete Murray and Another NNO v FirstRand Bank Ltd t/a Wesbank* 2015 (3) SA 438 (SCA) para 31 held that 'legal proceeding' bears the meaning of a lawsuit, for which it found support in *Van Zyl v Euodia Trust (Edms) Bpk* 1983 (3) SA 394 (T) at 399C-D and *Lister Garment Corporation (Pty) Ltd v Wallace NO* 1992 (2) SA 722 (D) at 723G-H.

746 The debtor is likely to rely on s 34 of the Constitution 108 of 1996, which contains the right to due process. Indeed, the courts have been critical of *parate executie* clauses in such security agreements; *SA Bank of Athens Ltd v Van Zyl* [2006] 1 All SA 118 (SCA); *Bock and Others v Duburoro Investments (Pty) Ltd* 2004 (2) SA 242 (SCA); *Juglal NO and Another v Shoprite Checkers (Pty) Ltd t/a OK Franchise Division* 2004 (5) SA 248 (SCA). See generally Berdou, 'The doctrine of *parate executie* or self-help by creditors in the present South African Law' [2010] De Rebus 28, 29.

747 ENS opinion (n 744) para 57.

748 There is also a possibility that s 136(2) could allow suspension and cancellation not only of obligations of the company, but also of 'provisions' of existing agreements generally. This is because s 136(2A) and (c) refer to 'provisions', but not 'obligations of the company' (see the discussion in PART B, Chapter 4, IV., 6., d. below.

(c). The material scope of s 136(2) will be considered further at 6.d. below.

Does the cancellation of a contract fall within s 133(1)?—It has recently been held by the SCA in *Cloete Murray and Another NNO v FirstRand Bank Ltd t/a Wesbank*[749] that the cancellation of an instalment sale agreement in respect of movable goods by a creditor after a company had been placed under rescue proceedings does not constitute 'enforcement action', and is therefore not precluded by s 133(1). According to the court, this is because read in the context of s 133(1), '"enforcement action" [must relate] to formal proceedings ancillary to legal proceedings, such as the enforcement or execution of court orders by means of writs of execution or attachment,'[750] Cancellation, by contrast, is a unilateral act by a party to an agreement and does not occur by means of a formal process within a 'forum', as is contemplated by s 133(1).

However, the court left open the question whether notwithstanding the valid cancellation of the agreement, the practitioner could have prevented the repossession of the movable goods, if he had relied on his right under s 134(1)(c) to prevent any person from exercising any right in respect of property in the lawful possession of the company during rescue proceedings.[751] The court also mentioned *obiter dictum* that the practitioner's right to suspend agreements under s 136(2)(a) could prevent a creditor from instituting action and repossessing or attaching property in the company's 'lawful possession'.[752] We will revisit the relationship of s 133(1), s 134(1)(a) and s 136(2) below.[753]

749 2015 (3) SA 438 (SCA) paras 31–2.
750 See para 32.
751 See para 22ff.
752 See para 35.
753 See PART B, Chapter 4, IV., 6., b. below.

bb. Types of assets caught by the phrase 'property belonging to the company'

The phrase 'property belonging to the company' would seem to catch property encumbered by most forms of real security,[754] since in most forms of real security the debtor retains title to the encumbered assets. Primary examples in South African law are the mortgage bond, the (general and special) notarial bond, the pledge, the cession of rights *in securitatem debit*, tacit hypothecs over particular movables in respect of arrear rent (landlord's tacit hypothec) and the balance of the purchase price outstanding in respect of an instalment sale agreement (creditor grantor's tacit hypothec) and liens[755]. The tacit hypothecs arise by operation of law, while the other forms of security mentioned are based on agreement.[756]

By use of the word 'or' (instead of 'and') between the two relevant phrases describing the type of property that fall within s 133(1), the moratorium also catches legal proceedings brought in respect of assets owned, but not possessed, by the company (ie, where the assets are in the possession of a third party). Common examples of security that would fall under such description are the pledge of corporeal movable assets and, arguably, a particular construction of a cession of incorporeal assets in security of the underlying debt, referred to as the 'pledge construction' of the cession

---

754 South African law distinguishes between real security and personal security. Real security is where assets of the debtor are reserved for the satisfaction of the creditor's claim. Here the creditor generally has a limited real right in respect of such assets. In relation to personal security, the third party binds itself contractually to the creditor for the performance of the debtor's obligation to the creditor; accordingly, the creditor obtains merely a personal right against the security provider (see eg, Lubbe (revised by Scott), 'Mortgage and Pledge' LAWSA (2nd edn, 2008) vol 17(2), paras 324ff; Boraine, 'Security' in Nagel (ed), *Commercial Law* (4th edn, Lexis Nexis Butterworths 2011) para 27.01ff). On the application of the moratorium to enforcement against personal security, see PART B, Chapter 4, IV., 3., a. above.

755 A lien is a right of retention of a thing by the creditor until compensated by the owner of the thing for expenses incurred by the creditor in the performance of his contractual obligations in relation to the thing; see, eg, Boraine, 'Hypothecs and Liens' in Nagel (ed), *Commercial Law* (4th edn, Lexis Nexis Butterworths 2011) para 29.01ff.

756 See generally on the types of security, Boraine, 'Security', 'Mortgage, Pledge and Cession in Security' and 'Hypothecs and Liens' in Nagel (ed), *Commercial Law* (4th edn, Lexis Nexis Butterworths 2011) paras 27.01ff, 28.01ff, 29.01ff.

in securitatem debiti. According to the pledge construction, the cedent does not transfer 'ownership' of its rights so ceded, but rather 'control' over such rights to the cessionary, by vesting in the cessionary the exclusive right to enforce such rights. The cedent is said to retain the '*bare dominium*', or at least a reversionary interest in, the ceded rights in question. The courts have sometimes referred to the transfer of 'control' over such rights from the cedent to the cessionary as the transfer of fictional or 'quasi-possession'.[757]

An important example of a security form where both ownership and 'quasi-possession' to the encumbered asset passes to the creditor (*fiducia cum creditore contracta*) is the alternative construction of a cession *in securitatem debiti* under South African law, referred to as the 'out-and-out transfer construction'.[758] Here, in contrast to the pledge construction of the cession *in securitatem debiti*, 'ownership' of the ceded rights in question transfers to the cessionary, while the cessionary undertakes (*pactum fiduciae*) to retransfer such 'ownership' so ceded upon satisfaction of the secured debt.[759] Since here the debtor neither retains title to, nor is in 'quasi-possession' of, the secured assets, this construction of the cession in *securitatem debiti* falls outside the scope of s 133(1).[760]

Apart from assets encumbered by security, an example of a type of asset that would be caught by the phrase 'belonging to the company' is any asset leased by the company to another person.

---

757 See, eg, WA Joubert, 'Cession' LAWSA (3rd edn, 2013) vol 3, para 53 (including n 15 and the cases cited therein, namely *Guman v Latib* 1965 4 SA 715 (A) 722; *Oertel v Brink* 1972 3 SA 669 (W) 674; *Muller v Trust Bank of Africa Ltd* 1981 2 SA 117 (N) 125).

758 For further security devices in which ownership passes to the creditor, see, eg, Lubbe (n 754) paras 325.

759 See, eg, WA Joubert, 'Cession' (n 757) para 53.

760 ENS opinion (n 744) para 62. It should be noted, however, that because some of the latest SCA decisions have endorsed the pledge construction in such emphatic fashion (see the cases cited in WA Joubert, 'Cession' (n 757) para 53 n 10.), some authors have expressed doubts as to whether the out-and-out transfer construction still forms part of the law; see, eg, WA Joubert, 'Cession' (n 757) para 1, para 53.

cc. Types of (security) arrangements caught by 'property in the company's lawful possession'

The phrase 'in the lawful possession of' is novel to the South African corporate insolvency law.[761] An important example in practice of the type of arrangement where the company would not have title to, but be in the lawful possession of, the applicable asset, is any lease and/or sale agreement that has the commercial effect of secured financing, often referred to as 'quasi-security'. Common examples of quasi-security arrangements in South African practice are sale and leaseback, factoring, hire purchase, retention of title and sale and repurchase agreements of fungible assets (repo transaction).[762]

4. The exercise of any right by a person against property owned and/or lawfully possessed by the company (s 134(1)(b), (c) and (2))

a. Relationship between s 133(1), on the one hand and s 134(1)(b), (c) and s 134(2), on the other hand

The relationship between s 134(1)(b) and (c) and sub-s 2, on the one hand and s 133(1), on the other hand is not entirely clear. S 134 is headed 'protection of property interests' and sub-s 1(b), (c) and sub-s 2 read as follows:

> (b) any person who, as a result of an agreement made in the ordinary course of the company's business before the business rescue proceedings began, is in lawful possession of any property owned by the company and may

761 The phrase 'in lawful possession' is also used under the Australian voluntary administration procedure. Under s 440BA Corporations Act 2001, where a holder of a lien or pledge over property of the company that is in voluntary administration is in the 'lawful possession' of such property, the holder of such lien or pledge may continue to possess the property, but is precluded from enforcing against the security. The situation contemplated by this provision is the equivalent to property owned, but in the possession of a third party, as discussed above, and, arguably, as contemplated by s 134(1)(b). This is considered further at 4. below.

762 Naumann and Shawe, 'South Africa' (2012) PLC – Multi-Jurisdictional Guide Finance <http://www.bowman.co.za/FileBrowser/ArticleDocuments/PLC%20Handbook%20%96%202012%20Edition.pdf> accessed 10 January 2017.

continue to exercise any right in respect of that property as contemplated in that agreement, subject to section 136; and

(c) despite any provision of an agreement to the contrary, no person may exercise any right in respect of any property in the lawful possession of the company, irrespective of whether the property is owned by the company, except to the extent that the rescue practitioner consents in writing.

(2) The rescue practitioner may not unreasonably withhold consent in terms of subsection (1) (c), having regard to—

(a) the purposes of this Chapter;
(b) the circumstances of the company; and
(c) the nature of the property, and the rights claimed in respect of it.

S 134(1)(b) and (c) applies to the same type of property as s 133(1), namely (i) property owned by the company, but in the lawful possession of a third party (s 134(1)(b)) and (ii) property in the lawful possession of the company, but owned by a third party (s 134(1)(c)).

However, the legal actions under s 134(1)(b) and (c), on the one hand and s 133(1), on the other hand are different: the legal action under s 134(1)(b) and (c) is the *exercise of any right* in respect of the relevant property (hereafter, '*the exercise of a right*'), while under s 133(1) it is *any legal proceeding, including enforcement action* in relation to the relevant property (hereafter, '*the bringing of legal proceedings*'). The difference between the two is that although 'the bringing of legal proceedings' is certainly a form of 'the exercise of a right', 'the exercise of a right' includes actions that go beyond 'the bringing of legal proceedings'. An example would be the right of a third party lessee of immovable property leased from the company-lessor to continue occupying the immovable property; put differently, the exercise of a right is broader than the bringing of legal proceedings.

There are two possibilities of interpreting the relationship s 134(1)(b) and (c) and s 133(1). On the one hand, s 134(1)(b) and (c) could be read to include in their ambit the bringing of legal proceedings, which would cause such provisions to overlap with s 133(1) in respect of the act of bringing legal proceedings. On the other hand, they could be read to be restricted to the exercise of any right *other than* the bringing of legal proceedings. In that case, the bringing of legal proceedings would be solely regulated under s 133(1)).

The last-mentioned construction is preferable. This is because if s 134(1)(b)[763] were read to overlap with s 133(1) in respect of the bringing of legal proceedings, then the bringing of legal proceedings would be permitted under s 134(1)(b),[764] but stayed under s 133(1). On the general rules of interpretation of statutes, two conflicting provisions should be reconciled, where possible.[765] Accordingly, s 133(1) and s 134(1)(b) could be reconciled by reading the reference to 'the exercise of a right' in s 134(1)(b) to exclude the bringing of legal proceedings. If it is correct that the relevant action under s 134(1)(b) should be read to exclude the bringing of legal proceedings, then a contextual reading of s 134(1)(c) – which is worded identically to s 134(1)(b) – would mean that the relevant action under s 134(1)(c) should have the same meaning as that under s 134(1)(b).

b. The scope of s 134(1)(b) and (c)

According to s 134(1)(b), a person to a contract with the company under which the person is in lawful possession of the company's property may only 'continue' to exercise any right in respect of such property. On a strict reading, this means that the person would only be entitled to exercise its rights in respect of the relevant property if it has begun to do so before the commencement of rescue proceedings, but not once rescue proceedings have commenced. This limitation seems absurd, and this provision should be therefore be read purposively, as is generally permitted by the general rules of interpretation under South African law.[766]

The rescue practitioner's power under s 134(1)(c) to prevent any person from exercising any right in relation to property in the lawful possession of the company during rescue proceedings potentially constitutes a rather drastic encroachment on such other person's (contractual) rights. This is somewhat alleviated by the fact that the rescue practitioner's discretion in exercising such power is restricted. According to s 134(2), the rescue prac-

---

763 This provision regulates the exercise of the company's rights in respect of property owned by the company, but lawfully in the possession of a third party.

764 This is subject to the company's right to cancel uncompleted contracts pursuant to s 136. That provision will be considered at 6. below

765 See generally Devenish, *Interpretation of Statutes* (Juta 1992) 279.

766 On the general rules of interpretation, see the *locus classicus Venter v R* 1907 TS 910; see generally Devenish (n 765) 177ff.

titioner must exercise his discretion under s 134(1)(c) reasonably, having regard to the purposes of business rescue,[767] the circumstances of the company and the nature of the property and the rights claimed in respect of it.

Needless to say, where a contractual relationship had been cancelled prior to the commencement of business by a creditor, the company can no longer be considered to be 'in lawful possession' of property that is subject to the contract for purposes of s 134(1)(c), and such property accordingly does not fall within the scope of the moratorium.[768]

However, the courts have gone further. *Kythera Court v Le RendezVous Café CC T/A Newscafe Bedfordview (in business rescue)*[769] held that once a lease agreement has been cancelled after the company was placed under rescue proceedings, the company would likewise no longer be in lawful possession of the property that had been leased for purposes of s 134(1)(c). Proceedings for the repossession of the applicable property was accordingly permitted on that basis.[770]

---

767 When considering the 'purposes of Chapter 6', rescue practitioners and the courts should either look to s 7(k), which sets out the purpose of rescue proceedings as '[providing] for the efficient rescue and recovery of financially distressed companies, in a manner that balances the rights and interests of all relevant stakeholders', or to the objectives of rescue as contained in s 128(1)(b)(iii); see the discussion in PART B, Chapter 4, IV., 1. above.

768 It has been held by *JVJ Logistics (Pty) Ltd v Standard Bank of South Africa Ltd and Others* [2016] JOL 36313 (KZD) that the cancellation of an instalment sale agreement by the seller of a vehicle prior to the commencement of rescue proceedings, means that the vehicle cannot be regarded as being in the 'lawful possession' of the company, and thus falls outside the scope of the moratorium. See also *Southern Value Consortium v Tresso Trading 102 (Pty) Limited (Klopper NO and Another as intervening business rescue practitioners)* [2015] JOL 34787 (WCC) paras 26ff. That court came to the same conclusion, but placed the emphasis on a purposive reading of ss 133(1) and 134(1)(c), by arguing that the moratorium does not prevent the exercise of real rights. The court held that, on the facts, the attempted ejection by the creditor of the tenant-company that had been placed under business rescue after the the cancellation by the creditor of the applicable lease agreement, constituted the exercise of real rights.

769 2016/11853) [2016] GJ (22 June 2016) paras 9ff.

770 See also the full bench in *LA Sport 4x4 Outdoor CC v Broadsword Trading 20 (Pty) Ltd* & others (A513/2013 [2015] ZAGPPHC 78 (26 February 2015) para 52. For the opposite view, see Elliot, 'Cancellation or suspension of agreements during business rescue' (2009) <https://www.hoganlovells.com/en/publications/cancellation-or-suspension-of-agreements-during-business-rescue> accessed 16 January 2017.

5. Disposal of the company's assets during business rescue proceedings (s 134(1) and (3))

During rescue proceedings, the rescue practitioner is not entitled to dispose of the company's assets, unless it is (i) in the ordinary course of business, (ii) in a *bona fide* transaction at arm's length[771] for fair value approved in advance and in writing by the rescue practitioner or (iii) as contemplated by a rescue plan.[772] The prohibition of the disposal of assets not in the ordinary course of business has been carried over from judicial management.[773] The rationale for this prohibition under judicial management was arguably to prevent the judicial manager from using the formal rescue procedure to carry out 'disguised' liquidations.[774]

The requirement that the sale be at arm's length and for a fair value is meant, arguably, to control the problem of asset dilution. The use of the conjunction 'or' before the final requirement (namely, that the sale be made as part of a rescue plan), suggests that the first two conditions need not be fulfilled under such a sale. This is important, particularly in respect of the first requirement (namely, that the sale be in the ordinary course of business), since a going concern sale of the company's business might not pass that requirement, while it is clearly envisaged by the secondary objective of rescue, as indicated above.

The rescue practitioner is entitled to sell assets that are encumbered by 'title interests',[775] if the proceeds would cover the company's outstanding

---

771 On the possible meaning of 'at arm's length', see *Henochsberg Companies Act* (n 592) s 134, 478(1).

772 S 134(1)(a)(i)-(iii).

773 S 434(1) Companies Act 1973.

774 See PART B, Chapter 3, III., 5. above.

775 The term 'title interest' in s 134(3)(passage before para (a)) and s 134(3)(a) is foreign to South African law and is one of various examples of the involvement of foreign drafters in drafting the Companies Act 2008. For evidence of the use of foreign drafters, see Mongalo, 'Preface' in Mongalo (ed), *Modern Company Law for a Competitive South African Economy* (AJ – Special Volume 2010). In a foreign context, 'title interest' would appear to mean quasi-security interests (see generally Wood (n 700) 14–019). This also seems to be the intended meaning of the term under the Companies Act 2008. Similarly, see *JVJ Logistics (Pty) Ltd v Standard Bank of South Africa Ltd and Others* 2016 (6) SA 448 (KZD); [2016] 3 All SA 813 (KZD). However, see *Henochsberg Companies Act* (n 592) s 134, 478(1)–478(2), where the term is regarded to be synonymous with 'security interests'.

indebtedness to the relevant creditor,[776] after which the rescue practitioner must, either satisfy the outstanding debt or promptly provide security for the amount outstanding.[777]

According to s 136(2A)(c), the limits on a rescue practitioner's powers to dispose of assets encumbered by security interests pursuant to s 134(3) cannot be circumvented by a rescue practitioner's power under s 136(2)(a) to suspend any provision of an agreement relating to security. It could be argued that this implies that a rescue practitioner's general power to *suspend* (and, arguably, also the court's power to *cancel*) obligations/provisions of security agreements, is not restricted to obligation-creating provisions of an agreement (the 'narrow interpretation'), but rather extends to transfer provisions of an agreement (the 'broad interpretation').[778] This is because there would simply have been no need for s 136(2A)(c), had the narrow interpretation applied, since under the narrow interpretation the rescue practitioner would, by definition, have been precluded from suspending transfer provisions of an agreement.[779]

6. Uncompleted contracts (s 136)

a. General

The rescue practitioner has the power to generally suspend, or apply urgently to court, to cancel agreements that the company had entered into

---

776 S 134(3)(a). If the proceeds of the assets would not cover the creditor's outstanding claim, the rescue practitioner requires the prior consent of the creditor to sell the assets.

777 S 134(3)(b).

778 'Obligation-creating' or 'obligationary provisions' have merely contractual effect, while transfer, or real, provisions have proprietary effect; see, eg, van der Merwe, 'Things' LAWSA (2nd edn, 2014) vol 27, para 191, para 365–6; WA Joubert, 'Cession' (n 757) para 1, para 8; see also ENS opinion (n 744) para 23–4.

779 By contrast, before the insertion of s 136(2A)(c) by s 87 of the Amendment Act 3 of 2011, the narrow interpretation might have been plausible on policy grounds, given the potential drastic consequences of the broad interpretation on the sanctity of security agreements during rescue proceedings (see, eg, ENS opinion (n 744)). Provisions in a security agreement, which create the limited real right of the creditor in the encumbered asset, are of a transfer nature rather than of an obligationary nature (ENS opinion (n 744) para 23).

prior to the commencement of rescue proceedings which continue during rescue proceedings. This is referred to as 'uncompleted contracts'[780] in South Africa.[781] Generally speaking, the ability of the rescue practitioner to suspend, and the court to cancel, uncompleted contracts is thought (within certain limitations) to be a justified departure from the common law principle of *pacta servanda sunt* because it allows the company to rid itself of contracts that would hamper the chances of success of rescuing the company.

There are certain functional overlaps between s 136, the statutory moratorium under s 133(1) and the restrictions placed on contractual counterparties on exercising their proprietary rights in respect of property owned by, or in the lawful possession of, the company, as contemplated by s 134(1)(b) and (c). These functional overlaps will be considered at b. below.

Although the scope of s 136 seems very broad at first glance, it has some contractual and material restrictions, which will be discussed at c. and d., respectively.

Some types of contracts are exempted from the power of suspension and cancellation. These are employment contracts (with a few exceptions)[782] and agreements relating to listed shares to which the rules of a 'stock exchange' (as defined) apply and listed securities under a 'master agreement' (as defined). Examples are derivatives, which, *inter alia*, provide for the termination and netting of unperformed obligations on the insolvency of one of the parties to such an agreement.[783] The special protection of employment contracts, particularly where the company's business is sold as a going concern to a third party out of insolvency proceedings, is not unusual from a comparative perspective. In saying that, the protection of employee contracts during rescue proceedings is particularly strong in South Africa, as will be discussed at e. below.

As briefly mentioned above, the suspension of contracts is further disapplied where the company sells assets that are encumbered by security interests of creditors.[784] This ensures that pre-insolvency security rights of

---

780 See, eg, Loubser, 'LLD thesis' (n 512) 87.

781 S 136(2).

782 S 136(2A)(a) and (b).

783 S 136(2A)(a)(i) and (b)(ii) read with ss 35A and 35B Insolvency Act 1936 and s 1 Financial Markets Act 18 of 2012.

784 S 136(2A)(c).

creditors are preserved during rescue proceedings despite the rescue practitioner's right of suspending uncompleted contracts.

S 136(3) provides that the awarding of damages is the remedy of a counterparty where the suspension and cancellation under s 136 has been exercised. Interesting questions arise around the relationship to the common law remedies for breach of contract, which will be discussed at f. below.

It should be noted that the requirements for the *cancellation* of uncompleted contracts are more onerous than for their *suspension*. This is because cancellation requires that the court find that cancellation of an uncompleted contract be 'just and reasonable' under the circumstances,[785] while no court approval is required for the suspension of such contracts. This is understandable, given that cancellation constitutes a more serious intrusion than suspension on the principle of the sanctity of contracts. Interestingly, these additional requirements for the cancellation of contracts were only introduced at a relatively late stage in the drafting process of the Companies Act 2008.[786]

b. Relationship of s 136 with the statutory moratorium under s 133(1)

To be sure, ss 136 and 133(1) are separate and distinct legal mechanisms, both in type and in scope. First, s 136 only comes into operation if exercised by the rescue practitioner, while the moratorium under s 133(1) operates automatically. Second, the power of suspension under s 136 applies only to proceedings based on contract, whereas the moratorium under s 133 can stay non-contractual proceedings, such as delictual claims brought against the company. And third, the counterparty under a suspended contract is entitled to damages,[787] whereas there is no remedy available for a party prevented from bringing legal proceedings under s 133(1).

785 S 136(2)(b).

786 By s 87(b) Companies Amendment Act 3 of 2011 (hereafter, the '*Companies Amendment Act 2011*'). Before this amendment, cancellation, like suspension, did not require court approval; see s 136(2) of the version of the Companies Act 2008 before the amendments made to such Act by the Companies Amendment Act 2011.

787 S 136(3).

Nevertheless, to the extent that the rescue practitioner makes use of his powers to suspend provisions of, or obligations of the company under,[788] uncompleted contracts under s 136,[789] and the suspension has the effect of preventing the counterparty from bringing 'legal proceedings' against the company (as contemplated by s 133(1)), there could be a functional overlap between these two provisions in certain situations.

Since the SCA's decision in *Cloete Murray and Another NNO v FirstRand Bank Ltd t/a Wesbank*, in which it held that the cancellation of an agreement does not fall within the scope of the moratorium,[790] the question arises whether the right of the creditors to cancel an agreement would be precluded by the practitioner's suspension of such agreement pursuant to s 136(2)(a). The court in *178 Stanfordhill CC v Velvet Star Entertainment*[791] held that it did not, on the basis that the grounds upon which the agreement was cancelled subsisted prior to the commencement of rescue proceedings, and the right of suspension applies only to obligations that would otherweise become due during rescue proceedings as provided under s 136(2)(b).[792]

c. Contractual restrictions on suspension and cancellation of contracts

A strong case could be made that the suspension and cancellation of uncompleted contracts under s 136 is subject to the common law doctrines of reciprocity and severability in the South African law of contract. With regard to the doctrine of reciprocity, non-performance of an obligation by the company as a result of the suspension or cancellation of such obligation should ordinarily entitle the counterparty to withhold its own obligations, provided the obligations are reciprocal and, where the company

---

788 On the question whether the company may suspend and cancel 'provisions' of, or just its 'oligations' under uncompleted contracts, see the discussion in d. below.

789 Since the moratorium merely prevents the bringing of legal proceedings during the course of rescue proceedings, it is functionally equivalent to s 136 only to the extent that such provision allows for the suspension, and not the cancellation, of uncompleted contracts.

790 See the discussion in PART B, Chapter 4, IV., 3., b., aa. above.

791 Unreported case no 1506/15 [2015] KZD (1 April 2015)) paras 23ff.

792 For a view that the right of suspension applies also to pre-commencement obligations, see Elliot (n 770).

seeks to enforce performance by the counterparty in court, to raise the *exceptio non adimpleti contractus*.[793]

With regard to the doctrine of severability, such doctrine provides that failure of a part of a contract that is not severable from the entire contract brings the contract to an end.[794] The test for severability is essentially whether the parties would have entered into the contract without the part of the contract that has failed.[795] Accordingly, where the suspended or cancelled provision is not severable from the entire contract, the entire contract would be terminated.[796]

d. Material scope of suspension and cancellation of contracts

As alluded to above, due to the inconsistent use of terminology, the material scope of application of s 136 is unclear. Thus under s 136(2) (which is the enabling provision of the right of suspension and cancellation), the practitioner's right to suspend and cancel is referred to as applying to 'obligations of the company'. By contrast, s 136(2A) provides that the powers of suspension and cancellation under s 136(2) may not be exercised in respect of 'provisions' of certain types of contracts. Moreover, under s 136(3) (which provides for the sanctions of a counterparty to a suspended or cancelled contract), the relevant counterparty is referred to, *inter alia*, as a party to an agreement, the 'provisions' of which have been suspended or cancelled under s 136(2). The term 'provisions' includes not just performance obligations of the company,[797] but also any provisions that do not oblige the company to do anything or refrain from doing any-

793 ENS opinion (n 744) para 25. Generally on the principle of reciprocity and the *exceptio non adimpleti contractus* defence, see *BK Tooling (Edms) Bpk v Scope Precision Engineering (Edms) Bpk* 1979 1 SA 391 (A) 416A; *Farmers' Co-operative Society v Berry* 1912 AD 343, 350; *Ese Financial Services (Pty) Ltd v Cramer* 1973 2 SA 805 (C) 808; see also van der Merwe and others (n 741) 359; de Wet and van Wyk, *Die Suid-Afrikaanse Kontraktereg en Handelsreg* (4th edn, Butterworths 1978) 196; DJ Joubert, *General Principles of the Law of Contract* (Juta 1987) 229.

794 See, eg, WA Joubert, 'Contract' LAWSA (3rd edn, 2014) vol 9, para 414.

795 *Sasfin (Pty) Ltd v Beukes* 1989 1 SA 1 (A) 16.

796 ENS opinion (n 744) para 26, 27.2.

797 To be sure, the term 'obligations' – which, intuitively, appears to entail provisions of contracts under which the company is required to render performance of something – could also be understood in its broader sense as derived from the

thing. This would presumably include provisions that grant the counterparty the right to perform an act that does not require performance from the company. An example would be *parate executie* enforcement by the counterparty, as indicated above.[798] Accordingly, provisions of a contract would appear to be broader than obligations of the company. If the exceptions from the powers of suspension and cancellation under s 136(2A) relate to 'provisions' of contracts, this might be regarded to imply that the same should be true for the powers of suspension and cancellation under s 136(2). There is accordingly a conflict between whether 'provisions' of a contract or (merely) 'obligations of the company' under such contract may be suspended or cancelled under s 136.[799]

The better view is that s 136 contemplates only obligations of the company under, and not 'provisions', of a contract. This is because both s 136(2A) and s 136(3) are subject to the enabling provision of the suspension and cancellation powers under s 136(2) and it would cause less disruption to the scheme of s 136 if sub-ss (2A) and (3) were read down to contemplate the narrower meaning under sub-s (2).[800]

It is also not entirely clear whether in addition to 'obligations of the company', entire contracts may be suspended and cancelled under s 136. That this may be so is suggested by s 136(3), which provides that damages may be claimed by a party to 'any agreement that has been suspended or cancelled [...] in terms of subsection (2)'. This presupposes that the suspension or cancellation of the agreement itself is allowed under s 136.

---

law of contract. In that sense, 'obligations' derives from the Latin term '*obligare*' (meaning 'to tie' or 'to bind' together) and entails both a right and a duty (van der Merwe and others (n 741) 2–3). It seems, however, that the determination of this question has no practical relevance for purposes of s 136 since. This is because even if 'obligations' were used in the broad sense, the company would hardly benefit from suspending or cancelling its own rights under an uncompleted contract.

798 See the discussion in PART B, Chapter 4, IV., 6., d. above.

799 A cynical explanation for this conflict is that it is the product of sloppy drafting by the legislature. S 136(2) (which contains the reference to obligations of the company) was only introduced at a later stage in the legislative process by s 87 Companies Amendment Act 2011. Before this amendment, the suspension and cancellation of contracts related consistently to provisions of agreements (see the version of the Companies Act before the amendments made by the Companies Amendment Act 2011).

800 The same conclusion is drawn by Hutchison, ENS internal memorandum, 17 August 2010, para 2.1.

Moreover, there is presumably no conflict between the power of suspension and cancellation of 'obligations of the company' under an uncompleted contract, on the one hand and entire contracts, on the other hand;[801] these two meanings of s 136 can thus exist concurrently.

e. General exemption of employment contracts from s 136 – some comparative perspectives from the UK, US and Australia

Employment contracts are exempted unconditionally from the power of the rescue practitioner to suspend uncompleted contracts.[802] Any retrenchment of employees is only possible by way of a dismissal based on operational requirements under the Labour Relations Act 66 of 1995 (hereafter, '*LRA*'). Broadly speaking, such requirements impose far-reaching consultation, consensus-seeking, and information-disclosure duties on the employer. Moreover, the employer is required to pay severance pay[803] and employees are given recourse in cases where the dismissal was unfair or amounted to 'unfair labour practices'.[804]

Unlike the dismissal of employees generally, it appears as though the authority for the dismissal of *managerial* employees vests in the rescue practitioner (rather than the court) and that it is not required that such a dismissal be 'just and reasonable in the circumstances'. This is because s 140(1)(c) specifically provides that the rescue practitioner 'may' remove managerial employees from office without any reference to s 136.[805] However, the managerial employees appear to enjoy the same labour law protections against terminations relating to retrenchments as non-managerial employees, notwithstanding the lack of a reference to the applicable provi-

801 This is also implied by Hutchison (n 800) para 2.11.

802 S 136(2A)(a)(i). Changes to the terms and conditions of employment contracts are only acceptable if these occur in the 'ordinary course of attrition' and if agreed to between the parties (s 136(1)(a)(i) and (ii), respectively). Neither of these options contemplate the unilateral suspension of employment contracts by the rescue practitioner.

803 S 191(5)(b)(ii) LRA.

804 See s 189 LRA in respect of companies with fewer than 50 employees and s 189A for companies with more than 50 employees.

805 *Clarke/EH Walton Packaging* [2014] JOL 31234 (CCMA) para 101. See generally *Meskin Insolvency Law* (n 576) para 18.9.3.

sion under s 136.[806] This is because the legal basis for the retrenchment rights of employees is labour law, whereas the legal basis for the question in whom the authority to cancel uncompleted contracts vests, is company law.

In contrast to the UK, Australia and the US,[807] in South Africa, the termination of employee contracts is not allowed while the rescue plan is being developed (which could take more than 3 months in South Africa);[808] instead, such termination must form part of the rescue plan. This plan must then be adopted by a majority vote of creditors and implemented after its adoption by the company under the direction of the rescue practitioner.[809] Given that employees are entitled to vote on the plan, the South African approach provides employees with a more direct influence over their continued employment by the company.[810]

The protection of employment interests in respect of the suspension and cancellation of uncompleted contracts must be seen in the context of the general employee-friendly approach of the South African rescue regime.

f. Remedies available to counterparty

In relation to the question as to the available remedies to the counterparty following the suspension or cancellation of its contract with the company,

806 *Meskin Insolvency Law* (n 576) para 18.13.3.

807 For the UK, see generally Fletcher, Higham and Trower, *Corporate Administration and Rescue Procedures* (2nd edn, Lexis Nexis 2004) para 7.19; for Australia, see s 437A Corporations Act; see also generally Harris, Hargovan and Adams, *Australian Corporate Law* (2nd edn, Lexis Nexis Butterworths 2009) para 24.50; for the US, see 11 USC § 1113 (in relation to collective bargaining agreements) and § 365 (in relation to employment contracts other than collective bargaining agreements). See generally Korobkin, 'Employee Interests in Bankruptcy' (1996) 4 Am. Bankr. Inst. L. Rev. 5, 7.

808 S 132(3).

809 S 136(2A)(b)(i) read with s 136(2) and s 152(2) and (5).

810 On the other hand, the influence of employees over dismissals is ensured by other means in the UK and the US: in the UK, a company is generally required to consult with employees where proposing to dismiss more than 20 employees in the UK (s 188 Trade Union and Labour Relations (Consolidation) Act 1992); and in the US, where proposing to terminate collective bargaining agreements (11 USC § 1113).

such party 'may assert a claim against the company *only*[811] for damages'. This remedy gives rise to interpretational difficulties, as its legal nature is not entirely clear The question is whetherthe company's failure to perform its suspended or cancelled obligation constitutes a breach of contract or a special statutory cause of action. It might be argued that the obligation of the company to perform does not become due, given that such obligation has been suspended or cancelled during rescue proceedings. On this interpretation, the right to damages for the suspension or cancellation under s 136(3) could be seen as a statutory right to compensation for the harm caused as a result of the suspension or cancellation.

However, such an interpretation is called into question by the absence of any further legislative guidance on the nature and the measure of such claim, and by the use of the word 'only' in s 136(3). Such word suggests that but for s 136(3), the delay or failure to perform by the company (*mora*)[812] would entitle the counterparty to remedies other than damages. This, in turn, implies that the suspension and cancellation constitutes breach of contract. However, because of the word 'only', the general remedies for breach of contract other than damages – namely, specific performance, cancellation and an interdict to prevent the impending breach[813] – are not available in respect of a suspension or cancellation under s 136.[814]

7. Post-commencement finance and general ranking of claims (s 135)

Any remuneration, reimbursement for expenses or other monies relating to employment that become due and payable to employees during rescue proceedings are treated as post-commencement finance.[815] Such claims rank ahead of any external post-commencement financing whether or not it is secured,[816] but behind the costs of rescue proceedings, including the

811 Emphasis added.
812 See van der Merwe and others (n 741) 297ff.
813 On the remedies for breach of contract under South African law generally, see van der Merwe and others (n 741) 250ff.
814 The above discussion on whether suspension or cancellation constitutes breach of contract paraphrases Hutchison (n 800) para 2.5.
815 S 135(1)(a).
816 S 135(3)(a)(i) read with sub-s 2.

rescue practitioner's remuneration.[817] All post-commencement finance will be preferred to any unsecured pre- and post-commencement claims.[818] This order of preference remains in force if rescue proceedings are converted to liquidation proceedings, except that the costs of liquidation rank ahead of post-commencement finance.[819] There is thus no super-preference for post-commencement finance of companies under the South African rescue procedure as found under Chapter 11 in the US.[820]

With regard to the general ranking of claims, any outstanding pre-commencement claims for remuneration, reimbursement for expenses or other claims relating to employment are preferred unsecured creditors.[821] This mirrors the position in winding-up.[822] Any outstanding pre-commencement employment claims in respect of a medical scheme or pension scheme, including a provident scheme, rank as unsecured creditors in rescue proceedings.[823]

The business rescue provisions under the Companies Act 2008 do not explicitly provide for the ranking of secured claims. The fact that the rescue practitioner is required to pay to the secured creditors the proceeds of the disposal of the collateral or otherwise provide security therefor, would seem to imply that secured claims retain the preferential status they are afforded in winding-up.[824] Certain security claims have a super-priority,

---

817 S 135(3)(before para a). The rescue practitioner's remuneration is regulated in s 143.

818 S 135(3)(a)(ii) and para (b).

819 S 135(4).

820 11 USC § 364; See generally, eg, Skeel Jr, 'The Past, Present and Future of Debtor-in-Possession Finance' [2004] Cardozo L.Rev. 1905.

821 S 144(2). It would appear that the equivalent provision applicable to liquidation (s 339 Companies Act 1973 read with s 98A(1)(a)(i) to (iii) Insolvency Act 1936) would also apply under rescue proceedings, to the extent that s 144(2) is silent on particular issues and the applicable insolvency provision is consistent with the general scheme of the rescue procedure.

822 Item 9 Sche 5 read with s 339 Companies Act 1973 read with s 98A Insolvency Act 1936.

823 S 144(4). The relationship between the equivalent provision under liquidation proceedings (s 339 Companies Act 1973 read with s 98A(1)(b) Insolvency Act 1936) and s 144(4) under rescue proceedings would appear to be the same as the aforementioned relationship between s 98A(1)(a)(i) to (iii) Insolvency Act 1936 and s 144(2) in relation to employment-related claims.

824 According to Item 9 Sche 5 read with s 339 Companies Act 1973 read with ss 95–103 Insolvency Act 1936.

even over the costs of liquidation,[825] while others rank after all other statutorily preferred creditors, such as claims secured by a general notarial bond.[826]

The case of *CSARS v Beginsel*[827] has held that the South African Revenue Service ('*SARS*') ranks as a general unsecured creditor in business rescue. This deviates from the position in winding-up, where SARS receives preferential status.[828] It would seem the position in business rescue is an appropriate concession to general unsecured creditors. This approach is also in line with UK's administration procedure, where the Crown's preferential status was abolished by the Enterprise Act of 2002.[829] Interestingly, the same Act also introduced a 'ring-fenced fund', according to which the office holder is obliged to pay a proportion of the company's 'net property'[830] – defined as assets that would otherwise be available to satisfy the claims of floating charge-holders – to unsecured creditors.[831] It has been argued that the ring-fenced fund is a *quid pro quo* for the abolition of the Crown preference.[832]

8. Governance of rescue proceedings

a. Operation of the management-displacing system of governance

As mentioned previously, South Africa has opted for a management-displacing, instead of a debtor-in-possession, system of governance in rescue proceedings.[833] However, although the rescue practitioner 'has full man-

825 See the order of ranking in s 339 Companies Act 1973 read with ss 95–103 Insolvency Act 1936. For the types of secured and quasi-secured claims that have a super-priority, see s 339 Companies Act 1973 read with s 95 Insolvency Act 1936.

826 Item 9 Sche 5 read with s 339 Companies Act 1973 read with s 102 Insolvency Act 1936.

827 2013 (1) SA 307 (WCC).

828 S 339 Companies Act 1973 read with s 99 Insolvency Act 1936.

829 S 251.

830 Of a minimum amount of £10,000, and generally 50% of net property up to £10,000, and 20% of any amounts exceeding this up to a global maximum to be set aside of £600,000; Insolvency Act 1986 (Prescribed Part) Order 2003, para 3.

831 Insolvency Act 1986, s 176A. Exceptions are set out in s 176A(3) to (5).

832 Armour and Mokal (n 609).

833 See the discussion in PART B, Chapter 4, IV., 1., a above.

agement control of the company in substitution for [the company's] board and pre-existing management',[834] the incumbent directors and persons in managerial positions are not automatically removed from their positions in rescue proceedings, but rather remain in office.[835] In fact, they have a duty to continue to exercise their directorial functions 'subject to the authority of the rescue practitioner' and their managerial functions 'in accordance with the express instructions or direction of the practitioner'.[836] The rescue practitioner is entitled to delegate any of his powers or functions to the directors or persons in managerial positions[837] and appoint any external person as an advisor to the company or as part of the company's management.[838] However, the rescue practitioner has the power to remove from office persons in managerial positions and is entitled to apply to court for the removal of directors from office.[839] Directors are required to attend to the practitioner's requests at all times[840] and provide the practitioner with relevant information.[841]

It would seem that these requirements seek to balance the need for the effective management of the company with the need for overcoming information deficits of the rescue practitioner.[842] Reducing such information deficits are necessary in order to reduce what we will refer to as 'familiarisation costs' of the rescue practitioner – ie, his time and resources in ob-

---

834 S 140(1)(a).

835 Directors are also exempted from their duties and liabilities under ss 76 and 77 (which include some of the codified directors' duties and liabilities at common law), save for the codified directors' common law duty to disclose a personal financial interest to the board under s 75 and the liabilities imposed on directors for knowingly acting in the name of the company without authority, fraud and, somewhat bizarrely, for reckless trading under s 77(3)(a) to (c)).

836 S 137(2)(a) and (b), respectively.

837 *Henochsberg Companies Act* (n 592) s 140, 490–1.

838 S 140(1)(c)(ii). However, such external person may have a relationship with the company that would compromise his impartiality (s 140(1)(c)(ii) read with s 140(2)).

839 Ss 140(1)(c)(i) and 137(5), respectively.

840 S 137(3).

841 S 137(3)) and s 142(1) to (3).

842 The need of reducing information deficits would not be required where the company had attempted an informal workout and negotiated a pre-packaged plan prior to invoking formal rescue proceedings, and the rescue practitioner had been involved as an advisor in such workout or pre-packaged plan negotiations.However, it is not clear whether such a person would be entitled to be appointed as a rescue practitioner under s 138(1)(e) and (f).

taining the necessary information about the company in order to perform his functions satisfactorily.[843]

Effective management of the company is ensured by the following requirements: (i) the entitlement of the rescue practitioner to take decisions both at the managerial and the board level unilaterally – which is implied by the fact that he has full management control of the company (s 140(1)(a)) and that directors must continue to exercise their functions subject to the authority of the rescue practitioner (s 137(2)(a)) –, as this reduces the decision-making costs; (ii) the authority of the rescue practitioner to instruct directors in relation to management functions (s 137(2)(b)) and to require that directors attend to his requests in relation to directorial functions (s 137(3)), as this ensures that the managers and directors co-operate with the rescue practitioner, which they may be reluctant to do, given that the practitioner may expose weaknesses of the company's pre-commencement management; (iii) the power of the rescue practitioner to remove from office persons in management positions and apply to court for the removal of directors from office on specified grounds (ss 137(5) and s 140(1)(c)(i), respectively), as this allows the practitioner to remove incompetent managers and obstructive directors; and (iv) the entitlement of the rescue practitioner to delegate tasks to directors and/or persons in management positions and appoint external persons as advisors or managers (s 140(1)(b) and para (c)(i), respectively), as this allows the practitioner to utilise expertise and distribute tasks efficiently.

The familiarisation costs of the rescue practitioner are reduced by a combination of 'carrots' and 'sticks'. The 'carrot' is that directors remain in office and may only be removed from office by the court on the grounds specified in s 137(5) and on application of the rescue practitioner. These requirements include situations where directors are impeding the management of the company.[844] The 'sticks' are that directors have a duty to continue to exercise their directorial and management functions and to pro-

843 See also Armour and Mokal (n 609).

844 See s 137(5)(b). Although this 'carrot' loses its *ex ante* effect where it becomes clear during rescue proceedings that the rescue practitioner is going to pursue a going concern sale of the company's business, as, in that case, the directors will have no prospect of retaining their positions after the implementation of the rescue plan. In the UK and Australia, removal of the incumbent directors is less onerous, in that the administrator can do so extra-judicially and without having to give reasons after the applicable court application (for the UK, see Insolvency Act 1986, Sch B1, para 61; for Australia, see s 442A Corporations Act 2001).

vide the practitioner with any information about the company's affairs generally (s 137(3)), with books and records that relate to the company's affairs[845] and with a statement of affairs containing certain specified information in respect of the company (s 142(1) to (3)).

b. Rescue practitioners' duties

aa. General

The rescue practitioners' duties broadly fall into two categories. One category of duties relates to very specific requirements under rescue proceedings. These are: (i) the procedural duties that enable the claimants to participate in the development of the rescue plan, which consist primarily of the duty to provide relevant information to the claimants[846] and make certain determinations in relation to the voting rights of claimants;[847] (ii) duties in relation to whether the company continues to be eligible for rescue proceedings, in particular whether the company continues to have a reasonable chance of being rescued, communicate his findings to the creditors' meeting and, should he find that the company has no reasonable

---

This allows the administrator to deal with incompetent directors more emphatically (Armour and Mokal (n 609)).

845 And the whereabouts of such books and records where they are not in the possession of the directors.

846 Eg, the duty (i) to give notice to all claimants of court proceedings, decisions, meetings or other relevant events (ss 144(3)(a) and 148(2) (in relation to employees), ss 145(1)(a) and 147(5)) (in relation to creditors), s 146(a) (in relation to security-holders) and s 151(2) (notice of the meeting in which the plan is voted on); (ii) to prepare reports relating to the proceedings for the creditors' committee and employees' committee (s 149(1)(b)); and (iii) to consult employees' representatives on the progress of the rescue plan and afford them sufficient opportunity to review the rescue plan and prepare a submission to the claimants' meeting considering the rescue plan (s 144(3)(d)). Notice given under the above-mentioned provisions does not replace the common law requirement of joining all interested parties to an application for setting aside a rescue plan; see *Golden Dividend v Absa Bank* (569/2015) [2016] ZASCA 78 (30 May 2016); *Absa Bank Ltd v Naude NO & others* (20264/2014) [2015] ZASCA 97 (1 June 2015).

847 In relation to voting on the plan, the practitioner must determine the voting entitlements, including whether a creditor is independent pursuant to s 128(1)(g)(ii), and request the independent appraisal of whether a general unsecured creditors would be subordinated in a liquidation (s 145(5)(a) and (b)).

chance of being rescued, take appropriate measures, including applying to court to place the company under winding-up proceedings;[848] and (iii) the duty to investigate relevant contraventions by the company or the directors that occurred prior to the commencement of rescue proceedings, and take appropriate measures.[849]

Practitioners are liable for any act or omission in the performance of their functions[850] according to the standards set out under s 140(3)(c). All the above-mentioned duties would appear to fall within s 140(3)(c). According to that section a practitioner

> '(i) is not liable for any act or omission in good faith in the course of the exercise of the powers and performance of the functions of practitioner
> (ii) but may be held liable in accordance with any relevant law for the consequences of any act or omission amounting to gross negligence in the exercise of the powers and performance of the functions of practitioner.'

Broadly speaking, the intention of this provision is to lower the standard for practitioners in respect of the relevant duties.[851] According to the first limb of the test, practitioners are only liable for any breaches of the relevant duties if they do so in bad faith and according to the second limb, only if they are grossly negligent. It is suggested that this rather curious provision should be read cumulatively, so that a practitioner is liable if he

---

848 S 141(1) and (2)(a) and (b), s 147(1)(a)(i) and s 148(1)(a). This duty could be seen as a legal strategy to counteract the perverse incentive of company controllers to either place economically distressed companies under rescue proceedings or, in exceptional circumstances, invoke rescue proceedings prematurely. This will be discussed in Chapter 7 below.

849 s 141(2)(c). It is not clear whether s 141(2)(c) requires a rescue practitioner to investigate breaches of the reckless trading duty under s 22(1) and whether the remedies provided under s 141(2)(c) include bringing reckless trading claims against directors. This question is relevant for the effectiveness of the reckless trading duty as a legal strategy to ameliorate the perverse incentive of company controllers to inappropriately delay the invocation of formal rescue proceedings, which will be examined in Chapter 5 below.

850 Other than the second category of rescue practitioner's duties discussed below.

851 For a criticism of this approach, see Bradstreet, 'The leak in the Chapter 6 lifeboat: Inadequate regulation of business rescue practitioners may adversely affect lenders' willingness and growth of the economy' (2010) 22 SA Merc LJ 195, 209; Jacobs and Neethling, 'Die sorgsame ondernemingspraktisyn: 'n ondersoek na die gepaste maatstaf' (2016) 13(3) LITNet Akademis 773, 787; Jacobs, *Die vertrouensverpligtinge van ondernemingsreddingspraktisyns: 'n Regsvergelykende studie* (unpublished LLD thesis, University of the Free State 2015) 247–8.

fails only one of the two limbs of the test and, conversely, is only safe from liability if he meets both limbs of the test. Of course, where a relevant duty does not require fault, liability is judged only on whether or not the practitioner acted in good faith.

The second category of rescue practitioners' duties are the directors' duties and liabilities contained under ss 75 to 77, which apply analogously to rescue practitioners by virtue of s 140(3)(b). Ss 75 to 77 contain both general directors' duties including the codified common law fiduciary duties and duty of care, skill and diligence, and duties specific to company law.[852]

The following directors' duties relevant for our discussion are contained in ss 75 to 77[853]

(i) *To act in good faith and for a proper purpose (s 76(3)(a));*
(ii) *To act in the best interests of the company (s 76(3)(b));*
(iii) *To act with care, skill and diligence (s 76(3)(c));*
(iv) *To not use the position, or any information obtained while acting in the capacity, of a director to gain an advantage for the director, or for another person or wholly-owned subsidiary of the company; or to knowingly cause harm to the company or a subsidiary of the company (s 76(2)(a));*
(v) *To communicate (certain) information to the company (s 76(2)(b)); and*
(vi) *To disclose any personal financial interest or any financial interest of a 'related person' (s 75).*

The duties set out in (i) to (iii) above are codifications of the common law directors' duties to act for a proper purpose, to act in the best interests of the company (both fiduciary duties) and to act with care, skill and diligence, respectively.

---

852 S 77(3)(e). The duties specific to company law are clearly not capable of analogous application to rescue practitioners.

853 It is true that some of the grounds of liability under s 77(3), other than the grounds that are generally not capable of analogous application to practitioners mentioned above, refer to corresponding duties under provisions of the Companies Act 2008 that fall outside of ss 75–77 (eg, rather oddly, the reckless trading duty under s 22(1) (see s 77(3)(b))), while other provisions under s 77 impose liability for (non-statutory) fraudulent acts (eg, s 77(3)(c)). These duties are not relevant for our discussion as they are unproblematic in their application, save perhaps for the reckless trading duty.

The limb of the duty set out in (iv) above that requires directors to not gain an advantage for themselves or a third person[854] would seem to include the strand of the common law duties to avoid a conflict of interest that deal with the use of a director of information, property and opportunities that 'belong' to the company.[855] This is so since a director who uses his position and information to which he is privy by virtue of that position to make a profit and pursue business opportunities for himself (or a third party) typically 'gains an advantage' (for himself or a third person) as contemplated by s 76(2)(a)(i).[856] The ability of the general meeting to waive compliance with the no-profit and corporate opportunities duties after disclosure by the affected director to it at common law,[857] would seem to still apply under the Companies Act 2008.

The other limb of the duty set out in (iv) above, which requires that directors do not knowingly cause harm to the company or a subsidiary of the

---

854 A similar duty is contained in s 182(1)(a) and 183(1)(a) of the Australian Corporations Act 2001.

855 For the no-conflict duty relating to the taking of the company's profits, see, eg, *Bray v Ford* [1896] AC 44, 51 (HL); *Boardman v Phipps* [1967] AC 46 213; [1966] 3 All ER 721, 756 (HL); *Consul Development Pty Ltd v DPC Estates Pty Ltd* (1975) 132 CLR 373, 393 (HC of A); *Regal (Hastings) Ltd v Gulliver* [1967] 2 AC 134n, 137; [1942] 1 All ER 378, 381 (HL). For the no-conflict duty relating to the taking of corporate opportunities, see, eg, *Transvaal Cold Storage Co Ltd v Palmer* 1904 TS 4 33; *Goldberg v Trimble and Bennett* 1905 TS 255; *Consul Development Pty Ltd v DPC Estates Pty Ltd* (1975) 132 CLR 373, 393 (HC of A); *Hospital Products Ltd v United States Surgical Products* (1984) 156 CLR 41, 103 (HC of A); *Chan v Zacharia* (1983) 154 CLR 178, 198–9 (HC of A).

856 See FHI Cassim, 'The Duties and the Liability of Directors' in FHI Cassim and others (man ed), *Contemporary Company Law* (2nd edn, Juta 2012) 505, 550ff. This conclusion is further supported by the fact that the statutorily-created remedy for breaches of s 76(2)(a)(i) – namely, the disqualification of the director(s 162(5)(c)(ii)) – refers to a director taking a 'personal advantage of *information* or an *opportunity*, contrary to s 76(2)(a)'. The reference to 'information' and 'opportunity' suggests that the equivalent common law no-conflict rules are caught by s 76(2)(a)(i).

857 *Robinson v Randfontein Estates Gold Mining Co Ltd* 1921 AD 168; *Gray v New Augarita Porcupine Mines Ltd* (1952) 3 DLR 1, 14 (PC); *Regal (Hastings) Ltd v Gulliver* [1967] 2 AC 134n, 150; [1942] 1 All ER 378, 389 (HL); *Gencor ACP Ltd v Dalby* [2000] 2 BCLC 734, 741; *Woolworths Ltd v Kelly* (1991) 4 ACSR 431, 438 CA(NSW); *Guinness plc v Saunders* [1988] 2 All ER 940, 944 (CA). See generally Blackman, Everingham and Jooste, *Commentary on the Companies Act* (loose-leaf) (Juta 2002) Ch 8, 161–2, 178.

company,[858] does not seem to codify a common law fiduciary duty. This is because such duty is conceptually different from any of the common law fiduciary duties and it requires the company to have suffered loss, which is not required under any of the common law fiduciary duties. It is actually quite incompatible with the absolute, strict and prophylactic nature of fiduciary duties generally.[859] This nature of the fiduciary duties derived from the fact that such duties originally developed in the law of trusts in order to protect the vulnerable position of the beneficiary to the fiduciary's position of having unmonitored control over the beneficiary's affairs and

---

858 A similar duty is contained in s 182(1)(b) and 183(1)(b) of the Australian Corporations Act 2001.

859 Eg, in relation to the duty to not take for himself profits or corporate opportunities for the company, the director is not required to be at fault or have acted in bad faith (*Matabele Syndicate v Lippert* (1897) 4 OR 372, 385, 386, 388; *Costa Rica Railway Co Ltd v Forwood* [1900] 1 Ch 746, 753 (CA); *Transvaal Cold Storage Co Ltd v Palmer* 1904 TS 4, 23; *Horn's Executor v The Master* 1919 CPD 48, 51; *Regal (Hastings) Ltd v Gulliver* [1967] 2 AC 134n, 137, 144; [1942] 1 All ER 378, 381, 386 (HL); *Boardman v Phipps* [1967] AC 46, 86, 116; [1966] 3 All ER 721, 732, 751 (HL); *O'Sullivan v Management Agency and Music Ltd* [1985] 3 All ER 351, 363–4, 370 (CA); *Guinness plc v Saunders* [1990] 2 AC 663, 690–2; [1990] 1 All ER 652, 659–60 (HL); *Woolworths Ltd v Kelly* (1991) 4 ACSR 431, 447 CA(NSW); *Du Plessis v Phelps* 1995 (4) SA 165 (C) 171; *Gencor ACP Ltd v Dalby* [2000] 2 BCLC 734, 741). Moreover, the director is liable regardless of whether the company could have earned the profit itself (*Boston Deep Sea Fishing and Ice Co v Ansell* (1888) 39 ChD 339; [1886-90] All ER Rep 65 (CA); *Parker v McKenna* (1874) 10 Ch App 96, 118, 124; [1874-80] All ER 443, 455, 456; *Transvaal Cold Storage Co Ltd v Palmer* 1904 TS 4 34; *Costa Rica Railway Co Ltd v Forwood* [1900] 1 Ch 746, 760 (CA); *Magnus Diamond Mining Syndicate v Macdonald and Hawthorne* 1909 ORC 65, 77; *Furs Ltd v Tomkies* (1936) 54 CLR 583 (HC of A); *Regal (Hastings) Ltd v Gulliver* [1967] 2 AC 134n, 144, 154; [1942] 1 All ER 378, 386, 392 (HL); *Boardman v Phipps* [1967] 2 AC 46, 108–9; [1966] 3 All ER 721, 746–7 (HL); *Woolworths Ltd v Kelly* (1991) 4 ACSR 431, 44–8 CA(NSW); *Gencor ACP Ltd v Dalby* [2000] 2 BCLC 734, 741); or whether the company was able to exploit the corporate opportunity (*Aberdeen Railway Co v Blaikie Bros* (1854) 1 Macq 461, 471; *Regal (Hastings) Ltd v Gulliver* [1942] 1 All ER 378, 385–6; [1967] AC 134; *Boardman v Phipps* [1966] 3 All ER 721, 756H; *Bhullar v Bhullar* [2003] 2 BCLC 241 (CA); *Robinson v Randfontein Estates Gold Mining Co Ltd* 1921 AD 168; *Gencor ACP Ltd v Dalby* [2000] 2 BCLC 734, 741; *Phillips v Fieldstone Africa (Pty) Ltd* 2004 (3) SA 465 (SCA) 483E).

the means of concealing his actions.[860] Since s 76(2)(a)(ii) appears to be irreconcilable with the common law no-conflict notion, it is better seen as a statutorily created duty, and any temptation to construe it as a codification of the common law fiduciary duty should be resisted.[861]

The duty set out in (v) above, which requires that directors communicate (certain) information to the company, appears to provide for a general duty of disclosure to the board of information that is likely to influence the company's decisions.[862] Although the requirement that 'any information' be disclosed to the board is broad enough to include facts that may give rise to a conflict situation contemplated by s 76(2)(a)(i), the better view is that disclosure to the board under s 76(2)(b) of such conflict situations, including taking the company's profits and opportunities for themselves, does not absolve the directors from the duty contemplated by s 76(2)(a)(i).

The duty set out in (vi) above, which requires directors to disclose personal financial interests to the board, is the codification of the common law duties that address situations in which a director has a personal interest in a transaction entered into by a company or a duty towards another person or company (typically in cases of multiple directorships or nominee directors).[863] This was referred to at common law as the 'self-dealing rule'[864].[865] S 75 replaces, and in certain respects amends, ss 234-241 Com-

---

860 See, eg, *Bray v Ford* [1896] AC 44, 51 (HL); *Boardman v Phipps* [1967] AC 46 213; [1966] 3 All ER 721, 756 (HL); *Consul Development Pty Ltd v DPC Estates Pty Ltd* (1975) 132 CLR 373, 393 (HC of A); *Regal (Hastings) Ltd v Gulliver* [1967] 2 AC 134n, 137; [1942] 1 All ER 378, 381 (HL) See generally *Blackman Companies Act* (n 857) Ch 8, 36, 149ff.

861 For a contrary view, see FHI Cassim (n 856) 551.

862 Ibid 553.

863 See, eg, *Movitex Ltd v Bulfield* [1988] BCLC 104, 117; *Commonwealth Bank of Australia v Smith* (1991) 102 ALR 453, 477 (Fed C of A); *Duke Group Ltd v Pilmer* (1999) 31 ACSR 213, 356 SC(SA); *Pilmer v Duke Group Ltd* [2001] 2 BCLC 773, 797–802 (Aust HC); *Transvaal Lands Co v New Belgium (Transvaal) Land and Development Co* [1914] 2 Ch. 488.

864 *Aberdeen Railway Co v Blaikie Bros* (1854) 1 Macq 461, 471–3; [1843-1860] All ER Rep 249, 252-253 (HL); *North-West Transportation Co Ltd v Beatty* (1887) App Cas 589, 593–4 (PC); *Cohen v Directors of Rand Collieries Ltd* 1906 TS 197, 201–2; *Robinson v Randfontein Estates Gold Mining Co Ltd* 1921 AD 168, 178; *Gundelfinger v African Textile Manufacturers Ltd* 1939 AD 314, 323; *Movitex Ltd v Bulfield* [1988] BCLC 104; *Neptune (Vehicle Washing Equipment) Ltd v Fitzgerald* [1995] 3 All ER 811, 814.

865 See FHI Cassim (n 856) 567.

panies Act 1973.[866] As under its predecessor, disclosure to, rather than approval by, the board of a personal financial interest is regarded to be sufficient to safeguard the interests of the company. In relation to a personal financial interest in a proposed transaction, the director may not participate in and vote on the board meeting deciding the matter.[867]

The South African approach of making some of the directors' duties applicable to rescue practitioners is not found in the UK or Australia, where the duties of administrators are contained either in the rescue legislation itself or in the common law.[868] A few questions arise in relation to the application of the directors' duties to rescue practitioners, which will be examined below.

bb. Interpretational difficulties regarding non-codified common law duties

It seems that not all common law fiduciary duties have been codified under ss 75 to 77. For example, the duty of the directors to act within the powers conferred upon them[869] and the duty to exercise an independent judgment,[870] are not specifically referred to under these sections.[871] Moreover, it is clear that only the common law remedy of damages for breach

866 Ibid; *Henochsberg Companies Act* (n 592) s 75, 281.

867 S 75(5).

868 For the UK, see, eg, Insolvency Act 1986, Sch B1, para 3 and 4 (in relation to the choice of which objective of rescue to pursue and to act quickly and efficiently); *Re Charnley Davies (No.2)* [1990] BCLC 760 (in relation to the duty of care); see generally Armour and Mokal (n 609). For Australia, see, eg, *Wood v Laser Holdings Ltd* (1995) 19 ACSR 245, 266 (in relation to general fiduciary duties); see generally, Keay, 'Corporate Governance During Administration and Reconstruction Under Part 5.3A of the Corporations Act' (1997) 15 C&SLJ 145, 157–8.

869 *Ashbury Railway Carriage and Iron Co v Riche* (1875) LR 7 HL 653.

870 For a leading case, see *Kregor v Hollins* (1913) 109 LT 225 (KB and CA).

871 For the view that the duty to act within the powers conferred might be covered by the duty to act in the best interests of the company and for a proper purpose under s 76(3)(a) and (b), and that the duty to exercise independent judgment is an aspect of the duty to act in the best interests of the company under s 76(3)(b), see FHI Cassim (n 856) 534 and 529, 532, respectively. It should also be noted that the imposition of personal liability on directors under s 77(3)(a) for having acted in the name of the company, signed anything on behalf of the company, or purported to bind the company or authorise the taking of any action by or on behalf of the company, despite knowing that the director lacked the authority to do so,

of fiduciary duties has been codified,[872] but none of the other common law remedies, namely disgorgement of profits;[873] to cancel a transaction entered into in breach of a fiduciary duty – that is, the contract is voidable against the fiduciary at the instance of the beneficiary;[874] and injunctive relief either to prevent the breach from occurring in the first place or to prevent it from continuing.[875] This raises the question whether the common law duties and remedies not codified under ss 75 to 77 apply to rescue practitioners. It could be argued that since s 140(3)(b) specifically only makes the duties and liabilities under ss 75 to 77 applicable to rescue practitioners, the uncodified duties and liabilities cannot apply to rescue practitioners lest s 140(3)(b) be redundant. On the other hand, such a conclusion might lead to absurd results in that the duty to exercise independent judgment might be relevant in reducing agency costs arising from the inter-creditor conflict during rescue proceedings for example,[876] insofar as the judgment of the rescue practitioner might be fettered by a bias in favour of one class of creditors. A strict reading of s 140(3)(b), however, would preclude courts from applying such a duty to the rescue practitioner.[877] This calls for a purposive (or contextual) reading of s 140(3)(b), as has been recently established in *Natal Joint Municipal Pension Funds v*

---

could functionally cover aspects of the common law fiduciary duty dealing with acts outside the authority conferred.

872 In s 76(2)(a).

873 Davies and Worthington (n 714) para 16–114f; *Blackman Companies Act* (n 857) Ch 8, 42(1)ff and cases cited therein.

874 *Transvaal Lands Co v New Belgium (Transvaal) Land and Development Co* (1934) 3 DLR 465 (PC); *EMB Co Ltd v Dominion Bank* [1937] 3 All ER 555, 569 (PC); *Rolled Steel Products (Holdings) Ltd v British Steel Corporation* [1986] Ch 246; [1985] 3 All ER 52 (CA); *Guinness plc v Saunders* [1990] 2 AC 663, 697; [1990] 1 All ER 652, 664–5 (HL); *Cowan de Groot Properties Ltd v Eagle Trust plc* [1992] 4 All ER 700, 763–7.

875 *Cyberscene Ltd v i-Kiosk Internet and Information (Pty) Ltd* 2000 (1) SA 806 (C) 820.

876 See Chapter 1 above.

877 To be sure, the rescue procedure provides for ample controls on the independence of the practitioner, in particular the removal grounds where a practitioner has a conflict of interest or lacks independence (s 139(2)(e)) and where the practitioner's relationship with the company would objectively raise doubts about his integrity, impartiality or objectivity (compromised relationship) (s 139(2)(d) read with s 138(1)(e)). However, it is not clear whether the material scope of the above removal grounds are the same as that of the duty to exercise independent judgment. Eg, the removal grounds of a lack of independence and for having a

Endumeni Municipality.[878] When applying this method of interpretation, any common law fiduciary duties and remedies that may reasonably admit of analogous application to the rescue practitioner to ensure appropriate protection of the beneficiaries of such duties during rescue proceedings, irrespective of whether they have been codified under ss 75 to 77, should be included into the ambit of that provision.

cc. Duty to act in the best interests of the company and to act for a proper purpose

Distinguishing the two duties—Both the best interests and the proper purpose duties are relevant to regulating the rescue practitioner's conduct as a *fiduciary* for the creditors of the company. Although these two duties may overlap,[879] they are separate and distinct duties. The proper purpose duty, properly understood, derives from the general duty to act within powers. Accordingly, both the proper purpose duty and the within powers duty require the directors to act within the authority conferred upon them. However, the within powers duty prohibits conduct outside the conferred powers themselves, while the proper purpose duty prohibits the exercise of the conferred powers for unauthorised purposes.[880] Given that the source of the proper purpose duty is therefore specifically the rules set out in the

---

compromised relationship would seem to presuppose a prior relationship between the rescue practitioner and the company, whereas the independent judgment duty would seem to cover situations where the discretion of the rescue practitioner is fettered for reasons other than any *prior* relationship with relevant persons. Moreover, the removal ground of a compromised relationship does not apply to a relationship between the company and affected persons. And finally, a conflict of interest might be conceptually different to a failure to exercise independent judgment.

878 2012 (4) SA 593 (SCA) para 18ff.

879 See, eg, *Punt v Symons & Co Ltd* [1903] 2 Ch 506; *Treasure Trove Diamonds Ltd v Hyman* 1928 AD 464; *Ngurli v McCann* (1954) 90 CLR 425 (HC of A); *Harlowe's Nominees Pty Ltd v Woodside (Lakes Entrance) Oil NL* (1967) 121 CLR 483, 493 (HC of A).

880 Davies and Worthington (n 714) para 16-23ff. Thus, s 171 of the British Companies Act 2006, which lists the duty to act within the company's constitution and the duty to act for a proper purpose under the heading 'duty to act within powers', probably gives a better conceptual and doctrinal account of the common law than its South African counterpart.

constitutional documents of the company and the company law legislation, actions by a director that fall outside the purpose of a particular rule are in breach of the proper purpose duty. This is notwithstanding that the directors may have honestly intended for such actions to promote the interests of the company (and would thus be in compliance with the best interests duty). By the same token, actions taken by directors consciously in their own, rather than the company's interests could be in breach of the best interests duty notwithstanding that they may be within the purpose for which they have been conferred.[881]

Reversal of the standard of the two duties at common law under the Companies Act 2008?—It follows from the relationship between the two duties that at common law the proper purpose duty is objective.[882] By contrast, the courts have always understood the best interest duty to be subjective: directors were required to act *bona fide* in what they considered – not what a court may have considered – to be in the best interest of the company, and it was not for the courts to review the merits of a directorial decision honestly arrived at.[883] In assessing whether the directors had done what they believed to be right, the courts would only conclude in the negative if satisfied that the directors had not acted as honest men of business might

---

881 Davies and Worthington (n 714) paras 16-26.

882 See, eg, *Extrasure Travel Insurance Ltd v Scattergood* [2003] 1 BCLC 598, 613; *Howard Smith Ltd v Ampol Ltd* [1974] A.C. 821, 834, PC; citing *Fraser v Whalley* (1864) 2 H.C.M. & M. 10; *Punt v Symons & Co Ltd* [1903] 2 Ch. 506; *Piercy v S Mills & Co Ltd* [1920] 1 Ch. 77; *Ngurli v McCann* (1954) 90 C.L.R. 425, Aust. HC; *Hogg v Cramphorn Ltd* [1967] Ch. 254, 267.

883 See, eg, *Carlen v Drury* (1820) Ves & B54; *Percival v Wright* [1902] 2 Ch 421, 425; *Re Bell Bros, ex parte Hodgson* (1891) 65 LT 245; *Punt v Symons & Co Ltd* [1903] 2 Ch 506, 515; *Richard Brady Franks Ltd v Price* (1937) 58 CLR 112 135 (HC of A); *Re Smith & Fawcett Ltd* [1942] Ch 304, 306; [1942] 1 All ER 542 (CA); *Levin v Felt and Tweeds Ltd* 1951 (2) SA 401 (A); *Ngurli Ltd v McCann* (1953) 90 CLR 425, 438 (HC of A); *R v Herholdt* 1957 (3) SA 236 (A); *Parke v Daily News Ltd* [1962] Ch 927; [1962] 2 All ER 929; *SA Fabrics Ltd v Millman* 1972 (4) SA 592 (A) 596; *Howard Smith v Ampol Petroleum* [1974] AC 821, 835–6; [1974] 1 All ER 1126, 113–4 (PC); *Novick v Comair Holdings Ltd* 1979 (2) SA 116 (W) 129–30; *Atlas Organic Fertilizers (Pty) Ltd v Pikkewyn Ghwano (Pty) Ltd* 1981 (2) SA 173 (T) 197; *Australian Growth Resources Corporation Pty v Van Reesema* (1988) 13 ACLR 261, 268 SC(SA); *Darvall v North Sydney Brick & Tile Co Ltd* (1989) 15 ACLR 230, 24–8 CA(NSW); *Equiticorp Finance Ltd v Bank of New Zealand* (1993) 11 ACSR 642, 72–8 CA(NSW); *Teck Corporation Ltd v Millar* (1973) 33 DLR (3d) 288, 331.

be expected to act.[884] Thus, in the context of the best interests duty, the 'good faith' concept had the effect of limiting the directors' liability, as it imposed on the plaintiff the difficult task of showing the director to have acted in bad faith when taking the decision under scrutiny.

Against this background it is somewhat surprising that the duty in s 76(3)(a) provides that a director must exercise his powers 'in good faith and for a proper purpose', while the codified best interest duty in s 76(3)(b) does not make reference to 'good faith'.[885] Does this imply that the scant common law authority that the proper purpose duty is subjective,[886] has found its way into the Companies Act 2008?[887]

Moreover, the business judgment rule,[888] which was introduced to South African law under the Companies Act 2008 does not only apply to the duty of care, but also to the best interest duty.[889] Under the business judgment rule, a director is taken to have complied with the s 76(3)(b) duty if he, *inter alia*, 'has taken reasonably diligent steps to become informed about the matter' (sub-para (i)) and he 'had a rational basis for believing, and did believe, that the decision was in the best interests of the company' (sub-para (ii)). The business judgment rule is generally intended to *relieve* directors from liability for breaches of applicable duties. However, if the duty to act in the best interest of the company was subjective, it is difficult to see how the fact that the director has properly informed himself about the matter, or that he had a rational basis for his belief, would *lower* the standard of the duty. The fact that the legislature has made the codified business judgment rule applicable to the best interest duty might therefore imply that such duty must have become objective.

---

884 Davies and Worthington (n 714) para 16-40.

885 Cf the codifications of the common law best interest and proper purpose duties in Australia (s 181(1)(a), (b) Corporations Act 2001) and the UK s 172(1) of the British Companies Act 2006. Both are in line with the majority view that the best interests duty is subjective and the proper purpose duty objective.

886 *Teck Corporation Ltd v Millar* (1973) 33 DLR (3d) 288, 312. See also *Blackman Companies Act* (n 857) Ch 8, 80, following Birds, 'Proper Purposes as a Head of Directors' Duties' (1974) 37 MLR 580.

887 One way to get around this anomaly is that the reference to 'good faith' and 'proper purpose' under s 76(3)(a) are cumulative, meaning that there is a separate and distinct duty to act in good faith; see, FHI Cassim (n 856) 525.

888 S 76(4)(a).

889 See s 76(4)(a)(passage before sub-para (i)).

This would of course make the best interests duty much more demanding on directors.

The content of the 'company's best interest' and the 'proper purpose' in rescue proceedings—While in South African company law the best interest of the company is arguably constituted by the long-term interests of the shareholders and the interests of stakeholders to the extent that these promote the interests of the shareholders ('enlightened shareholder value' approach),[890] in rescue proceedings the rescue practitioner must act in the best interest of the company's creditors (or, stated more precisely, the affected persons). Moreover, unlike in company law, there is no room for taking into account the long-term interests of affected persons, given the definite duration of rescue proceedings and, arguably, less room than in company law to have regard for wider interests, such as the community and the environment. Indeed, since the overarching objective of the company in rescue proceedings is the rescue outcomes as set out in the statutory objectives of rescue under s 128(1)(b)(iii), it would seem that in rescue proceedings the content of the best interest duty of a rescue practitioner is essentially the promotion of the rescue objectives. Seen in this sense, the practitioner will be in breach of his fiduciary duties to act in the best interest of the company for any conduct which is contrary to the rescue objectives.

Subtly distinct from staying within the boundaries of the objectives of rescue generally is the question, which of the rescue objectives should be followed and how long the practitioner should spend pursuing a particular objective. As we have seen, the South African objectives clause gives some guidance on this aspect by providing that the secondary objective (ie, the going concern sale of the company's business) may only be pursued if it is 'not possible' to achieve the primary objective (reorganisation).[891] In deciding when the primary objective is no longer possible to

---

890 FHI Cassim (n 856) 517ff. See, however, the current version of the Corporate Governance Code of South Africa ('King Code of Governance Principles for South Africa' (2009), Institute of Directors in Southern Africa ('*IoDSA*') <http://c.ymcdn.com/sites/www.iodsa.co.za/resource/collection/94445006-4F18-4335-B7FB-7F5A8B23FB3F/King_III_Code_for_Governance_Principles_.pdf> accessed 10 January 2017), which recommends that a 'stakeholder-inclusive' approach be adopted, pursuant to which the interests of stakeholders are to be given equal importance to those of shareholders.

891 S 128(1)(b)(iii). See further discussion in PART B, Chapter 4, IV., 1 above.

achieve, and in deciding how many costs the practitioner should be prepared to impose on the company in trying to achieve the primary objective before concluding that it is no longer possible to achieve, it would seem that the practitioner would be judged either with reference to the duty to act in the best interests of the company or the duty to act with care, skill and diligence[892] (particularly in relation to the practitioner's costs). The standard of proof of the practitioners' decision as to which objective to pursue, depends on which duty would apply: while the best interest duty is subjective[893], the duty of care is negligence-based.[894] In selecting the appropriate rescue objective in compliance with his duty to act in the best interests of the company and his duty of care, the practitioner would, as noted above, be shielded by the business judgment rule under s 76(4)(a). It is not clear whether the practitioner is, in addition, under a duty to act *rationally* when exercising his discretion in selecting the appropriate rescue objective. In recent years, there have been some developments under the administration procedure in the UK to this effect.[895] The question is whether the office holder can be held accountable for taking into account irrelevant considerations and failing to take into account relevant considerations and whether, based on the more demanding rationality requirements in public law, the office holder has a duty to give reasons for his decision. The creditors further have a right to be heard.[896] While there is some evidence under the South African rescue provisions of a right to be heard,[897] there is no basis for a duty of the practitioner to give reasons for his decisions.

892 Discussed at ee. below.

893 However, as we have seen this duty may have become objective under the Companies Act 2008.

894 See ee. below.

895 See Mokal and Armour, 'The New UK Corporate Rescue Procedure – The Administrator's Duty to Act Rationally' (2004) SSRN <http://papers.ssrn.com/sol3/papers.cfm?abstract_id=546624> accessed 16 January 2017.

896 Ibid.

897 In the form of the employees' right to be consulted by the rescue practitioner, to be afforded the opportunity to review the rescue plan and make a submission to the meeting to vote on the rescue plan before such a vote is taken (ss 144(d) and (e) read with s 152(1)(c)), the creditors' right to make proposals for a rescue plan to the practitioner (s 145(1)(d)) and generally through the consultation duties of the practitioner to the creditors' and employees' committees (s 149).

With regard to the proper purpose duty, in company law the source of the powers – and thus the purposes for which such powers may be exercised – is the applicable company law legislation (primarily the Companies Act) and the constitutional documents of the company.[898] In rescue law, by contrast, these authorities cannot be the sources of the office holder's powers and purposes of exercising such powers, since the shareholders (in whose interests such laws and documents are drafted) are typically no longer the company's residual claimants when the company has been placed under rescue proceedings. Rather, the practitioner's powers are based on the applicable rescue provisions and any authority given by the required majority of the creditors' meetings.

dd. Difficulties with the analogous application of applicable directors' duties to disclose relevant information to the board

As discussed above, some of the directors' duties under ss 75 to 77 that apply to rescue practitioners are either expressly formulated as a duty to disclose relevant information to the board (ie, the disclosure of a personal financial interest under s 75 and of information generally under s 76(2)(b)) or the common law entitles the general meeting to waive liability for breaching certain no-conflict duties, in particular the no-profit and corporate opportunities rules. These arguably fall under s 76(2)(a)(i). When such duties are applied to rescue law, the rescue practitioner would be required to disclose a conflict of interest pursuant to s 75 and relevant information pursuant to s 76(2)(b) to the board.

It is not clear, however, whether disclosure to the board particularly of a personal financial interest would be appropriate, given the weak position of directors during rescue proceedings to safeguard the company's interests adequately. This is because the directors' powers are subject to the authority of the rescue practitioner and their continued employment with the company is, to a large extent, at the discretion of the rescue practitioner. Being subject to the authority of the rescue practitioner however, make directors reluctant to take a decision unfavourable to the rescue practitioner when called upon to do so under the s 75-machinery. It might be more appropriate to place the decision as to whether the company should enter in-

898 Davies and Worthington (n 714) para 16-24.

to a conflicted contract in the beneficiaries of this fiduciary duty themselves, – ie, the creditors' meeting (as would seem to be the position by analogous application to company law under s 76(2)(a)(i)).[899]

It should also be noted that the type of conflict of interest situations contemplated by s 75 and s 76(2)(a)(i) could also fall within the ground of removal of a rescue practitioner for having a conflict of interest under s 139(2)(e).[900] This removal ground is enforced by the court upon application by an affected person and would, in any event, appear to provide for a stronger remedy (removal) than s 75 (damages to the company as a result of the breach).[901]

ee. The duty of care, skill and diligence

While the rationale of the fiduciary duties is the scope for abuse that is inherent to the fiduciary relationship, the duty of care ensures that the directors act with competence. Unlike the fiduciary duties, the duty of care requires negligence. While the courts at common law were rather lax in enforcing the duty of care at first, and formulated it largely in subjective terms,[902] the Companies Act 2008 has adopted a dual test which contains both an objective and a subjective element. The objective limb requires a director to exercise his functions with a degree of care that may be expected reasonably of a person carrying out the same functions in relation to the company as those carried out by that director.[903] Under the subjective limb, by contrast, whether or not the above applies will be measured against the general knowledge, skill and experience of that director.[904] The objective element constitutes a minimum standard of care and the subjec-

---

899 Under such duty the general meeting has to absolve the fiduciary from the application of the duty.

900 The removal ground for a conflict of interest might even be broader in scope than the conflict of interest duties; see the discussion in PART B, Chapter 4, IV., 8., c., cc below.

901 S 76(2)(a).

902 FHI Cassim (n 856) 555.

903 S 76(3)(c)(i).

904 S 76(3)(c)(ii). It would thus seem as though a different standard of care and skill will be required depending on whether the practitioners is a 'senior', an 'experienced' or a 'junior practitioner' pursuant to reg 127(2)(c); see Jacobs and Neethling (n 851) 778; Jacobs (n 851)200.

tive element can only raise, never lower, the standard of care required by the objective element.[905]

The newly introduced business judgment rule provides a safe harbour for directors when exercising the duty of care.[906] The business judgment rule recognises the cost benefits of swift directorial decision-making on less than perfect facts, and seeks to guard against the hindsight-bias of courts reviewing such decisions.[907] The South African business judgment rule presumes that directors have complied with the duty of care[908] if it can be shown that the directors (i) informed themselves about the matter reasonably diligently, (ii) had no interest in the subject matter of the decision as contemplated by s 75 (and, if they did, complied with the disclosure requirements under s 75) and (iii) that there was a rational basis for believing that the decision would be in the best interests of the company.[909]

With regard to the material scope of the duty of care, 'skill' has been described as technical competence, 'care' as the manner in which the skill is applied[910] and 'diligence' has been argued to mean 'attending to one's duties properly.[911]

The duty of care is expected to play a meaningful role in rescue law, particularly in ensuring the rescue practitioner's efficiency in managing the company and developing a rescue plan.

---

905 See *Henochsberg Companies Act* (n 592) s 76, 295; FHI Cassim (n 856) 509; Bouwman, 'An Appraisal of the Modification of the Directors' Duty of Care and Skill' (2009) 21 SA Merc LJ 509, 513–4; Bekink, 'A Historical Overview of the Directors' Duty of Care and Skill: From the Nineteenth Century to the Companies Bill 2007' (2008) 20 SA Merc LJ 95, 111–2; presumably also Jacobs and Neethling (n 851) 778–9; Jacobs (n 851) 201. For the opposite view, see du Plessis, 'A Comparative Analysis of Directors' Duty of Care, Skill and Diligence in South Africa and Australia' in Mongalo (ed), *Modern Company Law for a Competitive South African Economy* (Juta 2010) 263, 269–70, 288–9.

906 S 76(4)(a).

907 Roth, 'Business Judgment Rule' *Max Planck Encyclopedia of European Private Law* (2012).

908 And, rather unusually, the fiduciary duty to act in the best interest of the company; s 76(4)(passage before sub-para (i)).

909 S 76(4)(a)(i), (ii) and (iii), respectively.

910 *Daniels (formerly practising at Deloitte Haskins & Sells) v Anderson* (1996) 16 ASCR 607 (NSW); (1995) 37 NSWLR 438.

911 FHI Cassim (n 856) 560.

c. Rescue practitioners' removal from office

aa. General

The rescue practitioner may be removed from office on the grounds set out in s 130(1)(b), s 138 and s 139. There are two removal grounds that are only available in respect of out-of-court entry, namely those set out in s 130(1)(b)(ii) and (iii), while the balance of the removal grounds under the mentioned provisions can be invoked under both entry routes.[912] A rescue practitioner may be removed by the court until the adoption of a business rescue plan.[913] Affected persons have *locus standi* to bring an application to the court for removal. In respect of the removal grounds under s 139, the court may also remove the rescue practitioner on its own motion.[914]

As indicated by the fairly large number of removal grounds, the South African rescue procedure relies heavily on the remedy of the removal of the rescue practitioner. The general function of this remedy is to ensure the quality and accountability of the rescue practitioner. A further function of the removal grounds is the prevention of the appointment of a friendly rescue practitioner, which could be seen, in particular, to reduce the risk of the invocation by the directors of formal rescue proceedings for strategic purposes, as further discussed in Chapter 7 below. Three removal grounds could be seen to address the risk of the appointment of a friendly rescue practitioner, namely:

---

912 The grounds under s 138 are actually positive qualification requirements that a rescue practitioner has to fulfil *ex ante* when appointed under both out-of-court entry and entry by court order (see s 129(3)(b) and s 131(5), respectively). However, non-fulfilment of the requirements under s 138(1) also operate as grounds of removal of a rescue practitioner in respect of both entry routes by virtue of s 130(1)(b)(i) (out-of-court entry) and s 139(2)(d) (entry by court order).

913 See s 130(1)(passage before para (a)). See also *African Banking Corporation of Botswana Ltd v Kariba Furniture Manufacturers (Pty) Ltd and Others* 2013 (6) SA 471 (GNP) para 62. This is not stated explicitly in relation to the removal grounds under s 139; however, there is no reason why such removal grounds should not also be available until the adoption of a rescue plan.

914 See s 130(1)(passage before para (a)), s 139(2) and s 139(2)(passage before para (a)), respectively.

(i) *where the rescue practitioner, regarded from an objective perspective,*[915] *has a relationship with the company that compromises his integrity, impartiality or objectivity ('compromised relationship') (s 138(1)(e));*
(ii) *where the rescue practitioner has a conflict of interest or lacks independence (s 139(2)(e));*
(iii) *where the rescue practitioner is not independent of the company or its management (s 130(1)(b)(ii));*[916]

These removal grounds will now be considered in turn.

bb. Removal for having a compromised relationship (s 138(1)(e))

Meaning of 'relationship'—On a strict reading of the word 'relationship' in s 138(1)(e), this ground of removal would only apply if either the rescue practitioner or the company exercised 'control' of the other person in a way that allows the first person to materially influence the (corporate) policy of the other person in the ways contemplated by the definition of 'relationship'.[917] On such a construction of the word 'relationship', this removal ground would accordingly only be available if the rescue practitioner and the company were actually connected in a shareholder-company, director-company or functionally equivalent relationship of 'control' as contemplated in the applicable definition.[918] However, if that were the meaning of 'relationship' in s 138(1)(e), the description of such a relationship as one that compromises the rescue practitioner's integrity, impartiality or objectivity would be superfluous, as a relationship between two persons as contemplated by the applicable definition would by its very nature have the compromising effect described in s 138(1)(e). Nor would it be plausible to argue that the description of a compromised relationship is meant to clarify, for the avoidance of doubt, the meaning of the definition of 'relationship'. A compromised relationship is broader in scope than a 'relationship' (as defined). This is because it does not require a relationship of

915 As expressed by '[...] such as would lead a reasonable and informed third party to conclude [...]'.
916 This removal ground is only available in the out-of-court entry route.
917 See the definition of 'relationship' and 'related' in s 1 read with s 2 and s 3. For an explanation of the term 'related persons', see nn 651 to 654 above.
918 See also Loubser, 'LLD thesis' (n 512) 104–5.

'control' of one person over the other as contemplated in the applicable definition for the integrity, impartiality or objectivity of any of the two persons of such relationship to be compromised as contemplated by s 138(1)(e). Accordingly, the term 'relationship' under s 138(1)(e) should be given the broader meaning as mentioned above. Such an interpretation could be based on the lead-in language of the definitions section under the Companies Act 2008, which provides that the definitions do not apply where the context indicates that a defined term should have a different meaning.

What type of persons fall within s 138(1)(e)?—It would certainly be conceivable that such provision could catch any persons who had a close professional relationship with the company prior to the commencement of rescue proceedings, such as the company's auditors, attorneys, tax consultants and general financial advisors, provided a compromised relationship is found to exist on the relevant facts of each case.[919]

It would also seem that s 138(1)(e) is, in principle, broad enough to include third party professionals who might have assisted the company in restructuring its affairs before the company had been placed under rescue proceedings, such as advisors who are involved in a pre-packaged plan, to the extent that, on the relevant facts, their integrity, objectivity and impartiality has been compromised.[920] When called upon to determine compliance with s 138(1)(e), the courts will need to balance the need for protecting the company's creditors from biased rescue practitioners and the need for not unduly discouraging pre-insolvency contractual restructuring arrangements, including pre-packaged plans, given their potential of reducing the direct costs of rescue, which would benefit primarily unsecured creditors.[921]

---

919 Ibid.

920 Ibid 105. The judgment of *Copper Sunset Trading 220 (Pty) Ltd v Spar Group Ltd and Another* 2014 (6) SA 214 (LP) paras 23–4 seems to suggest that attorneys of the company who had acted for the company before the commencement of rescue proceedings could, in principle, be held to have a compromised relationship with the company as contemplated by s 138(1)(e). However, on the facts the court held that there was no basis for coming to such a conclusion.

921 Ibid.

cc. Removal for having a conflict of interest and for a lack of independence (s 139(2)(e))

Difference between removal for having 'a conflict of interest' and for 'lacking independence'—S 139(2)(e) combines two separate grounds of removal, namely conflict of interest and lack of independence of the rescue practitioner. These two terms may be intuitively quite similar in content, and may indeed often be seen as aspects of each other.[922] The difference between them, however, appears to be that the rescue practitioner could have a conflict of interest with the company, even where he would seem to lack any relationship with the company, its management or any other constituent that would call his independence into question. An example of where a conflict of interest could arise where a rescue practitioner is not necessarily influenced by, or biased in favour of, the company or any constituent of the company, is where the company enters into a contract during rescue proceedings in which the rescue practitioner has a personal financial interest, thereby profiting personally from a contract entered into by the company. There is no indication in this scenario that the rescue practitioner would lack independence of the company, its management or any other constituent in this scenario, although he would clearly be seen as having a conflict of interest.

Material scope of a conflict of interest—It is not clear whether s 139(2)(e) should be read to be limited to, or whether it should be read to be broader than, the conflict of interest situations that would ordinarily be covered by the codified no-conflict fiduciary duties under s 75 and s 76(2)(a)(i). This gives rise to the question as to whether a conflict of interest under s 139(2)(e) would also include situations where the conflict of interest arises by virtue of a (prior) relationship between the practitioner and the company or any of its constituents, which is typically not covered by the no-conflict duties. This is an important question for purposes of this study, since the removal of practitioners for having a conflict of interest under s 139(2)(e) could only be seen as a legal strategy to control the appointment of a

922 See, eg, para 31 read with para 40ff of the Ethics Code of the Insolvency Practitioners Association, 'Code of Ethics' <http://www.insolvency-practitioners.org.uk/regulation-and-guidance/ethics-code> accessed 10 January 2017, for Members of the British Insolvency Practitioners Association and para 4.5 of the Insolvency Standards for Members of the Australian Accounting Professional & Ethical Standards Board (Revised September 2014).

friendly rescue practitioner if such provision includes a conflict of interest arising as a result of such a (prior) relationship. On the other hand, it is not clear how a conflict of interest arising from a prior relationship would differ in content from a 'lack of independence' (which is the other limb of s 139(2)(e)).

Relationship with independence removal ground under s 130(1)(b)(i)— The scope of 'independence' of the rescue practitioner under s 139(2)(e), unlike the similarly worded removal ground in respect of out-of-court entries under s 130(1)(b)(i), does not specify the persons from whom the rescue practitioner is required to be independent. Given that in the out-of-court entry route any affected person is entitled to nominate an interim rescue practitioner,[923] and that there is a significant risk of a dependent relationship between the rescue practitioner and the affected person by whom the rescue practitioner has been nominated, it would seem that s 139(2)(e) would at the very least require that the rescue practitioner be independent from any affected person or class of affected persons. In saying that, this provision could also be interpreted to require the rescue practitioner to be independent from every constituent of the company, including the management and the company itself. Accordingly, s 139(2)(e), as it relates to a lack of independence, is broader than the similarly worded removal ground under s 130(1)(b)(i).

This difference in scope of the two otherwise similarly worded removal grounds can probably be justified on the basis that removal of the rescue practitioner under s 130(1)(b)(i) is only available in respect of out-of-court entries by the board of directors. Since affected persons are not entitled to commence rescue proceedings out-of-court, there is not a high risk that a rescue practitioner, who is not independent from any class of claimants, is appointed under such entry route.

dd. Relationship between removal grounds for lack of independence and for having a compromised relationship

The precise content of the two relevant removal grounds has not yet been determined by the courts or the regulator, and, accordingly, their differ-

923 S 131(5). The interim rescue practitioner is subject to ratification by a majority of independent creditors; see below.

ence in scope is not clear. The difficulty in distinguishing the meaning of the two relevant removal grounds is largely due to the novelty of the compromised relationship removal ground in the South African company law and corporate insolvency law (and, as a consequence thereof, the lack of any judicial interpretation of its meaning). This is further enhanced by the fact that, at least on the plain language meanings of 'independence' and what we defined as 'compromised relationship', there is a significant overlap in meaning of such two terms. However, given the presumption of the interpretation of statutes that each provision must have a meaning that is not redundant or tautologous,[924] the better view is that the content of the two removal grounds must differ in content.[925]

There is some guidance on the meaning of 'independence'. A case in the 1970s has held that term, with regard to a relationship between an accountant and a company, to mean that the accountant must not be subjected to the supervision and control of the company concerning the manner in which his duties are performed.[926] In another case, that term has been interpreted to mean the ability to bring an independent mind to bear on a particular problem.[927] The Third King Code on Corporate Governance in South Africa, for example, defines independence as 'the absence of undue influence and bias, which can be affected by the intensity of the relationship between the director and the company.'[928] It would seem that all the aforementioned definitions of 'independence' could just as well entail a compromised relationship. However, it would intuitively seem that the converse need not necessarily be true, namely that a compromised relationship might exist, which would not likewise constitute a relationship of 'dependence' within the aforementioned meaning of such term. In other words, a compromised relationship might be broader than a lack of independence.[929] The precise determination of a compromised relationship should be left to the courts, although it is doubtful that this particular issue will be subject to frequent litigation.

924 Devenish (n 765) 207.

925 See, however, *Meskin Insolvency Law* (n 576) para 18.4.2.2 n 3 and Loubser, 'LLD thesis' (n 512) 360, who argue that these two removal grounds are so similar in content that having both is unnecessary.

926 *De Villiers and Others v Sports Pools (Pty) Ltd* [1976] 3 All SA 515 (R) 519.

927 *Potato Marketing Board v. Merricks*, (1958) 2 Q.B. 316, 33 as cited in *De Villiers and Others v Sports Pools (Pvt) Ltd* [1976] 3 All SA 515 (R) 519.

928 IoDSA (n 890).

929 See also Loubser, 'LLD thesis' (n 512) 105.

A clear difference between the two relevant removal grounds is that the lack of independence ground is broader than the compromised relationship ground in relation to the scope of persons with whom the rescue practitioner is prohibited from being connected. The removal of the rescue practitioner is only possible under the compromised relationship ground where the rescue practitioner has a compromised relationship with the *company* (which could include, indirectly, the management and shareholders). On the other hand, the lack of independence ground under s 130(1)(b)(ii) is triggered where the rescue practitioner is not independent of the management, while the lack of independence ground under s 139(2)(e) is triggered where the rescue practitioner is not independent of any constituent of the company. This effectively means that the compromised relationship ground cannot be seen as a legal strategy to ameliorate inter-creditor agency costs.[930]

d. Brief overview of the plan procedure

Another innovation under the new business rescue law is the plan procedure. The rescue practitioner's primary task is to develop and place before the relevant creditors' meeting a rescue plan on which the creditors are to vote. The procedure affords affected persons with extensive 'participation' rights and corresponding duties on the rescue practitioner, including disclosure duties at various stages of the plan procedure, to facilitate such participation.[931] The creditors and employees are entitled to form creditors' and employees' committees to this end.[932] Within 25 business days after the rescue practitioner's appointment, he must publish a rescue plan[933] and within ten business days thereof, a creditors' meeting must be called to consider and vote on the rescue plan.[934]

Approval of a plan requires a majority of 75% of the creditors' voting interest that were voted, which must include 50% of the 'independent

---

930 For a general overview, see Chapter 1.

931 See, eg, s 144 Companies Act 71 of 2008 (provisions cited in this Chapter refer to the Companies Act 2008, unless otherwise indicated) (in relation to employees), s 145 (in relation to creditors) and s 146 (in relation to shareholders).

932 See s 149.

933 S 150.

934 S 151.

creditors' voting interests'.[935] Unlike under the compromise with creditors procedure, creditors are not divided into classes for purposes of voting on the plan.[936] Interestingly, secured creditors have a voting interest to the full value of their claim, and not just the unsecured portion.[937] This would seem problematic as secured creditors only carry the risk of rescue proceedings to the extent of their unsecured portions.

The South African procedure provides for three remedies where a majority for passing a rescue plan has not been attained, namely (i) the preparation and publication of a revised plan by the practitioner;[938] (ii) the application to court by the practitioner and, failing that, by any affected person to have the vote on the plan set aside on the grounds that it was 'inappropriate';[939] and (iii) the right of any affected person to make a 'binding offer' to purchase the voting interest of a dissenting creditor.[940]

The second and third mentioned remedies introduce new concepts into the South African rescue law. With regard to the concept of an 'inappropriate vote', some guidance as to the meaning of that term is provided in s 153(7). It provides that in deciding on whether to set aside a vote on that ground, the court must be satisfied that it would be reasonable and just to do so, having regard to the interests of the persons voting against the proposed rescue plan, any provision made in the plan in respect of the persons voting against the proposed plan and the liquidation value of their claims.[941] The court in *Copper Sunset Trading 220 (Pty) Ltd v Spar Group Ltd and Another*[942] has held a vote to be inappropriate pursuant to s 153(1)(a)(ii) where a secured creditor and an unsecured creditor opposed the res-

---

935 s 145(4)(a).

936 See s 155(2)(passage before para (a)). The compromise with creditors procedure will be considered at PART B, Chapter 4, V below.

937 S 145(4)(a). The position is the same in Australia (Corporations Regulations 2001, reg 5.6.24(4)). In the UK, however, secured creditors are entitled to vote only the value of the unsecured portion of their claim (Insolvency Rules 1986, rule 2.24).

938 The practitioner must obtain the approval from presumably a majority of the creditors' voting interest (s 153(1)(a)(i)). Should the practitioner fail to to do so, any affected person present at the meeting may call for a vote of approval from the holders of voting interests, requiring the practitioner to prepare and publish a revised plan (s 153(1)(b)(i)(aa)).

939 S 153(1)(a)(ii) and s 153(1)(b)(i)(bb), respectively.

940 S 153(1)(b)(ii).

941 S 153(7)(a), (b), and (c), respectively.

942 2014 (6) SA 214 (LP) paras 35ff.

cue plan although there were reasonable grounds to believe that they would receive a higher return if the rescue plan were to be implemented than if the company were placed under liquidation proceedings. This judgment was criticised in *Shoprite Checkers (Pty) Ltd v Berryplum Retailers CC* and Others,[943] on the grounds that the enquiry into the inappropriateness of a vote should be judged purely from the persons who voted against the plan. Such enquiry did not entitle the court to replace its opinion of what was appropriate for that of the applicable creditor where the decision for the vote was taken in good faith and reflected what was in the best interests of that creditor.

The other new concept is that of a 'binding offer'. After there had previously been differing views about its meaning, the SCA in *African Banking Corporation of Botswana*[944] settled the matter. It held that such term contemplates that the offer binds the offeror (to the extent that once the offer has been made by the offeror, it may not be withdrawn), and not, as was held by the court at first instance,[945] the offeree (to the extent that once the offer has been made by the offeror, it must be accepted by the offeree).

S 154(2) provides that a creditor is precluded from enforcing any pre-commencement claims against the company unless otherwise provided in the rescue plan. This effectively functions as a cramdown mechanism, as it permits a plan to override the contractual rights of creditors who were out-voted in the vote on the plan.

The essential difference between s 154(1) and s 154(2) is that the former contemplates a situation where the creditor whose claim is reduced or discharged under the plan voted in favour, rather than against, the approval of the plan.[946] To the extent that here the creditor has consented to the dis-

943 [2015] JOL 34498 (GP) para 38.

944 *African Banking Corporation of Botswana v Kariba Furniture Manufacturers & others* (228/2014) [2015] ZASCA 69 (20 May 2015) para 12ff.

945 In the court *a quo*, *African Banking Corporation of Botswana v Kariba Furniture Manufacturers (Pty) Ltd and Others* 2013 (6) SA 471 (GNP) para 29.

946 If a creditor's debt has been discharged under s 154(1) or (2), a surety is released from any liability towards the creditor under a surety agreement due to the accessory nature of suretyships; see *Tuning Fork (Pty) Ltd t/a Balanced Audio v Jonker* 2014 4 SA 521 (WCC) rejecting the opposite conclusion by *African Banking Corporation of Botswana Ltd v Kariba Furniture Manufacturers (Pty) Ltd and Others* 2013 (6) SA 471 (GNP) para 68. For discussion of the Tuning

charge of his claim under the plan, s 154(1) does not contemplate a cram-down mechanism as such.

V. The scheme of arrangement (Chapter 6 Part E)

1. General

As mentioned earlier in this Chapter, the scheme of arrangement procedure under the Companies Act 1973 has been split into arrangements with shareholders (s 114) and with creditors (s 155) under the Companies Act 2008.[947] In this section we will only consider the compromise with creditors under s 155, not the scheme of arrangement with shareholders under s 114, as the latter is functionally not a restructuring procedure for distressed companies.

The discussion of the compromise with creditors procedure will proceed as follows. We will first consider the extent to which the new procedure differs from the previous procedure. Our focus here will be on the scope of restructuring arrangements available (see 2. below) and whether the new procedure has addressed the requirements of its predecessor that have been criticised for unduly raising its direct costs (see 3. below).[948] We will then examine issues in relation to the debt consolidation scheme under the new procedure (see 4. below).[949]

Fork case, see Lombard and Swart, 'Business rescue: The unsurety about sureties – *Tuning Fork (Pty) Ltd T/A Balanced Audio v Jonker*' (2015) 78 THRHR 521. However, it is possible to contract out of s 154(1) and (2) to the extent that it affects the liability of sureties; see *New Port Finance Company (Pty) Ltd and Another v Nedbank Ltd*; *Mostert and Another v Nedbank Ltd* [2015] 2 All SA 1 (SCA).

947 See PART B, Chapter 4, III., 2., b. above. We have also mentioned that this separation may raise the direct costs of capital restructuring mechanisms, and is thus undesirable.

948 See PART B, Chapter 4, II., 2. above.

949 For the use of the debt consolidation scheme under the scheme of arrangement under the Companies Act 1973, see PART B, Chapter 3, IV., 3. and PART B, Chapter 4, II., 4. above.

2. Scope of restructuring mechanisms available

The compromise with creditors under the Companies Act 2008 has retained the wide scope of arrangements under the scheme of arrangement under the Companies Act 1973. First, as under the scheme of arrangement, the compromise with creditors allows for both a 'compromise' and the slightly broader 'arrangement' of its obligations with its creditors.[950]

Second, the compromise with creditors appears to have retained the broad scope of restructuring mechanisms that were allowed under the scheme of arrangement. We have seen that under the scheme of arrangement, the requirement that a scheme may not usurp another procedure of the Companies Act 2008 was interpreted very broadly by the courts. For example, the courts went so far as approving schemes that effectively amounted to alternative means of liquidations of the companies' assets.[951] Although the compromise with creditors, unlike its predecessor, requires that certain information in relation to the manner of the compromise or arrangement be provided to the creditors,[952] none of such information implies that the scope of the manner of compromise or arrangement is narrower than under the previous compromise. Indeed, the fact that the type of mandatory information to be provided to creditors on the types of restructuring mechanisms is exactly the same for compromises as the information to be included in a rescue plan under rescue proceedings,[953] seems to suggest that the scope of restructuring mechanisms is equally broad under compromises as under a business rescue plan.

Case law on the scope of arrangements available under the scheme of arrangement therefore remains relevant in respect of the compromise with creditors.

---

950 See s 155(2) and (9) in relation to compromise with creditors and the headings of ss 311, 312 Companies Act 1973 in relation to the scheme of arrangement in which the terms 'compromise and arrangement' are used.

951 See PART B, Chapter 3, IV., 1. above.

952 See s 155(3)(b).

953 Compare s 155(3)(b) (in respect of compromises) and s 150(2)(b) (in respect of business rescue).

3. Procedural requirements

The compromise with creditors has abolished the requirement under its predecessor that a person with *locus standi* has to apply to court with a proposal and the court order a meeting of creditors or classes of creditors.[954] Under the compromise with creditors, the proposer of the compromise – ie, the company's board of directors or the liquidator (where the company is in liquidation), but no longer individual creditors[955] – can now deliver a copy of the proposal and a notice of the meeting to consider the proposal to the Commission and every creditor affected by it, without having to go through the onerous and costly court procedure.[956] It would seem that further onerous procedural requirements under the old Companies Act have been removed, such as the publication of the circular in local newspapers and the appointment of the Chairman to preside over the meetings.[957] This is expected to significantly lower the direct costs of the compromise procedure.[958]

It has been argued that even the additional costs imposed on the company by the requirement that the compromise be sanctioned by the court is not merited, as the right of an aggrieved creditor to challenge the compromise before the court *ex post* would afford sufficient protection to the minority.[959] Such an approach is relied on in the UK under the CVA, which is an alternative to the scheme of arrangement procedure.[960] It is clear that such an approach reduces the quality of enforcement of minority rights, since by removing the requirement that the court must sanction the scheme, the costs of enforcement of minority rights are effectively transferred from the general body of unsecured creditors to the affected minority creditors themselves, discouraging challenges to a scheme. Careful con-

954 S 311(1).

955 Creditors had *locus standi* to apply to court with a compromise proposal by virtue of s 311(1) Companies Act 1973.

956 S 155(2). The proposal must be accompanied by a certificate that the information contained in the proposal 'appears to be accurate, complete and up to date' and that the projections in the proposal are made in good faith; s 155(5)(a)-(b).

957 For these requirements under the previous scheme of arrangement, see PART B, Chapter 3, IV., 2. above.

958 See also Klopper and Bradstreet (n 513) 559.

959 Loubser, 'LLD thesis' (n 512) 161.

960 S 6(2) Insolvency Act 1986.

sideration should therefore be given before such a proposal is implemented.

The fact that the board of directors is now entitled to propose a compromise would seem to encourage use of the compromise procedure outside formal insolvency proceedings, as directors are generally in the best position to assess when a collective procedure of restructuring might be required when the company is still trading. However, the fact that the compromise does not provide for a moratorium reduces its effectiveness as a restructuring tool outside formal insolvency proceedings.[961]

The voting procedure from the previous procedure has largely been retained: 75% majority in value of the creditors or class of creditors present and voting;[962] moreover, creditors must still vote in their separate classes and the majority will still have to be attained in each class.[963]

Under the compromise with creditors, the court will only look into the merits of the compromise when being asked to sanction the scheme after the required majority has been obtained.[964] Although on a strict reading of s 155(7)(b) application to the court for sanctioning of the compromise seems optional,[965] this cannot be correct, since the compromise only has legal effect if sanctioned by the court.[966]

The new procedure requires that the scheme be just and equitable for the court to sanction it.[967] The courts are expected to draw on principles established by case law under the previous scheme of arrangement procedure in determining whether a scheme is just and equitable. These include considerations that the formalities were complied with, the classes of creditors were fairly represented, the statutory majority is acting *bona fide* in the best interest of the class of creditors, the creditors had sufficient information and time to consider the proposal, the scheme be in the public

---

961 The two regulatory approaches to providing a formal restructuring procedure suitable for small companies was set out at PART B, Chapter 4, III., 2., c. above.

962 S 155(6). See generally *Henochsberg Companies Act* (n 592) s 155, 537ff. However, see Loubser, 'LLD thesis' (n 512) 159–60.

963 See also Klopper and Bradstreet (n 513) 560–1.

964 S 155(7).

965 As is indicated by the term 'may' in s 155(7)(b).

966 Eg, it is the 'copy of *an order of the court sanctioning a compromise*' (s 155(8)) (emphasis added) that is final and binding on the company's creditors (s 155(8)(c)); see Loubser, 'LLD thesis' (n 512) 160; *Henochsberg Companies Act* (n 592) s 155, 542.

967 S 155(7)(b)(before sub-para (i)).

interest, whether it is fair and reasonable and whether a man of business would reasonably approve of the scheme.[968] At the same time, the courts are expected to follow the general reluctance of courts under the previous procedure to interfere with the will of the majority of creditors, on the basis that the majority are better judges of what is in their commercial interest than the court can be.[969]

4. The debt consolidation scheme

As we have seen, under the previous Companies Act, a form of the scheme of arrangement was often relied on in practice under the Companies Act 1973 where a third party (who was often a corporate insider) acquired the claims of existing creditors and typically became the sole shareholder of the company primarily for tax purposes ('debt consolidation scheme'). This form the scheme appears to still be allowed under the new compromise with creditors procedure.[970]

It should be noted that the provision under s 20(1)(a)(ii) Income Tax Act,[971] pursuant to which the amount of any assessed loss of a company that could be set off for tax purposes is reduced by any amount compromised or concession granted, has been repealed.[972] Because this amendment appears to obviate the need of ensuring that the creditors' claims are only reduced marginally from the liquidation value of the company in order to preserve the full amount of the assessed loss, it could be seen to raise the appeal of the debt consolidation scheme.[973]

A further controversial issue in respect of the variants of the scheme under the old regime was whether the court could sanction a scheme where, as was often the case, the original company would effectively carry on trading while being balance sheet insolvent.[974] The question was whether

---

968 See PART B, Chapter 3, IV., 2. above.

969 Ibid.

970 See also *Henochsberg Companies Act* (n 592) s 155, 534ff.

971 58 of 1962.

972 By the Taxation Laws Amendment Act 22 of 2012.

973 On the other hand, it is expected that creditors would typically not be amenable to have their claims compromised to much less than their liquidation value in practice, as that would place them in a worse position than they would be if the company were liquidated.

974 See PART B, Chapter 3, IV., 3., b. above.

reliance on existing creditor protection mechanisms, coupled with the power of the courts to impose conditions on the company, such as a re-capitalisation or a subordination of debt on a case-by-case basis, sufficiently protected future creditors of that company. The legislature has opted to maintain the previous approach rather than providing for mandatory regulation in this regard.

Subject to the aforementioned amendment to the Income Tax Act, case law on the debt consolidation scheme under the scheme of arrangement therefore remains relevant.[975]

VI. Forces that shape the South African corporate insolvency law – some comparative perspectives from the UK and the US

1. General

Legal culture, the historical evolution of the law (which is sometimes also referred to path dependence)[976] and the nature of the lending markets play an important role in shaping corporate insolvency law.[977] Moreover, par-

975 *Henochsberg Companies Act* (n 592) s 155, 534ff.

976 On path dependence generally, see Hathaway, 'Path Dependence in the Law: The Course and Pattern of Legal Change in a Common Law System' (2003) John M. Olin Center for Studies in Law, Economics, and Public Policy Working Papers, Paper 270, http://digitalcommons.law.yale.edu/lepp_papers/270 accessed 16 January 2017. In relation to specific areas of law, primarily corporate law, see Kahan and Klausnev, 'Path Dependence in Corporate Contracting' (1996) 74 Wash. U. L. Q. 347; Gilson, 'Corporate Governance and Economic Efficiency: When Do Institutions Matters?' (1996) 74 Wash. U. L. Q. 327; Bebchuk and Roe, 'A Theory of Path Dependence in Corporate Ownership and Governance' (1999) 52 Stan. L. Rev. 127. In relation to the field of law and economics, see Roe, 'Chaos and Evolution in Law and Economics' (1996) 109 Harv. L. Rev. 641.

977 It should be noted that all three factors are, in a sense, intra-jurisdictional. However, corporate insolvency law might, in principle, also be shaped by supra-jurisdictional forces, such as cross-jurisdictional co-ordination (for this concept in relation to corporate law, see Armour, Hansmann and Kraakman, 'What is Corporate Law' in Kraakman and others (eds), *Anatomy of Corporate Law – A Comparative and Functional Approach* (2nd edn, Oxford University Press 2009) 1, 33ff). This is frequently found in the EU through the EU Insolvency Regulation (EC) 1346/2000 and, more recently, the EU Bank Insolvency Directive 2014/59/EU. However, cross-jurisdictional co-ordination does not play a major role in shaping the South African corporate insolvency law. A further possible

ticularly the first two mentioned factors could influence how courts construe legal requirements that leave room for interpretation, which is inherently the case in relation to the *standards strategy*,[978] for example. All three factors do not only provide indications as to why corporate insolvency law is shaped in a particular way, but also why amendments to the law-on-the-books effecting a particular policy shift may often take time before taking effect in practice.[979] An understanding of how these factors correlate to corporate insolvency law is therefore essential to our analysis.

2. The impact of legal culture and path dependence

In relation to the factors of legal culture, we have already seen in Chapter 3 that the South African corporate insolvency law has historically been more biased in favour of liquidations rather than rescues and, accordingly, in favour of secured creditors. Examples of this bias are the narrow objectives of judicial management and the court's interpretation of the just and equitable ground for granting a provisional and final judicial management order, both of which significantly restricted the access of companies to judicial management.[980]

As we have seen throughout this Chapter, judicial reluctance towards fully embracing a rescue culture has also occasionally shone through under the new rescue regime, for example the restrictive interpretation of the

supra-jurisdictional force shaping company law, namely international competition (see Armour, Hansmann and Kraakman (see above in this footnote) 32ff), appears to be of less relevance to shaping national corporate insolvency law. International best practice guides, such as the World Bank Insolvency and Creditor/ Debtor Rights Systems (*revised 2015*) <http://siteresources.worldbank.org/EXTGILD/Resources/5807554-1357753926066/2015_Revised_ICR_Principles%283%29.pdf> accessed 10 January 2017 and the UNCITRAL Model Guide on Insolvency Law (Parts 1–4) <http://www.uncitral.org/uncitral/en/uncitral_texts/insolvency/2004Guide.html> accessed 10 January 2017, would also appear to have a lesser bearing on developing more established insolvency jurisdictions.

978 On the *standards strategy*, see PART A, Chapter 1, II., 2., a., bb. above.

979 Martin, 'Common-Law Bankruptcy Systems: Similarities and Differences' (2003) 11 Am. Bankr. Inst. L. Rev. 367, 374–5.

980 See PART B, Chapter 3, III., 3., c. above. On the conservatism of the courts generally, see *Le Roux Hotel Management (Pty) Ltd v E Rand (Pty) Ltd* 2001 (2) SA 727, para 39. See also Burdette, 'LLD thesis' (n 537) 347.

rescuability entry ground by earlier courts.[981] An indication of path dependence is the difficulties demonstrated by earlier decisions in recognising the secondary objective of rescue (ie, the realisation of assets),[982] where the courts were presumably influenced by the absence of a similar objective under judicial management.

Moreover, South Africa has adopted the British general attitude of scepticism of entrepreneurial risk-taking and disapproval of business failure, while financiers are arguably regarded with respect and sympathy.[983] An important illustration of this attitude in the South African rescue procedure, unlike Chapter 11 in the US, for example, is the management-displacing system of governance: since the incumbent directors are generally perceived to be responsible for the company's problems in the first place, they are seen as the least suited persons to lead a company out of its financial problems during rescue proceedings.[984] Moreover, although under the new rescue procedure the board of directors is entitled to place the company under rescue proceedings out-of-court, they may only do so when the company is close to a state of insolvency (ie, 'financial distress').[985] This contrasts with the absence of an insolvency ground for the commencement of Chapter 11 proceedings in the US.[986] Nor does the South African rescue procedure provide for priority ranking of post-commencement external

---

981 See the discussion in PART B, Chapter 4, IV., 2., a., dd. above.

982 See the cases in n 599 above in this Chapter and accompanying text.

983 See generally Rochelle, 'Lower the Penalties for Failure: Using the Insolvency Law as a Tool for Spurring Economic Growth; the American Experience, and Possible Uses for South Africa' (1996) 2 TSAR 315. On the sympathy for financiers in the UK, see Moss, 'Comparative Bankruptcy Cultures: Rescue or Liquidations? Comparisons of Trends in National Law—England' (1997) 23 Brook. J. Int'l L.; McCormack, 'Control and Corporate Rescue – An Anglo-American Evaluation (2007) 56 ICLQ 515, 525.

984 For the US and the UK, see Goode, *Principles of Corporate Insolvency Law* (3rd edn, Sweet & Maxwell, 2005) 328; Martin (n 979) 374; Moss, 'Chapter 11: An English Lawyer's Critique' (1998) 11 Insolv.Int. 17, 18–19; Moss, 'Comparative Bankruptcy Cultures' (n 983) 115; Carruthers and Halliday, *Rescuing Business: The Making of Corporate Bankruptcy Law in England and the United States* (Clarendon Press, 1998) 246; Westbrook, 'A Comparison of Bankruptcy Reorganization in the US With the Administrative Procedure in the UK' [1990] I.L. & P. 86. See generally McCormack (n 983) 522.

985 For a discussion of the financial distress entry ground, see PART B, Chapter 4, IV., 2., a., cc. and PART B, Chapter 4, IV., 2., b., cc. above.

986 We will revisit this difference in approach to entry again in Chapter 7 where we consider the legal strategies controlling the problem of premature entry.

funders, thereby preferring not to encourage such funding. This could be seen as a rejection of the potential that such a priority could prolong rescue proceedings at the expense of secured creditors' rights. The opposite is true for the Chapter 11 in the US, where such super-preference external funding (which is referred to as 'debtor-in-possession finance') is provided .[987]

In the US, the strong rights awarded to the incumbent directors and shareholders (debtor-in-possession and exclusivity period), the emphasis on the maintenance of the corporate entity through capital reorganisation over its dissolution through a going concern sale (at least up until the 1990s) and the general distrust of banks, appear to have their roots in a strong entrepreneurial culture of society in general.[988] The particular circumstances of the railroad receiverships of the mid- to late 18th Century appear to have played an important tole in this regard. The relevance of the railroad receiverships is predicated on several factors.[989] First, given the particular nature of the railroads, there was uncertainty at the time whether Congress or the States had jurisdiction over them. As a result, when many of the railroad companies went bankrupt, a regulatory vacuum existed.[990] This opened the opportunity for the railroad managers to turn to

---

987 11 USC § 364(c), (d). Yet, somewhat ironically, debtor-in-possession finance has been argued to be the reason for a power shift from shareholder-regarding directors to financiers under Chapter 11 proceedings in recent years. This has apparently resulted in a stronger emphasis on quick going concern sales in Chapter 11 proceedings; see, eg, Warren and Westbrook, 'Secured Party in Possession' (2003) 11 Am. Bankr. Inst. L. Rev. 12; Baird and Rasmussen, 'Four (or Five) Easy Lessons From Enron' (2002) 55 Vand.L.Rev 1787, 1807; Skeel Jr, 'Creditors' Ball: The "New" New Corporate Governance of in Chapter 11' (2003) 152 U.Pa.L.Rev. 917; Skeel Jr, 'The Past, Present and Future of Debtor-in-Possession Finance' [2004] Cardozo L.Rev. 1905; Baird, 'The New Face of Chapter 11' (2004) 12 Am. Bankr. Inst. L. Rev. 69. See generally McCormack (n 983) 546ff.

988 See the references in n 984 above in this Chapter and accompanying text.

989 For a comprehensive discussion of the impact of the railroad bankruptcies on bankruptcy law in the US, see, eg, McCormack (n 983) 536ff; Skeel Jr, 'An Evolutionary Theory of Corporate Law and Corporate Bankruptcy' (1998) 51 Vand.L.Rev. 1325; Skeel Jr, *Debt's Dominion* (Princeton University Press, 2001); Armour, Cheffins and Skeel Jr, 'Corporate Ownership Structure and the Evolution of Bankruptcy Law: Lessons from the United Kingdom' (2002) 55 Vand.L.Rev 1699.

990 McCormack (n 983) 537; Hansen, 'The people's welfare and the origins of corporate reorganization: The Wabash receivership reconsidered' (2000) 74 Bus. Hist. Rev. 377.

the courts for negotiated *ad hoc* restructuring proposals, often with little creditor involvement. Moreover, the railroad managers were often appointed as receivers.[991] The combination of these factors might be seen as the origin of the powers of the incumbent directors under Chapter 11 proceedings today.[992]

The second factor is that due to the major importance of the railroads for the US economy at the time, their continued existence was regarded to be in the public interest. Moreover, due to the intrinsic nature of railroads, the companies owning them were clearly worth more as a going concern than broken up. Moreover, a market for the underlying business of such companies presumably did not exist at the time. This is often seen as the source of the bias for capital reorganisations over going concern sales under Chapter 11 proceedings in the US.[993]

A further factor that appears to have shaped British and Australian corporate insolvency law is floating charge security, which was never received in South Africa. This might explain why secured creditors have never been granted the same level of control in corporate insolvency proceedings as they do in the UK and Australia.[994] The administration procedures in both the UK and Australia have been heavily influenced by the administrative receivership procedure. This procedure is designed specifically for a receiver to realise the security of floating charge-holders (usually banks) solely in their interests. The control rights of floating charge-holders over the initiation procedure of administration and, arguably, the bias in practice for going concern sales over capital reorganisations under administration might be seen as a legacy of administrative receivership.[995]

Instead, the South African rescue procedure affords strong rights to employees, as we have seen before, notably strong protection of employment

991 Although it is said that the trend that railroad managers were appointed as receivers only started with the notorious bankruptcy of the Wabash railroad (*Central Trust Co v Wabash* (1886) 29 Fed 618, 626), it has been shown that this trend had started long before that; see Hansen (n 990) 377. See generally McCormack (n 983) 537.

992 See generally McCormack (n 983) 536ff.

993 Ibid. However, for evidence that directors are frequently replaced during Chapter 11 proceedings, see references cited in n 86 in Chapter 1.

994 On the control awarded to floating charge-holders in corporate insolvency procedures in the UK and Australia, see PART B, Chapter 4, IV., 2., c.

995 McCormack (n 983) 535ff; Armour and Mokal (n 609).

contracts during rescue proceedings;[996] super-preference of pre-commencement employment claims;[997] and particularly strong participation rights.[998] It would seem, however, that the emphasis on protecting employees is more a result of a need to combat current socio-economic realities (notably the high unemployment rate)[999] and the political influence of trade unions, than of legal culture or path dependence.

3. The nature of the lending markets

Apart from the legal culture and path dependence, the nature of the lending markets has been suggested as a further force that may possibly shape corporate insolvency law. A theory has been advanced that predicts every market will evolve in a way that results in a correlation between the structure of the lending markets and the governance structure of insolvency proceedings, on the one hand and the debt structure and ownership structure, on the other hand. It is argued that in jurisdictions where the lending is concentrated in the hands of a few banks, one would expect to see a management-displacing system of governance in corporate insolvency proceedings. This is because the banks can use the threat of placing the company under insolvency proceedings as a useful 'lever' to cause the directors to have regard for the banks' interests. In that way, banks are able to reduce company-creditor agency costs in the vicinity of insolvency. In debtor-in-possession jurisdictions, however, the directors of distressed companies are able to respond to the demands of the concentrated lenders by invoking rescue proceedings. This would increase company-creditor agency costs in the vicinity of insolvency. Moreover, due to information advantages and low monitoring costs, in a management displacing system of governance, banks would be able to respond appropriately by instigating an informal workout. Failing that, banks would be in a position to dis-

996 See PART B, Chapter 4, IV., 6., e. above.
997 See PART B, Chapter 4, IV., 7. above.
998 See PART A, Chapter 1, III. above. For a view that executive directors fall within the meaning of 'employees' for purposes of the business rescue procedure, see Joubert and Loubser, 'Executive directors in business rescue: employees or something else?' (2016) 49 De Jure 95.
999 The latest statistics show that in the third quarter of 2015, the unemployment rate in South Africa was 27.1%; Statistics South Africa <http://www.statssa.gov.za/?page_id=737&id=1> accessed 10 January 2017.

tinguish between good and poor management, and make the most costs-effective decision as to the management of the company during formal rescue proceedings, thereby minimising office holder-company agency costs. Why would banks want to keep the incumbent management on board in cases of exogenous causes to the company's decline? Because management will generate lower costs in familiarising themselves with the company's affairs and the industry in which the company operates than an external office holder (hereafter, '*familiarisation costs*').

The opposite is true for jurisdictions with dispersed debt. Due to collective action problems, the creditors will face high co-ordination costs, limiting their ability to use the threat of initiating insolvency proceedings as a 'lever' to keep the incumbent directors in check. Moreover, in cases where the company's distress is due to exogenous factors, dispersed creditors will find it difficult to co-ordinate an informal workout due to the collective action problem. This means that the company is likely to be placed under formal insolvency proceedings where the incumbent directors are likely to be sidelined by an external office holder, giving rise to high familiarisation costs, even in cases where the company's financial troubles were not caused by management. For this reason, one would expect a debtor-in-possession system of governance in jurisdictions with dispersed debt.[1000]

Moreover, it is argued that a market with concentrated share ownership will always go together with concentrated lending structures, while dispersed ownership will go together with dispersed debt. The reason for the first-mentioned relationship is that concentrated debt will be more readily available to a company with concentrated ownership, given the collective action problems of dispersed lenders in controlling company-creditor agency costs. By contrast, the second-mentioned relationship comes about because companies with dispersed ownership will be able to obtain debt finance at lower costs from the public debt market, as the need to monitor the directors will be low, given that company-creditor agency costs are also likely to be low. Furthermore, a company with dispersed debt should be able to raise equity at lower costs than a company with concentrated debt, as the executives of a company with concentrated debt might be too risk averse.[1001]

1000 This paraphrases Armour, Cheffins and Skeel (n 989) 1699.
1001 Ibid 1763.

However, this theory does not seem to always accord with reality. For example, the UK has a concentrated debt structure, but an insolvency regime with a management-displacing system of governance and dispersed share ownership.[1002] It is argued, however, that the UK is increasingly moving towards a more dispersed debt structure, which will ultimately result in a debtor-in-possession system of governance of its insolvency procedure.[1003]

What does seem to be clear, is that the co-operation of lenders in informal restructuring efforts (such as the London Approach) would be more likely in a concentrated lending market, as the lenders' investments in companies will be large enough to justify the costs of monitoring and coordinating informal rescue mechanisms.[1004]

The South African corporate insolvency law might fit the theory, as it would seem to have relative concentration in share ownership,[1005] a concentrated lending market[1006] and its rescue procedure has a management displacing governance system. It is expected that the concentrated debt patterns would encourage the development of an informal rescue market.

VII. Summary and conclusion

The procedural separation of insolvency procedures raises the direct costs of moving between different procedures. The decision as to whether to move between procedures is made by the court and the rescue practitioner is prohibited from remaining in office after a conversion. This raises the procedural costs and the costs of the office holder to familiarise himself with the company's affairs ('familiarisation costs'). A preferable approach would be to permit extra-judicial conversion, either by the rescue practitioner or the creditors' meeting by majority vote, as in the UK and Australia, respectively.

1002 McCormack (n 983) 543ff.

1003 Armour, Cheffins and Skeel (n 989) 1775–6.

1004 Ibid 1774.

1005 Alves, 'Corporate Ownership: Some International Evidence' (2010) International Research Journal of Finance and Economics Issue 41 SSRN http://papers.ssrn.com/sol3/papers.cfm?abstract_id=1304197 accessed 16 January 2017.

1006 This is merely a conjecture based on personal observations.

The separation of the scheme of arrangement with creditors and with shareholders under the new Companies Act could lead to duplicative procedural costs, and as a result raise the costs of capital restructuring measures.

Since the current rescue procedure would seem to provide for certain procedural requirements that are not strictly necessary for the restructuring of small companies, the introduction of a rescue procedure for small companies should be considered by the legislature. Two possible approaches are (i) introducing a separate and self-contained procedure for small companies (such as the CVA in the UK) or (ii) specific provisions that apply to small companies under the main rescue proceedings (as in the US).

Unlike under judicial management, rescue practitioners are now regulated under a two-tiered system of regulation – ie, required licensing of persons who are not members of the accounting, legal and business management professions, and accreditation of relevant institutions within such professions. However, the Commission is currently granting licences on an *ad hoc* and conditional basis pending research on an appropriate licensing and accreditation approach.

The business rescue procedure allows for both reorganisation and going concern sales. This significantly broadens the rescue objectives compared to judicial management. The two objectives of rescue are structured in a hierarchy of importance.

The courts have leaned towards excluding break-up sales from the objectives of rescue. However, this conclusion is questionable. As long as there is a sound factual basis that break-up sales would fetch higher returns for creditors if they were conducted under rescue proceedings instead of under winding-up proceedings, the creditors should not be denied of such higher returns.

It would seem that the adoption of a rescue plan is mandatory under business rescue in South Africa, on the grounds that the rescue practitioners' powers are derived primarily from the plan procedure, including the creditors' meeting, rather than from the rescue objectives in conjunction with the rescue practitioners' duties *ex post*. Accordingly, a quick sale of the company's business outside the plan procedure, and thus without the authority of the creditors' meeting, does not seem to be allowed under the South African procedure, notwithstanding their commercial appeal. This contrasts with the position in the UK.

In contrast to judicial management, the South African rescue procedure provides for a dual entry route. The addition of the out-of-court entry route by the directors could promote the timeous invocation of rescue proceedings.

The two primary requirements for the commencement of rescue proceedings are that the company is 'financially distressed' (ie, in a state of impending insolvency) and that there is a reasonable prospect of success of rescue, which is defined with reference to the two objectives of rescue mentioned above.

South Africa does not afford secured creditors the same level of control over the appointment and management of rescue proceedings as that afforded to floating charge-holders (primarily banks) in the UK and Australia.

The statutory moratorium under the South African rescue procedure gives rise to four pertinent issues. First, the fact that the moratorium (s 133 Companies Act 2008) applies to legal proceedings brought 'within a forum' would seem to suggest that contractual private enforcement (for example, *parate executie*) falls outside its scope. Second, the moratorium does not preclude cancellation of a contract by a creditor after the company has been placed under rescue proceedings. Third, the description of the type of property that falls within the moratorium ('property belonging to the company or lawfully within in its possession') would seem to catch all types of real security and quasi-security, save, arguably, for the 'out-and-out transfer construction' of the *cession in securitatem debiti,* since under such construction 'ownership' of the ceded rights passes to the cessionary. And fourth, the moratorium does not preclude enforcement by creditors of the company against third party sureties of the company's obligations.

S 134(1)(b), (c) Companies Act 2008 provides that no person may exercise any rights against property belonging to the company and in its lawful possession. The cancellation of property in the lawful possession of the company by a creditor before, and probably also after, the commencement of rescue proceedings deprives the property of its 'lawfulness', and such property accordingly falls outside the scope of the moratorium.

The power of the practitioner to suspend, and the court to cancel, uncompleted contracts under s 136(2)(a) and (b) Companies Act 2008 gives rise to five interpretational difficulties, which have been proposed to be resolved as follows.

First, the right of the creditors to cancel an agreement would not be precluded by the practitioner's suspension of such agreement pursuant to s 136(2)(a), where the grounds upon which the agreement was cancelled subsisted prior to the commencement of rescue proceedings.

Second, suspension and cancellation under s 136(2)(a) would seem to be subject to the contractual doctrine of reciprocity and severability. Under the doctrine of reciprocity, a counterparty would be entitled to raise the common law defence of *exceptio non adimpleti contractus* where the company does not perform a reciprocal obligation as a result of the suspension and cancellation. Under the doctrine of severability, the entire contract would fail if the suspended or cancelled part is not severable from the entire contract.

Third, the better view is that s 136(2)(a), (b) permit the suspension and cancellation of entire agreements and 'obligations of the company', but not individual 'provisions' of an agreement.

Fifth, the exemption of employees from the practitioners' powers of suspension and cancellation (s 136(2A)) would not seem to include managerial employees (see s 140(1)(c)).

And sixth, it would seem that a suspension or cancellation under s 136(2)(a), (b) would constitute a breach of contract, but that only the statutory remedy of damages under s 136(3) is available for such breaches.

In contrast to liquidation proceedings, the State does not rank as a preferential creditor under rescue proceedings. Moreover employees are given a super-preference ranking in respect of post-commencement employees' claims.

The South African rescue procedure uses a management-displacing system of governance.

In order to ensure that the rescue practitioner is accountable to the claimants, he is saddled with several duties, which include relevant codified common law fiduciary duties and the duty of care.

The application of the directors' duties to practitioners raises three pertinent issues. First, although some of the common law fiduciary duties (for example, the duty to act within powers and the duty to exercise independent judgment), and some of the remedies for breach of the relevant duties, do not appear to have been codified, s 140(3)(b) should be read in a way which does not preclude the application of such non-codified common law duties and remedies.

Second, it could be argued that the fact that the business judgment rule applies to the duty to act in the best interest of the company, implies that it is no longer subjective, as at common law, but rather objective under the Companies Act 2008. This would make the best interests duty much more demanding on rescue practitioners.

Third, the content of the 'best interests' of the company would appear to be the interests of the creditors as a whole and the promotion of the rescue objectives in the order of preference stipulated. How much time and how many costs the practitioner should spend in pursuing the chosen rescue objective, is likely to be mediated either through the best interests duty or the duty of care.

The South African rescue procedure relies heavily on the remedy of the removal of a rescue practitioner. The removal grounds in s 138(1)(e) (compromised relationship with company), s 139(2)(e) (conflict of interest and lack of independence) and s 130(1)(b)(ii) (lack of independence from company and management) can be seen to ameliorate the risk of the appointment of a friendly rescue practitioner, which will be discussed in Chapter 7.

A 'relationship with the company that compromises [the practitioners'] integrity, impartiality or objectivity' ('compromised relationship') under s 138(1)(e) would seem to be broader in scope than a relationship of dependence under s 130(1)(b)(ii) and s 139(2)(e). On the other hand, the persons with whom the practitioner is not allowed to have a relevant relationship is broader under s 139(2)(e) than under s 138(1)(e) (pursuant to which the relationship needs to be with the company) and s 130(1)(b)(ii) (pursuant to which the relationship needs to be with the company or its management).

It would seem that any person who had a close professional relationship with the company before it was placed under rescue proceedings, for example, the company's auditors, attorneys, tax consultants and general financial advisors could, in principle, fall within the ambit of s 138(1)(e), particularly where such persons had assisted the company in a pre-rescue workout and a pre-packaged plan. The courts will need to be sensitive to the advantages of informal rescue measures in reducing the direct and indirect costs of financial distress when interpreting this provision.

Part D of the Companies Act 2008 provides for the development of a rescue plan on which creditors vote. A cramdown mechanism is provided to counteract holdout creditors.

It is not clear why secured creditors are entitled to vote the full portion of their claims on the rescue plan, given that they would only carry the risk of the rescue outcome to the extent of their unsecured portion. This could increase inter-creditor agency costs during rescue proceedings.

The new compromise procedure has reduced some of the direct costs of the previous procedure: (i) removal of court approval to convene meetings of creditors; (ii) dispensing with the need of a Chairman to preside over meetings; and (iii) placing publications in newspapers.

Although directors are now entitled to propose a compromise with creditors procedure, a significant drawback to its utilisation outside formal insolvency proceedings is the lack of a moratorium.

The new compromise procedure has introduced the requirement that the scheme be 'just and equitable' when the court is asked to sanction it. In interpreting this requirement, courts are expected to draw on principles established by case law under the previous scheme of arrangement procedure, including considerations regarding procedural irregularities and the reasonableness and fairness of the scheme.

The debt consolidation scheme seems to still be available under the compromise with creditors. The Companies Act 2008 has not introduced any specific remedy for the protection of post-scheme creditors of a debt consolidation scheme.

Legal culture and path dependencies could explain some of the features of the new rescue law, such as the management-displacing system of governance and the absence of super-preference external funding during rescue proceedings, while the strong employee rights under the new procedure appear to be an outgrowth of socio-economic realities.

Since the proprietary rights of secured creditors are restrained to a much greater degree under the new rescue procedure than under judicial management, it is expected that banks will play a bigger role in promoting informal rescue mechanisms. The costs of doing so may be reduced by the fact that South Africa appears to have a concentrated lending market.

Although the South African procedure has certain characteristics that suggests it will favour going concern sales over reorganisations (legal cultural factors, management-displacing governance system, absence of super-preference ranking for external funding), the strong rights of employees under business rescue would seem to hinder such a development.

PART C
CRITICAL EVALUATION OF LEGAL RESPONSES TO THE THREE MANIFESTATIONS OF THE COMPANY-CREDITOR AGENCY CONFLICT IN THE VICINITY OF INSOLVENCY

Chapter 5 The First Manifestation of the Company-Creditor Agency Conflict in the Vicinity of Insolvency: Company Controllers' Perverse Incentive in Respect of Trading Decision in the Vicinity of Insolvency

I. Introduction

As we saw in Chapter 1, one of the manifestations of the company-creditor agency conflict in the vicinity of insolvency is where the company controllers have a perverse incentive to either continue trading, notwithstanding that the company's assets would have been placed to their highest value use if the company would be placed under formal rescue or liquidation proceedings, or to pursue excessively risky projects. This perverse incentive arises where the shareholders' economic interest in the company has been depleted and is unlikely to be restored through the company's established business model. The reason for this is that at that point, shareholders no longer carry the risk of corporate projects and can look solely to the upside of such projects, regardless of the chances of their success, given that the doctrine of limited liability protects shareholders' personal assets from the failure of the company. Instead, the risk of corporate projects falls solely on creditors. (Because the risk of any losses incurred by the company as a result of continued trading *shifts* from the shareholders to the creditors, this perverse incentive will be referred to as the '*risk-shifting incentive*'.)

The manifestation of this perverse incentive is slightly different from the other value-minimising action explained by the risk-shifting incentive – namely the extension of shareholder loans (which we will consider in Chapter 6). This is because under the action of concern in this Chapter, it is the strategic trading decision whether to continue trading in the vicinity of insolvency and to embark on overly risky projects that could harm the creditors. Under the problem of shareholder loans, by contrast, it is the advancement of funds in the form of the shareholder loan that might enable the company controllers to embark on the strategic decision to continue trading inappropriately.[1007]

The emphasis on the *strategic* nature of the decision is also the reason why the primary focus of this Chapter is not transactions by company controllers out of the assets of the company with the aim or effect of harming the body of (unsecured) creditors (which generally fall under the heading of 'asset dilution' transactions). Nor is the main focus transactions favouring some creditors over others (which, to the extent that the favoured creditors exert influence over the company controllers without being connected to them, forms part of the inter-creditor agency conflict outside insolvency proceedings).[1008]

The most common approach relied on by South Africa and the other management-displacing jurisdictions to control the company controllers' risk-shifting incentive is a number of *ex post standards* strategies. In addition, South Africa also employs, rather unusually, an *ex ante initiation rights strategy*.

The most common *ex post standards strategy* in this regard is the statutory creditor-regarding duties in the vicinity of insolvency. In South Africa, this is the reckless trading duty under ss 22(1) read with s 77(3)(b) Companies Act 2008.[1009] Equivalent legal strategies, which also impose creditor-regarding duties on directors in the vicinity of insolvency, are found in the UK, Australia and Germany. The US, by contrast, relies on a *reward strategy*, in the form of the debtor-in-possession, as mentioned in Chapter 1. We will examine the creditor-regarding duties of the abovementioned jurisdictions from a comparative perspective at II below.

We will then consider three further possible *ex post standards* strategies found in the jurisdictions in question in III below.

First, it has been argued that the rationale of the British statutory clawback of undervalue transactions (s 238 Insolvency Act 1986) is to address the problem of the application of low risk assets to high risk projects (ie,

---

1007 See also Davies, 'Directors' Creditor-Regarding Duties in the Vicinity of Insolvency' (2006) 7 EBOR 301, 302–3.

1008 Ibid 303. Notwithstanding this differentiation, we will consider a type of such transactions under German law under § 62 *GmbH-Gesetz* and § 92(2) *Aktiengesetz* mainly because these provisions are systematically closely connected with the creditor-regarding duty to refrain from the strategic decision in question under § 15a *Insolvenzordnung*.

1009 Each section cited in this Chapter, both in the body of the text and in the footnotes, will be a section of the Companies Act 2008, unless otherwise indicated.

'asset substitution').[1010] We will briefly look into whether the equivalent South African provision (the setting aside of transactions 'without value' under s 26 Insolvency Act 1936) and the equivalent German provisions (the setting aside of transactions disadvantaging creditors and gratuitous benefits under §§ 132 and 134 *Insolvenzordnung*, respectively) could be seen to perform a similar purpose (see III.1. below).

Second, South African law provides for delictual liability for the incurrence of debt without a reasonable expectation of discharging such liability. We will explore to what extent such liability might ameliorate the risk-shifting incentive (see III.2. below).

Third, some common law jurisdictions have developed a directors' common law duty to creditors in the vicinity of insolvency. However, an equivalent directors' duty has apparently not yet been introduced in South Africa. We will examine the merits of this duty for purposes of controlling the perverse incentive in question, and the role such a duty could play in South African law (see III.3. below).

We will finally examine the peculiar *ex ante initiation rights strategy* employed in South Africa in IV. below.

II. The primary ex post standards strategy: Statutory creditor-regarding duty of directors in the vicinity of insolvency – comparative perspectives from the UK, Australia and Germany

1. Some theoretical aspects of the directors' statutory creditor-regarding duty

a. The target of the duty

The imposition of liability for wrongful trading in the vicinity of insolvency generally targets directors even though it is actually the shareholders whose perverse incentive gives rise to the potential for value-minimising trading. This approach is justified on the basis that shareholders can only implement their actions through the directors, given the separation of management and control in company law. By imposing liability on directors, the law provides a counter-incentive to directors for taking shareholder-re-

1010 For the meaning of the term 'asset substitution', see Chapter 1 above.

garding actions in the vicinity of insolvency and, in that way, counteract the risk-shifting incentive of shareholders.[1011]

The fact that the risk-shifting incentive actually emanates from the shareholders does mean, however, that it is probably stronger in companies in which directors are effectively accountable to shareholders, such as in closely-held companies. This is because shareholders in such companies either sit on the boards themselves or typically have better information and lower co-ordination costs than widely dispersed shareholders, which enables them to influence the management of the company to a greater extent than in widely-held companies.[1012]

However, even where directors are not accountable to shareholders, their interests may be aligned with the risk-shifting incentive of shareholders, as directors may risk losing their jobs in insolvency. Of course, the extent of the perverse incentive of directors is greater in jurisdictions that employ a management-displacing, rather than a debtor-in-possession, system of governance, since directors are effectively removed from office under the former system of governance.[1013] The US uses a different legal strategy in this regard: the retention of control awarded to directors during Chapter 11, coupled with the absence of an insolvency ground of entry, could be seen as *rewarding* (shareholder-regarding) directors with a continued stake in the company for the early invocation of rescue proceedings; this could thus be seen as an *ex ante reward strategy*.[1014] From the perspective of legal culture, the US could be seen to have greater confidence than South Africa,e UK and Australia in the formal rescue procedure to resolve the company-creditor agency conflict in the vicinity of insolvency.[1015]

The fact that in management-displacing systems of governance of insolvency proceedings the degree of the risk-shifting incentive may vary according to the ownership structure of companies, raises the theoretical

1011 Davies, 'Directors' Creditor-Regarding Duties' (n 1007) 312.

1012 Davies, 'Directors' Creditor-Regarding Duties' (n 1007) 308; Mokal, *Corporate Insolvency Law* (Oxford University Press 2005) 289ff.

1013 Davies, 'Directors' Creditor-Regarding Duties' (n 1007) 308.

1014 Armour, Hertig and Kanda, 'Transactions with Creditors' in Kraakman and other (eds), *The Anatomy of Corporate Law – A Comparative and Functional Approach* (2nd edn, Oxford University Press 2009) 116, 145ff.

1015 For a possible explanation on the grounds of borrowing patterns for the adoption of management-displacing vs debtor-in-possession governance regime in certain common law jurisdictions, see PART B, Chapter 4, VI., 3. above.

question about the need for modifying the intensity of liability according to the ownership structures of companies.[1016] However, the introduction of such varying degrees of liability seem undesirable, since it may not significantly reduce the cost of compliance of directors *ex ante*, but is likely to significantly increase the cost of litigation *ex post*.[1017]

Notwithstanding that the focus of liability of the statutory creditor-regarding duty is the (shareholder-regarding) directors, it is obviously not in the public interest that persons (shareholders and others) who act as a director or exercise significant influence over the management of the company without being formerly appointed as such should escape liability. Jurisdictions are therefore generally prepared to extend liability to such persons.[1018]

In the UK (and presumably also South Africa), liability to such other persons is generally extended through the concepts of '*de facto*' and 'shadow' directors.[1019] A *de facto* director actually exercises the functions of a director, whether or not he has been appointed to that position, while a shadow director (merely) directs the actions of the board so that the board becomes accustomed to act in accordance with such directions on a continuing basis.[1020] The distinction between these two concepts thus turns on how the person presents himself to the public: while a *de facto* director claims to act and purports to act as a director, a shadow director exercises

---

1016 See Mokal (n 1012) 285ff.

1017 See also Davies, 'Directors' Creditor-Regarding Duties' (n 1007) 308ff.

1018 Ibid 312.

1019 The British law concepts of *de facto* and shadow directors would appear to fall within the definition of directors under the South African Companies 2008, according to which a director '[…] includes any persons occupying the position of a director [...] by whatever name designated'. See R Cassim, 'Governance and the Board of Directors' in FHI Cassim (man. ed), *Contemporary Company Law* (2nd edn, Juta 2012) 372, 375–6. There is even some evidence in the common law (*S v De Jager* 1965 (2) SA 616 (A)) that shadow directors were recognised even though they were not referred to as such; see R Cassim (as cited in this footnote) 382.

1020 For the UK, see ss 214(7) and the definition of 'director' in s 251 Insolvency Act 1986, s 251 Companies Act 2006. Particularly on shadow directors see also *Secretary of State for Trade and Industry v Becker* [2003] 1 B.C.L.C. 565; *Secretary of State for Trade and Industry v Deverell* [2000] 2 B.C.L.C. 133, CA; see generally Davies and Worthington, *Gower and Davies Principles of Modern Company Law* (10th edn, Sweet & Maxwell 2016) para 9-7ff.

control over the board 'behind the scenes'.[1021] In saying that, the difference sometimes becomes blurred by the fact that in practice the influence of a person on the board may be open at times and concealed at others.[1022] However, it seems that it is generally not necessary to distinguish between the two concepts for purposes of directors' creditor-regarding statutory duties in the vicinity of insolvency.[1023]

The creditor-regarding duties in the vicinity of insolvency could in theory also be extended to banks for exerting influence over the management of the company in the vicinity of insolvency with the aim or effect of enhancing the chances of the recovery of their claims at the expense of unsecured creditors.[1024] Possible actions of banks that could give rise to liability in this regard are, most obviously, the appointment of a bank representative to the board of directors or the imposition of restrictions on the management of the company by more subtle means, for example by way of contractual covenants in funding agreements governing the provision of bank funding to distressed companies.[1025]

The regulation of liability of banks for losses to the company or other classes of creditors in the vicinity of insolvency needs to balance the need to protect unsecured creditors from self-interested actions of banks and the need to promote the use of informal rescue measures, particularly since the provision of further bank funding may in practice often be crucial for the success of a private workout.[1026]

1021 Davies and Worthington (n 1021) para 16-9.

1022 See, eg, the English case *Re Kaytech International Plc; Portier v Secretary of State Trade and Industry* [1999] BCC 390, 402.

1023 In this regard on English law, see Davies, 'Directors' Creditor-Regarding Duties' (n 1007) 312, n 27. See also Steffek, *Gläubigerschutz in der Kapitalgesellschaft* (Mohr Siebeck 2011) 390ff, 500.

1024 See Davies, 'Directors' Creditor-Regarding Duties' (n 1007) 312. See also Steffek, 'Gläubigerschutz' (n 1023) 390ff, 506ff.

1025 For the UK, see Davies, 'Directors' Creditor-Regarding Duties' (n 1007) 312. For Germany, see Wagner, '§ 826' in Habersack (ed), *Münchener Kommentar zum Bürgerlich Gesetzbuch* (vol. 5) (6th edn, C.H. Beck 2013) recitals 112ff. It should be noted, as we saw in Chapter 1, this more subtle form of banks exerting influence over directorial decision-making in order to extract benefits for themselves at the expense of unsecured creditors could also be regarded as a manifestation of the inter-creditor agency problem in the vicinity of insolvency (see PART A, Chapter 1, II., 3., b. above).

1026 Davies, 'Directors' Creditor-Regarding Duties' (n 1007) 312; Prentice, 'Corporate Personality, Limited Liability and the Protection of Creditors' in Grantham

It seems that in the UK the scales are tipped in favour of promoting a rescue culture in that banks are generally not classified as shadow directors if their influence on management serves to safeguard their own interests, provided the company retained the power to decide whether to accept the restrictions posposed by the bank.[1027] It is suggested that the South African courts apply the same degree of sensitivity to this question.

In Germany, banks could be held liable either as an accessory for the commission of a delict by another under §§ 830, 840 *BGB* ('*Teilnehmerhaftung*')[1028] or for causing intentional damage to another contrary to public policy under § 826 *BGB* ('*sittenwidrige vorsätzliche Schädigung*').[1029] Since both provisions require subjective intention on the part of the defendant,[1030] the level of liability of banks appears to be similarly low as in the UK.[1031]

b. The recipients of the duty

Since the risk-shifting incentive generally arises when the shareholders' funds have been wiped out, and assuming that at such time the secured creditors are not undersecured, the losses incurred by the company as a result of the opportunistic trading will primarily fall on unsecured creditors. The focus of protection of any regulation should therefore also be unsecured creditors, particularly in respect of recoveries from liable directors.[1032] Moreover, due to the collective action problem of unsecured cred-

---

and Rickett (eds), *Corporate Personality in the 20th Century* (Hart Publishing 1998) 99, 114–5. From a German perspective, see Wagner (n 1025) recital 113; Kuder and Unverdorben, 'Die Rolle der Kreditinstitute' in Schmidt and others (eds), *Die GmbH in Krise, Sanierung und Insolvenz* (5th edn, Otto Schmidt 2015) 309.

1027 *Hydrodan (Corby Ltd, Re* [1994] 2 BCLC 180; *Re PFTZM Ltd* [1995] 2 BCLC 354. See generally Davies and Worthington (n 1021) para 9-7; Steffek, 'Gläubigerschutz' (n 1023) 506–7.

1028 See generally Steffek, 'Gläubigerschutz' (n 1023) 507.

1029 Hopt, 'Bankgeschäfte' in Hopt (ed), *Baumbach/Hopt Handelsgesetzbuch Kommentar* (36th edn, C.H. Beck 2014) recitals G6, G31–2; Wagner (n 1025) recitals 112ff.

1030 In respect of §§ 830, 840 *BGB*, this is the majority view; see BGH NJW 2005, 3137, 3139; see generally Steffek, 'Gläubigerschutz' (n 1023) 502, 507.

1031 Steffek, 'Gläubigerschutz' (n 1023) 506ff.

1032 Davies, 'Directors' Creditor-Regarding Duties' (n 1007) 307.

itors, it is more appropriate for the protection to be in the form of mandatory law, rather than leaving it to creditors to protect themselves by contract.[1033]

However, where unsecured creditors would no longer have an economic interest in the company at the time that the perverse incentive arises (ie, where the assets of the company are not sufficient to provide a dividend for unsecured creditors in insolvency), unsecured creditors may themselves have a perverse incentive to embark on value-minimising projects. In such a situation, the law should therefore deny recoveries to unsecured creditors who are proved to have consented to or encouraged the company controllers' decision to continue trading, as is the case in Australia, for example.[1034]

2. The South African reckless trading duty

a. General

In South Africa, the statutory duty that could be seen as addressing the company controllers' risk-shifting incentive is contained in s 22(1) read with s 77(3)(b) Companies Act 2008. This section provides that 'a company must not carry on its business recklessly, with gross negligence, with intent to defraud any person or for any fraudulent purpose'. The duty under s 22(1) is similar to the duty under s 424 Companies Act 1973. The relevant part of the reckless trading duty under s 424 is contained in sub-s 1 and reads as follows: 'When it appears, whether it be in a winding-up, judicial management or otherwise, that any business of the company was or is being carried on recklessly or with intent to defraud creditors of the company or creditors of any other person or for any fraudulent purpose, the court may, on the application of the Master, the liquidator, the judicial manager, any creditor or member or contributory of the company, declare that any person who was knowingly a party to the carrying on of the business in the manner aforesaid, shall be personally responsible, without any limitation of liability, for all or any of the debts or other liabilities of the company as the court may direct.' S 424 is contained in Ch 14 of the

1033 Ibid.

1034 According to s 588Y(2)(b) Corporations Act 2001. See generally Davies, 'Directors' Creditor-Regarding Duties' (n 1007) 307.

Companies Act 1973. This Chapter continues to apply under the Companies Act 2008 by virtue of item 9 of Sch 5 Companies Act 2008. This raises the question whether s 424 continues to apply despite the enactment of s 22(1) read with s 77(3)(b) under the new Companies Act. It would seem that it does not. The continued application of Ch 14 is limited to the provisions contained therein 'with respect to the winding-up and liquidation of companies under the new Companies Act'. S 424 arguably does not form part of the statutory winding-up scheme, as the liability that arises thereunder relates to directorial conduct that occurred prior to the invocation of winding-up proceedings. S 424 claims were generally only enforced during winding-up proceedings not because of its doctrinal nature, but rather because information deficits of potential claimants made it difficult to detect breaches of s 424 outside insolvency proceedings.[1035]

It would seem that this conclusion is supported by policy considerations. The temptation to argue that the differences between s 424 and s 22 read with s 77(3)(b)[1036] would ensure the widest scope of protection possible should be resisted. If both provisions would apply in parallel, any policy changes intended to be implement by the legislature under the new reckless trading provision[1037] would be reduced to absurdity if the previous provision were to continue to apply.

1035 Drawing the same conclusion, however for different reasons, see *Grancy Property Limited and Another v Gihwala and Others*; *In Re: Grancy Property Limited and Another v Gihwala and Others* (1961/10; 12193/11) [2014] ZAWCHC 97 (26 June 2014) para 42. For the opposite view, see Delport and others, *Henochsberg on the Companies Act 71 of 2008* (loose-leaf) (Lexis Nexis 2015) s 22, 104; Stevens and de Beer, 'The duty of care and skill, and reckless trading: Remedies in flux' (2016) 28 SA Merc LJ 250, 282–3; Phulunga, 'Lessons to be learned from reckless and fraudulent trading by a company: Section 424(1) of the Companies Act 61 of 1973 and sections 22 and 77(3)(b) of the Companies Act 71 of 2008' (2016) 28 SA Merc LJ 238, 239ff. For the view that s 424 still applies during liquidation proceedings, see *obiter dictum* in *Blue Farm Fashion Limited v Rapitrade 6 (Pty) Ltd and Others* (22288/2014) [2016] ZAWCHC 35 (1 April 2016) para 26.

1036 For the differences, see PART C, Chapter 5, II., 2., b. below.

1037 See with respect ot the recipients of the duty PART C, Chapter 5, II., 2., b., aa. and with respect to the nature of liability PART C, Chapter 5, II.,2., b., bb below.

It should be noted that s 22(1), like s 424, is not limited to the *continued trading in the vicinity of insolvency* that causes losses to the company.[1038] The duty under s 22(1) also includes *fraudulent conduct* by directors.[1039] It is the former conduct of s 22(1) that will primarily concern us in this Chapter, as such conduct could be seen to functionally control the risk-shifting incentive of the company controllers in the vicinity of insolvency.

The remedy for breaches of the duty under s 22(1) is the imposition of personal liability on directors under s 77(3)(b) 'for any loss, damages or costs sustained by the company as a direct or indirect consequence of [a] director having acquiesced in the carrying on of the company's business despite knowing that it was being conducted in a manner prohibited by section 22(1).'[1040] Civil liability for breaches of the duty under s 424 was contained in that section itself, which read in relevant parts: '[...] shall be personally responsible, without any limitation of liability, for all or any of the debts or other liabilities of the company as the court may direct.' There are two important differences between civil liability for breaches under the new and the old reckless trading duties, which may have important implications for the scope of new reckless trading duty. These will be discussed in section b below. The conduct prohibited, and the action required, by the duty under s 22(1), as well as its standard (ie, the applicable fault element) are also relevant to its function of ameliorating the company controllers' risk-shifting incentive. This will be considered in sections c and d, respectively. Finally, contravention of s 22(1) gives rise to remedies in addition to civil liability under s 77(3)(b), which will be discussed in section e below.

1038 This is covered by the limb of the duty that requires directors not to carry on the business of the company 'recklessly' (and 'with gross negligence'). As we will see below, the better view of the relationship between 'recklessness' and 'gross negligence' under s 22(1) is that 'gross negligence' constitutes the fault element of the reckless limb of the duty under s 22(1).

1039 This is covered by the limb of the duty that requires directors not to carry on the business of the company 'with intent to defraud any person or for any fraudulent purpose'.

1040 Further remedies for breaches of the duty under s 22(1) will be discussed at PART C, Chapter 5, II., 2., e below.

b. Pertinent differences between the new and the previous reckless trading duties

The first important difference between s 22(1) and s 424 is that the duty under s 22(1) appears to be owed only to the company,[1041] whereas the duty under s 424(1) was, in addition to being owed to the company, also owed to individual creditors. Second, liability under s 22(1) is solely compensatory, whereas liability under s 424 contained an additional punitive element.[1042]

We will consider these differences in turn.

aa. The recipients of the duty

While s 22(1) is owed only to the company, s 424 was owed to both the company and individual creditors.[1043] This follows from the fact that individual creditors and individual members (in addition to the insolvency office holder (hereafter, the '*office holder*') had *locus standi* to bring s 424 claims,[1044] and that they could do so not only during, but also outside

1041 For a discussion on this isse, see PART C, Chapter 5, II., 2., e., aa.

1042 It should be noted that an argument could be made that s 214(1)(c) provides for an additional basis of criminal liability for the 'fraud' limb of the prohibited conduct under s 22(1). S 214(1)(c) provides that 'a person is guilty of an offence if the person was knowingly a party to an act or omission by a company to defraud a creditor or employee of the company, or a holder of the company's securities, or with another fraudulent purpose.' The 'carrying on of [a company's] business' could be argued to constitute 'an act or omission by a company' under s 214(1)(c) and the fraudulent elements are almost identical in both sections. On the other hand, a contrary interpretation could be inferred from the fact that s 214(1)(c) does not specifically refer to s 22(1). This interpretation is supported by the fact that a specific reference to s 22(1) in an earlier version of s 214(1)(c) was deleted by the Companies Amendment Act 2011. As the fraud limb of s 22(1) does not contemplate conduct arising from the risk-shifting incentive, it is not necessary to determine this issue for purposes of our discussion.

1043 For a justification of this conclusion under the new reckless trading duty on law and economics grounds, see Stevens and de Beer (n 1035) 275ff.

1044 See s 424(1).

of,[1045] formal insolvency proceedings.[1046] Of course, where the office holder brought a successful claim under s 424 during insolvency proceedings, the collective scheme of insolvency[1047] required that the proceeds of the recoveries from the relevant directors were generally in favour of the creditors *pari passu*, rather than any particular creditors whose positions might have been prejudiced by the reckless trading conduct.[1048] By contrast, s 77(3) of the new Act explicitly makes directors in breach of s 22(1) personally liable for 'any loss, damage or costs sustained by the *company*'.[1049]

In light of this, it might be asked what practical difference it makes that s 424 was owed to the individual creditors and s 22(1) to the company. The answer is that if the duty is owed to creditors rather than the company, it widens the scope of liability and lowers the burden of proof. This makes it easier to bring claims against the directors for reckless trading and potentially increases the *ex ante* deterrent effect of the civil liability remedy for reckless trading. This point will be illustrated with reference to liability

---

1045 Which is implied by the term '[whether it be in a winding-up, judicial management] *or otherwise*'; see, eg, *Bowman NO v Sacks and Others* 1986 (4) SA 459 (W) 462.

1046 See *Body Corporate of Greenwood Scheme v 75/2 Sandown (Pty) Ltd* 1999 (3) SA 480 (W) 488–9. But see *Ex Parte Liquidator, Vautid Wear Parts (Pty) Ltd* 2000 (3) SA 96 (W) paras 9.1–9.2, where the court held that the duty under s 424 is owed solely to the creditors/members, and not to the company. A strong argument against such a conclusion is that liability to individual creditors presupposes a causal link between the breach of the duty and the harm to the creditor, a result that is inconsistent with the punitive element of liability under s 424; see Blackman, Everingham and Jooste, *Commentary on the Companies Act* (loose-leaf) (Juta 2002) Ch 14, 548.

1047 For which the basis is the common law institution of *concursus creditorum*. The *locus classicus* in this regard is *Walker v Syfret* 1911 AD 141. For a presumably exhaustive list of case law on the *concursus creditorum*, see Bertelsmann and others, *Mars The Law of Insolvency in South Africa* (9th edn, Juta 2008) 171 n 11. On the role of the *concursus creditorum* in the South African insolvency law generally, see Swart, *Die Rol van die concursus creditorum in die Suid-Afrikaanse Insolvensiereg* (unpublished LLD thesis, University of Pretoria 1990).

1048 See Blackman, 'Companies' in WA Joubert (ed) LAWSA (1st Re-issue, 1995) vol 4, para 170, nn 14, 15, as confirmed by *Terblanche NO v Damji* 2003 (5) SA 489 (C) 515–6. But see *Bowman v Sacks* 1986 (4) 459 (W) 464–5 held *obiter dictum* that the court has a discretion to allocate recoveries to particular creditors where this was required by 'special equitable considerations'.

1049 Emphasis added. See also Stevens and de Beer (n 1035) 270ff.

under the equivalent German duty in the comparative evaluation below.[1050]

From a policy perspective, in focussing on any diminution of the net asset position of the company, rather than losses to individual creditors as the basis for civil liability, the new reckless trading duty has moved towards recognising the value of reasonable informal rescue measures for the interests of companies' creditors as a whole.[1051] Since the continued application of s 424 would contradict this policy shift, the better view is that such provision no longer applies despite item 9 Sch 5.

bb. The nature of liability

The other difference between s 22(1) and s 424 is the punitive element of liability under s 424(1).[1052] S 424 imposed liability on the wrongdoer 'for all or any of the debts or other liabilities of the company'.[1053] The degree of liability for a breach of the s 22(1) duty, by contrast, is restricted by the causal requirement between the prohibited conduct and the loss, damages or costs sustained by the company, as evidenced by the term 'as a conse-

---

1050 See the discussion in PART C, Chapter 5, II., 3., b. below.

1051 See the discussion in PART C, Chapter 5, II., 3., b. below.

1052 The punitive element follows from s 424(1) imposing liability on the wrongdoer 'for all or any of the debts or other liabilities of the company'. The phrase 'as the court may direct' indicates the court's wide discretion in determining the extent of the liability.

1053 S 424(1). The phrase 'as the court may direct' indicates the court's wide discretion in determining the extent of the liability. For earlier case law confirming this position, see *Howard v Herrigel* 1991 (2) SA 660 (A) 672; *Philotex (Pty) Ltd v Snyman* 1998 (2) SA 138 (SCA) 142; *Kalinko v Nisbet* [2002] 3 All SA 294 (W) 303; *Nel NNO v McArthur* 2003 (4) SA 142 (T) 155–6; *Terblanche NO v Damji* 2003 (5) SA 489 (C) 511. See also *Corinth Trading (Pty) Limited v Greunen and Others* (27635/2010) [2014] ZAGPPHC 101 (20 March 2014) para 3. For the same position in regard to British fraudulent trading provision on which s 424 is based, see *Cyona Distributers Ltd* [1967] Ch 889, 902; [1967] 1 All ER 281, 284 (CA); *Re a Company* (No 001418 of 1988) [1991] BCLC 197, 203. This was recently confirmed in *Fourie v FirstRand Bank Ltd* [2012] ZASCA 119 (578/2012) (18 September 2012) para 28ff in a situation where the conduct that gives rise to the reckless trading occurred while the company was unable to pay its debts.

quence of'.[1054] As with the difference between s 22(1) and s 424 relating to the recipient of the duty, the lack of a causal element under s 424 lightens the plaintiff's burden of proof, and thus makes liability under s 22(1) narrower in application than s 424.

However, when taking the lack of a causal element in s 424 to its logical conclusion, directors could, in principle, be held liable for the company's debts or liabilities that were not incurred during the period of reckless trading or for debts that had been paid off in the meantime. These implications of the punitive element were arguably justified in respect of the 'fraud' limb of s 424. This is because it did not specifically relate to the inappropriate continued trading of companies in the vicinity of insolvency,[1055] as it is in the public interest that fraudulent conduct by directors be punished regardless of whether such conduct causes financial losses to the company or creditors.

However, for conduct that fell short of fraud, but was nevertheless caught by the 'reckless' limb under s 424 (for example, where creditors incurred losses while the company was inappropriately continuing to trade in the vicinity of insolvency), the above-mentioned policy considerations would be less relevant. To the contrary, it would seem questionable that directors should be held liable for taking trading decisions that fell within the 'reckless' limb (and were thus short of fraudulent conduct), where such conduct did not cause losses to creditors. Recognising that such a result was irreconcilable with the underlying purpose of s 424 insofar as the duty was owed to creditors, the concurring judgment of Judge Harms in *Saincic v Industro-Clean (Pty) Ltd*[1056] read into s 424 a causal link between the prohibited conduct and the losses incurred by the creditors. While under *Saincic* this causal link was arguably discretionary,[1057] the new reckless trading duty has now made the causal link mandatory. This change has a similar effect as the change in recipients of the duty, namely that this has made bringing reckless trading claims more onerous. It also

---

1054 See s 77(3) (b). It should be noted that an *indirect* causal connection is sufficient for the imposition of liability.

1055 As we will see below, the range of directorial conduct that was caught by s 424 was indeed broader than the continued trading of the company in the vicinity of insolvency.

1056 2009 (1) SA 538 SCA para 29. The SCA's earlier judgment (*L & P Plant Hire BK en Andere v Bosch en Andere* 2002 (2) SA 662 (SCA) paras 39–40) laid the foundation for this principle.

1057 See para 29 of the judgment.

indicates a similar policy shift towards the recognition that informal rescue measures in the vicinity of insolvency could promote the interests of companies' creditors as a whole.

c. The type of conduct prohibited and the course of action required to be undertaken

The prohibited conduct under s 22(1) is the '[reckless or fraudulent] carrying on of the company's business'. The wording is essentially the same as under s 424, save that s 424 referred to reckless trading as '*any of* the company's business', while s 22(1) has omitted the word 'any' and refers merely to the 'carrying on of (the company's) business'. Relying on an Australian case decided in the 1960s,[1058] an argument could be advanced that the omission of the word 'any' has limited the scope of the phrase 'the business of the company' to continuous courses of action and has excluded single (isolated) transactions or acts from the ambit of s 22(1).[1059]

However, none of the South African cases holding that reckless trading liability under s 424 is incurred in respect of single transactions based this finding on the word 'any'. Rather, most courts based their finding on the broad scope of the phrase 'carrying on of (the company's) business' as such,[1060] while others did so on the fact that the duty under s 424 was owed to individual creditors.[1061] The better view is, therefore, that the omission of the word 'any' under s 22(1) does not mean it does not cover isolated transactions. However, since the duty under s 22(1) is owed to the company rather than individual creditors, isolated transactions will only be caught by s 22(1) if such transactions diminish the net asset position of the company, which is not likely to occur often in practice.

It is clear that s 424 also included conduct that went beyond the 'reckless' (and 'fraudulent') continued trading of companies in the vicinity of

---

1058 *Hardie v Hanson* (1960) 105 CLR 451, 456 (HC of A).

1059 The court in *Hardy v Johnson* held that the word 'any' in the equivalent provision to s 424 broadened the scope of the phrase's ordinary meaning, which the court held to mean the company's external activities as a whole.

1060 *Body Corporate of Greenwood Scheme v 75/2 Sandown (Pty) Ltd* 1999 (3) SA 480 (W) 486.

1061 *Gordon NO and Rennie NO v Standard Merchant Bank* 1984 (2) 519 (C) 524–9; *Ex Parte Lebowa Development Corporation Ltd* 1989 (3) SA 71 (T) 110–1; *Du Plessis NO v Oosthuyzen* 1999 (2) SA 191 (O) 200–1.

insolvency,[1062] and generally included conduct relating to aspects of the company's business that went beyond the financial affairs of the company. This was also held to follow from the broad scope of the prohibited conduct as contemplated by the phrase 'carrying on any of [the company's] business'. It was further implied by the fact that liability for breaches of the duty under s 424 could also arise while the company was still solvent[1063].[1064] Since the description of the prohibited conduct under s 22(1) is essentially the same as under s 424, it would seem that, in theory, its scope embraced by s 22(1) is as broad as it was under s 424. However, one important limitation under s 22(1) is that it would need to be shown that such conduct has resulted in loss to the *company*. Under s 424, by contrast, the loss could have been incurred by an individual creditor without having to prove a causal link between the prohibited conduct and the loss.

A further important feature of s 22(1) is that like s 424, it does not prescribe a particular course of action to be taken by directors once the duty is triggered. S 22(1) presumably contemplates courses of action other than placing the company under insolvency proceedings. This necessarily follows from the fact that the duty arises in advance of insolvency. Interestingly, a previous version of s 22(1) still imposed a particular course of action on directors,[1065] namely to cease trading once the company is in a state of insolvency.[1066]

1062 On the standard, and thus the trigger, of the duty under s 22(1) (which is the same as the standard of the duty under s 424) in respect of the 'reckless' (and 'fraudulent') trading in the vicinity of insolvency, see section d below.

1063 This, in turn, is implied by the fact that the duty is available to be enforced by individual creditors outside of formal insolvency proceedings.

1064 See, eg, *Harri NO v On-Line Management CC* 2001 (4) SA 1097 (T) 1099, relying on *Body Corporate of Greenwood Scheme v 75/2 Sandown (Pty) Ltd* 1999 (3) SA 480 (W) 487.

1065 See the Companies Bill 61 of 2008.

1066 Under s 22(1) Companies Bill, the equivalent duty to s 22(1) under the Companies Act 2008 was contained in para a. The additional duty appeared in para b, and read: '[The company must not] trade under insolvent circumstances.' As we will see below, the previous version of s 22(1) is similar to the approach found in Germany and Australia. The question whether a particular action is prescribed may be significant, as it determines the freedom of directors to embark on informal rescue measures.

d. The standard of the duty

aa. The applicable element of fault and its impact on the standard of the duty

The standard of duty under s 22(1) is broadly the same as under s 424, save that under s 22(1) the phrase 'with gross negligence' appears in addition to the word 'recklessly'. The use of a comma to separate the phrase 'with gross negligence' and the term 'recklessness' might suggest that 'gross negligence' introduces a new element of fault which is separate and distinct from the element of recklessness. However, such a reading of s 22(1) would contradict the judicial interpretation of the term 'reckless' under s 424, which held that gross negligence constitutes the applicable fault element of recklessness under s 424.[1067] Moreover, although s 64 Close Corporations Act, which is the equivalent provision to s 424 and s 22(1),[1068] also treats 'gross negligence' and 'recklessness' as two distinct elements of fault, the courts have nevertheless treated them as meaning the same under s 64 Close Corporations Act.[1069] In light of the above, the better view is that 'gross negligence' serves to clarify the meaning of 'recklessness' rather than to introduce an additional element of the duty under s 22(1).[1070] One would have wished for more precise drafting in this regard.[1071] It follows that despite the slight deviation in diction between s 22(1) and s 424, the standard of the duty should still be the same in both

1067 See *S v Goertz* 1980 (1) SA 269 (C) 272; *S v Dorklerk Investments (PTY) Ltd v Bhyat* 1980 (1) SA 443 (W) 444; *S v Parsons* 1980 (2) SA 397 (D) 440–1; *Fisheries Development Corporations of SA Ltd v Jorgensen* 1980 (4) SA 156 (W) 169–70; *S v Harper* 1981 (2) SA 639 (D); *Anderson v Dickson and Another NNO* 1985 (1) SA 93 (N) 110; *Ex Parte Lebowa Development Corporation Ltd* 1989 (3) SA 71 (T) 111; *Ozinsky v Lloyd* 1992 (3) SA 396 (C) 413; *Mafikeng Mail (Pty) Ltd v Centner* (No 2) 1995 (4) SA 607 (W) 613–4; *Philotex (Pty) Ltd v Snyman* 1998 (2) SA 138 (SCA) 144; *Triptomania Twee (Pty) Ltd v Connolly* [2003] 1 All SA 374 (C).

1068 S 22 does not apply to close corporations, and the equivalent provision under the Close Corporations Act (s 64) therefore remains in force.

1069 *L & P Plant Hire BK en Andere v Bosch en Andere* 2002 (2) SA 662 (SCA) 696–70.

1070 See also Wainer, 'The new Companies Act: Peculiarities and Anomalies' (2009) 126 SALJ 806, 812.

1071 For a criticism of the poor drafting of s 64 in this respect, see Cassim and Larkin, 'Company Law' [2002] A.S.S.L. 627, 651–63.

provisions, and case law on the standard of s 424 therefore remains relevant to the interpretation of s 22(1).

In relation to the reckless and fraudulent continued trading in the vicinity of insolvency, it has emerged from case law on s 424 that the duty is triggered when, seen from the perspective of a reasonable businessman, there would be no reasonable prospect that the company would be able to pay its debts when these become due. The Appellate Division (as it then was) in *Philotex (Pty) Ltd v Snyman*[1072] held that for purposes of s 424 'reasonable prospect' means a *strong chance* of non-payment of debts. According to the court, this is less onerous than non-payment as a *virtual certainty* (which the court believed to place too heavy a burden on the plaintiff), but more onerous than a *material (but not a high) risk* of non-payment.[1073] The court held that the latter criterion distinguishes gross negligence from plain negligence.[1074] This, then, is the degree of risk the s 22(1) duty permits directors to take in respect of the decision as to whether or not to continue carrying on the company's business.

The court in *Philotex* further held that the courts should have regard to the following factors in determining whether reckless trading under s 424 existed, namely: the scope of operations of the company; the role, functions and powers of the directors; the amount of the debts; the extent of the company's financial difficulties and the prospect, if any, of recovery.[1075] Such factors would appear to remain relevant to the enquiry under s 22(1).

As we have seen, s 22(1) has followed s 424 insofar as it includes both the reckless (ie, gross negligent) and the fraudulent[1076] carrying on of the company's business. Moreover, the standard of fraud has been held generally to require a showing of 'actual dishonesty involving, according to current notions of fair trading among commercial men, real moral blame'.[1077] In relation to the continued trading in the vicinity of insolvency, such con-

---

1072 *Philotex (Pty) Ltd v Snyman* 1998 (2) SA 138 (SCA) 145–6, citing *Ozinsky N O v Lloyd and Others* 1992 (3) SA 396 (C).

1073 At 144.

1074 At 146. Note that the court stressed this test is merely evidential and not substantive.

1075 See also *Fisheries Development Corporation of SA Ltd v Jorgensen* 1980 (4) SA 156 (W) 170.

1076 Which is described as 'with intent to defraud any person or for any fraudulent purpose' in s 22(1).

1077 *Patrick Lyon Ltd, Re* [1933] Ch. 786, 790, 791.

duct would be regarded as fraudulent if a company continues to carry on its business and to incur debts at a time when, to the knowledge of its directors, there is no reasonable prospect of the creditors *ever receiving* payment.[1078]

bb. The applicable test

Under s 424, the test for measuring the controller's state of mind when taking the decision to carry on the business in the critical period is objective, since the defendant's conduct is measured against the standard of the notional reasonable person. This gives the 'reckless' limb of s 424 a slightly broader meaning than its established meaning in criminal law, where recklessness requires *dolus eventualis* – that is, the person subjectively foreseeing harm to the victim and nonetheless persisting in this conduct or, stated differently, the company controller consciously or wilfully disregarding the consequences of his actions.[1079] Consciousness of the consequences of one's actions is thus not required for breach of s 424.[1080] The same principle should apply to s 22(1).

The new reckless trading provision introduces an objective element into the test. According to s 77(3)(b), any director *knowingly* acquiescing in the prohibited conduct incurs liability. The Companies Act 2008 defines the term 'knowingly' (as well as 'knowing' and 'know'), when used in respect to a person, and in relation to a particular matter, to mean that the person

---

1078 *In re William C Leitch Brothers Ltd* [1932] 2 Ch 71 at 77, as approved by *Heneways Freight Services (Pty) Ltd v Grogor* 2007 (2) SA 561 (SCA) para 4; *R v Wax* 1957 (4) SA 399 (C) 404–405; *Dorklerk Investments (Pty) Ltd v Bhyat* 1980 (1) SA 443 (W) 444; *Fisheries Development Corporation of SA Ltd v Jorgensen* 1980 (4) SA 156 (W) 169; *S v Harper* 1981 (2) SA 639 (D) 681; and see *Orkin Bros Ltd v Bell* 1921 TPD 92; *Ex parte Lebowa Development Corporation Ltd* 1989 (3) SA 71 (T) 101–6; *Simon NO v Mitsui and Co Ltd* 1997 (2) SA 475 (W) 525.

1079 *S v Goertz* 1980 (1) SA 269 (C) 269; *Ex Parte Lebowa Development Corporation Ltd* 1989 (3) SA 71 (T) 111; *Ozinsky v Lloyd* 1992 (3) SA 396 (C) 413; *Philotex (Pty) Ltd v Snyman* 1998 (2) SA 138 (SCA) 143; *Triptomania Twee (Pty) Ltd v Connolly* [2003] 1 All SA 374 (C) 378.

1080 *Philotex (Pty) Ltd v Snyman* 1998 (2) SA 138 (SCA) 143, following *S v Van Zyl* 1969(1) SA 553 (A), 559.

either had actual knowledge of the matter or was in a position in which the person reasonably ought to have had knowledge.[1081]

Based on case law on s 424, the test under s 22(1) should also have a subjective limb insofar as the notional person is considered to move in the same spheres and have the same access to knowledge as the party in question.[1082] The better view of the relationship between the objective and subjective elements is that the subjective element can only increase the level of the duty required by the objective test. This means that the subjective test can only impose liability on a controller who would otherwise not be liable under the objective element of the test, but it can never save a controller from liability who would otherwise be liable under the objective element of the test.[1083] This would be consistent with the approach in relation to the codified duty of care under s 76(3)(c)[1084] and the British approach under the wrongful trading provision.[1085]

cc. The time at which the duty arises

In relation to the *reckless* trading in the vicinity of insolvency, the trigger point of the duty under s 424 was based on the standard of the duty. Accordingly, the duty kicked in when there was no reasonable prospect that

---

1081 See s 1. The definition requires a person to have acquired knowledge either through investigating the matter to an extent that would have provided that person with actual knowledge of the matter or to have taken other measures which would reasonably be expected to have provided the person with actual knowledge of the matter (see para (b)(i)-(ii) of the definition).

1082 *S v Van As* 1976 (2) SA 921 (AD) 928; *Philotex (Pty) Ltd v Snyman* 1998 (2) SA 138 (SCA) 143; *Triptomania Twee (Pty) Ltd v Connolly* [2003] 1 All SA 374 (C) 378.

1083 See *Philotex (Pty) Ltd v Snyman* 1998 (2) SA 138 (SCA) 148.

1084 See *Henochsberg Companies Act* (n 1035) s 76, 295; FHI Cassim, 'The Duties and the Liabilities of Directors' in FHI Cassim and others (man. ed), *Contemporary Company Law* (2nd edn, Juta 2012) 459, 509; Bouwman, 'An Appraisal of the Modification of the Directors' Duty of Care and Skill' (2009) 21 SA Merc LJ 509, 513–4; Bekink, 'A Historical Overview of the Directors' Duty of Care and Skill: From the Nineteenth Century to the Companies Bill 2007' (2008) 20 SA Merc LJ 95, 111–2. For the opposite view, see du Plessis, 'A Comparative Analysis of Directors' Duty of Care, Skill and Diligence in South Africa and Australia' in Mongalo (ed), *Modern Company Law for a Competitive South African Economy* (Juta 2010) 263, 269–70, 288–9.

1085 Davies and Worthington (n 1021) paras 9-6, 16-16.

the company would meet its debts when these became due.[1086] Since the standard of the s 22(1)-duty is the same as that under s 424, case law in respect of the trigger point of the s 424-duty remains relevant to the interpretation of s 22(1).

The phrase '(reasonable) prospect' implies that the inability to pay must necessarily be a future event, which places the trigger point of the duty into the period leading up to the actual point of (cash flow) insolvency. On the other hand, because the inability to pay debts when these would fall due is required to be approaching for the duty to bite, the duty only arises when the company is in the vicinity of insolvency.

Moreover, under s 424, the courts formulated the point at which the company would be unable to pay its debts when these became due as cash flow insolvency.[1087] It seems that cash flow insolvency was assessed on a commercial reality basis, meaning that the factual non-payment of debts did not necessarily amount to cash flow insolvency.[1088] Accordingly, the better view is that contingent and prospective debts had to be taken into account for such an enquiry.[1089] The position should be the same under s 22(1).

e. Remedies and enforcement

aa. Civil liability

As noted above, the designated remedy for contraventions of s 22(1) is s 77(3)(b). This provision provides the legal basis for civil liability for breaches of the duty under s 22(1) relating both to the 'reckless' and the 'fraud' limbs of the prohibited conduct.

1086 As most recently confirmed in *Fourie v FirstRand Bank Ltd* [2012] ZASCA 119 (578/2012) (18 September 2012) para 28ff.

1087 *Ex parte De Villiers and another NNO: In re Carbon Developments (Pty) Ltd (In Liquidation)* 1993 (1) SA 493 (A) 504; *Fourie* v *Newton* 2010 *JDR* 1437 (SCA) para 30. See also *Heneways Freight Services (Pty) Ltd v Grogor* 2007 (2) SA 561 (SCA) 569.

1088 *Blackman Companies Act* (n 1046) Ch 14, 130, citing Australian case law (see nn 889–91). This view was relied on *obiter dictum* in *Fourie* v *Newton* 2010 *JDR* 1437 (SCA) para 30.

1089 S 345(2) Companies Act 1973. See generally *Blackman Companies Act* (n 1046) 132ff.

Does s 218(2) provide for additional ground of liability for contraventions of s 22(1)?—It has been argued that the general ground for civil actions under s 218(2) might provide for an additional ground of liability for contraventions of s 22(1).[1090] According to s 218(2), any person who contravenes any provision of the Companies Act 2008 is liable to any other person for any loss or damage suffered by that person as a result of such contravention. It would have serious implications for the scope of civil liability that would arise from breaches of the duty under s 22(1) if s 218(2) applied to s 22(1) contraventions. This is because the duty under s 22(1) would then also be owed, *inter alia*, to individual creditors, which would broaden the scope of, and lower the burden of proving, civil liability as explained above.[1091] Given these significant implications if s 218(2) were to be interpreted to provide for an additional ground of civil liability for s 22(1) contraventions, the better view is that civil liability is exhaustively provided for under s 77(3)(b); in other words, such section operates as *lex specialis* of s 218(2).[1092] In general, s 218(2) is best seen as a general ground of liablity for any contravention of the Companies Act 2008 that only applies to the extent the Companies Act 2008 does not provide for a specific ground of liability.

Defence—Under s 77(3)(b), a company controller can only be held liable for reckless trading if he acquiesced to the prohibited conduct, which forms the basis of a defence for directors. The term 'acquiesce' is not used in s 424, nor is there any meaningful guidance in different contexts of the Companies Act 2008 or the common law. Some commentators have used the judicial interpretation of the phrase '(knowingly) a party to' (which was the term which attributed liability to directors for the prohibited conduct by the company under s 424) to give meaning to the term 'acqui-

---

1090 See the court in *Rabinowitz v Van Graan and Others* 2013 (5) SA 315 (GSJ) which found support for this view in FHI Cassim (n 1084) 459, 530, 534. See also *Sanlam Capital Markets (Pty) Ltd v Mettle Manco (Pty) Ltd and Others* [2014] 3 All SA 454 (GJ) para 42. Interpreting s 22(1) read with s 77(3)(b) to afford third parties *locus standi*, see *Blue Farm Fashion Limited v Rapitrade 6 (Pty) Ltd and Others* (22288/2014) [2016] ZAWCHC 35 (1 April 2016) para 31.

1091 See PART C, Chapter 5, II., 2., b., aa above.

1092 Coming to the same conclusion but for different reasons, see Stevens and de Beer (n 1035) 274–5; for the opposite view, see Gerber, 'Reckless Trading and Building Contracts' (2016) (79) THRHR 121, 124–5.

esce'.[1093] In interpreting this phrase under s 424, the courts have held that 'knowingly a party to' means something less than taking positive steps and that mere concurrence in the reckless trading (which may even be satisfied by a director's supine attitude) is sufficient to trigger liability.[1094] However, regard should also be had to the ordinary dictionary meaning of 'acquiesce', which is 'to assent tacitly' or to 'submit or comply silently or without protest'.[1095] Such meaning would seem, in essence, to come close to the meaning of 'knowingly a party to'.[1096] In effect, it would appear that a director will only escape liability if the director can show that he distanced himself from the prohibited conduct.

Relief from liability, indemnification and insurance—The court may relieve a director from liability on any grounds under s 77 (except for wilful misconduct or wilful breach of trust) if the latter has acted honestly and reasonably or on the grounds of fairness.[1097] It is not clear whether or not company controllers can be relieved from personal liability imposed pursuant to s 77(3)(b). A literal reading of s 77(9) suggests that relief from liability for reckless trading under s 77(3)(b) should be available, since s 77(9) relieves directors from 'any liability set out in this section', and liability for reckless trading under s 77(3)(b) appears in the same section.

However, this conclusion is contradicted by the position under the Companies Act 1973, where it has been argued that the equivalent provision (s 248) did not provide for relief from liability for reckless trading under s 424.[1098] One of the reasons advanced in favour of this proposition appears to apply to the new regime. This is that the objective element to measure the director's conduct under s 22(1) (as was the case under s 424(1)) and the (essentially) subjective enquiry as to whether the director acted honestly and reasonably under s 77(9)(a) (as was the case under

1093 See FHI Cassim (n 1084) 536–7.

1094 See, eg, *Howard v Herrigel* 1991 (2) SA 660 (A) 674; *Philotex (Pty) Ltd v Snyman* 1998 (2) SA 138 (SCA) 142; *Nel v McArthur* 2003 (4) SA 142 (T).

1095 Oxford Online Dictionary < http://www.oxforddictionaries.com> accessed 20 December 2016.

1096 See also Stevens and de Beer (n 1035) 266; Van der Linde, 'Personal liability of directors for corporate fault – An exploration' (2008) 20 SA Merc LJ 439, 443.

1097 Relief may be granted *ex officio*, in the course of proceedings against the director (s 77(9)) or upon an application by the director pre-empting possible proceedings brought against that director (s 77(10)).

1098 *Blackman Companies Act* (n 1046) Ch 8, 363, n 4.

s 248), renders the standard of the reckless trading duty and the standard of the conduct against which the relief is measured effectively irreconcilable.[1099] It would be appropriate to argue, in light of the above, that there should be no relief for reckless trading liability under the Companies Act 2008.

With regard to the company's ability to indemnify or insure directors, the company is not allowed to indemnify a director for liability under s 77(3)(b)[1100] or for the litigation expenses of the proceedings brought against the director[1101]; nor is the company allowed to insure the director for liability under s 77(3)(b).[1102]

Enforcement—The Companies Act 2008, unlike the Companies Act 1973,[1103] does not expressly authorise office holders to bring claims for civil sanctions for reckless trading breaches within liquidation and rescue proceedings. Although the rescue provisions under the Companies Act 2008 provide that if the rescue practitioner discovers evidence of, *inter alia*, reckless trading, he (i) must forward this evidence to the appropriate authority and (ii) direct the management to take any necessary steps to rectify the matter.[1104] However, neither of these modes of enforcement appear to contemplate the bringing of reckless trading claims under s 77(3)(b). The question therefore arises whether the enforcement of s 22(1) under s 77(3)(b) is in fact allowed in insolvency.

It is clear from the relevant provisions that such claims are available outside insolvency, as they are located squarely under the company law sections of the Companies Act 2008, and there is no other wording that would suggest a contrary meaning. However, as the duty is owed to the *company*, the only way in which to bring such a claim outside insolvency is by means of the derivative action under s 165,[1105] which would often

1099 See the UK case *Re Produce Marketing Consortium Ltd* [1989] 3 All ER 1 (Ch), regarding the equivalent UK provisions (see s 727 Companies Act 1985 (now s 1157 Companies Act 2006) and s 214 Insolvency Act 1986). Endorsing this reasoning in South Africa, see *Blackman Companies Act* (n 1046) Ch 8, 363, n 4.

1100 S 78(6)(a)(i).

1101 S 78(4)(b)(ii) read with s 78(6)(a)(i).

1102 S 78(7)(a).

1103 S 424(1) Companies Act 1973.

1104 S 141(2)(c)(ii)(aa) and (bb).

1105 A creditor would presumably use the ground under s 165(2)(d) to bring the derivative action.

seem unfeasible, given the onerous nature of the derivate action.[1106] In any event, since s 22(1) is couched as a standard rather than a rule, breaches are unlikely to be detected outside insolvency due to information asymmetries of parties that would generally have an interest in bringing reckless trading claims, namely unsecured creditors. Within insolvency proceedings, by contrast, office holders are generally afforded fairly extensive powers of investigation of transactions before the opening of insolvency proceedings,[1107] which could be used to investigate compliance with the reckless trading duty, provided the costs of such an investigation (which fall primarily on unsecured creditors) would be justified by the likelihood that reckless trading breaches could be proved. It follows from this that the enforceability of reckless trading claims would be significantly hampered if such claims were not available during insolvency proceedings, a result that would seem contrary to public policy. This is particularly true for winding-up proceedings (where the liquidator's *locus standi* could be based on the general power of the liquidator to bring legal proceedings in the name of the company under s 386(4) Companies Act 1973); however, less so for rescue proceedings, as a case could be made that the unavailability of reckless trading claims during rescue proceedings could contribute to promoting a rescue culture for two primary reasons.[1108] First, the removal of the threat of personal liability for reckless trading during rescue proceedings could encourage directors to utilise the out-of-court entry route as soon as the need for it arises, which seems worth encouraging. This is because directors are better placed to take this decision than creditors, given that they have the best information as to the company's need for rescue proceedings.[1109] Second, and related to the first reason, since the success of rescue proceedings will, in practice, depend heavily on the co-operation of the pre-existing management (notably the sharing of com-

1106 For a recent extensive analysis of the South African derivative action, see MF Cassim, *The statutory derivative action under the Companies Act of 2008: Guidelines for the exercise of the judicial discretion* (unpublished PhD thesis, University of Cape Town 2014).

1107 In winding-up proceedings, s 400 Companies Act 1973; in rescue proceedings, s 141(2)(c) Companies Act 2008.

1108 This is not to say that there could be no legal basis for such power, as bringing legal action would surely fall generally into the general management powers of the rescue practitioner under s 140(1)(a) Companies Act 2008.

1109 In relation to British law, see Davies, 'Directors' Creditor-Regarding Duties' (n 1007) 323–4.

pany-specific information with the rescue practitioner), the rescue practitioner's duty to investigate the directors' conduct in relation to reckless trading prior to insolvency could discourage the directors' willingness to cooperate with the rescue practitioner. This would reduce the chances of success of rescue, primarily due to the rescue practitioner's costs of investigation and having to familiarise himself with the company's affairs, which would be much higher if the pre-existing managers are unwilling to co-operate.[1110]

bb. Disqualification of directors

Placing the provision into its legislative and historical context—As was the case under the Companies Act 1973, reckless trading liability is a ground for disqualification of a director under the Companies Act 2008.[1111] Directors are liable to be disqualified from office if they have been found personally liable for breaches of the duty under s 22(1) under s 77(3)(b),[1112] which, in turn, will automatically lead to their disqualification.[1113]

There are, however, two important differences between the disqualification remedies under the Companies Act 1973 and the Companies Act 2008. First, under the Companies Act 2008, the liability for reckless trading is a ground of disqualification for managing-members of close corporations,[1114] which was not the case under the Companies Act 1973. Sec-

1110 Ibid.

1111 Compare s 219(1)(d) Companies Act 1973 with s 162(5)(c)(iv)(bb) read with s 69(8)(a) Companies Act 2008. For a South African case where directors were disqualified under the Companies Act 2008, see *Kukama v Lobelo and Others* (GSJ) (unreported case no 38587/2011 (12 April 2012).

1112 S 162(5)(c)(iv)(bb).

1113 S 69(8)(a). Note that a declaration of delinquency is only one of several grounds of disqualification; the other grounds are set out in s 69(8)(b). However, a declaration of delinquency is the only ground of disqualification from which a director may not be exempted by the court (s 69(11)). It should further be noted that the statutory grounds of disqualification set a minimum standard and that the Memorandum of Incorporation of the company may impose additional grounds and provide for minimum qualifications to be met by directors (s 69(6)).

1114 By virtue of s 47(1C) Close Corporations Act. Delinquency under the Companies Act (s 162) is a ground of disqualification for managing-members of close corporations. Because s 47(1C) Close Corporations Act authorises

ond, the persons who have *locus standi* in bringing an application for a declaration of delinquency are different under the Companies Act 2008. The Master, the Director of Public Prosecutions and, quite significantly, creditors no longer have *locus standi*.[1115] By contrast, the company, a director, the company secretary or the prescribed officer of a company, and a registered trade union that represents employees of the company or another representative of the employees of the company have been added to the group of persons with *locus standi*.[1116] Liquidators and rescue practitioners should have *locus standi* despite the fact that they are no longer expressly mentioned under s 162(2),[1117] on the basis that they are authorised to act for the company during winding-up proceedings and rescue proceedings, respectively. The fact that the reckless trading duty is no longer owed to individual creditors under the Companies Act 2008 could perhaps explain that creditors no longer have *locus standi* to enforce the remedy of disqualification. This could have a chilling effect on the enforcement of the disqualification remedy, particularly for situations where the directors have been disqualified for reckless trading in the vicinity of insolvency. This is because in such situations it would have been primarily the creditors who incurred losses as a result of the reckless trading, and would therefore have a strong incentive to bring a disqualification remedy.

Extent and duration of the disqualification—Once disqualified, the director is removed, with immediate effect, from the boards of all the companies on which he serves and from all participations in the management of a close corporation.[1118] The director is also precluded from accepting new board appointments.[1119]

changes to s 162 'required by the context', reckless trading liability under s 64 Close Corporations Act (which is the equivalent provision of s 22(1) read with s 77(3)(b)) should be the applicable ground of disqualification.

1115 It should be noted that under the Companies Act 1973, the Director of Public Prosecutions, creditors (and, in fact, members) only had standing in respect of a company in liquidation or under judicial management; s 219(2)(a)(i) Companies Act 1973.

1116 Compare s 162(2) with s 219(2)(a)(i) Companies Act 1973.

1117 They were, however, mentioned in s 219(2)(a)(i) Companies Act 1973.

1118 S 69(4) and s 47(1)(c) Close Corporations Act. The proviso in s 70(2), which allows the director to have his disqualification order reviewed by the court, does not apply to a disqualification on the ground of a declaration of delinquency; see s 70(2) read with ss 71(3)(a)(i) and 69(8)(a).

1119 S 69(2)(b).

The scope of the disqualification is fairly broad, which is presumably intended to also catch persons that act as directors in substance, but not in form. Accordingly, the Companies Act 2008 specifically precludes the disqualified person from serving or acting as an alternate director, as prescribed officers, board committee members, audit committee members,[1120] and *ex officio* directors.[1121] Moreover, given the lack of any limitation in the relevant section on the generally broad meaning of 'director'[1122] in the Companies Act 2008, it would appear that conduct recognised by the Companies Act 2008 as that of *de facto* and shadow directors is also caught by the disqualification. The extent of the disqualification appears to have been similarly broad under the Companies Act 1973 in that under such Act, the director was precluded from directly or indirectly taking part in the management of the company or close corporation.[1123]

Under the Companies Act 2008, the court may impose further conditions to a declaration of delinquency, which are set out in s 162(10).

While the duration of disqualification under the Companies Act 1973 was entirely at the court's discretion,[1124] the Companies Act 2008 prescribes a period of 7 years,[1125] which may, however, be reduced by the court in the prescribed circumstances.[1126]

Sanctions for contravening the disqualification order—The imposition of criminal liability and personal liability on directors who contravene the disqualification order under the Companies Act 1973[1127] has been dropped under the Companies Act 2008. In the case of criminal liability, this is

1120 S 69(1).
1121 S 66(5)(a).
1122 See s 1.
1123 S 219(1) and s 47(2) Close Corporations Act.
1124 See also Pretorius and Du Plessis, 'Enkele Aspekte Rakende die Diskwalifikasie van Direkteure en Andere in die Suid-Afrikaanse en die Engelse Reg' (1993) 4 SA Merc LJ 144, 147.
1125 The period starts from the date of the order of disqualification; s 162(6)(b)(ii).
1126 S 162(12)(b).
1127 For directors, see ss 219(5) Companies Act 1973. The imposition of personal liability was introduced in 2004 (s 4 Companies Amendment Act 20 of 2004), presumably as an additional deterrent for non-compliance with disqualification orders. Non-compliant managing-members of close corporations suffered criminal liability, but no personal liability (s 47(2) Close Corporations Act). The maximum sentence for criminal liability under this section was a fine or imprisonment for 2 years; s 414(1)(d) Companies Act 1973.

consistent with the legislature's stated policy of decriminalising company law.[1128] The current law instead sanctions non-compliance with a disqualification order by imposing a life-long ban on the non-compliant director to serve as a director of a company or to manage a close corporation.[1129]

The Companies Act 2008 also imposes civil liability on the company if it knowingly[1130] permits a disqualified person to serve as director.[1131] Liability would presumably be based on s 218(2). According to this provision, the person contravening the duty is held liable to the extent of any loss or damage suffered by any other person as a result of such contravention.

Evaluation of disqualification remedy—The disqualification remedy constitutes a useful additional remedy to civil sanctions for ameliorating the risk-shifting incentive of company controllers in the vicinity of insolvency. This is because the prospect that directors, once disqualified, are banned from their profession for a number of years, as well as the reputational damage and stigma caused by the disqualification,[1132] could have a stronger deterrent effect than the imposition of personal liability. This is because directors may often not have available the funds required to meet the liability claim under s 77(3)(b).[1133]

The position is similar in the UK. There a court, upon application of relevant persons or of its own accord, can make a disqualification order against a director who has been held personally liable for compensation

1128 See DTI Policy Framework, *South African Company Law for the 21st Century: Guidelines for Corporate Law Reform* (GG 26493, Notice 26493 of 2004) 12, 46 and the Explanatory Memorandum to the Companies Bill (2007) 5, 14.

1129 S 162(6)(a) read with s 162(5)(a) and (b). The same applies to directors having contravened an order of probation, which will be considered in greater detail below.

1130 The term 'knowingly' introduces an objective standard; see text to n 1081 above.

1131 S 69(3).

1132 R Cassim, 'Delinquent directors under the Companies Act 71 of 2008' (2013) De Rebus <http://www.saflii.org/za/journals/DEREBUS/2013/14.html> accessed 30 December 2016.

1133 See generally Hirte, Lanzius and Mock, 'Tätigkeitsverbote für Organmitglieder als Gläubigerschutzintrument' in Lutter (ed), *Das Kapital der Aktiengesellschaft in Europa* (De Gruyter 2006) 301, 304. See further the text to n 1207 below and references cited therein.

under ss 213 and 214 Insolvency Act 1986 (which are the equivalent provisions to s 22(1) of the South African Companies Act).

cc. Issue of compliance notice by company law regulator

According to s 22(2) and (3), if the Commission has reasonable grounds to believe that a company is contravening s 22(1) or that the company is unable to pay its debts as they become due in the normal course of business, the Commission may issue a notice to the company to show cause why it should be permitted to continue carrying on its business, or to trade, as the case may be. If the company fails to so notify the Commission within 20 business days of receiving the notice, the Commission may issue a compliance notice to the company, ordering it to cease carrying on its business or to cease trading. [1134]

Four points arise in relation to this remedy. First, although this remedy is triggered both when the Commission has reasonable grounds to believe that a company is engaging in reckless trading under s 22(1) and when the company is (essentially) cash flow insolvent, only the first-mentioned trigger addresses the company controller opportunism in question, as that trigger arises in advance of insolvency, which is when the perverse incentive arises, while the second-mentioned trigger would generally be too late.

Second, in describing which actions the company may be required to adopt by the Commission if the company fails to satisfy the Commission that it is not engaging in reckless trading, s 22(3) draws a distinction between the actions of 'carrying on business' and of 'trading'. Although there is common law authority that the 'carrying on of the company's business' is wider than '(*active*) trading',[1135] it would seem that both actions in circumstances contemplated by s 22(2) and (3) would, in practice, generally amount to the requirement that the company initiate formal insolvency proceedings.

Third, this remedy, in theory, has two advantages over compensation under s 77(3)(b) and disqualification. First, to the extent that the Commission relies on the trigger in advance of insolvency, it is envisaged that the compliance notice is issued shortly after the breach of the duty. This could

1134 Note that s 22(2) and (3) do not apply to close corporations, nor does the Close Corporation Act contain an equivalent provision.

1135 See *Re Sarflax Ltd* [1979] 1 All ER 529 (Ch) 534.

reduce the loss to the company when compared to s 77(3) and the disqualification remedy, given that these last two mentioned remedies typically operate only in insolvency proceedings (in the case of s 77(3)) or even after the company's dissolution (in the case of disqualification). Second, the costs of enforcement of the remedy fall on the companies' regulator, rather than on the unsecured creditors (in the case of s 77(3)) or by the person bringing the action (in the case of disqualification). To the extent that the costs of s 77(3) and disqualification claims might discourage reliance on such remedies, this could, *ceteris paribus*, mean that s 22(2) and (3) could play a useful supplementary role for the enforcement of reckless trading breaches.

However, it would seem that the compliance notice remedy will not play a significant role in practice. This is because the Commission will primarily have to rely on the filing of complaints by affected persons in respect of companies' financials in order to be in a position to determine companies' compliance with s 22(1). Secured creditors are likely to be the only class that will have the necessary information to become aware of s 22(1) contraventions. However, secured creditors will have little incentive to involve the Commission in the manner contemplated by s 22(2) and (3), as they are likely to have protected themselves by contract.

dd. Gatekeeper control enforcement: The auditor's and independent reviewer's duty to report any 'reportable irregularities'

Under s 45(1) of the Auditing Profession Act 26 of 2005[1136] (hereafter, '*Auditing Profession Act*'), a registered auditor of an entity is obliged to report on any 'reportable irregularity' in respect of the entity. A 'reportable irregularity' is defined as

a) any unlawful act or omission committed by any person responsible for the management of any entity, which—
b) has caused or is likely to cause material financial loss to the entity or to any partner, member, shareholder, creditor or investor of the entity in respect of his, her or its dealings with that entity; or
c) is fraudulent or amounts to theft; or

1136 26 of 2005. It replaced the Public Accounts' and Auditors' Act 80 of 1991; the equivalent provision of s 45 was s 20(5).

d) represents a material breach of any fiduciary duty owed by such person to the entity or any partner, member, shareholder, creditor or investor of the entity under any law applying to the entity or the conduct or management thereof. [1137]

According to the Accounting and Auditing Guide on 'Trading Whilst Factually Insolvent' ('The Guide') by the South African Institute of Chartered Accountants,[1138] reckless trading pursuant to s 424 constituted a reportable irregularity where it satisfied the conditions set out in the definition,[1139] including that the reckless trading caused or was likely to cause 'material financial loss'[1140] to the company or any of the persons mentioned in the section (including a single creditor).[1141]

Where the auditor had reason to believe that reckless trading had taken place or was taking place, he had to report this to the Regulatory Board without delay.[1142] If upon notifying the management of the company of the report[1143] and discussing it with the management,[1144] and the reportable irregularity continued, the auditor had to send another report to the Regulatory Board. The latter had to, in turn, notify the appropriate regulator.

S 45 Auditing Profession Act could be seen as the enforcement of the reckless trading duty by conscripting the auditor as a monitor (or 'gatekeeper') of companies in the vicinity of insolvency to ensure compliance with the reckless trading duty by directors. However, the recruitment of auditors to perform this function gives rise to a new principal-agent relationship (where the auditor acts as agent of the company). The temptation of the auditor to shirk on his monitoring duties is controlled by the imposi-

---

1137 Definition of 'reportable irregularity', s 1 Auditing Profession Act.

1138 South African Institute of Chartered Accountants ('*SAICA*'), 'Trading Whilst Factually Insolvent' (1999) < https://www.saica.co.za/Portals/0/Technical/auditing/documents/Guide%20on%20Trading%20Whilst%20Factually%20Insolvent.pdf> accessed 14 January 2017.

1139 See paras 6, 15–9 of the Guide.

1140 Which term is not defined in the Auditing Profession Act.

1141 Para (a) of the definition of 'reportable irregularity', s 1 Auditing Profession Act.

1142 S 45(1) Auditing Profession Act.

1143 S 45(2) Auditing Profession Act.

1144 S 45(3)(a) Auditing Profession Act.

tion of *ex post* civil and criminal sanctions on the auditor for failure to report in accordance with s 45 Auditing Profession Act.[1145]

Under the Companies Act 2008, breaches of the duty under s 22(1) will likewise constitute 'any unlawful act or omission committed [by a director]' and, to the extent that the continued trading has caused 'material financial loss' to the company, it will constitute a 'reportable irregularity' under s 45 Auditing Profession Act, and accordingly trigger the duty of the auditor to report such breaches. Although the Guide has not yet been amended to take account of the changes brought about by the Companies Act 2008,[1146] it would seem that the Guide will remain relevant. This is because the standard of the new reckless trading duty (including the fault element of gross negligence and the interplay between the objective and subjective tests) and that the duty arises in advance of cash flow insolvency has remained unchanged from the previous reckless trading duty. Of course, the narrower scope of liability for breaches of the new reckless trading duty (since it is now owed to the company and no longer to individual creditors) is expected to likewise reduce the scope of transactions that the auditor will be required to report under s 45.

However, the effectiveness of the gatekeeper control remedy might be undermined by the fact that the mandatory audit generally only applies to public companies and to certain private companies that are above a certain size threshold.[1147] The size of a company is determined according to the number of employees, the amount of third party liability, the amount of the annual turnover and the number of shareholders and the assets held in a fiduciary capacity.[1148] Companies falling under the applicable threshold only require an 'independent review' but not an audit under the Auditing Profession Act.[1149] Since an independent review is specifically excluded

---

1145 S 46(7) and s 52(1)(a) Auditing Profession Act. Criminal sanctions amounted to a fine or to imprisonment for a term not exceeding ten years or both; s 52(3) Auditing Profession Act.

1146 The is acknowledged by the Guide itself; see the note on the cover page of the Guide under the heading 'Errata: June 2009'.

1147 S 30(2)(b)(i) read with sub-s 7 and reg 28(2)(a), (c) Companies Regulations, 2011. The size threshold is a public interest score of 350 (reg 28(2)(c)(i)) or 100 in respect of a public company that compiled its annual financial statements internally (reg 28(2)(c)(ii)).

1148 Regs 26(2), 28(2)(a) Companies Regulations, 2011.

1149 S 30(2)(b)(ii), reg 28(2) Companies Regulations, 2011 (*argumentum e contrario*).

from the definition of an audit,[1150] the person conducting an independent review is not required to report a 'reportable irregularity' under s 45 Auditing Profession Act.[1151]

Instead the Companies Act 2008 provides for a separate regime for reporting 'reportable irregularities' in respect of independent reviews. According to that regime, an 'independent reviewer'[1152] has to report a 'reportable irregularity' to the Commission. The procedure of the reporting largely mirrors that under s 45 Auditing Profession Act.

One occurrence that gives rise to a 'reportable irregularity' under the Companies Act 2008 is 'an act or omission which causes or has caused the company to trade under insolvent circumstances',[1153] which is not required under s 1 read with s 45 Auditing Profession Act. From a textual and contextual perspective, the meaning of 'insolvent circumstances' would seem to refer to balance sheet insolvency.[1154] This would however be contrary to the general policy underlying the reckless trading duty that under South African law, balance sheet insolvency does not *a priori* give rise to creditor protective mechanisms in respect of trading decision of directors in the vicinity of insolvency. It is therefore expected that the courts will interpret this provision purposively to refer to cash flow insolvency.[1155]

It would appear, however, that the *gatekeeper control strategy* under the Companies Act 2008 would be less effective than under the Auditing Profession Act. Importantly, there do not seem to be any sanctions for the failure of the independent reviewer to comply with his duty to report. This would weaken this legal strategy's effect in realigning the independent re-

1150 See the definition of 'audit' in s 1, s 30(8).

1151 See also Maroun and Wainer, 'To report or not to report: In what context is a 'reportable irregularity' reportable?' (2013) 16 South African J. Econ. Manage. Sci.13, 18.

1152 Ie, an auditor or equivalent professional specified in reg 29(1)(a) read with subreg 4 Companies Regulations, 2011.

1153 Reg 29(1)(b)(iii) Companies Regulations, 2011.

1154 See also Wainer, 'The Insolvency Conundrum in the Companies Act' (2015) 132 SALJ 509, 513.

1155 This would still beg the question of the functional difference with the reportable irregularity under reg 29(1)(b)(i), namely the unlawful cause of material financial loss to the entity or to any partner, member, shareholder, creditor or investor of the entity, which have traditionally given rise to the reporting duties for reckless trading breaches under s 1 read with s 45 Auditing Profession Act; see also Wainer (n 1154) 513.

viewer's incentive to perform his reporting duties diligently *ex ante*. Further factors that are likely to hinder its effectiveness are (i) legal uncertainties about interpretational difficulties of the meaning of some of the reportable irregularities (as explained above), (ii) the inefficiencies of having to report to two separate institutions under the Companies Act and the Auditing Profession Act and (iii) the lack of experience and resources of the Commission to fulfil its functions efficiently in receiving and processing reports and notifying relevant regulators.[1156] The weakness of this legal strategy is reinforced by the fact that it is the reporting duty in respect of the independent review that applies to smaller-sized private companies and close corporations, notwithstanding that the risk-shifting incentive of directors may be particularly high in such companies given the close alignments of the interests of directors and shareholders.

A further inherent weakness of the reporting duties under both the Companies Act and the Auditing Profession Act is that both the independent review and the audit are only required to be made once a year.[1157]

3. Comparative evaluation of the South African reckless trading duty with equivalent statutory duties under British, Australian and German law

a. The time at which the duty arises and the course of action to be undertaken

As indicated above, to the extent that the South African reckless trading duty applies to the 'reckless' trading of the company in the vicinity of insolvency,[1158] such duty is triggered only when the company is in distress, but sometime in advance of insolvency. Moreover, it does not specify a particular course of action to be taken by directors once the duty arises.

A similar approach can be found in the UK. The equivalent British provision, s 214 of the Insolvency Act 1986, bites when the company con-

1156 Maroun and Wainer (n 1151) 18.

1157 See s 30(1), (2), reg 29(3) Companies Regulations, 2011.

1158 As mentioned above, s 22(1) also covers conduct that goes beyond the type of actions that arise as a result of the risk-shifting incentive (and generally also catches conduct relating to 'non-financial' matters). It also applies to 'fraudulent' trading. However, both of these aspects of s 22(1) are irrelevant for our analysis in this section. Accordingly, any reference to the South African duty under s 22(1) in this section relates only to the risk-shifting incentive.

trollers knew or ought to conclude that there is no reasonable prospect that the company would avoid going into insolvent liquidation.[1159] Like s 22(1), this is necessarily forward-looking and the duty thus bites in advance of insolvency.[1160] The British courts have defined this point with reference to cash flow insolvency,[1161] despite the fact that s 214(6) Insolvency Act 1986 defines 'insolvent liquidation' on a balance sheet basis. The explanation for this is that balance sheet insolvency operates as a necessary condition for the enforcement, rather than as a trigger, of the duty. This distinction is important as there is no reason to impose liability on the directors if the company is balance sheet solvent when it goes into formal insolvency proceedings, since the creditors would, in principle, receive their full claim in insolvency proceedings.[1162] The courts in the UK, like their South African counterparts, take a commercial, rather than a technical, view of cash flow insolvency. This means that *failure* to pay debts does not necessarily amount to the *inability* to pay debts when considering the company's financial position as a whole.[1163]

Furthermore, like the South African provision, the British provision does not specify the course of action to be taken by directors. The British duty is more explicit than its South African counterpart in that it mandates – indeed, arguably *requires* – continued trading in the vicinity of insolvency if a reasonable person would have concluded that this would be in the best interests of creditors. This would include a situation where informal rescue mechanisms would have been value-maximising to the (unsecured) creditors. This follows from the defence from wrongful trading liability under s 214(3), which permits the directors to prove that they took

1159 S 214(2)(b) Insolvency Act 1986.

1160 Davies, 'Directors' Creditor-Regarding Duties' (n 1007) 316ff.

1161 See *Re Purpoint* [1991] BCLC 491; R*e Road Gunner Organisation* [2004] 2 BCLC 110. See generally Davies, 'Directors' Creditor-Regarding Duties' (n 1007) 319.

1162 Davies, 'Directors' Creditor-Regarding Duties' (n 1007) 319. A company may sometimes be cash flow insolvent while still being balance sheet solvent when the company has a large proportion of illiquid assets; Goode, *Principles of Corporate Insolvency Law* (3rd edn, Sweet & Maxwell 2005) para 4-06; Steffek, 'Insolvenzgründe in Europa – Rechtsvergleich, Regelungsstrukturen und Perspektiven der Rechtsangleichung' [2009] KTS 317, 317ff.

1163 For the UK, see *Sandell v Porter* (1966) 115 C.L.R. 666, 670–1; Re *Brian D Pearson (Contractors) Ltd* [1999] BCC 26. See generally Goode (n 1162) paras 4-16, 4-21ff. For South Africa, see the sources cited in n 1088 above.

every step with a view to minimising the potential loss to the company's creditors. By focussing on the 'loss to the company's creditors', the British provision leaves the door open for the argument that directors are entitled – or, rather, *required* – to embark on informal rescue measures in the vicinity of insolvency if there is a reasonable chance that such measures would succeed, as this would avoid imposing the costs of formal insolvency proceedings on the (unsecured) creditors unnecessarily.[1164]

Since the trigger of the South African duty is defined solely with reference to the company's (impending) cash flow insolvency, it is less obvious whether the interests of (unsecured) creditors in value-maximising informal rescue measures are to be taken into account by directors under s 22(1). The term 'reckless trading' might leave some scope for considerations of weighing up the 'costs' of informal rescue measures compared to formal rescue measures. Moreover, the introduction of the new business rescue procedure is expected to promote the development of a rescue culture in South Africa. This is likely to increase the relevance of the merits of informal rescue measures for the judicial interpretation of s 22(1). However, it is expected that it will take some time before this paradigm shift will occur.

A different approach can be found in Germany and Australia. The equivalent German provisions are the duty of directors to place a company under formal insolvency proceedings (§ 15a *Insolvenzordnung*) and a prohibition on making payments out of the company's assets, unless such payments are reasonable under the circumstances (§ 64 *GmbH-Gesetz* and § 92(2) *Aktiengesetz*).[1165] Both duties arise when the company is either cash flow or balance sheet insolvent.[1166] In Australia, the equivalent provision requires that directors refrain from incurring a debt when the compa-

1164 See generally Davies, 'Directors' Creditor-Regarding Duties' (n 1007) 316ff. See also Steffek, 'Gläubigerschutz' (n 1023) 453ff.

1165 The payment prohibition pursuant to § 64 *GmbH-Gesetz* and § 92(2) *Aktiengesetz* could also be seen as specifically addressing the problem of asset dilution, ie, siphoning assets out of the company, rather than the taking of value-minimising strategic trading decisions by the company controllers. For a distinction of these two manifestations of the risk-shifting incentive, see PART A, Chapter 1, II., 3., a., bb above.

1166 In respect of the duty to invoke insolvency proceedings, see § 15a (1) read with § 17 and § 19 *Insolvenzordung*. To be precise, directors have 3 weeks after the onset of cash flow and balance sheet insolvency to invoke formal insolvency proceedings. In respect of the duty to refrain from making payments, see § 64

ny is cash flow insolvent at the time or becomes cash flow insolvent by incurring the debt (s 588G Corporations Act 2001).[1167]

In contrast to the duties in South Africa and the UK, both the German and Australian duties bite only when the company has reached a state of insolvency. In Germany, this is defined both in cash flow and in balance sheet terms and in Australia solely in cash flow terms.[1168]

Both the German and Australian provisions are also more specific as to the course of action to be taken by directors. In Germany, it is the placing of the company under formal insolvency proceedings and refraining from making payments, while in Australia it is refraining from incurring any further debts.[1169] Although directors are given slightly more freedom to manoeuvre in Australia, its rationale seems to come close to the German provisions, which is that once the company reaches a state of insolvency, the decision as to the company's future should be placed in the hands of the creditors, not the directors,[1170] as is the case in the UK and, arguably, also South Africa.[1171]

In saying that, the attempt of the applicable duties in the UK and South Africa to carefully balance the company controllers' risk-shifting incentive and enhance the chances of value-enhancing informal rescue measures, might be undermined by two provisions in those jurisdictions. First, both in the UK and South Africa, failure to pay a particular undisputed debt after payment has been demanded provides sufficient evidence of

---

(1st sentence) *GmbH-Gesetz* and § 92(2) (1st sentence) *Aktiengesetz*. The trigger of the duty to refrain from making payments to shareholders arises where such payments would cause the company to become cash slow insolvent (see § 64 (3rd sentence) *GmbH-Gesetz* and § 92(2) (3rd sentence) *Aktiengesetz*.

1167 The trigger of the duty arises from s 558G(1)(b) and (c) read with s 95A Corporations Act 2001.

1168 However, we will see below that the German provisions may nevertheless bite earlier than the South African and British provisions.

1169 For Germany, § 15a (1) *Insolvenzordnung* and for Australia, s 558G(1)(b) Corporations Act 2001. In Australia, the 'incurrence of debt' has a broad meaning, and includes several transactions that could be seen as distributions generally, such as paying dividends and buying back shares (see s 588G(1A) Corporations Act 2001.

1170 Davies, 'Directors' Creditor-Regarding Duties' (n 1007) 313–4, citing Austin and Ramsay, *Ford's Principles of Corporations Law* (16th edn, LexisNexis Butterworths 2005) para 24.360 in relation to the Australian provision.

1171 In relation to the British provision, see Davies, 'Directors' Creditor-Regarding Duties' (n 1007) 316–7.

cash flow insolvency, at which point a creditor of the company is entitled to place it under formal insolvency proceedings.[1172] Since failure to pay may often occur before the occurrence of cash flow insolvency, the ability of creditors to invoke insolvency proceedings at that point may, in applicable circumstances, pre-empt the pursuance of informal rescue measures.[1173]

Second, as indicated in Chapter 4, the new South African Companies Act has under s 129(7) introduced a peculiar duty on directors of 'financially distressed' companies to disclose to all affected persons[1174] that the company has become financially distressed and to provide reasons for not having commenced rescue proceedings under the out-of-court entry route, notwithstanding that the company meets the impending insolvency entry ground.[1175]

Such a disclosure is likely to greatly reduce – perhaps even eliminate – the chances of a pre-insolvency workout. This is because the disclosure is likely to place affected persons in a position either to look for opportunities to enforce on their claims, leading to a value-destroying 'race to collect' (the prevention of which has been argued to be one of the justifications for formal insolvency law);[1176] or affected persons might apply to court for the commencement of rescue proceedings under the court entry route. Moreover, particularly in respect of public (listed) companies, the market is likely to (over)react negatively to such disclosure, which is likely to lead to a dramatic reduction in the company's value, expediting the company's demise.[1177]

1172 For the UK, see *Re Globe New Patent Iron & Steel Co* (1875) L.R. 20 Eq. 337; *Mann v Goldstein* [1968] 2 All E.R. 769, 773; *Cornhill Insurance plc v Improvement Services Ltd* [1986] 1 W.L.R. 114. See generally Goode (n 1162) paras 4-23; Davies, 'Directors' Creditor-Regarding Duties' (n 1007) 315. For South Africa, see s 345(1)(a) and (b) Companies Act 1973. That provision still applies under the Companies Act 2008 by virtue of Sch 5 item 9 Companies Act 2008. See also, eg, *S v Rosenthal* 1980 (1) SA 65 (A) 75.

1173 In relation to the British provision, see Davies, 'Directors' Creditor-Regarding Duties' (n 1007) 315. It has therefore been argued that the British deeming provision of insolvency is a functional equivalent of § 15a *Insolvenzordnung*; Schall, 'The UK Limited Company Abroad' (2005) 16 E.B.L.R. 1577, 1581.

1174 On the meaning of 'affected persons', see PART B,Chapter 4,IV.,2.,a.,aa above.

1175 S 129(7) Companies Act 2008.

1176 See the discussion in Chapter 2 above.

1177 See also Wainer (n 1154) 512, 515.

When s 129(7) is regarded as a legal strategy that has the effect of counteracting the company controllers' risk-shifting incentive, its rationale would seem to be diametrically opposed to that of s 22(1). This is because it regards not the board of directors, but rather the creditors, as the appropriate constituent to decide on the merits of formal rescue proceedings. Because of this tension between the underlying principles of s 22(1) and s 129(7), the introduction of s 129(7) seems difficult to justify.[1178]

Another debate is to be had about the desirability of s 129(7) as a self-standing provision. On the one hand, the purpose of the disclosure duty appears to be the removal of information asymmetries between the company controllers and unsecured creditors and employees, which generally prevents such constituents to make effective use of their right to apply for the commencement of rescue proceedings under s 131 Companies Act 2008. At face value, this seems perfectly reasonable: if the law affords affected persons with the right to place companies under rescue proceedings, then it would seem only consistent with such entitlement that affected persons are provided with the necessary information to exercise that right properly.

On the other hand, the aforementioned likely adverse effects of the disclosure under s 129(7) for the success of value-maximising informal rescue measures raises serious doubts about its desirability.

Since s 129(7) could be seen as a distinct legal strategy, it will be discussed in a separate section further below in this Chapter.[1179]

It should be noted that because German insolvency law defines insolvency both in cash flow and balance sheet terms, the German provision would appear to bite earlier than the respective provisions under the other jurisdictions in question.[1180] This is because balance sheet insolvency generally occurs before cash flow insolvency, since in efficient credit markets, companies are generally able to obtain finance even where they are overindebted.[1181] In saying that, the qualification in § 19(2) *Insolvenzordnung* stating that despite the existence of a technical excess of liabilities

---

1178 However, as we will see below, s 129(7) is not likely to play a significant role in practice due to problems with its enforcement.

1179 See III. below.

1180 Bachner, 'Wrongful Trading – A New Model for Creditor Protection?' (2006) EBOR 293, 300ff.

1181 Steffek, 'Insolvenzgründe' (n 1162) 317–34; Eidenmüller, 'Trading in Times of Crisis: Formal Insolvency Proceedings, Workouts and the Incentives for Share-

over assets, balance sheet insolvency does not arise where it is 'highly likely' (*überwiegend wahrscheinlich*) that the company will be able to continue in business (*positive Fortführungsprognose*),[1182] would seem to push the trigger of the respective German provisions to a later stage.[1183] This forward-looking element requires the directors to make a projection on the ability of the company to pay its debts and the company's financial performance in the medium term.[1184] It is considered 'highly likely' that the company will 'continue in business' where the chance that the company will be able to service its debts is greater than 50%.[1185] The diretors are given a margin of discretion (*Beurteilungsspielraum*) when making this projection.[1186]

---

holders/Managers' (2006) 7 EBOR 239, 242. For case law under the South African Companies Act 1973 implicitly endorsing this view, see *Heneways Freight Services (Pty) Ltd v Grogor* 2007 (2) SA 561 (SCA) 569. This general sequence of events is reversed where the credit market fails due to a financial crisis or where the debtor has an unusual high proportion of illiquid assets; Steffek, 'Insolvenzgründe' (n 1162) 317ff.

1182 This qualification was introduced as a result of the financial crisis in 2008 by Art 5 *Finanzmarktstabiliserungsgesetz* (FMStG) of 17 October 2008, BGBl. I 2008, S. 1982 initially as an interim arrangement until 31 December 2010. However, in 2009 it was extended to 1 April 2014 by the *Gesetz zur Erleichterung der Sanierung der Unternehmen* of 24 April 2009. Based on a study by Bitter and Hommerich, *Die Zukunft des Überschuldungsbegriffs Expertenbefragung im Auftrag des Bundesministeriums der Justiz - Abschlussbericht* (RWS Verlag Kommunikationsforum 2012), it was finally made permanent by the *Gesetz zur Einführung einer Rechtsbehelfsbelehrung im Zivilprozess und zur Änderung anderer Vorschriften* of 23 November 2012 (BGBI. I, 2012, S. 2418).

1183 The effectiveness of the earlier trigger of insolvency in Germany may however be undermined in practice by the fact that particularly directors of small companies may often lack the financial experience, expertise and resources that would enable them to determine balance sheet insolvency timeously (see Frastanlis, *Insolvenzverschleppungshaftung und Gläubigerschutz in der Insolvenzkrise – Ein rechtsvergleichender Blick aus Sicht des deutschen, griechischen und US-amerikanischen Rechts* (unpublished doctoral thesis, copy on file with author, University of Hamburg 2015) 232 and further references cited therein; from a US perspective, see Korobkin, 'Vulnerability, Survival and the Problem of Small Business Bankruptcy' (1994) 23 Cap. U. L. Rev. 413, 427).

1184 See Hübert, *Sorgfaltskonforme Prognosen und Pflichten der Geschäftsleiter im Vorfeld der Insolvenz; ein Beitrag mit rechtsvergleichenden Bezügen* (unpublished doctoral thesis, University of Hamburg 2015) 216ff, 229ff.

1185 Hübert (n 1184) 242 with further references cited in n 1278 therein.

1186 See generally Hübert (n 1184) 242. The boundaries of this discretion (which is not based on the German business judgment rule pursuant to § 93(1)(2nd sen-

To be sure, balance sheet insolvency probably comes closer than cash flow insolvency to identifying the point at which the shareholders' equity has been wiped out and at which creditors are no longer protected by the fact that losses will fall on shareholders first.[1187] However, the earlier trigger of the German provisions does not save them from the criticism that the narrowly defined courses of action required to be pursued by directors leave them with little freedom to take value-enhancing informal rescue measures.[1188] In fact, the limited actions available to company controllers under the German provisions, means that the earlier trigger has the opposite effect to what it would have had if the South African and British provisions were activated earlier; it reduces the scope for informal rescue measures even more.[1189]

Furthermore, particularly in light of the fact that in practice informal workouts are generally only commenced when the company reaches a state of insolvency,[1190] the three week window period within which directors in Germany have to place the company under insolvency proceedings[1191] is generally too short for the implementation of informal rescue measures.[1192] It has therefore been suggested that the period for invoking

---

tence) *Aktiengesetz*) has been exceeded where the projection is found to be unreasonable when judged from an *ex ante* perspective against the standard of care particularly in relation to the procurement of relevant information on which the projection was based (see Hübert (n 1184) 382ff; Klöhn, '§ 15a' in Kirchhof, Eidenmüller and Stürner (eds), *Münchener Kommentar zur Insolvenzordnung* (3rd edn, C.H. Beck 2013) recital 179.

1187 Davies, 'Directors' Creditor-Regarding Duties' (n 1007) 317ff.

1188 For a critique of both the German and the Australian provisions in this regard, see Davies, 'Directors' Creditor-Regarding Duties' (n 1007) 314ff. For a a critique of the German provision as a mechanism for re-balancing the risk-shifting incentive generally, see Eidenmüller (n 1181) 250.

1189 Davies, 'Directors' Creditor-Regarding Duties' (n 1007) 320.

1190 Eidenmüller, *Finanzkrise, Wirtschaftskrise und das deutsche Insolvenzrecht* (De Gruyter 2009) 22. See also Frastanlis (n 1183) 235-6, 240.

1191 § 15a(1) *Insolvenzordnung*.

1192 Hirte, ‚§ 15a' in Uhlenbruck and Hirte (eds), *Kommentar Insolvenzordnung* (14th rev. edn, Vahlen 2015) recital 16ff; Hirte, 'Ökonomische Überlegungen zur zwingenden Insolvenzantragspflicht des deutschen Rechts', in Eger and others (eds), *Internationalisierung des Rechts und seine ökonomische Analyse/ Internationalization of the Law and its Economic Analysis, Festschrift für Hans-Bernd Schäfer zum 65. Geburtstag* (Springer 2008) 605, 608ff; Eidenmüller, *Unternehmenssanierung zwischen Markt und Gesetz: Mechanismen der Un-*

formal insolvency proceedings under the German provision be extended to up to three months.[1193]

It should be noted that the company controllers' costs of interpretation are generally higher in respect of a general duty to creditors in the vicinity of insolvency than a clearly and precisely formulated duty.[1194] This is particularly true for directors of small companies as they may often lack the experience, expertise and resources to determine their compliance with the duty.[1195] As these higher interpretation costs are inevitable to the use of legal standards, the common way to reduce them from within such a system of regulation is that the courts develop and, if necessary, update guidelines for compliance that reflect the current mores of good business practice recognised by the business community.[1196]

b. Civil liability and enforcement

In South Africa, since civil liability for breaches of the reckless trading duty under s 77(3)(b) arises for *losses to the company*, directors would seem to only be liable for the reduction in the net asset position of the company, rather than any damages incurred by the creditors. In principle, this follows the position under the British wrongful trading duty, under which contributions from the directors are limited to the diminution on the company's net asset position during the period of wrongful trading.[1197]

Whether civil liability for breaches of the applicable duty takes account of losses to the *company*, as opposed to losses to the company's *creditors*, is important for the scope of liability and for the evidentiary burden of proving breaches of the duty. In relation to the scope of liability, liability is

ternehmensreorganisation und Kooperationspflichten im Reorganisationsrecht (Otto Schmidt 1999) 691; Richter and Pluta, 'Haftungssprung Insolvenzreife – ein Plädoyer für die integrierte Unternehmensplanung' (2009) InsVZ 31, 33; Frastanlis (n 1183) 234, 240.

1193 Frastanlis (n 1183) 239ff and further references cited therein.

1194 Ulen, 'Standards und Direktiven im Lichte begrenzter Nationalität' in Ott and Schäfer (eds), *Die Präventivwirkung zivil- und strafrechtlicher Sanktionen* (Mohr 1999) 356ff; Frastanlis (n 1183) 234.

1195 Schall, *Kapitalgesellschaftsrechtlicher Gläubigerschutz* (Beck 2009) 102; Steffek, 'Gläubigerschutz' (n 1023) 548; Frastanlis (n 1183) 237ff.

1196 Davies, 'Directors' Creditor-Regarding Duties' (n 1007) 327.

1197 Davies, 'Directors' Creditor-Regarding Duties' (n 1007) 324–5.

potentially broader in scope where the duty is owed to the creditors. This is because breaches of the duty might in certain circumstances impair the position of individual creditors, while having no effect on the net asset position of the company. A conspicuous example of this is where one creditor is paid off after the duty has arisen. Here the creditors that were not paid would suffer a loss to the extent that their dividend in relation to their full claims against the company would be reduced. The company's net asset position, on the other hand, remains stable, given that the decrease in assets (ie, the cash outflow) on the debit side of the balance sheet is matched by a reduction in debt on the credit side of the balance sheet.[1198] Accordingly, such an action would not trigger liability under the South African and British provisions. In contrast, payment of one creditor after the duty has set in would presumably give rise to liability under the German duty to initiate insolvency proceedings after the company has reached a state of insolvency (§ 15a *Insolvenzordnung*), as damages for breaches of such duty[1199] are based on the reduction of any individual creditor's dividend in insolvency as a result of the wrongful conduct, referred to as '*Quotenschaden*'.[1200]

A further example illustrating the wider scope of liability under § 15a *Insolvenzordnung* is that directors are liable for losses to creditors who extended credit to the company after it has reached a state of insolvency ('new creditors'). This liability consists of the difference between the new creditors' position had they not extended credit to the company and their actual position in having to share in the insolvent estate *pari passu*. This is referred to as '*Vertrauensschaden*' or 'reliance loss'.[1201] In contrast, since the injection of the new funds after the duty is triggered would have no impact on the company's net asset position (as the increase in credit is matched by a corresponding increase in cash), such transaction would presumably not give rise to liability under the South African and British duties. Similarly, directors are liable to make contributions for pay-

1198 See Bachner (n 1180) 312, who makes this point by way of illustrative examples.

1199 § 823(2) *BGB*.

1200 BGHZ 138, 211, 221. See generally Steffek, 'Gläubigerschutz' (n 1023) 444.

1201 BGHZ 126, 181. See generally Steffek, 'Gläubigerschutz' (n 1023) 444; Fleischer, 'The Responsibility of the Management and its Enforcement' in Ferrarini and others (eds), *Reforming Company and Takeover Law in Europe* (Oxford University Press 2004) 399, 400.

ments out of the assets of the company in breach of § 64 *GmbH-Gesetz* and § 92 *Aktiengesetz*, regardless of whether such payments reduced the net asset position of the company.[1202]

In relation to the evidentiary burden of proving breaches of the duty, where the duty is owed to creditors (as under the German provisions), rather than the company (as under the South African and British provisions), the office holder is entitled to focus on isolated (single) transactions prejudicing specific creditors. Similarly, the fact that new creditors can claim for their reliance loss under the German provisions permits the office holder to consider the position of an individual creditor having suffered reliance loss. Both these scenarios are easier to prove than proving negative developments in the company's overall net asset position during the wrongful trading period, which would be required where the duty is owed to the company, as under the South African and British provision.[1203]

The wider scope of liability of company controllers and the lower evidentiary burden of the German provisions means that it has a greater *ex ante* effect on company controllers' risk-shifiting incentive than the South African and British provisions.[1204]

From the perspective of legal policy, the German approach of taking account of negative developments of individual creditors would seem to be consistent with the policy that insolvent companies are best removed from the market place.[1205] By contrast, the British and South African approach of limiting liability to losses to the *company* could be seen as a further illustration of their reluctance to restrict the directors' freedom of manoeuvre in steering the company out of its financial difficulties in the vicinity of insolvency.[1206]

1202 See Steffek, 'Gläubigerschutz' (n 1023) 448 and further references cited therein.

1203 Bachner (n 1180) 313, 318.

1204 See Steffek, 'Gläubigerschutz' (n 1023) 539; Frastanlis (n 1183) 228. See generally on the effect of the likelihood of success of the enforcement of *ex post* liability on compliance *ex ante*, Eckert, Grechening and Stremitzer, 'Ökonomische Analyse der Kapitalhaftung' in Kalss (ed), *Vorstandshaftung in 15 europäischen Ländern* (Linde Verlag 2005) 101.

1205 See BGH 6 June 1994, NJW 1994 p. 2220. See also Fleischer, 'The Responsibilities of the Management and its Enforcement' in Ferrarini and others (eds), *Reforming Company and Takeover Law in Europe* (Oxford University Press 2004) 399.

1206 Davies, 'Directors' Creditor-Regarding Duties' (n 1007) 325.

It would seem that the sanction of civil liability has a general limitation, particularly in respect of small companies. This is because owner-managers may have invested their entire wealth in the company, and would, therefore, not be able to contribute any funds from their personal estate if found liable ('judgment-proof-problem'). This would reduce the incentive of company controllers to comply with this duty.[1207] The availability of the disqualification of directors remedy in South Africa and the UK[1208] and criminal sanctions in Germany[1209] would appear to increase the deterrent effect of the respective provisions.[1210]

A question that has occupied the British, but apparently not (yet) the South African, courts, is the class of creditors that should be entitled to the proceeds of a successful wrongful trading claim. Under the British provision, this question has been settled in favour of the unsecured creditors (including the statutory preferential creditors), on the grounds that s 214 recoveries are not caught by security interests granted prior to insolvency.[1211] It might be argued that because under South African insolvency law, secured creditors are essentially entitled to realise their claims outside the collective procedure in liquidation proceedings,[1212] any proceeds of litigation during such proceedings should also fall into the free residue available to unsecured (and statutory preferred) creditors. Such a result would be justified, as it is the unsecured creditors (as residual claimants) that ulti-

1207 Frastanlis (n 1183) 228ff; Eckert, Grechening and Stremitzer (n 1204) 108; Shavell, *Foundations of Economic Analysis of Law* (Harvard University Press 2004) 518ff.; Schall (n 1195) 103. See also Klöhn (n 1186) recital 39; Bachmann and others, 'Rechtsregeln für die geschlossene Kapitalgesellschaft' (2012) ZGR Sonderheft 18 93; Shavell (n 1207) 230ff.

1208 See the discussion in PART C, Chapter 5, II., 2., e., bb. above.

1209 § 15a(4) and (5) *Insolvenzordnung*.

1210 However, the deterrent effect of criminal sanctions have been questioned in Germany; see, eg, Frastanlis (n 1183) 242; Bork, *Sanierungsrecht in Deutschland und England* (RWS-Verlag Kommunikationsforum 2011) recital 24.4.

1211 *Re Oasis Merchandising Ltd* [1998] Ch. 170, CA. This has been argued to be supported by the general principle that causes of action not created until insolvency proceedings are commenced, and enforceable only in the liquidator's name, benefit the unsecured creditors (*Re Yagerphone Ltd* [1935] 1 Ch. 395); see Davies, 'Directors' Creditor-Regarding Duties' (n 1007) 316–7, 325–6, including n 72.

1212 Sch 5 item 9 Companies Act 2008 read with s 339 Companies Act 1973 and with s 83 Insolvency Act 1936.

mately bear the risk of any losses imposed on the company by the risk-shifting incentive of company controllers.[1213]

A major criticism of the British provision is that too few cases are pursued due to a lack of funding.[1214] A low rate of enforcement of the creditor-regarding duty of directors could reduce the effect of the duty on rebalancing the risk-shifting incentive, since the lower the likelihood of sanctions being enforced for non-compliance, the lower the incentive of making an effort and expending costs to comply.[1215] The reasons for the lack of funding for wrongful trading litigation in the UK is that because unsecured creditors will essentially bear the investigation and litigation costs of a wrongful trading claim, the office holder, acting in the best interests of the company, will be reluctant to pursue cases that do not have a good chance of being successful,[1216] and it is in the nature of the standards approach that many cases would fall into that category. Moreover, the obvious alternative source of funding of wrongful trading litigation, namely third-party financing,[1217] has been held to be precluded by the civil procedure rule against champerty.[1218] This is an agreement where an outsider provides finance to enable a party to litigate in return for a share of the proceeds of the action if that party was successful.[1219]

No similar concerns have yet been raised in respect of the South African reckless trading duty. It might be argued that if the answer to the question, which creditors are entitled to the recoveries from directors from a successful reckless trading claim, is unsecured creditors, then secured creditor – who are generally better resourced than unsecured creditors – would have no incentive to fund such litigation.[1220] However, although the

---

1213 See the discussion in PART C, Chapter 5, II., 1., b. above.

1214 For further procedural problems of wrongful trading claims, see Steffek, 'Gläubigerschutz' (n 1023) 421ff and further references cited therein.

1215 See reference cited in n 1204.

1216 Ibid 326.

1217 Because third parties can spread their risk over a number of claims, they are likely to be more willing to pursue risky claims than an office holder; see Davies, 'Directors' Creditor-Regarding Duties' (n 1007) 326.

1218 *Re Oasis Merchandising Ltd* [1998] Ch. 170, CA. See generally Davies, 'Directors' Creditor-Regarding Duties' (n 1007) 325-7.

1219 *Pricewaterhouse Coopers Inc v National Potato Cooperative Ltd* 2004 (6) SA 66 (SCA) para 26.

1220 In relation to the British provision, see Davies, 'Directors' Creditor-Regarding Duties' (n 1007) 326.

law against champertous agreements does form part of South African law,[1221] the SCA in *PricewaterhouseCoopers Inc v National Potato Cooperative Ltd*[1222] has moved away from the scepticism of champertous agreements of earlier cases,[1223] by holding that such agreements are generally not contrary to public policy or unenforceable,[1224] unless they amount to an abuse of process (ie, where the court process is used in bad faith). This requirement is not specific to champertous agreements, and the courts will accordingly apply the general rules on abuse of process in this context.[1225] Following this judgment, it would seem that the common law rule against champerty would no longer generally prohibit third-party funded litigation, which would include reckless trading claims, and the legal certainty provided by the judgment is expected to encourage third-party funding of claims.[1226] This will increase the effect of the reckless trading duty on ameliorating the company controller's risk-shifting incentive. However, recent developments that the third-party funder may be joined as a party to the proceedings so that he can be made liable to contribute to the costs of

---

1221 As received from Roman and Roman-Dutch law (*pacta de quota litis*) and English law (maintenance and champerty) (see *PricewaterhouseCoopers Inc v National Potato Cooperative Ltd* 2004 (6) SA 66 (SCA) para 25). See *Green v De Villiers, Dr Leyds, N.O., and The Rand Exploring Syndicate* [1895] 2 OR 289; *Thomas Hugo and Fred J Möller NO v The Transvaal Loan, Finance and Mortgage Company* [1894] 2 OR 336; *Schweizer's Claimholders' Rights Syndicate, Limited v The Rand Exploring Syndicate, Limited* [1896] 2 OR 140; *C.V.J.J. Platteau v S.P. Grobler* [1897] 4 OR 389; *Page v Malcomess Ltd* 1922 EDL 295; *Campbell v Welverdiend Diamonds, Ltd* 1930 TPD 287.

1222 2004 (6) SA 66 (SCA) para 27ff.

1223 Eg, that champertous agreements are generally unlawful and that litigation pursuant to such agreements should not be entertained; *Lekeur v Santam Insurance Co Ltd* 1969 (3) SA 1 (C); *Goodgold Jewellery (Pty) Ltd v Brevadau CC* 1992 (4) SA 474 (W).

1224 The court based its decision on the right of access to justice under s 34 of the Constitution 108 of 1996, the freedom of contract and that a strict appliance of the champerty rule was no longer justified, given that the civil justice system has, in the meantime, become strong enough to withstand the perceived abuses of third-party funding for a share in the proceeds of a successful suit; at paras 43ff.

1225 Burger, 'Let the Litigation Funder beware' (2014) Werksmans Attorneys Legal Brief <http://www.werksmans.com/legal-briefs-view/let-litigation-funder-beware/> accessed 14 January 2017.

1226 Indeed, the last few years has seen an increase in third-party funded litigation; Burger (n 1225).

an unsuccessful suit,[1227] would raise the costs of third-party funding for the funded party (ie, how much of the share of the proceeds the funded party surrenders to the financier). It is not clear what effect this might have on the overall prevalence of third-party funding of litigation.

III. Alternative ex post standards strategies – comparative perspectives from the UK and Germany

1. Gatekeeper control enforcement: Amelioration of 'asset substitution' by relevant insolvency claw-back remedies?

a. The claw back of 'undervalue transactions' in insolvency under British law

aa. The function and basic requirements of the undervalue transactions claw-back remedy

S 238 of the British Insolvency Act 1986 entitles the office holder to impugn antecedent transactions made for an undervalue.[1228] The proper domain of the claw-back of undervalue transactions in insolvency has convincingly been argued to be the amelioration of 'asset substitution'.[1229] As explained in Chapter 1, asset substitution is a subtle form of the perverse incentive of company controllers to pursue excessively risk projects in the vicinity of insolvency. It constitutes the transfer of wealth, in an expected value sense, from the creditors to the company controllers through the application of low-risk assets to high-risk corporate projects. In such a trans-

1227 *PricewaterhouseCoopers Inc v IMF (Australia) Ltd and Another* 2013 (6) SA 216 (GNP); *EP Property Projects (Pty) Ltd v Registrar of Deeds, Cape Town, and Another* 2014 (1) SA 141 (WCC). See generally Burger (n 1225).

1228 On the meaning of 'undervalue transaction', see s 238(4) Insolvency Act 1986.

1229 Armour, 'Transactions at an Undervalue' in Armour and Bennett (eds), *Vulnerable Transactions in Corporate Insolvency Law* (Hart Publishing 2003) paras 2.14, 2.28. See generally See generally Clark, 'The Duties of the Corporate Debtor to its Creditors' (1977) 90 Harv.L.Rev. 505; Jackson, 'Avoiding Powers in Bankruptcy' (1984) 36 Stan.L.Rev. 725, 777-86; Baird and Jackson, 'Fraudulent Conveyance Law and its Proper Domain' (1985) 38 Vand.L.Rev. 829; Prentice, 'The Effect of Insolvency on Pre-Liquidation Transcations' in Pettet (ed), *Company Law in Change* (4th edn, Stevens & Son 1987) 69, 75-78.

action the company would receive less consideration than what the assets are worth, in expected value terms. This difference in value is likely to be caught by the second limb of the definition of 'undervalue transactions' under s 238,[1230] namely that the consideration received by the company is 'significantly less' than that which it has given.[1231] 'Significantly less' value has been held to contemplate the difference of anything more than 15% of the true value.[1232]

None of the other rationales for s 238 that have been advanced over the years – namely the avoidance of fraud,[1233] the reversal of unjust enrichment[1234] and the support of the *pari passu* principle[1235] – provide a better account of 238 than the curbing of asset substitution.[1236]

It would seem that none of the further requirements for attacking undervalue transaction in insolvency under s 238 detract significantly from regarding that provision as a legal strategy to counteract asset substitution transactions.

First, undervalue transactions can only be attacked if they occurred at 'the relevant time'. This concept has a temporal and financial element. The temporal element is that the transaction must have been entered into within two years of the onset of insolvency proceedings.[1237] The financial element is that the transaction must have taken place when the company was unable to pay its debts within the meaning of s 123 Insolvency Act 1986, or the company must have become so as a result of entering into the transaction.[1238]

1230 S 238(4)(b) Insolvency Act 1986.

1231 Armour (n 1229) paras 2.14, 2.28. The first limb of the definition deals with gifts or transactions for no consideration (s 238(4)(a) Insolvency Act 1986). This limb does not seem to catch asset substitution transactions.

1232 See *National Westminster Bank plc v Jones* [2001] 1 BCLC 98 at 129 (affirmed [2001] EWCA Civ 1541, [2002] 1 BCLC 55); *McDonald & Anor v Hanselmann* (1998) 28 ACSR 49 at 56.

1233 See Armour (n 1229) paras 2.19, 2.20.

1234 Birks and Mitchell, 'Unjust Enrichment' in Birks (ed), *English Private Law* Vol II (Oxford University Press 2000) 525, 529.

1235 See Bridge, 'Insolvency' in Birks (ed), *English Private Law* Vol II (Oxford University Press 2000); Keay, 'In Pursuit of the Rationale Behind the Avoidance of Pre-Liquidation Transactions' (1996) 18 Syd LR 55, 65.

1236 Armour (n 1229) paras 2.14ff.

1237 S 238(2) read with 240(1) Insolvency Act 1986.

1238 S 238(2) read with s 240(2) Insolvency Act 1986.

The financial element of 'the relevant time' could be seen to come close to identifying the point at which the risk-shifting incentive arises.[1239] 'Inability to pay debts' within the meaning of s 123 contemplates both the cash flow and the balance sheet tests of insolvency. Since balance sheet insolvency ordinarily occurs before cash flow insolvency[1240] and, as we have seen, the wrongful trading duty under s 214 Insolvency Act is pegged to cash flow insolvency, s 238 potentially bites before s 214, and thus closer to the point at which the risk-shifting incentive arises.[1241]

However, the temporal element of 'the relevant time' is less useful as a gauge of when the risk-shifting incentive arises. The presence of the twilight period under s 238 is best seen as an historical descendant of those fraudulent conveyances under the Statute of Elizabeth[1242] that arose only in insolvency proceedings, and were accordingly actionable only by the office holder, as opposed to 'pure' fraudulent conveyance actions that had no retrospective effect and could be brought by any person prejudiced by it.[1243] This historical purpose does not transfer seamlessly to viewing s 238 as reducing company-creditor agency costs. This is because any time period in advance of the commencement of insolvency proceedings says very little about when the shareholders have lost their economic interest in the company, which is the reason for the perverse incentive to pursue excessively risky projects, including the subtle form of asset substitution in question. The problem with this is, of course, that potentially value-minimising transactions will not be caught by s 238 where the risk-shifting incentive arises before the two year twilight period. However, it

1239 On the point at which the risk-shifting incentive arises, see Chapter 1 and the theoretical discussion above in this Chapter on the statutory creditor-regarding duties.

1240 Armour (n 1229) paras 2.34.

1241 The company is presumed to have been unable to pay its debts at the time of the transaction where the counterparty is a connected person to the company (s 240(2)(passage after para 2) Insolvency Act 1986). This presumption is thought to be a legacy of the applicable fraudulent conveyance provision, as a close relationship between the parties to a transaction provides a strong inference of collusion between the parties to a transaction, and thus fraud on the part of both parties. This could harm creditors irrespective of whether the transaction took place when the company was insolvent or became insolvent as a result of the transaction; Armour (n 1229) paras 2.19–20.

1242 Statute of 13 Elizabeth 1, c.5 of 1571.

1243 Armour (n 1229) paras 2.7ff.

would seem unlikely that the risk-shifting incentive would arise that far in advance regularly.

Second, the requirements that there must be mutuality of intent of the parties entering into the transaction, apart from cases where a gift is made by the company,[1244] supports the view that s 238 is best seen as curbing asset substitution transactions. Since s 238 recruits potential counterparties of companies as monitors to be wary of 'generous bargains' with companies in distress (as further explained at bb. below), the counterparties can only be expected to do so if they are aware that the transactions could be harmful to the company, and the mutuality requirement goes a long way to ensuring this to be the case.[1245]

Third, the counterparty can raise two defences to an action brought by the office holder under s 238, namely that (i) the debtor-company entered into the transaction in good faith and for the purpose of carrying on its business; and (ii) there were reasonable grounds for believing that it would benefit the debtor-company.[1246]

The first defence appears to combine the directors' fiduciary duties to act *bona fide* in the best interests of the company and to exercise their directorial powers for purposes for which they were conferred.[1247] The purpose is specified in the section as the carrying on of the company's business, which would appear to include once-off transactions in special circumstances, for example during informal rescue operations.[1248] However, since the standard of this defence appears to be subjective,[1249] combined with the fact that the onus of proof of establishing both defences is on the counterparty, the practical relevance of this defence appears to be limited.[1250]

1244 See *Re Taylor Sinclair (Capital) Ltd* [2001] 2 BCLC 176. For a critique on that decision and on the mutuality approach in general, see Mokal and Ho, 'Consideration, Characterisation, Evaluation: Transactions at an Undervalue after *Phillips v Brewin Dolphin*' (2001) 1 J. Corp. L 359, 360ff.

1245 Armour (n 1229) paras 2.59.

1246 S 238(5) Insolvency Act 1986.

1247 Armour (n 1229) paras 2.111.

1248 See the relevant Parliamentary debates on s 238 as part of the insolvency law reforms of 1985/86: HC Debts (6th Series) 84 col 687, 28 October 1985. See generally Armour (n 1229) paras 2.111.

1249 Keay and Walton, *Insolvency Law – Corporate and Personal* (2nd edn, Jordans 2008) 553.

1250 Armour (n 1229) paras 2.112.

The second defence requires a showing that at the time of the undervalue transaction there were reasonable grounds for believing that it would benefit the company's business, which is an objective enquiry.[1251]

Both defences could be seen to encourage informal rescue measures by recognising that unsecured creditors could benefit in the long run from the ability of companies in distress to sell non-core assets quickly, albeit at an undervalue.[1252] This policy does not contradict the argument that s 238's ultimate purpose is to control asset substitution transactions.

bb. Explaining the gatekeeper control standards strategy with reference to the negligence-based trading standards strategy under the wrongful trading provision

S 238 could be seen to complement the imposition of *ex post* liability on directors for wrongful trading under s 214 Insolvency Act 1986 considered above. This is because s 238 specifically targets asset substitution transactions, while s 214 catches the value-reducing trading in the vicinity of insolvency as a result of the risk-shifting incentive more generally. Like s 214, s 238 also operates as an *ex post standards strategy*: while the standard under s 214 is negligence-based trading of the company in the critical period, under s 238 it is the conclusion of undervalue transactions at the relevant time between the company and a third party.

However, s 238 seeks to counteract creditor-harming actions by the company controllers as a result of the risk-shifting incentive in a rather different manner to s 214. Rather than targeting directors for wrongful trading in the vicinity of insolvency, s 238 conscripts potential counterparties of undervalue transactions as gatekeepers and forces them to think twice about entering into such transactions with an ailing company.[1253] Moreover, rather than seeking to ensure compliance by directors with their wrongful trading duty by imposing personal liability on them *ex post*, compliance of the gatekeepers with s 238 is reinforced by the risk that the

---

1251 Ibid.

1252 Parry, *Corporate Rescue* (Sweet & Maxwell 2008) para 18-03.

1253 Kraakman and other (eds), *Anatomy of Corporate Law – A Comparative and Functional Approach* (2nd edn, Oxford University Press 2009) 141–2; Armour (n 1229) paras 2.29.

counterparty may have to return the amount or asset received to the debtor during insolvency proceedings *ex post*.[1254]

b. The claw-back in insolvency of 'dispositions without value' under South African law and relevant remedies under German law

aa. General; relevance of further types of claw-back remedies to the problem of asset substitution

The equivalent statutory provisions to s 238 in South Africa is found in s 26 Insolvency Act 1936[1255] and in Germany in §§ 132 and 134 *Insolvenzordnung*. Similar to s 238, both the South African and German provisions allow the office holder to claw back amounts or assets disposed of within relevant time frames before the opening of insolvency proceedings for less than their true value. Since one of the characteristic features of an asset substitution transaction is a disparity between the true value of the asset and the expected value of the projects to which such assets are applied, both the South African and German claw-back remedies could be relevant.

It does not appear as though other types of claw-back remedies are relevant to the problem of asset substitution. First, as already noted in Chapter 1, claw-back remedies that allow the attack of transactions which are aimed at, or have the effect of, preferring certain creditors over others, deal with the problem of inter-creditor agency costs in the vicinity of insolvency,[1256] rather than company-creditor agency costs, which is at issue here.

Second, there is a type of claw-back remedies that requires fraudulent intent on the part of the debtor-company and sometimes also the counterparty.[1257] However, these type of claw-back remedies are generally not

1254 Armour (n 1229) paras 2.29.

1255 This section applies to entities falling under the Companies Act 2008 by virtue of s 340 Companies Act 1973, which, in turn, continues to apply under the new company law regime by virtue of Sch 5 item 9 Companies Act 2008.

1256 See the discussion in PART A, Chapter 1, II., 3., b. above.

1257 Examples of such remedies are the common law *actio Pauliana* in South Africa, which allows for the rescission of transactions by the insolvent in fraud of creditors both outside and within insolvency (Bertelsmann and others (n 1047) 281ff); Boraine, 'Toward Codifying the Actio Pauliana' (1996) 8 SA Merc LJ 227); transaction intended to disadvantage creditors under § 133(1) *Insolven-*

suitable for controlling the problem of asset substitution, as the parties to an asset substitution transaction would seem to enter into such transactions regardless of fraudulent intent.

A final type of claw-back remedies is transactions with a third party connected to the company, which is not a necessary feature of the problem of asset substitution.[1258] This is because such transactions can be, and often are, concluded with counterparties that are not connected to the company.

We will now consider the applicable South African and German claw-back remedies mentioned above.

bb. The South African claw-back remedy

According to s 26 Insolvency Act 1936, the office holder may set aside any disposition not made for value by the debtor-company if the disposition caused the debtor-company to become balance sheet insolvent. Where the relevant disposition was made more than two years before the onset of insolvency proceedings, then the office holder bears the onus of proof. However, where the disposition was made within two years of the onset of insolvency proceedings, then the counterparty benefitting from the disposition bears the onus proof.[1259]

Only dispositions *without* value are liable to be impugned under s 26. The term 'without value' has been interpreted to mean either *no* value[1260] (for example, a donation) or merely *illusory* or *nominal* value.[1261] The meaning of 'illusory' value is not defined and appears to mean value that seems to exist, but actually does not exist. 'Nominal' value is used in its plain language meaning, ie, consideration as a mere matter of form, being

---

zordnung in Germany; and the transactions defrauding creditors under ss 423–425 Insolvency Act 1986 in the UK.

1258 Examples of such type of claw-back remedies are found in the US (see 11 USC § 548(a)(1)) and Germany (see § 133(2) *Insolvenzordung*).

1259 S 26(1) Insolvency Act 1936.

1260 The term 'value' must be interpreted in its ordinary sense; *Estate Wege v Strauss* 1932 AD 76, 82.

1261 *Swanee's Boerdery (Edms) Bpk (in Liquidation) v Trust Bank of Africa Ltd* 1986 (2) SA 850 (A) 860; *Terblanche v Baxtrans CC* 1998 3 SA 912 (C) 917.

far below the real value,[1262] and does not refer to its economic meaning, ie, face value or book value.[1263] The types of transactions the courts have thus far found to fall within s 26 generally fall squarely within the restrictive meaning of 'without value'. They include relinquishing or mortgaging of assets without any legal obligation to do so;[1264] payment under an invalid or illegal contract;[1265] the sale of property for a trifling consideration;[1266] and a surety or guarantee.[1267] It would therefore seem that the difference between an asset's market value and the value received as required by the terms 'illusory' and 'nominal' is too big for the relevant South African claw-back provision to catch the more subtle difference in value between the market value of assets and consideration typically found in an asset substitution transaction.[1268]

1262 Oxford Online Dictionary < http://www.oxforddictionaries.com> accessed 20 December 2016.

1263 It should also be noted that 'value' is not confined to a monetary or tangible material consideration, nor need it be arithmetically calculable (*Goode Durrant & Murray Ltd v Hewitt & Cornell NNO* 1961 (4) SA 286 (N); *Enyati Resources Ltd v Thorne NO* 1984 (2) SA 551 (C) 563; *Rousseau v Visser* 1989 2 289 (C), as confirmed on appeal in *Visser v Rousseau* 1990 1 SA 139 (AD*); Rousseau v Malan* 1989 2 SA 451 (C)). Thus, eg, the financial stability of a group of companies may constitute value under s 26; *Langeberg Koöperasie Bpk v Inverdoorn Farming and Trading Co Ltd* 1965 (2) SA 587 (A). However, this is not a hard and fast rule, and would depend on the circumstances of each case; *Swanee's Boerdery (Edms) Bpk (in Liquidation) v Trust Bank of Africa Ltd* 1986 (2) SA 850 (A) 860.

1264 *Swadif (Pty) Ltd v Dyke NO* 1978 (1) SA 928 (A).

1265 *Estate Jager v Whittaker & another* 1944 AD 246; *Harcourt v Eastman NO* 1953 (2) SA 424 (N); *Rousseau en andere v Malan en'n ander* 1989 (2) SA 451 (C).

1266 *Bloom's Trustee v Fourie* 1921 TPD 599.

1267 *Swanee's Boerdery (Edms) Bpk (in Liquidation) v Trust Bank of Africa Ltd* 1986 (2) SA 850 (A) 53.

1268 It has been suggested, however, that s 26 includes transactions made for 'inadequate value' (see the *obiter dictum* in *Cronje v De Paiva* [1997] 2 All SA 80 (B) 86, citing Bertelsmann and others (n 1047) 254, para 13.6), which might perhaps be a helpful concept for the problem of asset substitution. However, the better view is that it does not, as the courts have predominantly insisted on the restrictive interpretation as expressed by 'illusory' and 'nominal' value, which leaves little scope for the (intuitively) broader meaning of 'inadequate'; see, eg, *Terblanche v Baxtrans CC* 1998 3 SA 912 (C) 917, where the court rejected the argument that less than equivalent value was *prima facie* proof of no value,

From the above it would seem that the better rationale of s 26 is the prevention of blatant instances of asset dilution, rather than the more subtle form of asset substitution. As elucidated in Chapter 1 and in the introduction of this Chapter, asset dilution transactions fall outside the scope of the analysis, as they occur independent of the risk-shifting incentive in the vicinity of insolvency and, strictly-speaking, are best seen as isolated transactions, rather than forming part of the company controllers' general strategic decision to continue trading and embarking on overly risky projects in the vicinity of insolvency.

cc. The German claw-back remedies

§ 134 Insolvenzordnung—It is appropriate to start the discussion on the German remedies with § 134 *Insolvenzordung*, as this is the claw-back remedy that deals specifically with transactions for a lesser value, although it is § 132 *Insolvenzordnung* that actually comes functionally closer to curbing asset substitution transactions. According to § 134, the insolvency officer holder may contest any gratuitous benefit ('*unentgeltliche Leistung*') granted by the debtor-company to a third party within four years of the opening of insolvency proceedings and which disadvantages the insolvency creditors.[1269] The receiver of a gratuitous benefit within the meaning of § 134 has to restore such benefit only to the extent of his enrichment, unless the receiver knew or must have known under the circumstances that the gratuitous benefit disadvantaged the insolvency creditors.[1270]

For purposes of § 134, a benefit is gratuitous if the value of the benefit granted by the debtor-company is not matched by the value of the counter-performance of the counterparty;[1271] the scope of § 134 is therefore broader than the making of donations.[1272]

---

as this may nevertheless amount to *illusory or nominal* value; see also *Freeman and Another v Germishuys* [2006] JOL 18632 (T) 18.

1269 § 134(1) read with § 129(1) *Insolvenzordnung*.

1270 § 143(2) *Insolvenzordnung*.

1271 Ede and Hirte, '§ 134' in Uhlenbruck and Hirte (eds), *Kommentar Insolvenzordnung* (14th rev. edn, Vahlen 2015) recital 27ff.

1272 Ibid recital 33.

Whether or not the value of the debtor company's performance and the value of the counterparty's counter-performance are commensurate is judged first from an objective perspective.[1273] Where the objective enquiry does not provide a clear answer, the subjective perceptions of the parties may be considered; here they are said to be given 'reasonable scope for judgment' ('*angemessener Beurteilungsspielraum*').[1274] This subjective limb to the enquiry is meant to ensure that commercial conditions and market realities are taken into account.[1275] Thus, forced sales below true value generally fall outside § 134, provided the parties have not overstepped the reasonable scope for judgment.[1276] In saying that, the subjective scope of judgment of the parties may not be too far removed from the objective realities.[1277]

It would seem that in contrast to the South African claw-back provision, the required difference between the value of the performance and the value of the counter-performance under § 134 may in certain instances be sufficiently small to catch asset substitution transactions.

However, two aspects of § 134 do not sit well with regarding it as a legal strategy to ameliorate asset substitution transactions. First, to be sure, the enquiry as to whether or not the counterparty to the gratuitous benefit is regarded to have agreed to commensurate counter-performance is subjective in principle.[1278] However, misconceptions on the part of counterparties, such as the mistaken belief that performance was received from a third party rather than from the debtor-company, generally do not save the counterparty from the claw-back remedy.[1279] This detracts from the ability

---

1273 BGH NZI 2010, 439.

1274 BGHZ 71, 61, 66 = NJW 1978, 1326, 1327; BGHZ NZI 2004, 376, 378; BGHZ 113, 98, 102ff = NJW 1991, 560, 561.

1275 Ede and Hirte, '§ 134' (n 1271) recital 29.

1276 Ibid 29; Kayser, '§ 134' in Kirchhof, Eidenmüller and Stürner (eds), *Münchener Kommentar zur Insolvenzordnung* Vol 2 (3rd edn, C.H. Beck 2013) recitals 25, 41.

1277 See generally Ede and Hirte, '§ 134' (n 1271) recital 29ff; Kayser, '§ 134' (n 1276) recital 40ff. It is also possible that a benefit granted to a counterparty is partially gratuitous; see generally Ede and Hirte, '§ 134' (n 1271) recital 34; Kayser, '§ 134' (n 1276) recital 41.

1278 Kayser, '§ 134' (n 1276) recitals 17, 40.

1279 GH 11.12.2008 IX ZR 195/07 ZIP 2009, 186 = ZInsO 2009, 185 = NZI 2009, 103; BGH 21.12.2010 IX ZR 199/10 Tz 12 f NZI 2011, 107 = ZInsO 2011, 183; BGH 18.7.2013 IX ZR 198/10 Tz 21 ZIP 2013, 1504. See also Kayser, '§ 134'

of potential contractual counterparties to exercise their monitoring function under the *gatekeeper control strategy*.

Second, and more importantly, the four year period up until the opening of insolvency proceedings within which a gratuitous benefit is vulnerable does not appropriately identify the point at which the risk-shifting incentive arises. Insofar as the risk-shifting incentive is generated only after the start of the twilight period, § 134 may give rise to unnecessary monitoring costs of potential contractual counterparties of debtor-companies in certain circumstances.

§ 132 Insolvenzordnung—According to § 132, the office holder may contest any legal transaction that directly disadvantages creditors of the company (§ 132(1)) and any other legal act by which the debtor-company loses a right or is unable to assert such right or by which a proprietary claim against the debtor-company is maintained or becomes enforceable (§ 132(2)). § 132(2) is supposed to provide for a catch-all provision for all legal acts disadvantaging creditors (i) that are not caught by paying off, or granting pre-existing security to, creditors pursuant to §§ 130 and 131, (ii) that lack an intentional element pursuant to § 133 and (iii) that fall short of a gratuitous benefit pursuant to § 134.[1280]

§ 132(2) is not directly relevant to the problem of asset substitution. § 132(1), on the other hand, has been held to include the 'emergency' sale of assets at an undervalue in order to restore the debtor company's liquidity and equivalent transactions.[1281] To the extent that undervalue transactions disadvantage creditors, and thus fall within the underlying purpose of § 132,[1282] this remedy addresses the problem of asset substitution to a greater degree than § 134, since undervalue transactions comes closer to describing the problem of asset substitution than gratuitous benefits.

(n 1276) recital 17; Ede and Hirte, '§ 134' (n 1271) recital 32. The good faith belief of the counterparty that the gratuitous benefit did not disadvantage the insolvency creditors merely reduces the size of the amount to be returned to the company under § 143(2) (Kayser, '§ 134' (n 1276) recital 17).

1280 Ede and Hirte, '§ 132' in Uhlenbruck and Hirte (eds), *Kommentar Insolvenzordnung* (14th rev. edn, Vahlen 2015) recita 12.; Kayser, '§ 132' in Kirchhof, Eidenmüller and Stürner (eds), *Münchener Kommentar zur Insolvenzordnung* Vol 2 (3rd edn, C.H. Beck 2013) recital 20.

1281 Ede and Hirte, '§ 132' (n 1280) recital 2; Kayser, '§ 132' (n 1280) recital 1.

1282 Kayser, '§ 132' (n 1280) recital 1.

Transactions falling under § 132 can only be attacked when they have occurred when the company was cash flow insolvent and within three months of the opening of insolvency proceedings.[1283] Since cash flow insolvency generally occurs after the risk-shifting incentive arises,[1284] and generally before three months within the onset of insolvency proceedings, § 132 is probably triggered too late for it to counteract asset substitution effectively. To be sure, similar to the mutuality of intent under the applicable British claw-back remedy, the requirement that the counterparty must have known that the company was cash flow insolvent,[1285] could be seen to acknowledge that third parties can only exercise their gatekeeper functions adequately if they are aware that the debtor-company is in financial difficulties. However, the requirement that such knowledge is presumed where the third party is connected to the debtor-company (as described in § 138) does not specifically address the risk-shifting incentive that gives rise to asset substitution.

c. Conclusion

Since the specific problem of asset substitution is merely a more specific form of the strategic decision in relation to the continued trading in the vicinity of insolvency, it is (indirectly) covered by the threat of personal liability of directors under the reckless trading duty. What is more, the imposition of personal liability on directors has a stronger re-balancing effect on the risk-shifting incentive than undervalue transactions enforced by gatekeeper control. It would therefore seem more effective than the claw-back remedy.

On the other hand, the British claw-back provision of undervalue transactions is the more specific legal strategy for the problem of asset substitution. This means that broadening the scope of the applicable South African claw-back provision could play a useful (supplementary) role in South Africa in controlling the problem of asset substitution.

1283 § 132(1)(no 1). The ability of the office holder to contest applicable transactions after insolvency proceedings have commenced (§ 132(1)(no 2)) is obviously not relevant in this context.

1284 See PART C, Chapter 5, II., 3., a above

1285 § 132(1)(no 1).

2. Control of risk-shifting incentive by relevant delictual liability under South African law and British law?

a. The elements of the delict

Since *Kern Trust (Edms) Bpk v Hurter*[1286] South African law recognises a delictual action against any debtor that has incurred debts without a reasonable expectation of discharging it. The debtor's misrepresentation of its financial position to the creditor constitutes the wrongful conduct. By incurring the debt, the debtor (impliedly) misrepresents to the creditor its ability to discharge it.[1287] The fault element is negligence (*culpa*).[1288] Insofar as this misrepresentation induces the creditor to extend credit to the company and the creditor suffers (patrimonial) loss[1289] as a result, the debtor could be held liable in delict.[1290]

b. Tensions between the law of delict and company law – perspectives from the UK

However, where this delictual action is applied to directors acting on behalf of companies, the default position in company law is that the company, not the director, is the perpetrator of the delict. This is the position in

---

1286 1981 (3) SA 607 (C) 616 followed, *inter alia*, by *Bayer South Africa (Pty) Ltd v Frost* 1991 4 SA 559 (A).

1287 See the *obiter dictum* in *Ex parte De Villiers and another: In re Carbon Developments (Pty) Ltd (in liquidation)* 1992 (2) SA 95 (W) 145. The court based this contention on the general principle pronounced by *Kern Trust (Edms) Bpk v Hurter* 1981 (3) SA 607 (C) that delictual liability for negligent misstatements that induces a person to a contract does exist under South African law; see generally also de Koker, *Die Roekelose en Bedrieglike Dryf van Besigheid in die Suid-Afrikaanse Maatskappyereg* (unpublished LLD thesis, University of the Orange Free State 1996) 61–2.

1288 Yet it has been held that where a reasonable expectation of discharging the debt is absent, it will be very difficult for the debtor to prove the honesty of the belief; see, eg, *Frankel Pollak Vinderine Inc v Sandton NO* 1996 2 All SA 582 (W) 596.

1289 See, eg, *Administrateur van Natal v Trust Bank van Afrika Bpk* 1979 3 SA 824 (A) 832–3.

1290 See generally, eg, *Administrateur van Natal v Trust Bank van Afrika Bpk* 1979 3 SA 824 (A); *Bayer South Africa (Pty) Ltd v Frost* 1991 4 SA 559 (A).

British law, where due to the 'identification' or 'alter ego' theory, the directing mind and will of the person acting on behalf of the company is ascribed to the company.[1291] It has been argued that the policy consideration underlying this approach is the promotion of the corporate form as a vehicle for corporate risk-taking.[1292]

However, in seeking to give effect to the opposing consideration from the law of tort – namely that every person should answer for their own tortious acts –, the British courts have imposed liability on directors or other agents of the company where on the facts, the plaintiff can prove that the director has assumed personal responsibility for the negligent misstatement (on either an actual or imputed basis), and the plaintiff has reasonably relied on the director's misstatement. The test in determining whether the director had accepted personal responsibility for the negligent misstatement is objective, ie, whether it was reasonable for the third party to conclude that the director accepted responsibility.[1293]

However, in South Africa, the court in *Pinshaw's* case rejected the 'assumption of responsibility' test as applied in British law.[1294] In line with earlier criticism of the British position in South African academic writing,[1295] the point of departure for determining directorial liability in this

---

1291 On the 'identification' or 'alter ego' theory, see, eg, *Lennard's Carrying Company Ltd v Asiatic Petroleum Company Ltd* [1915] AC 705 (HL) 713; *HL Bolton (Engineering) Co Ltd v TJ Graham and Sons Ltd* [1957] 1 QB 159 (CA); *Tesco Supermarkets Ltd v Nattrass* [1972] AC 153 (HL); *Meridian Global Funds Management Asia Ltd v Securities Commission* [1995] 2 AC 500 (PC).

1292 See *C Evans & Sons v Spritebrand Ltd* 1985 2 All Er 415, 424. For classical academic accounts of this policy consideration, see Sealy, 'Directors' "wider" responsibilities - problems conceptual, practical and procedural' 1987 Mon LR 164, 186; Grantham and Rickett, 'Directors' 'Tortious' Liability: Contract, Tort or Company Law?' 1999 MLR 133, 139 and Link Newcomb, 'The limitation of directors' liability: a proposal for legislative reform' [1987] Tex. L. Rev. 411, 412–3; from a South African perspective, see du Plessis, *Maatskappyregtelike Grondslae van die Posisie van Direkteure en Bestuurende Direkteure* (unpublished LLD thesis, University of the Orange Free State 1990) 266.

1293 See Davies and Worthington (n 1021) para 7-31.

1294 *Pinshaw v Nexus Securities (Pty) Ltd* 2002 (2) SA 510 (C) 535.

1295 See de Koker, 'Die Aanspreekliheid van Direkteure vir Delikte Gepleeg in Ampsverband' (2002) 1 TSAR 18, 35–7; de Koker, 'Die Roekelose en Bedrieglike Dryf' (n 1287) 117–25; see also Havenga, 'Directors' Co-liability for Delicts' (2006) 18 SA Merc LJ 229, 236. For earlier sympathies of this approach, see du Plessis and Henning, 'Die Deliktuele Aanspreeklikheid van Persone wat as Maatsappyorgane Opgetree het' [1989] THRHR 540. Generally, the

regard now appears to be the law of delict. Although no clear principles have emerged as yet, one criterion that appears to have been accepted by the courts is that where circumstances suggest that there is a relationship between the company's director/employee and the third party, in which the director/employee can be said to owe a particular duty of care or skill to the third party, personal liability of the director/employee is possible.[1296] *Pinshaw*'s case also stated that despite the fact that the 'assumption of responsibility' doctrine does not apply in South Africa, considerations underlying the doctrine – namely proximity between the director and the third party, the directors' professed skills and the third party's reliance thereon – are relevant in determining the wrongfulness of the director's purported misrepresentation.[1297]

However, despite the broader scope of the delictual action against directors in South Africa than in the UK, the company controllers' perverse incentive in the vicinity of insolvency is not likely to be caught by delictual liability under South African law. The opportunism at issue, as it would typically arise, would not appear to regularly involve behaviour by the company controllers giving rise to the 'special relationship' between the director and the affected creditor, so as to found a particular duty of care owed by the director to the affected creditor, as is required by the delictual action.

3. The development of a general directors' duty to creditors in various common law jurisdictions

In various common law jurisdictions (but apparently not yet in South Africa), the law of directors' duties has, over the last few decades, de-

British position was criticised for being unduly harsh on the victims of the delict: where the company is not available to be sued (notably because it is insolvent), the creditor would be left empty-handed, which – applied to the scenario laid out above – disadvantages particularly the least informed (trade) creditors, the type of creditors that the law ought to grant special protection to. The general law of delict (and particularly the element of wrongfulness) would seem to be sufficiently flexible to strike an appropriate balance between the opposing policy considerations mentioned above.

1296 See *Pinshaw v Nexus Securities (Pty) Ltd and another* 2002 (2) SA 510 (C) 535 and *Durr v ABSA Bank Ltd and another* 1997 (3) SA 448 (SCA).

1297 At 535.

veloped toward the recognition of a general duty to take account of the interests of creditors in circumstances near insolvency.[1298] The general duty to creditors has been developed by extending to creditors the common law duties traditionally owed by directors to the company. However, no clear trend has emerged from the case law yet as to which of the two strands of the traditional common law duties – fiduciary or care and skill – should be the preferred basis for such a development, as it is conceptually possible to found the general duty of creditors on both such strands.[1299] The fundamental difference between these two strands of common law directors' duties, is that fiduciary duties require the directors, in exercising their discretionary powers, to promote the interests of the beneficiary. The duty of care and skill, by contrast, requires directors to avoid harm to the beneficiary, which means that fiduciary duties are conceptually more demanding than the duty of care. In other words, where the fiduciary duties are extended to creditors, directors would, from a particular point in the company's decline towards insolvency, be required to promote the interests of

1298 The trend started in Australia in the 1970s by *Walker v Wimborne* (1976) 137 CLR 1, 6–7, and was subsequently followed by other common law jurisdictions. For a further influential case in Australia, see *Kinsela v Russell Kinsela Pty Ltd (in liq)* (1986) 4 NSWLR 722; for the UK, see, eg, *Lonrho Ltd v Shell Petroleum Co Ltd* [1980] 1 WLR 627, 634; *Liquidator of West Mercia Safetywear Ltd v Dodd* (1988) 4 BCC 30; for New Zealand, see, eg, *Hilton International Ltd (in liq) v Hilton* [1989] NZLR 442; for the US, see, eg, *Credit Lyonnais Bank Nederland, NV v Pathe Communications Corp* No 12150 1991 WL 277613 (Del Ch Dec 30, 1991), reprinted in (1992) 17 *Del.J.Corp.L.*1099; and for Canada, see, eg, *Dylex Ltd (Trustee of) v Anderson* (2003) 63 OR (3rd) 659, 32 BLR (3rd) (Ont SCJ Comm List); *Peoples Department Stores Inc v Wise* [1998] Q.J. No. 3571 (Bankruptcy and Insolvency Division) (Quebec Supreme Court); however, the Peoples Department Stores decision was overturned on appeal (*Peoples Department Stores Inc v Wise* (2003) 224 DLR (4th) 509), and there is thus some doubt as to the continued existence of the principles of the general duty of creditors developed in the court of first instance; see generally on this debate Morgan and Underwood, 'Directors' Liability to Creditors on a Corporation's Insolvency in Light of the *Dylex* and *Peoples Department Stores* Litigation' (2004) 39 C.B.L.J. 336. For a useful overview of the legal position in the common law at the time, see Keay, 'Another way of skinning a cat: enforcing directors' duties for the benefit of creditors' (2004) 17 Insolv. Int. 1. For a a comprehensive study on the development of a duty to creditors in South Africa, see Lombard, *Directors' Duties to Creditors* (unpublished LLD thesis, University of Pretoria 2006).

1299 Davies, 'Directors' Creditor-Regarding Duties' (n 1007) 327–8; Lombard (n 1298) 129.

creditors (either exclusively or along with those of shareholders). However, where the duty of care and skill is extended to creditors, directors – in promoting primarily the interests of the shareholders – [1300] would be required to ensure that their actions do not prejudice the interests of creditors.[1301]

The burden of proving both strands of directors' duties is potentially lower than the South African statutory creditor-regarding duty. This is because liability for breaches of fiduciary duties is typically strict[1302] and the fault element of the duty of care and diligence is negligence. By contrast, because the fault element for reckless trading in the vicinity of insolvency is gross negligence, it is slightly more difficult to prove,[1303] although the directors may raise the defence of the business judgment rule where they are charged with breaching the duty of care, skill and diligence.[1304] The lower burden of proof of the common law duties than the statutory creditor-regarding duty could raise the level of protection of the body of creditors from value-minimising trading by companies as a result of the risk-shifting incentive.

Although it is clear that the duty generally bites in advance of insolvency (and not only once the company has reached a state of insolvency), the courts have experimented with different trigger points. There is even some authority that the duty may arise while the company is still solvent and

---

1300 The South African company arguably adopts an 'enlightened shareholder value' approach – ie, that the long-term interests of shareholders are to be primarily promoted, but the interests of stakeholders are to be taken into account to the extent that such interests promote the long-term interests of the shareholders (see generally FHI Cassim (n 1084) 467–70). See, however, the current version of the Corporate Governance Code of South Africa ('King Code of Governance Principles for South Africa' (2009), IoDSA, <http://c.ymcdn.com/sites/www.iodsa.co.za/resource/collection/94445006-4F18-4335-B7FB-7F5A8B23F-B3F/King_III_Code_for_Governance_Principles_.pdf> accessed 10 January 2017), which recommends that a 'stakeholder-inclusive' approach be adopted, pursuant to which the interests of stakeholders are to be given equal importance to those of shareholders.

1301 Davies, 'Directors' Creditor-Regarding Duties' (n 1007) 328.

1302 Lombard (n 1298) 399. The duty to act in the best interests of the company probably comes closest to ameliorating value-minimising continued trading in the vicinity of insolvenc. However, as noted above, this duty is subjective, which of course raises the burden of proof considerably.

1303 See PART C, Chapter 5, II., 2., d., aa. above.

1304 S 76(4)(a) Companies Act 2008.

where the directors take actions that would push the company into insolvency.[1305] It would seem that the courts' flexibility in determining when the duty would arise might be an advantage over the more static trigger point of the statutory creditor-regarding duty, as it would allow the courts some freedom to adapt the trigger to the circumstances of each case. Particularly the ability to push the trigger to an earlier stage in the company's path to insolvency would seem useful, given that the trigger of the statutory duty arguably has the potential to kick in after the shareholder's economic interest in the company has been extinguished, and thus too late.[1306]

Although some courts have toyed with the idea that the modified common law duty is owed directly to creditors,[1307] the majority view is that the recipient of the duty is the company.[1308] As we have seen in relation to the same debate in respect of the statutory creditor-regarding duties, this means that the duty can only be enforced by the company (through a derivative action) outside of insolvency proceedings and by the office holder during insolvency proceedings.

1305 *Nicholson v Permakraft (NZ) Ltd* [1985] 1 NZLR 242. See generally Davies, 'Directors' Creditor-Regarding Duties' (n 1007) 328; Lombard (n 1298) 106ff.

1306 In relation to the British statutory creditor-regarding duty, see Davies, 'Directors' Creditor-Regarding Duties' (n 1007) 329. On the trigger point generally, see Keay, 'The Directors' Duty to Take into Account the Interests of Company Creditors: When is it Triggered?' (2001) 25 MULR 315.

1307 *Winkworth v Edward Baron Development Ltd* [1986] 1 WLR 1512; *Jeffree v National Companies and Securities Commission* (1989) 7 ACLC 556; *Hilton International Ltd (in liq) v Hilton* [1989] NZLR 442; (1988) 4 NZCLC 64, 721, 64, 751; *Peoples Department Stores Inc v Wise* [1998] Q.J. No. 3571 (Bankruptcy and Insolvency Division) (Quebec Supreme Court). This approach has been heavily criticised in academia; see, eg, Prentice, 'Creditor's Interests and Director's Duties' (1990) 10 OJLS 265, 275; Worthington, 'Directors' Duties, Creditors' Rights and Shareholder Intervention' (1991) 18 MULR 121, 151; Sealy, 'Personal Liability of Directors and Officers for Debts of Insolvent Corporations : A Jurisdictional Perspective (England)' in Ziegel (ed), *Current Developments in International and Comparative Corporate Insolvency Law* (Oxford University Press 1994) 486. The arguments against the view that the duty be owed to creditors directly are conveniently summarised in Keay, 'Another way of skinning a cat' (n 1298) 4.

1308 See, eg, the English case *Yukong Lines Ltd of Korea v Rendsburg Investments Corporation* [1998] BCC 870 and the Australian case *Spies v The Queen* (2000) 201 CLR 603. See generally Davies, 'Directors' Creditor-Regarding Duties' (n 1007) 328.

Moreover, it is the general view of the courts that the general right of shareholders (as 'owners' of the company) to authorise or ratify breaches of the common law duties is not available in respect of the modified common law duty to creditors at some time before the company is placed under insolvency proceedings.[1309] This is an important adjustment of the law, as the shareholders' right of ratification had the potential of undermining the effectiveness of the modified common law duty, given that creditor-harming actions by directors, by necessary implication, would typically have promoted the interests of the shareholders, and the shareholders would therefore only be too happy to ratify such actions *ex post*.[1310]

In contrast to the statutory creditor-regarding duties, the proceeds of the enforcement of the common law duty would appear to not flow primarily to unsecured creditors, but are rather caught by the security interests of secured creditors.[1311] This would seem problematic, as it is the unsecured creditors, not the secured creditors, that bear the primary risk of value-minimising strategic trading decisions by directors.[1312]

IV. The ex ante initiation rights strategy in South Africa: Disclosure of 'financial distress' to affected persons (s 129(7) Companies Act 2008)

1. Explaining the legal strategy

As noted above, the disclosure duty under s 129(7) Companies Act 2008 is presumably intended to provide unsecured creditors and employees with the necessary information that would put them in a position to utilise their

1309 Davies, 'Directors' Creditor-Regarding Duties' (n 1007) 329 and cases cited in n 86. See also Lombard (n 1298) 125ff, particularly 130.

1310 Davies, 'Directors' Creditor-Regarding Duties' (n 1007) 329. It should be noted, however, that if the modified common law duty to creditors were to be developed in South Africa by extension of the codified fiduciary duties to act for a proper purpose and in the best interests of the company (under s 76(3)(a) and (b) Companies Act 2008) or the duty of care, skill and diligence (under s 76(3)(c) Companies Act 2008), breaches of such a duty would be subject to the power of the court of relieving such directors from liability and the right of the company to indemnify from, and purchase directors' insurance for the eventuality of, such breaches.

1311 Davies, 'Directors' Creditor-Regarding Duties' (n 1007) 329.

1312 See the discussion in PART C, Chapter 5, II.,1., b. above.

right under s 131(1) Companies Act 2008 to place the company under rescue proceedings. This effectively enables individual unsecured creditors and employees to *initiate* the managerial decision as to the appropriate format in which the company should be rescued. It is for this reason that s 129(7), together with s 131(1), could be regarded as an *initiation rights strategy*.[1313]

2. A critique of s 129(7) Companies Act 2008

Placing affected persons in a position to exercise managerial rights in relation to the appropriate format for rescuing a distressed company is problematic for two reasons. First, affected persons (apart from perhaps secured creditors) generally lack relevant managerial and financial expertise for taking effective managerial decisions. Moreover, the fact that such constituents are likely to be widely dispersed gives rise to the collective action problem. This is generally the reason for the separation of management and control in companies. Accordingly, save for the most fundamental decisions such as where the company proposes to enter into fundamental transactions, company law generally refrains from affording the owners (acting as principals) so-called 'decision rights'. Even then, company law ordinarily limits the intervention by principals to ratification rights *ex post*, but hardly ever enables principals to initiate managerial decisions *ex ante*.[1314]

Thus, the first reason why s 129(7) is problematic is that it gives rise to high decision-making costs.

Second, because s 129(7) effectively places affected persons in a position where they act as the agents for the company, a new agency relationship comes into being. Particularly unsecured creditors and employees are likely to have a strong perverse incentive to invoke formal rescue proceedings in situations where informal rescue measures would be value-maximising.[1315]

1313 On the *initiation rights strategy* (as a subset of so-called 'decision rights') generally, see PART A, Chapter 1, II., 2., a., cc. above.

1314 Ibid.

1315 Although the term 'affected persons' also includes shareholders and secured creditors, neither of these two constituents will generally be tempted to place a company under rescue proceedings inefficiently. Rather, shareholders have a

The intensity of the opportunism of unsecured creditors depends on the extent of their economic interest in the company at the point at which they are placed in a position to invoke rescue proceedings: the lower their economic interest in the company, the greater the chance that they will take an inefficient decision, as in such a scenario they will carry a smaller share of the downside risk of their decision. Unsecured creditors in such a scenario and employees generally may be tempted to invoke formal rescue proceedings inappropriately, *inter alia*, because rescue proceedings generally afford these two constituents with stronger rights to oversee the management of the company (for example, through disclosure and consultation requirements of the rescue practitioner and the right to form a creditors'/ employees' committee) than in an informal workout. Formal rescue proceedings also afford such constituents a stronger say in the outcome of the restructuring mechanisms through voting rights on the rescue plan than in informal rescue mechanisms. Employees would further favour formal rescue proceedings because of the protection afforded to their employment contracts,[1316] and that their post-commencement claims will be given a super-preference[1317] under rescue proceedings.

Therefore, the second reason why s 129(7) is problematic is because it is likely to generate high agency costs.

Since s 129(7) essentially enhances the ability of affected persons to make use of their right under s 131(1) to place financially distressed companies under formal rescue proceedings, but is for the aforementioned reasons nevertheless problematic, the question arises whether the right of unsecured creditors and employees to invoke rescue proceedings in advance of insolvency generally is justified at all. The only readily apparent justification appears to be that the chance that an affected person may invoke rescue proceedings in advance of insolvency (and the almost certain result that this would eliminate the prospects of informal rescue measures), is to encourage the company's management to pursue informal rescue measures

---

perverse incentive to inappropriately delay the invocation of formal rescue proceedings (risk-shifting incentive) and secured creditors would be tempted either to enforce on their claims outside formal insolvency proceedings or, where that is not possible, to place economically viable companies in liquidation proceedings inefficiently, as both options maximise the chances of returning the full value of their claims.

1316 See the discussion in PART B, Chapter 4, IV., 6., e above.

1317 See the discussion in PART B, Chapter 4, IV., 7 above.

before the point at which the company is 'financially distressed'. Seen in this sense, s 131(1) operates to control the risk-shifting incentive of company controllers in the vicinity of insolvency.

However, this rationale could be queried on two grounds. First, the *ex ante* effect of s 131(1) on the board's decision at what point in the company's path to decline the board is to pursue informal rescue measures, depends heavily on the likelihood that such right of initiation will be utilised. However, due to information asymmetries (and in the absence of disclosure requirements as found under s 129(7)), such right is not likely to be utilised often in practice, which raises doubts as to its effectiveness in achieving its objective.

Second, the effect of s 131(1) to encourage company controllers to embark on informal rescue measures before the company is 'financially distressed' appears to be arbitrary. This is because the question whether formal or informal rescue proceedings should be employed does not in principle depend on the closeness of a company to insolvency. Even if it did, it is doubtful whether six months before cash flow or balance sheet insolvency appropriately identifies the ideal point in time after which informal rescue measures should no longer be taken.[1318]

3. Weak enforcement of s 129(7) Companies Act 2008

S 129(7) operates by way of mandatory disclosure by the board of directors. The type of disclosure under s 129(7) is not periodic (where the disclosure is expected, but not the content, so-called 'known unknowns'); rather, it is *ad hoc* (where the disclosure is not expected, so-called 'unknown unknowns').[1319] Compliance with periodic disclosure generally does not need to be enforced *ex post*, as non-disclosure itself could already arouse the principal's attention.[1320] Because here the danger for the princi-

---

1318 We will encounter this argument again in Chapter 7, where we will consider the financial distress entry ground as a legal strategy for controlling premature entry.

1319 On the two types of disclosure mentioned generally, see Kraakman and others (eds), *Anatomy of Corporate Law – A Comparative and Functional Approach* (2nd edn, Oxford University Press 2009) 50.

1320 For periodic disclosure, the focus of compliance is thus less on whether disclosure is made at all, and more on the disclosure's quality; see Kraakman and others (n 1319) 50.

pal is that the disclosure itself is faulty, the standard legal strategy is for gatekeepers (for example, auditors in respect of financial statements) to ensure the quality of the information. By contrast, compliance with *ad hoc* disclosure relies on vigorous enforcement.[1321]

The Companies Act 2008 does not provide for a specific remedy for non-compliance with s 129(7). In spite of this, non-compliance with s 129(7) may (possibly) give rise to two remedies: (i) compensation for losses incurred by the company or any creditor as result of contravening s 129(7) under s 218(2) Companies Act 2008; or (ii) the auditor's duty to report under s 45 Auditing Profession Act (where the non-compliance with s 129(7) would presumably constitute an 'unlawful omission' under the definition of 'reportable irregularity').[1322]

However, such remedies are unlikely to be effective in practice, as both require that the contravention of s 129(7) has caused 'harm or loss' to the company or any particular affected person (under s 218(2)) or 'material financial loss' to the company (under s 45 Auditing Profession Act), both of which would seem very difficult to prove in practice.

Perhaps due to the weak enforcement of s 129(7), there is anecdotal evidence that it has not played a significant role in practice.[1323]

V. Summary and Conclusion

All jurisdictions in question rely primarily on *ex post* standards strategies to ameliorate the perverse incentive of company controllers in respect of taking value-minimising strategic trading decisions in the vicinity of insolvency, namely: (i) a creditor-regarding statutory duty on directors duty in the vicinity of insolvency; (ii) the claw-back remedy to set aside transactions for less than reasonable equivalent value; and (iii) the development of a general directorial duty owed to creditors in the vicinity of insolvency. A further unique legal strategy is found in South Africa in the form of a disclosure duty of the board of directors to affected persons of the impending insolvency of the company, defined as 'financial distress' (s 129(7) Companies Act 2008). Together with the right of affected persons to apply to court for the commencement of rescue proceedings (s131(1) Companies

1321 Bhattacharya and Daouk, 'The World Price of Insider Trading' (2002) 57 JF 75.
1322 S 1 Auditing Profession Act.
1323 See also Wainer (n 1154) 515.

Act 2008), this disclosure duty can be regarded as an *ex ante initiation rights strategy*.

In relation to the statutory creditor-regarding directorial duty, although directors' risk-shifting incentive is stronger in closely-held companies, it would be present in widely-held companies as well, given that directors would want to avoid losing their jobs under formal insolvency proceedings. However, the fact that directors generally remain in control in debtor-in-possession rescue regimes might explain the absence of an equivalent *ex post standards strategy* in the US. The preferred approach in the US is rather an *ex ante reward strategy*, which effectively transfers the resolution of the company-creditor agency conflict to within formal rescue proceedings.

Although the statutory creditor-regarding duty targets the directors, jurisdictions regularly also impose liability on persons (shareholders and others) who either act as *de facto* directors or influence the directorial decision-making on a continued basis. There is a danger, however, of over-deterrence in relation to imposing liability on banks for their involvement in informal workouts, given the crucial importance of bank funding for the success of such workouts. The UK allays that danger by generally not classifying banks as 'shadow directors' for protecting their own interests in workouts. It is suggested that this position be followed in South Africa. In Germany, the subjective elements of §§ 830, 840 *BGB* (accessory delictual liability) and § 826 *BGB* (intentional damage to another contrary to public policy) appear to effectively result in the same level of liability being imposed as in the UK.

The applicable creditor-regarding duty in South Africa is contained in s 22(1) read with s 77(3)(b) Companies Act 2008, which impose personal liability on directors for knowingly allowing their company to carry on its business recklessly or fraudulently. Since the risk-shifting incentive of company controllers giving rise to the pursuance of excessively risky projects in the vicinity of insolvency arises independently from fraudulent intent, only the 'reckless'-limb of s 22(1) is relevant for our purposes.

Personal liability is imposed on directors for any losses to the company as a result of the reckless trading. Accordingly, in contrast to the predecessor of s 22(1), s 424 Companies Act 1973, a causal link between the prohibited conduct and the company's loss must be established, and losses to individual creditors are irrelevant if the company's net asset position remained stable. These amendments are likely to have reduced the scope, and raised the burden of, proving reckless trading liability.

The range of the prohibited conduct and the actions that directors are required to take once the reckless trading kicks in is determined largely by the meaning of the phrase 'carrying on the company's business recklessly' and the fault element of gross negligence. While s 22(1) would clearly catch strategic trading decisions in the vicinity of insolvency that cause losses to the company, its scope arguably goes beyond that. Accordingly, s 22(1) would, in theory, seem to also catch individual transactions and conduct relating to non-financial matters.

The reckless trading duty does not prescribe a particular course of conduct to the directors when the duty arises, such as placing the company under formal insolvency proceedings. Based on case law under the previous reckless trading duty, directors would be in breach of the reckless trading when, seen from an objective perspective, there would be *no reasonable prospect that the company would be able to pay its debts when these become due*. 'Reasonable prospect' has been held to mean a *strong chance* of non-payment, which is more onerous than a *material (but not a high)* risk of non-payment, but less onerous than where non-payment is a *virtual certainty*.

The applicable test for measuring the directors' conduct has an objective element (ie, reasonable notional person) and a subjective element (ie, the notional person is considered to move in the same spheres and to have the same access to knowledge as the director in question). The better view is that the subjective element can only increase, but never decrease, the level of the duty required by the objective element.

With regard to the trigger of the duty, the phrase '(reasonable) prospect' under the aforementioned judicially formulated test implies that the inability to pay must necessarily be a future event, which places the trigger point of the duty into the period leading up to the actual point of (cash flow) insolvency. By the same token, because the inability to pay debts when these would fall due is required to be approaching for the duty to bite, the duty only arises when the company is in the vicinity of insolvency.

It would seem that the state of insolvency under the judicially formulated test refers to cash flow insolvency, which appears to be assessed on a commercial reality, rather than a technical, basis. Moreover, the better view is that contingent or prospective debts should be taken into account.

Breaches of the reckless trading duty give rise to four remedies: (i) compensation for losses incurred by the company as a result of such breach (s 77(3)(b)); (ii) the disqualification of directors; (iii) the issuing of a compliance notice by the companies regulator; and (iv) the duty to report by the auditor of the company under s 45 Auditing Profession Act.

The second remedy available for breaches with the reckless trading duty is the disqualification of directors. The disqualification remedy is a useful supplement to the personal liability remedy, as it might have a stronger deterrent effect than personal liability, given that directors may often lack the required funds to pay. Unlike under the Companies Act 1973, individual creditors do not have *locus standi* to bring a disqualification application. This may have a chilling effect on the enforcement of the disqualification remedy.

The third remedy for contraventions with s 22(1) is the right of the Commission to send a compliance notice to companies where such companies are contravening the reckless trading duty or where they are in a state of cash flow insolvency. This remedy is expected to play a limited role in practice, since the Commission is likely to generally lack the requisite information.

The final remedy for breaches of the reckless trading duty is the duty of the auditor or the independent reviewer, acting as gatekeeper, to report on reckless trading contraventions under s 45 Auditing Profession Act and s 30(2)(b)(ii)(bb) Companies Act 2008 (read with applicable provisions under the Companies Regulations, 2011). The disadvantages of this *gatekeeper control strategy* is the infrequency of the audit and the independent review, the fact that the mandatory audit under the Auditing Profession Act does not apply to smaller-sized private companies and close corporation, notwithstanding that the risk-shifting incentive of directors in such companies may be particularly pervasive, given the closely aligned interests of directors and shareholders. Although the independent review under the Companies Act applies to smaller companies, problems with its effectiveness arise.

When evaluating s 22(1) from a comparative perspective, it becomes clear that its rationale is similar to the British wrongful trading provision under s 214 Insolvency Act 1986. Both provisions regard the board of directors as the appropriate constituent to determine the future of the company. They seek to internalise the negative externalities of the risk-shifting incentive in the directors' strategic trading decisions, by requiring – sometime before the company has reached a state of insolvency – that the directors act in the (unsecured) creditors' best interests, but do not determine the course of action to be taken for them.

By contrast, the German provision (§ 15a *Insolvenzordnung* (duty to invoke insolvency proceedings), § 92(2) *Aktiengesetz* (prohibition on making payments)) and the Australian provision (s 558G Corporations Act 2001 (duty not to incur further debts)) take as their point of departure that once a company has reached a state of insolvency, it is the creditors, not the directors, in whom the decision as to the company's future should be vested.

From the perspective of rescue law, all other things being equal, the British and South African provisions thus leave the directors with greater scope to embark on informal rescue measures than the German and Australian provisions. This conclusion is not affected by the fact that upon closer inspection the German provision bites earlier, since it defines insolvency both in cash flow and in balance sheet terms; the specific nature of the action prescribed still gives directors little room for manoeuvre. The higher interpretation costs inevitable to legal standards as found in South Africa and the UK could be reduced by the development of guidelines by the courts that reflect the current mores of good business practice recognised by the business community.

In saying that, the scope left for informal rescue measures by the South African and British provisions might be undermined by provisions in both jurisdictions that deem the company to be in a state of insolvency and, in South Africa, by the directors' duty of disclosure to affected persons of the company's financial distress under s 129(7). This is because these provisions could have the effect of pre-empting the pursuance of informal rescue measures.

In relation to liability for, and enforcement of, the statutory creditor-regarding duty, the scope of liability appears to be slightly broader, and the burden of proving liability lower, in Germany than in the UK and South Africa, given that the Germany duty takes account of the impairment of the positions of single creditors (through the concepts of *Quotenschaden* and *Vertrauensschaden*). The availability of the disqualification of directors remedy in South Africa and the UK and, to a lesser extent, of criminal sanctions in Germany would seem to compensate for the low deterrent effect of civil liability.

It would seem that in South Africa, unlike apparently in the UK, third parties generally are entitled to fund reckless trading claims in return for a share in the proceeds of a successful suit. This is likely to raise the likelihood of the enforcement of reckless trading breaches, thereby increasing the chilling effect of the reckless trading duty on the company controllers' risk-shifting incentive.

There are three possible further *ex post* standards strategies that could be seen to control (aspects of) the risk-shifting incentive of company controllers in the vicinity of insolvency: (i) the claw-back remedy in insolvency proceedings of transactions for less than reasonable equivalent value; (ii) delictual liability for the incurrence of a debt without a reasonable expectation of discharging it; and (iii) a general duty of directors owed to 'creditors' at common law.

With regard to the claw-back remedy, the British insolvency claw back of 'transactions at an undervalue' (s 238 Insolvency Act 1986), which employs a gatekeeper control mechanism, could be seen to address the problem of asset substitution (ie, the application of low risk assets to high risk projects). The German claw-back of transactions disadvantaging creditors (§ 132 *Isolvenzordung*) contains some features (in particular, that it includes undervalue transactions and requires knowledge of cash flow insolvency by a third party) goes in the same direction, however the trigger of when transactions are vulnerable is much too late to make § 132 *Insolvenzordung* an effective remedy for asset substitution. The equivalent South African claw-back of 'transactions without value' (s 26 Insolvency Act 1936) and the German claw-back of gratuitous benefits (§ 134 *Insolvenzordnung*), however, cannot be seen to control the problem of asset substitution satisfactorily.

With regard to the applicable delictual liability, it will typically not catch value-reducing trading decisions in the vicinity of insolvency. This is because the risk-shifting incentive will generally arise even where no special relationship exists between the director/employee of the company and the prospective third party creditor, which is required for liability to arise under this delict.

With regard to a general directorial duty to creditors in the vicinity of insolvency, such a duty has been developed over the last few decades in various common law jurisdictions (but not yet in South Africa) by extension of the traditional common law directors' duties. From a South African perspective, the development of such a duty could potentially have the following advantages over the statutory creditor-regarding duty. First, the lighter standard of the duty (subjective for the fiduciary duties, negligence for the duty of care vs. gross negligence for reckless trading) could make this duty more demanding on directors. And second, while the trigger of the reckless trading duty is fixed and too late, the common law duty leaves the courts with some flexibility to adapt the trigger point of the duty to the circumstances of each case. However, one major disadvantage of the common law duty is that any proceeds of enforcement would be caught by security interests, meaning that unsecured creditors are not the primary beneficiaries of this duty, notwithstanding that the risk of value-reducing strategic trading decisions fall primarily on them.

The final legal strategy addressing the company controllers' risk-shifting incentive is an *ex ante initiation rights strategy* relied on only in South Africa: disclosure under s 129(7) coupled with involuntary entry of rescue proceedings under s 131(1). Its aim is presumably to reduce the information asymmetries of affected persons that enable them to utilise their right to invoke formal rescue proceedings. Aside from the adverse practical effects of a s 129(7)-disclosure on the chances of success of an informal workout, this provision may be flawed as a self-standing provision, as it is likely to generate high decision-making and agency costs. However, it seems that s 129(7) will not play a significant role in practice due to problems with its enforcement.

Chapter 6 The Second Manifestation of the Company-Creditor Agency Conflict in the Vicinity of Insolvency: Company Controllers' Perverse Incentive in Respect of the Extension of Shareholder Loans

I. Introduction

The advancement of a loan by shareholders to their company in the vicinity of insolvency could in certain circumstances constitute a further manifestation of the company-creditor agency conflict. This Chapter will examine the legal strategies controlling creditor-harming shareholder loans.

The focus of our analysis in this Chapter will be the *advancing*, and not the *securing* or *paying back*, of shareholder loans in the vicinity of insolvency. The source of the last two mentioned actions (apart perhaps from the securing of shareholder loans for purposes of eliminating the downside risk of projects, as discussed above) is generally that the lending shareholder secures preferred treatment over other (external) creditors in respect of recovering his loan, thereby contravening the *par condicio creditorum*.[1324] Shareholders are in a stronger position than external creditors to obtain this preferred treatment, as they have an information advantage over external creditors, and – especially in majority-owned closely-held companies – are able to influence the management of the company to a greater extent than external creditors.[1325] The standard legal strategy to counteract this problem is the insolvency claw-back of transactions prefer-

1324 Eidenmüller, 'Gesellschafterdarlehen in der Insolvenz' in Heldrich and others (eds), *Festschrift für Claus-Wilhelm Canaris zum 70. Geburtstag Band II* (C.H. Beck 2007) 49, 61–2.

1325 Ibid. See also Westermann and Mock (eds), *Festschrift für Gerold Bezzenberger zum 70. Geburtstag am 13. März 2000* (Walter de Gruyter 2000) 43ff; Mülbert, 'A Synthetic View of Different Concepts of Creditor Protection' (2006) 7 EBOR 357, 397; Cahn, 'Equitable Subordination of Shareholder Loans?' (2006) 7 EBOR 287, 296ff.

ring certain creditors over others.[1326] As indicated in Chapter 1, this type of legal provision falls outside the scope of this study.

As we will see below, South Africa does not specifically regulate shareholder loans, however, they could be seen to be covered by a provision aimed at the reckless trading duty. The German and US approach to shareholder loans will be used for the comparative analysis. Those jurisdictions do not only specifically deal with shareholder loans (unlike the UK, for example), but also approach the problem of shareholder loans very differently from each other and from the approach under South Africa. This promises to yield interesting results for the discussion.

This Chapter will proceed as follows. The theoretical foundations of the regulation of shareholder loans will be consider in II below. This will be followed by an analysis of the German, US and South African legal strategies in III below. The comparative analysis will follow in IV below.

II. Theoretical foundations

As we saw in Chapter 1, shareholders of companies that are in the vicinity of insolvency may have a perverse incentive to advance a loan to their companies that would inappropriately delay the invocation of formal liquidation or rescue proceedings. As with the first manifestation of the company-creditor conflict in the vicinity of insolvency discussed in Chapter 5 above, this perverse incentive arises when the shareholders have lost their economic interest in the company and there is no prospect of it being rebuilt in the near future.[1327] At this point, shareholders might be tempted to advance a loan to their company (such a shareholder, hereafter, '*lending shareholder*') that would enable the company to continue trading by postponing or removing the cash flow or balance sheet insolvency of the company, and thus the immediate threat that a creditor could place the company under liquidation or rescue proceedings,[1328] even where the company's

---

1326 See, eg, Eidenmüller (n 1324) 61ff, who suggests the introduction of a specific claw-back provision for the above-mentioned problem under German law.

1327 See the discussion and references cited in PART A, Chapter 1, II., 3., a., aa above.

1328 The shareholder loan may prevent creditors from showing that the debtors are not paying their debts as they become due (eg, in the US, see 11 USC § 303h (see generally, Skeel Jr. and Krause-Vilmar (n 1330) 271)) or to avert the occurrence of certain situations that allow the company to be deemed cash flow insol-

assets would have been placed to their highest value use if the company had been placed under rescue or liquidation proceedings. A shareholder loan could furthermore enable the company to pursue excessively risky projects (ie, projects with a negative net value).[1329] A project would have a negative net value if its expected value, calculated with reference to the expected returns and the probability of success less the costs of pursuing the project (in this case, the shareholder loan), would be negative.[1330]

However, shareholder loans advanced in the vicinity of insolvency could also be value-enhancing. This would be the case where shareholder loans could provide a distressed company with the necessary cash flow to pursue a project with a positive net value or, more generally, implement informal rescue measures with a reasonable prospect of success.[1331] What is more, in those two situations, the funding of a distressed company through shareholder loans would, *ceteris paribus*, serve the interests of the company's (unsecured) creditors better than the raising of debt from exter-

---

vent (eg, in South Africa, see Sch 5 item 9 Companies Act 2008 read with s 345 Companies Act 1973 (see, generally, Delport and others, *Henochsberg on the Companies Act 71 of 2008* (loose-leaf) (Lexis Nexis 2015) s 345, 706(2)ff)). In jurisdictions that provide for balance sheet insolvency as a stand-alone test of insolvency, such as Germany (§ 19 (1) *Insolvenzordnung*, BGHZ 146, 264, 269ff), a shareholder loan could, theoretically, make a company balance sheet insolvent where the loan would raise the company's liabilities to an amount that exceeds the company's assets. This would, however, only be the case where the loan is used for a purpose (eg, servicing ongoing expenses) *other than* acquiring further assets and where the lending shareholder has not contractually subordinated his loan (§ 19 (2) *Insolvenzordnung*. In saying that, the German test of balance sheet insolvency requires that, in addition to the company's overindebtedness, it must also be unlikely that the company will be able to continue in existence, despite its overindebtedness (§ 19 (2) *Insolvenzordnung*). This means that where a shareholder loan has made a company balance sheet insolvent, this does not, by itself, trigger the balance sheet test of insolvency. The ground of impending insolvency that is required in some jurisdictions for the commencement of rescue proceedings would not be affected in South Africa and Germany, as only the directors are entitled to trigger rescue proceedings on such ground (for South Africa, s 129 Companies Act 2008; for Germany, § 18 *Insolvenzordnung*) and directors generally have a disincentive to invoke formal rescue proceedings (see PART A, Chapter 1, II., 3., a., bb above).

1329 See the discussion and references cited in PART A, Chapter 1, II., 3., a., bb above.

1330 For a numerical example, see Skeel Jr. and Krause-Vilmar, 'Recharacterization and the Non-Hindrance of Creditors' (2006) 7 EBOR 259, 270.

1331 For a further numerical example, see Skeel Jr. and Krause-Vilmar (n 1330) 271.

nal creditors, as they would have at such point typically become the company's residual claimants (or its 'owners'). This is because shareholder loans are likely to provide the company with lower borrowing costs than loans from external creditors for two primary reasons: (i) the close proximity between the company and shareholders allows shareholders to contract with the company at lower transaction costs than external creditors;[1332] and (ii) the fact that shareholders typically have better information about the company's chances of recovery than external creditors, means that external creditors would estimate the risk of funding too conservatively.[1333] In these situations, therefore, shareholder loans could solve an underinvestment problem.[1334]

Of course, the company could also generate funds through the sale of non-core or loss-making assets. However, the market may often undervalue such assets for two primary reasons. First, potential buyers might, in light of the company's distress, doubt the quality of the company's business, and therefore discount its assets.[1335] Second, where there is an industry-wide downturn, the potential buyers, because they have been similarly affected by the downturn, may either not be in a position to acquire the assets (low demand for the assets) or may also be looking to sell similar assets (over-supply of assets). Both these effects would push down the price of the company's assets.[1336]

1332 Eidenmüller (n 1324) 49 and n 1; Skeel Jr. and Krause-Vilmar (n 1330) 275.

1333 Eidenmüller (n 1324) 57; Drukarczyk, 'Gesellschafterdarlehen, Rechtsprechungsgrundsätze des BGH und § 32a GmbHG – Einige kritische Anmerkungen' in Elschen, Siegel and Wagner (eds), *Unternehmenstheorie und Besteuerung – Festschrift zum 60. Geburtstag von Dieter Schneider* (Gabler 1995) 171, 191ff.

1334 For an explanation of the term underinvestment, see n 528 in Chapter 4.

1335 Webb, 'An Economic Evaluation of Insolvency Procedures in the United Kingdom: Does the 1986 Insolvency Act Satisfy the Creditors' Bargain?' (1991) 43 Oxford Econ. Pap. 193, 149; Armour and Frisby, 'Rethinking Receivership' (2001) 21 OJLS 73, 83.

1336 Shleifer and Vishny, 'Liquidation Values and Debt Capacity: A Market Equilibrium Approach' (1992) 47(4) J. Finance 1343; Crystal and Mokal, 'The Valuation of Distressed Companies – A Conceptual Framework' (2006) SSRN <http://papers.ssrn.com/sol3/papers.cfm?abstract_id=877155> accessed 16 January 2017. For empirical evidence, see Pulvino, 'Do Asset Fire-sales Exist? An Empirical Investigation of Commercial Aircraft Transactions' (1998) 53 J. Finance 939; D Brown, 'Liquidity and Liquidation: Evidence from Real Estate Investment Trusts" (2000) 55 J. Finance 469; Strömberg, 'Conflicts of Interest and

It should be noted, however, that the perverse incentive of the lending shareholder is counteracted by the fact that he does not only act as *shareholder*, but also as *creditor*. As creditor, the lending shareholder would participate in the downside risk of the company's continued trading and projects pursued following the advancement of the shareholder loan. The extent of the perverse incentive would depend on the relationship between the lending shareholder's percentage share of the company's (unsecured) debt and his percentage share in the company's value as owner, which will vary according to the relevant circumstances of each case.[1337]

However, there are situations where shareholders generally would not have a perverse incentive, on the one hand and where shareholders would always have a perverse incentive when advancing a loan to their company, on the other hand. Shareholders generally would not have a perverse incentive where the shareholders' funds have not been used up or, where they have been used up, they are likely to be restored in the near future through the company's established business model. In that situation, the losses of any projects financed by the shareholder loan will fall on the shareholders first, not on the creditors. This gives the shareholder-regarding managers a disincentive to pursue excessively risky projects.[1338] By contrast, where the lending shareholder fully secures his loan, he would generally have a perverse incentive when advancing a loan to the shareholder. The fact that his loan is secured means that he does not share in the downside risk of the continued trading or projects pursued by the company,[1339] save for the risk that the secured assets might lose in value due to changes in trading conditions.[1340]

Market Illiquidity in Bankruptcy Auctions: Theory and Tests' (2000) 55 J. Finance 2641.

1337 Eidenmüller (n 1324) 56; Engert, 'Die ökonomische Begründung der Grundsätze ordnungsgemäßer Unternehmensfinanzierung' [2004] ZGR 813, 82ff; Westermann and Mock (n 1325) 38ff.

1338 In relation to the strategic decision to continue trading in the vicinity of insolvency, see Davies, 'Directors' Creditor-Regarding Duties in the Vicinity of Insolvency' (2006) 7 EBOR 301, 303ff.

1339 Skeel Jr. and Krause-Vilmar (n 1330) 272ff; Engert (n 1337) 824, 830ff; Eidenmüller (n 1324) 56.

1340 This is the reason why it has been suggested that securities over shareholder loans should be disallowed and that the loan should be treated as a general unsecured loan in insolvency; Skeel Jr. and Krause-Vilmar (n 1330) 275, 284. On the risk of devaluation of the secured assets in insolvency, see Armour and Mokal, 'Reforming the Governance of Corporate Rescue: The Enterprise Act 2002'

It becomes clear from the above that shareholder loans advanced in the vicinity of insolvency are generally not *per se* harmful to the company's creditors. In fact, they could, in applicable circumstances, even be in the creditors' best interests, as indicated above. Accordingly, the threat to creditors' interests is not the mere advancing of a shareholder loan (ie, the financing decision by the lending shareholder), but rather how and for what purpose such funding is invested (ie, the investment decision by the company's management).[1341] As we have seen, only shareholder loans that inappropriately enable the company to continue trading, or that are used to pursue excessively risky projects, in principle, harm creditors. In line with the above-mentioned suggestion that the focus of regulation should be on the investment rather than the financing decision, a criterion has been developed in literature which distinguishes value-enhancing and value-reducing shareholder loans according to whether it is expected *ex ante* that the projects pursued after the advancement of the shareholder loan would increase or decrease the value of the company's assets. This test, which is referred to as the '*ex ante* efficiency test', holds that where the shareholder loan is expected to decrease the company's assets, it should be subordinated. However, where the shareholder loan is expected to increase the assets, it should be treated as an unsecured creditor in insolvency.[1342] One potential problem of this approach is that courts would not be well placed to assess compliance with the *ex ante* efficiency test *ex post*. This is because making such calculations would not fall into judges' natural field of expertise (and hence would increase the procedural costs due to the need for obtaining expert opinions). Moreover, adjudication after the fact is subject to the problem of hindsight bias.[1343]

Having considered these theoretical considerations on the distinction between creditor-harming and creditor-advancing shareholder loans, we will now examined the legal strategies relied on in Germany, the US and South Africa.

(2004) ESRC Centre for Business Research Working Paper 288 <http://papers.ssrn.com/sol3/papers.cfm?abstract_id=567306> accessed 16 January 2017.

1341 Eidenmüller (n 1324) 58ff. It is for this reason that an automatic and blanket subordination of all shareholder loans, as is provided for under German law, is problematic; see the discussion below.

1342 Gelter, 'The subordination of shareholder loans in bankruptcy' (2006) 26 Int. Rev. Law Econ 478, 499.

1343 Skeel Jr. and Krause-Vilmar (n 1330) 271.

III. Legal strategies to control the perverse incentive in respect of shareholder loans relied on in Germany, the US and South Africa

1. The ex ante rules strategy: Automatic statutory subordination of shareholder loans under German law

a. Setting out the legal strategy

Under German law, *any* shareholder debt claim (or any commercially equivalent claim) is subordinated in the company's insolvency.[1344] Before the reforms to the law applicable to private limited companies (hereafter, '*GmbH*') of 2008,[1345] a shareholder loan was subject to mandatory subordination only if it had been advanced (or left in place) at a time when a prudent businessperson would have financed the company by means of equity capital. This explains why such loans were referred to as having the 'character of substituting equity' (*kapitalersetzender Charakter des Gesellschafterdarlehens*). A shareholder loan was characterised as 'substituting equity' when it was advanced at a time when the company was in a state of crisis (*Krise der Gesellschaft*).[1346] This state existed if the company was unable to obtain credit from external lenders at fair market rates – that is, when the company was no longer creditworthy (*Kreditunwürdigkeit*). However, the practical significance of this requirement was negligible, as a shareholder's failure to call a loan that was advanced when the company was still in a sound financial state was also subject to

1344 See § 39(1)(no. 5) *Insolvenzordnung*. This applies to all entities except for those forms in which a natural person is personally liable or in which a corporate entity is liable, which, in turn, has a personally liable natural person; § 39 (4) (1st sentence) InsO.

1345 These reforms are contained in 'Gesetz zur Modernisierung des GmbH-Rechts und zur Bekämpfung von Missbräuchen ('*MoMiG*')' (2008) Bundesgesetzblatt 48 2026.

1346 See § 32a (1) *GmbH-Gesetz a.F.* The legal definition was codified by Art 10 No 1 'Gesetz zur Kontrolle und Transparenz im Unternehmensbereich (KonTraG)' (1998) Bundesgesetzblatt 24 5702 after it had been developed by the judiciary; BGH 14/12/1959 Z 31, 258, 268ff ['Luft-Taxi']; BGH v. 24. 3. 1980 – II ZR 213/77, BGHZ 76, 326, 330 = NJW 1980, 1524, 1525; BGH v. 13. 7. 1981 – II ZR 256/79, BGHZ 81, 252, 255 = NJW 1981, 2570, 2571; BGH v. 19. 9. 1988 – II ZR 255/87, BGHZ 155, 168, 185 = NJW 1988, 3143, 3147.

statutory subordination.[1347] This is why the removal of the requirement under the new law that the loan must have been advanced when the company was no longer creditworthy, or left in place where it had been advanced previously,[1348] may not have broadened the scope of the new provision as much as might appear at first glance.[1349] In saying that, this amendment has lowered the procedural costs, as there will no longer be a need to prove that the company was in a state of crisis when the loan was advanced.[1350]

There are two situations in which the subordination does not apply. One is where the shareholder giving the loan is not the managing director of the company and holds 10% or less of the company's shares (which is referred to as the 'exemption for shareholders with small holdings' (*Kleinbeteiligtenprivileg*)).[1351] The other situation is where a creditor has, after any of the tests of insolvency have occurred,[1352] acquired a members' interest in the company for purposes of rescuing the company (which is referred to as the 'rescue exemption' (*Sanierungsprivileg*).[1353]

1347 See Cahn (n 1325) 292. On the fact that loans granted before the state of 'crisis' also fell within the statutory subordination, see BGHZ 75, 334, 338 = NJW 1980, 592 = ZIP 1980, 115; BGHZ 105, 168, 185 = NJW-RR 1989, 33 = ZIP 1988, 1248 = KTS 1989, 114 = EWiR § 32a *GmbH-Gesetz* 1/88, 1095 (Fleck); BGH NJW-RR 1990, 290 = ZIP 1990, 98 = KTS 1990, 258 = EWiR § 32a *GmbH-Gesetz* 2/90, 373 S *(Roeseler)*.

1348 § 39 (1) No. 5 *Insolvenzordnung*.

1349 See also the explanation by the German Government on the MoMiG, Deutscher Bundestag, 'Begr Beschlussempfehlung und Bericht des Rechtsausschusses' (DruckS 16/6140) 56.

1350 Schmidt, 'Reform der Kapitalsicherung und Haftung in der Krise nach dem Regierungsentwurf des MoMiG' [2007] GmbHR 1072, 1077.

1351 § 39 (5) *Insolvenzordnung*.

1352 The tests of insolvency appear in § 17 *Insolvenzordnung* (cash flow insolvency (*Zahlungsunfähigkeit*)), § 18 *Insolvenzordnung* (impending cash flow insolvency (*drohende Zahlungsunfähigkeit*)) and § 19 *Insolvenzordnung* (balancesheet insolvency (*Überschuldung*)).

1353 § 39 (4) (2nd sentence) *Insolvenzordnung*.

b. Discussion: Failure to distinguish appropriately between value-enhancing and value-reducing shareholder loans

The automatic statutory subordination of all shareholder loans under German law is problematic. This is because even shareholder loans that would enable the company to continue trading where informal rescue measures would have a reasonable chance of success or where the projects pursued would have a positive net value and would fall to be subordinated under the relevant provision. Since the subordination provides a disincentive to a shareholder to advance a loan and outside creditors might, particularly near insolvency, be unwilling to fund the company on reasonable terms, the company might be deprived of funds to invest in value-enhancing informal rescue measures and projects.[1354]

It would appear as though the rescue exemption (*Sanierungsprivileg*) does not remove the disincentive posed by the subordination for the advancement of value-enhancing loans. This is because the relevant situation does not generally fall within the exemption, as it envisages a situation where the creditor must acquire the shares after having advanced the loan to the company (which must also be after the statutory tests of insolvency have occurred) for purposes of rescuing the company. Since under the rescue exemption, the loan is advanced at a time when the creditor is not (yet) also a shareholder of the company, there is no perverse incentive at play.[1355]

The exemption for shareholders with small holdings, on the other hand, might be helpful. This is because lending shareholders with a small holding might generally not have a strong perverse incentive, as their respective percentage shares in the company's equity and debt – and thus their upside benefit and downside risk – might be aligned. However, as the lending shareholder's percentage share in the company's debt would vary in each case, it is generally not possible to say that the lending shareholder would have a perverse incentive if he would hold up to 10% – or any other percentage share, for that matter – in the company's equity.[1356]

1354 Eidenmüller (n 1324) 57. See also Drukarczyk, 'Gesellschafterdarlehen' (n 1333) 191ff, 201; Skeel Jr. and Krause-Vilmar (n 1330) 282; Gelter (n 1342) 490ff.

1355 On this scenario generally, see Skeel Jr. and Krause-Vilmar (n 1330) 275.

1356 To be sure, the purpose of this exemption when it was initially enacted (§ 32a(3) *GmbH-Gesetz a.F.*) was not to reduce the effect of the subordination on the in-

2. The ex post standards strategy enforced by the courts: Discretionary subordination or recharacterisation of shareholder loans as equity under US law

a. Distinguishing recharacterisation and equitable subordination

Under US law, there are two provisions that could be seen as addressing the lending shareholder's perverse incentive in question: (i) the statutory remedy of equitable subordination, which entitles the court to subordinate a shareholder loan (or a loan by an outside creditor) to other creditors' debt claims in insolvency;[1357] (ii) and the recent judge-made remedy which allows courts to recharacterise shareholder loans as equity in insolvency, which is of more recent origin than the equitable subordination doctrine.[1358] Due to the generally similar nature in content of the two remedies, some courts have denied their equitable jurisdiction to recharacterise shareholder loans, given that such loans are already dealt with by the statutory equitable subordination remedy.[1359] However, critics have argued this fails to acknowledge that the two doctrines are distinguishable in content and in the consequences arising from their contravention.[1360] Under the equitable subordination doctrine, the focus of the enquiry is on the propriety of the lending shareholder's conduct (ie, whether he has engaged in 'inequitable' conduct). It is, accordingly, not relevant that the inequitable

centive of (minority) shareholders to give value-enhancing loans to the company, but presumably rather generally to protect minority shareholders from the harsh consequences of a subordination on the insolvency of the company in which they held those shares; see, eg, Hirte, '§ 39' in Uhlenbruck and Hirte (eds), *Kommentar Insolvenzordnung* (14th rev. edn, Vahlen 2015) recital 72.

1357 11 U.S.C. § 510(c). The equitable subordination remedy was codified in the Bankruptcy Code of 1978 after it had been developed by the courts from its introduction in 1939 by *Taylor v Standard Gas & Electric*, 306 US 307 (1939) (referred to as the 'Deep Rock case') and *Pepper v Litton*, 308 US 295 (1939). See generally Skeel Jr. and Krause-Vilmar (n 1330) 263ff.

1358 See the leading case *In re Autostyle Plastics Inc.*, 269 F.3d 726 (6th Cir. 2001).

1359 See the leading case *In re Pacific Express, Inc.*, 69 Bankr. 112 (9th Cir. BAP 1986) 115. See also *In re Pinetree Partners, Ltd.*, 87 B.R. 481, 491 (Bankr. N.D. Ohio 1988). This position was followed recently by *Straightshot Communications v Telekenex*, 2010 U.S. Dist. Lexis 123390 (W.D. Wash. 2010).

1360 See particularly *In re Autostyle Plastics Inc.*, 269 F.3d 726, 748 (6th Cir. 2001).

conduct is related to the shareholder loan.[1361] Under recharacterisation, by contrast, the focus of the enquiry is on the 'character' of the funds advanced by the shareholder to the company – ie, whether such funding is, in substance, debt or equity.[1362] This distinction follows, *inter alia*, from the fact that inequitable conduct of the shareholder is a prerequisite for equitable subordination,[1363] but not for recharacterisation. Recharacterisation on the other hand, generally requires some evidence that the transaction was intended (and was discernible to the public) as debt, not equity.[1364]

However, this distinction is by no means consistently applied by the courts. For example, some courts have taken the shareholder's conduct into account in recharacterisation cases.[1365] By the same token, the nature of funding by the shareholder has played a role in equitable subordination cases.[1366]

The other difference between the two doctrines, of course, is their legal consequences. In practice, this would mean that a shareholder whose claim was subordinated would rank ahead of a shareholder whose claim was recharacterised as equity.[1367]

1361 On the fact that there need not be a correlation between the conduct and the loan, see *In re Kansas City Journal-Post Co.*, 144 F.2d. 791, 804 (8th Cir. 1944). See also Cahn (n 1325) 293; Gelter (n 1342) 482.

1362 See generally Skeel Jr. and Krause-Vilmar (n 1330) 275. See also Sprayregen and others, 'Recharacterization of Debt to Equity: An Overview, Update and Practical Guide to an Evolving Doctrine' [2004] Ann.Surv.Bankr.L. 1, 12 who define the determining factor as whether the transaction in question was at arm's length.

1363 *In re Lifschultz Fast Freight*, 132 F.3d 339, 345 (7th Cir. 1997); *Sender v Bronze Group, Ltd.* 380 F.3d. 1292, 1302 (10th Cir. 2004); *In re Fabricators*, 926 F.2d 1458, 1469 (5th Circ. 1991). See generally Gelter (n 1342) 482.

1364 Generally on the differences between these two doctrines, see Skeel Jr. and Krause-Vilmar (n 1330) 262ff. See also Nozemack, 'Making Sense Out of Bankruptcy Courts' Recharacterization of Claims: Why Not Use § 510(c) Equitable Subordination?' (1999) 56 Wash. S Lee L. Review 689.

1365 See, eg, *In re Micro-Precision Technologies, Inc.*, 303 Bankr. 238 (Bankr. D. N.H. 2003) 247.

1366 Notably that one of the factors relevant for determining whether to recharacterise – ie, whether the company was adequately capitalised at its formation – has also been taken account of by the courts in equitable subordination; see *In re Mobile Steel Corp.*, 563 F.2d 692, 703 (5th Cir. 1977). See generally Skeel Jr. and Krause-Vilmar (n 1330) 267; Gelter (n 1342) 481.

1367 See generally on this distinction Sprayregen and others (n 1362) 4. See also Skeel Jr. and Krause-Vilmar (n 1330) 265.

Despite the subtle differences in content between these two doctrines, both could, in principle, be seen as covering the lending shareholder's perverse incentive in question: equitable subordination through the requirement that the shareholder must not have engaged in inequitable conduct; and recharacterisation through the requirement that the funding by the shareholder must have the character of a loan rather than equity.[1368] However, for purposes of demonstration, we will focus on the recharacterisation remedy. Of the two doctrines, it appears to address the perverse incentive more specifically than equitable subordination, insofar as it focuses on the nature of the loan rather than on the conduct of the shareholder, which is the criterion used by the equitable subordination remedy. As the conduct of the shareholder need not be related to the shareholder's claim, it could cover a broader range of creditor-harming actions, such as the abuse of the corporate form, which is not at issue for purposes of this study.[1369]

b. Factors determining whether shareholder loans should be recharacterised

Over the years, the courts have developed various multi-factor tests to determine whether a shareholder's debt claim should be recharacterised as equity and the following eleven-factor test has prevailed:[1370]

1368 In relation to equitable subordination, see Cahn (n 1325) 293. This is also implied by the numerical examples and discussion thereon in relation to the Deep Rock doctrine in Roe, *Bankruptcy and Corporate Reorganization – Legal and Financial Materials* (2nd edn, Foundation Press 2007) 290ff. In relation to recharacterisation, see, eg, Skeel Jr. and Krause-Vilmar (n 1330) 270ff.

1369 See, eg, the commingling of assets, which appeared to be a factor in the *Deep Rock* case. It would seem that such actions might also covered by the veil-piercing remedy. Indeed, it has been argued that both the veil-piercing and the equitable subordination remedies could be seen to have grown out of fraudulent conveyance law. They were developed because they eased the burden of proof given that they obviate the need that creditors have to point to a particular transaction or transactions that harm creditors; Clark, *Corporate Law* (Little Brown 1986) 52–72; Clark, 'The Duties of the Corporate Debtor to Its Creditors' (1977) 90 Harv. L. Rev. 505. See generally Skeel Jr. and Krause-Vilmar (n 1330) 261–2.

1370 The test was first articulated by *Roth Steel Tube Co. v Commissioner of Inland Revenue*, 800 F.2d 625, 630 (6th Cir. 1986). See also *In re Autostyle Plastics, Inc.*, 269 F.3d 726, 747–3 (6th Cir. 2001); *In re SubMicron Sys. Corp.*, 432 F.3d

1. the names given to the instruments, if any, evidencing the indebtedness;
2. the presence or absence of a fixed maturity date and schedule of payments;
3. the presence or absence of a fixed interest rate and interest payments;
4. the source of repayments;
5. the adequacy or inadequacy of capitalisation;
6. the identity of interests between the creditor and stockholder;
7. the security, if any, for the advances;
8. the corporation's ability to obtain financing from outside lending institutions;
9. the extent to which the advances were subordinated to the claims of outside creditors;
10. the extent to which the advances were used to acquire capital assets; and
11. the presence or absence of a sinking fund to provide repayments.

The factors fall broadly into two categories. One category of factors (factors one to three) addresses the problem where shareholders conceal the loan from creditors (often through refraining from properly documenting the loan) or mislead the creditors of the existence of the loan. This problem is referred to as 'ambiguous loans'. Ambiguous loans are problematic because they enable the company to overstate its financial position, which may result in creditors providing credit to the company, which they would have otherwise withheld.[1371] However, ambiguous loans are not a product of the shareholder opportunism, and therefore need not concern us further.[1372]

The other category of factors (factors four to eleven), on the other hand, seeks to determine whether the character of the shareholders' claim is debt or equity, which could be relevant for the shareholder opportunism in

448, 455 n.8 (3d Cir. 2006); *In re Official Comm. of Unsecured Creditors for Dornier Aviation (North America), Inc.*, 453 F.3d 225, 233 (4th Cir. 2006); *In re Hedged-Invs. Assocs., Inc.*, 380 F.3d 1292, 1298 (10th Cir. 2004).

1371 Skeel Jr. and Krause-Vilmar (n 1330) 268–9, 277.

1372 Save to the extent that the courts have been criticised for focussing too much on the requirement that a loan be properly documented at the expense of the factors that might, in principle, address the shareholder opportunism in question, as discussed below.

question. Such factors will therefore be examined in greater detail in the comparative evaluation below.

It should be noted that the eleven-factor analysis involves an open-ended enquiry. Courts have varied on the number of factors and the choice of factors they have reviewed.[1373] Moreover, no single factor prevails and the weight given to each factor in any particular case is within the court's discretion.[1374] This approach has been criticised for making the recharacterisation remedy unpredictable and uncertain.[1375] Moreover, as we will see below, the fact that some of the factors have been interpreted with reference to previous court decisions on similar factors used in the tax law context – where the underlying concerns may be very different from those in the insolvency law context – has resulted in misguided judicial interpretation of some of the factors.[1376]

c. Effectiveness of eleven factor test in distinguishing value-enhancing from value-reducing shareholder loans

Unlike the blanket subordination of shareholder loans, the above-mentioned factors under the recharacterisation remedy in the US do provide for criteria on which shareholder claims are assessed by the courts as to whether they are, in substance, loans or rather equity. If they are found to be equity, those shareholder claims should be recharacterised as such in insolvency.[1377]

Factors five (adequacy of capitalisation) and eight (creditworthiness) are similar in nature in that they both use as a benchmark the company's

---

1373 *In re SubMicron Sys. Corp.*, 432 F.3d 448, 455 n.8 (3d Cir. 2006) the court reviewed the (reported) case law on recharacterisation and found these cases to have used various numbers of tests.

1374 See *In re SubMicron Sys. Corp.*, 432 F.3d 448, 456 (3d Cir. 2006), *In re Official Comm. of Unsecured Creditors for Dornier Aviation (North America), Inc.*, 453 F.3d 225, 234 (4th Cir. 2006), *In re Hedged-Invs. Assocs., Inc.*, 380 F.3d 1292, 1298–9.

1375 Wilton and Moeller-Sally, 'Debt Recharacterization Under State Law' (2007) 62 Bus. Law. 1257, 1263ff.

1376 Wilton and Moeller-Sally (n 1375) 1265–7; Skeel Jr. and Krause-Vilmar (n 1330) 268ff.

1377 We have seen above that the first three factors deal with the ambiguous loan problem, which is a problem separate from the shareholder opportunism in question, and will therefore not be considered further in this study.

financial state at the time of the advancement of the loan. Indeed, such factors are not uncommon in international comparison, as the previous German law on shareholder loans also employed a creditworthiness criterion for determining when loans should be subordinated. However, both factors are ultimately unhelpful, as neither provides an accurate barometer for when shareholder loans may enhance or reduce value to the company's creditors. Undercapitalisation fails to accurately identify when the shareholder's perverse incentive arises. As we have seen, the shareholder opportunism will only arise when shareholders have lost their economic interest in the company, and shareholders may very often still have an economic interest in companies that are overindebted.[1378] Whether or not an outside creditor would extend a loan to the company (creditworthiness) is also unsatisfactory for this enquiry. This is because the interests of outside creditors when taking that decision (ie, the probability of repayment) do not necessarily correspond with whether the proceeds of their loan are put to value-maximising uses.[1379]

Factors four and eleven (whether there is a source of repayment of the claim), factor seven (whether the shareholder has insisted on security) and factor nine (whether the loan claim is subordinated) all seem to address the tax concern that shareholders designate their advance as debt, although they are equity in substance, in order to take advantage of the tax benefits of debt (for example, the deductibility of interest payments).[1380]

However, when applied to the insolvency context, none of these factors appropriately address the shareholder opportunism in question. Even where there is no designated source of repayment of a loan (factors four and eleven), this does not necessarily mean that the shareholders no longer have an economic interest in the company (and thus whether or not they would have a perverse incentive to embark on value-minimising trading or corporate projects). Nor are the factors that enquire whether the shareholder has insisted on security (factor seven) or whether the shareholder's claim has been subordinated (factor nine) relevant for the question at hand. To the contrary, the seventh factor might get it exactly the wrong

1378 See also Skeel Jr. and Krause-Vilmar (n 1330) 278.

1379 Gelter (n 1342) 495–7. The creditworthiness criterion under the previous German provision (§ 32a(1) *GmbH-Gesetz*) was criticised on a similar basis; see Drukarczyk, 'Gesellschafterdarlehen' (n 1333) 191ff, 201ff.

1380 See Skeel Jr. and Krause-Vilmar (n 1330) 278; Wilton and Moeller-Sally (n 1375) 1265.

way round. This is because, where the shareholder has secured his loan in the vicinity of insolvency (which would under the test be an indication that the advance was intended as debt, not equity, and thus weigh against recharacterisation), he is likely to have a perverse incentive regardless of the relationship between his equity and debt shares in the company. Factor ten (whether the shareholder advance was used to acquire capital assets) is a further example where reliance on the judicial interpretations on the equivalent factors in the tax sphere has resulted in misguided judgments in the insolvency context. In tax law, the use of advances by shareholders to meet ongoing operational expenses, rather than to acquire capital assets, indicates that such advances were intended as debt, and should therefore not be recharacterised.[1381] However, this says nothing about whether the funds are used for value-enhancing purposes – ie, whether servicing ongoing operational expenses may form part of a value-maximising or minimising informal rescue strategy, and whether or not the acquisition of new assets may be excessively risky.[1382]

Moreover, it seems that, broadly speaking, courts are reluctant to interfere with shareholder loans that are properly documented. This approach is problematic, as the documentation of a loan might address the problem of ambiguous loans, but it certainly does not say anything about the shareholder opportunism in question.[1383]

3. Ex post standards strategy enforced by gatekeeper control: Contractual subordination of certain shareholder loans insisted on by the auditor

a. Setting out the legal strategy

Unlike Germany and the US, South Africa does not provide for a remedy that specifically addresses the problem of shareholder loans. However, a practice developed under the previous company law regime pursuant to which auditors, in complying with their duty to report a 'reportable irregu-

1381 *In re Autostyle Plastics Inc.*, 269 F.3d 752.

1382 However, see Skeel Jr. and Krause-Vilmar (n 1330) 278, who argue that the opposite interpretation by the courts may be helpful in distinguishing between desirable and undesirable shareholder loans.

1383 Skeel Jr. and Krause-Vilmar (n 1330) 279.

larity' under the Auditing Profession Act[1384] in relation the company under audit, would accept (or insist on the conclusion of) a subordination agreement. According to such an agreement, a creditor (who was often an existing shareholder) would subordinate his claim to other unsecured creditors.[1385] The Guide on Trading Whilst Factually Insolvent by the South African Institute of Chartered Accountants[1386] (hereafter, '*Guide*') provided that the conclusion of such a subordination agreement was a factor in the enquiry whether the company's directors were engaging in reckless trading under s 424 Companies Act 1973. Reckless trading generally constituted a reportable irregularity,[1387] and could, if all the relevant requirements were met, relieve the auditor from such reporting duty.[1388]

The Guide's reasons why a subordination agreement might bring directors in compliance with the reckless trading duty are not easy to comprehend. The Guide provides that a subordination agreement 'is relevant in determining the subjective state of mind' of the directors.[1389] However, the reckless trading duty uses an objective standard,[1390] and, accordingly, the state of mind of the director is not relevant to the enquiry. A more plausible explanation could be that the subordination would improve the company's (short-term) cash flow position, as the subordinated debt would not

1384 26 of 2005. The term reportable irregularity is defined in s 1 of such Act and, in relevant parts, means any unlawful act or omission by a manager of an entity which has caused material financial loss to the entity, see Chapter 5 above.

1385 As we have seen in Chapter 3, a subordination agreement was also often insisted on by the courts when sanctioning the debt consolidation scheme. We will deal with this issue again in Chapter 7. Subordination agreements were held to be enforceable in insolvency by *Ex parte De Villiers and another: In re Carbon Developments (Pty) Ltd (in liquidation)* 1993 (1) SA 493 (A). This conclusion is consistent with other common law jurisdictions; for the UK, see *Re Maxwell Communications Corporation plc* No 2) [1994] 1 BCLC 1; for Australia, see *Horne v Cherster & Fein Property Developments Pty Ltd & Ors* [1986] 11 ACLR 485 (Supreme Court of Victoria).

1386 South African Institute of Chartered Accountants (SAICA), 'Trading Whilst Factually Insolvent' (1999) < https://www.saica.co.za/Portals/0/Technical/auditing/documents/Guide%20on%20Trading%20Whilst%20Factually%20Insolvent.pdf > accessed 14 January 2017.

1387 Para 17 of the Guide.

1388 Paras 28–53 of the Guide.

1389 Para 35 of the Guide.

1390 See the discussion in Chapter 5 above.

have to be serviced during the currency of the subordination agreement.[1391] This might bring the continued trading of the company within the acceptable confines of the reckless trading duty, as that duty – besides other relevant factors – effectively requires the directors to take appropriate measures when there is no reasonable prospect that the creditors would receive payment when due.[1392] However, a subordination agreement would, of course, only have such effect on the reckless trading duty if it operated both outside insolvency proceedings (ie, where the repayment of the interest and capital of the subordinated loan is not permitted until the happening of an event, for example, the restoration of the company's balance sheet solvency) and within insolvency proceedings (ie, where the subordinated creditor ranks below other unsecured creditors). Auditors would accordingly only have accepted subordination agreements that also operated outside of insolvency, despite the fact that parties are in principle free to agree on either of the two mentioned options.[1393]

As we saw in Chapter 5, the Guide should remain relevant for the interpretation of whether the reckless trading of companies under s 22(1) of the

1391 The fact that the subordination would also reduce the risk of advances made by subsequent creditors (as such creditors would rank ahead of the subordinated creditors in an insolvency if the insolvency would occur while the subordination agreement is still in place), does not appear to impact on the reckless trading duties of directors.

1392 See generally PART C, Chapter 5, II., 2., c. above. That this is how a subordination could remove reckless trading liability is hinted at by the Guide when it states that 'a subordination agreement represents a valuable concession to the undertaking to which it is given' (para 36). The South African courts have also indicated that appropriate subordination agreements in respect of existing (shareholder) loans could bring directors in compliance with the reckless trading duty; See *Cooper v A & G Fashions (Pty) Ltd: Ex parte Millman NO* 1991 (4) SA 204 (C) 207–8, *Ex parte De Villiers and another: In re Carbon Developments (Pty) Ltd (in liquidation)* 1993 (1) SA 493 (A) 505. But see, eg, Stegman J in the court *a quo* of *Ex parte De Villiers and another: In re Carbon Developments (Pty) Ltd (in liquidation)* 1992 (2) SA 95 (W) 114–8. It should be noted, however, that these cases concerned the subordination of shareholder loans as a condition for the sanctioning of the debt consolidation scheme (see generally PART B, Chapter 3, IV., 3. above). The statements on the subordination of shareholder loans in the vicinity of insolvency were thus merely *obiter*.

1393 On the different types of subordination agreements from a South African perspective, see McLennan, 'Abuse of Limited Liability, "Insider" Debts and Subordination Agreements' (1993) 110 SALJ 686, 690. See generally, eg, Nicolaides, 'Priorities for Subordinated Debt' [1989] JIBFL 247.

new Companies Act would fall within s 45 Auditing Profession Act and presumably also under the equivalent reporting regime under the Companies Act.[1394] Accordingly, it is expected that the practice will continue under the new Companies Act where auditors, and presumably also independent reviewers as contemplated under the Companies Act reporting regime, insist on the contractual subordination of shareholder loans, if this would avoid the directors being in breach of the reckless trading duty.

As with the duty of the auditor or the independent reviewer to report reckless trading breaches discussed in Chapter 5, here the auditor or independent reviewer is recruited as a gatekeeper to monitor companies in order to ensure that the directors comply with their reckless trading duties. The gatekeeper thus acts as the enforcer of the legal standard – ie, the reckless trading duty. In thUS, by contrast, the applicable legal standards are enforced by the court.

b. Problems of gatekeeper control enforcement

However, the *gatekeeper control strategy* has serious drawbacks in ameliorating the perverse incentives of shareholders to fund creditor-harming projects in the vicinity of insolvency. First, as indicated in Chapter 5, both the audit under the Auditing Profession Act, and the independent review under the Companies Act, are only required to occur once a year.[1395] This means that some time might pass after the extension of a (value-minimising) shareholder loan before the auditor or the independent reviewer may be in a position to suggest a contractual subordination. Second, we also saw in Chapter 5 that the audit under the Auditing Profession Act does not apply to private companies and close corporations that fall under a certain size threshold.[1396] This means that this legal strategy simply does not apply to the types of companies that may in practice be financed frequently

1394 See the discussion in PART C, Chapter 5, II., 2., e., dd. above.
1395 See the discussion in PART C, Chapter 5, II., 2., e., dd. above.
1396 As pointed out in Chapter 5, the size of private companies is determined by annual turnover, annual third party liability, the number of employees and shareholders and assets held by the company in a fiduciary capacity.

by shareholder loans.[1397] Although the independent review applies to such smaller companies, it has been shown above to lack effectiveness as a legal strategy.[1398]

The third weakness of this legal strategy is inherent to contractual subordinations. Since the subordination agreement would generally be concluded between the shareholder advancing the funds and the company (as it might be impractical for creditors to contract among each other), there is a risk that the agreement might be cancelled subsequently. This risk is even greater where the subordinated creditor is a shareholder who controls the company.[1399] In saying that, such action might be discouraged by the reputational costs arising from cancellation, as there is a chance that it will be exposed in the subsequent mandatory audit or independent review.

And finally, neither of the two reporting regimes allow for the auditor or the independent reviewer to distinguish between shareholder loans that were advanced in the vicinity of the insolvency of the company, on the one hand and loans that had been advanced while the company was still solvent, on the other hand. Since – for reasons explained above – shareholders generally do not have a perverse incentive while the company is still solvent, the fact that the auditor might insist on the subordination of such loans when the company would fall into distress outside insolvency proceedings, could discourage perfectly justifiable shareholder loans. Accordingly, this legal strategy could deprive companies of an important source of funding.

All these drawbacks appear to arise because the *gatekeeper control strategy* in South Africa is not specifically designed for the purpose of ameliorating the lending shareholder's perverse incentive to advance value-diminishing loans in the vicinity of insolvency. It is rather the problem discussed in Chapter 5, namely the company controllers' perverse incen-

---

1397 On the fact that small companies are frequently financed by shareholder loans, see, eg, *Ex parte Strydom NO: In re Central Plumbing Works (Natal) (Pty) Ltd; Ex parte Spendiff NO: In re Candida Footwear Manufacturers (Pty) Ltd; Ex parte Spendiff NO: In re Jerseytex (Pty) Ltd* 1988 (1) SA 616 (D) 623, which was confirmed by the Appellate Division (as it then was) in *Ex parte De Villiers and another: In re Carbon Developments (Pty) Ltd (in liquidation)* 1993 (1) SA 493 (A) 503. See also McLennan (n 1393) 700.

1398 See the discussion in PART C, Chapter 5, II., 2., e., dd. above.

1399 See the judgment of Stegmann J in the trial court of *Ex parte De Villiers and another: In re Carbon Developments (Pty) Ltd (in liquidation)* 1992 (2) SA 95 (W) 118–9. See also McLennan (n 1393) 697–9; para 42 of the Guide.

tive in respect of the strategic decision in the vicinity of insolvency to pursue value-minimising projects.

IV. Comparative evaluation – perspectives from Germany and the US

The three relevant jurisdictions rely on different legal strategies to reduce agency costs arising from the extension of shareholder loans in the vicinity of insolvency: Germany uses a *rules strategy* in the form of an automatic and blanket subordination of all shareholder loans *ex ante;* the US, a *standards strategy* in the form of equitable subordination and recharacterisation of shareholder loans enforced by courts *ex post*; and South Africa, a *standards strategy* in the form of contractual subordination of shareholder loans enforced by gatekeeper control *ex post*.

A statutory automatic subordination of all shareholder loans, as found in Germany, creates a high degree of legal predictability.[1400] By contrast, legal standards, such as the open-ended enquiry pursuant to the multi-factor test under the recharacterisation remedy and the determination of inequitable behaviour under the equitable subordination remedy in the US, are inherently less certain. The varying weight the courts have accorded to the different factors under the recharacterisation doctrine arguably raises the legal uncertainty of this strategy even further. The South African approach is similarly unpredictable, as the auditor's determination whether a contractual subordination relieves him of his duty to report depends on whether such subordination would bring the continued trading of the company within the legal confines of the reckless trading duty.

A further advantage of the German *rules strategy* is that it lowers the adjudication costs, as compliance with the requirement is easily ascertainable. By contrast, the standards *strategy* of the US and South Africa give rise to higher adjudication costs, as compliance would have to be determined by the court and the auditor, respectively.

However, the approaches of all three jurisdictions are ultimately unsuccessful in distinguishing between value-enhancing and value-diminishing shareholder loans. As we have seen, the German blanket subordination of

1400 Indeed, one of the reason given by the legislature for removing the 'creditworthiness' criterion in 2008 was that this would simplify the law and accordingly create more legal certainty; see the explanation by the German Government on the MoMiG (n 1349) 56.

all shareholder loans does not attempt to draw such a distinction: all shareholder loans are subordinated, irrespective of whether such loans could be value-maximising (and therefore in the best interests of the company's creditors). However, as subordination would always discourage the advancement of a shareholder loan, the company would be deprived of an important source of funding for value-maximising informal rescue measures or corporate projects, at the expense of the company's unsecured creditors.

The rescue exemption (*Sanierungsprivileg*) does not apply to loans advanced by shareholders, but rather to existing lenders acquiring shares in the company (for purposes of rescuing the company), and is therefore not relevant to the perverse incentive in question. To be sure, the exemption for shareholders with small holdings (*Kleinbeteiligtenprivileg*) might allow for value-enhancing shareholder loans because the disincentive posed by the automatic subordination falls away. By contrast, the risk of value-reducing loans by minority shareholders is low. This is because such shareholders are not likely to have a strong perverse incentive, given that their respective shares in the company's debt and equity are likely to be aligned. However, since the relationship of the shareholder's interest in the company's debt and equity will vary according to the circumstances of each case, it is impossible to predict *ex ante* whether the perverse incentive will *always* arise if a shareholder holds less than a certain amount of the company's shares.

A blanket subordination of shareholder loans *ex ante* would inherently seem to be an inappropriate strategy for ameliorating the shareholder opportunism in question. This is because it is not the *advancement* of the shareholder loan itself, but rather the management decision as to how to *invest* the proceeds of the loan, which could harm the company's creditors.

The US' *ex post* standards strategies – equitable subordination and recharacterisation – do not suffer from the inherent defect of the German blanket subordination approach. The US remedies attempt to distinguish between desirable and undesirable loans by means of the standard of inequitable behaviour of the lending shareholder (in respect of equitable subordination) and by means of whether the character of advancement is debt or equity in the form of the eleven-factor test (in respect of recharacterisation). However, in respect of recharacterisation (to which we restricted our analysis for purposes of demonstration), none of the eleven factors are particularly helpful, and some are even misguided, for purposes of identifying value-reducing shareholder loans. The reasons for this are, first, that some of the factors have been influenced by judicial interpretation of relevant equivalent factors used in the tax context, where the underlying concerns are often very different from those in insolvency law. Second, the courts have tended to conflate the problem of the advancement of ambiguous shareholder loans and value-minimising shareholder loans. They have also tended to give undue weight to the factors addressing ambiguous loans. As a result, shareholder advancements have often not been tested sufficiently against the factors dealing with the substance of the loan.

Although the standard of reckless trading under the South African *gatekeeper control strategy* probably comes closer to identifying the perverse incentive in question than the factors under the US recharacterisation remedy, the South African legal strategy is inherently flawed. This is because, first, the independent review under the the Auditing Profession Act and the Companies Act are only required to occur once a year. Second, the mandatory audit does not apply to smaller-sized private companies and close corporations, notwithstanding that such companies would be particularly amenable to the shareholder opportunism in question, given that such companies are often heavily financed by shareholder loans . Although the independent review applies to such smaller companies, it has been shown above to lack effectiveness as a legal strategy. Third, contractual subordination might, in principle, not be an appropriate remedy, as it gives rise to the risk that the subordination may be terminated subsequently (although such risk might be alleviated somewhat by possible reputational costs arising from such action). And fourth, because the auditor's duty to report 'reportable irregularities' under s 45 Auditing Profession Act does not distinguish between loans advanced in the vicinity of insolvency and loans while the company is still solvent, companies might be deprived of a perfectly legitimate and useful source of funding.

All three weaknesses of the South African approach seem to derive from the fact that the contractual subordination remedy is not specifically designed for the purpose of ameliorating the lending shareholder's perverse incentive to advance value-diminishing loans in the vicinity of insolvency, but rather the company controllers' perverse incentive in respect of strategic trading decision in the vicinity of insolvency.

The comparative examination illustrates the difficulty of developing criteria that appropriately distinguishes value-enhancing from value-reducing shareholder loans. Given this difficulty, it would seem, in principle, that an *ex post* standards approach would be preferable to an *ex ante* rules approach, as the former approach may allow for the problem of shareholder loans to be addressed with greater sensitivity.

In devising an appropriate legal strategy for South Africa, an *ex post* subordination of shareholder loans by the court based on criteria that focus on the consequences of the investment decision or perhaps a development of the directors' duty of care that caters for the problem of shareholder loans should be considered.[1401]

V. Summary and conclusion

The regulation of shareholder loans must have regard for the fact that they are not *per se* harmful to the company's creditors. In fact, shareholder loans could be an important source of funding, particularly for closely-held companies, as they may often be available at lower costs than external debt funding.

Generally-speaking, it is not simply the *advance* of a shareholder loan, but rather for what purposes such loan is *invested*, which holds the risk of value-minimisation for creditors.

The major problem for regulation is the difficulties of determining appropriate criteria for distinguishing between value-enhancing and value-reducing shareholder loans.

It would seem that none of the three jurisdictions examined draw that distinction successfully.

The German *ex ante rules strategy* – a blanket subordination of all shareholder loans (§ 39(1)(5) *Insolvenzordnung*) – does not attempt to draw such a distinction in the first place. Nor do the two exemptions from the blanket subordination (loans for purposes of rescue ('*Sanierungsprivileg*') and for shareholders with small holdings ('*Kleinbeteiligtenprivileg*')) introduce appropriate criteria for making that distinction. The problem with the German approach is that even value-enhancing shareholder loans are subordinated, which provides a disincentive for an important source of funding during informal rescue proceedings.

The *ex post* standards strategies enforced by the court – equitable subordination and recharacterisation – relied on in the US attempts to distin-

1401 For a suggestion of bringing the problem of shareholder loans under the German duty of care, see Eidenmüller (n 1324) 60.

guish by means of the standard of inequitable behaviour of the lending shareholder (in respect of equitable subordination) and by means of whether the character of advancement is debt or equity in the form of the eleven-factor test (in respect of recharacterisation). However, the eleven factors under the recharacterisation remedy (to which we limited our discussion) are ultimately inadequate in identifying creditor-harming shareholder loans.

The South African *ex post* standards approach enforced by the auditor and presumably the independent reviewer acting as gatekeeper, also falls short in controlling the problem of shareholder loans. Reasons for this are (i) the infrequency of the audit and the mandatory review, (ii) the inapplicability of the audit to smaller companies, notwithstanding that the risk of value-reducing shareholder loans is greatest in such companies, (iii) the ineffectiveness of the independent review regime, (iv) the possibility that subordination agreements may be subsequently cancelled and (v) the lack of a requirement that the auditor or independent reviewer distinguish between value-enhancing and value-reducing shareholder loans when exercising their respective reporting duties.

In general, an *ex post* standards approach would appear to allow for the problem of shareholder loans to be addressed with greater sensitivity than an *ex ante* rules approach, and therefore seems preferable.

Normatively, a judicially imposed *ex post* subordination remedy of shareholder loans on criteria focussing on the merits of the projects that are funded by such shareholder loans or perhaps a development of the directors' duty of care, should be considered.

Chapter 7 The Third Manifestation of the Company-Creditor Agency Conflict in the Vicinity of Insolvency: Company Controllers' Perverse Incentive in Respect of the Value-Minimising Invocation of Formal Business Rescue Proceedings

I. Introduction

As we saw in Chapter 1, company controllers might in certain circumstances be tempted to initiate formal rescue proceedings where this would be value-diminishing to the company, rather than delaying the invocation of formal rescue proceedings through the extension of shareholder loans and pursuing overly risky – and thus value-minimising – projects. We identified two general instances and one particular instance of this manifestation of the company controller opportunism in the vicinity of insolvency. The two general instances are premature entry and the entry of economically distressed companies,[1402] while the specific instance arises under the South African debt consolidation scheme. Because the proposer of the scheme is normally an existing shareholder or connected to the company, he could be seen as a company controller. Under the debt consolidation scheme, the company, acting through the proposer, has a perverse incentive to acquire the claims of all existing creditors at an undervalue and to apply such assets for value-reducing purposes in the post-scheme period. This gives rise primarily to three actions that reduce value to creditors of the company, as will be explored in greater detail further below in this Chapter.

As we have seen, there are different sources of the three types of company controller opportunism in question. In premature entry, somewhat ironically, it is the contractual protections and privileges under rescue proceedings – in particular the moratorium and cramdown – that could give rise to the problem of premature entry in certain situations. There are two

1402 For a comprehensive theoretical discussion and the relevant literature of the two general forms of this manifestation of the company controller opportunism in the vicinity of insolvency, see PART A, Chapter 1, II., 3., a., cc above.

standard examples of such situations. One is where the company is faced by a contingent claim that is large enough to jeopardise the company's continued existence if it arises, which has so far been most prevalent in the US. The other is where the company is faced with particularly onerous prospective claims under an employee redundancy scheme, which has been reported in the Netherlands, but apparently not yet in any of the jurisdictions examined in this study.

It will depend on the particular circumstances of each case whether the company controllers' decision to place the company under rescue proceedings is value-minimising, and therefore undesirable. Useful considerations in this regard are (i) the size of the prospective claim against the company, (ii) the significance of the threat that the claim poses to the company's continued existence if it would arise, (iii) the number of classes of creditors that would be affected by a potential restructuring outside of formal rescue proceedings (the fewer the number of creditor classes affected, the lower the potential costs of restructuring informally, as this would entail lower bargaining and co-ordination costs) and (iv) a comparison of the likely costs of dealing with such threat outside, as opposed to within, formal rescue proceedings.

Rescue regimes that use a debtor-in-possession governance system are, in principle, more vulnerable to the problem of premature entry, given that such rescue regimes generally encourage early entry of formal rescue proceedings.

As explained in Chapter 1, the sources of the perverse incentive of company controllers to place economically distressed companies under formal rescue proceedings are (i) that the financial state of an economically distressed company is likely to have deteriorated to a degree where rescue measures outside of formal insolvency proceedings may no longer be feasible, (ii) a cognitive state of rational optimism on the part of company controllers and (iii) a perception of directors that there is a smaller chance of being held liable for relevant pre-insolvency directorial duties, largely due to the general shorter time periods of rescue proceedings than liquidation proceedings.

The sources of the strategic use of the South African debt consolidation scheme are (i) the tax benefit under s 20(1)(a) Income Tax Act, which allowed the acquirer of the existing creditors' debt claims to set off the loss of the company against the profits generated from the same trade as the acquirer's other business entities and (ii) the weakness of the market for distressed businesses in South Africa.

The problems of premature entry and the entry of economically distressed companies are dealt with in South Africa, the UK and Australia broadly by a combination of *ex ante* entry requirements and relevant *ex post* strategies, namely (i) directorial sanctions *ex post* for non-compliance with the entry grounds (which could be seen as a *standards strategy*), (ii) the right of creditors to challenge the invocation of rescue proceedings (which could be seen as a *ratification rights strategy*) and (iii) the duties of the office holder to investigate the company's financial affairs and take relevant steps where he finds that the company should remain in rescue proceedings (which could be seen as an *ex ante trusteeship strategy*). The US, on the other hand, addresses the value-minimising invocation of Chapter 11 proceedings by means of the judge-made good faith requirement *ex post*. These legal strategies will be considered at II.

In rescue regimes that use a management-displacing system of governance, the effectiveness of the above-mentioned legal strategies addressing the perverse incentive of company controllers giving rise to the two types of value-minimising invocations of formal rescue proceedings could be undermined, where the directors appoint an office holder who is related, or sympathetic, to the directors or the shareholders of the company (hereafter, '*friendly office holder*'). The applicable jurisdictions rely on several legal strategies in this regard, namely: (i) relevant *ex ante* minimum qualification requirements that relate generally to office holders' independence of, *inter alia*, the shareholders and directors of the company (which can be regarded as a *rules strategy*); (ii) *ex ante* duties of disclosure of office holders of their independence (and both (i) and (ii)) are supplemented by applicable *ex post* sanctions for non-compliance with such requirements); and (iii) the *ex post* removal of office holders, *inter alia*, in situations where the office holder is unable to exercise an independent and unfettered judgment (which can be seen as a *removal rights strategy*). These legal strategies will be considered at III. The legal strategies controlling the strategic use of the South African debt consolidation scheme will be examined at IV.

Since this Chapter will explore legal strategies controlling the perverse incentives of company controllers to invoke formal rescue proceedings for strategic purposes, only the commencement of rescue proceedings out-of-court *by directors* will concern us. Moreover, the entry route by court application is either not available to directors, as is the case in South Africa,[1403] or, where it is available, as in the UK, is rarely used by directors. Given the lower costs of out-of-court entry, only the legal strategies available under this entry route will form part of our analysis in this Chapter.[1404] By the same token, the risk of the appointment of a friendly office holder is greater where the directors appoint the office holder out-of-court, given the lack of court supervision in such entry route.

That is why the focus of our analysis will also be on the relevant legal strategies available under the out-of-court entry route.

Where a company has been placed under formal rescue proceedings inappropriately, the costs of remedying the situation are likely to be very high. Such costs typically would entail the costs of the office holder to investigate the company's affairs and the costs of court proceedings (where applicable) and conversion to liquidation proceedings (in the case of the entry of economically distressed companies). Since in such situations the company ought not to have been placed under rescue proceedings in the first place, the costs of remedying the inappropriate invocation of rescue proceedings would be wasteful from the perspective of the company's unsecured creditors. This makes it all the more important that the legal strategies controlling the three mentioned forms of this manifestation of the company controller opportunism be effective.

In saying that, 'tough' rules on ameliorating the perverse incentive of company controllers to invoke rescue proceedings 'prematurely' and of the entry of economically distressed companies could discourage the timeous invocation of rescue proceedings by directors.[1405] Such legal strategies must thus balance the company controller opportunism that gives rise to the problem of premature entry, on the one hand and the value-minimising delay of formal rescue proceedings, on the other hand, in

---

1403 Eg, the Australian procedure does not provide for entry by court application at all.

1404 Thus, entry by court application (which is available in, eg, South Africa and the UK) and out-of-court entry by, eg, the floating charge-holders in the UK and Australia or by creditors in the US (11 USC §§ 301, 303) will be excluded from our analysis.

1405 The other manifestation of the company controller opportunism, where formal rescue proceedings are used for strategic purposes – namely, where companies are economically distressed – is less relevant in this context, as in such a situation the scope for continued trading is likely to be small.

particular the pursuit of risky projects in the vicinity of insolvency and asset dilution.

There is a further tension in relation to the rules regulating the risk of the appointment of a friendly rescue practitioner between the potential of value reduction as a result of the existence of bias of the rescue practitioner in favour of one particular constituent of the company during rescue proceedings, on the one hand and the costs of having to appoint a person as rescue practitioner other than the professional who assisted the company in the period leading up to the invocation of formal restructuring proceedings, on the other hand. The latter costs consist of the resources that need to be expended by the office holder to obtain the information required to perform his responsibilities to the company during rescue proceedings satisfactorily ('familiarisation costs').

Unlike the company controller opportunism to pursue excessively risky projects at the expense of the company's creditors in the vicinity of insolvency (discussed in Chapter 5) and the extension of value-minimising shareholder loans in the vicinity of insolvency (discussed in Chapter 6), the various types of perverse incentives of the company controllers that will be discussed in this Chapter have not received much attention in the literature so far. The problems around the use of the South African debt consolidation scheme have, to the knowledge of this author, not been analysed from a law and economics perspective before.

II. Comparative evaluation of legal strategies controlling premature entry and entry by economically distressed companies – comparative perspectives from the UK, Australia and the US

1. Applicable grounds of entry in conjunction with relevant ex post legal strategies: The approach generally relied on in South Africa, the UK and Australia

a. The entry grounds

aa. Counteracting premature entry: The impending insolvency entry ground

General—The procedures of South Africa, the UK and Australia provide that directors may only place the company under rescue proceedings if the company meets the applicable test of impending insolvency, ie, the impending insolvency entry ground.[1406] The impending insolvency entry ground could be thought to control the company controller opportunism that gives rise to premature entry (hereafter, '*premature entry opportunism*'), insofar as such opportunism often arises in respect of *solvent* companies. It appears that the reason for this – at least from an economics perspective – is that, so long as companies are *solvent*, a prospective threat to their continued existence, through a large contingent delictual claim for example, could generally be resolved at lower overall costs outside formal rescue proceedings (or perhaps under a less onerous alternative formal rescue proceeding) than under the main formal rescue proceeding.[1407] This is largely because solvent companies, even when faced with a potential threat to their solvency, are generally not in immediate danger of a general default by the company. Accordingly, both the costs of creditor enforcement and the bargaining costs between the company and the creditors and between the affected creditors *inter se* that arise when the anticipated threat to the company's continued existence is resolved outside formal insolvency proceedings, is likely to be lower than the costs arising when such threat is resolved within formal insolvency proceedings. The main reason for this would appear to be the generally high direct and indirect costs of formal rescue proceedings.[1408]

Differences in impending insolvency entry grounds of relevant jurisdictions—The formulations of the impending insolvency entry ground differ slightly in the three jurisdictions: in South Africa, the test is that it appears reasonably likely that the company becomes unable to pay its debts as they become due and payable in the immediately ensuing six months or become insolvent within the immediately ensuing six months; in the UK, the test is that the company is or is likely to become unable to pay its

1406 For South Africa, see ss 129(1)(a), 131(4)(a)(i) read with s 128(1)(f) Companies Act 2008; for the UK, see Insolvency Act 1986, Sch B1, para 27(2)(a); for Australia, see s 436A(1)(a) Corporations Act 2001.

1407 However, as we will see below, it is unlikely that the impending insolvency entry grounds under the jurisdictions considered in this context were enacted for the purpose of ameliorating premature entry opportunism.

1408 However, as we will see below, there might be exceptions to this general position, and the impending insolvency entry ground must, *inter alia* as a result of this, be seen as ultimately inadequate in controlling the company controllers' opportunism in question.

debts; and in Australia, the test is that the company is insolvent or is likely to become insolvent at some future time. The South African and British grounds use both a cash flow test and a balance sheet test. This is expressly so in South Africa: the second-mentioned test that the company becomes insolvent within the immediately ensuing six months must refer to balance sheet insolvency, given that the first-mentioned test clearly entails cash flow insolvency.[1409] In the UK, although intuitively the balance sheet test does not fall within the meaning of the phrase 'inability to pay debts', it nevertheless forms part of such ground, by reading it together with para 111 of Sch B and s 123 Insolvency Act 1986.[1410] The Australian ground, by contrast, defines insolvency only in cash flow terms.[1411] The enquiry in relation to the Australian ground is whether the company is able to pay debts generally (as opposed to a particular debt), and it is forward-looking. For example, if the company is able to pay its debts generally through the sale of liquid assets and further debt funding, then the company would meet the cash flow test.[1412] This brings the cash flow test closer to the balance sheet test.[1413] Moreover, given the element of futurity in the impending insolvency entry grounds in all three jurisdictions, the

1409 *Henochsberg on the Companies Act 71 of 2008*, s 129, 452. This conclusion also follows from a contextual reading of the second-mentioned test. The 'solvency' test under s 4 Companies Act 2008 (which, together with the 'liquidity' test, *inter alia*, distinguishes admissible from inadmissible distributions and related transactions under Part D Companies Act 2008) is formulated in balance sheet terms, namely 'the assets of the company, as fairly valued, equal or exceed the liabilities of the company, as fairly valued'. (The liquidity test, on the other hand, constitutes cash flow insolvency.) The fact that the solvency test under s 4 means balance sheet insolvency implies that the reference to 'insolvency' under the applicable test of 'financial distress' in s 128(1)(f) should also mean balance sheet insolvency.

1410 See also Keay and Walton, *Insolvency Law – Corporate and Personal* (2nd edn, Jordans 2008) 98 n 7.

1411 S 436A(1)(a) read with s 95A(1) Corporations Act 2001.

1412 See, eg, *Crema Pty Ltd v Landmarl Property Developments Pty Ltd* (2006) 58 ACSR 632, 652 citing *Hymix Concrete Pty Ltd v Garritty* (1977) 2; *Jetaway Logistics Pty Ltd v Deputy Commissioner of Taxation* [2009] VSCA 319, para 14; *Southern Cross Interiors Pty Ltd (in liqu) v Deputy Commissioner of Taxation* (2001) 53 NSWLR 213; ACLR 559; *Sandell v Porter* (1966) 115 CLR 666. See generally Gronow and Mason, *McPhersons Law of Company Liquidations* (loose-leaf) (Thomson Reuters 2012) 15ff.

1413 Goode, *Principles of Corporate Insolvency Law* (3rd edn, Sweet & Maxwell 2005) 4–16.

differences between the cash flow and balance sheet tests become less significant.

A conspicuous difference between the South African and the Anglo-Australian impending insolvency entry grounds is that the South African provision provides for a particular time frame within which the state of insolvency must occur, namely within the immediately ensuing six months. By contrast, both the British and Australian provisions provide that the state of insolvency must be 'likely' to occur. In the UK, the word 'likely' in this context means 'more probable than not'.[1414] Even when judged from the perspective of legal doctrine, the 6-months period under the South African impending insolvency entry ground is arbitrary.[1415]

The absence of a fixed time period under the British and Australian versions of the impending insolvency entry ground allows the courts to select the companies for which restructuring measures within, rather than outside, formal rescue proceedings would be value-maximising with greater sensitivity. This would apply to companies, for which rescue proceedings would be value-enhancing. Such companies are likely to become insolvent pursuant to the Anglo-Australian versions of the impending insolvency ground, but would (only) reach the state of insolvency under the South African ground later than six months from the time of assessment. On that basis, those companies would inappropriately be denied access to rescue proceedings in South Africa.

Impending insolvency entry ground ultimately inadequate in controlling premature entry opportunism—However, seen as a legal strategy to control premature entry, the impending insolvency entry ground as such is ultimately inadequate, at least when regarded in isolation from other rele-

1414 *Re Colt Telecom Group plc (No2)* [2003] BPIR 324. See generally, Keay and Walton (n 1410) 98–9. The South African version of the impending insolvency entry ground also requires a 'reasonable likelihood' that the two tests be met within the next six months. Although its meaning has not been determined by the courts in this context, it is likely to be very close to the British meaning of 'likely'.

1415 It has been suggested that a 12 month period would have been preferable, on the grounds that this is the general time period over which companies usually plan in advance as evidenced, eg, by financial statements; Loubser, *Some Comparative Aspects of Corporate Rescue in South African Company Law* (LLD thesis, University of South Africa 2010) 337.

vant legal strategies.[1416] This is because the source of premature entry opportunism is not the threat of insolvency as such (which is the benchmark used for entry of rescue proceedings under the impending insolvency entry ground), but rather the availability of certain protective measures under the formal rescue procedure, in particular the statutory ranking of claims coupled with the cramdown mechanism. Thus, where the company is faced by a large contingent claim, premature entry opportunism arises because of the prospect of being able to block enforcement by the affected (and other) creditors against the company and to cram down the plan on lower ranking classes of creditors (including the holders of the contingent claims). In that way, the company controllers secure value for shareholders.[1417] It is because of such protective measures that company controllers of companies that are, for example, faced with a prospective, but potentially devastating claim, are tempted to place companies under formal rescue proceedings, without regard for whether resolving such claim would be more efficient outside or within formal rescue proceedings.

To be sure, given that the state of solvency is generally a reliable indicator that the costs of formal rescue proceedings would be higher than the costs of informal rescue measures (or alternative formal rescue proceedings) in dealing with a prospective claim, the impending insolvency entry ground may often appropriately address the premature entry problem.[1418] This would be the case under the South African impending insolvency entry ground to the extent that premature entry occurs earlier than six months before insolvency, and in the UK and Australia, where premature entry occurs before the company is 'likely' to reach the state of insolvency provided under the respective Anglo-Australian impending insolvency entry grounds.

However, the state of solvency of a company is not the only factor in determining whether informal or formal rescue measures are the most cost-effective means by which to deal with a prospective threat to the

1416 As we will see in PART C, Chapter 7, II., 1., c., aa below, some jurisdictions in question provide for grounds of challenging the out-of-court entry into rescue proceedings that might have the effect of remedying part of the limitation of the impending insolvency entry ground in resolving premature entry opportunism.

1417 And possibly for secured creditors, particularly where the management is responsive to secured creditors' interests primarily through covenants in loan agreements.

1418 See text to n 1408 above.

company's continued existence. Other relevant factors in this regard are, for example, the severity of the prospective threat to a company's solvency and the complexity of a company's (debt) capital structure. The more serious the threat and the more complex the company's capital structure, the higher the applicable bargaining costs and the greater the chance that the costs of informal rescue measures might exceed those of formal rescue proceedings in dealing with the anticipated threat to the company's continued existence. This means that depending on whether, *inter alia*, the above-mentioned factors are present, there could be situations where *insolvent* companies[1419] might be restructured more cost-effectively outside formal rescue proceedings or under a less onerous alternative formal turnaround proceeding. Although such companies should, accordingly, be denied access to the main formal rescue proceeding, they are, *ceteris paribus*,[1420] granted access to formal rescue proceedings inappropriately under the impending insolvency entry ground. Conversely, in some situations, *solvent* companies[1421] might be restructured more cost-effectively under formal rescue proceedings, and, accordingly, require access to formal rescue proceedings. Yet, such companies are inappropriately denied access to formal rescue proceedings under the impending insolvency entry ground.[1422] It should be noted, however, that in this second-mentioned situation the company is denied access to formal rescue proceedings irrespective of the presence of premature entry opportunism.

To the extent that the impending insolvency entry ground, *ceteris paribus*, fails to provide for the above-mentioned exceptional situations, it ultimately constitutes an imperfect legal strategy for controlling premature

1419 Or, to be more precise, companies that have reached, and are possibly beyond, the state of impending insolvency as defined under the applicable provision in the jurisdictions in question.

1420 See the qualification noted in n 1416 above.

1421 Or, to be more precise, solvent companies that have not yet reached the state of impending insolvency as defined under the applicable provision in the jurisdictions in question.

1422 The adverse effects of this appear to be greater under the South African version of the impending insolvency entry ground than under the Anglo-Australian versions, given the more flexible test of the Anglo-Australian versions than the South African version, which arguably grant companies access to formal rescue proceedings earlier than six months before the onset of the state of insolvency, as is the case under the South African version.

entry opportunism and the value-maximising invocation of formal rescue proceedings, in respect of the second-mentioned situation.

The reason for the unsatisfactory nature of the impending insolvency entry ground in restraining the premature entry problem is that it was most probably not primarily designed for that purpose in the relevant jurisdictions. A better explanation for the existence of the impending insolvency entry ground in those jurisdictions is presumably a general (legal cultural) belief that corporate insolvency procedures should not be available to *solvent* companies.[1423] This conviction is underlined by a (secured) creditor-friendly legal culture in those jurisdictions.[1424] The only concession to the debtor and unsecured creditors that those jurisdictions are prepared to make, is to allow entry into rescue proceedings sometime before the onset of insolvency. This is thought to cater for the need to allow companies access to rescue proceedings before it is too late for such companies to be rescued. To be sure, in the UK and Australia, floating charge-holders are exempted from having to show impending insolvency when placing the company under administration and voluntary administration, respectively. However, the basis for this exemption is the safeguarding of the interests

1423 For a doctrinal explanation from a German perspective however, see Grünewald, *Mehrheitsherrschaft und insolvenzrechtliche Vorauswirkung in der Unternehmenskrise* (Mohr Siebeck 2015) 111ff, 166ff, 355ff and further references cited therein. Grünewald argues that collective decision-making by creditors is only justified at the onset of insolvency (ie, cash flow and balance sheet insolvency pursuant to §§ 17 and 19 *Insolenzordung*, respectively). This is because only from this point on the debtor's cash flow and net assets are no longer sufficient to satisfy the outstanding claims of all its creditors. This means that at this point it is no longer possible for creditors to pursue their interests against the debtor without affecting the interests of the other creditors. He goes on to argue that here majority decision-making among the creditors is the only way of safeguarding the equal treatment of creditors ('*Gläubigergleichbehandlung*') and the relative weighting of interests of creditors ('*Wahrung der relativen Interessengewichte*'), which exists because of the different strengths of interests of the different creditors based on pre-insolvency contractual rights (eg, secured, unsecured and contractually subordinated creditors). This is the reason why, according to Grünewald, the entry ground of immiment insolvency pursuant to § 18(1) and § 270b(1)(1st sentence) *Insolvenzordung* is contrary to the German system of insolvency law ('*systemwidrig*').

1424 See the discussion in PART B, Chapter 4, VI., 2 above.

of the floating charge-holder, rather than the promotion of an inclusive rescue procedure.[1425]

An analysis of the impending insolvency entry ground, then, constitutes a vivid illustration of the divergence between legal doctrine and legal culture, on the one hand and the agency cost theory, on the other hand in explaining and evaluating the law. However, as already mentioned in Chapter 1, this does not mean that the two methodologies are mutually exclusive; the principal-agent theory can rather be seen to exist alongside legal doctrine if the former is understood as a heuristic device for thinking about the functional role of rescue law.

bb. Counteracting the entry of economically distressed companies: Economic distress entry ground

The *ex ante* strategy relied on in South Africa and the UK (but not Australia) to control the problem of the entry of economically distressed companies is a ground of entry which requires that, at the time of entry, there is a reasonable likelihood that the company will meet the economic distress entry ground. There are three potentially important differences in the approaches taken by these three jurisdictions in relation to this *ex ante* strategy. First, in South Africa, the *board of directors* must satisfy itself of the likelihood of the success of rescue *ex ante* by means of a board resolution that the company be placed under rescue proceedings.[1426] In the UK, by contrast, the administrator is given the responsibility of reassuring the company's claimants of the likelihood of success of administration proceedings, by way of a public statement.[1427]

It is not clear whether the South African or the British approach is more effective in reducing the likelihood of the entry of economically distressed companies in rescue proceedings. On the one hand, because office holders are by law required to be independent, *inter alia*, of the company and its

1425 Armour and Mokal, 'Reforming the Governance of Corporate Rescue: The Enterprise Act 2002' (2004) ESRC Centre for Business Research Working Paper 288 <http://papers.ssrn.com/sol3/papers.cfm?abstract_id=567306> accessed 16 January 2017.

1426 S 129(1)(b) read with s 128(1)(b) and (h) Companies Act 2008.

1427 The administrator must, soon after his appointment, make a statement in which he must declare, *inter alia*, that 'in his opinion, the purpose of administration is reasonably likely to be achieved' (Insolvency Act 1986, Sch B1, para 29(3)(b)).

directors,[1428] office holders ought to be more objective than the directors (whose perverse incentive is the very reason for this value-minimising action) in determining whether or not the company meets the economic distress entry ground. On the other hand, office holders – by acting as agents for the body of creditors –,[1429] may generally have a perverse incentive to refrain from terminating formal rescue proceedings, given that they receive a time-based remuneration. This explains why office holders may generally be reluctant to conclude that rescue proceedings be discontinued on the basis that the company does not comply with the economic distress entry ground. To be sure, it might be argued that this perverse incentive of office holders could be counteracted by an incentive that they are seen by the market as dealing responsibly with companies in order to secure more future appointments.[1430] However, it is not clear that such long-term benefits are tangible enough to sufficiently re-balance office holders' perverse incentive in question.[1431]

Moreover, due to the general lack of information of office holders and the requirement that office holders make the relevant determination soon after their appointment (as, for example, in the UK[1432]) office holders are, in any event, not in a strong position to make an informed judgment as to whether the company meets the economic distress entry ground.[1433] The danger is rather that office holders would simply rubber-stamp the direc-

1428 This is primarily to prevent the appointment of an office holder who is connected to, *inter alia*, the company controllers, which reduces the likelihood that the two general value-minimising actions discussed here could, in a sense, be circumvented. We will consider the legal strategies counteracting the appointment of a friendly office holder at III below.

1429 For a more detailed theoretical explanation of this agency conflict, see Chapter 1.

1430 A similar argument has been advanced in respect of the perverse incentive of company controllers to pursue excessively risky projects in the vicinity of insolvency (Mokal, *Corporate Insolvency Law* (Oxford University Press 2005) 285–8), which could be applied analogously in this context.

1431 See a similar argument in respect of the perverse incentive of company controllers to pursue excessively risky projects in the vicinity of insolvency, declining the contrary argument by Mokal (n 1430) 285–8; Davies, 'Directors' Creditor-Regarding Duties in the Vicinity of Insolvency' (2006) 7 EBOR 308.

1432 Insolvency Act 1986, Sch B1, para 29.

1433 Indeed, this is implicitly acknowledged by the provision that permits the administrator to rely on information supplied by the directors of the company in making the relevant declaration; Insolvency Act 1986, Sch B1, para 29(4).

tors' determination that the company does indeed meet the economic distress entry ground.

Second, while in the UK, the objectives of administration explicitly include the piecemeal sale of the company's assets where such sale would return a greater value under administration than under liquidation proceedings,[1434] the law, as it currently stands in South Africa, presumably does not allow for the break-up sale of companies' assets.[1435] While the UK approach is more rigorous than the South African approach in relation to the (monetary) interests of the company's creditors as a whole, the South African approach probably leaves less scope for the perverse incentive of company controllers that gives rise to the entry of economically distressed companies.

Third, although Australia does not provide for an economic distress entry ground *ex ante*, as we will see in greater detail further below in this Chapter, the company can still be released from voluntary administration *ex post*, on the grounds that it is in the creditors' interests for the voluntary administration to end. This ground arguably includes a situation where the company is not likely to meet the objectives of voluntary administration.[1436] At face value, the absence of requiring the board of directors (as in South Africa) or the administrator (as in the UK) to declare the company's compliance with the economic distress entry ground *ex ante*, effectively moves the entire costs of the enforcement of the economic distress entry ground to within formal rescue proceedings. The fact that such costs are essentially borne by the unsecured creditors seems undesirable, particularly given that unsecured creditors are the very constituent that is meant to be protected from the problem of the entry of economically distressed companies.

In saying that, since neither South Africa nor the UK impose *ex post* sanctions on the board of directors for placing the company under rescue proceedings in violation of the economic distress entry ground, the costs of such enforcement may often fall within rescue proceedings, and therefore on the unsecured creditors.

1434 Insolvency Act 1986, Sch B1, para 3(1)(c).

1435 This issue was considered in Chapter 4.

1436 Such objectives of rescue are set out in s 435A Corporations Act 2001. As we will see below, both South Africa and the UK also allow for various grounds of releasing the company from rescue proceedings in the event of non-compliance with both entry grounds in question.

However, imposing *ex post* sanctions on the applicable decision-takers at the entry stage may not be appropriate either, as the *ex ante* effect of such sanctions may generally discourage the decision-takers from utilising rescue proceedings where this would be value-maximising, and thus desirable.

b. The ex post standards strategy: Directorial sanctions for non-compliance with the impending insolvency entry ground

In South Africa and the UK, the impending insolvency entry ground is supplemented by directorial sanctions *ex post*. In South Africa, such directorial sanctions are in the form of a cost-order against any director who voted in favour of the board resolution commencing rescue proceedings in violation of the cash flow limb of the impending insolvency entry ground.[1437] In the UK, such directorial sanctions are in the form of criminal sanctions for a false statement in the statutory declaration made by the directors who have appointed the administrator. In such statement, the directors must, *inter alia*, declare that the company meets the British version of the impending insolvency entry ground.[1438] The threat of *ex post* sanctions gives greater force to the impending insolvency entry ground. It could, accordingly, reduce the likelihood that the costs of enforcement of compliance with the impending insolvency entry ground are moved to within formal rescue proceedings, where they would, essentially, fall on the unsecured creditors. *Ex post* sanctions would seem to be particularly important in respect of out-of-court entries, given the lack of court scrutiny in that entry route.

However, the need to control premature entry opportunism must be balanced with the need to encourage the timeous commencement of rescue proceedings. Company controllers are, *ceteris paribus*, best placed to determine the appropriate time at which economically viable, but temporarily distressed, companies ought to be placed under formal rescue proceedings, since they have the best information about the company's affairs.[1439] However, as we saw above, company controllers have a perverse incentive

1437 S 130(5)(c)(ii).

1438 Insolvency Act 1986, Sch B1, paras 27(2)(a), 27(4).

1439 Apart from perhaps major secured creditors; see Armour and Mokal (n 1425); Armour and Frisby, 'Rethinking Receivership' (2001) 21 ojls 73, 75.

to inappropriately delay the invocation of formal rescue proceedings, in particular through the pursuance of overly risky projects in the vicinity of insolvency and the extension of shareholder loans.[1440] Accordingly, 'tough' rules on controlling premature entry opportunism might promote the above-mentioned perverse incentives of company controllers in the vicinity of insolvency to inappropriately delay the invocation of formal rescue proceedings.

The balancing mechanism used in South Africa in this regard is that any director who voted in favour of the board resolution that commenced rescue proceedings contrary to the impending insolvency entry ground, may raise a defence that he acted in good faith and on the basis of information that he obtained by taking reasonable diligent steps and that was provided to him by specified persons, including professional advisors of the company. This statutory defence forms part of the South African version of the 'business judgment rule' that was introduced under the Companies Act 2008.[1441] The balancing mechanism relied on in the UK is that the question whether a director should be held criminally liable for declaring that the company met the impending insolvency entry ground, is judged from a subjective perspective.[1442]

Both the above-mentioned South African business judgment rule and the British subjective test raise the standard of proof, and thereby make successful suits more difficult to obtain. This arguably alleviates the possible adverse *ex ante* effect of the relevant *ex post* directorial sanctions on the company controllers' premature entry opportunism.

c. The ex post ratification rights strategy: Applicable grounds of challenging the commencement of business rescue proceedings by claimants

aa. Challenges to the invocation of business rescue proceedings that counteract premature entry

All three jurisdictions in question allow for challenges by claimants to the commencement, and, occasionally, the termination, of rescue proceedings

1440 See the discussion in Chapter 5 and Chapter 6, respectively.
1441 S 130(5)(c)(ii) read with s 76(4) and (5) Companies Act 2008.
1442 Insolvency Act 1986, Sch B1, para 27(4)(b), 29(7)(b).

in situations where the company would be restructured more cost-effectively outside formal rescue proceedings (or under a less onerous alternative formal turnaround proceeding). Insofar as here the claimants (acting as principals) are entitled to *ratify* the management decision as to the most appropriate forum of dealing with the ailing company, this mechanism could be seen as a *ratification rights strategy*. Although the *decision rights strategy* is generally used sparingly in company law, given the efficiencies of delegating decision-making to a small group of experts, fundamental decisions, such as the initiation of, and ('premature') exit[1443] from, formal corporate insolvency proceedings, are often placed in the hands of the principals themselves. To be sure, where the decision rights are granted to a single principal acting on behalf of the group of principals,[1444] a new agency relationship arises between the single principal (now acting as agent) and the entire group of principals. However, the scope of agent opportunism is generally quite limited in respect of challenging the initiation of rescue proceedings by a single claimant, as all of the jurisdictions in question require the court to have the final word on this decision.

The modes of challenging the commencement of rescue proceedings by claimants fall into two broad categories. One relates to non-compliance with the impending insolvency entry ground itself. As mentioned above, to the extent that the impending insolvency entry ground often appropriately denies access to companies for which informal turnaround mechanisms would be value-maximising, the right to challenge the entry of companies that do not meet such entry ground could also be seen to counteract premature entry. Indeed, the right to challenge entry into rescue proceedings *ex post* in such circumstances is an important remedy, particularly for out-of-court entries, given the lack of court oversight in respect of such entry route. Examples of challenges to the initiation of rescue proceedings on the impending insolvency entry grounds are found in South Africa and

1443 Another typical example of where ratification rights are granted to the principals that allow for the exit from rescue proceedings is the right of the claimants to vote on the rescue plan that has been developed and proposed by the office holder; see generally Armour, Hertig and Kanda, 'Transactions with Creditors' in Kraakman and others (eds), *The Anatomy of Corporate Law – A comparative and Functional Approach* (2nd edn, Oxford University Press 2009) 144.

1444 Another means by which ratification rights could be exercised is where the decision rights are given to the entire group of principals, who then decide by means of majority vote. The most obvious example of this in the context of rescue law is the right of the claimants to vote on the rescue plan.

Australia. In South Africa, each affected person is entitled to apply to court for an order terminating rescue proceedings for the lack of a reasonable basis for believing that the company is 'financially distressed.[1445] In Australia, each claimant of the company is entitled to apply to court for an order to end voluntary administration on the grounds that the company is 'solvent',[1446] which presumably includes the state of impending insolvency that constitutes the Australian version of the premature entry ground.[1447]

The other broad mode of challenging the entry of companies into rescue proceedings potentially include instances where companies have met the impending insolvency entry ground and have been granted access to rescue proceedings on that basis, notwithstanding that such companies would be restructured more cost-effectively outside formal rescue proceedings (or under a less onerous alternative formal turnaround proceeding).[1448] Such mode of challenge may, accordingly, provide recourse to the company's creditors in the situations where the impending insolvency entry ground is inadequate in controlling premature entry opportunism.[1449]

Differences in the relevant jurisdictions in relation to this second mode of challenging the commencement of rescue proceedings can be found in respect of the persons who are entitled to initiate such challenge and the grounds upon which the invocation of rescue proceedings can be challenged (if any).

1445 S 130(1)(a)(i) Companies Act 2008.

1446 S 447A(2)(a) read with sub-s 4(b) Corporations Act 2001. Other persons that are entitled to apply to court for the termination of rescue proceedings are the company, the administrator, the Australian Securities and Investment Commission and 'any other interested person' (s 447A(4) Corporations Act 2001).

1447 Pursuant to s 436A(1)(a) Corporations Act 2001.

1448 On the reasons for this value-minimising action, see PART C, Chapter 7, II., 1., a., aa above.

1449 See the discussion under the heading "*Impending insolvency ground ultimately inadequate in controlling premature entry opportunism*" in PART C, Chapter 7, II., 1., a., aa. It should be noted that, as we have seen, there is another situation where the impending insolvency entry ground fails to appropriately deal with the problem of premature entry. This is where it would be value-enhancing for a company that faces a contingent claim to be restructured within formal rescue proceedings, but where such company is still 'solvent' according to the impending insolvency ground, and would, on that basis, be denied access to rescue proceedings. This problem is not addressed in any of South Africa, the UK or Australia.

The UK procedure provides for two avenues by which administration can be challenged and set aside by the court. Under the one avenue, the administrator must apply to court for the termination of administration if required to do so by the creditors' meeting.[1450] It appears as though the mere instruction by the creditors' meeting without the need for the administrator to satisfy applicable (objective) requirements is sufficient for allowing the administrator to make the application. This is consistent with the economic principle that a constituency bearing the ultimate risk of a particular decision is best placed in taking such decision.[1451] Given the lack of any objective requirements for the court application by the administrator to terminate administration, this avenue of challenge would be broad enough to catch instances of premature entry of companies that would have been inappropriately granted access to administration under the impending insolvency entry ground.

Under the second relevant avenue of challenge, a creditor of the company can apply to court for the termination of administration on the grounds of an 'improper motive' on the part of the person who appointed the administrator.[1452] The term 'improper motive' has been held to include the invocation of administration for a collateral purpose,[1453] and it seems to be wide enough to also encompass premature entry. However, given that the persons who appointed the administrator (in this case, the directors) were actually motivated by an improper purpose when commencing administration – which appears to require an examination of his subjective state of mind –, this ground will often be difficult to prove.[1454]

1450 Insolvency Act 1986, Sch B1 para 79(2)(c).

1451 Armour, 'The Law and Economics of Corporate Insolvency Law: A Review' (2001) ESRC Centre for Business Research Working Paper 197 <http://disciplinas.stoa.usp.br/pluginfile.php/35886/mod_resource/content/1/CHY%20The%20Law%20and%20Economics%20of%20Corporate%20Insolvency.pdf> accessed 16 January 2017.

1452 Insolvency Act 1986, Sch B1, para 81. Although this ground of challenge is available in respect of all entry routes, because premature entry is a manifestation of directorial opportunism at the expense of the company, we are only concerned here with the application of para 81 where an administrator had been appointed by the directors out-of-court (according to para 22).

1453 Fletcher, Higham and Trowers, *Corporate Administrations and Rescue Procedures* (2nd rev edn, Lexis Nexis 2004) 411.

1454 Ibid.

The avenues of challenging the commencement of voluntary administration in Australia are similar to those in the UK. Accordingly, Australia also allows for the creditors as a group to end voluntary administration by resolution.[1455] The lack of any ground of termination ensures that the above discussed manifestation of premature entry would, in principle, be caught by this mode of termination. In contrast to the equivalent mode of challenge in the UK, however, the creditors can terminate voluntary administration themselves, presumably extra-judicially, whereas in the UK, the administrator must apply to court to terminate administration on the instruction of the creditors' meeting. Moreover, in Australia, an individual creditor[1456] is entitled to apply to court for ending voluntary administration on the grounds that any provisions of Part 5.3A of the Corporations Act 2001 (which deals with voluntary administration) are being abused or 'for some other reason'.[1457] The fact that the above-mentioned further ground on which an application can be made to the court under this provision – namely that the company is 'solvent'[1458] – suggests that the first two mentioned grounds must contemplate instances other than where the company was 'insolvent' when invoking voluntary administration. Both grounds seem to be broad enough, in principle, to include premature entry. Particularly the ground that the administration provisions are being abused seems relevant in this regard. It has been held to include situations where the directors are found to use the procedure to frustrate creditors or where the administrator had been appointed for an improper purpose.[1459] Both

---

1455 S 439C(b) Corporations Act 2001. The administrator has a duty to investigate whether termination of administration would be in the best interests of creditors and inform the creditors of his conclusion in relation thereto; s 438A(b)(ii) and s 439(A)(4)(b)(ii) Corporations Act 2001. Such duties of the administrator are also found in South Africa and the UK. Here the office holder could be seen as gatekeeper. This mode of enforcement of the grounds of challenge is discussed at d. below.

1456 Among other parties; see s 447A(4) Corporations Act 2001.

1457 S 447A(2)(b) and (c) Corporations Act 2001.

1458 S 447A(2)(a) Corporations Act 2001.

1459 *Aloridge Pty Ltd (provisional liquidator appointed) v Christianos* (1994) 12 ACLC 237. Although the administrator had been appointed by a floating charge-holder in that case, there is no reason why this principle cannot apply to appointments by directors. See also *Re Bartlett Researched Securities Pty Ltd; Re Nova Corp Ltd* (1994) 12 ACSR 707. See generally Crutchfield, *Annotated Corporate Voluntary Administration Law* (Law Book Company Ltd 1994) 150.

these grounds could include situations where the company does not meet the impending insolvency ground.

In South Africa, the SCA in *Panamo Properties (Pty) Ltd and Another v Nel and Others NNO*[1460] has effectively closed the door on the development of the just and equitable ground to provide for a ground of challenging the premature out-of-court entry by the board of directors which is not dealt with by the impending insolvency ground. The SCA did this by holding – arguably incorrectly – that the just and equitable concept in s 130(5)(a)(ii) should be read to constitute not an alternative ground of challenge, but rather a requirement in addition to each of the grounds of challenge specified in s 130(1)(a).[1461]

bb. Conversion to liquidation proceedings where the company is economically distressed

The modes of challenges relating to the entry of economically distressed companies found in the three jurisdictions are broadly the same as those employed by each jurisdiction to counteract premature entry: in South Africa, by the court on application by any affected person on non-fulfilment of the economic distress entry ground;[1462] in the UK, by the court on application of the administrator as instructed by the creditors' meeting[1463] and, possibly, by the court on application of a single creditor on the grounds of an improper motive on the part of the directors who appointed the administrator;[1464] and in Australia, by creditors' resolution[1465] and by

1460 2015 (5) SA 63 (SCA) paras 20ff. For similar sentiments in previous decisions, see *Ex Parte Van den Steen NO (Credit Suisse Group AG Intervening)* 2014 (6) SA 29 (GJ)M; *ABSA Bank Ltd v Caine NO, In Re: Absa Bank Ltd v Caine NO* [2014] ZAFSHC 46. See also *MAN Financial Services SA (Pty) Ltd v Blouwater Boerdery CC* (GNP case no 72522/2012).

1461 See the discussion in PART B, Chapter 4, IV., 2., a., ee. above. The development of a good faith requirement in respect of out-of-court entry and challenge to such entry by affected persons by *Griessel and Another v Lizemore and Others* [2015] 4 All SA 433 (GJ) paras 82–7 does not help either, as the court presumably also meant for this requirement to apply *in addition to* the applicable statutory grounds.

1462 S 130(1)(a)(ii) Companies Act 2008.

1463 Insolvency Act 1986, Sch B1 para 79(2)(c).

1464 Insolvency Act 1986, Sch B1, para 81.

1465 S 439C(b) Corporations Act 2001.

the court on application of a single creditor, arguably on the same grounds as the ones applicable to premature entry.[1466]

cc. Conclusion

Conspicuous general differences between the *ratification rights* strategies of the three jurisdictions are that South Africa relies solely on challenges by individual claimants by means of a court application. By contrast, both the UK and Australia provide for an additional avenue of challenge by creditors collectively, although only in Australia is the creditors' meeting entitled to terminate voluntary administration extra-judicially. In the UK, by contrast, the creditors' meeting must instruct the administrator, who, in turn, must apply to court to terminate administration.

From an economics perspective, extra-judicial termination by the creditors collectively appears to have certain advantages. First, the fact that the creditors' meeting acts by a majority vote in this instance largely overcomes the collective action and holdout problem.

Second, such mode of termination avoids the involvement of the court, which is generally a costly process, and such costs are likely to generally exceed the costs of execution of, and voting during, a creditors' meeting.

Third, placing the decision to apply for the termination of rescue proceedings in individual creditors could give rise to agency costs, particularly insofar as secured creditors are entitled to bring a termination application. This is because secured creditors (acting as agents on behalf of the general body of creditors when bringing a termination application) have a general perverse incentive to take the course of action that would favour realising their security, irrespective of whether this would be in the best interests of the company's creditors as a whole. Thus, secured creditors would generally favour the release of the company from rescue proceedings, irrespective of whether the company was placed under rescue proceedings prematurely, and the conversion to liquidation proceedings, irrespective of whether the company is financially distressed. It would be easier for secured creditors to realise their security under both alternative op-

1466 These provisions are that the objectives of rescue in s 435A Corporations Act 2001 are being abused) and 'for some other reason' (s 447A(2)(b) and (c) Corporations Act 2001).

tions than under formal rescue proceedings.[1467] Granted, the fact that courts are the final arbiter in respect of termination applications by individual claimants reduces the likelihood that a company is released from rescue proceedings inappropriately. However, the company would still incur the procedural costs of the court application, which it would not incur if extra-judicial termination by a majority of creditors were the sole termination route available.

And finally, where the creditors act collectively, there might not even be a need for external control of such action. This means, for example, that the additional avenue of termination by the court upon application of a single creditor in Australia and the UK, and the requirement that the creditors' meeting instruct the administrator, who then has to apply to court, are superfluous. This is because the decision by the collective body of creditors is unlikely to generate negative externalities, as it ultimately bears the risk of the relevant decision.[1468] Moreover, since the applicable determination will often require commercial considerations, the courts may not be best placed to make such a determination.

In saying that, the extra-judicial termination of rescue proceedings by creditors collectively gives rise to the risk that secured creditors may generally impose their above-mentioned perverse incentive on unsecured creditors, insofar as secured creditors may obtain the majority in an applicable creditors' vote. The lack of court supervision in this termination route means that agency costs are more likely to arise than in the above-mentioned scenario where the same type of secured creditor opportunism gives rise to inappropriate termination applications to the court. Two possible strategies to counteract this problem are found in Australia and the UK. First, a creditors' resolution requires a majority both in value of debts owed by the company and the number of creditors.[1469] This could protect

---

1467 Since companies are expected to be generally balance sheet insolvent by the time they apply for formal rescue proceedings – meaning that unsecured creditors would not receive their full claim if the company were liquidated –, unsecured creditors are expected to have a general incentive that the company remains in formal rescue proceedings. This is because the primary objectives of such procedure would provide them with a prospect of returning a greater portion of their initial claims. It is for this reason that there are likely to be no negative externalities where a secured creditor brings a termination application to the court.

1468 Eidenmüller (n 1451).

1469 Reg 5.6.21(1)–(3) Corporations Regulations 2001.

unsecured creditors to the extent that secured creditors are, in practice, often likely to make up less than half of the creditors in number (Australia). And second, secured creditors are not entitled to vote the value of their claim that is covered by the value of their security (UK).[1470]

d. The ex ante trusteeship strategy: Office holders' duties in relation to taking relevant measures in cases of premature entry and the entry of economically distressed companies

aa. General

All three jurisdictions in question require that the board of directors of the company be replaced by an independent office holder during rescue proceedings and that the office holder is by law required to be independent of the company and the directors who have appointed him. Accordingly, office holders could possibly be seen generally to act as 'trustees'[1471] in respect of their duties to take the relevant measures aimed at counteracting premature entry and the entry of economically distressed companies.[1472] Two primary mechanism are used by the three jurisdictions in this regard, namely: (i) a duty of the office holder to investigate the company's affairs in order to determine whether the company should be released from rescue proceedings or be placed under a less onerous formal turnaround proceeding; and (ii) the conversion of rescue proceedings to liquidation proceedings in cases where the company is economically distressed. Where the office holder comes to such conclusion, he is required to take the relevant steps, including informing the claimants of his conclusions and, in some instances, terminating rescue proceedings of his own accord.

Office holders could be seen as trustees with respect to the above-mentioned function to the extent that, as mentioned above, they are required by law to be independent of the company (ie, its shareholders), the direc-

1470 Rule 2.24 Insolvency Rules 1986. In Australia, this only applies in respect of winding-up proceedings, not voluntary administration proceedings or the scheme of arrangement (see reg 5.6.24 Corporations Regulations 2001).

1471 On the *trusteeship strategy* generally, see Chapter 1.

1472 However, as we will see below, the classification of the office holder as a 'trustee' in respect of the relevant functions is not entirely unproblematic.

tors and each of the classes of creditors.[1473] Moreover, they may to a certain degree respond to non-monetary incentives, such as reputation, conscience and pride, when performing the relevant functions.

However, the categorisation of office holders as trustees in this regard is not perfect, as their actions may often also be motivated by monetary incentives. Indeed, since office holders are remunerated based on the time they spend on a particular rescue case, they may themselves be subject to a perverse incentive to prolong rescue proceedings, irrespective of whether this would be in the best interests of the company's creditors. This could contribute to the prevention of the timeous termination of rescue proceedings by the office holders where such course of action would be value-maximising. Examples of this are (i) where the company had been placed under rescue proceedings prematurely, it must be released or be placed under a less onerous rescue proceeding and (ii) where the company is economically distressed, it must be liquidated.

What is more, not only is such perverse incentive a monetary one, it is also diametrically opposed to the office holder's duties of investigation, disclosure and terminating rescue proceedings of his own accord. It is presumably for this reason that none of the relevant jurisdictions rely solely on reputational incentives of the office holders in ensuring that they perform these duties, but rather provide for relevant mandatory requirements.

It would seem that the reason why office holders do not respond solely to non-monetary incentives is that they are solely responsible for managing the company during rescue proceedings. Accordingly, acting as agent, they profit directly from applicable actions they take that are value-reducing to the company's creditors (acting as principals). This is unlike the typical example of trustees found in company law who are, like office holders, involved in the management of the company, rather than exercising external control,[1474] namely the 'independent director'. By contrast, because independent directors perform more of a supervisory function, the

1473 It follows from this that, eg, administrative receivers in Australia and the UK, who are required to act in the primary interest of the secured creditors that have appointed them, can hardly be seen as trustees in the sense contemplated by the *trusteeship strategy*.

1474 Typical examples of trustees who exercise external control are auditors (in approving financial statements and certain corporate actions), investment banks (in assessing offers in shareholder control transactions) and the courts (in deciding on the deployment of assets in bankruptcy proceedings, eg, in France); see Armour, Hansmann and Kraakman, 'Agency Problems and Legal Strategies' in

gains from the value-minimising effects of the actions by the non-independent (executive) directors are not reaped by the independent directors.[1475]

bb. Relevant mechanisms in South Africa, the UK and Australia

In South Africa and Australia, the duty of the office holder to investigate the affairs of the company[1476] and, in Australia, report his findings to the claimants,[1477] is specifically provided for. In the UK, on the other hand, at least the duty to investigate is arguably implied by the administrators' duty to apply to court for the termination of administration where he thinks that the company should not have entered administration or that the purpose of

---

Kraakman and others (eds), *Anatomy of Corporate Law – A Comparative and Functional Approach* (2nd edn, Oxford University Press 2009) 35, 43–4; Armour, Hertig and Kanda (n 1443) 145–6; Davies and Hopt, 'Control Transactions' in Kraakman and others (eds), *Anatomy of Corporate Law – A Comparative and Functional Approach* (2nd edn, Oxford University Press 2009) 250–1.

1475 See Enriques, Hansmann and Kraakman, 'The Basic Governance Structure: Minority Shareholders and Non-Shareholder Constituencies' in Kraakman and others (eds), *Anatomy of Corporate Law – A Comparative and Functional Approach* (2nd edn, Oxford University Press 2009) 64ff.

1476 For South Africa, s 141(1); for Australia, s 438(A)(b)(ii) Corporations Act 2001. To be sure, in South Africa, the duty to investigate the presence of the impending insolvency entry ground is not specifically mentioned in s 141(1); that section only refers to the investigation of the entry ground as to whether or not the company is economically viable. However, the duty to investigate the impending insolvency entry ground is implied by the duty of the rescue practitioner to terminate rescue proceedings, on the grounds that the company does not meet the impending insolvency entry ground; see s 141(2)(b).

1477 S 438D and s 439A Corporations Act 2001. In South Africa, the rescue practitioner is only required to inform the first meeting of creditors, the first meeting of employees' representatives and the meeting to consider the rescue plan whether he continues to believe that there is a likelihood of success of rescue (s 147(1)(a)(i), s 148(1)(a), s 152(1)(b) Companies Act 2008, respectively). A case could be made that the duty to report to affected persons on whether the company meets the impending insolvency entry ground does, in fact, exist by virtue of the practitioners' duty to act in the best interests of the company (see s 140(3)(b) read with s 76(3)(b) Companies Act 2008). Such an argument could be based on the grounds that the continuation of rescue proceedings would not be in the company's best interest where the above-mentioned grounds are not met.

administration cannot be achieved.[1478] As we saw above, in Australia, only the creditors as a group by resolution,[1479] or by an individual creditor on the specified grounds,[1480] can resolve to terminate administration specifically on the strength of the information that the administrator is required to provide to the creditors.[1481] By contrast, in South Africa and in the UK, the office holder himself is entitled to apply to court for the release of the company from rescue proceedings. This step can be taken where he concludes that the entry grounds relating to impending insolvency[1482] and to the economic viability of the company[1483] are not met (in South Africa) and 'thinks' that the company should not have entered administration or that the purpose of administration cannot be achieved[1484] (in the UK).

1478 Insolvency Act 1986, Sch B1, para 79(2)(a) and (b). In any event, the duty of investigation by the administrator in this regard would arguably fall within the duty of care which the administrator in principle owes to the company at common law; see *Re Charnley Davies (No.2)* [1990] BCLC 760; see also Armour and Mokal (n 1425), and further references cited at n 91.

1479 S 439C(b) and (c) Corporations Act 2001.

1480 S 447A(2)(b) read with sub-s 4 Corporations Act 2001.

1481 On the applicable requirements, this is, strictly speaking, only true for the termination of voluntary administration by creditor resolution. However, it is expected that an individual creditor will, as a matter of practice, often rely on the information of the administrator in bringing an application to court for the termination of voluntary administration under s 447A(2)(b) Corporations Act 2001.

1482 S 141(2)(b). It should be noted that the provision states that the rescue practitioner must terminate rescue proceedings where the company 'no longer' meets the impending insolvency entry ground. On a strict reading, this provision is only available in the unlikely event where the company's distress has been resolved before the implementation of a rescue plan and not where the company had failed to meet the impending insolvency entry ground at the time of commencement of rescue proceedings. If that is the correct interpretation, then this provision cannot be seen to address the problem of premature entry. To be sure, the use of 'no longer' could be argued to be deliberate, especially when one compares s 141(2)(b) to the functionally equivalent Australian provision (s 447A(1)(2)(b) Corporations Act 2001), which entitles the court to end voluntary administration if the company 'is solvent'. However, given that such a reading of s 141(2)(b) would forbid the rescue practitioner to protect the interests of the companies' claimants adequately and, indeed, compel the rescue practitioner to breach his duties to act with care and in the best interests of the company, this provision should be read purposively.

1483 S 141(2)(a).

1484 See the discussion in n 1478 above and the references cited therein.

It becomes clear from the above that both South Africa and the UK generally require the office holder to *apply to court* for the termination of rescue proceedings (rather than terminating of his own accord) where he has concluded that the company should be released from rescue proceedings.[1485] This general reliance on the court as final arbiter in this regard is somewhat surprising, given the high costs of court proceedings generally and the general absence of a perverse incentive of the office holder to release the company from rescue proceedings in cases where this would be value-minimising for the company's creditors.[1486] Nor is it clear whether the Australian approach – namely that the creditors, by majority vote, collectively terminate rescue proceedings on the strength of the recommendations provided by the administrator[1487] – is justified, as this disregards the general efficiencies of delegated management.

In South Africa, the duties of the rescue practitioner in relation to premature entry do not appear to provide recourse where premature entry occurs after the point at which the South African version of the impending insolvency entry ground commences (namely six months before reaching the applicable state of insolvency). This is because, first, unlike with the right of affected persons to challenge the commencement of rescue proceedings, the rescue practitioner does not have a duty to apply to court for the termination of rescue proceedings where this would be otherwise just and equitable. As explained above, the scope of this conceopt arguably includes the above-mentioned manifestation of premature entry.[1488]

And second, the rescue practitioner does not, on a strict reading of the applicable provisions, have a duty to investigate the company's affairs in respect of whether the continuation of rescue proceedings would be otherwise just and equitable. Nor does he have a duty to inform affected persons where he comes to this conclusion. This would enable individual affected persons to challenge the commencement of rescue proceedings by

1485 One exception to this is found under the South African procedure where the rescue practitioner concludes that the company does not meet the impending insolvency entry ground and where rescue proceedings had been commenced out-of-court, and this was not subsequently challenged by an affected person; s 141(2)(b)(i) Companies Act 2008.

1486 To the contrary, as we have seen above, the office holder rather has a perverse incentive to refrain from releasing the company from rescue proceedings where taking such course of action would be value-maximising.

1487 S 439C read with s 439A Corporations Act 2001.

1488 See the discussion in b. above.

the board on such ground. It could be argued that such duties nevertheless arise by virtue of the rescue practitioner's duty to act in the best interests of the company,[1489] insofar as the termination of rescue proceedings would be in the company's best interests where this would otherwise be just and equitable as required by the applicable statutory provision. However, even if such a duty on the rescue practitioner does exist, the practical effect of this duty is reduced by the problems relating to its enforcement. This includes the difficulties of proving the requirements that the company has suffered a loss as a consequence of the breach of the duty by the rescue practitioner for purposes of being awarded damages[1490] and the procedural difficulty with the fact that the company must bring the action.

e. Minimising the direct costs of formal insolvency proceedings: Possibility of swift transition to alternative rescue procedures and liquidation procedure upon premature termination of business rescue proceedings

aa. Transition to alternative rescue procedures in cases of premature entry

In cases of premature entry, the release of the company from rescue proceedings in order to resolve the company's anticipated threat to its solvency by way of informal rescue measures outside rescue proceedings may not always be the appropriate remedy. It may often be the case that the company's prospective distress is best resolved in an alternative rescue procedure. This is because, on the one hand, the company may require the advantages of a collective rescue procedure,[1491] the possibility of impos-

1489 See s 140(3)(b) read with s 76(3)(b) Companies Act 2008.

1490 See s 77(2)(a) Companies Act 2008, which is the codification of the remedy for damages for breaches of the directors' fiduciary duties at common law.It applies to rescue practitioners by virtue of s 140(3)(b) Companies Act 2008.

1491 Eg, in the UK, a moratorium is effectively available under the alternative rescue measures, insofar as such measures can be invoked while the company is under administration, and thus protected from creditor enforcement by the moratorium of such procedure. This will be considered further below. In addition, in the UK, the company voluntary arrangement procedure contains a moratorium for small companies; s 1A Insolvency Act 1986.

ing the rescue measures on a minority class of creditors[1492] and the likely lower costs of claimant co-ordination and bargaining that is provided by a collective or streamlined process. On the other hand, alternative restructuring procedures are typically less onerous and less costly than the main rescue procedure. Moreover, where rescue proceedings are terminated on the grounds that the company is economically distressed,[1493] then the company should be placed under liquidation proceedings.

In both scenarios mentioned above, it would be in the best interests of the company's claimants that the transition to the alternative corporate insolvency procedure take place at the lowest (direct) costs possible. This is because from the moment the decision has been taken that rescue proceedings be converted to an alternative turnaround proceeding, there are no countervailing considerations.[1494]

The UK provides for a particularly cost-effective mode of transition from the main rescue proceeding to alternative rescue procedures, which would also be available in cases of premature entry.[1495] This is that the alternative rescue procedures, the CVA and the scheme of arrangement are available while the company is under administration.[1496] This generally reduces the procedural costs, such as additional court/administrative proceedings for the premature termination of administration and the subsequent initiation of the alternative procedures. Moreover, where administration is converted to a CVA and the administrator intends to remain in of-

1492 As is available, eg, under the scheme of arrangement in all three jurisdictions considered here: for South Africa, see s 155(8)(c) Companies Act 2008; for the UK, see s 899(3) Companies Act 2006; for Australia, see s 444D Corporations Act 2001.

1493 Or it is concluded that the return of a fire sale of the company's assets would be greater in winding-up proceedings than in rescue proceedings, to the extent that a fire sale of the assets is an alternative goal of rescue, which is certainly the case in the UK and possibly in South Africa.

1494 For a consideration of possible countervailing considerations in respect of moving between insolvency procedures in the South African legal framework, see PART B, Chapter 4, III., 2 above.

1495 This is primarily because neither of the two alternative rescue procedures requires that the company be insolvent or close to insolvency. See also Parry, *Corporate Rescue* (Sweet & Maxwell 2008) para 2–08.

1496 Insolvency Act 1986, Sch B1, para 49(3)(a) and (b), respectively. See also Insolvency Act 1986, s 1(1) and (3)(a) (in relation to the CVA) and s 896(2)(c) Companies Act 2006 (in relation to the scheme of arrangement). See generally, eg, Goode (n 1413) paras 11–109, 11–115; Parry (n 1495) paras 2–06, 5–08.

fice and oversee the CVA procedure,[1497] the costs of familiarisation with the relevant facts and devising a restructuring proposal would be much lower than where a new person would be appointed to administer the CVA. And finally, the fact that the two alternative procedures are available during administration means that the company is also protected from creditor enforcement by the moratorium that is available under administration, which reduces the general costs associated with the race to collect, as discussed in Chapter 2 above.

In South Africa and Australia, by contrast, the only alternative formal rescue procedures – 'compromise with creditors' and the 'scheme of arrangement', respectively – are not available under the main rescue procedure.[1498] The above-mentioned cost savings and the procedural or structural advantage resulting from the ability of combining various rescue procedures under the British formal rescue scheme are accordingly not available under those procedures. In addition, the alternative rescue procedures in Australia and South Africa[1499] are in any event generally not particularly well suited for restructuring a company's affairs, as they are fairly cumbersome, inflexible and costly.[1500]

bb. Transition to liquidation proceedings in cases of the entry of economically distressed companies

In relation to the need for a swift and cost-effective conversion from rescue proceedings to winding-up proceedings where the company has been found to be economically distressed, both the UK and Australia allow for

1497 This option is possible by virtue of Insolvency Act 1986, s 3(2). The office of overseeing a CVA is referred to as 'nominee' (see Insolvency Act 1986, s 1(2)).

1498 In South Africa, use of the compromise with creditors procedure during rescue proceedings is expressly prohibited by s 155(1) Companies Act 2008. In Australia, the same conclusion presumably follows from the absence of a statutory right to the contrary.

1499 The same would, in principal, be true for the scheme of arrangement in the UK. However, the fact that the court have recently softened their discretionary jurisdiction in sanctioning the scheme has made the use of the scheme more feasible; Parry (n 1495) paras 2–04, 246.

1500 In relation to the South African procedure, see PART B, Chapter 4, V. above; in relation to the Australian procedure, see Crutchfield (n) 3–4.

a transition to a creditors' voluntary liquidation (hereafter, '*CVL*')[1501] on the application of the administrator (in the UK)[1502] and by a creditors' resolution (in Australia).[1503] This obviates the need of a typically costly and time-consuming court application. The fact that the administrator is allowed to act as the liquidator after the transition to a CVL in both jurisdictions[1504] reduces the costs of familiarisation with the company's affairs for purposes of liquidating such company's assets. On the one hand, the fact that in the UK, the administrator is entitled to place the company under a creditors' voluntary liquidation saves the costs of the creditors' meeting and of taking a creditors' resolution, as is required under the Australian procedure. On the other hand, placing the decision whether to convert administration to a CVL solely in the hands of the administrator might, as we have seen, give rise to agency costs, as administrators may have a perverse incentive to delay the conversion to liquidation proceedings, given that they generally receive a time-based remuneration.

By contrast, such agency costs would not arise under the Australian approach, since by placing such decision on the principals themselves (ie, the body of creditors, who decide by a majority vote), the negative externalities of such decision are internalised. However, the fact that in the UK, the office holder is allowed to act as liquidator in a subsequent CVL might counteract their perverse incentive to inappropriately prolong administration proceedings, insofar as the administrator has the prospect of earning further fees in a subsequent liquidation.

In contrast to the UK and Australia, rescue proceedings in South Africa may only be converted to liquidation proceedings by a court application,[1505] and a person other than the rescue practitioner is required to act as the liquidator in a subsequent liquidation proceedings.[1506] Accordingly, the above-mentioned efficiencies of the transition to liquidation proceed-

1501 For the UK, Insolvency Act 1986, Sch B1, para 83; for Australia, Div 12 Corporations Act 2001.

1502 The administrator may place the company under the CVL where he 'thinks' that the amount to be received by secured creditors has been paid to him or set aside for him and that there are sufficient funds to make a distribution to unsecured creditors; Insolvency Act 1986, Sch B1, para 83(1)(a) and (b).

1503 S 446A(1)(a) Corporations Act 2001.

1504 For the UK, Insolvency Act 1986, Sch B1, para 83(7)(b); for Australia, s 446A Corporations Act 2001.

1505 Ss 130(5)(c)(i) and 141(3) Companies Act 2008.

1506 S 140(4) Companies Act 2008.

ings under the Anglo-Australian main rescue procedures are not available under the South African procedure.

2. The ex post standards strategy: Dismissal of Chapter 11 proceedings on the grounds of bad faith filings in the US

One important feature of the general pro-debtor approach of Chapter 11 is that it allows debtors easy access to Chapter 11 proceedings.[1507] The absence of *ex ante* entry requirements, including that the debtor be in the state of impending insolvency, is a manifestation of this underlying philosophy.[1508] However, the US resorts to an *ex post standards strategy* to control the perverse incentive of company controllers to place debtors under Chapter 11 prematurely and where such debtors are economically distressed. According to this *standards strategy*, a court is entitled to dismiss Chapter 11 proceedings *ex post*, where the debtor is found to have commenced rescue proceedings in 'bad faith'. Although the Bankruptcy Code 1978 does not provide for a good faith requirement, many courts read such a requirement into the provision that bankruptcy proceedings may be dismissed for 'cause' under § 1112(b)(1) Bankruptcy Code 1978.[1509]

Examples of where Chapter 11 filings have been dismissed on the grounds of bad faith are (i) where the debtor had no realistic chance or hope of being rescued,[1510] (ii) where the debtor was financially healthy and where its normal business operations would continue regardless of its

1507 Armour, Hertig and Kanda, 'Transactions with Creditors' in Kraakman and others (eds), *Anatomy of Corporate Law – A Comparative and Functional Approach* (2nd edn, Oxford University Press 2009).

1508 Ibid.

1509 11 USC § 1112(b). This section allows the court to convert Chapter 11 reorganisation proceedings to Chapter 7 liquidation proceedings. See generally, eg, *In re* Victory Constr. Co., 42 B.R. 145, 146 (Bankr. C.D. Cal. 1984), citing *In re* Victory Constr. Co., 9 B.R. 549 (Bankr. C.D. Cal. 1981). See also Flaccus, 'Have Eight Circuits Shorted? Good Faith and Chapter 11 Bankruptcy Petitions' (1993) 67 Am. Bankr. L.J. 401; Mojdehi and Gertz, 'The Implicit Good Faith Requirement in Chapter 11 Liquidations: A Rule in Search of a Rationale?' (2006) 14 Am. Bankr. Inst. L. Rev. 143, 150.

1510 *C-TC 9th Ave. P'ship v. Norton Co.* (*In re* C-TC 9th Ave P'ship), 113 F.3d 1304, 1310–11 (2d Cir. 1997); *Little Creek Dev. Co. v. Commonwealth Mtg. Corp.* (*In re* Little Creek Dev. Co.), 779 F2.d 1068, 1073 (5th Cir. 1986).

bankruptcy,[1511] (iii) where the debtor has ceased all operations,[1512] (iv) where the debtor failed to show that Chapter 11 proceedings were needed to implement the proposed rescue measures[1513] and (v) where the debtor failed to show that Chapter 11 proceedings would preserve some value that would otherwise be lost outside bankruptcy proceedings.[1514] It is clear from the above-mentioned decisions that the good faith test addresses both premature entry (for example, where the debtor was financially healthy)[1515] and entry of economically distressed companies (for example, where the debtor had no realistic chance of being rescued).[1516] Moreover, courts have construed this requirement not necessarily in terms of financial distress or solvency.[1517] Accordingly, companies have been found to be in good faith and, consequently, granted access to Chapter 11 where they were solvent[1518] and, conversely, denied access to Chapter 11 on the ground of bad faith where they were insolvent.[1519]

The underlying criterion of the good faith standard that emerges from the case law appears to be whether placing the debtor under rescue proceedings would achieve the underlying purpose of Chapter 11, namely preserving the going concern of the company and maximising value for the claimants of the company.[1520] One manifestation of this criterion is that the courts have been willing to compare the merits of informal rescue

---

1511 *In re* SGL Carbon Corp., 200 F.3d 154, 164 (3d Cir. 1999).

1512 *In re* SB Props., 185 B.R., 205 (Bankr. E.D. Pa. 1995).

1513 *In re* Liberate Technologies 314 B.R. 206, 215 (Bankr. N.D. Cal. 2004).

1514 NMSBPCSLDHB; *L.P. v. Integrated Telecom Express Inc.* (*In re Integrated Telecom Express Inc.*) 384 F.3d 108, 129 (3d Cir. 2004).

1515 See n 1511 above and accompanying text.

1516 See n 1510 above and accompanying text.

1517 But see Brunstad, Jr., 'Good Faith, Solvent Debtors, and the Subject of Bankruptcies' in 79' Annual Meeting Of The National Conference Of Bankruptcy Judges (2005) 4–5, arguing that the doctrine of good faith demonstrates that the bankruptcy procedure is restricted to *insolvent* debtors, and citing an equitable receivership case in support thereof, namely *First National Bank of Cincinnati v. Flershem* 290 U.S. 504, 517 (1934).

1518 See, eg, *In re Chameleon Sys., Inc.* 306 B.R. 666, 668 (Bankr. N.D. Cal. 2004).

1519 See, eg, *In re* Integrated Telecom Express, Inc., No.02-12945, (Bankr. D. Del. Jan. 30, 2003).

1520 *Bank of Am. Nat'l Trust & Sav. Ass'n v. 203 N. La Salle St. P'ship*, 526 U.S. 434, 453 (1999); *Toibb v. Radloff*, 501 U.S. 157, 163–64 (1991). See also H. Rep. No. 95-595, 220 (1977). See generally Mojdehi and Gertz (n 1509) 151–2. However, measuring good faith against the preservation of the going concern has been argued to be problematic where a debtor files for Chapter 11 for purposes of a

measures with formal rescue measures.[1521] Such an enquiry is particularly helpful, as it goes to the heart of the distinction between desirable and undesirable uses of formal rescue proceedings.

3. Conclusion

Two important points arise when comparing the combination of *ex ante* and *ex post* strategies relied on in South Africa, the UK and Australia, on the one hand and the *ex post standards* approach used in the US, on the other hand, in addressing the two general value-minimising uses of formal rescue proceedings. First, since the true source of premature entry opportunism is the protective measures under formal rescue proceedings (rather than the financial state of a company), the impending insolvency ground is, by definition, an inappropriate mechanism for purposes of addressing the problem of premature entry. The *ex post* good faith standard under Chapter 11 would seem to leave more scope for courts to take into account pertinent considerations, such as a comparison of the costs of informal and formal rescue measures. This is the central enquiry in distinguishing between value-minimising and value-maximising commencements of rescue proceedings, particularly in cases where the company is faced with a large contingent claim.

Second, unlike with the legal strategies of the relevant jurisdictions that address the problem of premature entry, there does not seem to be a difference in content of the legal strategies that address the problem of the entry of economically distressed companies of the relevant jurisdictions. Under both the economic distress entry ground (and the relevant further strategies discussed above) in South Africa, the UK and Australia, and the good faith standard in the US, the primary enquiry is whether the company has a likely chance of achieving the goals of the respective rescue procedures.

It is not clear whether the *ex ante* together with the relevant *ex post* approaches used in South Africa and the UK will necessarily prevent that a large proportion of the costs of enforcement of the mechanisms curbing the entry of economically distressed companies are transferred to within

fire-sale of its assets, which, although formally the purpose of Chapter 7, is nevertheless an accepted goal under Chapter 11 as well; see 11 U.S.C. § 1123(a)(5)(B), (D), (b)(4). See generally Mojdehi and Gertz (n 1509) 144ff, 152ff, 166ff.

1521 See nn 1513-1514 and accompanying text.

rescue proceedings and, accordingly, fall primarily on unsecured creditors. This is because of the absence of the imposition of *ex post* sanctions on the relevant decision-takers *ex ante*. There might therefore not be a significant difference in this regard with the sole reliance on *ex post* strategies in Australia and the US.

It should be noted that the risk of premature entry is expected to be generally lower in the UK and Australia than in South Africa due to the strong rights afforded to floating charge-holders to initiate and control administration. The reasoning is as follows. In both jurisdictions, directors have to notify the floating charge-holders that they have commenced administration, and the floating charge-holders are then entitled to appoint an administrator of their own choice to manage the company during administration (in the UK) or to realise their security in a special procedure to the exclusion of the other creditors of the company (in Australia). The prospect of directors having to relinquish control over the appointment of the administrator to the floating charge-holder (in the case of the UK) and that the floating charge-holder is entitled to circumvent the formal voluntary administration (in the case of Australia),[1522] is expected to significantly curtail the directors' appetite for using administration for strategic purposes generally. At the same time, the strong rights of secured creditors in the UK and Australia in relation to the initiation and control of formal administration, might give directors a greater incentive to resort to rescue measures outside the formal procedure.[1523]

1522 On the types of legal strategies explained in Chapter 1, the British approach could be seen as an *initiation rights strategy* and the Australian approach as an *exit strategy*.

1523 Having said that, in jurisdictions where creditors lack equivalent initiation and control rights as in the UK and Australia, such as South Africa, creditors could – and particularly in large companies that are heavily financed by debt often in fact do – ensure their control over companies outside of formal rescue proceedings through applicable contractual measures, eg, through undertakings, covenants and events of default, which may often equally give such companies an incentive to pursue informal rescue measures; see Baird and Rasmussen, 'Control Rights, Property Rights and the Conceptual Foundations of Corporate Reorganizations' (2001) 87 Va. L. Rev. 921.

III. Comparative evaluation of legal strategies mitigating the risk of the appointment of a 'friendly' office holder – comparative perspectives from the UK, Australia and the US

1. Ex ante rules strategy: Minimum qualification and disclosure requirements and relevant ex post sanctions for non-compliance

a. Minimum qualification requirements of rescue practitioners in South Africa

In South Africa, the rescue practitioner must fulfil certain minimum qualification requirements when being appointed. There are two, perhaps three, qualification requirements that are relevant to the risk that the board of directors appoints a friendly rescue practitioner, namely: (i) where the rescue practitioner lacks independence of the company and its management;[1524] (ii) where the rescue practitioner has a relationship with the company that would lead a reasonable and informed third party to conclude that such relationship would compromise his integrity, impartiality or objectivity (herafter, 'compromised relationship')[1525] or is related to a person who has a compromised relationship;[1526] and, arguably, (iii) where the rescue practitioner has a conflict of interest.[1527] Although the last two mentioned grounds are not expressly required as prerequisites for the appointment of the rescue practitioner *ex ante*, the fact that the rescue practitioner can be removed on those grounds *ex post* implies that they also constitute such prerequisites *ex ante*.[1528]

The removal grounds essentially address the situation where there is a strong chance that the rescue practitioner does not exercise independent and unfettered discretion in managing the company during rescue proceedings. This gives rise to the risk that the practitioner will take decisions in the best interests of the management (acting in the interests of the shareholders), rather than the group of claimants during rescue proceedings, which, *inter alia*, increases the likelihood that premature entries and en-

1524 S 130(1)(b)(ii).
1525 S 130(1)(b)(i) read with s 138(1)(e).
1526 S 130(1)(b)(i) read with s 138(1)(e) and (f).
1527 S 139(2)(e).
1528 See generally on the removal grounds the discussion in PART B, Chapter 4, IV., 8., c. above.

tries of economically distressed companies are not detected and dealt with appropriately.

b. The Australian approach: minimum qualification and mandatory disclosure requirements supplemented by ex post sanctions for non-compliance

Australia, like South Africa, provides for minimum qualification requirements relating to the administrator's independence *ex ante*. However, such qualification requirements are framed in more specific terms than the South African ones. S 448C Corporations Act 2001 sets out specific types of positions held by a person that places him in a relationship with the company or its creditors, which prohibits such person from being appointed as the administrator of a company during voluntary administration. Examples of such prohibited positions are where the person is the auditor of the company or a partner or an employee of the auditor of the company and where the administrator is a partner, employer or employee of a 'shadow' director of the company.[1529] Non-compliance with such qualification requirements will result in strict criminal liability for the administrator.[1530]

Australia provides for a further legal strategy that could be seen as minimising the risk of appointing a friendly administrator, namely the disclosure of any 'relevant relationships' and 'indemnities' to as many creditors of the company as reasonably practicable.[1531] A 'relevant relationship' is broadly defined as any relationship that existed in the previous 24 months between an administrator, other persons within the administrator's organisation and related persons of the administrator or of the administrator's organisation. It also refers to a relationship with the company (including a director or related persons of the company or a director of the related person), a former liquidator of the company and a floating charge-holder.[1532] If there is such a relationship, the administrator must state his reasons for believing that the relationship does not result in the administrator having a

1529 S 448C (1)(e) and (f) and s 448C(1)(g) read with paragraph b(iii) of the definition of 'officer' in s 9 Corporations Act 2001, respectively.

1530 S 448C(1A) Corporations Act 2001.

1531 S 436DA(2) and (3) Corporations Act 2001.

1532 S 60(1)(a) Corporations Act 2001.

conflict of interest or duty.[1533] This could be seen as a type of 'comply or explain' mechanism often used in corporate governance codes in company law. Failure to make such a disclosure gives rise to criminal liability of the administrator.[1534] The requirement that the administrator must disclose any indemnities provided to him arguably addresses the risk that the administrator's judgment is fettered by financial incentives.

In contrast to the types of positions held by the administrator, who by virtue of that position clearly has a relationship with the company or its creditors under the minimum qualification requirements mentioned above, the meaning of 'relevant relationships' under the mandatory disclosure requirements leaves some scope for interpretation. Although the persons of the relationship are specified, the independence of the administrator depends on the nature and 'closeness' of the relationship between such persons. Some guidance on this question has been given by *Re Monarch Gold Mining Co Ltd.*[1535] In that case, the court broadly identified three types of relationships that fall within the meaning of 'relevant relationships', namely: (i) where the administrator has in the preceding 24 months provided professional services to the company or the creditors of a sufficiently material nature (in relation to creditors) and a degree of magnitude and of such a nature (in relation to the company), as to put in doubt his ability to act independently; (ii) where there is a clear evidence of bias; and (iii) where there is a close relationship with a creditor such that there is a clear tendency to prefer that creditor.[1536]

Furthermore, guidance is provided by the professional codes of conduct for insolvency office holders (hereafter, the '*office holders*') of professional bodies, for example, by the Australian Restructuring Insolvency and Turnaround Association ('*ARITA*'), on the nature and closeness of the relationship required for triggering the mandatory disclosure requirement.[1537] Although such professional codes of conduct do not constitute legal enforceable rules, they nevertheless provide useful guidance both to the courts and the regulator (the Australian Securities and Investments Com-

1533 S 60(1)(b) Corporations Act 2001
1534 S 436DA(2) Corporations Act 2001.
1535 [2008] WASC 201.
1536 See generally Lipton, Herzberg and Welsh, *Understanding Company Law* (17th edn, Lawbook 2014) para 24.55.
1537 ARITA, *Code of Professional Practice* (3rd edn, 2014).

mission ('*ASIC*'))[1538] for purposes of enforcing the independence requirements of administrators.[1539] However, one significant limitation of professional codes of conducts is that they only bind the members of the applicable professional body.

The mandatory disclosure of relevant relationships addresses the problem of the appointment of a friendly administrator in two ways. First, it forces administrators to apply their minds as to whether they are independent of the company or its management. And second, given that the disclosure itself does not remedy or cure a relevant relationship, mandatory disclosure could serve to provide the creditors with relevant information that enables them to protect their interests through resolving to remove the administrator[1540] or through an individual creditor applying to the court for the removal of the administrator.[1541]

1538 ASIC can bring complaints against administrators before the Companies Auditors and Liquidators Disciplinary Board ('*CALDB*') (s 1292 Corporations Act 2001), which can be appealed to the Administrative Appeals Tribunal and thereafter to the court on matters of law. See generally D Brown and Symes, 'Insolvency Practitioner Regulation: Providing Practice Standards Through the Use of Codes of Conduct' [2013] 3 (hard copy on file with author).

1539 See, eg, *Dean-Willcocks v CALDB* [2006] FCA 475; *Wylie and CALDB* (1998) 54 ALD 523; *Goodman v ASIC* [2004] FCA 1000; *Gould v CALDB* [2009] FCA 475; *Re Monarch Gold Mining Co Ltd ex p Hughes* [2008] WASC 201. See generally D Brown and Symes (n 1538) 13ff. The primary mechanism for the enforcement through self-regulation is the bringing of complaints by ASIC against non-compliant administrators before CALDB (see n 1538 above). The ultimate sanction is the withdrawal of professional licences for acting as office holders; see D Brown and Symes (n 1538) 3.

1540 S 436E(4) Corporations Act 2001.

1541 S 449B Corporations Act 2001. Administrators have also been removed under s 447A(1). According to this provision, the court has a general power to make any order, as it deems appropriate, for the proper operation of any voluntary administration provision of the Corporations Act 2001 (Harris, Hargovan and Adams, *Australian Corporate Law* (2nd edn, Lexis Nexis Butterworths 2009) 717). It has also been suggested that an administrator could be removed under the more specific powers of the court under s 447E. According to this provision, the court may make any order, as it deems just, where the administrator is managing the company or has done or failed to do an act or proposes to do an act that is or would be prejudicial to the company (Cassidy, *Corporations Law – Text and Essential Cases* (4th edn, The Federal Press 2013) para 13.310).

c. Professional self-regulatory mechanisms in the UK

Unlike in South Africa and Australia, the UK does not provide for mandatory minimum independence requirements for office holders *ex ante*, but rather addresses the risk of the appointment of a friendly administrator by relevant mechanisms contained under the professional self-regulatory regimes governing office holders. The UK, similar to the proposed system of professional regulation of rescue practitioners in South Africa, uses a dual approach to professional regulation.[1542] It licences recognised professional bodies ('*RPBs*') (of which there are currently eight) and thereby makes such bodies responsible for the self-regulation and supervision of their members acting as office holders.[1543] Persons who do not belong to an RPB may be licensed individually by the competent government institution itself, the Secretary of State, acting through the Insolvency Service.[1544]

Each of the RPBs will have their own set of professional standards that will be enforced through the internal complaints procedures of the respective RPBs. All of the RPBs have adopted, in substantially similar terms, the Insolvency Code of Ethics,[1545] dealing primarily with ensuring the objectivity of the office holder ('Ethics Code'), which was produced by the Joint Insolvency Committee ('*JIC*'), a co-ordinating forum for the Insolvency Service and the RPBs.[1546] A further set of professional standards produced by the JIC apply to members of all the RPBs is the Statement of Insolvency Practice ('*SIPs*'). The SIPs deal with a wide range of matters relating to office holders.[1547]

1542 For the South African approach to professional regulation, see PART B, Chapter 4, III., 3. above.

1543 On the regulation of the rescue practitioners' profession in South Africa generally, see PART B, Chapter 4, III., 3. above.

1544 Finch, *Corporate Insolvency Law – Perspectives and Principles* (2nd edn, Cambridge University Press 2009) 182–3.

1545 Insolvency Practitioners Association, 'Code of Ethics' <http://www.insolvency-practitioners.org.uk/regulation-and-guidance/ethics-code> accessed 30 December 2016.

1546 See the Introduction of the Ethics Code for Members of one of the RPBs, the Insolvency Practitioners Association. See generally Finch (n 1544) 185.

1547 Finch (n 1544) 85.

The relevant requirements relating to the administrator's independence are contained in the Ethics Code.[1548] The Ethics Code sets out various types of threats to the objectivity of the office holder both generally and when being appointed, including (i) prior professional and personal relationships generally with the company, its management and employees, related persons of the company or any of the company's creditors,[1549] (ii) a relationship with any of the above-mentioned persons specifically due to a prior or subsequent appointment as office holders for the company (typically in respect of other insolvency procedures)[1550] and (iii) the offer by the company and relevant persons to the office holders, prior to and after being appointed as office holders, of any financial benefits over and above the statutory fees, for example, referral fees and commissions as well as gifts and hospitality.[1551]

The Ethics Code requires the office holder to take reasonable steps to evaluate any possible threats to his objectivity from an objective perspective (including whether any relationship with the company or relevant persons is 'significant' or not), introduce safeguards to reduce the threat to an acceptable level (including through internal procedures and policies that have been established *ex ante*) and only if this is not possible, decline the appointment as office holder.[1552] The Ethics Code requires that an office holder keep records of the steps taken and conclusions reached in identifying, evaluating and responding to threats[1553] and generally disclose any

---

1548 The SIPs also contain requirements with regard to the independence of the administrator in relation to pre-packaged sales in administration (which are dealt with in SIPs 16, version of 1 November 2013). However, the emergence of negative externalities as a result of the lack of independence of the office holder in relation to pre-packaged sales differs from the emergence of negative externalities as a result of the appointment of a friendly office holder, where this facilitates the perverse incentive of company controllers to place the company under administration prematurely and where the company is economically distressed. The lack of independence of the office holder in relation to pre-packaged sales is best seen as potentially facilitating the risk of undervalue sales of the company's business and, where such sales are made to incumbent managers, the problem of 'Phoenix' trading. The last-mentioned problem is a form of asset dilution, which generally falls outside the scope of this study.

1549 Ethics Code (n 1545) paras 40–48, 78–80.

1550 Ethics Code (n 1545) paras 81–86.

1551 Ethics Code (n 1545) paras 57–73.

1552 Ethics Code (n 1545) paras 17–19, 24–30, 43–75.

1553 Ethics Code (n 1545) paras 74–75.

threat to his objectivity to the creditors of the company. The mechanisms used in this regard are akin to the basic governance principle of 'comply or explain' which are often used in corporate governance codes.[1554] It further provides that a good indication of whether it is appropriate for the office holder to accept the appointment is if the creditors do not object to such appointment.[1555]

The above-mentioned requirements of disclosure (and record-keeping) reduce the likelihood of the appointment of a friendly administrator for the same reasons as the duty to disclose relevant relationships under the Australian rescue procedure: they compel the administrator to apply his mind as to whether he is independent of the company and the relevant persons. He further is compelled to provide the creditors with the necessary information enabling them to make use of the remedy of removal of the administrator (either by the court on application of, *inter alia*, an individual creditor[1556] or by the creditors' meeting).[1557]

Although the Ethics Code does not have the force of law, compliance with the Ethics Code is reinforced by its enforcement through the internal complaints procedures under the self-regulatory regimes of each of the RPBs, with one of the sanctions being the naming and shaming of non-compliant office holders.[1558]

1554 Milman, *Governance of Distressed Firms* (Edward Elgar 2013) 85.

1555 Ethics Code (n 1545) para 24(a). The Ethics Code also suggests that the office holder make disclosure to creditors specifically of any relationships with, and financial benefits offered by, the company and relevant persons (para 46(a), 59 and 62).

1556 Insolvency Act 1986, Sch B1, para 88 read with rule 2.112 Insolvency Rules 1986.

1557 Insolvency Act 1986, Sch B1, para 97. Of course, the requirement of record-keeping itself – without additional disclosure of such records, which is not required under the Ethics Code – does not provide the creditors with information enabling them to remove the administrator.

1558 Milman (n 1554) 86–7. A further way in which compliance with the professional standards is strengthened is through judicial recognition and, to a degree, application of professional standards. Eg, a pre-packaged sale is likely to be approved by the court if it was conducted in compliance with SIPs 16 (see Milman (n 1554) 85).

2. Ex post removal rights strategy: Removal of office holder for lack of independence and related ex post grounds

Of the three relevant jurisdictions, the *removal rights strategy* is relied on most extensively in South Africa.[1559]

Both the UK and Australia provide for removal remedies that do not specify the grounds on which an administrator may be removed. Theoretically, this leaves scope for the removal of an administrator on the grounds relating to a lack of independence or for a conflict of interest. Indeed, in Australia, there is some authority (albeit *obiter dictum*) that an administrator could be removed by the court on the grounds of a lack of independence from, *inter alia*, the company and the directors.[1560] It has been suggested that the grounds on which an administrator can be removed by the court in the UK could also be based, by analogy, on the equivalent removal ground of the liquidator in liquidation proceedings. Accordingly, an administrator might be removed, for example, for having a conflict of interest or duty[1561] and where there is a well-founded perception of bias,[1562] both of which could be seen to address the problem of the appointment of a friendly administrator.[1563]

1559 The three removal grounds were mentioned above in PART C, Chapter 7, III., 1., a.

1560 *Commonwealth of Australia v Irving* (1996) 19 ACSR 459, 465. The other constituent from whom the administrator must be independent lest he be removed, according to the court, is the company's creditors. For further general judicial pronouncements that an administrator is required to be independent, see *Re Bartlett Researched Securities Pty Ltd* (1994) 12 ACSR 707, 710; *Re St George Builders' Hardware Pty Ltd* (1995) 13 ACLC 1, 801. Interestingly, the 'Harmer Report' (see Australian Law Reform Commission General Insolvency Inquiry (Harmer Report) 1988 < http://www.alrc.gov.au/sites/default/files/pdfs/publications/alrc45_Summary.pdf> accessed 10 January 2017) had proposed that a lack of independence constitutes an explicit ground of removal by the court. See generally Keay, 'Corporate Governance during Administration and Reconstruction under Part 5.3A of the Corporations Law' (1997) 15 C&SLJ 145, 155.

1561 Cf *Re Corbenstone Ltd (No 2)* [1990] BCLC 60; *Deloitte and Touche AG v Johnson* [2000] 1 BCLC 485.

1562 *Re Gordon & Breach Science Publishers Ltd* [1995] 2 BCLC 189.

1563 On the position in the UK, see generally Fletcher, Higham and Trower (n 1453) para 17.29.

In both the UK and Australia, an administrator can be removed either by the court, upon application of, *inter alia*, an individual creditor,[1564] or by the creditors' meeting by majority vote.[1565] However, in the UK, a removal by the creditors' meeting is only available where administration had been commenced out-of-court and where there is no qualifying floating charge-holder, which is expected to rarely be the case in practice.[1566]

3. Conclusion

In controlling the risk of the appointment of friendly office holders, South Africa relies most heavily on the *removal rights strategy ex post*. By contrast, Australia's primary legal strategy in this regard is the mandatory disclosure of relevant information relating to the administrator's independence, supplemented by relevant *ex post* criminal sanctions for non-compliance with such disclosure requirements. As in Australia, the UK primarily resorts to disclosure of relevant information relating to the administrators' independence, supplemented by *ex post* sanctions (namely internal disciplinary procedures of the regulatory bodies). However, unlike in Australia, the regulation and enforcement of office holders in the UK is located entirely in 'soft law'. The benefit of the UK approach in this regard is that the costs of adjudication and enforcement of the relevant requirements are largely moved to the regulatory bodies, while in Australia and South Africa, a large portion of such costs are borne by the unsecured creditors. However, self-regulation requires strong, well-organised and pro-active professional bodies. In South Africa, the legislature has put further development of the role of self-regulation on hold for the time being.

There are three further potentially important differences between the approaches of the relevant jurisdictions in reducing the risk of the appointment of a friendly rescue practitioner. In the first place, the applicable

1564 S 449B Corporations Act 2001. Creditors may arguably also bring a removal application under s 447E, pursuant to which the court can make any order, as it deems just, where the administrator is managing the company or has done an act or omission that is prejudicial to the company (see Cassidy (n 1541) para 13.310). For the UK, Insolvency Act 1986, Sch B1, para 88 read with rule 2.112 Insolvency Rules 1986.

1565 For Australia, s 436E(4) Corporations Act 2001; for the UK, Insolvency Act 1986, Sch B1, para 97.

1566 Insolvency Act 1986, Sch B1, para 97.

qualification requirements in Australia and the UK are more specific than the South African qualification requirements. Moreover, the Anglo-Australian qualification requirements are framed as *legal rules*, while the South African qualification requirements are framed as *legal standards*. In Australia, non-compliance with such requirements is sanctioned by the imposition of criminal liability on the administrator, and such liability is strict. Both mechanisms are likely to reduce the scope for non-compliance with such requirements.

The UK and Australia (but not South Africa) provide that the office holder take certain procedural steps to deal with potential threats to the office holder's independence (and keep records of such steps) (in the UK) and disclose any potentially improper relationships to the creditors (in the UK and Australia). These *ex ante* strategies force the administrator to apply his mind to whether he is able to exercise independent and unfettered judgment before he accepts the appointment, thereby reducing the likelihood of costly enforcement *ex post* and the costs of a new administrator to familiarise himself with the company's affairs. By contrast, such procedural costs and familiarisation costs are more likely to occur in South Africa, given the absence of *ex ante* requirements equivalent to those in the UK and Australia. Moreover, the duties to disclose the relevant information reduce the general information asymmetries of unsecured creditors, and places them in a position to utilise their remedies of removal of the office holder that are available under the UK and Australia.

And finally, both the UK and Australia provide for the extra-judicial enforcement of the removal of directors by a majority vote of the creditors collectively, in addition to removal of an office holder by the court, upon application of an individual creditor. On the other hand, South Africa only provides for the last-mentioned route of removal of an office holder. The reliance of all three jurisdictions on such route for the removal of an office holder is surprising, given the advantages of the extra-judicial removal by the creditors collectively. These advantages are largely the same as those of the extra-judicial termination of formal rescue proceedings by creditors collectively relied on in Australia,[1567] which are as follows. First, the collective action and holdout problems of the removal ground by creditors collectively is significantly mitigated by the requirement that the creditors are entitled to act by majority.

1567 See PART C, Chapter 7, II., 1., c., cc above.

Second, the costs of executing, and voting during, the applicable creditors' meeting are likely to be lower than the court proceedings under the alternative removal route.

Third, allowing individual creditors to remove the office holder could give rise to opportunistic removal applications by creditors, for example, where the rescue objective pursued by the office holder does not favour one class of creditors. The intensity of this perverse incentive depends on the party that is entitled to appoint the replacement office holder; the more power given to the party that brought the removal application to also appoint the replacement office holder, the greater the perverse incentive is likely to be, as this would enable the applicable creditor to appoint a friendly office holder. Of the relevant jurisdictions, South Africa affords the greatest power to the party removing the rescue practitioner to also appoint his replacement. This is because the majority of the independent creditors who were represented in the removal hearing before the court may nominate the replacement rescue practitioner who is ultimately appointed by the court.[1568] However, it would seem that there is a good chance that if the replacement rescue practitioner is acceptable to such majority independent creditors who attended the hearing, then the court is unlikely to second-guess such nomination. In the UK and Australia, by contrast, the replacement administrator is generally appointed by directors of the company,[1569] which would significantly reduce the perverse incentive of individual creditors to bring removal applications for strategic purposes.

It might be argued that this perverse incentive is already adequately dealt with by existing legal mechanisms in some of the applicable jurisdictions, obviating the need for further legal intervention. First, it would seem that, in the UK, the courts are expected to set a fairly high standard for the removal grounds. As a result, strategic removal applications are being discouraged, on the grounds that courts may well be reluctant to second-guess the administrator's commercial judgment, largely due to his superior commercial expertise and the risk associated with the benefit of hindsight. Second, courts are expected to recognise that there is bound to be dis-

---

1568 S 130(6)(a) Companies Act 2008. An 'independent creditor' is one who is not 'related' to the company (ie, who is not able to exercise any form of control over the company).

1569 For the UK, Insolvency Act 1986, Sch B1, para 94(1); for Australia, s 449C(2)(b)(i) read with s 436A Corporations Act 2001.

agreement among the classes of creditors in relation to the deployment of assets, given the strongly diverging interests of the different classes of creditors due to the general scarcity of available assets of companies located in administration.[1570] And third, courts might refuse the removal of an administrator if the benefits of this removal to the general body of creditors are outweighed by the costs of his replacement by a new administrator.[1571] The British courts, for example, have shown a general reluctance to remove directors, *inter alia*, on the above-mentioned grounds.[1572]

It is nevertheless conceivable, on the other hand, that in some situations, the potential strategic gain for the applicant in bringing a removal application may outweigh the risk that the application is dismissed with costs. One mechanism that should be considered in this regard is the imposition of damages *ex post* on applicants where it is found that the application is an abuse of the court's procedure or is malicious or vexatious. Such a provision could be based on the provision in the South African liquidation law, which entitles the court to award damages to the company against an applicant for bringing an abusive application for a winding-up order.[1573] A further possible mechanism in this regard is the dismissal of applications for the removal of office holders by creditors that have no economic interest in the company, for example, where an unsecured creditor has no prospect of a return, as has been proposed in the UK.[1574] This could be an effective legal strategy where the lack of an economic interest of the applicant can easily be ascertained (that is, at no or very low costs). It would not be appropriate, however, where a costly valuation is required to determine the economic interest of the applicant.

1570 Both arguments are based on Milman (n 1554) 114.

1571 Courts have relied on this reasoning in the UK; see *AMP Music Box Enterprises v Hoffmann* [2002] EWHC 1899 (Ch), [2002] BCC 996; *Re C E King Ltd* [2000] 2 BCLC 297. See generally Milman (n 1554) 114; Fletcher, Higham and Trower (n 1453) para 17.29.

1572 Removal was refused, eg, in *Re Abbey Forwarding Ltd* [2010] EWHC 1644 (Ch), [2010] BPIR; *Re Kimberley Scott Services Ltd* [2011] EWHC 1563 (Ch), [2012] BPIR 135; *Doffman and Isaacs v Wood and Hellard* [2011] EWHC 4008 (Ch), [2012] BPIR 972. See also *Finnerty v Clark* [2011] EWCA Civ 858, [2011] BCC 702 (CA). See generally Milman (n 1554) 114–5.

1573 S 347(1A) Companies Act 1973. See Loubser (n 1415) 55, who suggests this provision could be used for abusive applications by employees for the commencement of rescue proceedings.

1574 See Fletcher, Higham and Trower (n 1453) para 17.30 in relation to the British removal provision under Insolvency Act 1986, Sch B1, para 88).

And finally, since no negative externalities should, in principle, arise from placing the decision of removal of the administrator in the entire body of creditors, it could be argued that there might not be a need for the additional avenues of removal by the court, upon application by an individual creditor.[1575] The risk that secured creditors may impose their interests on unsecured creditors through the majority vote as a result of typical borrowing structures could be counteracted by the requirement that secured creditors may only vote the unsecured portion of their claim.[1576]

IV. Legal strategies ameliorating the use of the debt consolidation scheme for value-minimising purposes in South Africa

1. General

As discussed in Chapter 4,[1577] three potentially value-reducing actions arose under the debt consolidation scheme under the previous rescue regime, namely: (i) the underpayment of existing creditors; (ii) the inefficient deployment of the company's assets in the post-scheme period (underinvestment problem);[1578] and (iii) the adverse selection problem prejudicing new trade creditors in the post-scheme period.

It has been mentioned before that all three problems have in principle persisted under the new rescue regime.[1579]

The sources of the perverse incentive of the acquirer in pursuing these creditor-harming actions under the previous rescue regime were the following: (i) shortcomings of judicial management as a modern rescue procedure, resulting in many temporarily distressed but economically viable companies ending up in liquidation proceedings, where such companies

1575 For a more elaborate version of this argument and relevant references, see PART C, Chapter 7, II., 1., c., cc above, where it was discussed in relation to the creditors' meeting to resolve that administration be dismissed.

1576 Ibid.

1577 See PART B, Chapter 4, II., 4. above.

1578 Strictly speaking, the continued trading in the post-scheme period constituted an overinvestment where the company was economically viable, not where it was economically distressed; see n 528 in Chapter 4 and accompanying text. However, we will refer to this opportunistic action as overinvestment generally for the sake of convenience.

1579 See PART B, Chapter 4, V., 4. above.

were exposed to the perverse incentive of the acquirer pursuing the three value-minimising actions; (ii) the fact that the debt consolidation scheme was normally invoked during liquidation proceedings meant that at that stage there was generally little scope for capital restructuring measures; and (iii) as a result, the assets of economically viable companies would often have been placed to their highest value use if sold as a going concern. However, the legislative scheme did not generally cater for going concern sales, nor was there a high demand for such assets in the South African market. The last two mentioned causes explain why existing creditors were often left with little choice but to sell their claims at an undervalue. It further explains why, from the perspective of the acquirer, the tax benefit often exceeded the going concern value of economically viable companies. This gave rise to the acquirer's perverse incentive to embark on the debt consolidation scheme.

At 2. below, it will be argued that the more rescue-friendly new rescue procedure is likely to reduce the prevalence of the value-minimising use of the debt consolidation scheme, although some scope for this form of opportunism of the acquirer remains under the new Companies Act.

This raises the question about the appropriate legal responses to this residual risk. The previous rescue regime did not provide for any specific legal strategies addressing the problems of the underpayment of existing creditors during the debt consolidation scheme and the underinvestment problem in the post-scheme period. Nor have any legal strategies been introduced in this regard under the new rescue regime. Possible legal responses will be explored at 3. below.

The adverse selection problem, by contrast, was addressed by some courts by means of a court-imposed subordination agreement between the acquirer and the company, under which the acquirer subordinated his claim against the company to all future unsecured creditors.[1580] Presumably this is still the position under the new rescue regime. We will consider the effectiveness of this legal strategy at 4. below.

1580 See PART B, Chapter 3, IV., 3., b. above.

2. Impact of the new rescue procedure on the prevalence of value-minimising debt consolidation schemes

There are good reasons to believe that the use of the debt consolidation scheme for value-reducing purposes is likely to become less prevalent under the new rescue procedure.[1581] This conjecture is based on two related arguments, namely: (i) the replacement of judicial management with business rescue has resulted in overall fewer economically viable companies being placed under liquidation proceedings; and (ii) the risk that companies would be made subject to the perverse incentive of the acquirer is lower under the new business rescue proceedings. These two arguments will now be considered in turn.

With regard to the first argument, the new rescue regime has made major improvements as compared to judicial management in respect of providing economically viable companies with access to, and encouraging their use of, formal rescue proceedings. First, the introduction of an out-of-court entry route and an impending insolvency entry ground under the new procedure enable companies earlier access to the formal rescue procedure.[1582]

Second, the broader rescue objectives of the new procedure provide access to a wider range of economically viable companies than was the case under judicial management.[1583]

And third, the shortcomings of the governance regime under judicial management, relating mainly to the competence and independence of the judicial manager, resulted in a general lack of confidence in judicial management.[1584] The new rescue procedure appears to have addressed most of the problems indicated above, namely: (i) the regulation of the rescue practitioners' profession;[1585] (ii) removing the Master of the High Court from the appointment process and thereby the corrupt practices that this gave rise to;[1586] and (iii) tougher measures holding rescue practitioners to account, for example, a statutory fiduciary duty and duty of care, skill and diligence and an express right of removal from office on specific

1581 However, there are no relevant statistics to support this argument.
1582 See the discussion in PART B, Chapter 4, IV., 2., b., bb. and cc., respectively.
1583 See the discussin in PART B, Chapter 4, IV., 2., b., dd.
1584 See the discussion in PART B, Chapter 3, III., 5. and PART B, Chapter 4, II., 3.
1585 See the discussion in PART B, Chapter 4, III., 3.
1586 Ibid.

grounds.[1587] These factors are likely to instil greater confidence in the formal rescue procedure, reducing the number of temporarily distressed but economically viable companies being placed under liquidation proceedings. As a result, fewer economically viable companies are likely to be exposed to the perverse incentive of the third party acquirer under liquidation proceedings.

With regard to the second argument, although a debt consolidation scheme might theoretically be permitted under the capital reorganisation method of rescue under the new rescue procedure,[1588] the likelihood of this would appear to be reduced by certain requirements of the procedure for several reasons. First, permitting the acquirer to purchase the claims of existing creditors at liquidation value while allowing him the benefit of such claims at going concern value would hardly be compatible with the purpose of the Companies Act 2008, which requires that the interests of all relevant stakeholders be balanced.[1589]

Second, the new rescue procedure provides for extensive participation rights of the company's creditors. Pertinent examples are the right (i) to form a creditors' committee and be consulted by the rescue practitioner during the development of a rescue plan through that committee[1590] and (ii) the right of creditors generally to make proposals for a business rescue plan to the rescue practitioner.[1591] Such participation rights reduce the likelihood of the acquisition of the creditors' claims at an undervalue.

And finally, a stronger market for distressed businesses is likely to develop due to the possibility of going concern sales under the new business rescue procedure and an expected development of informal rescue mechanisms.[1592] The strengthening of a market for distressed businesses, in turn, is expected to reduce the likelihood of undervalue-acquisitions of the

1587 See the discussion in PART B, Chapter 4, IV., 8.

1588 The minimum information that is required to be provided to the company's claimants in a rescue plan pursuant to s 150(2)(b) Companies Act 2008 implies that the types of restructuring mechanisms contemplated by business rescue are broad enough to include the transaction that was concluded as part of a debt consolidation scheme.

1589 The purpose is that the Companies Act 2008 is to provide for an efficient rescue and recovery of financially distressed companies that balances the rights and interests of all relevant stakeholders S 7(k) Companies Act 2008.

1590 S 145(3) Companies Act 2008.

1591 S 145(1)(d) Companies Act 2008.

1592 See the discussion in PART B, Chapter 4, VI., 3. above.

existing creditors' claims by a prospective acquirer and discourage the value-minimising application of the assets of economically viable companies in the post-scheme period.

Nevertheless, the new rescue regime still provides for some limited scope for the value-minimising use of the debt consolidation scheme. First, there is still a minor risk that some temporarily distressed but economically viable companies would be placed under liquidation proceedings. Such companies would be exposed to a greater risk of falling subject to the acquirer's perverse incentive in question under liquidation proceedings than under rescue proceedings.

Second, the introduction of the new rescue regime and the expected development of a market for distressed businesses would only address the value-reducing use of the scheme of arrangement by economically viable companies, not economically distressed companies. Such companies are generally placed under liquidation proceedings,[1593] where they would be vulnerable to the acquirer's perverse incentive.

3. Normative analysis of appropriate legal response to the underpayment of creditors and the underinvestment problem

The requirement that schemes must be sanctioned by the court under the compromise with creditors procedure[1594] could be a suitable strategy for dealing with the underpayment of creditors and the underinvestment of assets. This would constitute a *trusteeship strategy*. In exercising its discretion as to whether or not to approve a scheme, the court may have regard to factors such as the commercial morality and the interests of the public.[1595] Since the set of facts and behaviour of the acquirer that give rise to the two value-reducing actions in question is likely to vary significantly in every given situation, the flexibility of the two factors allow the courts to address the acquirer's opportunism with the required degree of sensitivity.

1593 Except where they are placed under rescue proceedings inappropriately or where the rescue procedure allows for break-up sales, as is the case under administration in the UK.

1594 S 155(7) Companies Act 2008.

1595 Eg, the proposal of a debt consolidation scheme was not approved by the court on the grounds that it was clear from the facts that the acquirer had no intention of restoring the company's profitability in the post-scheme period in *Cooper v A & G Fashions (Pty) Ltd: Ex parte Millman* 1991 (4) SA 204 (C).

To be sure, these two factors would have to be developed in identifying the perverse incentive in question when deciding on whether or not to sanction schemes. As it will be argued that the *trusteeship strategy* could also serve to ameliorate the adverse selection problem, we will deal with this question under the next heading.

4. Ex ante trusteeship strategy: Insistence of contractual subordination by the court when called upon to sanction a scheme of arrangement

a. Explaining the acquirer's perverse incentive

The acquirer has a perverse incentive to propose a value-diminishing debt consolidation scheme in respect of economically distressed companies where, from the perspective of the acquirer, the value of the tax benefit exceeds the break-up value of the company. It is conceivable that this could be the case in certain situations. The general tendency would seem to be that the larger the margin by which the profit-making capability of the acquirer's other business entities exceeds the (potential) profit-generating capability of the company, the greater the likelihood that such a perverse incentive would arise. Economically distressed companies would *per se* have a less than probable chance of survival.

With regard to economically viable companies, the acquirer's perverse incentive would arise where from his perspective, the value of the tax benefit would exceed the going-concern value of the company, and for as long as such disincentive prevails, the company has a less than probable chance of surviving for a sustainable period. The general tendency would appear to be that the larger the margin by which the profit-making capability of the acquirer's other business entities exceeds the (potential) profit-generating capability of the company, the greater the likelihood that such a perverse incentive would arise, and the longer the period in which such perverse incentive would prevail. Accordingly, economically viable companies would have a less than probable chance of survival for as long as the value of the tax benefit exceeds the company's going concern value to the acquirer. In such a situation, the acquirer would have a disincentive to expend his efforts or invest funds in the company, making the survival of the company unlikely.

Although companies that have a less than probable chance of survival might often also be balance sheet insolvent, this need not be so.

b. The need for legal protection in the first place

South African company law does not generally protect creditors against situations akin to the adverse selection problem in question. It rather relies on creditor self-help in this regard. The absence of minimum capital requirements and the fact that the test of insolvency is generally cash flow insolvency (though sometimes together with balance sheet insolvency), bears testimony to this approach.[1596]

The question whether or not a legal response is required for the adverse selection problem therefore depends on whether the extension of trade creditors to companies emerging from a debt consolidation scheme is a different situation to a situation where a company extends credit while it is balance sheet insolvent generally. Indeed, some courts under the previous company law regime regarded there to be no difference between the two situations and, on that basis, held that, as would be the case generally, contractual self-help measures were sufficient for the protection of post-scheme trade creditors.[1597]

This is a complex matter. To be sure, the fact that a company had undergone a debt consolidation scheme before it was placed back on the open market, does not make the post-scheme creditors more vulnerable to extending risky credit to the company than when such creditors extend credit to balance sheet insolvent companies generally.

The actual source of the potential harm to the post-scheme creditors would rather seem to be the perverse incentive of the acquirer to put the company's assets to value-minimising uses in the post-scheme period and the resulting risk that the company resumes trading where it has a less than probable chance of survival on a sustainable basis. From the perspective of commercial morality, this is a risk to which no creditor ought to be exposed.

1596 S 344(f) read with s 345(1)(c) and 345(2) Companies Act 1973. The provisions in the Companies Act 1973, including the mentioned sections, still apply under the Companies Act 2008 by virtue of Sch 5, item 9 Companies Act 2008. In the context of the debt consolidation scheme, see, eg, *Ex parte Strydom NO: In re Central Plumbing Works (Natal) Pty Ltd* 1988 (1) SA 616 (D) 623. See also Luiz and van der Linde, 'Trading in Insolvent Circumstances – Its Relevance to Sections 311 and 424 of the Companies Act' [1993] SA Merc LJ 230ff.

1597 In particular, *Ex parte Strydom NO: In re Central Plumbing Works (Natal) Pty Ltd* 1988 (1) SA 616 (D) 623.

c. The merits of the court-imposed contractual subordination

Since the question whether or not post-scheme creditors require protection depends on the existence of the acquirer's perverse incentive, the question that should be asked is whether the court-imposed contractual subordination appropriately re-balances the acquirer's perverse incentive to underinvest such assets in the post-scheme period. This would ensure that debt consolidation schemes would be implemented, and the company be placed back on the open market, only in situations where the company has a more than probable chance of surviving for a sustainable period.

Whether the court-imposed contractual subordination would appropriately re-balance this perverse incentive depends on whether it would always ensure that the company's break-up value (where the company is economically distressed) and its going-concern value (where the company is economically viable) would exceed the value of the tax benefit to the acquirer. This is because in such situations the acquirer would have a disincentive to propose a value-diminishing debt consolidation scheme in the first place.

The applicable subordination might be argued to re-balance the acquirer's perverse incentive, insofar as it could be seen to effectively decrease the value of the acquirer's investment in the company (ie, the acquisition of the debt claims of the existing creditors) and, if such investment is seen as the 'consideration' for the tax benefit, also decreases the value of the tax benefit to the acquirer. Such decrease in value is due to the reduced likelihood that the acquirer's debt investment will be (fully) returned to him.[1598]

However, it is doubtful that this decrease in value of the tax benefit to the acquirer would always be sufficient to re-balance the acquirer's per-

1598 The type of subordination agreement that was commonly – and presumably still is – used in the context of the debt consolidation scheme is that the acquirer's debt claim was subordinated to the post-scheme unsecured creditors' claims until the company regained its balance sheet insolvency (whereby the subordinated debt claim was presumably recognised as a contingent liability in the company's balance sheet). Accordingly, both capital and interest payments on the acquirer's claim were not permitted during the subsistence of the subordination and the acquirer's entire debt claim would rank behind the claims of the post-scheme unsecured creditors if the company were to be placed under liquidation during the subsistence of the subordination; see, eg, McLennan, 'Abuse of Limited Liability, "Insider" Debts and Subordination Agreements' (1993) 110 SALJ 686, 690.

verse incentive. For example, where the profit-making capability of the company is significantly lower than the profit-making capability of the acquirer's other entities, the value of the tax benefit to the acquirer increases, which makes it less likely that a subordination would sufficiently re-balance the acquirer's perverse incentive in question.

A further problem with the subordination is that, as it is a contractual subordination, it is possible for the company and the acquirer to terminate the subordination agreement once the company resumes trading after its release from liquidation proceedings.[1599] This problem could, in theory, be remedied by the imposition of a mandatory (statutory) subordination.[1600] However, even mandatory subordination would not resolve the first mentioned shortcoming of subordination generally and, on that ground, should be rejected as an appropriate legal strategy to re-balance the acquirer's perverse incentive in question.

It would seem that, as was proposed in respect of the underpayment of creditors and underinvestment problem above, the existing *trusteeship strategy* could, with a few modifications, appropriately protect post-scheme creditors from the perverse incentive of the acquirer. This is so for several reasons.

First, as with the problem that the debt consolidation scheme could be utilised for value-reducing purposes generally, the existence and the intensity of the acquirer's opportunism would vary according to the facts of each case. The wide discretion of the court and its competence to require that the parties bring relevant facts before it in determining whether or not to sanction a scheme, allows the court to deal with the opportunism with the required sensitivity. This advantage of this *trusteeship strategy* derives from the fact that this question is determined by legal standards rather than mandatory rules.

Second, where the court decides to decline its approval of a scheme, any harm to post-scheme creditors is precluded. This advantage derives

---

1599 See the trial court in *Ex parte De Villiers & another NNO: In re Carbon Developments (Pty) Ltd (In Liquidation)* 1992 (2) SA 95 (W) 118. The imposition by the court of a requirement in the subordination agreement that precludes the parties from terminating such agreement would, of course, be contrary to contractual principles and would therefore not be permitted; McLennan (n 1598) 706.

1600 See, eg, Kloppers, *Judicial management as a technique for corporate rescue : a comparison with English and Australian law* (LLM thesis, University of Stellenbosch 2000) 199ff; McLennan (n 1598) 708ff.

from the *ex ante* application of the *trusteeship strategy*. It constitutes a clear advantage over another legal strategy that could be regarded as being appropriate in this regard, namely directorial liability *ex post*.[1601] This is because such directorial duties are enforceable *ex post*, thus at a time when post-scheme creditors would have already extended credit to the company. This means that even if, for example, a reckless trading suit is successful, such creditors would still share in the costs of the relevant litigation.

Of course, the considerations on which the courts have so far declined to sanction a scheme – most notably considerations of commercial morality and the interests of the general public – would need to be developed in order to deal with the perverse incentive of the acquirer specifically. Considerations that the courts should have regard to in this matter are, for example, evidence of the economic viability of the company and the profit-making capability of the company as compared to that of the other entities of the acquirer. Such considerations would assist the court in determining when the company would *per se* have a less than probable chance of sustainable trading. This would be the case where the court finds that the company is economically distressed. Moreover, the court might be able to determine where the value of the tax benefit to the acquirer is likely to exceed the value of going-concern value or the break-up value of the company. This would be the case where the court finds that the profit-making capabilities of the company are significantly less than those of the acquirer's other entities.

V. Summary and conclusion

The perverse incentive of the company controllers to use formal rescue proceedings for strategic purposes gives rise to two general value-minimising actions in South Africa, namely premature entry and the entry of economically distressed companies, and one value-minimising action under the debt consolidation scheme.

In management-displacing rescue regimes, there is a risk that legal responses to the problems of premature entry and the entry of economically distressed companies are undermined by the appointment of an office

1601 Eg, for the inappropriate extension of credit, which could fall within the existing directorial reckless trading duty, if such duty were developed accordingly.

holder related or sympathetic to the company controllers ('friendly office holder'). Most jurisdictions therefore address this risk by means of specific requirements.

Premature entry and the entry of economically distressed companies are generally addressed in South Africa, the UK and Australia by a combination of applicable entry requirements and relevant *ex post* legal strategies.

The impending insolvency ground in South Africa, the UK and Australia can be regarded as addressing the problem of premature entry.

The time period of six months under the South African version of the impending insolvency entry ground is arbitrary and is also more restrictive than the Anglo-Australian versions; the latter give the courts greater flexibility in determining for which companies restructuring measures would be more value-maximising within, as opposed to outside, formal rescue proceedings.

The impending insolvency ground is ultimately inadequate in controlling premature entry for two primary reasons. First, it is not necessarily the company's financial position, but rather the availability of certain protective measures under formal rescue proceedings (in particular, the moratorium and the cramdown mechanism) that give rise to premature entry opportunism. Second, it disregards variables other than the solvency of the company for determining whether or not formal rescue measures would be value-enhancing, namely the severity of the contingent claims and the complexity of the debt-capital structure of the company. Both these reasons explain why the impending insolvency ground fails to satisfactorily deny access to companies that would be restructured more cost-effectively outside formal rescue proceedings.

The economic distress entry ground used in the UK and South Africa can be regarded as addressing the problem of the entry of economically distressed companies. As the law currently stands in South Africa, the objectives of rescue are narrower in South Africa than in the UK, as South Africa arguably does not allow for the break-up sale of companies' assets during rescue proceedings. While the UK approach is a more rigorous application of the principle that rescue law should maximise the wealth of creditors, the South African approach probably leaves less scope for the entry of economically distressed companies.

In South Africa and the UK, compliance with the impending insolvency entry ground is reinforced by means of an *ex post standards strategy*, namely applicable directorial sanctions (South Africa: cost-order against directors; UK: criminal sanctions against directors). The mechanisms used in both jurisdictions to counteract the risk that the *ex post* directorial sanctions discourage the timeous invocation of rescue proceedings by company controllers are the analogous application of the business judgment rule (South Africa) and the use of a subjective test for proving liability (UK).

Moreover, South Africa, Australia and the UK entitle the company's claimants to challenge the invocation of rescue proceedings where the company does not meet the premature entry ground or the economic distress entry ground. Insofar as here the claimants (acting as principals) are entitled to effectively *ratify* a management decision during rescue proceedings, this mechanism could be seen as a *ratification strategy*.

One of the modes of challenge found in the UK and Australia could potentially include the premature entry of companies that is not caught by the premature entry ground, and thus might remedy the weakness of that ground of entry mentioned above. The possibility of the development of such a mode of challenge in South Africa has recently been ended by the SCA judgement of *Panamo Properties*.

Only Australia allows for the challenge to be made by the creditors collectively by majority vote. This has the advantage of saving on procedural, agency and decision-making costs. On the other hand, given the commercial realities of borrowing structures, this approach could give rise to secured creditors' agency costs. This could be controlled by requiring a majority, not only in value but also in number, of creditors or the exclusion from the vote of creditors that lack an economic interest in the outcome of the decision.

A further legal strategy found in all three jurisdictions is a duty of the office holder to take relevant steps to terminate rescue proceedings, or convert to liquidation proceedings where required. To the extent that an office holder responds primarily to non-monetary incentives in performing these duties, this mechanism could be seen as a *trusteeship strategy*.

The reliance on the court as final arbiter for terminating rescue proceedings in the UK and South Africa is somewhat surprising, given the high procedural costs of court proceedings and the low risk of agency costs if that decision were to be placed on the office holder.

Where the decision has been taken that the company be released from rescue proceedings or that rescue proceedings be converted to an alternative insolvency proceeding, the relevant requirements should ensure that this transition take place at the lowest costs possible. Both the UK and Australia provide for a more cost-effective transition than South Africa. The costs of conversion are lower (i) where it may be done extra-judicially, (ii) where the alternative insolvency procedures are procedurally integrated (both reducing procedural costs) and (iii) where the office holder remains in control (reducing 'familiarisation' costs).

The US addresses the problems of premature entry and the entry of economically distressed companies solely by means of the *ex post standards strategy* of the dismissal of Chapter 11 filings on the grounds of the judge-made good faith requirement.

The US *ex post standards strategy* has the advantage of leaving more scope for the important consideration of a comparison of costs of formal and informal rescue measures. Moreover, the absence of *ex post* sanctions on directors for invoking rescue proceedings in violation of the economic distress entry ground in the UK and South Africa could reduce the level of compliance with that entry ground. Hence the costs of enforcement of this entry ground are likely to be transferred to formal rescue proceedings, just as under the *ex post standards strategy* in the US.

The strong rights of floating charge-holders to initiate and control rescue proceedings is expected to reduce the perverse incentive of directors to use rescue proceedings for strategic purposes, and at the same time, encourage directors to pursue informal workouts.

The risk of the appointment of a friendly office holder is addressed in South Africa, the UK and Australia by *ex ante* qualification and disclosure requirements relating to the office holder's independence (ie, a *rules strategy*). This is supplemented by relevant *ex post* sanctions for non-compliance with such requirements as well as by the removal of the office holder *ex post*, *inter alia*, for a lack of independence (which can be seen as a *removal rights strategy*).

There are five potentially important differences in the approaches of the relevant jurisdictions to the risk of the appointment of a friendly office holder. First, the UK regulates such problem largely by way of 'soft' law, which moves the costs of adjudication and enforcement largely to the regulatory bodies.

Second, the specific formulation of the applicable qualification requirements in Australia and the UK and the imposition of criminal liability for non-compliance in Australia is expected to raise the level of compliance with the applicable qualification requirements.

Third, the *ex ante* procedural steps to deal with potential threats to the office holder's independence and *ex ante* disclosure of potentially improper relationships in the UK and Australia are likely to increase the level of screening out friendly rescue practitioners.

Fourth, the reliance by all three jurisdictions on the removal by court application of an individual claimant is surprising for essentially the same reasons as the termination of rescue proceedings by the court mentioned above, namely high procedural and agency costs. The extent of the agency costs would seem to be directly proportional to the extent of the power given to the creditor who has brought the removal application, to also appoint the replacement office holder.

One way to deal with the threat of agency costs is that courts set a fairly high standard for the removal grounds, which seems to be the preferred route in the UK. Further mechanisms that should be considered is the imposition of damages *ex post* for applications that are an abuse of the court's procedure or are malicious or vexatious and the dismissal of applications by claimants that have no economic interest in the company.

The three potentially value-reducing actions arising under the debt consolidation scheme are (i) the underpayment of existing creditors, (ii) the inefficient deployment of the company's assets in the post-scheme period (underinvestment problem) and (iii) the adverse selection problem prejudicing new trade creditors in the post-scheme period.

Although the more rescue-friendly new rescue procedure is likely to reduce the prevalence of the value-minimising use of the debt consolidation scheme, some scope for this form of opportunism of the acquirer will remain under the new Companies Act.

The underpayment of existing creditors during the debt consolidation scheme and the underinvestment problem in the post-scheme period has not been addressed under the new Companies Act. By contrast, the adverse selection problem is arguably addressed by the court-imposed contractual subordination of the acquirer's debt claim to all unsecured creditors of the company that is typically insisted on by the courts when sanctioning a scheme under the compromise for creditors procedure.

It would seem that the requirement that schemes must be approved by courts – an *ex ante trusteeship strategy* – could be developed so as to deal with the problems of the underpayment of creditors and the underinvestment of assets. The requirement that the court must have regard for the commercial morality and the interests of the public when sanctioning a scheme would allow for the required degree of sensitivity to address the perverse incentive of the acquirer in question. Of course, these two factors will need to be developed to cater for the acquirer's perverse incentive (see the discussion in relation to the adverse selection problem below).

In relation to the adverse selection problem, it would seem there is a need for protecting post-scheme creditors from the risk of extending credit on unfavourable terms to a company emerging from a debt consolidation scheme.

The aforementioned *ex ante trusteeship strategy* does not appear to address the adverse selection problem appropriately for two reasons. First, it does not appear to remove the acquirer's perverse incentive in every situation. Second, there is a risk that the acquirer terminates the subordination agreement in the post-scheme period.

It would seem that the same *ex ante trusteeship strategy* suggested to controlling the underpayment and the underinvestment problems might be appropriate for addressing the adverse selection problem as well. This is so for two primary reasons. First, as in relation to the desirability of the *trusteeship strategy* for the first two problems, this legal strategy allows for the required flexibility to take account of the varying circumstances in which the acquirer opportunism could arise. Second, the court's refusal to sanction a scheme would prevent any harm to creditors, which stems from the *ex ante* nature of this legal strategy.

In developing the concepts of commercial morality and the interests of the public to deal with the acquirer opportunism, the court should have regard to considerations concerning the economic viability and the profit-making capability of the company compared to the other entities of the acquirer.

OVERALL SUMMARY AND OUTLOOK

Since its inception in 2011 the South African business rescue regime received considerable attention in academia. So far, legal scholars have largely analysed the South African rescue law from a doctrinal, and occasionally a comparative, perspective. In contrast to this, the approach adopted in this study is primarily a functional one. The primary *function* against which the South African rescue law has been measured, is how successful it is in reducing so-called 'agency costs'.

The notion of agency costs stems from the field of economics. In basis terms, agency costs arise whenever the welfare of one person (the principal) depends on the actions of another person (the agent). The problem arises because a person is not likely to exert himself as much if he acts for someone else as where he acts for himself. This explains why an agent is tempted to skimp on the quality of his performance promised to the principal or positively take for himself some of the value that was promised to the principal. Here the agent is said to have a 'perverse incentives' or to act 'opportunistically'. Agency costs, then, constitute the value loss suffered by the principal as a result of his dependency on the actions of the agent.

This study has identified three principal-agent relationships (or conflicts) in relation to rescue law, based on the equivalent agency relationships in company law, namely: (i) the company-creditor conflict; (ii) the office holder-company conflict; and (iii) the secured creditors-unsecured creditors conflict. While the first-mentioned agency conflict arises in the vicinity of insolvency, the last two mentioned agency conflicts occur during rescue proceedings.

It has been shown that corporate insolvency law could be seen to respond to each of these agency conflicts by means of so-called 'legal strategies' – that is, substantive law rules that can be seen to ameliorate agency costs. When analysing rescue law from the perspective of these three agency relationships, various principal-harming actions were identified. Due to the large scope of the subject matter, the focus has been on the agency costs-generating actions arising under the company-creditor conflict.

Of course, the field of economics identifies types of inefficiencies other than agency costs. Of particular importance in the context of corporate insolvency law are the direct and indirect costs of insolvency – that is, the costs of the insolvency procedure and the negative market reaction to financial distress. Accordingly, such other types of efficiencies have formed part of the analysis. However, because the agency costs theory is capable of application across the entire set of rules of corporate insolvency law, it has been used as the primary analytical tool in examining the South African rescue law.

As with some of the conventional writings on the South African rescue law, this study has also adopted a comparative approach. Needless to say, in taking account of applicable foreign law rules, the primary focus has been on the extent to which they can be seen to address the relevant agency costs-generating actions under the company-creditor conflict. Due to the common legal heritage with South Africa, the UK, Australia and the US were primarily drawn on, while Germany was occasionally consulted as well.

The application of the agency costs analysis to the South African rescue law was the main objective of this study. It should appeal foremost to academics in the field of law and economics.

A further objective was to provide an overview of rescue law in South Africa and examine selected problems thereof. The historical and legal cultural context was taken into account for this analysis. This part should be of interest primarily to legal practitioners, students and judges.

The structure of the thesis reflects its dual objective. After a comprehensive theoretical discussion of the principal-agent theory in Chapter 1, an overview of the theoretical foundations of corporate insolvency law, largely from a law and economics perspective, was provided in Chapter 2.

Chapters 3 and 4 were devoted to the objective of providing an overview, and scrutinising selected problems, of the South African rescue law. While Chapter 3 set out the previous rescue regime, Chapter 4 dealt with the new rescue regime.

The other objective of this study, namely to analyse the the South African rescue law from a comparative and functional perspective, is contained in Chapters 5 to 7. The structure of the discussion in these Chapters is unconventional. The reason for this is that it follows the three actions identified as arising from the company-creditor conflict that are particularly relevant to rescue law. These are i) the perverse incentive of company controllers to delay the invocation of rescue proceedings or pursue excessively risky projects (Chapter 5), (ii) the extension of shareholder loans to the company (Chapter 6) and (iii) the strategic invocation of formal rescue proceedings (Chapter 7).

The main conclusions that emerged from the discussion could be summarised as follows.

The theoretical foundations of corporate insolvency law in Chapter 2 showed that (i) a mandatory insolvency procedure would seem to be necessary, given the prohibitively high costs of resolving financial distress by contract (duplicative enforcement costs, high monitoring costs, high co-ordination costs and holdout behaviour of creditors), (ii) there is no clear answer as to whether the preservation of the corporate entity through capital restructuring mechanisms or the sale of the company's assets should be the preferred outcome of rescue and (iii) despite the necessity of a mandatory corporate insolvency procedure, the high direct and indirect costs of insolvency proceedings raise the appeal of informal rescue measures.

A further important point that arose is that non-binding principles between banks, such as under the London Approach, hybrid devices, such as pre-packaged plans and the development of co-operation duties of creditors from the general law could reduce the free-rider/hold out problems.

The overview and analysis of selected problems of the South African rescue law in Chapters 3 and 4 highlighted that the new rescue procedures of business rescue and the compromise with creditors have been influenced by the historical and legal cultural context. Some features of the new procedure directly address the problems under the previous procedures, such as the broader objectives of rescue, earlier entry, lower involvement of the courts and regulation of the office holders' profession. Other features are an outgrowth of socio-economic conditions (employee protection) and of legal cultural attitudes towards risk-taking and business failures (for example, management-displacing system of governance).

Since secured creditors' proprietary rights are much more curtailed under business rescue than they had been under the previous rescue law, it is conjectured that there will be a stronger impetus from banks to drive informal rescue measures. This development is supported by the fact that South Africa would seem to have a concentrated lending market, making the costs of co-ordination worthwhile relative to the investments of each bank in the market.

Given that the South African rescue law provides for procedural requirements that would appear unnecessary for small companies, a procedurally less onerous mechanism for small companies should be considered. This could be shaped either as a self-standing procedure (as in the UK) or as separate provisions within the main procedure (as in the US).

The agency costs and comparative analysis of the South African rescue law is contained in Chapters 5 to 7. Chapters 5 and 6 deal with legal responses to manifestations of company controller opportunism to *delay* the invocation of rescue proceedings inappropriately, while Chapter 7 addresses legal responses to manifestations of company controller opportunism to *invoke* rescue proceedings inappropriately.

The company controller opportunism to delay rescue proceedings improperly arises when the shareholders have lost their economic interest in the company and therefore no longer bear the risk of failure. This gives them an incentive to take value-minimising trading decisions, in particular the pursuit of excessively risky projects (Chapter 5) or advance a loan to the company that enables it to fund value-reducing corporate projects (Chapter 6).

The primary legal strategy relied on by *management-displacing* rescue regimes to ameliorate the company controller opportunism to take creditor-harming trading decisions (generally discussed in Chapter 5), is the adoption of *ex post* statutory creditor-regarding duties (ie, a 'stick' approach). This is supplemented by further *ex post* legal strategies: insolvency claw back of 'undervalue transactions' enforced by 'gatekeepers' (found in the UK) and a directorial common law duty to creditors (found in some common law jurisdictions, though not (yet) in South Africa). Moreover, South Africa provides for an *ex ante* disclosure duty of directors to creditors of the impending insolvency of the company presumably aimed at enabling creditors to place companies under rescue proceedings.

Debtor-in-possession rescue regimes on the other hand, rely on a 'carrot' approach by offering directors control over rescue proceedings and the prospect of a continued stake in the reorganised company for invoking rescue proceedings early.

It would seem that the statutory creditor-regarding duties in the UK and South Africa are more promotive of informal rescue measures than the German and Australian duties. On the other hand, problems with the enforcement of the British duty in particular appear to reduce its effectiveness in controlling the perverse incentive in question.

The development of the common law duty to creditors should be encouraged in South Africa as it holds opportunities for resolving some of the weaknesses of the statutory duty (lower standard of proof, more flexible trigger).

The *ex ante* disclosure duty of directors in South Africa would appear to reduce the chances of informal workouts. However, its practical importance seems to be limited due to problems with its enforcement.

The regulation of shareholder loans (discussed in Chapter 6) must have regard for the fact that shareholder loans are not *per se* harmful to creditors. In fact, shareholder loans could be an important source of funding for closely-held companies in particular, as they may often be available at lower costs than external debt funding. Generally-speaking, it is not simply the *advance* of a shareholder loan, but rather for the purposes for which such loan is *invested*, which holds the risk of value-minimisation for creditors. The law must therefore be careful to distinguish between creditor-harming and creditor-enhancing shareholder loans, lest companies are deprived of an important source of funding when in distress.

It would seem that none of the legal strategies used in the examined jurisdiction draw that distinction successfully (*ex ante rules strategy* (Germany); *ex post standards strategy* enforced by the courts (US); and *ex post standards strategy* enforced by 'gatekeepers' (South Africa)).

In general, an *ex post standards* approach (which leaves the precise determination of compliance to adjudicators after the fact) would appear to be preferable, as this would allow for the problem of shareholder loans to be addressed with greater sensitivity.

Company controllers could in certain circumstances also have a perverse incentive to invoke formal rescue proceedings inappropriately (discussed in Chapter 7). This could occur either when informal rescue measures would be more efficient ('premature entry') or when the company is economically distressed, and liquidating its assets would place them to their highest value use ('entry of economically distressed companies'). A further form of this opportunism is found in the strategic use of a certain variant of the South African scheme of arrangement procedure ('debt consolidation scheme').

Premature entry and the entry of economically distressed companies are generally addressed in South Africa, the UK and Australia by a combination of relevant entry requirements and relevant *ex post* legal strategies (directorial liability for non-compliance with entry grounds; creditors' rights of challenging entry; and office holders' duties to take relevant steps, including terminating rescue proceedings).

In management-displacing rescue regimes, there is a risk that legal responses to the problems to control premature entry and the entry of economically distressed companies are undermined by the appointment of an office holder related or sympathetic to the company controllers ('friendly office holder'). This problem is controlled in South Africa, the UK and Australia by *ex ante* qualification and disclosure requirements relating to the office holder's independence, as supplemented by relevant *ex post* sanctions for non-compliance with such requirements and by the removal of the office holder from office *ex post*.

Three fundamental differences between these three jurisdictions emerged from the discussion, namely: (i) the UK and Australia provide for more cost-effective transition between insolvency procedures than South Africa (procedural costs and 'familiarisation costs' of office holder); (ii) the initiation and control rights afforded to floating charge-holders in the UK and Australia would seem structurally to reduce the company controller opportunism; and (iii) the stronger reliance on self-regulation by professional bodies of office holders ('soft law') in the UK than in the other two jurisdictions is likely to reduce the costs of enforcement of the problem of the appointment of a friendly office holder.

Looking to the other side of the Atlantic, the US solely relies on an *ex post standards strategy* (good faith requirement) in controlling premature entry and the entry of economically distressed companies. This has the advantage of leaving more scope for the important consideration of comparing the costs of formal and informal rescue measures and whether the company is economically viable.

The three potentially value-reducing actions arising under the debt consolidation scheme are (i) the underpayment of existing creditors, (ii) the inefficient deployment of the company's assets in the post-scheme period (underinvestment problem) and (iii) the adverse selection problem prejudicing new trade creditors in the post-scheme period. It would seem that all three problems would be most appropriately dealt with by developing the criteria used by courts in sanctioning schemes of arrangements.

The agency costs methodology adopted in this study was intended to provide a fresh perspective on how to think about corporate insolvency law in South Africa. There is certainly much scope for future law and economics research on the South African corporate insolvency law. This study has already laid the foundation for an agency costs analysis of the two agency conflicts within rescue proceedings, namely the office holder-creditors and the inter-creditor conflict during rescue proceedings. It is believed that a comparative approach would again be useful for this analysis. Particularly the traditional debtor-friendly US Chapter 11 governance system and the strong rights of floating charge-holders in the UK and Australia may provide for an interesting reference point.

It is hoped that this study will provide an impetus for the field of law and economics to grow in South Africa generally.

Bibliography

Acharya, Viral V, Amihud Yakov and Litov, Lubomir P, 'Creditor Rights and Corporate Risk Taking' (2008) SSRN <http://papers.ssrn.com/sol3/papers.cfm?abstract_id=1085195>

Adler, Barry E, 'Financial and Political Theories of American Corporate Bankruptcy' (1993) 45 Stan. L. Rev. 311

Aghion, Philippe, Hart, Oliver and Moore, John, 'A Proposal for Bankruptcy Reform in the UK' (1993) 9 I.L. & P. 103

–, 'The Economics of Bankruptcy Reform' (1992) 8 J.L. Econ. & Org. 523

Altman, Edward I, 'Evaluating the Chapter 11 Bankruptcy-Reorganization Process' [1993] Colum. Bus. L. Rev. 1

Alves, Paulo FP, 'Corporate Ownership: Some International Evidence' (2010) International Research Journal of Finance and Economics Issue 41 SSRN http://papers.ssrn.com/sol3/papers.cfm?abstract_id=1304197

Andrade, Gregor and Kaplan, Steven N, 'How Costly is Financial (not Economic) Distress? Evidence from Highly Leveraged Transactions that Became Distressed' (1998) 53 J. Finance 1443

Anonymous, 'Company Schemes of Arrangement: Preserving the Assessed Loss' [1989] The Taxpayer 26

Armour, John and Bennett, Howard (eds), *Vulnerable Transactions in Corporate Insolvency* (Hart Publishing 2003)

Armour, John and Deakin, Simon, 'Norms in Private Insolvency Procedures: The "London Approach" to the Resolution of Financial Distress' (2001) 1 JCLS 21

Armour, John and Frisby, Sandra, 'Rethinking Receivership' (2001) 21 OJLS 73

Armour, John and Mokal, Rizwaan J, 'Reforming the Governance of Corporate Rescue: The Enterprise Act 2002' (2004) ESRC Centre for Business Research Working Paper 288 <http://papers.ssrn.com/sol3/papers.cfm?abstract_id=567306>

Armour, John, 'Legal Capital: An Outdated Concept?' (2006) 7 EBOR 5

–, 'The 'The Law and Economics of Corporate Insolvency Law: A Review' (2001) ESRC Centre for Business Research Working Paper 197 <http://disciplinas.stoa.usp.br/pluginfile.php/35886/mod_resource/content/1/CHY%20The%20Law%20and%20Economics%20of%20Corporate%20Insolvency.pdf>

Armour, John, Cheffins, Brian and Skeel, David A, 'Corporate Ownership Structure and the Evolution of Bankruptcy Law: Lessons from the United Kingdom' (2002) 55 Vand.L.Rev. 1699

Asquith, Paul, Gertner, Robert and Scharfstein, David, 'Anatomy of Financial Distress: An Examination of Junk Bond Issuers' (1994) 109 Quart. J. Econ. 625

Austin, Robert P and Ramsay, Ian M, *Ford's Principles of Corporations Law* (16th edn, Lexis Nexis 2014)

Ayer, John D, Bernstein, Michael L and Friedland, Jonathan, 'Ch 11 – "101": Out-of-Court Workouts, Prepacks and Pre-arranged Cases: A Primer' (2005) 24 Abi Journal 16

Ayotte, Kenneth and Morrison, Edward R, 'Creditor Control and Conflict in Chapter 11' (2008) Columbia Law and Economics Research Paper No. 321 <http://ssrn.com/abstract=1081661>

Bachmann, Gregor, Eidenmüller, Horst, Engert, Andreas, Fleischer, Holger and Schön, Wolfgang, 'Rechtsregeln für die geschlossene Kapitalgesellschaft' (2012) ZGR Sonderheft 18

Bachner, Thomas, 'Wrongful Trading – A New Model for Creditor Protection?' [2006] EBOR 293

Baird, Douglas G and Jackson, Thomas H, 'Corporate Reorganisations and the Treatment of Diverse Ownership Interests: A Comment on Adequate Protection of Secured Creditors in Bankruptcy' (1984) 51 U. Chi. L. Rev. 97

—, 'Fraudulent Conveyance Law and its Proper Domain' (1985) 38 Vand.L.Rev. 829

Baird, Douglas G and Rasmussen, Robert K, 'Control Rights, Property Rights and the Conceptual Foundations of Corporate Reorganizations' (2001) 87 Va. L. Rev. 921

—, 'Four (or Five) Easy Lessons From Enron' (2002) 55 Vand.L.Rev 1787

—, 'The End of Bankruptcy' (2002) 55 Stan L Rev 751

Baird, Douglas G, 'A World without Bankruptcy' (1987) 50 Law & Contemp. Probs. 173

—, 'Bankruptcies Uncontested Axioms' (1998) 108 Yale L.J. 573

—, 'Loss Distribution, Forum Shopping, and Bankruptcy: A Reply to Warren' (1987) 54 U. Chi. L. Rev. 815

—, 'Revisiting Auctions in Ch 11' (1993) 36 J.L. & Econ. 633

—, 'Substantive Consolidation Today' (2005) 47 B.C. L. Rev. 5

—, 'The New Face of Chapter 11' (2004) 12 Am. Bankr. Inst. L. Rev. 69

—, 'The Uneasy Case for Corporate Reorganisations' (1986) 15 J. Legal Stud. 127

Barath, Sreedhar T, Panchapagesan, Venkatesh and Werner, Ingrid M, 'The Changing Nature of Chapter 11' (2010) Fisher College of Business Working Paper No. 2008-03-003 <http://ssrn.com/abstract=1102366>

Bebchuk, Lucian A and Chang, Howard F, 'Bargaining and the Division of Value in Corporate Reorganization' (1992) 8 J.L. Econ. & Org. 253

Bebchuk, Lucian A and Fried, Jesse M, 'The Uneasy Case for the Priority of Secured Claims in Bankruptcy' (1996) 105 Yale L.J. 857

Bebchuk, Lucian A and Roe, Mark J, 'A Theory of Path Dependence in Corporate Ownership and Governance' (1999) 52 Stan. L. Rev. 127

Bebchuk, Lucian A, 'A New Approach to Corporate Reorganizations' (1988) 101 Harv. L. Rev. 775

Bekink, Mildred, 'An Historical Overview of the Directors' Duty of Care and Skill: From the Nineteenth Century to the Companies Bill 2007' (2008) 20 SA Merc LJ 95

Berdou, Jean, 'The doctrine of *parate executie* or self help by creditors in the present South African Law' [2010] De Rebus 28

Berle, Adolf and Means, Gardiner, *The Modern Corporation and Private Property* (Macmillan 1932)

Bertelsmann, Elizabeth M, Evans, Roger G, Harris, Adam, Kelly-Louw, Michelle, Loubser, Anneli, Roestoff, Melanie, Smith, Alastair, Stander, Leonie and Steyn, Lee, *Mars: The Law of Insolvency in South Africa* (9th edn, Juta 2008)

Bhandari, Jagdeep S and Weiss, Lawrence A (eds), *Corporate Bankruptcy – Economic and Legal Perspectives* (Cambridge University Press 1996)

Bhattacharya, Utpal and Daouk, Hazem, 'The World Price of Insider Trading' (2002) 57 JF 75

Birds, John, 'Proper Purposes as a Head of Directors' Duties' (1974) 37 MLR 580

Birks, Peter (ed), *English Private Law* Vol II (Oxford University Press 2000)

Blackman, Michael S, Everingham, Geoff and Jooste, Richard, *Commentary on the Companies Act* (loose-leaf) (Juta 2002)

Bodenstein, Helgard D J, 'English Influences on the Common Law of South Africa' (1915) 32 SALJ 337

Bolton, Patrick and Scharfstein, David, 'Optimal Debt Structure and the Number of Creditors' (1996) 104 J. Polit. Economy 1

Bonthuys, Elsje, 'Reciprocity in Relation to The Exceptio Non Adimpleti Contractus: The Intentions of the Parties' [2001] TSAR 180

Boraine, André, 'Toward Codifying the Actio Pauliana' (1996) 8 SA Merc LJ 227

Boraine, André, Burdette, David A, Kunst, Jennifer A and Magid, Pam, *Meskin Insolvency Law and its Operation in Winding-up* (loose-leaf) (Lexis Nexis Butterworths 2006)

Bork, Reinhard, *Sanierungsrecht in Deutschland und England* (RWS-Verlag Kommunikationsforum 2011)

Botha, Graham C, 'The Early Influence of the English Law Upon the Roman-Dutch Law in South Africa' (1923) 40 SALJ 396

Bouwman, Natasha, 'An Appraisal of the Modification of the Directors' Duty of Care and Skill' (2009) 21 SA Merc LJ 509

Bradstreet, Richard S, 'Business Rescue Proves to be Creditor-friendly: Claassen J's Analysis of the New Business Rescue Procedure in *Oakdene Square Properties*' (2013) (130) SALJ 44

—, 'The leak in the Chapter 6 lifeboat: Inadequate regulation of business rescue practitioners may adversely affect lenders' willingness and growth of the economy' (2010) 22 SA Merc LJ 195

Bratton, William W, 'Bond Covenants and Creditor Protection: Economics and Law, Theory and Practice, Substance and Process' (2006) 7 EBOR 39

Bris, Arturo and Welch, Ivo, 'The Optimal Concentration of Creditors' (2005) 60 J. Finance 2193

Brown, David T, 'Liquidity and Liquidation: Evidence from Real Estate Investment Trusts' (2000) 55 J. Finance 469

—, *Corporate Rescue – Insolvency Law in Practice* (John Wiley & Sons 1996)

Brown, David T and Symes, Christopher, 'Insolvency Practitioner Regulation: Providing Practice Standards Through the Use of Codes of Conduct' [2013] (hard copy on file with author)

Brudney, Daniel, 'Hypothetical Consent and Moral Force' (1991) 10 Law & Phil. 235

Brunner, Antje and Krahnan, Jan Peter, Multiple Lenders and Corporate Distress: Evidence on Debt Restructuring (2008) 75 Rev. Econ. Stud. 415

Brunstad, Eric G, 'Bankruptcy and the Problems of Economic Futility: A Theory on the Unique Role of Bankruptcy Law' (2000) 55 Bus. Law. 449

—, 'Good Faith, Solvent Debtors, and the Subject of Bankruptcies' in 79' Annual Meeting Of The National Conference Of Bankruptcy Judges' (2005) 4

Burdette, David A, 'Some Initial Thoughts on the Development of a Modern and Effective Business Rescue Model for South Africa (Part 1)' (2004) 16 SA Merc LJ 241

—, 'Unified Insolvency Legislation in South Africa: Obstacles in the Path of the Unification Process' (1999) 32 DJ 44

—, *A Framework for Corporate Insolvency Law Reform in South Africa* (LLD thesis, University of Pretoria, 2002)

Burger, 'Let the Litigation Funder beware' (2014) Werksmans Attorneys Legal Brief <http://www.werksmans.com/legal-briefs-view/let-litigation-funder-beware/>

Cahn, Andreas, 'Equitable Subordination of Shareholder Loan' (2006) 7 EBOR 287

Calitz, Juanitta and Burdette, David A, 'The Appointment of Insolvency Practitioners in South Africa: Time for a Change?' (2006) 4 TSAR 721

Carlson, David Gray, 'Philosophy in Bankruptcy' (1987) 85 Mich. L. Rev. 1341

Carruthers, Bruce G and Halliday, Terrence C, *Rescuing Business: The Making of Corporate Bankruptcy Law in England and the United States* (Clarendon Press, 1998)

Cassidy, Julie, *Corporations Law – Text and Essential Cases* (4th edn, The Federal Press 2013)

Cassim, Farouk H I and Larkin, Michael P, 'Company Law' [2002] A.S.S.L. 627

Cassim, Farouk H I, Cassim, Maleka F, Cassim, Rehana, Jooste, Richard, Shev, Joanne, Yeats, Jaqueline, *Contemporary Company Law* (2nd ed, Juta 2012)

Cassim, Maleka F, *The statutory derivative action under the Companies Act of 2008: Guidelines for the exercise of the judicial discretion* (unpublished PhD thesis, University of Cape Town 2014)

Cassim, Rehana, 'Delinquent directors under the Companies Act 71 of 2008' (2013) De Rebus <http://www.saflii.org/za/journals/DEREBUS/2013/14.html>

Cheffins, Brian R, *Company Law – Theory, Structure and Operation* (Clarendon Press 1997)

Cilliers, Hendrik S and Benade, *1985 Noter-up, including commentary on the Close Corporations Act 1984* (Butterworths 1986)

Clark, Robert C, 'The Duties of the Corporate Debtor to Its Creditors' (1977) 90 Harv. L. Rev. 505

–, *Corporate Law* (Little Brown 1986)

Coase, Ronald, 'The New Institutional Economics' (1998) 88(2) Americ. Econ. Rev. 72

Cohen, Lloyd R, 'Holdouts and Free Riders' (1991) 20 J. Legal Stud. 351

Coleman, Jules L, *Markets, Morals and the Law* (Cambridge University Press 1988)

Cranston, Ross (ed), *Banks and Remedies* (2nd edn, Taylor Francis 1999)

–, *Pre-packaged Business Disposals: White Knight or Thief in the Night?* (ILA Annual Conference 2006)

Crutchfield, Phillip, *Annotated Corporate Voluntary Administration Law* (Law Book Company Ltd 1994)

Crystal, Michael and Mokal, Rizwaan J, 'The Valuation of Distressed Companies – A Conceptual Framework' (2006) SSRN <http://papers.ssrn.com/sol3/papers.cfm?abstract_id=877155>

Daigle, Katherine H and Maloney, Michael T, 'Residual Claims in Bankruptcy: An Agency Theory Explanation' (1994) 37 J.L. & Econ. 157

Davids, Ezra, Norwitz, Trevor and Yuill, David, 'A microscopic analysis of the new merger and amalgamation provisions in the Companies Act 71 of 2008' [2010] AJ 337

Davies, Paul L and Worthington, Sarah, *Gower and Davies Principles of Modern Company Law* (10th edn, Sweet & Maxwell 2016)

Davies, Paul L, 'Directors' Creditor-Regarding Duties in the Vicinity of Insolvency' (2006) 7 EBOR 301

–, *An Introduction to Company Law* (2nd edn, Clarendon Press 2010)

Davies, Stephen, 'Pre-pack – He Who Pays the Piper Calls the Tune' [2006] Recovery 16

Davydenko, Sergei A and Franks, Julian R, 'Do Bankruptcy Codes Matter? A Study of Defaults in France, Germany, and the UK' (2008) 63 J. Finance 565

De Koker, Louis, 'Die Aanspreeklikeid van Direkteure vir Delikte Gepleeg in Ampsverband' (2002) 1 TSAR 18

–, *Die Roekelose en Bedrieglike Dryf van Besigheid in die Suid-Afrikaanse Maatskappyereg* (unpublished LLD thesis, University of the Orange Free State 1996)

De la Rey, Elisabeth M, 'Aspekte van die Vroeë Maatskapyereg: 'n Vergelykende Oorsig (Deel 1)' (1986) 27 Codicillus 4

–, 'Aspekte van die Vroeë Maatskapyereg: 'n Vergelykende Oorsig (Slot)' (1986) 27 Codicillus 18

–, *Skikkings in die Suid-Afrikaanse Maatskappyereg* (LLD thesis, University of Pretoria 1983)

De Wet, Johannes C and van Wyk, Andreas H, *Die Suid-Afrikaanse Kontraktereg en Handelsreg* (4th edn, Butterworths 1978)

Delport, Piet A, 'Die Appèlhof en Standaardskemas in die Maatskappyereg' [1996] SA Merc LJ 377

Delport, Piet A, Vorster, Quintus, Esser, Irene-Marie, Lombard, Sulette, Burdette, David, *Henochsberg on the Companies Act 71 of 2008* (loose-leaf) (Lexis Nexis 2015)

Devenish, George E, *Interpretation of Statutes* (Juta 1992)

Dickerson, A Mechele, 'A Behavioral Approach to Analyzing Corporate Failures' (2003) 38 Wake Forest L. Rev. 1

Du Plessis, Jean J and Henning, Johan J, 'Die Deliktuele Aanspreeklikheid van Persone wat as Maatsappyorgane Opgetree het' [1989] THRHR 540

Du Plessis, Jean J, *Maatskappyregtelike Grondslae van die Posisie van Direkteure en Bestuurende Direkteure* (unpublished LLD thesis, University of the Orange Free State 1990)

Dworkin, Ronald, 'Why Efficiency? A Response to Professor Calabresi and Posner' (1981) 8 Hofstra L. Rev. 563

Easterbrook, Frank H and Fischel, Daniel, *The Economic Structure of Corporate Law* (Harvard University Press 1996)

Easterbrook, Frank H, 'Is Corporate Bankruptcy Efficient? (1990) 27 J. Finan. Econ. 411

Eger, Thomas, Ott, Klaus, Bigus, Jochen, von Wangenheim, Georg (eds), *Internationalisierung des Rechts und seine ökonomische Analyse/Internationalization of the Law and its Economic Analysis, Festschrift für Hans-Bernd Schäfer zum 65. Geburtstag* (Springer 2008)

Eidenmüller, Horst, 'Die GmbH im Wettbewerb der Rechtsformen' [2007] ZGR 181

–, *Finanzkrise, Wirtschaftskrise und das deutsche Insolvenzrecht* (De Gruyter 2009)

–, 'Trading in Times of Crisis: Formal Insolvency Proceedings, Workouts and the Incentives for Shareholders/Managers' (2006) 7 EBOR 239

–, *Unternehmenssanierung zwischen Markt und Gesetz: Mechanismen der Unternehmensreorganisation und Kooperationspflichten im Reorganisationsrecht* (Otto Schmidt 1999)

Eisdorfer, Assaf, 'Empirical Evidence of Risk Shifting in Financially Distressed Firms (2008) 63 J. Finance 609

Elliot, Alex, 'Cancellation or suspension of agreements during business rescue' (2009), <https://www.hoganlovells.com/en/publications/cancellation-or-suspension-of-agreements-during-business-rescue>

Elschen, Rainer, Siegel, Theodor and Wagner, Franz W (eds), *Unternehmenstheorie und Besteuerung – Festschrift für D. Schneider* (Gabler 1997)

Emmerich, Volker and Habersack, Mathias, *Konzernrecht* (10th edn, C.H. Beck 2013)

Engert, Andreas, 'Die ökonomische Begründung der Grundsätze ordnungsgemäßer Unternehmensfinanzierung' (2004) ZGR 813

Faber, Dennis, Vermunt, Niels and Kilborn, Jason (eds), *Commencement of Insolvency Proceedings* (Oxford University Press 2012)

Ferrarini, Guido, Hopt, Klaus J, Winter, Jaap, Wymeersch, Eddy (eds), *Reforming Company and Takeover Law in Europe* (Oxford University Press 2004)

Finch, Vanessa, *Corporate Insolvency Law – Perspectives and Principles* (2nd edn, Cambridge University Press 2009)

–, 'Security, Insolvency and Risk: Who Pays the Price?' (1999) 62 MLR 633

–, 'The Measures of Insolvency Law' (1997) 17 OJLS 227

Finnis, John, *Natural Law and Natural Rights* (Clarendon Press 1980)

Flaccus, Janet, 'Have Eight Circuits Shorted? Good Faith and Chapter 11 Bankruptcy Petitions' (1993) 67 Am. Bankr. L.J. 401

Fleischer, Holger, 'Grundfragen der ökonomischen Theorie im Gesellschafts- und Kapitalmarktrecht' (2001) 30 ZGR 1

Fletcher, Ian, Higham, John and Trower, William, *Corporate Administration and Rescue Procedures* (2nd edn, Lexis Nexis 2004)

Fletcher, Ian, *The Law of Insolvency* (4th edn, Sweet & Maxwell 2009)

Flood, John, Abbey, Robert, Skordaki, Eleni and Aber, Paul, 'The Professional Restructuring of Corporate Rescue: Company Voluntary Arrangements and the London Approach' (1995) ACCA Research Report 45 < http://johnflood.com/pdfs/Prof_Restructuring_of_Corp_Rescue_1995.pdf>

Flynn, Desmond, 'Pre-pack Administrations' – A Regulatory Perspective' [2006] Recovery 3

Franks, Julian and Sussman, Oren, 'Financial Distress and Bank Restructuring of Small to Medium Size UK Companies' (2005) 9 Review of Finance 65

Franks, Julian and Torous, Walter N, 'An Empirical Investigation of U.S. Firms in Reorganization' (1989) 44 J. Finance 747

Frastanlis, Stergios, *Insolvenzverschleppungshaftung und Gläubigerschutz in der Insolvenzkrise – Ein rechtsvergleichender Blick aus Sicht des deutschen, griechischen und US-amerikanischen Rechts* (unpublished doctoral thesis, copy on file with author, University of Hamburg 2015)

Friedman, Alan E, 'The Economics of the Common Pool: Property Rights in Exhaustible Resources' (1971) 18 UCLA L. Rev. 855

Furubotn, Eirik and Richter, Rudolf, *Institutions and Economic Theory: The Contribution of the New Institutional Economics* (2nd edn, University of Michigan Press 2005)

Galai, Dan and Masulis, Ronald W, 'The Option Pricing Model and the Risk Factor of Stock' (1976) 3 J. Finan. Econ. 53

Garrido, José M, 'The Distributional Question in Insolvency: Comparative Aspects' (1995) 4 I.I.R. 25

Gauthier, David, *Morals and Agreement* (Clarendon Press 1986)

Gelter, John M, 'The subordination of shareholder loans in bankruptcy' (2006) 26 Int. Rev. Law Econ. 478

Gerber, Sarita C, 'Reckless Trading and Building Contracts' (2016) (79) THRHR 121

Getz, Keith and Jooste, Richard, 'S 311 of the Companies Act: Preserving the Assessed Loss' [1995] AJ 58

Gewirth, Alan, *The Community of Rights* (University of Chicago Press 1996)

Gilson, Stuart C, 'Bankruptcy, Boards, Banks, and Blockholders: Evidence on Changes in Corporate Ownership and Control When Firms Default' (1990) 27 J. Finan. Econ. 355

–, 'Corporate Governance and Economic Efficiency: When Do Institutions Matters?' (1996) 74 Wash. U. L. Q. 327

–, 'Management Turnover and Financial Distress' (1989) 25 J. Finan. Econ. 241

–, 'Managing default: Some Evidence on how Firms choose between Workouts and Chapter 11' (1991) 4 J. Appl. Corp. Finance 62

Gilson, Stuart C, John, Kose and Lang, Larry, 'Troubled debt restructurings – An empirical study of private reorganisation of firms in default' (1990) 27 J. Finan. Econ. 315

Giovanoli, Mario and Heinrich, Gregor (eds), *International Bank Insolvencies, A Central Bank Perspective* (Kluwer Law International 1999)

Goode, Roy, *Principles of Corporate Insolvency Law* (4th edn, Sweet & Maxwell 2005)

Gower, Laurence C B, *Modern Company Law* (2nd edn, Sweet & Maxwell 1957)

Grantham, Ross and Rickett, Charles E F (eds), *Corporate Personality in the 20th Century* (Hart Publishing 1998)

–, 'Directors' 'Tortious' Liability: Contract, Tort or Company Law?' 1999 MLR 133

Gronow, Michael and Mason, Rosalind, *McPhersons Law of Company Liquidations* (loose-leaf) (Thomson Reuters 2013)

Gross, Karen, 'Taking Community Interests into Account in Bankruptcy: An Essay' (1994) 72 Wash. U. L. Q. 1031

Failure and Forgiveness: Rebalancing the Bankruptcy System (Yale University Press 1997)

Grünewald, Philipp, *Mehrheitsherrschaft und insolvenzrechtliche Vorauswirkung in der Unternehmenskrise* (Mohr Siebeck 2015)

Hansen, Bradley A, 'The people's welfare and the origins of corporate reorganization: The Wabash receivership reconsidered' (2000) 74 Bus. Hist. Rev. 377

Habersack, Mathias, *Münchener Kommentar zum Bürgerlich Gesetzbuch* (vol 5) (6th edn, C.H. Beck 2013)

Hansmann, Henry and Kraakman, Reinier, 'Toward Unlimited Shareholder Liability for Corporate Torts' (1991) 100 Yale L.J. 1879

Hansmann, Henry, 'When Does Worker Ownership Work? ESOPs, Law Firms, Codetermination and Economic Democracy' (1990) 99 Yale L.J. 1749

Hardin, Garrett, 'The Tragedy of the Commons' (1968) 162 Science 1243

Harris, Jason, Hargovan, Anil and Adams, Michael, *Australian Corporate Law* (2nd edn, Lexis Nexis Butterworths 2009)

Harvey, Neil (ed), *Turnaround Management & Corporate Renewal – A South African Perspective* (Wits University Press 2011)

Hathaway, Oona A, 'Path Dependence in the Law: The Course and Pattern of Legal Change in a Common Law System' (2003) John M. Olin Center for Studies in Law, Economics, and Public Policy Working Papers, Paper 270, http://digitalcommons.law.yale.edu/lepp_papers/270

Havenga, Michele, 'Directors' Co-liability for Delicts' (2006) 18 SA Merc LJ 229

—, 'Directors May Not – or May They? – Apply for the Liquidation of Their Company' (1993) 1 JBL 183

Heldrich, Andreas, Koller, Ingo, Prölss, Jürgen, Langenbucher, Katja, Grigoleit, Hans Christoph, Hager, Johannes, Hey, Felix, Neuner, Jörg, Petersen, Jens, Singer, Reinhard (eds), *Festschrift für Claus-Wilhelm Canaris zum 70. Geburtstag Band II* (C.H. Beck 2007)

Hicks, John R, 'The foundations of welfare economics' (1939) 49 Econ. J. 696

Hommelhoff, Peter, Hopt, Klaus and Lutter, Marcus (eds), *Konzernrecht und Kapitalmarktrecht* (Stämpfli 2001)

Hosten, Willy J, Edwards, Basil, Bosman, Francis and Church, Joan, *Introduction to South African Law and Legal Theory* (2nd edn, Butterworths 1995)

Hotchkiss, Edith S, 'Post-Bankruptcy Performance and Management Turnover' (1995) 50 J. Finance 21

Hübert, Evens, *Sorgfaltskonforme Prognosen und Pflichten der Geschäftsleiter im Vorfeld der Insolvenz; ein Beitrag mit rechtsvergleichenden Bezügen* (unpublished doctoral thesis, copy on file with author, University of Hamburg 2015)

Hudson, John, 'The Limited Liability Company: Success, Failure and Future' (2008) 26 Royal Bank of Scotland Review

Idensohn, Kathy, 'The Regulation of Shadow Directors' (2010) 22 SA Merc LJ 326

Jacobs, Lézelle, *Die vertrouensverpligtinge van ondernemingsreddingspraktisyns: 'n Regsvergelykende studie* (unpublished LLD thesis, University of the Free State 2015)

Jacobs, Lézelle and Neethling, Johann, 'Die sorgsame ondernemingspraktisyn: 'n ondersoek na die gepaste maatstaf' (2016) 13(3) LITNet Akademis 773

Jackson, Thomas H and Kronman, Anthony T, 'Secured Financing and Priorities Among Creditors' (1979) 88 Yale L.J. 1143

Jackson, Thomas H and Scott, Robert E, 'On the Nature of Bankruptcy: An Essay on Bankruptcy Sharing and the Creditors' Bargain' (1989) 75 Va. L. Rev. 155

Jackson, Thomas H, 'Avoiding Powers in Bankruptcy' (1984) 36 Stan.L.Rev. 725

—, 'Bankruptcy, Non-Bankruptcy Entitlements and the Creditors' Bargain' (1982) 91 Yale L.J. 857

—, *The Logics and Limits of Bankruptcy Law* (Harvard University Press 1986)

Jensen, Michael C and Meckling, William H, 'Theory of the Firm: Managerial Behaviour, Agency Costs and Ownership Structure' (1976) 3 J. Finan. Econ. 305

Jooste, Richard D, 'Schemes of Arrangement – a new Development' (1989) 28 Income Tax Reporter 7

Joubert, David J, *General Principles of the Law of Contract* (Juta 1987)

Joubert, Tronel, '"Reasonable possibility" versus "reasonable prospect": Did business rescue succeed in creating a better test than judicial management?' 2013 (76) THRHR 550

Joubert, Tronel and Loubser, Anneli, 'Executive directors in business rescue: employees or something else?' (2016) 49 De Jure

Joubert, Willem A, 'Cession' LAWSA (3rd edn, 2013) vol 3

–, 'Contract' LAWSA (3rd edn, 2014) vol 9

Kahan, Marcel, 'The Qualified case Against Mandatory Terms in Bonds' (1995) 89 Nw. U. L. Rev. 565

Kahan, Marcel and Klausnev, Michael, 'Path Dependence in Corporate Contracting' (1996) 74 Wash. U. L. Q. 347

Kaldor, Nicholas, 'Welfare propositions of economics and interpersonal comparisons of utility' (1939) 49 Econ. J. 549

Kalss, Susanne (ed), *Vorstandshaftung in 15 europäischen Ländern* (Linde Verlag 2005)

Kanda, Hideki, 'Debtholders and Equityholders' (1992) 21 J. Legal Stud. 431

Katz, Alan and Mumford, Michael, *Report to the Insolvency Service: Study of Administration Cases* (Insolvency Service 2008)

Keay, Andrew and Walton, Peter, *Insolvency Law – Corporate and Personal* (2nd edn, Jordans 2008) 3rd edn

Keay, Andrew, 'Another way of skinning a cat: enforcing directors' duties for the benefit of creditors', (2004) 17 Insolv. Int. 1

–, 'Corporate Governance During Administration and Reconstruction Under Part 5.3A of the Corporations Act' (1997) 15 C&SLJ 145

–, 'The Duty of Directors to Exercise an Independent Judgment' (2008) 29 Co Law 290

–, 'To Unify or not to Unify Insolvency Legislation: International Experience and the Latest South African Proposals' (1999) 32 De Jure 62

–, 'The Directors' Duty to Take into Account the Interests of Company Creditors: When is it Triggered?' (2001) 25 MULR 315

–, 'In Pursuit of the Rationale Behind the Avoidance of Pre-Liquidation Transactions' (1996) 18 Syd LR 55

Kent, Pen, 'Corporate Workouts: A UK Perspective' (1997) 6 I.I.R. 165

–, 'The London Approach: Distressed Debt Trading' (1994) B.E.Q.B. 110

–, 'The London Approach' (1993) 8 J.I.B.L. 81

Kirchhof, Hans-Peter, Eidenmüller, Horst and Stürner, Rolf (eds), *Münchener Kommentar zur Insolvenzordnung* (3rd edn, C.H. Beck 2013)

Klopper, Hans and Bradstreet, Richard S, 'Averting Liquidations with Business Rescue: Does a Section 155 Compromise Place the Bar too High?' (2014) 3 Stell LR 549

Kloppers, Pieter, 'Judicial Management – A Corporate Rescue Mechanism in Need of Reform?' (1999) 10 Stell LR 417

–, 'Judicial Management Reform – Steps to Initiate a Business Rescue' (2001) 13 SA Merc LJ 359

–, *Judicial management as a technique for corporate rescue: a comparison with English and Australian law* (LLM thesis, University of Stellenbosch 2000)

Korobkin, Donald R, 'Contractarianism and the Normative Foundations of Bankruptcy Law' (1993) 71 Tex. L. Rev. 541

–, 'Employee Interests in Bankruptcy' (1996) 4 Am. Bankr. Inst. L. Rev. 5

–, 'Rehabilitating Values: A Jurisprudence of Bankruptcy' (1991) 91 Colum. L. Rev. 717

–, 'The Role of Normative Theory in Bankruptcy Debate' (1996–7) 82 Iowa L. Rev. 75

–, 'Vulnerability, Survival and the Problem of Small Business Bankruptcy' (1994) 23 Cap. U. L. Rev. 413

Kraakman, Reinier, Armour, John, Davies, Paul, Enriques, Luca, Hansmann, Henry, Hertig, Gerard, Hopt, Klaus, Kanda, Hideki and Rock, Edward (eds), *Anatomy of Corporate Law – A Comparative and Functional Approach* (2nd edn, Oxford University Press 2009)

Kraus, Jody and Walt, Steven (eds), *The Jurisprudential Foundations of Corporate and Commercial Law* (Cambridge University Press 2000)

Larkin, Michael P, 'A Question of Management: Does it Include Ceasing to Manage?' (1987) 16 Businessman's Law 165

Lawson, Gary, 'Efficiency and individualism' (1992) 42 Duke L.J. 53

Leebron, David W, 'Limited Liability, Torts Victims, and Creditors' (1991) 91 Colum. L. Rev. 1565

Levmore, Saul, 'Monitors and Freeriders in Commercial and Corporate Settings' (1982) 92 Yale L.J. 49

Lipton, Phillip, Herzberg, Aibe and Welsh, Michelle, *Understanding Company Law* (17th edn, Lawbook 2014)

Lombard, Sulette, *Directors' Duties to Creditors* (unpublished LLD thesis, University of Pretoria 2006)

Lombard and Swart, Christiaan WJC, 'Business rescue: The uncertainty about sureties – *Tuning Fork (Pty) Ltd T/A Balanced Audio v Jonker*' (2015) 78 THRHR

LoPucki, Lynn M and Doherty, Joseph W, 'The Determinants of Professional Fees in Large Bankruptcy Reorganization Cases' (2004) 1 J. Emp. L. Stud. 111

LoPucki, Lynn M and Whitford, William C, 'Bargaining over Equity's Share in the Bankruptcy Reorganization of Large, Public Held Companies' (1990) 139 U. Pa. L. Rev. 125

–, 'Corporate Governance in the Bankruptcy Reorganisation of Large, Publicly Held Companies' (1993) 141 U.Pa.L.Rev. 669

Loubser, Anneli, 'An International Perspective on the Regulation of Insolvency Practitioners' (2007) 19 SA Merc LJ 123

—, 'Defining the Unincorporated Business in Financial Distress: Should It Be Treated as a Business or as a Consumer?' (2007) 19 SA Merc LJ 444

—, 'Judicial Management as a Business Rescue Procedure in South African Corporate Law' (2004) 16 SA Merc LJ 137

—, 'The Insolvency Practitioner – Professional Status at Last?' (1999) 7 JBL 53

Some Comparative Aspects of Corporate Rescue in South African Company Law (LLD thesis, University of South Africa 2010)

Lubbe, Gerhard F (revised by Scott), 'Mortgage and Pledge' LAWSA (2nd edn, 2008) vol 17(2)

Lubben, Stephen J, 'Chapter 11 Professional Fee Study' (2007) Am. Bankr. Ins. <http://ssrn.com/abstract=1020477>

—, 'Corporate Reorganization & Professional Fees' (2008) 82 Am. Bankr. L.J. 77

—, 'What we "Know" about Chapter 11 Cost is Wrong' (2012) 17 Fordham J. Corp. & Fin. L. 142

Luiz, Stephanie and van der Linde, Kathleen, 'Trading in Insolvent Circumstances – Its Relevance to Sections 311 and 424 of the Companies Act' [1993] SA Merc LJ 230

Lutter, Marcus (ed), *Das Kapital der Aktiengesellschaft in Europa* (De Gruyter 2006)

—, *Legal Capital in Europe* (De Gruyter 2006)

Maroun, Warren and Wainer, Harvey, 'To report or not to report: In what context is a 'reportable irregularity' reportable?' (2013) 16 South African J. Econ. Manage. Sci. 13

Martin, Nathalie, 'Common-Law Bankruptcy Systems: Similarities and Differences' (2003) 11 Am. Bankr. Inst. L. Rev. 367

McCahery, Joseph, Picciotto, Sol and Scott, Colin (eds), *Corporate Control and Accountability* (Clarendon Press 1993)

McCormack, Gerard, 'Control and Corporate Rescue – An Anglo-American Evaluation (2007) 56 ICLQ 515

McLennan, John S, 'Abuse of Limited Liability, "Insider" Debts and Subordination Agreements' 110 (1993) SALJ 686

—, 'Powers of Directors to Winding Up Insolvent Companies' (1987) 104 SALJ 232

Meckling, William H, 'Financial Markets, Default and Bankruptcy: The Role of the State' (1977) 41 Law & Contemp. Probs. 13

Mendelson, Nina A, 'A Control-Based Approach to Shareholder Liability' 102 (2002) Colum. L. Rev. 1203

Meskin, Philip M, Galgut, Justice B, Kunst, Jennifer A, *Henochsberg on the Close Corporations Act* (loose-leaf) (Lexis Nexis 1997)

Mevorach, Irit, 'The Appropriate Treatment of Corporate Groups in Insolvency' (2007) 8 EBOR 179

Milgrom, Paul and Roberts, John, *Economics, Organization and Management* (2nd edn, Prentice-Hall 1992)

Milman, David, *Governance of Distressed Firms* (Edward Elgar 2013)

Mojdehi, Ali M M and Gertz, Janet D, 'The Implicit Good Faith Requirement in Chapter 11 Liquidations: A Rule in Search of a Rationale?' (2006) 14 Am. Bankr. Inst. L. Rev. 143

Mokal, Rizwaan J, *Consistency of Principle in Corporate Insolvency* (Doctoral thesis, University College London 2001)

–, *Corporate Insolvency Law – Theory and Application* (Oxford University Press 2005)

Mokal, Rizwaan J and Ho, Chan, 'Consideration, Characterisation, Evaluation: Transactions at an Undervalue after Phillips v Brewin Dolphin' (2001) 1 J. Corp. L 359

Mongalo, Tshepo (ed), *Modern Company Law for a Competitive South African Economy* (Juta 2010)

Morgan, Brian and Underwood, Harry, 'Directors' Liability to Creditors on a Corporation's Insolvency in Light of the *Dylex* and *Peoples Department Stores* Litigation' (2004) 39 C.B.L.J. 336

Morrison, Edward R, 'The Economics of Bankruptcy: An Introduction to the Literature' (2009), Columbia Law and Economics Working Paper No. 366, 2 < http://papers.ssrn.com/sol3/papers.cfm?abstract_id=1529822>

Moss, Gabriel, 'Chapter 11: An English Lawyer's Critique' (1998) 11 Insolv.Int. 17

–, 'Comparative Bankruptcy Cultures: Rescue or Liquidations? Comparisons of Trends in National Law—England' (1997) 23 Brook. J. Int'l L.

Moulton, Jon, 'The Uncomfortable Edge of Propriety – Pre-packs or Just Stitch-ups?' [2005] Recovery 2

Mülbert, Peter O, 'A Synthetic View of Different Concepts of Creditor Protection' (2006) 7 EBOR 357

Myers, Stewart C, 'Determinants of Corporate Borrowing' (1977) 5 J. Fin. Econ. 147

Nagel, Chris J (ed), *Commercial Law* (4th edn, Lexis Nexis Butterworths 2011)

Naumann, Ulrike and Shawe, Lionel, 'South Africa' (2012) PLC – Multi-Jurisdictional Guide Finance <http://www.bowman.co.za/FileBrowser/ArticleDocuments/PLC%20Handbook%20%96%202012%20Edition.pdf>

Newcomb, R Link, 'The limitation of directors' liability: a proposal for legislative reform' [1987] Tex. L. Rev. 411

Newman, Peter (ed), *The New Palgrave Dictionary of Economics and the Law* (Palgrave Macmillan 1998)

Nicolaides, Mark C, 'Priorities for Subordinated Debt' [1989] JIBFL 247

Nozemack, Matthew, 'Making Sense Out of Bankruptcy Courts' Recharacterization of Claims: Why Not Use § 510(c) Equitable Subordination,' 56 Wash. S Lee L. Review (1999) 689

O'Connor, Marleen A, 'Restructuring the Corporation's Nexus of Contracts: Recognizing a Fiduciary Duty to Protect Displaced Workers' (1991) 69 North Car. L. Rev. 1189

Olver, 'Judicial Management – A Case For Law Reform' 1986 (49) THRHR 84

–, *Judicial Management in South Africa* (PhD thesis, University of Cape Town 1980)

Omar, Paul (ed), *International Insolvency Law – Themes and Perspectives* (Ashgate 2008)

Ott, Claus, Schäfer, Hans-Bernd (eds), *Die Präventivwirkung zivil- und strafrechtlicher Sanktionen* (Mohr 1999)

Pareto, Vilfredo, *Manual of Political Economy* (Schwier tr, Schwier and Page (eds), A. M. Kelly 1971)

Parry, Rebecca, *Corporate Rescue* (Sweet & Maxwell 2008)

Pettet, Ben G (ed), *Company Law in Change* (4th edn, Stevens & Son 1987)

Picker, Randal C, 'Security Interests, Misbehaviour and Common Pools' (1992) 59 U. Chi. L. Rev. 64

Phulunga, Simphiwe, 'Lessons to be learned from reckless and fraudulent trading by a company: Section 424(1) of the Companies Act 61 of 1973 and sections 22 and 77(3)(b) of the Companies Act 71 of 2008' (2016) 28 SA Merc LJ 238

Pointon, 'London Approach: A Look at its Application and its Alternatives' [1994] Insolv. B. 5

Posner, Richard, 'The Ethical and Political Basis of the Efficiency Norm in Common Law Adjudication' (1980) 8 Hofstra L.R. 487

Prentice, Daniel D, 'Creditor's Interests and Director's Duties' (1990) 10 OJLS 265

Pretorius, Johan A and Du Plessis, Jean J, 'Enkele Aspekte Rakende die Diskwalifikasie van Direkteure en Andere in die Suid-Afrikaanse en die Engelse Reg' (1993) 4 SA Merc LJ 144

Pulvino, Todd C, 'Do Asset Fire-sales Exist? An Empirical Investigation of Commercial Aircraft Transactions' (1998) 53 J. Finance 939

—, 'Effects of Bankruptcy Court Protection on Asset Sales' (1999) 52 J. Finan. Econ. 151

Rajak, Harry (ed), *Insolvency Law: Theory and Practice* (Sweet & Maxwell 1993)

Rajak, Harry and Henning, Johan J, 'Business Rescue for South Africa' (1999) 115 SALJ 262

Rasmussen, Robert K and Thomas, Randall S, 'Whither the Race? A Comment on the Effects of the Delawarization of Corporate Reorganizations' (2001) 54 Vand. L. Rev. 283

Rasmusen, Eric, *Games and Information: An Introduction to Game Theory* (4th edn, Blackwell 2007)

Rasmussen, Robert K, 'Debtor's Choice: A Menu Approach to Corporate Bankruptcy' (1992) 71 Tex. L. Rev. 51

—, 'Secured Debts, Control Rights and Options' (2004) 25 Cardozo L. Rev. 1935

Rawls, John, *A Theory of Justice* (Harvard University Press 1971)

Rich, Jefferey N and Moser, Eric T, 'Bankruptcy Claims Trading: Basic Concepts' (2013) Practical Law Company <http://www.r3mlaw.com/Articles/Bankruptcy-Claims-Trading-Basic-Concepts.pdf>

Richter, Bernd and Pluta, Maximllian, 'Haftungssprung Insolvenzreife – ein Plädoyer für die integrierte Unternehmensplanung' (2009) InsVZ 31

Ringleb, Al H and Wiggins, Steven N, 'Liability and Large-Scale, Long-Term Hazards' (1990) 98 J. Polit. Economy 574

Rochelle, Michael R, 'Lower the Penalties for Failure: Using the Insolvency Law as a Tool for Spurring Economic Growth; the American Experience, and Possible Uses for South Africa' (1996) 2 TSAR 315

Rock, Edward B and Wachter, Michael L, 'Islands of Conscious Power: Law, Norms, and the Self-Governing Corporation' (2001) 149 U. Pa. L. Rev. 1619

Roe, Mark J, 'Bankruptcy and Debt: A Model for Corporate Reorganization' (1983) 83 Colum. L. Rev. 527

Roe, Mark J, 'Chaos and Evolution in Law and Economics' (1996) 109 Harv. L. Rev. 641

Roth, Markus, 'Business Judgment Rule' *Max Planck Encyclopedia of European Private Law* (2012)

Schall, Alexander, 'The UK Limited Company Abroad' (2005) 16 E.B.L.R. 1577

—, *Kapitalgesellschaftsrechtlicher Gläubigerschutz* (Beck 2009)

Schermer, Barry S, 'Response to Professor Gross: Taking the Interests of the Community into Account in Bankruptcy' (1994) 72 Wash. U. L. Q. 1049

Schmidt, Karsten, 'Reform der Kapitalsicherung und Haftung in der Krise nach dem Regierungsentwurf des MoMiG' [2007] GmbHR 1072

Schmidt, Karsten, Uhlenbruck, Wilhelm, Grezelius, Georg, Maus, Karl H, Moll, Wilhelm, Schluck-Amend, Alexandra, Vallender, Heinz, Wellensiek, Jobst and Wittig, Arne (eds), *Die GmbH in Krise, Sanierung und Insolvenz* (5th edn, Otto Schmidt 2015)

Scholtz, Johan W, 'Suretyship' LAWSA (2nd edn repl. vol, 2015) vol 26

Schwartz, Alan, 'A Contract Theory Approach to Bankruptcy' (1998) 107 Yale L.J. 1807

—, 'Bankruptcy Workouts and Debt Contracts' (1993) 36 J.L. & Econ. 595

—, 'Relational Contracts in the Courts: An Analysis of Incomplete Agreements and Judicial Strategies' (1992) 21 J. Legal Stud. 271

—, 'Security Interests and Bankruptcy Priorities: A Review of Current Theories' (1981) 10 J. Legal Stud. 1

Scott, Susan, 'Lien' LAWSA (2nd edn, 2008) vol 15(2)

Sealy, Leonard S and Milman, David, *Annotated Guide to the Insolvency Legislation* (10th edn, Thomson/Sweet & Maxwell 2007)

Sealy, Leonard S, 'Directors' "wider" responsibilities – problems conceptual, practical and procedural' 1987 Mon LR 164

Segal, Nicholas A, 'Corporate Recovery and Rescue – Mastering the Key Strategies Necessary for Successful Cross Border Workouts' (2000) 13 Ins. Int. 17

Shavell, Steven, *Foundations of Economic Analysis of Law* (Harvard University Press 2004)

Shleifer, Andrei and Vishny, Robert W, 'Liquidation Values and Debt Capacity: A Market Equilibrium Approach' (1992) 47 J. Finance 1343

Shuchmann, Philip, 'An Attempt at a "Philiosophy of Bankruptcy"' (1973) 21 UCLA. L. Rev. 403

Skeel Jr., David A and Krause-Vilmar, Georg, 'Recharacterization and the Non-Hindrance of Creditors' (2006) 7 EBOR 259

Skeel Jr., David A, *Debt's Dominion: A History of Bankruptcy Law in America* (Princeton University Press 2001)

–, 'An Evolutionary Theory of Corporate Law and Corporate Bankruptcy' (1998) 51 Vand.L.Rev. 1325

–, 'Creditors' Ball: The "New" New Corporate Governance of in Chapter 11' (2003) 152 U.Pa.L.Rev. 917

–, 'The Past, Present and Future of Debtor-in-Possession Finance' [2004] Cardozo L.Rev. 1905

Smith, Clifford W and Warner, Jerold B, 'On Financial Contracting: An Analysis of Bond Covenants' (1979) 7 J. Finan. Econ. 117

Smits, Anthony, 'Corporate Administration: A Proposed Model' (1999) 32 DJ 80

Sprayregen, James H M, Friedland, Jonathan P, Brighton Jo Anne J, Bianca, Salvatore F, 'Recharacterization of Debt to Equity: An Overview, Update and Practical Guide to an Evolving Doctrine' [2004] Ann.Surv.Bankr.L. 1

Steffek, Felix, 'Insolvenzgründe in Europa – Rechtsvergleich, Regelungsstrukturen und Perspektiven der Rechtsangleichung' [2009] KTS 317

Gläubigerschutz in der Kapitalgesellschaft (Mohr Siebeck 2011)

Stevens, Richard and de Beer, Philip 'The duty of care and skill, and reckless trading: Remedies in flux' (2016) 28 SA Merc LJ 250

Strömberg, Per, 'Conflicts of Interest and Market Illiquidity in Bankruptcy Auctions: Theory and Tests' (2000) 55 J. Finance 2641

Swart, Barend H, *Die Rol van die concursus creditorum in die Suid-Afrikaanse Insolvensiereg* (unpublished LLD thesis, University of Pretoria 1990)

Sweeney, Richard J, Tollison, Robert D and Willett, Thomas D, 'Market Failure, The Common Pool Problem, and Ocean Resource Exploitation' (1974) 17 J.L. & Econ. 179

Tashjian, Elizabeth, Lease, Ronald C and McConnell, John J, 'Prepacks: An Empirical Analysis of Prepackaged Bankruptcies' (1996) 40 J. Finan. Econ. 135

Triantis, Georg G, 'Financial Slack Policy and the Law of Secured Transactions' (2000) 29 J. Legal Stud. 35

–, 'The Interplay between Liquidation and Reorganization in Bankruptcy: The role of screens, gatekeepers, and guillotines' (1996) 16 Int. Rev. Law Econ. 101

Uhlenbruck, Wilhelm and Hirte, Heribert (eds), *Kommentar Insolvenzordnung* (14th rev. edn, Vahlen 2015)

Van der Linde, Kathleen, 'Personal liability of directors for corporate fault – An exploration' (2008) 20 SA Merc LJ 439

Van der Merwe, Schalk W J, 'Things' LAWSA (2nd edn, 2014) vol 27

Van der Merwe, Schalk W J, van Huyssteen, Louis F, Reinecke, Machiel F B and Lubbe, Gerard F, *Contract – General Principles* (2nd edn, Juta 2003)

Vilaplana, Victor A, 'A Pre-Pack Bankruptcy Primer' (1998) 44 Ali-Aba The Practical Lawyer 33

Villiers, Charlotte, 'Employees as Creditors: A Challenge for Justice in Insolvency Law' (1999) 20 Co. Law. 222

Wainer, Harvey E, 'The new Companies Act: Peculiarities and Anomalies' (2009) 126 SALJ 806

—, 'The Insolvency Conundrum in the Companies Act' (2015) 132 SALJ 509

Walton, Peter, 'Pre-packaged Administrations – 'Trick or Treat' (2006) 19 Ins. Int. 113

Walzer, Michael, *Spheres of Justice* (Basil Blackwell 1995)

Warren, Elizabeth and Westbrook, Jay L, *The Law of Debtors and Creditors* (6th edn, Aspen 2009)

—, 'Secured Party in Possession' (2003) 11 Am. Bankr. Inst. L. Rev. 12

Warren, Elizabeth, 'Bankruptcy Policy in an Imperfect World' (1993) 92 Mich. L. Rev. 336

—, 'Bankruptcy Policy' (1987) 54 U. Chi. L. Rev. 775

Webb, David C, 'An Economic Evaluation of Insolvency Procedures in the United Kingdom: Does the 1986 Insolvency Act Satisfy the Creditors' Bargain?' (1991) 43 Oxford Econ. Pap. 193

Weiss, Lawrence, 'Bankruptcy Resolution: Direct Costs and Violation of Priority Claims' (1990) 27 J. Finan. Econ. 285

Weiss, Lawrence and Capkun, Vedran, 'Bankruptcy Resolution: Priority of Claims with the Secured Creditor in Control' (2007) American Law & Economics Association Annual Meetings <http://law.bepress.com/cgi/viewcontent.cgi?article=1929&context=alea>

Westbrook, Jay L, 'A Comparison of Bankruptcy Reorganization in the US With the Administrative Procedure in the UK' [1990] I.L. & P.

Westermann, Harm Peter and Mock, Klaus (eds), *Festschrift für Gerold Bezzenberger zum 70. Geburtstag am 13. März 2000* (Walter de Gruyter 2000)

White, James J, 'Harvey's Silence' (1995) 69 Am. Bankr. L.J. 467

—, 'The Ex Ante Effects of Bankruptcy Reform on Investment Incentives' (1994) 72 Wash. U. L.Q. 1159

White, Michelle J, 'Corporate Bankruptcy as a Filtering Device': Ch 11 Reorganization and Out-of-Court Restructuring' (1994) 10 J.L. Econ. & Org. 268

—, 'The Corporate Bankruptcy Decision' (1989) 3 J. Econ. Perspect. 129

Williamson, Oliver and Masten, Scott, *Transaction Cost Economics* (Edward Elgar 1995)

Williamson, Oliver *The Economic Institution of Capitalism* (The Free Press 1985)

—, 'The New Institutional Economics: Taking Stock, Looking Ahead' (2000) 38(3) J. Econ. Lit. 59

Willimse, 'Het die Klokke Gelui vir Skikkings Ingevolge a 311 van die Maatskappywet?' [1989] De Rebus 205

Wilton, James M and Moeller-Sally, Stephen, 'Debt Recharacterization Under State Law' (2007) 62 Bus. Law. 1257

Wood, Philip R, *Principles of International Insolvency* (2nd edn, Sweet & Maxwell 2007)

Worthington, Sarah, 'Directors' Duties, Creditors' Rights and Shareholder Intervention' (1991) 18 MULR 121

Ziegel, Jacob S (ed), *Current Developments in International and Comparative Corporate Insolvency Law* (Oxford University Press 1994)

Zimmer, Marcus, 'Overview of Specialized Courts' (2009) International Journal for Court Administration <http://www.iaca.ws/files/LWB-SpecializedCourts.pdf>

Zimmermann, Reinhard, *Das römisch-holländische Recht in Südafrika – Einführung in die Grundlagen und usus hodiernus* (Wissenschaftliche Buchgesellschaft 1983)

Commission reports, opinions, presentation, statistics

American Bankruptcy Institute Commission to Study the Reform of Chapter 11, *2012-2014 Final Report and Recommendations* (ABI, 2014) 242

Australian Law Reform Commission General Insolvency Inquiry (Harmer Report) 1988 <http://www.alrc.gov.au/sites/default/files/pdfs/publications/alrc45_Summary.pdf>

Bitter, Georg and Hommerich, Christoph, *Die Zukunft des Überschuldungsbegriffs Expertenbefragung im Auftrag des Bundesministeriums der Justiz – Abschlussbericht* (RWS Verlag Kommunikationsforum 2012)

Companies and Intellectual Property Commission Report (CIPC), 'Status of Business Rescue Proceedings in South Africa (March 2015)' (2015) <http://www.cipc.co.za/files/1914/3377/1988/Status_of_Business_Rescue_in_South_Africa_version1_0.pdf>

Department of Trade and Industry (DTI) Policy Framework, *South African Company Law for the 21st Century: Guidelines for Corporate Law Reform* (GG 26493, Notice 1183, 2004)

ENS opinion 28 April 2010

Frisby, Sandra, 'A Preliminary Analysis of Pre-packaged Administrations: Report to R3 – The Association of Business Recovery Professionals' 2007 R3 <https://www.r3.org.uk/media/documents/publications/press/preliminary_analysis_of_pre-packed_administrations.pdf>

Hutchison, Dale, ENS internal memorandum, 17 August 2010

INSOL International, 'Statement of Principles for a Global Approach to Multi-Creditor Workouts' (2000) <https://www.insol.org/pdf/Lenders.pdf >

Lotheringen, 21 September 2012, Power Point Presentation, slide 10 (on file with the author)

Millin Commission, *Report of the Commission of Enquiry on the Amendment of the Companies Act* (UG No. 69 of 1948) 93

South African Institute of Chartered Accountants (SAICA), 'Trading Whilst Factually Insolvent' (1999) < https://www.saica.co.za/Portals/0/Technical/auditing/documents/Guide%20on%20Trading%20Whilst%20Factually%20Insolvent.pdf>

Statistics South Africa <http://www.statssa.gov.za/?page_id=737&id=1>

UNCITRAL, *Legislative Guide on Insolvency Law* (New York, 2005) 23 <http://www.uncitral.org/pdf/english/texts/insolven/05-80722_Ebook.pdf>

Van Wyk – de Vries Commission, *Main Report of the Companies Act Commission of Enquiry* (RP 45 1970) 145

Dictionaries and Websites

Black's Law Dictionary <http://thelawdictionary.org/>

Business Day (28 August 2002) <https://www.businesslive.co.za/>

Oxford Online Dictionary <http://www.oxforddictionaries.com>